*The Editors*

RUDOLPH P. BYRD is the Goodrich C. White Professor of American Studies in the Graduate Institute of the Liberal Arts and the Department of African American Studies and the founding director of the James Weldon Johnson Institute for Advanced Interdisciplinary Studies at Emory University. He is the author and editor of ten books, including *Jean Toomer's Years with Gurdjieff; Essentials* by Jean Toomer with Charles Johnson; *Charles Johnson's Novels: Writing the American Palimpsest; The Essential Writings of James Weldon Johnson;* and with Alice Walker *The World Has Changed: Conversations with Alice Walker.* Among Professor Byrd's awards and fellowships are an Andrew W. Mellon Fellowship at Harvard University, Visiting Scholar at the Bellagio Study and Conference Center, and the Thomas Jefferson Award from Emory. He is a founding officer of the Alice Walker Literary Society.

HENRY LOUIS GATES, JR., is the Alphonse Fletcher University Professor and the Director of the W. E. B. Du Bois Institute for African and African American Research at Harvard University. He is the author of twelve books and has hosted and produced ten documentaries, including *Faces of America* and *African American Lives 1* and *2.* Professor Gates is co-editor, with Professor Evelyn Brooks Higginbotham, of the *African American National Biography,* and his recent work has been instrumental in popularizing African American genealogical research and DNA testing. His book *In Search of Our Roots: How 19 Extraordinary African Americans Reclaimed Their Past* won an NAACP Image Award in 2010. He is the recipient of fifty honorary degrees and many awards, including the MacArthur Foundation "genius grant" and the National Humanities Medal.

A NORTON CRITICAL EDITION

Jean Toomer
# CANE

AUTHORITATIVE TEXT
CONTEXTS
CRITICISM

**SECOND EDITION**

*Edited by*

RUDOLPH P. BYRD
EMORY UNIVERSITY

HENRY LOUIS GATES, JR.
HARVARD UNIVERSITY

W · W · NORTON & COMPANY · *New York* · *London*

W. W. Norton & Company has been independent since its founding in 1923, when William Warder Norton and Mary D. Herter Norton first published lectures delivered at the People's Institute, the adult education division of New York City's Cooper Union. The firm soon expanded its program beyond the Institute, publishing books by celebrated academics from America and abroad. By mid-century, the two major pillars of Norton's publishing program—trade books and college texts—were firmly established. In the 1950s, the Norton family transferred control of the company to its employees, and today—with a staff of four hundred and a comparable number of trade, college, and professional titles published each year—W. W. Norton & Company stands as the largest and oldest publishing house owned wholly by its employees.

This title is printed on permanent paper containing 30 percent postconsumer waste recycled fiber.

Book design by Antonina Krass
Production manager: Eric Pier-Hocking

Library of Congress Cataloging-in-Publication Data

Toomer, Jean, 1894–1967.
    Cane : authoritative text, contexts, criticism / Jean Toomer.—2nd ed. / edited
by Rudolph P. Byrd, Henry Louis Gates, Jr.
        p.   cm. — (A Norton critical edition)
    Includes bibliographical references.
    **ISBN 978-0-393-93168-6 (pbk.)**
    1. African Americans—Fiction.   2. Southern States—Fiction.   3. Toomer,
Jean, 1894–1967. Cane.   4. African Americans in literature.   I. Byrd,
Rudolph P.   II. Gates, Henry Louis.   III. Title.
    PS3539.O478C3 2010
    813' .52—dc22

                                                            2010039793

W. W. Norton & Company, Inc., 500 Fifth Avenue, New York, N.Y. 10110
wwnorton.com
W. W. Norton & Company Ltd., Castle House, 75/76 Wells Street,
London W1T 3QT

2   3   4   5   6   7   8   9   0

# Contents

# Criticism   175

# A Note on This Edition

"A man died in a rest home near Philadelphia on March 30 of this year [1967]. There have been no editorials in newspapers, no reminiscences in magazines. Probably few knew the name when they read the brief obituary in his hometown newspaper. He deserved more. In 1923 he was the most promising of them all."[1] Jean Toomer died of congestive heart failure in a nursing home outside of Philadelphia. Almost no one noticed. No one in the Harlem Renaissance could have possibly imagined that Jean Toomer, the author of that movement's most original work of literature, would one day die in obscurity. But as these things go, Toomer, in one of the great ironies in literary history, would be rediscovered in the Black Arts movement and canonized in the late 1960s and throughout the 1970s in African American Studies departments by scholars such as Darwin T. Turner and Charles T. Davis for creating one of the hallmarks of the African American literary tradition, a tradition from which Toomer did his best to flee. Building upon the example and scholarship of Turner, who edited the first Norton Critical Edition of *Cane* in 1988, we have sought, in this new edition, to map the expansion of scholarship on Toomer into the twenty-first century.

Part 1 of this Norton Critical Edition consists of the first edition of *Cane,* including the foreword by Toomer's friend, Waldo Frank, which introduced Toomer to a small, but nevertheless influential, contemporary readership, and which catalyzed the rupture among Frank, Toomer, and the book he had labored so diligently to produce.

Part 2 consists of two works of Toomer's autobiographical writing, and these illuminate important themes and phases in his development as an artist and as a teacher of the philosophy of Georges I. Gurdjieff, the Russian psychologist and mystic. These writings offer Toomer's own perspective on two vital stages in his search for what he termed an "intelligible scheme."[2] In "The Cane Years," a section

---

1. Darwin T. Turner, "And Another Passing," in *Jean Toomer: A Critical Evaluation,* ed. Thurman B. O'Daniel (Washington, D.C.: Howard University Press, 1988), 81.
2. "The Cane Years" was first published in Darwin T. Turner's *The Wayward and the Seeking: A Collection of Writings by Jean Toomer* (Washington, D.C.: Howard University Press, 1980), the first anthology of its kind that both answered questions and also generated new ones concerning the complex life of the author of *Cane.*

in the third version of an autobiography entitled "Outline of an Autobiography" (written between 1931 and 1932), Toomer reflects on his
life between 1920 and 1923. Here, he reconstructs his role as the
sole caretaker of his aging grandparents. He comments on his
struggle to find his voice during a critical phase in his apprenticeship as a writer; the challenges of becoming a writer; the range of
his readings in literature, religion, and philosophy; and race in
America. He also writes about his unpublished poem "The First
American," the ancestor of the epic "The Blue Meridian," both of
which elaborate his views on race. "The Cane Years" also contains
Toomer's quite lyrical reflections upon the Georgia landscape that
inspired his writing of *Cane* as well as reflections on the book's publication history and reception.

"Why I Entered the Gurdjieff Work," written in 1941, documents
the impact of his first encounters with Alfred Orage, the English
writer, editor, and teacher of the Gurdjieff method, and with Gurdjieff himself at Manhattan's Leslie Hall and the Neighborhood
Playhouse in January 1924. Here Toomer, accompanied by Margaret Naumburg (his lover and the estranged wife of Waldo Frank),
witnessed Gurdjieff's dances and exercises performed by the master himself. Toomer recalled that this experience "made me feel as a
wayfarer who was being recalled to his rightful way and destiny."
From January to July 1924, Toomer attended Orage's lectures in
New York, deepening his commitment to Gurdjieff. In July 1924,
he sailed from New York to Paris, and then traveled to Gurdjieff's
Institute for the Harmonious Development of Man, located in
Fontainebleau-Avon. Toomer was in residence at the institute
from July to October 1924. When he returned to New York that
fall, he began what would prove to be a lifelong commitment as a
teacher of this system, soon rivaling Orage himself in his knowledge and command of Gurdjieff's philosophy of psychological
transformation, and in the number of students and disciples he
attracted. Published together here for the first time, "The Cane
Years" and "Why I Entered the Gurdjieff Work" provide invaluable
testimony, in Toomer's own words, about crucial events between
1920 and 1924 that had profound consequences upon his emerging and quite fluid sense of himself as an artist and spiritual
reformer.

Our third section consists of correspondence written between
1919 and 1930. This eleven-year correspondence arranged in chronological order provides an illustrative context for the autobiographical writings of the previous section, especially for "The Cane Years."
In these letters, we acquire a clear sense of Toomer's relationship to
other writers and intellectuals of his generation. Put another way,
through these letters we begin to appreciate the depth and complex-

ity of his relationship to the two communities of writers in Washington, D.C., and New York to which Toomer belonged.

Toomer's letters to Alain Locke and Georgia Douglas Johnson provide us with a window into the black world of the Saturday Nighters, the literary salon hosted by Johnson in her Washington townhouse and attended by Locke, Countee Cullen, and other luminaries of the Harlem Renaissance. At the same time, in his letters to Waldo Frank, Sherwood Anderson, John McClure, and Gorham B. Munson, Toomer emerges as a figure of growing power and significance among the writers of the "Lost Generation." Through these letters, we have sought to reveal the nature and depth of the various relationships Toomer cultivated in both communities, and the particular value he placed upon these evolving relationships. Moreover, these letters reveal the thoughtful manner in which Toomer was conceptualizing the work that would become *Cane*. In the correspondence, his stance is one of an artist thinking deeply about the relationship between theme and form, as one of the leading experimentalists of his generation. Toomer emerges as a writer keenly aware of his gifts in relation to contemporaries whose work he respected.

We also acquire a portrait of Toomer as an artist of considerable ambition, particularly in his correspondence with Frank, McClure, and the poet and editor Claude McKay. Here we witness Toomer engaged in the necessary, unglamorous work of self-promotion, with his goal to persuade key figures in the American literary establishment to publish his work. The letters offer a unique way to think about Toomer's evolving positions on race. In his correspondence with his publisher, Horace Liveright, we encounter Toomer's opinion about the controversy regarding his racial self-fashioning, and witness how the marketing goals of a powerful publisher collided with his vision of himself as an emerging, raceless artist.

Similarly, in his letters to James Weldon Johnson and Georgia O'Keeffe, we become aware of the consistency of Toomer's position on his own racial identification, and the passionate manner in which he articulated and defended it to skeptical, even hostile, associates. Here we can begin to sense not only that Toomer was fleeing the Negro world, but he was also attempting to move toward something not merely or exclusively "white," a cosmopolitan world more broadly defined than traditional, received categories of "race" in America would allow. We can glean in these letters early signs of a certain fatigue engendered by the need to explain his unorthodox stance about race, again and again, sometimes defensively, sometimes like a prophet of a new way of seeing and thinking about ethnicity. Toomer's correspondence also allows us to compare his broader opinions about the function, value, and direction of the arts in civil society with those of his modernist contemporaries, black and white.

Our final section contains the reviews and articles that we think representative of the best criticism and scholarship published about Toomer. Arranged in chronological order, these texts span the period from 1923 to 2008; thus, they mark the effort of Toomer's contemporaries and those who came to his work after his death in 1967 to plumb the meanings of a dense and sometimes enigmatic work of art. The earliest assessments of *Cane* are all full of praise. Montgomery Gregory, a Harvard University graduate like his Howard University colleague Alain Locke, wrote the first substantive review of *Cane,* in 1923. Robert Littell's review followed a few weeks later in the *New Republic.* The chorus of praise continued from W. E. B. Du Bois, Alain Locke, Gorham Munson, and Paul Rosenfeld, among others. Toomer had made his mark upon both of the communities of writers and intellectuals who claimed him as their own.

The various articles by scholars address a range of vital questions, including Toomer's precise relationship to the writers of the New Negro movement and the Lost Generation, and thus to the project of modernism; his strengths and weaknesses as a dramatist; the thematic unity within *Cane*; the integral relationship of the poems to the various stories in the work; the impact of region upon imagination and identity; and Toomer's theories of race and his shifting positions on his own identity, which, of course, informed his vision of his life and art. These essays by Robert Bone, Darwin T. Turner, John M. Reilly, Catherine L. Innes, Bernard Bell, Charles T. Davis, Charles Scruggs, George B. Hutchinson, Barbara Foley, Emily Lutenski, Mark Whalan, and Nellie Y. McKay shaped the scholarly discourse on Toomer between his rediscovery in the late 1960s and his canonization in the classroom over the past forty years.

These views of scholars and critics are balanced by assessments of other creative writers. Waldo Frank's historic foreword, which is as much a record of a friendship as it is testimony of a writer's assessment of the achievement of a fellow writer, is the first of these, followed by the perspectives of such writers as Sterling A. Brown, Langston Hughes, and Arna Bontemps, all of whom were also Toomer's contemporaries. Bontemps arranged for the Toomer papers to be deposited at Fisk University in 1962, long before they became part of the James Weldon Johnson Memorial Collection of Negro Arts and Letters at Yale University in 1985, through discussions that Henry Louis Gates, Jr., initiated with Toomer's widow in 1980. Bontemps, moreover, wrote the introduction to the 1969 edition of *Cane,* and it was this edition that exposed the text to a new generation of readers, especially black writers and critics hungry for seminal precedents. Along with essays by Brown, Hughes, and Bontemps, we have included essays by Alice Walker, David Bradley, and Gayl Jones who in their collective testimony provide us with evidence of

Toomer's formal appeal to his literary heirs. A chronology of Toomer's life, created by Cynthia E. Kerman and Richard Eldridge, Toomer's biographers, follows the contemporary criticism and reviews.

The critical writings gathered here are evidence of the richness of *Cane*'s critical reception, and its continuing vitality as a seminal work in both the canon of American modernism and the canon of African American literature. They also testify to a certain fascination with one of the first black authors to question and attempt to deconstruct America's peculiar social definitions of race. How could a writer who wrote such a "black" text at the beginning of the Harlem Renaissance (a text that helped to catalyze that movement, really) seemingly then seek to flee it and the cultural heritage that his work of fiction enshrined, only to have his literary reputation revived by militant black cultural nationalists and African American scholars in the academy in the late 1960s?

The ironies of Toomer's life and death and literary resurrection abound. Perhaps a new generation of readers, in an era of multiculturalism and the self-conscious proclamation of mixed-race identities, will find in Jean Toomer both a prophet of the deconstruction of essentialized American definitions of "race," definitions rooted in a profoundly racist metaphysics, and a harbinger of the fluidity and multiplicity of our social identities, identities always and inevitably socially constructed, not biological or natural. Perhaps. The essays collected here provide a record of the fresh and original ways that generations of readers have interpreted Toomer's text and what we might think of as the text of Toomer. But they also, we hope, provide a framework for new and perhaps more sympathetic theorizing about Toomer's theories of race and about *Cane*, the magical, lyrical masterpiece of black literature that continues to intrigue us almost ninety years after it was published. As Toomer himself put it: "The setting was crude in a way, but strangely rich and beautiful. I began feeling its effects despite my state, or, perhaps, just because of it. There was the valley, the valley of 'Cane,' with smoke-wreaths during the day and mist at night . . ."

Rudolph P. Byrd                          Henry Louis Gates, Jr.
Emory University                         Harvard University

# Acknowledgments

We wish to acknowledge the support of friends and colleagues in bringing this Second Norton Critical Edition of *Cane* to publication: Elizabeth Alexander, Louise Bernard, the late Arna Bontemps, John F. Callahan, Glenda Carpio, Johnnetta B. Cole, the late Marjorie Content-Toomer, Adelaide Cromwell, Angela De Leon, Amy Gosdanian, Sharon Harley, Michael S. Harper, Evelyn Brooks Higginbotham, Cecelia Corbin Hunter, Dorcas Ford Jones, Joanne Kendall, Jeffrey B. Leak, Henry A. Leonard, Michael Page, Hollis Robbins, Seth Rosenbaum, Mark A. Sanders, Beverly Guy Sheftall, Megan Smolenyak Smolenyak, Jennifer Snodgrass, Werner Sollors, John Stauffer, Yolande Tomlinson, Natasha Trethewey, Alice Walker, Abby Wolf, Donald Yacovone, and the staff of the Manuscript, Archive and Rare Book Library of Emory University. The editors also would like to gratefully acknowledge Mark Whalan's *The Letters of Jean Toomer, 1919–1924* (2006), from which the majority of the letters that appear in this volume are reprinted.

# Introduction

## "Song of the Son": The Emergence and Passing of Jean Toomer

### by Rudolph P. Byrd and Henry Louis Gates, Jr.

Toomer[†]

I did not wish to "rise above"
or "move beyond" my race. I wished

to contemplate who I was beyond
my body, this container of flesh.

I made up a language in which to exist.
I wondered what God breathed into me.

I wondered who I was beyond
this complicated, milk-skinned, genital-ed body.

I exercised it, watched it change and grow.
I spun like a dervish to see what would happen. Oh,

to be a Negro is—is?—
to be a Negro, is. To be.

(*Jean Toomer*)

—Elizabeth Alexander

"The setting was crude in a way," Jean Toomer would recall of the rural Georgia landscape that inspired him to write *Cane*, "but strangely rich and beautiful. I began feeling its effects despite my state, or, perhaps, just because of it. There was a valley, the valley of 'Cane,' with smoke-wreaths during the day and mist at night." And in that valley, Toomer encountered, perhaps for the first time, the spirituals, the traditional music of the African American sacred

---

[†] "Toomer," from *Crave Radiance: New and Selected Poems 1990–2010*. Copyright © 2010 by Elizabeth Alexander. Reprinted with the permission of Graywolf Press and the author.

vernacular: "A family of back-country Negroes had only recently moved into a shack not too far away. They sang. And this was the first time I'd ever heard the folk-songs and spirituals. They were very rich and sad and joyous and beautiful."[1] In this lyrical remembrance of things all-too-soon to pass, Toomer suggests something of the beauty and poignancy of a landscape, a people, and an art form in transition in the first quarter of the twentieth century, a moment he would render in a loving yet searching experimental form, in the single work that would define his career and his legacy as a writer. *Cane*, a compelling, haunting amalgam of fiction, poetry, and drama unified formally and thematically and replete with leitmotifs, would elevate Toomer, virtually overnight, to the status of a canonical writer in two branches of American modernism: the writers and critics who compose the New Critics and the "Lost Generation," and those who compose the New Negro movement or the Harlem Renaissance. Toomer was an important, admired, influential figure in both of these articulations of high American modernism, which reached their zenith in the 1920s and which unfolded downtown and uptown, respectively, in New York City.

The man who would startle his small but enthusiastic readership with the originality of *Cane* entered the cultural world of the Lost Generation downtown in Greenwich Village primarily through his close friend, the writer and critic, Waldo Frank. Uptown, simultaneously, Toomer was emerging as one of the New Negro writers of the Harlem Renaissance, chiefly through the stewardship of its erstwhile "dean," Alain Locke, who edited the movement's signature manifesto, *The New Negro,* in 1925. In the two or three years preceding the publication of *Cane* in 1923, Toomer—perhaps more than any other black writer—moved seemingly effortlessly between these two cultural worlds. Both movements were shaped by their own vibrant and defiant theories of language, art, culture, and history, some of which they shared, some of which they did not. But both, in their ways, challenged, to an unprecedented degree, conventional American definitions of race and social strictures defined by the so-called color line. In so very many ways, these two movements were mutually constitutive, Janus faces of a larger, unfolding concept of American modernism, although they have been frequently and mistakenly cast as discrete, isolated formations in American literature and culture.[2]

1. Jean Toomer, "The Cane Years," in *The Wayward and The Seeking: A Collection of Writings by Jean Toomer,* ed. Darwin T. Turner (Washington, D.C.: Howard University Press, 1980), 123.
2. Perhaps the earliest scholar to query Toomer's relationship to the writers of the "Lost Generation" and the New Negro movement or Harlem Renaissance was Robert A. Bone in *The Negro Novel in America* (1958). Since then Toomer's relationship to the communities of writers who collectively constitute the various forms of American modernism has been examined by Rudolph P. Byrd, Charles T. Davis, Ann Douglas, Richard

Jean Toomer, circa 1932. Jean Toomer Papers, Yale Collection of American Literature, Beinecke and Rare Book Manuscript Library.

Raised as an African American but, to most observers, racially indeterminate, Toomer embodied in his person, in his disposition, and in his art many of the signal elements—hybridity, alienation,

Eldridge, Genevieve Fabre, Maria Farland, Michel Feith, Alice P. Fisher, Karen S. Ford, S. P. Fullwinder, Henry Louis Gates, Jr., Jane Goldman, Nathan Grant, Leonard Harris, Mark Helbling, George Hutchinson, Robert B. Jones, Cynthia R. Kerman, Catherine G. Kodat, Victor Kramer, Vera Kutzinski, Charles R. Larson, Nellie Y. McKay, Charles Molesworth, Arnold Rampersad, Frederick L. Rusch, Mark A. Sanders, Charles Scruggs, Robert B. Stepto, Alan Trachtenberg, Darwin T. Turner, Mark Whalan, and Jon Woodson, among other scholars.

fragmentation, dislocation, migration, fluidity, experimentation—
that define American modernism, and that he would so imaginatively
address in *Cane*. Throughout his life, Toomer displayed a marked
ambivalence toward his Negro ancestry, addressing it—or erasing
it—again and again in his posthumously published autobiographical writings. The relation of this deep and abiding ambivalence to
the various forms of fragmentation that wind their way through
*Cane* has intrigued critics virtually since *Cane* was published in
1923. Indeed, one could say that the great theme of *Cane* is fragmentation itself, rendered through close and careful encounters
between blacks and blacks, and blacks and whites, in an almost
mythic, transitional, pre-Jazz Age, Jim Crow rural South. Toomer tells
us that the impact of the southern agrarian setting upon his northern, urbane sensibility was dramatic, referring to the psychological
and emotional "state" created by his first encounters with southern
black culture in the town of Sparta, Georgia. Put another way,
Toomer is describing the particular structures of feeling and thought
generated when he encountered a region of the country that fundamentally shaped his parents and grandparents, a region about which
he would grow increasingly ambivalent almost as soon as, if not
before, he published *Cane*.

Jean Toomer was born Nathan Pinchback Toomer on December
26, 1894, in Washington, D.C., the first and only child of Nina
Pinchback and Nathan Toomer, both African Americans. Toomer's
name at birth was the source of some controversy in a family that,
from the start, seems to have been totally devoted to him. This controversy is, in its way, emblematic of what would become Toomer's
own preoccupation with naming and self-definition, with determining what to call himself and how to define himself ethnically, and
with exercising control over his public image in a society that favored
the shorthand of labels, especially when defining a person's color
or race.

Toomer's middle name, Pinchback, linked him directly to his
grandfather, Pinckney Benton Stewart Pinchback (1837–1921), the
husband of Nina Emily Hethorn, with whom he had four children.
P. B. S. Pinchback (as he was known) was the son of Major William
Pinchback, a white Virginia planter, and Eliza Stewart, a mulatto
slave, and the brother of an undetermined number of siblings, some
of whom disappeared into the white world. Born a free Negro in
Macon, Georgia, in 1837, Pinchback was a captain in the second
regiment of Louisiana's Native Guard, the black soldiers in the white
army who fought on the side of the Union during the Civil War,
from October 1862 to September 1863. As the only "cullid officer"
at Fort Pike, he served as the spokesman for his fellow black offi-
cers who were unrelenting in their protest of the discrimination

experienced by the black enlisted men under their command in the Union Army.[3] Pinchback would become, during Reconstruction, the first black lieutenant governor of Louisiana. For thirty-five days in December 1872 to January 1873, he even served as the Acting Governor.[4] Pinchback's "brief tenure as acting governor was the political high-water mark for Louisiana blacks during the nineteenth century."[5] A colorful and imperial figure who was sometimes mistaken for Andrew Carnegie, Pinchback derived his wealth from lucrative investments and political appointments, and derived his influence and standing within the deeply stratified society of Washington, D.C., to which he moved after his political career ended in Louisiana, from his historic achievements in office, and his light-skin privilege, often a visible marker of class.

The grandson would recount with some pride the grandfather's improbable, dramatic rise to power in the corrupting, byzantine, and multicultural world of the Pelican State, speculating that his motives for becoming a public servant were perhaps not entirely altruistic, even suggesting, incredulously, that Pinchback may have been a white man who only passed for black to facilitate his chances of being elected in Reconstruction Louisiana: "Then, the war ended and the black men freed and enfranchised, came Pinchback's opportunity in the political arena. He claimed he had Negro blood, linked himself with the cause of the Negro, and rose to power. How much he was an opportunist, how much he was in sincere sympathy with the freedmen, is a matter which need not concern us here . . . it would be interesting if we knew what Pinchback himself believed about his racial heredity. Did he believe he had some Negro blood? Did he not? I do not know. What I do know is this—his belief or disbelief would have had no necessary relation to the facts—and this holds true as regards his Scotch-Welsh-German and other bloods also."[6]

Nowhere, to our knowledge, was Pinchback ever ambivalent about being a Negro, even if, as W. E. B. Du Bois once wrote of him, to "all intents and purposes . . . [he] was an educated well-to-do congenial white man with but a few drops of Negro blood," as fair as, say, the novelist Charles W. Chesnutt or the civil rights leader Walter

3. James G. Hollandsworth, Jr., *The Louisiana Native Guards: The Black Military Experience During the Civil War* (Baton Rouge: Louisiana State University Press, 1995), 73.
4. Ibid., 111.
5. Ibid., 111. As a lawmaker, Pinchback sponsored civil rights legislation that granted blacks equal access in public transportation, business, and places of entertainment. He also introduced legislation in Louisiana's 1879 constitutional convention that would establish a "university for the education of persons of color." This legislation would lead to the establishment of Southern University in 1880. From 1883 to 1885, Pinchback served on the board of trustees of Southern University. See pp. 108 and 115 in Hollandsworth's *The Louisiana Native Guards*.
6. *The Wayward and the Seeking*, 23–24.

White.[7] In fact, elsewhere in his writings, when discussing why he attended an all-black elementary school, Henry Highland Garnet, in Washington, Toomer contradicts himself about Pinchback's racial identity: "For Pinckney Benston Stewart Pinchback to send his grandson to a white school, no, that will not do. It might look as if he were going back on his race and wanting me to be white."[8] Toomer is being disingenuous here, however; schools in Washington, D.C., were rigorously segregated; Pinchback would have had no choice, even if, as does not appear to be the case, he had sought to educate his grandson across the color line. Clearly the issue of his grandfather's ethnic ancestry was a vexed one for Toomer, one crucial for him to position and reposition as he sought to redefine his own racial identity.

And a large part of his strategy of strongly implying that his grandfather most probably was "passing for black" was rooted in Toomer's desire to paint the roots of this branch of his family tree white; to do so, he had to stress that Pinchback was the political opportunist par excellence: "I say he [Pinchback] was an adventurer. I think he was. I doubt that he saw himself bearing a mission to secure and maintain the rights of the freedmen."[9] His grandfather, moreover, Toomer reasoned, saw in the Louisiana of Reconstruction a certain fluidity of identity that allowed for an unprecedented amount of social mobility: "More than anything else Pinchback saw himself as a winner of a dangerous game. He liked to play the game. He liked to win. This—the reconstruction situation in Louisiana—was the chance his personal ambition had been waiting for. He was not a reformer. He was not primarily a fighter for a general human cause. He was, or was soon to become, a politician—but far more picturesque, courageous, and able than the majority of the men who bear that name."[1] If his grandfather had been a white man who passed for black, perhaps his grandson could be a black man who could pass for white.

Despite Toomer's highly dubious claim about his grandfather's racial identity, his assessment of his grandfather's career in politics is all the more compelling for being critical and unsentimental. Clearly, P. B. S. Pinchback was a man who inspired a great degree of awe, in Toomer and in just about everyone else: "For myself—I was fascinated by him. His goings and comings were the big events in the house . . . No one could speak to me and make me laugh and get me excited the way he could. He made me feel I was having a

---

7. Barbara Foley, "Jean Toomer's Washington and the Politics of Class: From 'Blue Veins' to Seventh-street Rebels," *Modern Fiction Studies* 42.2 (1996): 298.
8. Ibid., 313.
9. *The Wayward and the Seeking*, 24.
1. Ibid., 25.

part in everything he did. Sometimes he would take me downtown with him and I might even have lunch with 'the men,' who made much to-do over me, giving me the feeling that I was the scion of a great family."[2] "This was my grandfather as I knew him," Toomer writes with fond admiration. "I saw him as a dashing commanding figure, the centre of an unknown but exciting world. He created an atmosphere which thrilled me; and there is no doubt that his image, and the picture and sense of his life, were deeply impressed upon me, later to function as an unconscious ideal for myself, for how I wished to look and be; and also to serve as standards by means of which I measured men and life."[3]

Toomer's loving portrait of his grandfather as a bold and questing Victorian patriarch, however, is complicated by the fact that as he grew into adulthood, he was often at war with Pinchback, who grew increasingly bewildered and disappointed by his scion's seeming lack of purpose and direction. "Not till I was seven could I rule my mother and grandmother," Toomer tells us; but "Not till I was twenty-seven did I finally conquer my grandfather."[4] While his relationship with Pinchback would become increasingly fraught, Toomer, nevertheless, dutifully and lovingly cared for his grandfather in the final weeks of his life, immediately following his pivotal sojourn in Georgia. "Once again in Washington I had my grandfather brought back from the hospital. His condition there was too pitiable for me to bear. He touched my heart so strongly that I resolved to care for him till the very end. And this I did."[5] Precisely as Pinchback's health declined, Toomer found his voice as an artist: "He sank very rapidly. All during December I nursed him; and, at the same time, I wrote the materials of *Cane*. In these last days he seemed to know just what I meant to him. I knew and realized all he had done for me."[6]

In the small apartment he also shared with his resilient, long-suffering grandmother, Toomer and Pinchback reconciled in the days before his death, precisely as he was completing the powerful, final, haunting section of his first book: "Our almost life-long struggle and contest was finished, and all my love and gratitude for the once so forceful and dominant but now so broken and tragic man came to the fore. He died the day after I had finished the first draft of 'Kabnis,' the long semi-dramatic closing-piece of *Cane*."[7] Toomer would write to Waldo Frank that "Kabnis is *Me*," one of his last admissions of his awareness of the primacy of his own Negro ancestry in the

2. Ibid., 35–36.
3. Ibid., 30.
4. Ibid., 17.
5. Ibid., 124.
6. Ibid., 124.
7. Ibid., 124.

shaping of his cultural and ethnic identity. But it is altogether reasonable to speculate that the powerful, quasi-mythic encounter at *Kabnis*'s conclusion—between the northern, mulatto would-be intellectual and old, black Father John, the haunting figure of the slave past—was informed by this final, intense encounter and reconciliation between Toomer and Pinchback himself.

Toomer's Christian name and surname tie him to his father, Nathan Toomer. Born in 1839 in Chatham County, North Carolina, Nathan was the slave of Richard Pilkinson, who subsequently sold him to John Toomer.[8] When John Toomer died in 1859, his brother Henry Toomer purchased Nathan, his mother, Kit, and seven of her children from the estate. Nathan became the body servant of Henry Toomer, and adopted the surname of the family who had purchased him and most of his family. In the 1860s, Nathan Toomer married Harriet, a mulatta with whom he had four daughters. After Harriet's death in 1890, Toomer married Amanda America Dickson, regarded as "the richest colored woman alive."[9] Dickson, born in 1849, was the daughter of David Dickson, a prosperous planter of Hancock County, Georgia, and Julia Frances Lewis Dickson, a mulatta. Amanda was reared in the Dickson household by Elizabeth Dickson, her paternal grandmother. When David Dickson died in 1885 he left much of his estate, valued at approximately $400,000, including 15,000 acres of land, to Amanda America Dickson. Nathan Toomer and Amanda Dickson married on August 7, 1891, and took up residence in her well-appointed mansion located on Telfair Street among the wealthy white elite in Augusta, Georgia. Almost two years later, on June 11, 1893, Amanda would die, from "complications of disease."[1] Since Amanda left no will, Nathan found himself in a protracted court battle over the disposition of the estate with his two stepchildren, Julian and Charles, whom Amanda bore in her first marriage to Charles Eubanks, a white Civil War veteran. Adhering to the terms of David Dickson's will, the court awarded the bulk of Amanda's estate to her children.[2]

Nathan Toomer was a handsome widower in search of new sources of income as well as a third wife. Both of these needs were met in the person of Nina Pinchback, whom he met in December 1893. They met at her Bacon Street home during a "housewarming reception" hosted by her parents.[3] Soon after, Nathan began courting Nina. Three months later on March 24, 1894, they were married by

8. Kent Anderson Leslie and Willard B. Gatewood, Jr., "'This Father of Mine . . . a Sort of Mystery': Jean Toomer's Georgia Heritage," *The Georgia Historical Quarterly* LXXVII. 4 (Winter 1993): 793.
9. Ibid., 790.
1. Ibid., 798.
2. Ibid., 794.
3. Ibid., 789.

none other than the Reverend Francis J. Grimké, the nephew of the South Carolina abolitionists and suffragettes Angelina Weld and Sarah Moore Grimké, a graduate of Lincoln, Howard, and Princeton universities, co-founder of the American Negro Academy, and the very able and famous pastor of Washington's 15th Street Presbyterian Church. Grimké was a celebrity himself, as grand and as well known as Pinchback.

Pinchback objected to the marriage volcanically, disapproving of Nathan Toomer for several reasons. First of all, Nathan was twenty-seven years older than Nina (Pinchback himself was only two years older than his son-in-law). Second, he had been previously married. Third, Nathan impressed Pinchback as being "unreliable,"[4] perhaps because Nathan engendered a certain disturbing sense of self-recognition of his own adventurous past and temperament. But the Governor was accurate, indeed, prophetic in his identification of this defect in his future son-in-law's character. Nathan deserted Nina within a year of their marriage. Nevertheless, their only child refused to cast the failed union in a disreputable light: "I have been told and have reason to believe it was a love marriage. This was the one clear affirmation of her [Nina's] life."[5] Without an income, she was unable to support herself in the home located on Twelfth Street, which her husband had irresponsibly purchased with $12,000 in cash for his bride and infant son. Converting the bridal nest into rental property, Nina was forced to return, most reluctantly, to the Bacon Street home of her parents.

Predictably, the Governor "set conditions for readmitting his wayward daughter and her infant son. The biggest stumbling block was the boy's name."[6] Intent upon nothing short of patronymic erasure of the errant Nathan Toomer, Pinchback insisted that "if he was to support the baby," the surname had to be "legally changed to Pinchback and the first name changed to anything else."[7] According to Cynthia Earl Kerman and Richard Eldridge, "Nina rejected that proposed legal action but accepted the family's informal adaptation. The first name was soon replaced by Eugene, after Eugene Laval, [Toomer's] godfather . . ."[8] Throughout his life, Toomer's grandparents addressed him as Eugene Pinchback, while his mother stubbornly addressed him as Eugene Toomer, though she herself had reverted to her family name, Pinchback. Toomer's playmates on Bacon Street, he writes, called him "Pinchy—short for Pinchback. To them I was a

---

4. *The Lives of Jean Toomer: A Hunger for Wholeness* (Baton Rouge: Louisiana State University Press, 1987), 26.
5. *The Wayward and the Seeking*, 33.
6. *The Lives of Jean Toomer*, 28.
7. Ibid., 28.
8. Ibid., 28.

Jean Toomer as a young boy. Undated. Jean Toomer Papers, Yale Collection of American Literature, Beinecke and Rare Book Manuscript Library.

Pinchback. They knew nothing of Toomer."[9] "In my own home there were still other names," he confides. "Mother called me Booty [after beauty]. Uncle Bis called me Kid. Uncle Walter—Snootz. And grandfather—the little whippersnapper. I was, then, well-supplied."[1]

9. Ibid., 35.
1. Ibid., 35.

When he made the commitment to become a writer, Toomer gave himself the androgynous name of Jean, which stemmed from his admiration of Romain Rolland's novel *Jean-Christophe*.[2] During the 1930s and the 1940s, Toomer published under the name of N. J. Toomer, initials for Nathan Jean, for two reasons: first, to distance himself from *Cane* and the racial identity of its author, since *Cane* was the work by which he had come to be known as a Negro writer; and second, to mark a rebirth in his life, following his conversion to Quakerism, a rebirth that marked a certain return. By taking the name Nathan Jean, Toomer himself had come full circle, finally rendering futile his family's efforts to banish the memory of his father, Nathan.

The memory of the father kindled the imagination of the son. For years, Toomer kept a photograph of his father, from which he constructed a rather fanciful portrait of Nathan as a "handsome stirring," wealthy planter from Georgia.[3] And Toomer, in the drafts of an autobiography that he never published, wistfully re-creates the first and only meeting between the two. It is clear that through this anecdote, Toomer sought to recuperate his father from grandfather Pinchback's relentless traducing. Nathan Toomer returned to Washington in 1900, six years after Toomer's birth, and during this visit, according to Jean, he materialized before the Bacon Street house, presumably to see his son. Because he refused to pay alimony of $60 per month and the court costs of his divorce from Nina, the Supreme Court of the District of Columbia on January 20, 1899, declared Nathan in contempt. Nathan's return to Washington, accordingly, carried with it considerable risk; he could have been arrested and jailed.

One afternoon while playing in his front yard, Toomer tells us that he found himself in the arms of a stranger he intuitively recognized as his father: "I do not know how I knew him. But, soon, I was running up the way a bit towards a large man who was holding out his arms to me. He took me in them, raised me and kissed me, and I liked him very much. He said things to me which I didn't understand, but I knew he was my father and that he was showing how much he loved me and what a fine little man I had grown to be. He raised me high in the air, and then he saw mother come out. He lowered me, pressed a bright silver half-dollar in my hand, kissed me again, and told me to run back to her. He went off."[4] It was their first and only meeting, and it is clear that Toomer carefully nurtured this memory of his father, which uncannily recalls the first encounter between the mixed-race protagonist and his white father in James

2. Ibid., 101.
3. For Toomer's portrait of his father Nathan Toomer see *The Wayward and the Seeking*, 32–33.
4. *The Wayward and the Seeking*, 34.

Weldon Johnson's novel, *The Autobiography of an Ex-Coloured Man* (1912), a novel about passing, itself "passing" as autobiography.[5]

Though he knew nothing of his father's marriage to Amanda America Dickson, over time Toomer's memory of his father acquired a certain luster through his inheritance of artifacts that once belonged to him: "The only worldly possessions that came to me from him were some beautiful large silk handkerchiefs, a set of small diamond shirt studs, and a slender ebony cane with a gold head."[6] While Nathan Toomer never saw his son again, in correspondence between the elder Toomer and an acquaintance, Whitefield McKinlay, of Washington, D.C., between 1898 and 1905, there is evidence of his father's continued, genuine interest in a son whom he called in his letters to McKinlay the "Little Colonel."[7] Some years later, in the very Sparta, Georgia, that inspired *Cane,* the "Little Colonel" would encounter someone who had actually known his father—a barber who claimed to have some knowledge of Nathan Toomer. According to Kerman and Eldridge, Toomer asked the barber "whether his father had been regarded by the community as white or 'colored,'" and the barber "replied that Nathan stayed at the white hotel, did business with white men, and courted a black woman."[8] Like his grandfather and his father, Jean Toomer would live in both the black and the white worlds over the course of his life, and in both worlds the act of naming and self-definition would remain an obsession with him. There is new evidence that, like the nameless protagonist of James Weldon Johnson's novel, Toomer did in fact pass for white, as many of his black literary contemporaries assumed or believed he did.

Toomer's uncle, Bismarck Pinchback, also played a profoundly important role in his development. Bismarck was the second of his grandfather's three sons, along with Pinckney and Walter. It was Uncle Bis who introduced the "Kid," as he called him, to the world of literature, science, and the life of the mind, gradually inculcating in him a desire to become a writer. Toomer lovingly acknowledged Bismarck's role in his larger education, recalling how his relationship with his uncle transformed itself into that of master and apprentice: "Then something happened which swiftly transferred my interests from the world of things to the world of ideas and imagination. Uncle Bis and I suddenly discovered each other. He had been there all along, and his sensitivity and affection had drawn me

5. See *Jean Toomer's Racial Self-Identification,* lxvi.
6. *The Lives of Jean Toomer,* 27.
7. "'This Father of Mine . . . a Sort of Mystery': Jean Toomer's Georgia Heritage," 802–809.
8. *The Lives of Jean Toomer,* 85.

to him. . . . All at once the veils of familiarity dropped from our eyes and each in his own way beheld the wonder of the other."[9]

Bismarck Pinchback, a civil servant, was an avid reader and possessed some literary ambitions of his own. According to Toomer, his uncle was his Virgil, his first nurturing guide to the far shores of the imagination. Toomer vividly recounts his uncle's evening ritual of reading and writing in bed: "There he would get in bed with a book, cigarettes, and a saucer of sliced peaches prepared with sugar in a special way, and read far into the night. Sometimes he would write, trying his hand at fiction. . . . This position—my uncle in bed surrounded by the materials of a literary man—was impressed upon me as one of the desirable positions in life."[1] Bismarck was the father figure that neither Nathan nor his grandfather could ever be, and to him Toomer gives all the credit for the life of thought and feeling that he would pursue: "By nature he was far more the artist and thinker than a man of action; and, as far as possible, he evoked the thinker in me."[2] Bismarck Toomer would be the last black man whom Toomer would acknowledge as a shaping influence on the man of letters he would become.

Bismarck introduced Toomer not only to literature but also to physics and to astronomy, especially the earth's relation to other planets in the universe. "It was all wonderful," Toomer so fondly remembers. "And, young though I was, I was growing a sense of and forming an attitude towards my and our position on earth and in the universe. I had a new way of seeing things. This was the beginning of my world view. And for this alone I will be forever grateful to my uncle for having taken such interest in me." Bismarck would read historical works to his nephew, as well as "myths and fables, folk tales, romances and adventures. Often he would phrase the tale in his own words and himself tell it. He liked to do this. . . . For myself—I eagerly absorbed them. My imagination took flight and I was thrilled to follow it into those worlds of wonder."[3] Bismarck's gas-light tutorials in the Bacon Street house constituted Toomer's first meaningful introduction to the wonders of learning. At a time when he perhaps most needed it, Uncle Bismarck functioned as both teacher and mentor to his nephew, and thus provided him with a means by which to apprehend his potential as an intellectual, and more especially as thinker and writer: "He was, in truth, my real teacher. In comparison with him and with what I learned from him, my formal teachers and schooling were as nothing. . . . I truly learned with and from Bismarck. . . . Our evenings together were

9. *The Wayward and the Seeking*, 41–42.
1. Ibid., 42.
2. Ibid., 42.
3. Ibid., 44.

periods of genuine education. . . . My mind was born and nurtured during those times with him."[4]

As we have seen, Toomer attended the all-black Henry Highland Garnet School (named in honor of the pioneering nineteenth-century black nationalist) for his elementary education, and then the famous Paul Laurence Dunbar High School, previously known as M Street High School, the District's first public high school for African Americans, named after the famous black poet, from which he graduated in 1914. Dunbar High School was more like a black private school, an Exeter or Andover for African Americans, than a normal public school. Its teachers and students, incredibly, included several members of the Negro intellectual elite, the group that W. E. B. Du Bois would call "the talented tenth," the "college-bred Negro." Among its stellar alumni were the poet Sterling A. Brown, the feminist Nannie Helen Burroughs, the physician Charles R. Drew, and the lawyer and civil rights advocate Charles Hamilton Houston. (Both Brown and Houston would take advanced degrees from Harvard.) Dunbar High School's distinguished faculty included many Ph.D.'s, such as the sociologist Kelly Miller and the Harvard-trained historian, Carter G. Woodson, along with the woman's rights activist Mary Church Terrell, poet Angelina Weld Grimké (the niece of Reverend Frances J. Grimké, who had married Toomer's parents), and Anna Julia Cooper, Toomer's Latin teacher, the first African American to earn a Ph.D. at the Sorbonne. Scholars who should have been professors in the Ivy League found their best job opportunities at this public high school.

Despite these extraordinarily well-trained teachers, however, Toomer's education at school was apparently not nearly as fulfilling as those evenings spent with his beloved Uncle Bismarck, when he was the center of attention and Bismarck's mesmerizing pedagogical methods opened his nephew's mind to facts and mysteries at a pace that suited him best. Toomer found in Bismarck a badly needed father figure, of course; but he also had learning difficulties that even a school as sophisticated as Dunbar would have been ill-prepared to meet: "I had difficulty in learning to read. For some reason or other, try as hard as I would I couldn't get on the inside of the thing: the letters and characters obstinately withheld their sense from me, and the lines of words behind which meaning lurked were like closed doors which stubbornly refused me entrance. I gazed with hopeless amazement at the older children, the teacher, the grownup members of my family who read so easily and seemed

4. Ibid., 45, 48.

to think nothing of it."[5] Whether Toomer was dyslexic or merely a slow reader it is difficult to know, but in due course he overcame this frustration with deciphering the written word: "In time, however, reading had become just an ordinary thing which I was compelled to continue. I found but little to attract me in the various school readers. Some of the stories I liked, but they were not half as wonderful as those told me by Bismarck, and moreover, whatever pleasure or interest they may have had for me was spoiled when they were put through the mill of classroom recitations."[6]

Toomer, like many people with learning disabilities embarrassed by their inability to learn at a pace with other students, created diversions in school: "I was the class-room cut up," he recalls, "and the teacher's problem."[7] Kerman and Eldridge speculate that Toomer's disruptive classroom behavior may have had its roots in his resentment at being separated from his white friends on Bacon Street and the shock of attending a black school: "Surely resentment at being arbitrarily shut out of his group, as well as the inevitable lack of resources at a black school in Washington at the height of the Jim Crow era, would have affected what was offered to him and how Jean would accept it."[8] Though highly unlikely, as we shall see, these factors could possibly explain why the "little whippersnapper," as his grandfather called him, was uncomfortable at the Garnet School, and necessarily at odds with its pedagogy: "I resented and resisted it. I had an almost constant feeling that I was being maltreated."[9] Nonetheless, as something of a self-consciously privileged child—a child with an almost mythic grandfather and an absent father whom he would seek to transform into a myth—living in a community in which light skin color could signify upper-class status, Toomer was able to use his class status to his advantage in the classroom: "At the same time, I had a lot of fun in school. Some of this fun was natural to the gay spirit of childhood. Some sprang from an instinctive resistance to authority. . . . I felt somewhat privileged and immune owing to grandfather's position and influence . . ."[1]

Toomer's matriculation at Garnet Elementary School and Dunbar High School afforded him the opportunity to acquire a very special education in what James Weldon Johnson, describing his years at Atlanta University (both the preparatory school and the university),

5. Ibid., 45.
6. Ibid., 46.
7. Ibid., 45.
8. *The Lives of Jean Toomer*, 36.
9. *The Wayward and the Seeking*, 47
1. Ibid., 47.

termed the "arcana of race."[2] For Johnson, who would later correspond with Toomer regarding the possibility of the inclusion of some
of his poems in a revised edition of his *The Book of American Negro
Poetry* (1922, 1931), "the initiation into the arcana of race" meant
"preparation to meet the tasks and exigencies of life as a Negro,
a realization of the peculiar responsibilities due to my own racial
group, and a comprehension of the application of American democracy to Negro citizens."[3] Toomer's initiation into the arcana of race
would mean something quite different altogether. As he claims in
his autobiography, he "formed and formulated" his racial position
in the summer of 1914 just before he left Washington to matricu-
late at the University of Wisconsin.[4] He took this important step
toward self-definition because he was keenly aware of his hybrid
racial background, the racial ambiguity of his physical appearance,
the questions and stares it elicited, the fact that he had lived in both
the white and black worlds, and that he could, if he chose, continue
to do so, or even choose one over the other.

When Toomer attended the Garnet School, he was living in the
home of his grandparents, which was located on Bacon Street in a
neighborhood that at the time was composed of wealthy whites. During these years between 1894 and 1906, Toomer's neighbors and
playmates were white, but his classmates at Garnet School were all
black. In 1906, Toomer's mother, Nina Pinchback, remarried and
moved to New York with her son and second husband, Archibald
Combes, a traveling salesman for the Metropolitan Life Insurance
Company. During this second and relatively brief marriage, Toomer
lived and attended schools for three years in the white neighborhoods in Brooklyn and also in New Rochelle. After his mother's
tragic, apparently avoidable death by appendicitis in the summer of
1909, Toomer returned to Washington, D.C.

Here, he lived with his Uncle Bismarck and his family on Florida
Avenue in a black neighborhood. A year later in 1910 he enrolled at
Dunbar High School. Now, for the second time in his life, Toomer
found himself attending school in what he described as "the colored
world."[5] But in fact, all of Toomer's primary and secondary educa-

2. James Weldon Johnson, *Along This Way* (New York: Penguin Books, 1933; 1990), 66.
3. Ibid., 66.
4. Darwin Turner, *The Wayward and the Seeking* (Washington, D.C.: Howard University
Press, 1980), 91. Toomer "formed and formulated" his racial position in the summer of
1914. This racial position is set forth in "Outline of an Autobiography," which Toomer
wrote, according to Darwin Turner, between 1931 to 1932. Toomer claims that as a
student at the University of Wisconsin that he "had no use" for his racial position
because the "question [of race] was never raised." He contradicts himself here for in a
later section of his autobiography he recounts the experience of having to contend with
the campus rumor that he was a "Hindu" and an "Indian," as well as the racism of a
white male classmate. See pp. 95–96 of *The Wayward and the Seeking*.
5. *The Wayward and the Seeking*, 84.

tion, except for the three years in New York, took place in "the colored world," under black teachers, surrounded by all-black classmates, in an all-black cultural environment. For Toomer, however, "the initiation into the arcana of race" did not mean preparation for "life as a Negro" and leadership among the race as it would be for Johnson and other members of Du Bois's talented tenth. Rather, Toomer would have us believe that this initiation would be a means of acquiring an understanding of social relations and the operations of power as a member of what he termed "an aristocracy—such as never existed before and perhaps never will exist again in America— midway between the white and Negro worlds."[6]

But Toomer and his family did not live "midway" between these two worlds; rather, they lived, to a greater or lesser degree, as light-skinned black people who, for a time, managed to defy the color line and live in white residential neighborhoods. The Pinchbacks were undoubtedly aristocrats within the black world, but more likely were visitors or voyeurs or interlopers within the white world. The fact that Toomer attended the Garnet School even when his family lived in a white neighborhood underscores how rigid racial boundaries, in fact, were in Washington. By no stretch of the imagination, despite Toomer's claims to the contrary, did this class of Negroes enjoy equal status with their white class peers, especially in racially stratified Washington, D.C., at the beginning of the twentieth century. Toomer, clearly, is asserting this claim—just as he had done about his grandfather passing as a Negro—to lay the autobiographical and sociological groundwork for his self-fashioning as a pioneering member of a new elite, an upper class of mixed-race individuals who would be points of mediation between white Americans and black Americans.

From 1909 to 1914, Toomer once again was a member of Washington's fabled colored aristocracy, a world he would analyze and critique to great effect. Toomer is at pains to assure us that the transition into this world involved no hardship for him: "It was not difficult to do so. I accepted this as readily as I had accepted living in Brooklyn and New Rochelle."[7] Writing in an elegiac mode, Toomer reconstructs the character of the world he entered when he took up residence with his Uncle Bismarck after returning from New York, along the way arguing implausibly that this class of Negroes just "happened" arbitrarily to be defined as Negroes, as if the history of their families' racial identification and the history of their participation in Negro culture had had no relevance on the shaping of their identities: "In the Washington of those days—and those days have gone now—there was a flowering of a natural but transient

6. Ibid., 84.
7. Ibid., 84.

aristocracy, thrown up by the, for them, creative conditions of the post-war period. These people, whose racial strains were mixed and for the most part unknown, happened to find themselves in the colored group. They had a personal refinement, a certain inward culture and beauty, a warmth of feeling such as I have seldom encountered elsewhere and again. . . . All were comfortably fixed financially, and they had a social life that satisfied them. . . . The children of these families became my friends."[8]

Because of the similarities in class, the transition from the white world into the colored world was, Toomer is arguing, a seamless one, in spite of the fact that, he would have us believe, he had effectively been "white" in New York and now was "black" in Washington. It is important to emphasize that Toomer is postulating an almost mythic class and racial formation, a "people, whose racial strains were mixed and for the most part unknown, and who happened to find themselves in the colored group," who have, alas, disappeared ("those days are gone now"). He writes here of a racially and culturally distinct group *within* the "colored group," "an aristocracy . . . midway between the white and Negro worlds,"[9] which enjoyed considerable economic privilege, a class of which he and his family were always a part. Toomer's depiction of this class-within-a-class, as it were, a point of mediation between black and white, is another component in his rhetorical strategy of declaring racial independence as a member of the vanguard of a raceless *tertium quid*.

In Washington, Toomer most certainly lived among the Negro elite, but it was disingenuous of him to suggest that its members were racially or culturally indeterminate; they were legally defined as Negroes, whether they liked it or not. And this would have been especially the case at the turn of the century following the *Plessy v. Ferguson* Supreme Court ruling of 1896, which declared "separate but equal" as the law of the land, the ruling itself a desperate attempt to police the boundaries that interracial sexual liaisons had hopelessly blurred. Toomer never tells us, if we but pause to think about it, why his family, living effortlessly as "white" in New York, found itself sending its child to an all-black school in Washington. Surely, no white family would have done that out of choice. But Toomer does this to establish the experiential justification for his subsequent decision to define himself as an "American."

Toomer assures us that he identified implicitly with this new way of life, and certainly his earlier life on Bacon Street had prepared him for it: "They were my kind, as much as children of my early

8. Ibid., 85.
9. Ibid., 84.

Washington years had been."[1] Toomer emphasizes their social, racial, and cultural uniqueness: "These youths had their round of activity, parties, interests—and were self-sufficient. In their world they were not called colored by each other. They seldom or never came in contact with members of the white group in any way that would make them racially self-conscious."[2] Occupying this liminal world of a mulatto elite, Toomer is arguing, it is not difficult to understand how he could define himself as "neither white nor black."[3]

And yet it is also difficult to understand how Toomer could even suggest that within this period of American racial history that any white American at the time would label him as any thing other than black. Anticipating the curiosity, confusion, and misunderstanding that his body, speech, and appearance would engender, and no doubt seeking to escape the boundaries imposed upon persons of African descent, Toomer tells us he formed his own "racial position" before leaving what he would have us believe was a "special" race world of Washington, D.C., to attend college in 1914. If so, he became one of the earliest proponents of the theory that "race" was socially constructed, even if his motives for doing so were quite mixed. Moreover, he would spend the rest of his life, following the publication of *Cane*, socially constructing his racial indeterminacy, and simultaneously deconstructing his Negro ancestry.

"By hearsay," writes Toomer, echoing W. E. B. Du Bois's famous description, in *The Souls of Black Folk*, of his own ancestry, "there were in my heredity the following strains: Scotch, Welsh, German, English, French, Dutch, Spanish, with some dark blood. [Let us] assume the dark blood was Negro—or let's be generous and assume that it was both Negro and Indian. I personally can readily assume this because I cannot feel with certain of my countrymen that all of the others are all right but that Negro is not. Blood is blood. . . . My body is my body, with an already given and definite racial composition."[4] After identifying the various racial "strains" in his ethnic heredity, Toomer raises the vital question of genetic ancestry, of race: "Of what race am I? To this question there can be but one true answer—I am of the human race. . . ." Rejecting the one-drop rule (one drop of Negro blood doth forever a Negro make) as well as the reigning preoccupation with racial purity that governed conceptions of race in the United States at the beginning of the twentieth century, Toomer claimed a social identity that would inevitably place

---

1. Ibid., 85.
2. Ibid., 86.
3. Ibid., 93.
4. Ibid., 92.

him at odds with the American mainstream and, in retrospect, make him a pioneering theorist of hybridity, perhaps the first in the African American tradition. Nevertheless, he remained indifferent to the consequences of this position, and quite determined to maintain and justify it, returning to the subject seemingly endlessly in his autobiographical writings. Adopting an unorthodox, progressive, and certainly idealistic position on race that would be the source of some suffering even now in the twenty-first century, he defined himself as an "American, neither black nor white, rejecting these divisions, accepting all people as people."[5]

Toomer's "racial position" anticipates by eleven years a complementary theory of race conceptualized by the Mexican writer and political leader Jose Vasconcelos in *La raza cosmica* (*The Cosmic Race*), published in 1925. In this treatise, Vasconcelos defines the Mexican people as a new race composed of *all* the races of the world. The central claim of *La raza cosmica* is that "the various races of the earth tend to intermix at a gradually increasing pace, and eventually will give rise to a new human type, composed of selections from each of the races already in existence."[6] According to Vasconcelos, the "new human type" or alternately "the fifth universal race," the "synthetic race," "the definitive race," or the "cosmic race" has its origins in the pre-Mayan legendary civilization of Atlantis.[7]

In prose that is marked by a mixture of philosophy, poetry, and mysticism, Vasconcelos asserts that this new cosmic race will be "made up of the genius and the blood of all peoples and, for that reason, more capable of true brotherhood and of a truly universal vision."[8] It will emerge from the continent of South America, thus fulfilling, according to Vasconcelos, the historic destiny of Latin American people or the "Hispanic race" to bring the races of the world to an advanced state of spiritual development.[9] Based in the "Amazon region," Vasconcelos calls the capital of this new empire of the spirit "Universopolis," which will rise on the banks of the Amazon River.[1] One of the "fundamental dogmas of the fifth race" is love as it is expressed within the framework of Christianity which, according to Vasconcelos, "frees and engenders life,

---

5. Ibid., 93.
6. Jose Vasconcelos, *The Cosmic Race: A Bilingual Edition* (Baltimore: The Johns Hopkins University Press, 1997), 3.
7. Ibid., for Vasconcelos the terms "the fifth race," "synthetic race," "definitive race," and "cosmic race" are fungible. *The Cosmic Race* 3, 7, 9, 18–19, 40.
8. Ibid., 20.
9. Ibid., 38
1. Ibid., 35.

because it contains universal, not national, revelation."[2] Writing as an idealist and a visionary, Vasconcelos argues that we "have all the races and all the aptitudes. The only thing lacking is for true love to organize and set in march the law of History."[3] Love, then, is the expanding floor upon which will rise "a new race fashioned out of the treasures of all the previous ones: The final race, the cosmic race."[4]

While there is no concrete evidence that Toomer was familiar with the writings of Vasconcelos, there are many affinities between their respective views on race.[5] But it is quite possible that Toomer knew Vasconcelos's work, given its wide popularity and given Toomer's sojourns in New Mexico. Toomer and Vasconcelos emerge as prophets of a new order in which the mixed-race person is a pivotal figure, a metaphor or harbinger of a hybrid culture and a fusion of many ethnic and genetic strands. The claims of both are based upon an appeal to the universal, the positive values associated with hybridity and thus a rejection of racial purity, and the belief that racial mixture or *mestizaje* possesses the potential to unify humankind. For Toomer and Vasconcelos, the mixed-race person or the mulatto emerges as a symbol of "cosmic" possibility, and the spiritual resolution of all human conflict rather than as a symbol of human conflict and degeneracy. Gilberto Freye would develop a related theory of "racial democracy" as a hallmark of Brazilian culture in his classic work, *Casa-Grande e Senzaca*,[6] published in 1933. Ferdinand Ortiz would elaborate a similar theory for Cuban culture a few years later in his book, *Contrapunteo cubano del tabaco y el azúcar*, published in 1940.[7] Vasconcelos's theory (either directly, or through Toomer) influenced Zora Neale Hurston as well. In "How It Feels to Be Colored Me," Hurston writes, "At certain times, I am no race, I am *me*. . . . The cosmic Zora emerges."[8]

Toomer arrived at his definition of his own race when most Americans implicitly accepted a "scientific" or biological definition of race, and believed that the world was composed of several distinct racial

2. Ibid., 35.
3. Ibid., 39.
4. Ibid., 40.
5. In her article "'A Small Man in Big Spaces': The New Negro, the Mestizo, and Jean Toomer's Southwestern Writing," Emily Lutenski asserts "there is no clear evidence that Toomer used Vasconcelos as a source when studying the Southwest. Regardless, there are clear parallels between Toomer's and Vasconcelos' writings." *MELUS* 33. 1 (Spring 2008) See this volume, p. 417.
6 This was translated as *The Masters and the Slaves* in 1946.
7 This was translated as *Cuban Counterpoint? Tobacco and Sugar* in 1947.
8. Zora Neale Hurston, "How It Feels to Be Colored Me," in *I love myself when I am laughing . . . and then again when I am looking mean and impressive: A Zora Neale Hurston Reader*, edited by Alice Walker, with an introduction by Mary Helen Washington (Old Westbury, NY: Feminist Press, 1979), 154.

groups, each with its own history, each with its own place in a racial hierarchy, each with its own special contribution to make to world civilization. W. E. B. Du Bois's essay, "The Conservation of Races" (1896), theorizes race as a biological or natural concept, but rejects a racial hierarchy, assigning to the Negro a positive value and function among the world's races: "We are that people whose subtle sense of song has given America its only American music, its only American fairy tales, its only touch of pathos and humor amid its mad money-getting plutocracy."[9] He would later dismiss "The Conservation of Races" as an instance of "youthful effusion."[1] In *Dusk of Dawn* (1940), Du Bois revisited the question of race, abandoning the biological or scientific concept of race: "Perhaps it is wrong to speak of it at all as 'a concept' rather than as a group of contradictory forces, facts and tendencies."[2] In this final definition, Du Bois theorized race as a social construct. In doing so, he prepared the ground for a subsequent generation of scholars—Kwame Anthony Appiah, Jacqueline Nassy Brown, Henry Louis Gates, Jr., Paul Gilroy, Stuart Hall, Patricia Williams—who would build upon Du Bois's insight, and theorize race as a social construction or floating signifier. In Du Bois's writing, we witness the evolution of race from a biological concept to a discursive concept. But unlike Toomer, Du Bois heartily embraced a Negro social and cultural identity, never using its constructed nature as an excuse to "transcend" it; rather to de-biologize or de-essentialize it.

Toomer observed that "it is even more difficult to determine the nature of a man; so most of us are even more content to have a label for him."[3] In an era when the views of such white supremacists as Lothrop Stoddard and Earnest Cox were in the ascendancy and referenced even in such fictional works as F. Scott Fitzgerald's *The Great Gatsby,* Toomer proclaimed that in "my body were many bloods, some dark blood, all blended in the fire of six or more generations. I was, then, either a new type of man or the very oldest. In any case I was inescapably myself. . . . As for myself, I would live my life as far as possible on the basis of what was true for me."[4] While Toomer's metaphor of "bloods" recalls a biological conception of race, the direction of his thinking is toward a discursive concept of race. Toomer developed the following plan for its use in

9. W. E. B. Du Bois, "The Conservation of Races," in *W. E. B. Du Bois: Writings* ed. Nathan Huggins (New York: Library of America, 1986), 822.
1. David Levering Lewis, *W. E. B. Du Bois: Biography of a Race* (New York: Henry Holt & Company, 1993), 174.
2. *W. E. B. Du Bois: Writings,* 651.
3. *The Wayward and the Seeking,* 91.
4. Ibid., 93.

the protean, contested world of social relations: "To my real friends of both groups, I would, at the right time, voluntarily define my position. As for people at large, naturally I would go my way and say nothing unless the question was raised. If raised, I would meet it squarely, going into as much detail as seemed desirable for the occasion. Or again, if it was not the person's business I would either tell him nothing or the first nonsense that came into my head."[5] It would be left to him, not to others, to define and to determine his location in the social world, or so he imagined. Toomer would soon come to realize the limitations of his own power to shape the manner in which he would be perceived and defined by others, notwithstanding the appeal of his person and personality, and his great confidence in his ability to explain and to rationalize himself.

After graduating from Dunbar High School in January 1914, Toomer matriculated at six colleges and universities between 1914 and 1918, but failed to earn a degree. He attended the University of Wisconsin at Madison, and the Massachusetts College of Agriculture to pursue his interests in scientific agriculture. No longer interested in becoming a farmer, he pursued his new passion for exercise and bodybuilding at the American College of Physical Training in Chicago in January 1916. Toomer remained in Chicago through the fall and enrolled in courses that introduced him to atheism and socialism at the University of Chicago. In the spring of 1917 he decided to travel to New York, and there enrolled in summer school at New York University and the City College of New York where, respectively, he took a course in sociology and history. "Opposed to war but attracted to soldiering," wrote Kerman and Eldridge, Toomer volunteered for the army, but he was "classified as physically unfit 'because of bad eyes and a hernia gotten in a basketball game.'"[6] As we reveal in "Jean Toomer's Racial Self-Identification," Toomer registered as a Negro.

In 1918, Toomer returned to the Midwest, where he held a series of odd jobs, including becoming a car salesman at a Ford dealership in Chicago. During this second period in Chicago, he wrote "Bona and Paul," his first short story, in which he explored questions of passing and mixed-race identity, a powerful work that would eventually find its way into the second section of *Cane*. In February 1918, Toomer accepted an appointment in Milwaukee as a substitute physical education director, and continued his readings in literature, especially the works of George Bernard Shaw.[7]

5. Ibid., 93.
6. *The Lives of Jean Toomer*, 69.
7. Ibid., 69.

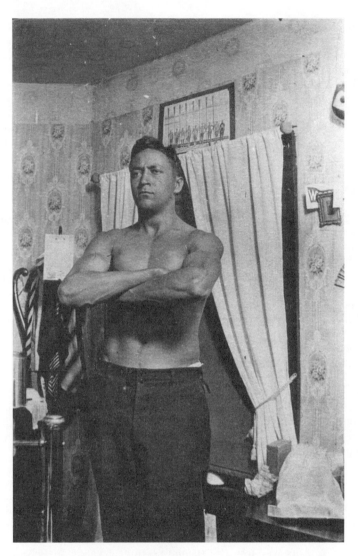

College photo of Jean Toomer, bare-chested with arms folded, 1916. Jean Toomer Papers, Yale Collection of American Literature, Beinecke and Rare Book Manuscript Library.

Group portrait with Toomer at center (four men in front blindfolded), from the Lunkentus Class of 1917 yearbook (American College of Physical Education). Jean Toomer Papers, Yale Collection of American Literature, Beinecke and Rare Book Manuscript Library.

Returning briefly to Washington, D.C., Toomer set out again for New York where he worked as a clerk with the grocery firm Acker, Merrall, and Condit Company. While in New York, his reading expanded to include Ibsen, Santayana, and Goethe; he attended meetings of radicals and the literati at the Rand School, as well as lectures by Alfred Kreymborg, who, a decade later, would describe Toomer as "one of the finest artists among the dark race, if not the finest."[8] In the spring of 1919, he left Manhattan to vacation in the resort town of Ellenville, New York. Indigent though somewhat rested, he then returned to Washington in the fall, where he was confronted by the condemnations of his grandfather who was far from pleased with his grandson's vagabond existence.

Unable to endure any longer the aging but vigorous Governor's harangues on personal responsibility, in December 1919, his twenty-fifth birthday only days away, Toomer was on the road again. With only ten dollars to his name, he walked from Washington, D.C., to Baltimore. Winter had arrived, and as Toomer recalled, it was "cold as the mischief."[9] After an overnight stay in Baltimore, he then walked to Wilmington, Delaware, and from there hitchhiked to Rahway, New Jersey, where he worked for a time as a fitter in the New Jersey shipyards for $22 per week.[1] This practical experience with the working class disabused him of his romantic notions about socialism. Toomer's destination was New York, and when he arrived there he once again took a job at Acker, Merrall and Condit. As he made his way from Washington to New York on Walt Whitman's open road, as it were, Toomer was alone; his only company was the ambitious, yet unrealized desire to become a writer.

In 1920, Pinchback sold the Washington home that Nathan Toomer had purchased as a wedding present for Nina Pinchback. In spite of his disappointment with his grandson, Pinchback sent Toomer $600, the small profit derived from the sale of the rental property after the payment of the mortgage and taxes. With this windfall, Toomer decided to remain in New York to continue what turned out to be the beginning of his apprenticeship as a writer: "I decided that I was at one of the turning points of my life, and that I needed all my time, and that the money would be well spent. I quit Acker Merrall. I devoted myself to music and literature."[2] And then, through yet another unexpected turn of events, he once again gained entrée into the rather closed world of New York's literati. In August 1920 he was invited by Helena DeKay, whose lectures on Romain Rolland and *Jean-Christophe* he had attended at the Rand School, to a party

8. Alfred Kreymborg, *Our Singing Strength* (New York: Coward-McCann, 1929), 575.
9. *The Wayward and the Seeking*, 111.
1. *The Lives of Jean Toomer*, 71.
2. *The Wayward and the Seeking*, 112.

hosted by Lola Ridge, editor of the new literary magazine *Broom.* "This was my first literary party," according to Toomer.[3] Actually, it would be more accurate for Toomer to claim that Ridge's soirée was his first "literary party" in New York, for he had attended the literary salons hosted by the black poet Georgia Douglas Johnson in Washington, D.C., as early as 1919.[4] Known among the cognoscenti of the nation's capital as Saturday Nighters, these gatherings attracted such luminaries of the Harlem Renaissance as Zora Neale Hurston, Richard Bruce Nugent, Sterling A. Brown, Countee Cullen, Langston Hughes, and Alain Locke.

Leonard Harris and Charles Molesworth suggest that it was within the charmed circle of the Saturday Nighters that Toomer came to know Locke, with whom he had a cordial relationship in the years preceding the publication of *Cane.* In search of a community of writers in his native Washington he found, to a certain extent, such a community among those black writers and artists who attended the Saturday Nighters. According to Kerman and Eldridge, Toomer shared some of his early writing with Johnson.[5] "Toomer was almost certainly the only writer in America," as Harris and Molesworth assert, with the possible exception of the Jamaican immigrant Claude McKay, who flowed easily between Harlem and socialist literary circles downtown, "who visited literary groups as diverse as Johnson's Saturday Nighters and the *Seven Arts* circle around Lewis Mumford, Sherwood Anderson, and Waldo Frank."[6] They are also correct in asserting that Toomer never conceived of himself as a bridge between these two discrete literary communities, both of which were committed to the project of American modernism.[7] Rather, he took what was useful from each in his efforts to create a work that expressed his own particular artistic and philosophical vision. Keenly aware of what he regarded as the differences and limitations of both artistic communities, Toomer, however, felt a much greater degree of affinity for those writers and artists whom he came to know through Ridge, chief among them Waldo Frank.

Toomer's attendance at Johnson's Saturday Nighters provided him with some preparation for the unmixable mix of banter, bravado, earnestness, narcissism, and posturing he would encounter at

---

3. Ibid., 113.
4. Leonard Harris and Charles Molesworth, *Alain L. Locke: The Biography of a Philosopher* (Chicago: The University of Chicago Press, 2008), 171. Toomer's correspondence with Georgia Douglas Johnson and Alain Locke reveals a level of familiarity absent in his autobiographical writings. For Toomer's correspondence with Douglas Johnson and Locke, see *The Letters of Jean Toomer, 1919–1924* (Knoxville: The University of Tennessee Press, 2006), edited by Mark Whalan. See also George Hutchinson's "Jean Toomer and the 'New Negroes of Washington,'" in *American Literature* 63 (December 1991).
5. *The Lives of Jean Toomer,* 94.
6. *Alain L. Locke: The Biography of a Philosopher,* 175.
7. Ibid., 175.

Ridge's "literary party" in Greenwich Village. In the main, he was not impressed by his first encounter with the literati of the Lost Generation which, on this particular occasion, was represented by Edwin Arlington Robinson, Witter Bynner, and Scofield Thayer, among others. Hungry to learn about this new world, Toomer felt "that there was far too much buzz about publishers, magazines, reviews, personalities; not enough talk of life and experience."[8] However, one "man stood out. . . . He had a fine animated face and a pair of lively active eyes. . . . I didn't know his name, but I marked him."[9] The man in question was none other than Waldo Frank, the celebrated author of *Our America,* a meditation on race, ethnicity, and spirituality in American culture. A few days after the party, Toomer encountered Frank while walking through Central Park. Both men stopped and introduced themselves, and thus began a friendship in letters that for Toomer would be instrumental in the publication of *Cane.* At this stage in his apprenticeship as a writer, Toomer had written the poem "The First Americans," the forerunner of his epic, "The Blue Meridian," and the short stories "Withered Skin of Berries" and "Bona and Paul." He shared his work with Frank, and was heartened by the encouragement he received from the older, established writer.

Shortly after this propitious meeting with Frank, Toomer returned to Washington, having spent his inheritance of $600. This was the end of the summer of 1920. Needless to say, Pinchback raged against Toomer's return. "Grandfather put up a fight but I beat him," Toomer remembers rather defiantly.[1] Possessing a sense of purpose and direction for the first time in five years, Toomer wrote, "I was wholly convinced that I had found my true direction in life, and no one was going to stop me. On the contrary, everyone, including grandfather, was going to help me. . . . I had matured considerably. And, I was filled with a purpose that was to keep me working for the next three years. But what terrible years they were!"[2]

And why would Toomer characterize the three years preceding the publication of *Cane* as "terrible"? The answer lies in part in the fact that during this period of his apprenticeship he lived in greatly reduced circumstances with his aging grandparents. "I was in the house with two old people whom," as Toomer wrote in his autobiography, "despite the continual struggle with grandfather—he never gave up completely; he was a game fighting cock to the end—I loved. And they were dying. No, they weren't dying. Grandfather gradually declined—a tragic sight—and, one day he broke. . . . I had to take

---

8. *The Wayward and the Seeking,* 114.
9. Ibid., 114.
1. *The Wayward and the Seeking,* 114.
2. Ibid., 114–15.

over whatever of his affairs needed attention. And I ran the house, even cooking meals and sweeping and cleaning. In a way, it was a good thing for them that I had returned."[3] Of his grandmother, Nina Emily Hethorn Pinchback, Toomer remembered her as strong, vivid, and humorous even as she declined amid circumstances of near poverty: "Yet she bore up. Not a whimper from her. She was glad to have me there . . . She would say every now and again that she only lived for me. But this was the miracle—as her body failed her, her spirit began taking on a more and more vivid life. Her mind became sharper—and also her tongue. She showed a vein of humor and satire that was the delight and amazement of all who came in."[4]

This was not the first time in his life when Toomer had responsibility for the care of his grandmother. In 1909 when Pinchback held an appointment in New York at the Department of Internal Revenue, Toomer and his grandmother lived with his Uncle Walter and his family. Owing to Pinchback's absence and the indifference of his uncle and wife, his grandmother, as he wrote, "becomes my responsibility. I look after her, and often, instead of going out at nights to play . . . I have to stay indoors and keep her company."[5] While he admired and loved his grandfather, Toomer also loved his grandmother. He understood her function and value in the household through its rise and decline: "She stood without flinching at Pinchback's side all through his stormy and dangerous political career. She saw the rise of the family and, outliving her husband and all but one of her children, she endured its rather tragic fall." Toomer also acknowledged the important fact of his grandmother's support, when everyone else, in particular his grandfather, had dismissed him as a ne'er-do-well: "She was the one person in my home who sustained her faith in me after I turned black sheep, who supported me through thick and thin. . . ."[6] Nina Emily Hethorn Pinchback lived to see the publication of *Cane,* which bears the dedication: "To my grandmother . . ." She died five years later.

Along with accepting the multiplying responsibilities of caring for his aging grandparents, Toomer also became the caretaker of his beloved Uncle Bismarck: "Bismarck got very sick. I took over the running of his house also, and each day I went over and massaged him. He was over a month recovering. This took it out of me."[7] Plainly, the responsibility of caring for aging relatives sapped Toomer's energy and strength, yet it also, paradoxically, introduced a certain discipline and structure that advanced his goal of becoming

3. Ibid., 116.
4. Ibid., 116.
5. Ibid., 89.
6. Ibid., 23.
7. Ibid., 118.

a writer. "My days were divided between attention to the house and my grandparents," as Toomer wrote of this period, "and my own work. At all possible times I was either writing or reading."[8]

Toomer inevitably came face to face with his own limitations and deficiencies as a writer. There was the dream, and there was the reality. To realize the potentialities of the one clear affirmation of his life at this juncture, he had to confront and overcome the division between his own aspirations and his abilities: "But what difficulties I had! I had in me so much experience so twisted up that not a thing would come out until by sheer force I had dragged it forth. Only now and again did I experience spontaneous writing. Most of it was will and sweat. And nothing satisfied me. . . . I wrote and wrote and put each thing aside, regarding it as simply one of the exercises of my apprenticeship. Often I would be depressed and almost despaired over the written thing."[9] These periods of despair were balanced by successes, few and far between though they were at the time. And these successes bolstered his confidence and renewed his faith in his capacity to become a writer: "But, on the other hand, I became more and more convinced that I had the real stuff in me. And slowly but surely I began getting the 'feeling' of my medium, a sense of form, of words, of sentences, rhythms, cadences, and rhythmic patterns. And then, after several years work, suddenly, it was as if a door opened and I knew without doubt that I was *inside, I knew literature*. And what was my joy! But many things happened before that time came!"[1]

Before he found his way "inside" literature, Toomer would have to endure another period when the accumulating responsibilities of being the sole caretaker of his aging grandparents would again drain him of his energy and focus. He had arrived at this state in the spring of 1922. "It was during this spring that I began feeling dangerously drained of energy," Toomer wrote. "I had used so much in my own work. So much had been used on my grandparents and uncles. I seldom went out. . . . Sometimes for weeks my grandmother would be laid up in bed, and by now my grandfather was almost helpless. The apartment seemed to suck my very life."[2] As the summer approached, Toomer's situation became even more desperate: "I felt I would die or murder someone if I stayed in that house another day."[3] Almost out of thin air, he managed to piece together enough funds for a week at Harpers Ferry, West Virginia, where he had often travelled to vacation. He made arrangements for the care of his grandparents during his absence. The time at Harpers Ferry

8. Ibid., 117.
9. Ibid., 117.
1. Ibid., 117.
2. Ibid., 122.
3. Ibid., 122.

was restorative, but all too short: "I returned with a small store of force which was soon spent . . . ," remembered Toomer. "The situation was slowly but steadily getting worse. . . . It was as if life were a huge snake that had coiled about me—and now it had me at almost my last breath."[4]

The much needed relief from this suffocating regimen would eventually come in the form of an invitation from Linton Stephens Ingraham, founder and principal of the Sparta Agricultural and Industrial Institute located in Sparta, Georgia. Ingraham was eager to hire an acting principal while he traveled to Boston to raise funds for his school. Toomer regarded this opportunity as a "Godsend." He accepted Ingraham's offer to serve as acting principal. Toomer again made arrangements for the care of his grandparents, and prepared for his fateful trip by train to Georgia. Girding himself for what he would encounter on "the southern road," as his contemporary, Sterling A. Brown, put it, Toomer recalled that "I had always wanted to see the heart of the South. Here was my chance."[5]

As acting principal of the Sparta Agricultural and Industrial Institute located in Hancock County, Georgia, Toomer provided continuity at an institution with an important history and mission. Ingraham was the institute's founder and principal. He was born a slave in Hancock County, Georgia, on August 24, 1855, the property of Judge Linton Stephens. He was taught to read and write by Alexander Stephens, the brother of Judge Stephens, and then matriculated at Atlanta University. He established the institute on October 10, 1910, on three acres of land on his former master's plantation. The institute was located one mile and a half west of Sparta, approximately eighty miles southwest of Atlanta, Georgia, in the county contiguous to Putnam County, Georgia, the birthplace of the writers Flannery O'Connor and Alice Walker.

At the time of Toomer's arrival in September 1921, the trustees of the institute had secured funding from the Julius Rosenwald Fund to erect a second building. By 1923 the institute was composed of two buildings perched on fifty-three acres with 210 students. A coeducational institution whose curriculum was a mix of industrial education and grade school instruction in reading, writing, and arithmetic, the institute prepared students for vocations in agriculture and industry. It served the African American community of Sparta, and the communities beyond it.[6] Toomer lived, like the teachers, in

4. Ibid., 123.
5. Ibid., 123.
6. The history of the Sparta Agricultural and Industrial Institute and its founder, Linton Stephens Ingraham, is derived from online sources composed of articles from the *Atlanta Constitution* and the *Augusta Chronicle* assembled by Eileen B. McAdams (2005). Ingraham died on September 20, 1935, after which his wife, Anna Turner Ingraham, became principal. The institute eventually became L. H. Ingraham High School. In addition to these sources, we recommend the overview of Sparta, Georgia, that

a residence provided by the institute. "As the [acting] principal, [he] was required to visit homes, businesses, and churches."[7]

Toomer was acting principal at the Institute from September to November 1921. This seminal, three-month sojourn in the South provided him with the materials, inspiration, and much of the setting for what became the first and third sections of *Cane*. Prior to his first visit to the South, Toomer's writing lacked a specific sense of place that could serve as the setting and foundation for his art. The landscape of Sparta, Georgia, with its history of slavery and an ancestral past that connected Toomer to his father, was precisely what the emerging writer needed at this vital juncture in his apprenticeship. Under the spell of an alien and yet somehow familiar landscape, Toomer eagerly embraced this new body of impressions and sensations and thoughts, immersing himself in a set of experiences that he would interpret with impressive originality, without being nostalgic in any way. He saw it as a world in transition, and a world of transition for himself. In Sparta, as we have noted, he heard for the first time, he claimed, the traditional Negro "folk-songs and spirituals." Because he was baptized as a Roman Catholic and reared in an upper-middle-class home in Washington, it is feasible that Toomer could have remained ignorant of the secular and sacred traditions in African American music whose origins were in slavery and that reached their maturity in the post-Reconstruction Jim Crow Deep South.

To be sure, these were not traditions often or openly embraced by the black men and women of Toomer's class or color background, even at the two all-black schools he attended in Washington. As the eponymous hero of his first play, *Natalie Mann*, written in 1922 following his stay in Georgia, would assert in almost self-righteous fashion: "What has become of the almost obligatory heritage of folk-songs? Jazz on the one hand, and on the other, a respectability which is never so vigorous as when it denounces and rejects the true art of the race's past. They are ashamed of the past made permanent by the spirituals."[8] Potentially, Toomer could have come to know the traditions emerging from the "race's past" in the person of Old Willis, a former slave who "did odd jobs" for the Pinchback family.[9] He writes that "I was very fond of [Old Willis]." But Toomer's encounters with him apparently did not introduce him to the black cultural past that was now unfolding all around him in Sparta.

---

appears in Charles Scruggs and Lee VanDemarr's *Jean Toomer and the Terror of American History* (Philadelphia: The University of Pennsylvania Press, 1998), 8–32. We also recommend Barbara Foley's "Jean Toomer's Sparta" in *American Literature* 67.4 (December 1995).

7. *The Lives of Jean Toomer*, 81.
8. Jean Toomer, *Natalie Mann*, in *The Wayward and the Seeking*, 290.
9. Ibid., 57.

Toomer discovered the slave and folk traditions of which Old Willis was doubtless a vessel as a young adult, precisely when he was struggling to find his voice as an artist, drawing upon these forms and traditions to illuminate his sense of his own identity and the historical experiences that had shaped that identity. As he went about his duties as acting principal in Sparta, he moved daily through a past that was also present, a past that helped him to understand the physical and cultural landscapes out of which he would shape the most original and seminal work of literature published in the entire Harlem Renaissance.

Like his contemporaries in the broad current of American modernism, Toomer was searching for—and ironically would discover in Sparta, Georgia, of all places—a "useable past," to summon a phrase much in circulation at the time and attributed to the critic Van Wyck Brooks (a classmate of Alain Locke at Harvard), which would give shape and heft to his art, but also allow him further to define his racial identity. As he observed in a letter to Sherwood Anderson, whose novel *Winesburg, Ohio* left its imprint upon *Cane*: "My seed was planted in the cane—and cotton-fields, and in the souls of the black and white people in the small southern town. My seed was planted in *myself* down there."[1] The image of the "seed" that Toomer uses to dramatic effect in his letter to Anderson would function as one of the unifying, fecund conceits in his poem "Song of the Son," in which he celebrates the ancestral past and cultural landscape of Sparta, the fictional community of Sempter in *Cane*.

In the same letter to Anderson, who asked Toomer's permission to write the introduction to *Cane*, Toomer elaborated upon the deep impact that the land, people, and music of Sparta had upon his sensibility and identity: "Here were cabins. Here Negroes and their singing. I had never heard the spirituals and work songs. They were like a part of me. At times, I identified with my whole sense so intensely that I lost my own identity."[2] Or, perhaps, we might say that here Toomer found his identity, if not his racial or cultural identity, then most certainly his identity as a creative writer, as the first American modernist writer to represent the complex culture of race in America in such a richly resonant and intricate manner. And because of this, Toomer's book stands as one of the truly great works of American modernism.

Toomer arrived in the South during a period of profound transformation. He witnessed firsthand the ebb and flow of the Great Migration. Beginning in the 1890s and then picking up the pace in 1915, African Americans were leaving rural communities like

1. *The Lives of Jean Toomer*, 84.
2. Ibid., 84.

Sparta for the urban centers of the South, first, and then the North, in search of expanding industrial economic opportunities, and a less repressive racial climate. As they left the southern agrarian way of life for modernity in the cities, some also sought to distance themselves from their slave past and its cultural traditions, which they regarded with a mixture of contempt, shame, and obsolescence. Regarding the "folk-songs and spirituals," Toomer lamented, "I learned that the Negroes of the town [Sparta] objected to them. They called them 'shouting.' They had victrolas and player-pianos. So, I realized with deep regret, that the spirituals, meeting ridicule, would be certain to die out. With Negroes also the trend was towards the small town and then towards the city—and industry and commerce and machines. The folk-spirit was walking in to die on the modern desert. That spirit was so beautiful. Its death so tragic."[3]

The poignancy of the passing of an era and the folk culture that defined it is a central theme of *Cane*. The speaker of "Song of the Son" exquisitely expresses this fateful sense of timing: "O land and soil, red soil and sweet-gum tree, / So scant of grass, so profligate of pines, / Now just before an epoch's sun declines / Thy son, in time, I have returned to thee. . . ."[4] In a subsequent line, the speaker explains why he has returned to the land of his ancestors: "To catch thy plaintive soul, leaving, soon gone. . . ."[5] This was Toomer's own purpose, too, in writing *Cane*, to bear witness to the passing of an epoch: "And this was the feeling I put into *Cane*. *Cane* was a swansong. It was a song of an end. And why no one has seen and felt that, why people have expected me to write a second and a third and a fourth book like *Cane*, is one of the queer misunderstandings of my life."[6] It is difficult to imagine that Toomer could be unaware that this urging that he write "a second and a third and a fourth book like *Cane*" stemmed both from that book's majesty and power and from his repeated failure to create anything that remotely approached it in sophistication throughout the remainder of his life, as he fruitlessly sought to find a language to express what being "neither white nor black" actually meant, without the soul-base of region that the deep black South had provided him in *Cane*.

At the end of his appointment in Sparta, Toomer wrote that on "the train coming north I began to write the things that later appeared in that book [*Cane*]."[7] As we have mentioned, he com-

---

3. *The Wayward and the Seeking*, 123.
4. Jean Toomer, *Cane, A Norton Critical Edition*, ed. Darwin T. Turner (New York: Norton, 1988), 14.
5. Ibid., 14.
6. *The Wayward and the Seeking*, 123.
7. Ibid., 124.

pleted the first draft of "Kabnis," the dramatic piece that composes the third section of *Cane,* in December 1921 in the last weeks of Pinchback's life. Toomer then wrote "Fern," which according to Kerman and Eldridge, would be published "almost without revision."[8] By April 1922 he had composed the parts of *Cane* in which Georgia is predominant. Having written so much, Toomer realized he had much more to write: "But I had not enough for a book. I had at most a hundred typed pages. These were about Georgia. It seemed that I had said all I had to say about it. So what, then? I'd fill out. The middle section of *Cane* was thus manufactured."[9]

The middle section of *Cane* began with "Bona and Paul," the story Toomer wrote in 1918 during his second stay in Chicago. He wrote many of the other stories and poems in this section throughout the summer of 1922. In July 1922, Toomer wrote to Waldo Frank and John McClure, editor of the New Orleans–based journal *Double Dealer,* to share with them his vision of the content and organization of *Cane.* Even at this early date, he imagined a book with a three-part structure. Toomer wrote that Part 1 would consist of all of the prose works in which Georgia is the setting; this first section he called "Cane Stalks and Choruses." Part 2 would consist of his poems, and at the time was entitled "Leaves and Syrup Songs." The third and final section would be prose works that now form the second section of *Cane,* and this section he entitled "Leaf Traceries in Washington."[1] Toomer was eager to assemble the various parts of his book into a unified whole for, as he declared to Frank and McClure, the "concentrated volume will do a good deal more than isolated pieces possibly could."[2]

Toomer's outline constituted a change of strategy. In the spring of 1922, he had sought help with publication of his work from two black writers: Alain Locke, professor of philosophy at Howard, and Claude McKay, the Jamaican immigrant poet who would be cast by Locke as a rising star, along with Toomer, among the younger generation of writers of the Harlem Renaissance. Locke had enormous influence within the black cultural world, and McKay was the associate editor of the white, socialist periodical, the *Liberator.*[3] Toomer wrote to them seeking their assistance in publishing the stories and poems that would eventually be published in *Cane.* As a result, Toomer's first and second appearances in print were in a black publication; with Locke's aid, "Song of the Son" was published in April 1922, in *Crisis,* the national monthly magazine of the National

8. *The Lives of Jean Toomer,* 86.
9. *The Wayward and the Seeking,* 125.
1. *The Lives of Jean Toomer,* 88.
2. Ibid., 88.
3. Ibid., 92.

Association for the Advancement of Colored People, edited by Du Bois. This was followed by the publication of the poem "Banking Coal" in the June issue of *Crisis*.

The outcome of Toomer's efforts to promote his work with McKay yielded slightly more in the way of results. McKay accepted "Carma," "Reapers," and "Becky" and published these in the September and October issues of the *Liberator*. Toomer enjoyed similar good fortune with other magazines. By the end of 1922, his growing list of publications included "Storm Ending," "Calling Jesus," and "Harvest Song" in *Double Dealer*; "Face," "Portrait in Georgia," and "Conversion" in *Modern Review*; and "Seventh Street" in *Broom*. In addition to appealing to Locke for guidance in publishing his writings, Toomer also solicited his assistance in securing a patron to support him as he continued to write *Cane*. Although a patron never materialized, Locke, who functioned as the midwife to so many young black writers, did exert himself on Toomer's behalf.[4]

As his poems and short stories began to appear, Toomer traveled with Frank back to the South, this time to Spartanburg, South Carolina. Toomer suggested the weeklong visit to Frank, in the fall of 1922, as a means of helping him to solidify his vision of the black world so central to *Holiday*, his novel-in-progress. Traveling as "blood brothers," the trip strengthened the friendship between the two writers as well as their shared belief that out of the materials of the black folk experience they were creating a new art that would transform American literature.[5] At a crucial point in their developing friendship, Toomer expressed just this view to Frank: "I cannot think of myself as being separated from you in the dual task of creating an American literature, and of developing a public, however large or small, capable of responding to our creations. Those who read and know me, should read and know you."[6]

When Toomer returned from Spartanburg, he worked for two weeks as an assistant to the manager of Washington's all-black Howard Theater. Out of this experience he wrote "Theater" and "Box Seat,"[7] and these beautifully written but nevertheless searching critiques of black middle-class Washington would appear in the middle section of *Cane*. Toomer sent these stories to Frank for his comments. Encouraged by his response, he sent Frank the complete manuscript of *Cane* in December 1922. He enclosed the now famous, widely quoted letter that reveals the latent design and theme of *Cane*: "My brother! CANE is on its way to you! For two weeks I have worked steadily at it. The book is done. From three

4. *Alain L. Locke: The Biography of a Philosopher*, 173.
5. *The Lives of Jean Toomer*, 89.
6. Ibid., 89.
7. Ibid., 91.

angles, CANE's design is a circle. Aesthetically, from simple forms
to complex ones, and back to simple forms. Regionally, from the
South up into the North, and back into the South again. Or, from
the North down into the South, and then a return North. From the
point of view of the spiritual entity behind the work, the curve
really starts with Bona and Paul (awakening), plunges into Kabnis,
emerges in Karintha etc. swings upward into Theatre and Boxseat,
and ends (pauses) in Harvest Song. Whew!"[8] Elated and expectant
that the book he had carried so long in his head would soon be in
the world because of the support of his best friend, Toomer provided Frank with clues as to the structure of a work that would
generate debates among scholars about its formal identity for
decades: "You will understand the inscriptions, brother mine: the
book to grandma; Kabnis, the spirit and the soil, to you. . . . Between
each of the three sections, a curve. These, to vaguely indicate the
design. I'm wide open to you for criticism and suggestion. Just these
few lines now. . . . love Jean."[9]

At the height of their friendship and doubtless appreciative of
Toomer's dedication of "Kabnis" to him, Frank shepherded the
manuscript to Horace Liveright, the co-founder of Boni and Liveright Publishers along with Albert Boni. On January 2, 1923, Frank
sent Toomer a telegram informing him that Liveright had accepted
*Cane* for publication. With Liveright as his publisher, Toomer
would make his literary debut in splendid modernist company: just
a year before, Liveright had published T. S. Eliot's *The Waste Land*.
In years to come, they would publish the first books of Ernest
Hemingway, William Faulkner, Hart Crane, Dorothy Parker, and
other bright stars in the firmament of American modernism.

In the months following Frank's excellent news, Toomer made
preparations for his departure from Washington to New York: "I saw
that it was very important for me to be in New York." He would never
again live in his native Washington. For the last time, Toomer dutifully made arrangements for the care of his beloved grandmother,
who spent her last years with her son Walter and his family. He then
boarded a train to New York, and "thus ended the three-year period
of death and birth in Washington."[1] Having left New York in the
summer of 1920 as an aspiring, unpublished writer, Toomer returned
to the nation's literary capital in the summer of 1923 as a published,
respected, and admired author through the sheer force of "will and
sweat," and through the support of McKay and especially Locke,

8. Jean Toomer to Waldo Frank, December 12, 1922.
9. Jean Toomer to Waldo Frank, December 12, 1922, Norton Critical Edition of *Cane*
(1988), 152.
1. *The Wayward and the Seeking*, 126.

though chiefly through the influence, counsel, and friendship of Frank.

In his recollection of this crucial period in his development as an artist, Toomer conveyed the excitement of his encounters with the major figures of white American modernism that summer: "In New York, I stepped into the literary world. Frank, Gorham Munson, Kenneth Burke, Hart Crane, Matthew Josephson, Malcom Cowley, Paul Rosenfield, Van Wyck Brooks, Robert Littell—*Broom,* the *Dial,* the *New Republic* and many more. I lived on Gay Street and entered into the swing of it. It was an extraordinary summer. . . . I met and talked with Alfred Stieglitz and saw his photographs. I was invited here and there."[2] In this recollection, Toomer is describing his pleasure at being introduced into a world populated by the key writers of the Lost Generation and the small, but influential magazines through which they shaped the mainstream of American modernism.

The sometimes overlapping, sometimes separate, other world of writers who contributed to the shape and direction of Afro-American modernism included most influentially Langston Hughes, Zora Neale Hurston, Claude McKay, Countee Cullen, and Sterling A. Brown, among two dozen others, coalescing around the slight, though formidable figure of Locke in his pied-à-terre in Harlem. But Toomer is largely silent about his encounters with them. These writers published in two magazines primarily: *Opportunity,* the monthly magazine of the Urban League, edited by the enterprising sociologist, Charles S. Johnson, who along with Locke, was one of the two midwives of the Harlem Renaissance; and in Du Bois's *Crisis.* Locke's *The New Negro* anthology, as we have seen, gave the nascent movement a form and a manifesto. A few other periodicals, such as *Fire,* the short-lived magazine founded by Hughes, Hurston, and Wallace Thurman, also played a role in shaping the course of the Renaissance, but none had the canonical presence of *Crisis* and *Opportunity.*

Perhaps a sign of Toomer's evolving thoughts about how he would identify himself racially, when he arrived in New York in that heady summer of 1923, is the fact that he did not seek lodging in Harlem but rather in Greenwich Village, sharing an apartment on Grove Street with Gorham Munson after the departure of his roommate Hart Crane. Munson's hospitality prepared the ground for a lifelong friendship with Toomer. Sometime later, he moved to the black section of the Village, renting a "small row-house apartment on Gay Street . . . distinctive then as being a predominantly black settlement in an otherwise white part of town." According to his biographers, "Toomer spent his days in the backyard reading or in the apartment

---

2. Ibid., 126.

writing. During that summer he was trying to establish himself as a freelance writer for various New York journals and little magazines."[3] At the end of that summer, Toomer's long-cherished dream of publishing a book—"I wanted a published book as I wanted nothing else"—became a reality. Liveright brought out *Cane* in September 1923.[4] Much to Toomer's delight, the reviews were uniformly positive. High praise came from the members of the two literary worlds who regarded him as a member. Comparing Toomer's debut work with Frank's fiction, Robert Littell offered this assessment of *Cane* in the *New Republic*: "Toomer's view is unfamiliar and bafflingly subterranean, the vision of a poet far more than the account of things seen by a novelist—lyric, symbolic, oblique, seldom actual."[5] Allen Tate, a member of the Fugitive Poets, also praised *Cane* in the pages of Nashville's *Tennessean*. Countee Cullen sent Toomer a congratulatory note in which he described *Cane* as a "classical portrayal of things as they are."[6] A month after the publication of *Cane*, the critic Edward O'Brien wrote from England requesting permission to reprint "Blood-Burning Moon" in the anthology *The Best Short Stories of 1923*.[7] Du Bois and Locke expressed their admiration for Toomer's achievement in an essay entitled "The Younger Literary Movement" in 1924 in *Crisis*. The influential African American critic William Stanley Braithwaite offered high praise of *Cane* in the pages of *The New Negro*: "*Cane* is a book of gold and bronze, of dusk and flame, of ecstasy and pain, and Jean Toomer is a bright morning star of a new day of the race in literature."[8] Two years later in the summer of 1927, Langston Hughes and Zora Neale Hurston paid homage to Toomer's artistic achievement by visiting Sparta, the inspiration for *Cane*, on their return North from a road trip through the South.[9]

Reflecting upon *Cane*'s reception and impact almost forty years after its publication, Arna Bontemps, a member of the younger generation of writers of the Harlem Renaissance, said this of Toomer's shaping influence on the forms his black contemporaries and literary heirs would craft: "*Cane*'s influence was by no means limited to the joyous band that included Langston Hughes, Countee Cullen, Eric Walrond, Zora Neale Hurston, Wallace Thurman,

3. *The Lives of Jean Toomer*, 105.
4. *The Wayward and the Seeking*, 124.
5. Robert Littell, *"Cane," New Republic* 37 (December 26, 1923): 126.
6. *The Lives of Jean Toomer*, 108.
7. Ibid., 108–09.
8. William Stanley Braithwaite, "The Negro in American Literature," *The New Negro*, ed. Alain Locke. (New York: Simon & Schuster, 1925; 1992), 44.
9. Arnold Rampersad, *The Life of Langston Hughes Volume I: 1902–1941; I, Too, Sing America* (New York: Oxford University Press), 152–53; Valerie Boyd, *Wrapped in Rainbows: The Life of Zora Neale Hurston* (New York: Scribner Books, 2003), 151; *The Lives of Jean Toomer*, 182.

Rudolph Fisher and their contemporaries of the Twenties. Subsequent writing by Negroes in the United States, as well as in the West Indies and Africa, has continued to reflect its mood and often its method and, one feels, it has also influenced the writing about Negroes by others. Certainly, no earlier volume of poetry or fiction or both had come close to expressing the ethos of the Negro in the Southern setting as *Cane* did."[1] While acknowledging his broad influence, Darwin T. Turner maintained that Toomer's signal contribution to American letters was to reverse years of stereotypical portrayals of rural, southern black language and life: "No matter how he influenced others, it cannot be denied that Jean Toomer was the first writer of the twenties to delineate southern black peasant life perceptively."[2]

Toomer's deft portrayal of southern black peasantry, his sensitive portrayal of black women, his power as a lyric poet, the manner in which he combined philosophy with fiction, and his exploration of the relationship between region and race directly influenced the shape of Zora Neale Hurston's *Their Eyes Were Watching God*, and through her, the theme of Ralph Ellison's *Invisible Man*. What's more, *Cane* has profoundly influenced both the fictions and the poetry of key African American writers who came of age since its republication in the late 1960s, including Alice Walker, Michael S. Harper, Rita Dove, Charles Johnson, Gloria Naylor, Elizabeth Alexander, and Natasha Trethewey. Though Ernest J. Gaines discovered *Cane* after he had developed his particular style of writing, he regards Toomer as a fellow artist with whom he shares a commitment to portray realistically the experiences of southern black farmers. Despite his desire to flee it, Toomer's literary legacy survives primarily because of *Cane's* canonization in the black literary tradition.

While *Cane* was clearly an artistic success, sales were disappointing. It sold only one thousand copies, but it was printed in a second edition. As Toomer himself remarked: "The reviews were splendid. It didn't sell well, but it made its literary mark—that was all I asked."[3] The strength of the reviews was doubtless a factor in Liveright's decision to reissue the second, smaller edition in 1927. While scholars would continue to praise *Cane*, it would remain out of print until the appearance of the third edition in 1967, followed by editions in 1969 and 1975. Doubtless, the renewed interest in the Harlem Renaissance by the writers of the Black Arts movement of the 1960s, the institutionalization of the field of African American Studies in 1969,

1. Arna Bontemps, "Introduction," *Cane* (New York: Harper & Row, 1923; 1969).
2. Darwin T. Turner, "Introduction," *Cane* (New York: Boni & Liveright, 1975); Norton Critical Edition of *Cane* (1988), 133.
3. *The Wayward and the Seeking*, 127.

and the dramatic growth of African American literary studies through the 1980s led to the first Norton Critical Edition in 1988, splendidly edited by Darwin T. Turner.

Though *Cane* had "made its literary mark," Toomer's relationship to the book he so much desired to be published began to shift as early as the fall of 1923. This shift, which would eventually result in his rejection of the book he once regarded as the "passport" that "would lead [him] from the cramped conditions of Washington which [he] had outgrown, into the world of writers and literature," would be catalyzed by his friend Waldo Frank and his publisher, Horace Liveright,[4] involving the launch of *Cane* itself and the efforts by Liveright to promote it. Frank had written, by all accounts, a beautiful foreword to *Cane*. He lavished praise upon his friend and protégé's debut book: "A poet has arisen among our American youth who has known how to turn the essences and materials of his Southland into the essences and materials of literature."[5] Quite perceptively, the ever-supportive Frank described *Cane* as "an aesthetic equivalent of the land." So far, so good.

However, the language that disturbed Toomer, was this: "A poet has arisen in that land who writes, not as a Southerner, not as a rebel against Southerners, not as a Negro, not apologist or priest or critic: who writes as a *poet*."[6] Moreover Frank's references to Toomer as "the gifted Negro" and "an American Negro" inadvertently only made matters worse so far as Toomer was concerned, undermining his desire to position himself publicly as a writer "neither white nor black." Frank's straightforward description of Toomer as a Negro, notwithstanding Toomer's belabored efforts to explain his racial sense of himself to his friend privately, felt first like disappointment, and then betrayal: "One day in the mail his [Frank's] preface [*sic*] to my book came. I read it and had as many mixed feelings as I have ever had. On the one hand, it was a tribute and a send-off as only Waldo Frank could have written it, and my gratitude for his having gotten the book accepted rose to the surface and increased my gratitude for the present piece of work in so far as it affirmed me as a literary artist of great promise. On the other hand, in so far as the racial thing went, it was evasive, or, in any case, indefinite."[7]

For reasons that are not clear to us, Toomer obsessed and fretted about Frank's references to his race in the foreword, as if Frank had either invented his black ancestry or publicly unmasked him as a Negro writer, leading him inevitably to question Frank's motives:

4. Ibid., 124.
5. Waldo Frank, "Foreword," *Cane* (New York: Boni and Liveright, 1923) as reprinted in the Norton Critical Edition of *Cane* (1988), 138 and 140.
6. Ibid., 138–39.
7. *The Wayward and the Seeking*, 125.

"Well, I asked myself, why should the reader know? Why should any such thing be incorporated in a foreword to *this* book? Why should Waldo Frank or any other be my spokesman in this matter? All of this was true enough, and I was more or less reconciled to let the preface [sic] stand as it was, inasmuch as it was so splendid that I could not take issue with it on this, after all, minor point, inasmuch as my need to have the book published was so great, but my suspicions as to Waldo Frank's lack of understanding of, or failure to accept, my actuality became active again."[8] Toomer would also claim that he learned from mutual friends that it was Frank who had constructed a portrait of him as a Negro in the literary circles of New York, a portrait that, he felt, misrepresented the "actuality" of his race, or his racelessness. Toomer, no doubt unfairly given his extensive contacts with other black writers in Washington and New York and his grandfather's historical status as the highest ranking black elected official in the whole of Reconstruction, claimed to believe that it was "through Frank's agency that an erroneous picture of me was put in the minds of certain people in New York before my book came out. Thus was started a misunderstanding in the very world, namely the literary art world, in which I expected to be really understood. I knew none of this at the time. . . ."[9] While Kerman and Eldridge write that Toomer and Margaret Naumburg, Frank's wife, "were entranced with each other from the first time they met," the unhappy poet of *Cane* may have ended his friendship with Frank by seeking his revenge, in part, by seducing his mentor's wife.[1]

While Toomer was still reeling from Frank's "betrayal," Liveright requested that Toomer capitalize upon his African American ancestry in the publicity for *Cane*, and this, as it turned out, would further complicate his relationship to his publisher and his first book. It is clear that Toomer wanted to write about the Negro, but not be regarded as a Negro. In fact, it is also clear that Toomer wanted to break out of the race itself through art, transcending the Negro world in a manner, say, that never would have occurred to Irish writers such as William Butler Yeats or James Joyce. Toomer objected to the oversimplification of what he seems, at times, genuinely to have believed was a truly complex, new racial identity, one too subtle, hybrid, or nuanced to be classified by those gross signifiers "black" and "white," especially to be exploited for the commercial purpose of selling the very book that he hoped would be his transport out of blackness. Accordingly, he refused to cooperate with

8. Ibid., 125–26.
9. Ibid., 126.
1. *The Lives of Jean Toomer*, 112.

Liveright, notwithstanding the risk that his refusal might jeopardize his book's publication. Toomer defiantly declared his position on race and marketing in a well-known letter to Liveright, dated September 23, 1923: "First, I want to make a general statement from which detailed statements will follow. My racial composition and my position in the world are realities which I alone may determine. . . . As a unit in the social milieu, I expect and demand acceptance of myself on their basis. I do not expect to be told what I should consider myself to be."[2] But Toomer did not stop there: "As a Boni and Liveright author, I make the distinction between my fundamental position, and the position which your publicity department may wish to establish for me in order that *Cane* reach as large a public as possible. In this connection I have told you . . . to make use of whatever racial factors you wish. Feature Negro if you wish, but do not expect me to feature it in advertisements for you. I have sufficiently featured Negro in *Cane*."[3] Toomer's dispute with Liveright over his book's marketing, following close upon his reaction to Frank's foreword, only added insult to injury, further alienating him from *Cane*.

It should not surprise us, then, that Alain Locke's decision to reprint excerpts from *Cane* in *The New Negro* without Toomer's permission just about drove Toomer to distraction: "But when Locke's book, *The New Negro*, came out, there was the [Winold] Reiss portrait, and there was a story from *Cane* [Locke reprinted the stories "Carma" and "Fern," as well as the poems "Georgia Dusk" and "Song of the Son"], and there in the introduction, were words about me which have caused as much or more misunderstanding than Waldo Frank's."[4] Toomer felt betrayed by the two major figures at the center of the literary worlds that claimed him, and by both he felt completely misunderstood. But between the two, Toomer reserved his greater scorn for Locke: "However, there was and is, among others, this great difference between Frank and Locke. Frank helped me at a time when I most needed help. I will never forget it. Locke tricked and misused me."[5] Toomer seriously considered contesting Locke's representation of him as a black writer, ultimately deciding against doing so because he was convinced that he probably could never correct the record, and fearing that his efforts at any sort of clarification would only contribute to the confusion. So Jean Toomer—despite his vehement objections— came to be known as a black writer through *Cane*, the book that

2. Jean Toomer to Horace Liveright, September 23, 1923, Norton Critical Edition of *Cane* (1988), 156–57.
3. Ibid., 156–57.
4. *The Wayward and the Seeking*, 132.
5. Ibid., 132.

ironically brought him the fame and acceptance in the literary world he had been seeking for so long.

Toomer's decision, just a few months after *Cane*'s publication, to become a student of Georges I. Gurdjieff, the Russian mystic and psychologist, and originator of the Gurdjieff system or method, also contributed to his estrangement from the book. Throughout much of his adult life, Toomer had been in search of what he called an "intelligible scheme, a sort of whole into which everything fit," and toward the end of 1923 he believed he had at last found this grand and unifying pattern in Gurdjieff's teachings. Toomer's introduction to Gurdjieff's philosphy came through P. D. Ouspensky's *Tertium Organum*, which he read in December 1923. Ouspensky's writings were the object of some fascination among the members of his literary community in Greenwich Village, particularly to Hart Crane, Gorham Munson, and Waldo Frank. After reading Ouspensky, Toomer acquired a pamphlet describing the history and mission of Gurdjieff's Institute for the Harmonious Development of Man in Fontainebleau, France. "In it I found expressed," he wrote, "more completely and with more authority than with anything possible from me, just the conditions of man which I myself realized. Moreover, a method, a means of *doing something about it* was promised. It was no wonder that I went heart and soul into the Gurdjieff work."[6]

It should be emphasized that in *Cane* we find ample evidence of an orientation toward spiritual and philosophical concerns that would assume a larger, more marked significance in Toomer's later writings. These concerns help to explain why he went "heart and soul into the Gurdjieff work." Even in his 1923 letter to Frank, Toomer had written of what he called the "spiritual entity behind the work." A few years before his introduction to Gurdjieff's theories, Toomer, an autodidact who early on saw himself as a philosopher-poet, found as his great theme modernity's attendant fragmentation and alienation. *Cane* is his most successful treatment of this theme, as it juxtaposes fragmentation with intense spirituality. Kerman and Eldridge describe the "spiritual entity" in the writing and in the writer thusly: "While others may have read *Cane* to see how a man could fit his human view into his blackness, Jean was trying to fit the blackness that was a part of him into a more comprehensive human view. Nor was he trying to 'pass' in a racial sense; rather, he was passing from preoccupations with external, visible reality to concentration on internal, invisible reality."[7] Perhaps. But Toomer *did* find a most original and compelling way to render the relation among fragmentation, alienation, and spirituality in the tripartite, lyrical form of *Cane*.

---

6. Ibid., 131.
7. *The Lives of Jean Toomer*, 115.

In fact, the grand achievement of Toomer is this: *Cane* is, per-haps, the first work of fiction by a black writer to take the historical experiences and social conditions of the Negro, and make them the metaphor for the human condition, in this case, the metaphor for modernity itself. Du Bois had, famously and brilliantly, redefined the concept of "double consciousness" as a metaphor for the Negro's duality, a duality created by racial segregation. For Du Bois, double consciousness was a malady, a malady that could be cured only by the end of segregation. For Toomer, however, fragmentation, or duality, is the very condition of modernity. It cannot be "cured," any more than the gap between the conscious mind and the uncon-scious can be obliterated. *Cane* is a book about nothing if not frag-mentation; it is a book about dualities, unreconciled dualities, and this theme is repeated in each of its sections, whether in the South or the North, whether in the country or the city, whether in the book's black characters or its white characters. Everybody and everything is hopelessly, inescapably fragmented. And nowhere is this better expressed than in the "Kabnis" section of *Cane,* in this exchange between Lewis and Kabnis, each other's alter egos, through Lewis's list of binaries:

> Kabnis: . . . My ancestors were Southern blue-bloods.
> Lewis: And black.
> Kabnis: Aint much difference between blue and black.
> Lewis: Enough to draw a denial from you. Cant hold them, can you? Master; slave. Soil; and the overarching heavens. Dusk; dawn. They fight and bastardize you. The sun tint of your cheeks, flame of the great season's multi-colored leaves, tar-nished, burned. Split, shredded; easily burned. No use . . .

The use of binary oppositions has a long history in African Ameri-can literature, going back at least to Frederick Douglass's *Narrative of the Life of Frederick Douglass* (1845). Du Bois transformed these in *The Souls of Black Folk* into the duality of the Negro citizen, a necessary and problematic by-product of anti-black racism and seg-regation. Toomer, however, takes Du Bois's concept of double con-sciousness, and boldly declares that this fragmentation is, ultimately, the sign of the Negro's modernity, first, and that the Negro, there-fore, is America's harbinger of and metaphor for modernity itself. It is a stunningly brilliant claim, this rendering by Toomer of the Amer-ican Negro as the First Modern Person. There is no end to the mani-festations of fragmentation in *Cane* and no false gestures to the unity of opposites at the text's end. No, in *Cane,* fragmentation is here to stay, for such is the stuff of modern life. When Kabnis ascends the stairs from his encounter with Father John in the base-ment at the end of the text, he carries a bucket of dead coals, undermining what would be the false nod to hope through reconciliation possibly suggested by the text's image of a rising sun. Zora Neale Hurston revises this very scene at the end of *Their Eyes Were Watching God,* having depicted her protagonist's coming to voice not as the result of reconciling binaries, but of developing the capacity to negotiate back and forth between them, acutely mindful of the fragmentation that Toomer defined as the necessary precondition for finding one's identity, an identity always split, or doubled, or divided. In *Cane,* Jean Toomer became a lyrical prophet of modernism. And then, abruptly, he decided to pursue other passages.

In January 1924, Toomer marked his passing from "external, visible reality" to "internal, invisible reality" by attending lectures by Gurdjieff and demonstrations of his method at Manhattan's Leslie Hall and the Neighborhood Playhouse. He writes about how deeply moved he was by his first encounter with Gurdjieff's teachings. Gurdjieff claimed that human beings are mechanical beings, and that they lack unity, and thus true consciousness. In the Gurdjieff system there are four levels of consciousness: the sleeping state, waking consciousness, self-consciousness, and objective or cosmic consciousness. Advanced levels of consciousness can only be attained through the practice of such exercises as self-remembering or self-observation as well as non-identification. Practiced in one's daily life, these exercises possessed the potential to liberate one from mechanical modes of thought and behavior, and to move one toward the attainment of higher levels of consciousness.

Toomer, to say the least, was captivated by the promise of Gurdjieff's teachings. By the summer of 1924 he had left New York to study at Gurdjieff's institute in France. Put another way, in less than a year after the publication of *Cane* and when the Harlem Renaissance and other expressions of high cultural modernism were approaching their apex, Toomer had passed into a vastly different cultural orbit. When he returned to New York in early 1925, he set about in almost priestly fashion to promote the Gurdjieff method through public lectures. It was as a Gurdjieff lecturer that Hughes and Hurston first met Toomer in Harlem in 1925.

Neither as a writer nor as a lecturer did Toomer earn an income substantial enough to support himself. Like his father Nathan Toomer, he was fortunate that he married well. In 1931, Toomer married the writer Margery Latimer, who died in 1932 after giving birth to their daughter, Margery Toomer. Two years later, Toomer married Marjorie Content, the daughter of a wealthy stockbroker, and the former wife of Harold Loeb, the founder of the magazine *Broom.* Marjorie Content and Toomer came close to meeting one another in 1923 at her East Ninth Street townhouse, in the basement of which were the offices of *Broom.* Lola Ridge attempted to introduce Content to Toomer, whose work she admired, but she shyly demurred. Toomer married her in Taos, New Mexico, on September 1, 1934, with his former lover Georgia O'Keeffe in attendance as witness. He would be her fourth and last husband.

Prior to his marriage to Content, however, Toomer had developed a reputation as the inamorato of two of the women who played central roles in the cultural world of American modernism. Its center of gravity shifted between *Seven Arts,* presided over to a very large degree by Waldo Frank, and the Photo-Secession Group, perhaps an even more exalted stratum of the arts, whose headquarters was Manhattan's 291 Gallery, of which the photographer Alfred Stieglitz was the imperious head. Shortly after the publication of *Cane* in the fall of 1923, Toomer had an affair with Margaret Naumburg, an educator who also happened to be Waldo Frank's wife, which not surprisingly led to the dissolution of their friendship.[8] Sometime later in 1933, Toomer also had an affair with the artist Georgia O'Keeffe during one of his visits to The Hill, Stieglitz and O'Keeffe's retreat on Lake George, New York.[9] Toomer was extraordinarily handsome and beguiling, and no doubt cut a striking figure, often finding himself one of the very few swarthy men in the inner sanctums of white American modernism.

As a result of his marriage to Marjorie Content, Toomer could continue with his work as a Gurdjieff lecturer without fear of impoverishment. He would lecture on the Gurdjieff method most intensely for the next two decades, not only in New York but in Chicago; Portage, Wisconsin; Taos, New Mexico; and Doylestown, Pennsylvania, his final home. Toomer continued to write novels, short stories, plays, aphorisms, and poems, but most of these bear the unmistakable imprint of Gurdjieff's philosophy and teachings, stimuli not nearly as fecund as the rural Georgian landscape. Except for autobiographical excerpts edited by Darwin T. Turner, including the poem "The Blue Meridian," and *Essentials,* edited by Rudolph P. Byrd, a collection of aphorisms, Toomer's post-*Cane* writings remain largely unpublished. Lacking *Cane*'s lyrical originality, Toomer's philosophical and psychological writings often read like sophomoric, prosaic, bloodless translations of Gurdjieff's philosophy and method.

As Toomer passed into Gurdjieff's world, he passed into literary obscurity. While his search for enlightenment or the "intelligible scheme" took him to India, through Jungian analysis, and to his conversion to the Society of Friends, Toomer's commitment to Gurdjieff, while fluctuating in its intensity, nevertheless remained the organizing

8. Ibid., 112.
9. Laurie Lisle, *Portrait of an Artist: A Biography of Georgia O'Keeffe* (New York: Seaview Books, 1981), 260–65.

principle of his life. He recommitted himself to this work in 1953, and remained a disciple until he passed away on March 30, 1967— the year in which the third edition of *Cane* was published.


## Jean Toomer's Racial Self-Identification: A Note on the Supporting Materials

Of course, we are still confronted with the vital question that has arisen in various ways throughout this introduction: Was Jean Toomer a Negro who passed for white?

Thanks to pioneering research conducted at the editors' request by the genealogist Megan Smolenyak Smolenyak, we can now understand more fully than ever before Jean Toomer's conflicted thinking about his racial identification, as he expressed them in public documents, including the federal census, two draft registrations, and on his marriage license to Margery Latimer. In addition, we also now know how Toomer's grandfather and grandmother, Pinckney Benton Stewart Pinchback and Nina Emily Hethorn, his mother, Nina Pinchback, and his father, Nathan Toomer, are all identified in federal census records.

In every census taken between 1850 and 1920, P. B. S. Pinchback and Nina Emily Hethorn are identified either as black or as mulattos. Between 1870 and her death in 1909, Nina Pinchback is identified as a mulatto or black. Likewise, Nathan Toomer is identified between 1870 and 1900 as either mulatto or black. (Nathan's previous wife, Amanda America Dickson, is also identified as a mulatto in the 1870 and 1880 censuses and as black on her marriage license with Nathan. Amanda's mother, Julia Frances Lewis Dickson, is also identified in the censuses taken between 1870 and 1910 as a mulatto or black.) In other words, Jean Toomer's mother, father, grandfather, and grandmother all self-identified as Negroes.

In the 1900 federal census, Eugene Toomer is listed as black. In the 1910 federal census he is listed as mulatto. In June 1917, Eugene Pinchback Toomer registered for the draft in Washington, D.C. He is recorded to be an unemployed student, single, as having an unspecified disability, and as being a "Negro." According to Kerman and Eldridge, the "unspecified disability" was actually "bad eyes and a hernia gotten in a basketball game."[1]

The 1920 United States Federal Census shows Toomer boarding with other lodgers in the home of an Italian couple on East Ninth Street in Manhattan. He is assigned New York as a birthplace,

---

1. *The Lives of Jean Toomer*, 69.

suggesting that someone else responded on his behalf, in his absence. His race is listed as "white."

In the 1930 United States Federal Census, Toomer is listed as a resident, with many others, at 11 Fifth Avenue, in Manhattan. Because of the accuracy of the other data contained in this document—including his birthplace, his parents' states of birth, and his occupation as a freelance writer—it is likely that he furnished these details himself. His race is listed as white.

A year later Toomer married "Marjery" or Margery Latimer on October 30, 1931, in Portage, Wisconsin. Both the bride and the groom are identified as "white" on the marriage license. According to Kerman and Eldridge, Margery Latimer was aware of what she terms "the racial thing," that is, that Toomer was black.[2] Though this is true and though she shared Toomer's vision of a new race in America, she was nevertheless unprepared for headlines such as this one published in the national press regarding her marriage to Toomer: "Negro Who Wed White Writer Sees New Race."[3] While Toomer proclaimed that his marriage to Margery Latimer was evidence of a "new race in America, . . . neither white nor black nor in-between," and that their marriage was simply one between "two Americans," the white press chose to focus upon only the most sensational aspects of their nuptials.[4]

In 1942, Toomer registered once again for the draft, as part of the World War II Draft Registration. He identified himself as Nathan Jean Toomer, and he was living with his second wife, Marjorie C. Toomer, in Doylestown, Pennsylvania. He is described as 5'10" tall, weighing 178 pounds, with black hair and eyes, and a "dark brown complexion." He identified himself as a "Negro."

These documents reveal that Jean Toomer self-identified as Negro in 1917, when he first registered for the draft. Then either he or a roommate decided to identify him as "white" in the federal census of 1920. Similarly, Toomer self-identified as "white" in the 1930 census and a year later on his marriage license with Margery Latimer. He then self-identified again as a Negro in 1942 on his second draft registration. Given the fact that draft boards at the time were local, Toomer's decision to identify himself as a black man is quite surprising. Since the draft board would have been unaware of Toomer's previous identification of himself as a Negro in 1917, we are left wondering why he did this after he had decided to pass as a white man.

In the course of the twenty-five years between his 1917 and 1942 army registrations, Toomer was endlessly deconstructing his Negro

2. Ibid., 199.
3. Ibid., 202.
4. Frederick L. Rusch, *A Jean Toomer Reader: Selected and Unpublished Writings* (New York: Oxford University Press, 1993), 105.

ancestry. We recall that during his childhood and adolescence in Washington, D.C., and New York, Toomer lived in both the white and the black worlds, and here we must emphasize the fact that during his adolescence he was educated and lived in the world occupied by Washington's black and mulatto elite. Based upon his experiences in this special world "midway between the white and Negro worlds,"[5] Toomer claimed that he developed his famous "racial position" in 1914, when he says he first defined himself as an "American, neither white nor black," just a year after declaring himself to be a Negro in his first draft registration. But given the fact that his parents and grandparents identified themselves and Toomer (in the 1900 and 1910 federal censuses) as black, it is apparent that Toomer's feelings about his racial identity were anomalous within his own family."[6] It is important to stress that the first short story Toomer ever wrote, "Bona and Paul," composed in 1918, takes passing as its central theme, and that this deeply autobiographical story reflects Toomer's early preoccupation with his racial identity.

Equally important, Toomer's assertion that "Kabnis is me," in his well-known December 1922 letter to Waldo Frank concerning his relationship to a character of mixed-race ancestry who is deeply conflicted about his Negro ancestry, is further evidence of his ambivalence regarding his racial identity. This ambivalence about his black ancestry is also reflected in the controversial launch of *Cane*, specifically his conflicted, indeed angry reaction to Waldo Frank's introduction, and later his refusal to cooperate with Horace Liveright, his publisher, in "featuring Negro" in the marketing of *Cane* in the fall of 1923. Indeed, he all but said to Liveright: "I was not a Negro."[7] According to Darwin Turner, Toomer, in his correspondence with the writer Sherwood Anderson just a year before the publication of *Cane*, "never opposed Anderson's obvious assumption that he was 'Negro.' In fact, Anderson began the correspondence because Toomer had been identified to him as a 'Negro.'"[8] Toomer's contradictory stance vis-à-vis Liveright and Anderson reveals the depth of his anguish about his race in the weeks before the publication of the work that would link him to a literary tradition from which he would flee.

We also must recall Toomer's anger with Alain Locke for reprinting excerpts of *Cane* in *The New Negro* in 1925 (he was silent regarding Locke's decision to reprint "Song of the Son" in the 1925 Harlem issue of *The Survey Graphic*), a reaction that smacks of denial and ingratitude, given Locke's early and consistent support

5. *The Wayward and the Seeking*, 84.
6. Ibid., 93.
7. Ibid., 127.
8. Ibid., 11–12.

of Toomer while he was still living in Washington, D.C. And then in 1934, almost ten years after the publication of *The New Negro*, Toomer, most improbably, observes to the *Baltimore Afro-American* newspaper that "I have not lived as [a Negro] nor do I really know whether there is colored blood in me or not."[9] During this same period, Toomer refuses to contribute to Nancy Cunard's anthology *The Negro* (1934) stating that "though I am interested in and deeply value the Negro, I am not a Negro."[1] This claim stands out as particularly disingenuous when we recall Toomer's week-long trip with Waldo Frank in the fall of 1922 in Spartanburg, South Carolina, where they masqueraded as "blood brothers," that is, as Negroes.[2] After serving as Frank's "host in a black world,"[3] Toomer returned to Washington, and for two weeks worked as an assistant to the manager of the Howard Theater, a theater that served the capital's African American community, and where he gathered material for such stories as "Box Seat" and "Theater." These shaping experiences in the black world, among many others, call into question Toomer's odd claim in the *Baltimore Afro-American* and to the anthologist Nancy Cunard that he was not, and had not been, black.

At this juncture, it is useful to return to Elizabeth Alexander's "Toomer," the splendid poem that opens our introduction and that also evokes Toomer's shifting, complex, contradictory stance on race: "I wished / to contemplate who I was beyond / my body, this container of flesh. / I made up a language in which to exist. / . . . Oh, / to be a Negro is—is? / to be a Negro, is. To be."[4] Alexander's key line is this: "I made up a language in which to exist." In this insightful line, Alexander captures not only Toomer's definition of race as a social construction, but also his anguished effort to liberate himself from his apparent anxiety and ambivalence about his black ancestry.

The several documents published here for the first time present a portrait of Toomer stained with contradictions, raising as many questions as they answer. Notwithstanding Toomer's definition of himself as an "American, neither white nor black,"[5] at crucial stages in his life he self-identified as Negro: as a young adult in 1917 at the age of 23, Toomer self-identified as Negro; again in 1942 as a mature adult at the age of 48, Toomer self-identified as Negro. While the

9. Barbara Foley, "Jean Toomer's Washington and the Politics of Class," *Modern Fiction Studies* 42.2 (1996): 289.
1. Ibid., 313.
2. Kerman and Eldridge, *The Lives of Jean Toomer*, 89.
3. Ibid., 90.
4. "Toomer," from *Crave Radiance: New and Selected Poems 1990–2010.* Copyright © 2010 by Elizabeth Alexander. Reprinted by permission of Graywolf Press and the author.
5. *The Wayward and the Seeking*, 93.

registration cards, the census data, and marriage certificate are contradictory, there is, nevertheless, a pattern. It is our carefully considered judgment, based upon an analysis of archival evidence previously overlooked by other scholars, that Jean Toomer—for all of his pioneering theorizing about what today we might call a multicultural or mixed-raced ancestry—was a Negro who decided to pass for white. Here we respectfully disagree with Toomer's biographers Kerman and Eldridge, who claim that Toomer never attempted "to 'pass' in a racial sense."[6]

And what is Toomer's relationship to American modernism and the African American literary tradition? Without question, *Cane* is a classic work of timeless significance in American and African American letters. In its pages we encounter again and again the arresting vision of an astonishingly original writer. And what shall be our generation's relationship to this great artist of the Harlem Renaissance and the Lost Generation, who rejected the very book by which he is destined to be remembered? Alice Walker expressed a perspective we would do well to reflect upon. Shortly after the publication of *Meridian*, her magisterial fictional meditation on the civil rights movement, and her own formal response to Toomer's call in *Cane*, Walker concluded: "I think Jean Toomer would want us to keep [*Cane*'s] beauty, but let him go."[7] Walker is probably correct in her assessment of Toomer's own wishes. However, since Toomer's *Cane* is arguably the most sophisticated work of literature created over the course of the Harlem Renaissance, we imagine that future generations of scholars will find his struggle with his racial identity as endlessly fascinating as we have.

---

6. *The Lives of Jean Toomer*, 115.
7. Alice Walker, "The Divided Life of Jean Toomer," in *In Search of Our Mothers' Gardens* (New York: Harcourt, Brace, and Jovanovich, 1983), 65.

Toomer's draft registration, June 5, 1917.

## REGISTRAR'S REPORT

1 | Tall, medium, or short (specify which)? _Tall_  Slender, medium, or stout (which)? _Slender_

2 | Color of eyes? _dark brown_ Color of hair? _black_ Bald? _no_

3 | Has person lost arm, leg, hand, foot, or both eyes, or is he otherwise disabled (specify)? _no_

I certify that my answers are true, that the person registered has read his own answers, that I have witnessed his signature, and that all of his answers of which I have knowledge are true, except as follows:

_Howell J. O'Brien_
(Signature of registrar)

Precinct **8**

City or County **Washington, D. C.**

State _____

JUN 5 1917
(Date of registration)

lxxiii

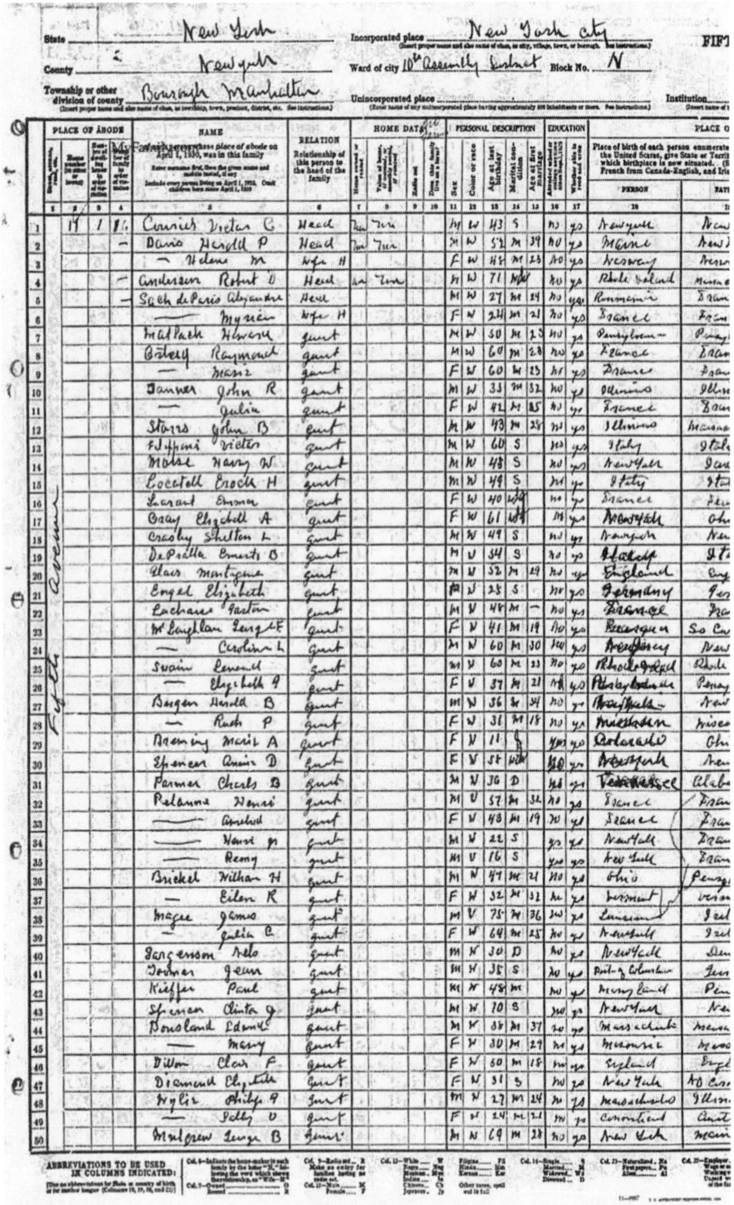

State: New York — Incorporated place: New York city — FIFT[…]
County: New York — Ward of city: 10th Assembly District — Block No. N
Township or other division of county: Borough Manhattan — Unincorporated place — Institution

| Line | Street, avenue, road, etc. | House number | Number of dwelling | Number of family | NAME | RELATION | Home owned or rented | Value of home | Sex | Color or race | Age at last birthday | Marital condition | Age at first marriage | Attended school | Whether able to read and write | Place of birth — PERSON | Place of birth — FATHER |
|---|---|---|---|---|---|---|---|---|---|---|---|---|---|---|---|---|---|
| 1 | Fifth Avenue | 14 | 1 | 1 | Couriet Victor C | Head | R | Ten | M | W | 43 | S | | no | yes | New York | New |
| 2 | | | | | Davis Harold P | Head | R | Ten | M | W | 52 | M | 39 | no | yes | Maine | New |
| 3 | | | | | — Helene M | Wife H | | | F | W | 48 | M | 23 | no | yes | Norway | Norw |
| 4 | | | | | Anderson Robert O | Head | R | Ten | M | W | 71 | Wd | | no | yes | Rhode Island | Massa |
| 5 | | | | | Sacheverell de Paris Alexandre | Head | | | M | W | 27 | M | 24 | no | yes | Roumania | Fran |
| 6 | | | | | — Mynie | Wife H | | | F | W | 24 | M | 21 | no | yes | France | Fran |
| 7 | | | | | Matlack Howard | guest | | | M | W | 50 | M | 23 | no | yes | Pennsylvania | Penn |
| 8 | | | | | Botsey Raymond | guest | | | M | W | 60 | M | 28 | no | yes | France | Fran |
| 9 | | | | | — Marie | guest | | | F | W | 60 | M | 23 | no | yes | France | Fran |
| 10 | | | | | Tanner John R | guest | | | M | W | 33 | M | 32 | no | yes | Illinois | Illin |
| 11 | | | | | — Julia | guest | | | F | W | 42 | M | 25 | no | yes | France | Fran |
| 12 | | | | | Starrs John B | guest | | | M | W | 43 | M | 28 | no | yes | Illinois | Massa |
| 13 | | | | | Filippini Victor | guest | | | M | W | 60 | S | | no | yes | Italy | Italy |
| 14 | | | | | Morse Harry W | guest | | | M | W | 48 | S | | no | yes | New York | [illegible] |
| 15 | | | | | Coccitelli Enoch H | guest | | | M | W | 49 | S | | no | yes | Italy | Ital |
| 16 | | | | | Lacarat Emma | guest | | | F | W | 40 | Wd | | no | yes | France | Fran |
| 17 | | | | | Gray Elizabeth A | guest | | | F | W | 61 | Wd | | no | yes | New York | Ohio |
| 18 | | | | | Crosby Shelton L | guest | | | M | W | 49 | S | | no | yes | New York | New |
| 19 | | | | | DePratta Ernesto B | guest | | | M | W | 34 | S | | no | yes | Italy | Ita |
| 20 | | | | | Glass Montague | guest | | | M | W | 52 | M | 29 | no | yes | England | Eng |
| 21 | | | | | Engel Elizabeth | guest | | | F | W | 25 | S | | no | yes | Germany | Ger |
| 22 | | | | | Lachaise Gaston | guest | | | M | W | 48 | M | — | no | yes | France | Fra |
| 23 | | | | | McLaughlan George F | guest | | | F | W | 41 | M | 19 | no | yes | Nicaragua | So Ca |
| 24 | | | | | — Caroline L | guest | | | M | W | 60 | M | 30 | no | yes | New Jersey | New |
| 25 | | | | | Swain Leonard | guest | | | M | W | 60 | M | 23 | no | yes | Rhode Island | Rhode |
| 26 | | | | | — Elizabeth A | guest | | | F | W | 37 | M | 21 | no | yes | Pennsylvania | Penn |
| 27 | | | | | Bergen Harold B | guest | | | M | W | 36 | M | 34 | no | yes | New York | New |
| 28 | | | | | — Ruth P | guest | | | F | W | 31 | M | 18 | no | yes | Michigan | Misso |
| 29 | | | | | Browning Marie A | guest | | | F | W | 11 | S | | yes | yes | Colorado | Ohio |
| 30 | | | | | Spencer Annie D | guest | | | F | W | 54 | Wd | | no | yes | New York | New |
| 31 | | | | | Farmer Charles B | guest | | | M | W | 36 | D | | no | yes | Tennessee | Alaba |
| 32 | | | | | Delaunne Henri | guest | | | M | W | 57 | M | 32 | no | yes | France | Fran |
| 33 | | | | | — Annabel | guest | | | F | W | 48 | M | 19 | no | yes | France | Fran |
| 34 | | | | | — Henri J | guest | | | M | W | 22 | S | | yes | yes | New York | Fran |
| 35 | | | | | — Remy | guest | | | M | W | 16 | S | | yes | yes | New York | Fran |
| 36 | | | | | Brickel William H | guest | | | M | W | 47 | M | 21 | no | yes | Ohio | Penn |
| 37 | | | | | — Eileen R | guest | | | F | W | 32 | M | 31 | no | yes | Vermont | Verm |
| 38 | | | | | Magee James | guest | | | M | W | 75 | M | 36 | no | yes | Louisiana | Irel |
| 39 | | | | | — Julia C | guest | | | F | W | 64 | M | 25 | no | yes | New York | Irel |
| 40 | | | | | Jorgensen Nels | guest | | | M | W | 30 | D | | no | yes | New York | Den |
| 41 | | | | | Tourner Jean | guest | | | M | W | 35 | S | | no | yes | District of Columbia | Fren |
| 42 | | | | | Kieffer Paul | guest | | | M | W | 48 | M | | no | yes | Maryland | Pen |
| 43 | | | | | Spencer Clinton J | guest | | | M | W | 70 | S | | no | yes | New York | New |
| 44 | | | | | Bousland Edward | guest | | | M | W | 38 | M | 37 | no | yes | Massachusetts | Mass |
| 45 | | | | | — Mary | guest | | | F | W | 30 | M | 29 | no | yes | Missouri | Miss |
| 46 | | | | | Dillon Clara F | guest | | | F | W | 60 | M | 18 | no | yes | England | Engl |
| 47 | | | | | Diamond Elizabeth | guest | | | F | W | 31 | S | | no | yes | New York | NO Car |
| 48 | | | | | Wylie Philip A | guest | | | M | W | 27 | M | 24 | no | yes | Massachusetts | Illin |
| 49 | | | | | — Sally D | guest | | | F | W | 24 | M | 21 | no | yes | Connecticut | Conn |
| 50 | | | | | Mulgrew George B | guest | | | M | W | 69 | M | 28 | no | yes | New York | Main |

ABBREVIATIONS TO BE USED IN COLUMNS INDICATED:

1930 census.

Form 15-6

DEPARTMENT OF COMMERCE—BUREAU OF THE CENSUS

TEENTH CENSUS OF THE UNITED STATES: 1930

POPULATION SCHEDULE

Enumeration District No. 31-118c

Sheet No.

Supervisor's District No. 21

22A

23

Enumerated by me on April 24d 1930. Franklin Howell, Enumerator.

| OF BIRTH | MOTHER TONGUE (OR NATIVE LANGUAGE) OF FOREIGN BORN | | CITIZENSHIP, ETC. | | | OCCUPATION AND INDUSTRY | | | | EMPLOYMENT | VETERANS | | |
|---|---|---|---|---|---|---|---|---|---|---|---|---|---|
| MOTHER | Language spoken in home before coming to the United States | A B C | | | | OCCUPATION | INDUSTRY | CODE | | | | | |
| New York | | 56 | | | yes | Attorney | Law | 5X94 E | yes | no | | | 1 |
| Maine | | 50 | | | yes | Writer | Journalist | 5444 E | | no | | | 2 |
| Norway | Hungarian | 65 65 | ✓ 1916 Na | | yes | none | | | | | | | 3 |
| Rhode Island | | | | | yes | Banker | Bank | 8563 W | yes | no | | | 4 |
| France | French | 18 74 | ✓ 1927 Al | yes | Orchard | Painting | 8304 O | yes | no | | | 5 |
| France | French | 13 13 | ✓ 1923 Al | | yes | none | 8241 O | | | | | 6 |
| Pennsylvania | | 58 | | | yes | Gen. manager | Storedge O | 7550 W | | no | | | 7 |
| France | French | 17 17 | ✓ 1852 Na | | yes | Manager | Hotel | 8491 E | yes | no | | | 8 |
| France | French | 17 17 | ✓ 1857 Na | | yes | none | | | | | | | 9 |
| Illinois | | 61 | | | yes | Architect | Building | 5234 | yes | yes WW | | | 10 |
| 8 France | French | 17 17 | ✓ 1930 Al | | yes | none | | | | | | | 11 |
| Canada | | 61 43 | ✓ | | yes | Sculptress | Art | 8394 O | yes | no | | | 12 |
| Italy | Italian | 71 71 | ✓ 1900 Al | | yes | Bank officer | Bank | 8553 VE | yes | no | | | 13 |
| Iowa | | 66 | | | yes | none | | | | | | | 14 |
| Italy | Italian | 24 24 | ✓ 1914 Na | yes | Merchant | Dry goods retail | 8591 E | | no | | | 15 |
| France | French | 13 13 | ✓ 1929 Al | | yes | none | | | | | | | 16 |
| Germany | | | | | yes | none | | | | | | | 17 |
| New York | | 58 | | | yes | Art dealer & antiques | Dealer | 4693 W | | no | | | 18 |
| Italy | Italian | 24 24 | ✓ 1902 Na | | yes | Sculptor | Art | 8394 O | | no | | | 19 |
| England | English | 60 60 | ✓ 1900 Na | | yes | Writer | Author | 8444 O | yes | no | | | 20 |
| Germany | German | 13 13 | ✓ 1913 Na | | yes | Hair dresser | Beauty shop | 8491 N | no | 1 | | | 21 |
| France | French | 13 13 | ✓ 1900 Na | | yes | Sculptor | Art | 8394 O | yes | no | | | 22 |
| So. Carolina | | 78 | | | yes | none | | | | | | | 23 |
| Pennsylvania | | 57 | | | yes | Physician | Practice | 4294 O | yes | yes WW | | | 24 |
| Rhode Island | | 54 | | | yes | Lawyer | Gen. Practice | 5X94 O | yes | no | | | 25 |
| New York | | 58 | | | yes | none | | | | | | | 26 |
| New York | | 58 | | | yes | Director | Soap works | 2389 E | yes | yes WW | | | 27 |
| Iowa | | 67 | | | yes | none | | | | | | | 28 |
| Germany | | 9 | | | yes | none | | | | | | | 29 |
| New Jersey | | 58 | | | yes | Salesman | Auto & Gas | 45X5 W | yes | | | | 30 |
| Alabama | | 81 | | | yes | Writer | Free lance | | | yes WW | | | 31 |
| France | French | 17 17 | ✓ 1844 Al | | yes | Merchant | Carpenter | 9441 O | yes | no | | | 32 |
| France | French | 17 17 | ✓ 1903 Al | yes | none | | | | | | | 33 |
| France | | 56 12 0 | | | yes | Salesman | Importing | 8591 W | yes | | | | 34 |
| France | | 56 12 0 | | | yes | none | | | | | | | 35 |
| Kentucky | | 61 | | | yes | Promoter | Independent | 9983 O | yes | yes WW | | | 36 |
| Vermont | | 57 | | | yes | none | | | | | | | 37 |
| England | | 85 64 0 | | | yes | Merchant | Silks | 8491 O | yes | no | | | 38 |
| Ireland | | 58 60 0 | | | yes | none | | | | | | | 39 |
| New York | | 56 60 1 | | | yes | Writer | Free lance | 8494 O | yes | yes WW | | | 40 |
| Louisiana | | 78 | | | yes | Writer | Free lance | 8491 O | yes | no | | | 41 |
| Pennsylvania | | 77 | | | yes | Lawyer | Practice | 5X94 E | yes | no | | | 42 |
| Maryland | | 58 | | | yes | none | | | | | | | 43 |
| Massachusetts | | 53 | | | yes | Advertising | Retail | 4183 O | yes | yes WW | | | 44 |
| Missouri | | 66 | | | yes | none | | | | | | | 45 |
| England | English | 60 60 | ✓ 1916 Na | | yes | none | | | | | | | 46 |
| Germany | German | 56 13 2 | | | yes | Stenographer | Public | 1193 O | yes | | | | 47 |
| Wisconsin | | 53 | | | yes | Writer | Free lance | 8494 O | yes | no | | | 48 |
| Austria | | 55 16 0 | | | na | none | | | | | | | 49 |
| New York | | 50 | | | yes | Messenger | Sawmill | 9244 E | | no | | | 50 |

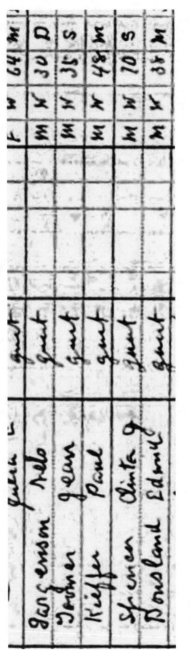

Detail of 1930 census.

COPY OF ORIGINAL

**STATE OF WISCONSIN**

Department of Health—Bureau of Vital Statistics    Register No. _____

**Certificate of Marriage**

License Number 4361

Place of Marriage

County of _____
Township of _____ or Village of _____ or City of _Portage_ in said County

I, _Daniel Cowiger_ hereby certify that I, _Oct. 30_ day of _A. D. 1931_, at _Portage_ of the State of Wis. _____ and _Marjory Latimer_ of _Portage_ state of Wis. _____ were by me united in marriage as authorized by Marriage License issued for that purpose by the County Clerk, _Columbia_ County and State of Wisconsin, numbered _4361_, dated the _21_ day of _Oct_ A. D. 19_31_ and

We, the undersigned, were present at the Marriage of _Jean Toomer_ _____ as set forth in the foregoing certificate, at their request, and heard their acknowledgments together with our _____ her husband and wife.

Witnesses: Two { _Marjory Latimer_ / _Maria Vigne_ }

Signature of person officiating and P.O. Address { _Daniel Cowiger_ / _Rev. Crawford Barnheart, Wis._ }

**Groom**

Name _Jean Toomer_
Residence _Chicago, Ill._
Age _36_  Color _W_  Single / Married / No. of Marriages _1_
Birthplace _Washington_  State _Wis_  Nationality
Occupation _Artist + Writer_
Relationship _____
Name of Father, Guardian or Curator _Nathan Toomer_
Maiden name of Mother _Nina Pinchback_

If previously Married {
Date of Marriage _____  To whom Married _____
Date of Death _____  Where Divorced _____
By What Court Divorced _____  To whom Divorce granted _____
}

Was a special dispensation issued? _No_
Date of Issue _10/21/31_
Filed _11/2/31_

**Bride**

Name _Marjory Latimer_
Residence _Portage Wis._
Age _32_  Color _W_  Single / Married / No. of Marriages _1_
Birthplace _Wis_  Nationality
Occupation _Writer_
Relationship _____
Name of Father, Guardian or Curator _Clark Latimer_
Maiden name of Mother _Laurie Brown_

If previously Married {
Date of Marriage _____  To whom Married _____
Date of Death _____  Date of Divorce _____
Where Divorced _____  By What Court Divorced _____
To whom Divorce granted _____
}

Maiden name of Bride If previously Married _____

_____ County Clerk. _H. C. Langton_
_____ Local Register. _John A. Bartley_

USE THIS FORM OF CERTIFICATE FOR REPORTING TO THE REGISTER OF DEEDS.

The _____ certificates marked duplicate and triplicate duly signed shall be given by the officiating person to the parties married by him, and the certificate marked original, legibly and completely filled out with indelible ink shall, if marriage was performed by any authorized or licensed person, or in case of a Marriage Ceremony performed without an official, be possessed by the parties to the Marriage Contract or either of them to the local registrar of vital statistics of the city, incorporated village or town in which said Marriage was performed within three days after the date of said marriage. Send all original certificates to the State Board of Health with the regular monthly reports.

1931 marriage certificate.

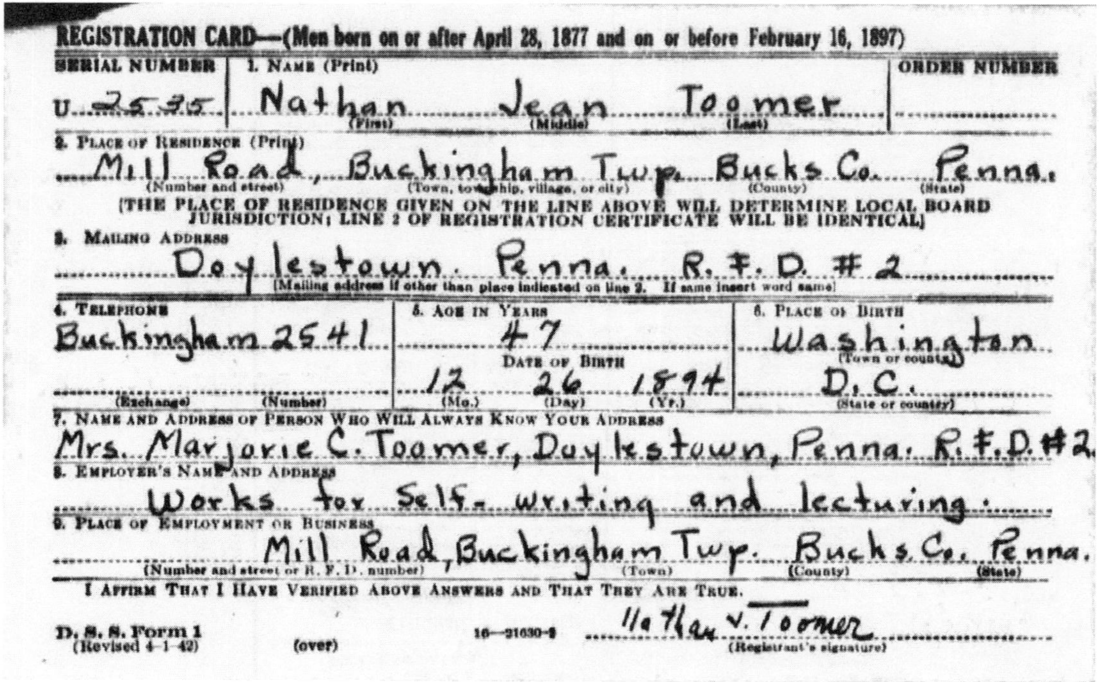
REGISTRATION CARD—(Men born on or after April 28, 1877 and on or before February 16, 1897)

SERIAL NUMBER U 2575 | 1. NAME (Print) Nathan (First) Jean (Middle) Toomer (Last) | ORDER NUMBER

2. PLACE OF RESIDENCE (Print)
Mill Road, (Number and street) Buckingham Twp. (Town, township, village, or city) Bucks Co. (County) Penna. (State)

[THE PLACE OF RESIDENCE GIVEN ON THE LINE ABOVE WILL DETERMINE LOCAL BOARD JURISDICTION; LINE 2 OF REGISTRATION CERTIFICATE WILL BE IDENTICAL]

3. MAILING ADDRESS
Doylestown. Penna. R. F. D. # 2
[Mailing address if other than place indicated on line 2. If same insert word same]

4. TELEPHONE
Buckingham 2541
(Exchange) (Number)

5. AGE IN YEARS
47
DATE OF BIRTH
12 (Mo.) 26 (Day) 1894 (Yr.)

6. PLACE OF BIRTH
Washington (Town or county)
D. C. (State or country)

7. NAME AND ADDRESS OF PERSON WHO WILL ALWAYS KNOW YOUR ADDRESS
Mrs. Marjorie C. Toomer, Doylestown, Penna. R. F. D. #2.

8. EMPLOYER'S NAME AND ADDRESS
Works for Self – writing and lecturing.

9. PLACE OF EMPLOYMENT OR BUSINESS
Mill Road, (Number and street or R. F. D. number) Buckingham Twp. (Town) Bucks Co. (County) Penna. (State)

I AFFIRM THAT I HAVE VERIFIED ABOVE ANSWERS AND THAT THEY ARE TRUE.

D. S. S. Form 1
(Revised 4-1-42)
(over)
16—21630-2
Nathan J. Toomer
(Registrant's signature)

Draft registration, April 24, 1942.

# REGISTRAR'S REPORT

## DESCRIPTION OF REGISTRANT

| RACE | | HEIGHT (Approx.) | | WEIGHT (Approx.) | | COMPLEXION | |
|---|---|---|---|---|---|---|---|
| White | | 5 ft. 10" | | 178 | | Sallow | |
| | | EYES | | HAIR | | Light | |
| Negro | X | Blue | | Blonde | | Ruddy | |
| | | Gray | | Red | | Dark | |
| Oriental | | Hazel | | Brown | | Freckled | |
| | | Brown | | Black | X | Light brown | |
| Indian | | Black | X | Gray | | Dark brown | X |
| | | | | Bald | | Black | |
| Filipino | | | | | | | |

Other obvious physical characteristics that will aid in identification

I certify that my answers are true; that the person registered has read or has had read to him his own answers; that I have witnessed his signature or mark and that all of his answers of which I have knowledge are true, except as follows:

*Edith V. Rider*
(Signature of registrar)

Registrar for Local Board   *34   Phila   Pa.*
(Number)        (City or county)      (State)

Date of registration   *4/27/42*

Local Board No. 34                      52

Philadelphia City                    101

                                     034

1613 North 28th Street              1

Phila.   STAMP OF LOCAL BOARD

(The stamp of the Local Board having jurisdiction of the registrant shall be placed in the above space)

16—21630—1

# The Text of
## CANE

To my grandmother . . .

# Karintha[1]

Her skin is like dusk on the eastern horizon,
O cant[2] you see it, O cant you see it,
Her skin is like dusk on the eastern horizon
. . . When the sun goes down.[3]

Men had always wanted her, this Karintha, even as a child, Karintha carrying beauty, perfect as dusk when the sun goes down. Old men rode her hobby-horse upon their knees. Young men danced with her at frolics when they should have been dancing with their grown-up girls. God grant us youth, secretly prayed the old men. The young fellows counted the time to pass before she would be old enough to mate with them. This interest of the male, who wishes to ripen a growing thing too soon, could mean no good to her.

Karintha, at twelve, was a wild flash that told the other folks just what it was to live. At sunset, when there was no wind, and the pine-smoke from over by the sawmill hugged the earth, and you couldnt see more than a few feet in front, her sudden darting past you was a bit of vivid color, like a black bird that flashes in light. With the other children one could hear, some distance off, their feet flopping in the two-inch dust. Karintha's running was a whir. It had the sound of the red dust that sometimes makes a spiral in the road. At dusk, during the hush just after the sawmill had closed down, and before any of the women had started their supper-getting-ready songs, her voice, high-pitched, shrill, would put one's ears to itching. But no one ever thought to make her stop because of it. She stoned the cows, and beat her dog, and fought the other children . . . Even the preacher, who caught her at mischief, told himself that she was as innocently lovely as a November cotton flower. Already, rumors were out about her. Homes in Georgia are most often built on the two-room plan. In one, you cook and eat, in the other you sleep, and there love goes on. Karintha had seen or heard, perhaps she had felt her parents loving. One could but

---

1. Originally included in *Natalie Mann*, a drama by Toomer, this piece was intended to illustrate the style and the thought of the literature written by Nathan Merilh, one of the major characters in the drama. Never published in Toomer's lifetime, *Natalie Mann* has now been published in *The Wayward and the Seeking: A Collection of Writings by Jean Toomer*, ed. Darwin T. Turner (Washington, D.C.: Howard UP, 1980). When "Karintha" was first published (*Broom* 4 [January 1923]: 83–85), a note instructed readers of the piece: "To be read, accompanied by the humming of a Negro folk-song."
2. Throughout *Cane*, apostrophes are generally omitted from contractions. When "Karintha" was published in *Broom*, however, this word was printed as "can't."
3. Throughout *Cane*, Toomer uses two or three periods to indicate a pause in the reading. Readers should not mistake these for ellipsis marks, which indicate an omission from the original text.

imitate one's parents, for to follow them was the way of God. She played "home" with a small boy who was not afraid to do her bidding. That started the whole thing. Old men could no longer ride her hobby-horse upon their knees. But young men counted faster.

> Her skin is like dusk,
> O cant you see it,
> Her skin is like dusk,
> When the sun goes down.

Karintha is a woman. She who carries beauty, perfect as dusk when the sun goes down. She has been married many times. Old men remind her that a few years back they rode her hobby-horse upon their knees. Karintha smiles, and indulges them when she is in the mood for it. She has contempt for them. Karintha is a woman. Young men run stills to make her money. Young men go to the big cities and run on the road. Young men go away to college. They all want to bring her money. These are the young men who thought that all they had to do was to count time. But Karintha is a woman, and she has had a child. A child fell out of her womb onto a bed of pine-needles in the forest. Pine-needles are smooth and sweet. They are elastic to the feet of rabbits . . . A sawmill was nearby. Its pyramidal sawdust pile smouldered. It is a year before one completely burns. Meanwhile, the smoke curls up and hangs in odd wraiths about the trees, curls up, and spreads itself out over the valley . . . Weeks after Karintha returned home the smoke was so heavy you tasted it in water. Some one made a song:

> Smoke is on the hills. Rise up.
> Smoke is on the hills, O rise
> And take my soul to Jesus.

Karintha is a woman. Men do not know that the soul of her was a growing thing ripened too soon. They will bring their money; they will die not having found it out . . . Karintha at twenty, carrying beauty, perfect as dusk when the sun goes down. Karintha . . .

> Her skin is like dusk on the eastern horizon,
> O cant you see it, O cant you see it,
> Her skin is like dusk on the eastern horizon
> . . . When the sun goes down.

> Goes down . . .

# Reapers

Black reapers with the sound of steel on stones
Are sharpening scythes. I see them place the hones
In their hip-pockets as a thing that's done,
And start their silent swinging, one by one.
Black horses drive a mower through the weeds,
And there, a field rat, startled, squealing bleeds,
His belly close to ground. I see the blade,
Blood-stained, continue cutting weeds and shade.

# November Cotton Flower[1]

Boll-weevil's coming, and the winter's cold,
Made cotton-stalks look rusty, seasons old,
And cotton, scarce as any southern snow,
Was vanishing; the branch, so pinched and slow,
Failed in its function as the autumn rake;
Drouth fighting soil had caused the soil to take
All water from the streams; dead birds were found
In wells a hundred feet below the ground—
Such was the season when the flower bloomed.
Old folks were startled, and it soon assumed
Significance. Superstition saw
Something it had never seen before:
Brown eyes that loved without a trace of fear,
Beauty so sudden for that time of year.

---

1. First published in *The Nomad* 2 (Summer 1923): 4.

# Becky[1]

Becky was the white woman who had two Negro sons. She's dead; they've gone away. The pines whisper to Jesus. The Bible flaps its leaves with an aimless rustle on her mound.

Becky had one Negro son. Who gave it to her? Damn buck nigger, said the white folks' mouths. She wouldnt tell. Common, God-forsaken, insane white shameless wench, said the white folks' mouths. Her eyes were sunken, her neck stringy, her breasts fallen, till then. Taking their words, they filled her, like a bubble rising— then she broke. Mouth setting in a twist that held her eyes, harsh, vacant, staring . . . Who gave it to her? Low-down nigger with no self-respect, said the black folks' mouths. She wouldnt tell. Poor Catholic poor-white crazy woman, said the black folks' mouths. White folks and black folks built her cabin, fed her and her growing baby, prayed secretly to God who'd put His cross upon her and cast her out.

When the first was born, the white folks said they'd have no more to do with her. And black folks, they too joined hands to cast her out . . . The pines whispered to Jesus . . . The railroad boss said not to say he said it, but she could live, if she wanted to, on the narrow strip of land between the railroad and the road. John Stone,[2] who owned the lumber and the bricks, would have shot the man who told he gave the stuff to Lonnie Deacon, who stole out there at night and built the cabin. A single room held down to earth . . . O fly away to Jesus . . . by a leaning chimney . . .

Six trains each day rumbled past and shook the ground under her cabin. Fords, and horse- and mule-drawn buggies went back and forth along the road. No one ever saw her. Trainmen, and passengers who'd heard about her, threw out papers and food. Threw out little crumpled slips of paper scribbled with prayers, as they passed her eye-shaped piece of sandy ground. Ground islandized between the road and railroad track. Pushed up where a blue-sheen God[3] with listless eyes could look at it. Folks from the town took turns, unknown, of course, to each other, in bringing corn and meat and sweet potatoes. Even sometimes snuff . . . O thank y Jesus . . . Old

---

1. First published in the *Liberator* 5 (October 1922): 26.
2. A suggestion of the common locale of the stories in the first section of *Cane* is the occasional recurrence of names. John Stone is the father of Bob Stone ("Blood-Burning Moon"). A person named Barlo, possibly the same one as in this story, appears in "Esther." David Georgia is a character in "Blood-Burning Moon" as well as in "Becky." The Dixie Pike is named in "Carma" and "Fern."
3. The locomotive.

David Georgia, grinding cane and boiling syrup, never went her
way without some sugar sap. No one ever saw her. The boy grew up
and ran around. When he was five years old as folks reckoned it,
Hugh Jourdon saw him carrying a baby. "Becky has another son,"
was what the whole town knew. But nothing was said, for the part
of man that says things to the likes of that had told itself that if
there was a Becky, that Becky now was dead.

    The two boys grew. Sullen and cunning . . . O pines, whisper to
Jesus; tell Him to come and press sweet Jesus-lips against their lips
and eyes . . . It seemed as though with those two big fellows there,
there could be no room for Becky. The part that prayed wondered if
perhaps she'd really died, and they had buried her. No one dared
ask. They'd beat and cut a man who meant nothing at all in mentioning that they lived along the road. White or colored? No one
knew, and least of all themselves. They drifted around from job to
job. We, who had cast out their mother because of them, could we
take them in? They answered black and white folks by shooting up
two men and leaving town. "Godam the white folks; godam the niggers," they shouted as they left town. Becky? Smoke curled up from
her chimney; she must be there. Trains passing shook the ground.
The ground shook the leaning chimney. Nobody noticed it. A creepy
feeling came over all who saw that thin wraith of smoke and felt the
trembling of the ground. Folks began to take her food again. They
quit it soon because they had a fear. Becky if dead might be a hant,[4]
and if alive—it took some nerve even to mention it . . . O pines,
whisper to Jesus . . .

    It was Sunday. Our congregation had been visiting at Pulverton,
and were coming home. There was no wind. The autumn sun, the
bell from Ebenezer Church, listless and heavy. Even the pines were
stale, sticky, like the smell of food that makes you sick. Before we
turned the bend of the road that would show us the Becky cabin,
the horses stopped stock-still, pushed back their ears, and nervously whinnied. We urged, then whipped them on. Quarter of a
mile away thin smoke curled up from the leaning chimney . . . O
pines, whisper to Jesus . . . Goose-flesh came on my skin though
there still was neither chill nor wind. Eyes left their sockets for the
cabin. Ears burned and throbbed. Uncanny eclipse! fear closed my
mind. We were just about to pass . . . Pines shout to Jesus! . . . the
ground trembled as a ghost train rumbled by. The chimney fell into
the cabin. Its thud was like a hollow report, ages having passed
since it went off. Barlo and I were pulled out of our seats. Dragged

4. A "haunt," a ghost.

to the door that had swung open. Through the dust we saw the bricks in a mound upon the floor. Becky, if she was there, lay under them. I thought I heard a groan. Barlo, mumbling something, threw his Bible on the pile. (No one has ever touched it.) Somehow we got away. My buggy was still on the road. The last thing that I remember was whipping old Dan like fury; I remember nothing after that—that is, until I reached town and folks crowded round to get the true word of it.

Becky was the white woman who had two Negro sons. She's dead; they've gone away. The pines whisper to Jesus. The Bible flaps its leaves with an aimless rustle on her mound.

# Face[1]

Hair—
silver-gray,
like streams of stars,
Brows—
recurved canoes
quivered by the ripples blown by pain,
Her eyes—
mist of tears
condensing on the flesh below
And her channeled muscles
are cluster grapes of sorrow
purple in the evening sun
nearly ripe for worms.

1. First published as number one of three "Georgia Portraits," *Modern Review* 1 (January 1923): 81.

# Cotton Song

Come, brother, come. Lets lift it;
Come now, hewit! roll away!
Shackles fall upon the Judgment Day
But lets not wait for it.

God's body's got a soul,
Bodies like to roll the soul,
Cant blame God if we dont roll,
Come, brother, roll, roll!

Cotton bales are the fleecy way
Weary sinner's bare feet trod,
Softly, softly to the throne of God,
"We aint agwine t wait until th Judgment Day!

Nassur; nassur,
Hump.
Eoho,[1] eoho, roll away!
We aint agwine t wait until th Judgment Day!"

God's body's got a soul,
Bodies like to roll the soul,
Cant blame God if we dont roll,
Come, brother, roll, roll!

1. A call.

# Carma[1]

Wind is in the cane. Come along.
Cane leaves swaying, rusty with talk,
Scratching choruses above the guinea's squawk,
Wind is in the cane. Come along.

Carma, in overalls, and strong as any man, stands behind the old brown mule, driving the wagon home. It bumps, and groans, and shakes as it crosses the railroad track. She, riding it easy. I leave the men around the stove to follow her with my eyes down the red dust road. Nigger woman driving a Georgia chariot down an old dust road. Dixie Pike is what they call it. Maybe she feels my gaze, perhaps she expects it. Anyway, she turns. The sun, which has been slanting over her shoulder, shoots primitive rockets into her mangrove-gloomed, yellow flower face. Hi! Yip! God has left the Moses-people for the nigger. "Gedap." Using reins to slap the mule, she disappears in a cloudy rumble at some indefinite point along the road.

(The sun is hammered to a band of gold. Pine-needles, like mazda, are brilliantly aglow. No rain has come to take the rustle from the falling sweet-gum leaves. Over in the forest, across the swamp, a sawmill blows its closing whistle. Smoke curls up. Marvelous web spun by the spider sawdust pile. Curls up and spreads itself pine-high above the branch, a single silver band along the eastern valley. A black boy . . . you are the most sleepiest man I ever seed, Sleeping Beauty . . . cradled on a gray mule, guided by the hollow sound of cowbells, heads for them through a rusty cotton field. From down the railroad track, the chug-chug of a gas engine announces that the repair gang is coming home. A girl in the yard of a whitewashed shack not much larger than the stack of worn ties piled before it, sings. Her voice is loud. Echoes, like rain, sweep the valley. Dusk takes the polish from the rails. Lights twinkle in scattered houses. From far away, a sad strong song. Pungent and composite, the smell of farmyards is the fragrance of the woman. She does not sing; her body is a song. She is in the forest, dancing. Torches flare . . . juju men, greegree,[2] witch-doctors . . . torches go out . . . The Dixie Pike has grown from a goat path in Africa.

*Night.*

Foxie, the bitch, slicks back her ears and barks at the rising moon.)

---

1. First published in the *Liberator* 5 (September 1922): 5. "Karma," from the Sanskrit word for "fate," is the force generated by a person's actions; it is believed in Hinduism and Buddhism to perpetuate the passage of the soul from one state to another and to determine a person's destiny in his or her next existence.
2. An African charm or amulet; *juju men*: conjurers, supposedly able to use powers of the supernatural.

> Wind is in the corn. Come along.
> Corn leaves swaying, rusty with talk,
> Scratching choruses above the guinea's squawk,
> Wind is in the corn. Come along.

Carma's tale is the crudest melodrama. Her husband's in the gang.[3] And its her fault he got there. Working with a contractor, he was away most of the time. She had others. No one blames her for that. He returned one day and hung around the town where he picked up week-old boasts and rumors . . . Bane accused her. She denied. He couldnt see that she was becoming hysterical. He would have liked to take his fists and beat her. Who was strong as a man. Stronger. Words, like corkscrews, wormed to her strength. It fizzled out. Grabbing a gun, she rushed from the house and plunged across the road into a canebrake . . . There, in quarter heaven shone the crescent moon . . . Bane was afraid to follow till he heard the gun go off. Then he wasted half an hour gathering the neighbor men. They met in the road where lamp-light showed tracks dissolving in the loose earth about the cane. The search began. Moths flickered the lamps. They put them out. Really, because she still might be live enough to shoot. Time and space have no meaning in a canefield. No more than the interminable stalks . . . Some one stumbled over her. A cry went up. From the road, one would have thought that they were cornering a rabbit or a skunk . . . It is difficult carrying dead weight through cane. They placed her on the sofa. A curious, nosey somebody looked for the wound. This fussing with her clothes aroused her. Her eyes were weak and pitiable for so strong a woman. Slowly, then like a flash, Bane came to know that the shot she fired, with averted head, was aimed to whistle like a dying hornet through the cane. Twice deceived, and one deception proved the other. His head went off. Slashed one of the men who'd helped, the man who'd stumbled over her. Now he's in the gang. Who was her husband. Should she not take others, this Carma, strong as a man, whose tale as I have told it is the crudest melodrama?

> Wind is in the cane. Come along.
> Cane leaves swaying, rusty with talk,
> Scratching choruses above the guinea's squawk,
> Wind is in the cane. Come along.

3. Chain gang: prisoners, chained at the feet, who repaired roads and performed other forms of labor.

# Song of the Son[1]

Pour O pour that parting soul in song,
O pour it in the sawdust glow of night,
Into the velvet pine-smoke air to-night,
And let the valley carry it along.
And let the valley carry it along.

O land and soil, red soil and sweet-gum tree,
So scant of grass, so profligate of pines,
Now just before an epoch's sun declines
Thy son, in time, I have returned to thee,
Thy son, I have in time returned to thee.

In time, for though the sun is setting on
A song-lit race of slaves, it has not set;
Though late, O soil, it is not too late yet
To catch thy plaintive soul, leaving, soon gone,
Leaving, to catch thy plaintive soul soon gone.

O Negro slaves, dark purple ripened plums,
Squeezed, and bursting in the pine-wood air,
Passing, before they stripped the old tree bare
One plum was saved for me, one seed becomes

An everlasting song, a singing tree,
Caroling softly souls of slavery,
What they were, and what they are to me,
Caroling softly souls of slavery.

1. First published in the *Crisis* 23 (June 1922): 65.

# Georgia Dusk[1]

The sky, lazily disdaining to pursue
   The setting sun, too indolent to hold
   A lengthened tournament for flashing gold,
Passively darkens for night's barbecue,

A feast of moon and men and barking hounds,
   An orgy for some genius of the South
   With blood-hot eyes and cane-lipped scented mouth,
Surprised in making folk-songs from soul sounds.

The sawmill blows its whistle, buzz-saws stop,
   And silence breaks the bud of knoll and hill,
   Soft settling pollen where plowed lands fulfill
Their early promise of a bumper crop.

Smoke from the pyramidal sawdust pile
   Curls up, blue ghosts of trees, tarrying low
   Where only chips and stumps are left to show
The solid proof of former domicile.

Meanwhile, the men, with vestiges of pomp,
   Race memories of king and caravan,
   High-priests, an ostrich, and a juju-man,
Go singing through the footpaths of the swamp.

Their voices rise . . . the pine trees are guitars,
   Strumming, pine-needles fall like sheets of rain . . .
   Their voices rise . . . the chorus of the cane
Is caroling a vesper to the stars . . .

O singers, resinous and soft your songs
   Above the sacred whisper of the pines,
   Give virgin lips to cornfield concubines,
Bring dreams of Christ to dusky cane-lipped throngs.

---

1. First published in the *Liberator* 5 (September 1922): 25.

# Fern[1]

Face flowed into her eyes. Flowed in soft cream foam and plaintive ripples, in such a way that wherever your glance may momentarily have rested, it immediately thereafter wavered in the direction of her eyes. The soft suggestion of down slightly darkened, like the shadow of a bird's wing might, the creamy brown color of her upper lip. Why, after noticing it, you sought her eyes, I cannot tell you. Her nose was aquiline, Semitic. If you have heard a Jewish cantor sing, if he has touched you and made your own sorrow seem trivial when compared with his, you will know my feeling when I follow the curves of her profile, like mobile rivers, to their common delta. They were strange eyes. In this, that they sought nothing—that is, nothing that was obvious and tangible and that one could see, and they gave the impression that nothing was to be denied. When a woman seeks, you will have observed, her eyes deny. Fern's eyes desired nothing that you could give her; there was no reason why they should withhold. Men saw her eyes and fooled themselves. Fern's eyes said to them that she was easy. When she was young, a few men took her, but got no joy from it. And then, once done, they felt bound to her (quite unlike their hit and run with other girls), felt as though it would take them a lifetime to fulfill an obligation which they could find no name for. They became attached to her, and hungered after finding the barest trace of what she might desire. As she grew up, new men who came to town felt as almost everyone did who ever saw her: that they would not be denied. Men were everlastingly bringing her their bodies. Something inside of her got tired of them, I guess, for I am certain that for the life of her she could not tell why or how she began to turn them off. A man in fever is no trifling thing to send away. They began to leave her, baffled and ashamed, yet vowing to themselves that some day they would do some fine thing for her: send her candy every week and not let her know whom it came from, watch out for her wedding-day and give her a magnificent something with no name on it, buy a house and deed it to her, rescue her from some unworthy fellow who had tricked her into marrying him. As you know, men are apt to idolize or fear that which they cannot understand, especially if it be a woman. She did not deny them, yet the fact was that they were denied. A sort of superstition crept into their consciousness of her being somehow above them. Being above them meant that she was not to be approached by anyone. She became a virgin. Now a virgin in a small southern town is by no means the usual thing, if you will

1. First published in *Little Review* 9 (Autumn 1922): 25–29.

believe me. That the sexes were made to mate is the practice of the South. Particularly, black folks were made to mate. And it is black folks whom I have been talking about thus far. What white men thought of Fern I can arrive at only by analogy. They let her alone.

Anyone, of course, could see her, could see her eyes. If you walked up the Dixie Pike most any time of day, you'd be most like to see her resting listless-like on the railing of her porch, back propped against a post, head tilted a little forward because there was a nail in the porch post just where her head came which for some reason or other she never took the trouble to pull out. Her eyes, if it were sunset, rested idly where the sun, molten and glorious, was pouring down between the fringe of pines. Or maybe they gazed at the gray cabin on the knoll from which an evening folk-song was coming. Perhaps they followed a cow that had been turned loose to roam and feed on cotton-stalks and corn leaves. Like as not they'd settle on some vague spot above the horizon, though hardly a trace of wistfulness would come to them. If it were dusk, then they'd wait for the search-light of the evening train which you could see miles up the track before it flared across the Dixie Pike, close to her home. Wherever they looked, you'd follow them and then waver back. Like her face, the whole countryside seemed to flow into her eyes. Flowed into them with the soft listless cadence of Georgia's South. A young Negro, once, was looking at her, spellbound, from the road. A white man passing in a buggy had to flick him with his whip if he was to get by without running him over. I first saw her on her porch. I was passing with a fellow whose crusty numbness (I was from the North and suspected of being prejudiced and stuck-up) was melting as he found me warm. I asked him who she was. "That's Fern," was all that I could get from him. Some folks already thought that I was given to nosing around; I let it go at that, so far as questions were concerned. But at first sight of her I felt as if I heard a Jewish cantor sing. As if his singing rose above the unheard chorus of a folk-song. And I felt bound to her. I too had my dreams: something I would do for her. I have knocked about from town to town too much not to know the futility of mere change of place. Besides, picture if you can, this cream-colored solitary girl sitting at a tenement window looking down on the indifferent throngs of Harlem. Better that she listen to folk-songs at dusk in Georgia, you would say, and so would I. Or, suppose she came up North and married. Even a doctor or a lawyer, say, one who would be sure to get along—that is, make money. You and I know, who have had experience in such things, that love is not a thing like prejudice which can be bettered by changes of town. Could men in Washington, Chicago, or New York, more than the men of Georgia, bring her

something left vacant by the bestowal of their bodies? You and I
who know men in these cities will have to say, they could not. See
her out and out a prostitute along State Street in Chicago. See her
move into a southern town where white men are more aggressive.
See her become a white man's concubine . . . Something I must do
for her. There was myself. What could I do for her? Talk, of course.
Push back the fringe of pines upon new horizons. To what purpose?
and what for? Her? Myself? Men in her case seem to lose their self-
ishness. I lost mine before I touched her. I ask you, friend (it makes
no difference if you sit in the Pullman or the Jim Crow[2] as the train
crosses her road), what thoughts would come to you—that is, after
you'd finished with the thoughts that leap into men's minds at the
sight of a pretty woman who will not deny them; what thoughts
would come to you, had you seen her in a quick flash, keen and
intuitively, as she sat there on her porch when your train thundered
by? Would you have got off at the next station and come back for
her to take her where? Would you have completely forgotten her as
soon as you reached Macon, Atlanta, Augusta, Pasadena, Madison,
Chicago, Boston, or New Orleans? Would you tell your wife or
sweetheart about a girl you saw? Your thoughts can help me, and I
would like to know. Something I would do for her . . .

   One evening I walked up the Pike on purpose, and stopped to say
hello. Some of her family were about, but they moved away to make
room for me. Damn if I knew how to begin. Would you? Mr. and
Miss So-and-So, people, the weather, the crops, the new preacher,
the frolic, the church benefit, rabbit and possum hunting, the new
soft drink they had at old Pap's store, the schedule of the trains,
what kind of town Macon was, Negro's migration north, bollwee-
vils, syrup, the Bible—to all these things she gave a yassur or nassur, without further comment. I began to wonder if perhaps my
own emotional sensibility had played one of its tricks on me. "Lets
take a walk," I at last ventured. The suggestion, coming after so
long an isolation, was novel enough, I guess, to surprise. But it
wasnt that. Something told me that men before me had said just
that as a prelude to the offering of their bodies. I tried to tell her
with my eyes. I think she understood. The thing from her that
made my throat catch, vanished. Its passing left her visible in a way
I'd thought, but never seen. We walked down the Pike with people

2. Noun or adjective, referring to the system of segregation or to the segregated facilities.
Here, it refers to the railway coach or coaches to which Blacks were assigned because
of Southern segregation. *Pullman*: the sleeping-car section of railway trains. During
the time when African Americans were legally segregated from whites on public transportation in the South (especially in the states that had formed the Confederacy during the Civil War), they were not permitted to ride in the sleeping-car section.
Therefore, the Pullman riders alluded to are white.

on all the porches gaping at us. "Doesnt it make you mad?" She meant the row of petty gossiping people. She meant the world. Through a canebrake that was ripe for cutting, the branch was reached. Under a sweet-gum tree, and where reddish leaves had dammed the creek a little, we sat down. Dusk, suggesting the almost imperceptible procession of giant trees, settled with a purple haze about the cane. I felt strange, as I always do in Georgia, particularly at dusk. I felt that things unseen to men were tangibly immediate. It would not have surprised me had I had vision. People have them in Georgia more often than you would suppose. A black woman once saw the mother of Christ and drew her in charcoal on the courthouse wall . . . When one is on the soil of one's ancestors, most anything can come to one . . . From force of habit, I suppose, I held Fern in my arms—that is, without at first noticing it. Then my mind came back to her. Her eyes, unusually weird and open, held me. Held God. He flowed in as I've seen the countryside flow in. Seen men. I must have done something—what, I dont know, in the confusion of my emotion. She sprang up. Rushed some distance from me. Fell to her knees, and began swaying, swaying. Her body was tortured with something it could not let out. Like boiling sap it flooded arms and fingers till she shook them as if they burned her. It found her throat, and spattered inarticulately in plaintive, convulsive sounds, mingled with calls to Christ Jesus. And then she sang, brokenly. A Jewish cantor singing with a broken voice. A child's voice, uncertain, or an old man's. Dusk hid her; I could hear only her song. It seemed to me as though she were pounding her head in anguish upon the ground. I rushed to her. She fainted in my arms.

There was talk about her fainting with me in the canefield. And I got one or two ugly looks from town men who'd set themselves up to protect her. In fact, there was talk of making me leave town. But they never did. They kept a watch-out for me, though. Shortly after, I came back North. From the train window I saw her as I crossed her road. Saw her on her porch, head tilted a little forward where the nail was, eyes vaguely focused on the sunset. Saw her face flow into them, the countryside and something that I call God, flowing into them . . . Nothing ever really happened. Nothing ever came to Fern, not even I. Something I would do for her. Some fine unnamed thing . . . And, friend, you? She is still living, I have reason to know. Her name, against the chance that you might happen down that way, is Fernie May Rosen.

# Nullo

A spray of pine-needles,
Dipped in western horizon gold,
Fell onto a path.
Dry moulds of cow-hoofs.
In the forest.
Rabbits knew not of their falling,
Nor did the forest catch aflame.

# Evening Song

Full moon rising on the waters of my heart,
Lakes and moon and fires,
Cloine tires,
Holding her lips apart.

Promises of slumber leaving shore to charm the moon,
Miracle made vesper-keeps,
Cloine sleeps,
And I'll be sleeping soon.

Cloine, curled like the sleepy waters where the
    moon-waves start,
Radiant, resplendently she gleams,
Cloine dreams,
Lips pressed against my heart.

# Esther[1]

*Nine.*

Esther's hair falls in soft curls about her high-cheek-boned chalk-white face. Esther's hair would be beautiful if there were more gloss to it. And if her face were not prematurely serious, one would call it pretty. Her cheeks are too flat and dead for a girl of nine. Esther looks like a little white child, starched, frilled, as she walks slowly from her home towards her father's grocery store. She is about to turn in Broad from Maple Street. White and black men loafing on the corner hold no interest for her. Then a strange thing happens. A clean-muscled, magnificent, black-skinned Negro, whom she had heard her father mention as King Barlo, suddenly drops to his knees on a spot called the Spittoon. White men, unaware of him, continue squirting tobacco juice in his direction. The saffron fluid splashes on his face. His smooth black face begins to glisten and to shine. Soon, people notice him, and gather round. His eyes are rapturous upon the heavens. Lips and nostrils quiver. Barlo is in a religious trance. Town folks know it. They are not startled. They are not afraid. They gather round. Some beg boxes from the grocery stores. From old McGregor's notion shop. A coffin-case is pressed into use. Folks line the curb-stones. Business men close shop. And Banker Warply parks his car close by. Silently, all await the prophet's voice. The sheriff, a great florid fellow whose leggings never meet around his bulging calves, swears in three deputies. "Wall, y cant never tell what a nigger like King Barlo might be up t." Soda bottles, five fingers full of shine, are passed to those who want them. A couple of stray dogs start a fight. Old Goodlow's cow comes flopping up the street. Barlo, still as an Indian fakir, has not moved. The town bell strikes six. The sun slips in behind a heavy mass of horizon cloud. The crowd is hushed and expectant. Barlo's under jaw relaxes, and his lips begin to move.

"Jesus has been awhisperin strange words deep down, O way down deep, deep in my ears."

Hums of awe and of excitement.

"He called me to His side an said, 'Git down on your knees beside me, son, Ise gwine t whisper in your ears.'"

An old sister cries, "Ah, Lord."

"'Ise agwine t whisper in your ears,' he said, an I replied, 'Thy will be done on earth as it is in heaven.'"

"Ah, Lord. Amen. Amen."

---

1. First published in *Modern Review* 1 (January 1923): 50–54.

"An Lord Jesus whispered strange good words deep down, O way down deep, deep in my ears. An He said, 'Tell em till you feel your throat on fire.' I saw a vision. I saw a man arise, an he was big an black an powerful—"

Some one yells, "Preach it, preacher, preach it!"

"—but his head was caught up in th clouds. An while he was agazin at th heavens, heart filled up with th Lord, some little white-ant biddies came an tied his feet to chains. They led him t th coast, they led him t th sea, they led him across th ocean an they didnt set him free. The old coast didnt miss him, an th new coast wasnt free, he left the old-coast brothers, t give birth t you an me. O Lord, great God Almighty, t give birth t you an me."

Barlo pauses. Old gray mothers are in tears. Fragments of melodies are being hummed. White folks are touched and curiously awed. Off to themselves, white and black preachers confer as to how best to rid themselves of the vagrant, usurping fellow. Barlo looks as though he is struggling to continue. People are hushed. One can hear weevils work. Dusk is falling rapidly, and the customary store lights fail to throw their feeble glow across the gray dust and flagging of the Georgia town. Barlo rises to his full height. He is immense. To the people he assumes the outlines of his visioned African. In a mighty voice he bellows:

"Brothers an sisters, turn your faces t th sweet face of the Lord, an fill your hearts with glory. Open your eyes an see th dawnin of th mornin light. Open your ears—"

Years afterwards Esther was told that at that very moment a great, heavy, rumbling voice actually was heard. That hosts of angels and of demons paraded up and down the streets all night. That King Barlo rode out of town astride a pitch-black bull that had a glowing gold ring in its nose. And that old Limp Underwood, who hated niggers, woke up next morning to find that he held a black man in his arms. This much is certain: an inspired Negress, of wide reputation for being sanctified, drew a portrait of a black madonna on the courthouse wall. And King Barlo left town. He left his image indelibly upon the mind of Esther. He became the starting point of the only living patterns that her mind was to know.

2

*Sixteen.*

Esther begins to dream. The low evening sun sets the windows of McGregor's notion shop aflame. Esther makes believe that they really are aflame. The town fire department rushes madly down the road. It ruthlessly shoves black and white idlers to one side. It whoops. It clangs. It rescues from the second-story window a dimpled infant which she claims for her own. How had she come by it? She thinks of it immaculately. It is a sin to think of it immaculately. She must dream no more. She must repent her sin. Another dream comes. There is no fire department. There are no heroic men. The fire starts. The loafers on the corner form a circle, chew their tobacco faster, and squirt juice just as fast as they can chew. Gallons on top of gallons they squirt upon the flames. The air reeks with the stench of scorched tobacco juice. Women, fat chunky Negro women, lean scrawny white women, pull their skirts up above their heads and display the most ludicrous underclothes. The women scoot in all directions from the danger zone. She alone is left to take the baby in her arms. But what a baby! Black, singed, woolly, tobacco-juice baby—ugly as sin. Once held to her breast, miraculous thing: its breath is sweet and its lips can nibble. She loves it frantically. Her joy in it changes the town folks' jeers to harmless jealousy, and she is left alone.

*Twenty-two.*

Esther's schooling is over. She works behind the counter of her father's grocery store. "To keep the money in the family," so he said. She is learning to make distinctions between the business and the social worlds. "Good business comes from remembering that the white folks dont divide the niggers, Esther. Be just as black as any man who has a silver dollar." Esther listlessly forgets that she is near white, and that her father is the richest colored man in town. Black folk who drift in to buy lard and snuff and flour of her, call her a sweet-natured, accommodating girl. She learns their names. She forgets them. She thinks about men. "I dont appeal to them. I wonder why." She recalls an affair she had with a little fair boy while still in school. It had ended in her shame when he as much as told her that for sweetness he preferred a lollipop. She remembers the salesman from the North who wanted to take her to the movies that first night he was in town. She refused, of course. And he never came back, having found out who she was. She thinks of Barlo. Barlo's image gives her a slightly stale thrill. She spices it by telling herself his glories. Black. Magnetically so. Best cotton picker in the county, in the state, in the whole world for that matter. Best man with his fists, best man with dice, with a razor. Promoter of church benefits. Of colored fairs. Vagrant preacher. Lover of all the women for miles and miles around. Esther decides that she loves him. And with a vague sense of life slipping by, she resolves that she will tell him so, whatever people say, the next time he comes to town. After the making of this resolution which becomes a sort of wedding cake for her to tuck beneath her pillow and go to sleep upon, she sees nothing of Barlo for five years. Her hair thins. It

looks like the dull silk on puny corn ears. Her face pales until it is
the color of the gray dust that dances with dead cotton leaves.

### 3

*Esther is twenty-seven.*

Esther sells lard and snuff and flour to vague black faces that drift
in her store to ask for them. Her eyes hardly see the people to whom
she gives change. Her body is lean and beaten. She rests listlessly
against the counter, too weary to sit down. From the street some one
shouts, "King Barlo has come back to town." He passes her window,
driving a large new car. Cut-out open.[2] He veers to the curb, and steps
out. Barlo has made money on cotton during the war.[3] He is as rich as
anyone. Esther suddenly is animate. She goes to her door. She sees
him at a distance, the center of a group of credulous men. She hears
the deep-bass rumble of his talk. The sun swings low. McGregor's
windows are aflame again. Pale flame. A sharply dressed white girl
passes by. For a moment Esther wishes that she might be like her. Not
white; she has no need for being that. But sharp, sporty, with get-up
about her. Barlo is connected with that wish. She mustnt wish. Wishes
only make you restless. Emptiness is a thing that grows by being
moved. "I'll not think. Not wish. Just set my mind against it." Then the
thought comes to her that those purposeless, easy-going men will possess him, if she doesnt. Purpose is not dead in her, now that she comes
to think of it. That loose women will have their arms around him at
Nat Bowle's place to-night. As if her veins are full of fired sun-bleached
southern shanties, a swift heat sweeps them. Dead dreams, and a forgotten resolution are carried upward by the flames. Pale flames. "They
shant have him. Oh, they shall not. Not if it kills me they shant have
him." Jerky, aflutter, she closes the store and starts home. Folks lazing
on store windowsills wonder what on earth can be the matter with
Jim Crane's gal, as she passes them. "Come to remember, she always
was a little off, a little crazy, I reckon." Esther seeks her own room,
and locks the door. Her mind is a pink meshbag filled with baby toes.

Using the noise of the town clock striking twelve to cover the
creaks of her departure, Esther slips into the quiet road. The town,
her parents, most everyone is sound asleep. This fact is a stable thing
that comforts her. After sundown a chill wind came up from the
west. It is still blowing, but to her it is a steady, settled thing like the
cold. She wants her mind to be like that. Solid, contained, and blank
as a sheet of darkened ice. She will not permit herself to notice the

2. A valve in the exhaust pipe of an internal combustion engine through which exhaust
gases may escape without going through the muffler.
3. World War I (1914–18).

peculiar phosphorescent glitter of the sweet-gum leaves. Their movement would excite her. Exciting too, the recession of the dull familiar
homes she knows so well. She doesnt know them at all. She closes
her eyes, and holds them tightly. Wont do. Her being aware that they
are closed recalls her purpose. She does not want to think of it. She
opens them. She turns now into the deserted business street. The
corrugated iron canopies and mule- and horse-gnawed hitching posts
bring her a strange composure. Ghosts of the commonplaces of her
daily life take stride with her and become her companions. And the
echoes of her heels upon the flagging are rhythmically monotonous
and soothing. Crossing the street at the corner of McGregor's notion
shop, she thinks that the windows are a dull flame. Only a fancy. She
walks faster. Then runs. A turn into a side street brings her abruptly
to Nat Bowle's place. The house is squat and dark. It is always dark.
Barlo is within. Quietly she opens the outside door and steps in. She
passes through a small room. Pauses before a flight of stairs down
which people's voices, muffled, come. The air is heavy with fresh
tobacco smoke. It makes her sick. She wants to turn back. She goes
up the steps. As if she were mounting to some great height, her head
spins. She is violently dizzy. Blackness rushes to her eyes. And then
she finds that she is in a large room. Barlo is before her.

"Well, I'm sholy damned—skuse me, but what, what brought you
here, lil milk-white gal?"

"You." Her voice sounds like a frightened child's that calls home-
ward from some point miles away.

"Me?"

"Yes, you Barlo."

"This aint th place fer y. This aint th place fer y."

"I know. I know. But I've come for you."

"For me for what?"

She manages to look deep and straight into his eyes. He is slow at
understanding. Guffaws and giggles break out from all around the
room. A coarse woman's voice remarks, "So thats how th dictie[4]
niggers does it." Laughs. "Mus give em credit fo their gall."

Esther doesnt hear. Barlo does. His faculties are jogged. She sees
a smile, ugly and repulsive to her, working upward through thick
licker fumes. Barlo seems hideous. The thought comes suddenly,
that conception with a drunken man must be a mighty sin. She
draws away, frozen. Like a somnambulist she wheels around and
walks stiffly to the stairs. Down them. Jeers and hoots pelter bluntly
upon her back. She steps out. There is no air, no street, and the
town has completely disappeared.

---

4. Slang term referring to educated, middle-class African Americans who behave as
   though they consider themselves socially superior to other African Americans—similar
   to "stuck-up," "snobbish."

# Conversion[1]

African Guardian of Souls,
Drunk with rum,
Feasting on a strange cassava,[2]
Yielding to new words and a weak palabra[3]
Of a white-faced sardonic god—
Grins, cries
Amen,
Shouts hosanna.

1. First published as number three of three "Georgia Portraits," *Modern Review* 1 (January 1923): 81. Earlier, Toomer had intended to use the first five lines of this poem as part of a longer, untitled poem in a short story, "Withered Skin of Berries." Not published in Toomer's lifetime, the story now appears in *The Wayward and the Seeking: A Collection of Writings by Jean Toomer,* pp. 138–65. The entire poem (p. 161) is as follows:

> Court-house tower,
> Bell-buoy of the Whites,
> Charting the white-man's channel,
> Bobs on the agitated crests of pines
> And sends its mellow monotone,
> Satirically sweet,
> To guide the drift of barges . . .
> Black barges . . .
>
> African Guardian of Souls,
> Drunk with rum,
> Feasting on a strange cassava,
> Yielding to new words and a weak palabra
> Of a white-faced sardonic God—

2. A tuberous root of the West Indies and tropical America and a staple vegetable; also the name for the starch or flour obtained from the plant's roots; bread and tapioca are made from it.
3. Talk.

# Portrait in Georgia[1]

Hair—braided chestnut,
    coiled like a lyncher's rope,
Eyes—fagots,
Lips—old scars, or the first red blisters,
Breath—the last sweet scent of cane,
And her slim body, white as the ash
    of black flesh after flame.

1. First published as number two of three "Georgia Portraits," *Modern Review* 1 (January 1923): 81.

# Blood-Burning Moon[1]

Up from the skeleton stone walls, up from the rotting floor boards and the solid hand-hewn beams of oak of the pre-war cotton factory, dusk came. Up from the dusk the full moon came. Glowing like a fired pine-knot, it illumined the great door and soft showered the Negro shanties aligned along the single street of factory town. The full moon in the great door was an omen. Negro women improvised songs against its spell.

Louisa sang as she came over the crest of the hill from the white folks' kitchen. Her skin was the color of oak leaves on young trees in fall. Her breasts, firm and up-pointed like ripe acorns. And her singing had the low murmur of winds in fig trees. Bob Stone, younger son of the people she worked for, loved her. By the way the world reckons things, he had won her. By measure of that warm glow which came into her mind at thought of him, he had won her. Tom Burwell, whom the whole town called Big Boy, also loved her. But working in the fields all day, and far away from her gave him no chance to show it. Though often enough of evenings he had tried to. Somehow, he never got along. Strong as he was with hands upon the ax or plow, he found it difficult to hold her. Or so he thought. But the fact was that he held her to factory town more firmly than he thought for. His black balanced, and pulled against, the white of Stone, when she thought of them. And her mind was vaguely upon them as she came over the crest of the hill, coming from the white folks' kitchen. As she sang softly at the evil face of the full moon.

A strange stir was in her. Indolently, she tried to fix upon Bob or Tom as the cause of it. To meet Bob in the canebrake, as she was going to do an hour or so later, was nothing new. And Tom's proposal which she felt on its way to her could be indefinitely put off. Separately, there was no unusual significance to either one. But for some reason, they jumbled when her eyes gazed vacantly at the rising moon. And from the jumble came the stir that was strangely within her. Her lips trembled. The slow rhythm of her song grew agitant and restless. Rusty black and tan spotted hounds, lying in the dark corners of porches or prowling around back yards, put their noses in the air and caught its tremor. They began plaintively to yelp and howl. Chickens woke up and cackled. Intermittently, all over the countryside dogs barked and roosters crowed as if heralding a weird dawn or some ungodly awakening. The women sang

---

1. First published in *Prairie* (March–April 1923): 18.

lustily. Their songs were cotton-wads to stop their ears. Louisa came
down into factory town and sank wearily upon the step before her
home. The moon was rising towards a thick cloud-bank which soon
would hide it.

> Red nigger moon. Sinner!
> Blood-burning moon. Sinner!
> Come out that fact'ry door.

### 2

Up from the deep dusk of a cleared spot on the edge of the forest a mellow glow arose and spread fan-wise into the low-hanging
heavens. And all around the air was heavy with the scent of boiling
cane. A large pile of cane-stalks lay like ribboned shadows upon the
ground. A mule, harnessed to a pole, trudged lazily round and round
the pivot of the grinder. Beneath a swaying oil lamp, a Negro alternately whipped out at the mule, and fed cane-stalks to the grinder. A
fat boy waddled pails of fresh ground juice between the grinder and
the boiling stove. Steam came from the copper boiling pan. The scent
of cane came from the copper pan and drenched the forest and the
hill that sloped to factory town, beneath its fragrance. It drenched
the men in circle seated around the stove. Some of them chewed at
the white pulp of stalks, but there was no need for them to, if all they
wanted was to taste the cane. One tasted it in factory town. And
from factory town one could see the soft haze thrown by the glowing
stove upon the low-hanging heavens.

Old David Georgia stirred the thickening syrup with a long ladle,
and ever so often drew it off. Old David Georgia tended his stove
and told tales about the white folks, about moonshining and cotton
picking, and about sweet nigger gals, to the men who sat there about
his stove to listen to him. Tom Burwell chewed cane-stalk and
laughed with the others till some one mentioned Louisa. Till some
one said something about Louisa and Bob Stone, about the silk
stockings she must have gotten from him. Blood ran up Tom's neck
hotter than the glow that flooded from the stove. He sprang up.
Glared at the men and said, "She's my gal." Will Manning laughed.
Tom strode over to him. Yanked him up and knocked him to the
ground. Several of Manning's friends got up to fight for him. Tom
whipped out a long knife and would have cut them to shreds if they
hadnt ducked into the woods. Tom had had enough. He nodded to
Old David Georgia and swung down the path to factory town. Just
then, the dogs started barking and the roosters began to crow. Tom
felt funny. Away from the fight, away from the stove, chill got to
him. He shivered. He shuddered when he saw the full moon rising
towards the cloud-bank. He who didnt give a godam for the fears of

old women. He forced his mind to fasten on Louisa. Bob Stone. Better not be. He turned into the street and saw Louisa sitting before her home. He went towards her, ambling, touched the brim of a marvelously shaped, spotted, felt hat, said he wanted to say something to her, and then found that he didnt know what he had to say, or if he did, that he couldnt say it. He shoved his big fists in his overalls, grinned, and started to move off.

"Youall want me, Tom?"

"Thats what us wants, sho, Louisa."

"Well, here I am—"

"An here I is, but that aint ahelpin none, all th same."

"You wanted to say something? . . ."

"I did that, sho. But words is like th spots on dice: no matter how y fumbles em, there's times when they jes wont come. I dunno why. Seems like th love I feels fo yo done stole m tongue. I got it now. Whee! Louisa, honey, I oughtnt tell y, I feel I oughtnt cause yo is young an goes t church an I has had other gals, but Louisa I sho do love y. Lil gal, Ise watched y from them first days when youall sat right here befo yo door befo th well an sang sometimes in a way that like t broke m heart. Ise carried y with me into th fields, day after day, an after that, an I sho can plow when yo is there, an I can pick cotton. Yassur! Come near beatin Barlo yesterday. I sho did. Yassur! An next year if ole Stone'll trust me, I'll have a farm. My own. My bales will buy yo what y gets from white folks now. Silk stockings an purple dresses—course I dont believe what some folks been whisperin as t how y gets them things now. White folks always did do for niggers what they likes. An they jes cant help alikin yo, Louisa. Bob Stone likes y. Course he does. But not th way folks is awhisperin. Does he, hon?"

"I dont know what you mean, Tom."

"Course y dont. Ise already cut two niggers. Had t hon, t tell em so. Niggers always tryin t make somethin out a nothin. An then besides, white folks aint up t them tricks so much nowadays. Godam better not be. Leastawise not with yo. Cause I wouldnt stand f it. Nassur."

"What would you do, Tom?"

"Cut him jes like I cut a nigger."

"No, Tom—"

"I said I would an there aint no mo to it. But that aint th talk f now. Sing, honey Louisa, an while I'm listenin t y I'll be makin love."

Tom took her hand in his. Against the tough thickness of his own, hers felt soft and small. His huge body slipped down to the step beside her. The full moon sank upward into the deep purple of the cloud-bank. An old woman brought a lighted lamp and hung it

on the common well whose bulky shadow squatted in the middle of
the road, opposite Tom and Louisa. The old woman lifted the well-
lid, took hold the chain, and began drawing up the heavy bucket.
As she did so, she sang. Figures shifted, restlesslike, between lamp
and window in the front rooms of the shanties. Shadows of the figures fought each other on the gray dust of the road. Figures raised
the windows and joined the old woman in song. Louisa and Tom,
the whole street, singing:

> Red nigger moon. Sinner!
> Blood-burning moon. Sinner!
> Come out that fact'ry door.

### 3

   Bob Stone sauntered from his veranda out into the gloom of fir
trees and magnolias. The clear white of his skin paled, and the
flush of his cheeks turned purple. As if to balance this outer change,
his mind became consciously a white man's. He passed the house
with its huge open hearth which, in the days of slavery, was the
plantation cookery. He saw Louisa bent over that hearth. He went in
as a master should and took her. Direct, honest, bold. None of this
sneaking that he had to go through now. The contrast was repulsive
to him. His family had lost ground. Hell no, his family still owned
the niggers, practically. Damned if they did, or he wouldnt have to
duck around so. What would they think if they knew? His mother?
His sister? He shouldnt mention them, shouldnt think of them in
this connection. There in the dusk he blushed at doing so. Fellows
about town were all right, but how about his friends up North? He
could see them incredible, repulsed. They didnt know. The thought
first made him laugh. Then, with their eyes still upon him, he
began to feel embarrassed. He felt the need of explaining things to
them. Explain hell. They wouldnt understand, and moreover, who
ever heard of a Southerner getting on his knees to any Yankee, or
anyone. No sir. He was going to see Louisa to-night, and love her.
She was lovely—in her way. Nigger way. What way was that? Damned
if he knew. Must know. He'd known her long enough to know. Was
there something about niggers that you couldnt know? Listening to
them at church didnt tell you anything. Looking at them didnt tell
you anything. Talking to them didnt tell you anything—unless it
was gossip, unless they wanted to talk. Of course, about farming,
and licker, and craps—but those werent nigger. Nigger was something more. How much more? Something to be afraid of, more?
Hell no. Who ever heard of being afraid of a nigger? Tom Burwell.
Cartwell had told him that Tom went with Louisa after she reached
home. No sir. No nigger had ever been with his girl. He'd like to

see one try. Some position for him to be in. Him, Bob Stone, of the old Stone family, in a scrap with a nigger over a nigger girl. In the good old days . . . Ha! Those were the days. His family had lost ground. Not so much, though. Enough for him to have to cut through old Lemon's canefield by way of the woods, that he might meet her. She was worth it. Beautiful nigger gal. Why nigger? Why not, just gal? No, it was because she was nigger that he went to her. Sweet . . . The scent of boiling cane came to him. Then he saw the rich glow of the stove. He heard the voices of the men circled around it. He was about to skirt the clearing when he heard his own name mentioned. He stopped. Quivering. Leaning against a tree, he listened.

"Bad nigger. Yassur, he sho is one bad nigger when he gets started."

"Tom Burwell's been on th gang three times fo cuttin men."

"What y think he's agwine t do t Bob Stone?"

"Dunno yet. He aint found out. When he does—Baby!"

"Aint no tellin."

"Young Stone aint no quitter an I ken tell y that. Blood of th old uns in his veins."

"Thats right. He'll scrap, sho."

"Be gettin too hot f niggers round this away."

"Shut up, nigger. Y dont know what y talkin bout."

Bob Stone's ears burned as though he had been holding them over the stove. Sizzling heat welled up within him. His feet felt as if they rested on red-hot coals. They stung him to quick movement. He circled the fringe of the glowing. Not a twig cracked beneath his feet. He reached the path that led to factory town. Plunged furiously down it. Halfway along, a blindness within him veered him aside. He crashed into the bordering canebrake. Cane leaves cut his face and lips. He tasted blood. He threw himself down and dug his fingers in the ground. The earth was cool. Cane-roots took the fever from his hands. After a long while, or so it seemed to him, the thought came to him that it must be time to see Louisa. He got to his feet and walked calmly to their meeting place. No Louisa. Tom Burwell had her. Veins in his forehead bulged and distended. Saliva moistened the dried blood on his lips. He bit down on his lips. He tasted blood. Not his own blood; Tom Burwell's blood. Bob drove through the cane and out again upon the road. A hound swung down the path before him towards factory town. Bob couldnt see it. The dog loped aside to let him pass. Bob's blind rushing made him stumble over it. He fell with a thud that dazed him. The hound yelped. Answering yelps came from all over the countryside. Chickens cackled. Roosters crowed, heralding the bloodshot eyes of southern awakening. Singers in the town were silenced. They shut their

windows down. Palpitant between the rooster crows, a chill hush
settled upon the huddled forms of Tom and Louisa. A figure rushed
from the shadow and stood before them. Tom popped to his feet.

"Whats y want?"

"I'm Bob Stone."

"Yassur—an I'm Tom Burwell. Whats y want?"

Bob lunged at him. Tom side-stepped, caught him by the shoulder, and flung him to the ground. Straddled him.

"Let me up."

"Yassur—but watch yo doins,[2] Bob Stone."

A few dark figures, drawn by the sound of scuffle, stood about
them. Bob sprang to his feet.

"Fight like a man, Tom Burwell, an I'll lick y."

Again he lunged. Tom side-stepped and flung him to the ground.
Straddled him.

"Get off me, you godam nigger you."

"Yo sho has started somethin now. Get up."

Tom yanked him up and began hammering at him. Each blow
sounded as if it smashed into a precious, irreplaceable soft something. Beneath them, Bob staggered back. He reached in his pocket
and whipped out a knife.

"Thats my game, sho."

Blue flash, a steel blade slashed across Bob Stone's throat. He
had a sweetish sick feeling. Blood began to flow. Then he felt a
sharp twitch of pain. He let his knife drop. He slapped one hand
against his neck. He pressed the other on top of his head as if to
hold it down. He groaned. He turned, and staggered towards the
crest of the hill in the direction of white town. Negroes who had
seen the fight slunk into their homes and blew the lamps out. Louisa, dazed, hysterical, refused to go indoors. She slipped, crumbled,
her body loosely propped against the woodwork of the well. Tom
Burwell leaned against it. He seemed rooted there.

Bob reached Broad Street. White men rushed up to him. He collapsed in their arms.

"Tom Burwell. . . ."

White men like ants upon a forage rushed about. Except for the
taut hum of their moving, all was silent. Shotguns, revolvers, rope,
kerosene, torches. Two high-powered cars with glaring searchlights.
They came together. The taut hum rose to a low roar. Then nothing
could be heard but the flop of their feet in the thick dust of the road.
The moving body of their silence preceded them over the crest of the
hill into factory town. It flattened the Negroes beneath it. It rolled to
the wall of the factory, where it stopped. Tom knew that they were

2. "Doings," actions.

coming. He couldnt move. And then he saw the search-lights of the two cars glaring down on him. A quick shock went through him. He stiffened. He started to run. A yell went up from the mob. Tom wheeled about and faced them. They poured down on him. They swarmed. A large man with dead-white face and flabby cheeks came to him and almost jabbed a gun-barrel through his guts.

"Hands behind y, nigger."

Tom's wrists were bound. The big man shoved him to the well. Burn him over it, and when the woodwork caved in, his body would drop to the bottom. Two deaths for a godam nigger. Louisa was driven back. The mob pushed in. Its pressure, its momentum was too great. Drag him to the factory. Wood and stakes already there. Tom moved in the direction indicated. But they had to drag him. They reached the great door. Too many to get in there. The mob divided and flowed around the walls to either side. The big man shoved him through the door. The mob pressed in from the sides. Taut humming. No words. A stake was sunk into the ground. Rotting floor boards piled around it. Kerosene poured on the rotting floor boards. Tom bound to the stake. His breast was bare. Nails' scratches let little lines of blood trickle down and mat into the hair. His face, his eyes were set and stony. Except for irregular breathing, one would have thought him already dead. Torches were flung onto the pile. A great flare muffled in black smoke shot upward. The mob yelled. The mob was silent. Now Tom could be seen within the flames. Only his head, erect, lean, like a blackened stone. Stench of burning flesh soaked the air. Tom's eyes popped. His head settled downward. The mob yelled. Its yell echoed against the skeleton stone walls and sounded like a hundred yells. Like a hundred mobs yelling. Its yell thudded against the thick front wall and fell back. Ghost of a yell slipped through the flames and out the great door of the factory. It fluttered like a dying thing down the single street of factory town. Louisa, upon the step before her home, did not hear it, but her eyes opened slowly. They saw the full moon glowing in the great door. The full moon, an evil thing, an omen, soft showering the homes of folks she knew. Where were they, these people? She'd sing, and perhaps they'd come out and join her. Perhaps Tom Burwell would come. At any rate, the full moon in the great door was an omen which she must sing to:

> Red nigger moon. Sinner!
> Blood-burning moon. Sinner!
> Come out that fact'ry door.

# Seventh Street[1]

> Money burns the pocket, pocket hurts,
> Bootleggers in silken shirts,
> Ballooned, zooming Cadillacs,
> Whizzing, whizzing down the street-car tracks.

Seventh Street is a bastard of Prohibition and the War.[2] A crude-boned, soft-skinned wedge of nigger life breathing its loafer air, jazz songs and love, thrusting unconscious rhythms, black reddish blood into the white and whitewashed wood of Washington. Stale soggy wood of Washington. Wedges rust in soggy wood . . . Split it! In two! Again! Shred it! . . . the sun. Wedges are brilliant in the sun; ribbons of wet wood dry and blow away. Black reddish blood. Pouring for crude-boned soft-skinned life, who set you flowing? Blood suckers of the War would spin in a frenzy of dizziness if they drank your blood. Prohibition would put a stop to it. Who set you flowing? White and whitewash disappear in blood. Who set you flowing? Flowing down the smooth asphalt of Seventh Street, in shanties, brick office buildings, theaters, drug stores, restaurants, and cabarets? Eddying on the corners? Swirling like a blood-red smoke up where the buzzards fly in heaven? God would not dare to suck black red blood. A Nigger God! He would duck his head in shame and call for the Judgment Day. Who set you flowing?

> Money burns the pocket, pocket hurts,
> Bootleggers in silken shirts,
> Ballooned, zooming Cadillacs,
> Whizzing, whizzing down the street-car tracks.

1. First published in *Broom* 4 (December 1922): 3.
2. World War I.

# Rhobert

Rhobert wears a house, like a monstrous diver's helmet, on his head. His legs are banty-bowed and shaky because as a child he had rickets. He is way down. Rods of the house like antennæ of a dead thing, stuffed, prop up in the air. He is way down. He is sinking. His house is a dead thing that weights him down. He is sinking as a diver would sink in mud should the water be drawn off. Life is a murky, wiggling, microscopic water that compresses him. Compresses his helmet and would crush it the minute that he pulled his head out. He has to keep it in. Life is water that is being drawn off.

Brother, life is water that is being drawn off.
Brother, life is water that is being drawn off.

The dead house is stuffed. The stuffing is alive. It is sinful to draw one's head out of live stuffing in a dead house. The propped-up antennæ would cave in and the stuffing be strewn . . . shredded life-pulp . . . in the water. It is sinful to have one's own head crushed. Rhobert is an upright man whose legs are banty-bowed and shaky because as a child he had rickets. The earth is round. Heaven is a sphere that surrounds it. Sink where you will. God is a Red Cross man with a dredge and a respiration-pump who's waiting for you at the opposite periphery. God built the house. He blew His breath into its stuffing. It is good to die obeying Him who can do these things.

A futile something like the dead house wraps the live stuffing of the question: how long before the water will be drawn off? Rhobert does not care. Like most men who wear monstrous helmets, the pressure it exerts is enough to convince him of its practical infinity. And he cares not two straws as to whether or not he will ever see his wife and children again. Many a time he's seen them drown in his dreams and has kicked about joyously in the mud for days after. One thing about him goes straight to the heart. He has an Adam's-apple which strains sometimes as if he were painfully gulping great globules of air . . . air floating shredded life-pulp. It is a sad thing to see a banty-bowed, shaky, ricket-legged man straining the raw insides of his throat against smooth air. Holding furtive thoughts about the glory of pulp-heads strewn in water . . . He is way down. Down. Mud, coming to his banty knees, almost hides them. Soon people will be looking at him and calling him a strong man. No doubt he is for one who has had rickets. Lets give it to him. Lets call him great when the water shall have been all drawn off. Lets build a monument and set it in the ooze where he goes down. A monument of hewn oak, carved in nigger-heads. Lets

open our throats, brother, and sing "Deep River"[1] when he goes
down.

> Brother, Rhobert is sinking.
> Lets open our throats, brother,
> Lets sing Deep River when he goes down.

1. African American spiritual.

# Avey

For a long while she was nothing more to me than one of those skirted beings whom boys at a certain age disdain to play with. Just how I came to love her, timidly, and with secret blushes, I do not know. But that I did was brought home to me one night, the first night that Ned wore his long pants. Us fellers were seated on the curb before an apartment house where she had gone in. The young trees had not outgrown their boxes then. V Street was lined with them. When our legs grew cramped and stiff from the cold of the stone, we'd stand around a box and whittle it. I like to think now that there was a hidden purpose in the way we hacked them with our knives. I like to feel that something deep in me responded to the trees, the young trees that whinnied like colts impatient to be let free . . . On the particular night I have in mind, we were waiting for the top-floor light to go out. We wanted to see Avey leave the flat. This night she stayed longer than usual and gave us a chance to complete the plans of how we were going to stone and beat that feller on the top floor out of town. Ned especially had it in for him. He was about to throw a brick up at the window when at last the room went dark. Some minutes passed. Then Avey, as unconcerned as if she had been paying an old-maid aunt a visit, came out. I dont remember what she had on, and all that sort of thing. But I do know that I turned hot as bare pavements in the summertime at Ned's boast: "Hell, bet I could get her too if you little niggers weren't always spying and crabbing everything." I didnt say a word to him. It wasnt my way then. I just stood there like the others, and something like a fuse burned up inside of me. She never noticed us, but swung along lazy and easy as anything. We sauntered to the corner and watched her till her door banged to. Ned repeated what he'd said. I didnt seem to care. Sitting around old Mush-Head's bread box, the discussion began. "Hang if I can see how she gets away with it," Doc started. Ned knew, of course. There was nothing he didnt know when it came to women. He dilated on the emotional needs of girls. Said they werent much different from men in that respect. And concluded with the solemn avowal: "It does em good." None of us liked Ned much. We all talked dirt; but it was the way he said it. And then too, a couple of the fellers had sisters and had caught Ned playing with them. But there was no disputing the superiority of his smutty wisdom. Bubs Sanborn, whose mother was friendly with Avey's, had overheard the old ladies talking. "Avey's mother's ont her," he said. We thought that only natural and began to guess at what would happen. Some one said she'd marry that feller on the top floor. Ned called that a lie because Avey was going to marry nobody but him. We had our doubts about that, but we did agree that she'd soon leave school and marry some one. The gang broke up, and I went home, picturing myself as married.

Nothing I did seemed able to change Avey's indifference to me. I played basket-ball, and when I'd make a long clean shot she'd clap with the others, louder than they, I thought. I'd meet her on the street, and there'd be no difference in the way she said hello. She never took the trouble to call me by my name. On the days for drill, I'd let my voice down a tone and call for a complicated maneuver when I saw her coming. She'd smile appreciation, but it was an impersonal smile, never for me. It was on a summer excursion down to Riverview that she first seemed to take me into account. The day had been spent riding merry-go-rounds, scenic-railways, and shoot-the-chutes. We had been in swimming and we had danced. I was a crack swimmer then. She didnt know how. I held her up and showed her how to kick her legs and draw her arms. Of course she didnt learn in one day, but she thanked me for bothering with her. I was also somewhat of a dancer. And I had already noticed that love can start on a dance floor. We danced. But though I held her tightly in my arms, she was way away. That college feller who lived on the top floor was somewhere making money for the next year. I imagined that she was thinking, wishing for him. Ned was along. He treated her until his money gave out. She went with another feller. Ned got sore. One by one the boys' money gave out. She left them. And they got sore. Every one of them but me got sore. This is the reason, I guess, why I had her to myself on the top deck of the *Jane Mosely* that night as we puffed up the Potomac, coming home. The moon was brilliant. The air was sweet like clover. And every now and then, a salt tang, a stale drift of sea-weed. It was not my mind's fault if it went romancing. I should have taken her in my arms the minute we were stowed in that old lifeboat. I dallied, dreaming. She took me in hers. And I could feel by the touch of it that it wasnt a man-to-woman love. It made me restless. I felt chagrined. I didnt know what it was, but I did know that I couldnt handle it. She ran her fingers through my hair and kissed my forehead. I itched to break through her tenderness to passion. I wanted her to take me in her arms as I knew she had that college feller. I wanted her to love me passionately as she did him. I gave her one burning kiss. Then she laid me in her lap as if I were a child. Helpless. I got sore when she started to hum a lullaby. She wouldnt let me go. I talked. I knew damned well that I could beat her at that. Her eyes were soft and misty, the curves of her lips were wistful, and her smile seemed indulgent of the irrelevance of my remarks. I gave up at last and let her love me, silently, in her own

way. The moon was brilliant. The air was sweet like clover, and
every now and then, a salt tang, a stale drift of sea-weed . . .

   The next time I came close to her was the following summer at
Harpers Ferry. We were sitting on a flat projecting rock they give
the name of Lover's Leap. Some one is supposed to have jumped off
it. The river is about six hundred feet beneath. A railroad track runs
up the valley and curves out of sight where part of the mountain
rock had to be blasted away to make room for it. The engines of this
valley have a whistle, the echoes of which sound like iterated gasps
and sobs. I always think of them as crude music from the soul of
Avey. We sat there holding hands. Our palms were soft and warm
against each other. Our fingers were not tight. She would not let
them be. She would not let me twist them. I wanted to talk. To
explain what I meant to her. Avey was as silent as those great trees
whose tops we looked down upon. She has always been like that. At
least, to me. I had the notion that if I really wanted to, I could do
with her just what I pleased. Like one can strip a tree. I did kiss her.
I even let my hands cup her breasts. When I was through, she'd
seek my hand and hold it till my pulse cooled down. Evening after
evening we sat there. I tried to get her to talk about that college
feller. She never would. There was no set time to go home. None of
my family had come down. And as for hers, she didnt give a hang
about them. The general gossips could hardly say more than they
had. The boarding-house porch was always deserted when we
returned. No one saw us enter, so the time was set conveniently for
scandal. This worried me a little, for I thought it might keep Avey
from getting an appointment in the schools. She didnt care. She
had finished normal school. They could give her a job if they wanted
to. As time went on, her indifference to things began to pique me; I
was ambitious. I left the Ferry earlier than she did. I was going off
to college. The more I thought of it, the more I resented, yes, hell,
thats what it was, her downright laziness. Sloppy indolence. There
was no excuse for a healthy girl taking life so easy. Hell! she was no
better than a cow. I was certain that she was a cow when I felt an
udder in a Wisconsin stock-judging class. Among those energetic
Swedes, or whatever they are, I decided to forget her. For two years
I thought I did. When I'd come home for the summer she'd be
away. And before she returned, I'd be gone. We never wrote; she
was too damned lazy for that. But what a bluff I put up about forgetting her. The girls up that way, at least the ones I knew, havent
got the stuff: they dont know how to love. Giving themselves completely was tame beside just the holding of Avey's hand. One day I
received a note from her. The writing, I decided, was slovenly. She
wrote on a torn bit of note-book paper. The envelope had a faint

perfume that I remembered. A single line told me she had lost her school and was going away. I comforted myself with the reflection that shame held no pain for one so indolent as she. Nevertheless, I left Wisconsin that year for good. Washington had seemingly forgotten her. I hunted Ned. Between curses, I caught his opinion of her. She was no better than a whore. I saw her mother on the street. The same old pinch-beck, jerky-gaited creature that I'd always known.

Perhaps five years passed. The business of hunting a job or something or other had bruised my vanity so that I could recognize it. I felt old. Avey and my real relation to her, I thought I came to know. I wanted to see her. I had been told that she was in New York. As I had no money, I hiked and bummed my way there. I got work in a ship-yard and walked the streets at night, hoping to meet her. Failing in this, I saved enough to pay my fare back home. One evening in early June, just at the time when dusk is most lovely on the eastern horizon, I saw Avey, indolent as ever, leaning on the arm of a man, strolling under the recently lit arclights of U Street. She had almost passed before she recognized me. She showed no surprise. The puff over her eyes had grown heavier. The eyes themselves were still sleepy-large, and beautiful. I had almost concluded—indifferent. "You look older," was what she said. I wanted to convince her that I was, so I asked her to walk with me. The man whom she was with, and whom she never took the trouble to introduce, at a nod from her, hailed a taxi, and drove away. That gave me a notion of what she had been used to. Her dress was of some fine, costly stuff. I suggested the park, and then added that the grass might stain her skirt. Let it get stained, she said, for where it came from there are others.

I have a spot in Soldier's Home to which I always go when I want the simple beauty of another's soul. Robins spring about the lawn all day. They leave their footprints in the grass. I imagine that the grass at night smells sweet and fresh because of them. The ground is high. Washington lies below. Its light spreads like a blush against the darkened sky. Against the soft dusk sky of Washington. And when the wind is from the South, soil of my homeland falls like a fertile shower upon the lean streets of the city. Upon my hill in Soldier's Home. I know the policeman who watches the place of nights. When I go there alone, I talk to him. I tell him I come there to find the truth that people bury in their hearts. I tell him that I do not come there with a girl to do the thing he's paid to watch out for. I look deep in his eyes when I say these things, and he believes me. He comes over to see who it is on the grass. I say hello to him. He greets me in the same way and goes off searching for other black splotches upon the lawn. Avey and I went there. A band in one of the buildings a fair distance off was playing a march. I wished they would stop. Their playing was like a tin spoon in one's mouth. I wanted the Howard Glee Club to sing "Deep River,"[1] from the road. To sing "Deep River, Deep River," from the road . . . Other than the first comments, Avey had been silent. I started to hum a folk-tune. She slipped her hand in mine. Pillowed her head as best she could upon my arm. Kissed the hand that she was holding and listened, or so I thought, to what I had to say. I traced my development from the early days up to the present time, the phase in which I could understand her. I described her own nature and temperament. Told how they needed a larger life for their expression. How incapable Washington was of understanding that need. How it could not meet it. I pointed out that in lieu of proper channels, her emotions had overflowed into paths that dissipated them. I talked, beautifully I thought, about an art that would be born, an art that would open the way for women the likes of her. I asked her to hope, and build up an inner life against the coming of that day. I recited some of my own things to her. I sang, with a strange quiver in my voice, a promise-song. And then I began to wonder why her hand had not once returned a single pressure. My old-time feeling about her laziness came back. I spoke sharply. My policeman friend passed by. I said hello to him. As he went away, I began to visualize certain possibilities. An immediate and urgent passion swept over me. Then I looked at Avey. Her heavy eyes were closed. Her breathing was as faint and regular as a child's in slumber. My passion died. I was afraid to move lest I disturb her. Hours and hours, I guess it was, she lay there. My body grew numb. I shivered. I coughed. I wanted to get up and whittle at the boxes of young trees. I withdrew my hand. I raised her head to waken her. She did not stir. I got up and walked around. I found my policeman friend and talked to him. We both came up, and bent over her. He said it would be all right for her to stay there just so long as she got away before the workmen came at dawn. A blanket was borrowed from a neighbor house. I sat beside her through the night. I saw the dawn steal over Washington. The Capitol dome looked like a gray ghost ship drifting in from sea. Avey's face was pale, and her eyes were heavy. She did not have the gray crimson-splashed beauty of the dawn. I hated to wake her. Orphan-woman . . .

---

1. African American spiritual; *Howard*: Howard University.

# Beehive

Within this black hive to-night
There swarm a million bees;
Bees passing in and out the moon,
Bees escaping out the moon,
Bees returning through the moon,
Silver bees intently buzzing,
Silver honey dripping from the swarm of bees
Earth is a waxen cell of the world comb,
And I, a drone,
Lying on my back,
Lipping honey,
Getting drunk with silver honey,
Wish that I might fly out past the moon
And curl forever in some far-off farmyard flower.

# Storm Ending[1]

Thunder blossoms gorgeously above our heads,
Great, hollow, bell-like flowers,
Rumbling in the wind,
Stretching clappers to strike our ears . . .
Full-lipped flowers
Bitten by the sun
Bleeding rain
Dripping rain like golden honey—
And the sweet earth flying from the thunder.

1. First published in *Double Dealer* 4 (September 1922): 118.

# Theater

Life of nigger alleys, of pool rooms and restaurants and near-beer saloons soaks into the walls of Howard Theater[1] and sets them throbbing jazz songs. Black-skinned, they dance and shout above the tick and trill of white-walled buildings. At night, they open doors to people who come in to stamp their feet and shout. At night, road-shows volley songs into the mass-heart of black people. Songs soak the walls and seep out to the nigger life of alleys and near-beer saloons, of the Poodle Dog and Black Bear cabarets. Afternoons, the house is dark, and the walls are sleeping singers until rehearsal begins. Or until John comes within them. Then they start throbbing to a subtle syncopation. And the space-dark air grows softly luminous.

John is the manager's brother. He is seated at the center of the theater, just before rehearsal. Light streaks down upon him from a window high above. One half his face is orange in it. One half his face is in shadow. The soft glow of the house rushes to and compacts about, the shaft of light. John's mind coincides with the shaft of light. Thoughts rush to, and compact about it. Life of the house and of the slowly awakening stage swirls to the body of John, and thrills it. John's body is separate from the thoughts that pack his mind.

Stage-lights, soft, as if they shine through clear pink fingers. Beneath them, hid by the shadow of a set, Dorris. Other chorus girls drift in. John feels them in the mass. And as if his own body were the mass-heart of a black audience listening to them singing, he wants to stamp his feet and shout. His mind, contained above desires of his body, singles the girls out, and tries to trace origins and plot destinies.

A pianist slips into the pit and improvises jazz. The walls awake. Arms of the girls, and their limbs, which . . . jazz, jazz . . . by lifting up their tight street skirts they set free, jab the air and clog the floor in rhythm to the music. (Lift your skirts, Baby, and talk t papa!) Crude, individualized, and yet . . . monotonous . . .

John: Soon the director will herd you, my full-lipped, distant beauties, and tame you, and blunt your sharp thrusts in loosely suggestive movements, appropriate to Broadway. (O dance!) Soon the audience will paint your dusk faces white, and call you beautiful. (O dance!) Soon I . . . (O dance!) I'd like . . .

Girls laugh and shout. Sing discordant snatches of other jazz songs. Whirl with loose passion into the arms of passing show-men.

1. A theater in the African American section of Washington, D.C.; the audiences and the performers were also African American.

John: Too thick. Too easy. Too monotonous. Her whom I'd love I'd leave before she knew that I was with her. Her? Which? (O dance!) I'd like to . . .

Girls dance and sing. Men clap. The walls sing and press inward. They press the men and girls, they press John towards a center of physical ecstasy. Go to it, Baby! Fan yourself, and feed your papa! Put . . . nobody lied . . . and take . . . when they said I cried over you. No lie! The glitter and color of stacked scenes, the gilt and brass and crimson of the house, converge towards a center of physical ecstasy. John's feet and torso and his blood press in. He wills thought to rid his mind of passion.

"All right, girls. Alaska. Miss Reynolds, please."

The director wants to get the rehearsal through with.

The girls line up. John sees the front row: dancing ponies. The rest are in shadow. The leading lady fits loosely in the front. Lack-life, monotonous. "One, two, three—" Music starts. The song is somewhere where it will not strain the leading lady's throat. The dance is somewhere where it will not strain the girls. Above the staleness, one dancer throws herself into it. Dorris. John sees her. Her hair, crisp-curled, is bobbed. Bushy, black hair bobbing about her lemon-colored face. Her lips are curiously full, and very red. Her limbs in silk purple stockings are lovely. John feels them. Desires her. Holds off.

John: Stage-door johnny; chorus-girl. No, that would be all right. Dictie,[2] educated, stuck-up; show-girl. Yep. Her suspicion would be stronger than her passion. It wouldnt work. Keep her loveliness. Let her go.

Dorris sees John and knows that he is looking at her. Her own glowing is too rich a thing to let her feel the slimness of his diluted passion.

"Who's that?" she asks her dancing partner.

"Th manager's brother. Dictie. Nothin doin, hon."

Dorris tosses her head and dances for him until she feels she has him. Then, withdrawing disdainfully, she flirts with the director.

Dorris: Nothin doin? How come? Aint I as good as him? Couldnt I have got an education if I'd wanted one? Dont I know respectable folks, lots of em, in Philadelphia and New York and Chicago? Aint I had men as good as him? Better. Doctors an lawyers. Whats a manager's brother, anyhow?

Two steps back, and two steps front.

"Say, Mame, where do you get that stuff?"

"Whatshmean, Dorris?"

---

2. Slang term referring to educated, middle-class African Americans who behave as though they consider themselves socially superior to other African Americans—similar to "stuck-up," "snobbish."

"If you two girls cant listen to what I'm telling you, I know where I can get some who can. Now listen."

Mame:  Go to hell, you black bastard.

Dorris:  Whats eatin at him, anyway?

"Now follow me in this, you girls. Its three counts to the right, three counts to the left, and then you shimmy—"[3]

John:—and then you shimmy. I'll bet she can. Some good cabaret, with rooms upstairs. And what in hell do you think you'd get from it? Youre going wrong. Here's right: get her to herself—(Christ, but how she'd bore you after the first five minutes)—not if you get her right she wouldnt. Touch her, I mean. To herself—in some room perhaps. Some cheap, dingy bedroom. Hell no. Cant be done. But the point is, brother John, it can be done. Get her to herself somewhere, anywhere. Go down in yourself—and she'd be calling you all sorts of asses while you were in the process of going down. Hold em, bud. Cant be done. Let her go. (Dance and I'll love you!) And keep her loveliness.

"All right now, Chicken Chaser.[4] Dorris and girls. Where's Dorris? I told you to stay on the stage, didnt I? Well? Now thats enough. All right. All right there, Professor?[5] All right. One, two, three—"

Dorris swings to the front. The line of girls, four deep, blurs within the shadow of suspended scenes. Dorris wants to dance. The director feels that and steps to one side. He smiles, and picks her for a leading lady, one of these days. Odd ends of stage-men emerge from the wings, and stare and clap. A crap game in the alley suddenly ends. Black faces crowd the rear stage doors. The girls, catching joy from Dorris, whip up within the footlights' glow. They forget set steps; they find their own. The director forgets to bawl them out. Dorris dances.

John:  Her head bobs to Broadway. Dance from yourself. Dance! O just a little more.

Dorris' eyes burn across the space of seats to him.

Dorris:  I bet he can love. Hell, he cant love. He's too skinny. His lips are too skinny. He wouldnt love me anyway, only for that. But I'd get a pair of silk stockings out of it. Red silk. I got purple. Cut it, kid. You cant win him to respect you that away. He wouldnt anyway. Maybe he would. Maybe he'd love. I've heard em say that men who look like him (what does he look like?) will marry if they love. O will you love me? And give me kids, and a home, and everything? (I'd like to make your nest, and honest, hon, I wouldnt run out on you.) You will if I make you. Just watch me.

Dorris dances. She forgets her tricks. She dances.

3. A popular dance movement that emphasized an erotic vibration of the torso.
4. Another dance.
5. A nickname for a band leader or pianist.

Glorious songs are the muscles of her limbs.

And her singing is of canebrake loves and mangrove feastings.

The walls press in, singing. Flesh of a throbbing body, they press close to John and Dorris. They close them in. John's heart beats tensely against her dancing body. Walls press his mind within his heart. And then, the shaft of light goes out the window high above him. John's mind sweeps up to follow it. Mind pulls him upward into dream.                                    Dorris dances . . .
John dreams:

> Dorris is dressed in a loose black gown splashed with lemon ribbons. Her feet taper long and slim from trim ankles. She waits for him just inside the stage door. John, collar and tie colorful and flaring, walks towards the stage door. There are no trees in the alley. But his feet feel as though they step on autumn leaves whose rustle has been pressed out of them by the passing of a million satin slippers. The air is sweet with roasting chestnuts, sweet with bonfires of old leaves. John's melancholy is a deep thing that seals all senses but his eyes, and makes him whole.
>
> Dorris knows that he is coming. Just at the right moment she steps from the door, as if there were no door. Her face is tinted like the autumn alley. Of old flowers, or of a southern canefield, her perfume. "Glorious Dorris." So his eyes speak. And their sadness is too deep for sweet untruth. She barely touches his arm. They glide off with footfalls softened on the leaves, the old leaves powdered by a million satin slippers.
>
> They are in a room. John knows nothing of it. Only, that the flesh and blood of Dorris are its walls. Singing walls. Lights, soft, as if they shine through clear pink fingers. Soft lights, and warm.
>
> John reaches for a manuscript of his, and reads. Dorris, who has no eyes, has eyes to understand him. He comes to a dancing scene. The scene is Dorris. She dances. Dorris dances. Glorious Dorris. Dorris whirls, whirls, dances . . .

Dorris dances.
The pianist crashes a bumper chord. The whole stage claps. Dorris, flushed, looks quick at John. His whole face is in shadow. She seeks for her dance in it. She finds it a dead thing in the shadow which is his dream. She rushes from the stage. Falls down the steps into her dressing-room. Pulls her hair. Her eyes, over a floor of tears, stare at the whitewashed ceiling. (Smell of dry paste, and paint, and soiled clothing.) Her pal comes in Dorris flings herself into the old safe arms, and cries bitterly.

"I told you nothin doin," is what Mame says to comfort her.

# Her Lips Are Copper Wire[1]

whisper of yellow globes
gleaming on lamp-posts that sway
like bootleg licker[2] drinkers in the fog

and let your breath be moist against me
like bright beads on yellow globes

telephone the power-house
that the main wires are insulate

(her words play softly up and down
dewy corridors of billboards)

then with your tongue remove the tape
and press your lips to mine
till they are incandescent

1. First published in *S4N* (May–August 1923).
2. Liquor illegally distilled, especially during Prohibition, a period during the 1920s and early 1930s when federal laws in the United States prohibited the manufacture, transportation, sale, and possession of alcoholic beverages. The term "bootleg liquor" now applies to liquor that manufacturers distill and distribute without paying the required state and federal taxes.

# Calling Jesus[1]

Her soul is like a little thrust-tailed dog that follows her, whimpering. She is large enough, I know, to find a warm spot for it. But each night when she comes home and closes the big outside storm door, the little dog is left in the vestibule, filled with chills till morning. Some one . . . eoho[2] Jesus . . . soft as a cotton boll brushed against the milk-pod cheek of Christ, will steal in and cover it that it need not shiver, and carry it to her where she sleeps upon clean hay cut in her dreams.

When you meet her in the daytime on the streets, the little dog keeps coming. Nothing happens at first, and then, when she has forgotten the streets and alleys, and the large house where she goes to bed of nights, a soft thing like fur begins to rub your limbs, and you hear a low, scared voice, lonely, calling, and you know that a cool something nozzles moisture in your palms. Sensitive things like nostrils, quiver. Her breath comes sweet as honeysuckle whose pistils bear the life of coming song. And her eyes carry to where builders find no need for vestibules, for swinging on iron hinges, storm doors.

Her soul is like a little thrust-tailed dog, that follows her, whimpering. I've seen it tagging on behind her, up streets where chestnut trees flowered, where dusty asphalt had been freshly sprinkled with clean water. Up alleys where niggers sat on low door-steps before tumbled shanties and sang and loved. At night, when she comes home, the little dog is left in the vestibule, nosing the crack beneath the big storm door, filled with chills till morning. Some one . . . eoho Jesus . . . soft as the bare feet of Christ moving across bales of southern cotton, will steal in and cover it that it need not shiver, and carry it to her where she sleeps: cradled in dream-fluted cane.

1. Originally entitled "Nora" when first published in *Double Dealer* 4 (September 1922): 132.
2. A call.

# Box Seat[1]

I

Houses are shy girls whose eyes shine reticently upon the dusk body of the street. Upon the gleaming limbs and asphalt torso of a dreaming nigger. Shake your curled wool-blossoms, nigger. Open your liver lips to the lean, white spring. Stir the root-life of a with-ered people. Call them from their houses, and teach them to dream.

Dark swaying forms of Negroes are street songs that woo virginal houses.

Dan Moore walks southward on Thirteenth Street. The low limbs of budding chestnut trees recede above his head. Chestnut buds and blossoms are wool he walks upon. The eyes of houses faintly touch him as he passes them. Soft girl-eyes, they set him singing. Girl-eyes within him widen upward to promised faces. Floating away, they dally wistfully over the dusk body of the street. Come on, Dan Moore, come on. Dan sings. His voice is a little hoarse. It cracks. He strains to produce tones in keeping with the houses' loveliness. Cant be done. He whistles. His notes are shrill. They hurt him. Negroes open gates, and go indoors, perfectly. Dan thinks of the house he's going to. Of the girl. Lips, flesh-notes of a forgotten song, plead with him . . .

Dan turns into a side-street, opens an iron gate, bangs it to. Mounts the steps, and searches for the bell. Funny, he cant find it. He fumbles around. The thought comes to him that some one passing by might see him, and not understand. Might think that he is trying to sneak, to break in.

Dan:[2]   Break in. Get an ax and smash in. Smash in their faces. I'll show em. Break into an engine-house, steal a thousand horse-power fire truck. Smash in with the truck. I'll show em. Grab an ax and brain em. Cut em up. Jack the Ripper.[3] Baboon from the zoo. And then the cops come. "No, I aint a baboon. I aint Jack the Ripper. I'm a poor man out of work. Take your hands off me, you bull-necked bears. Look into my eyes. I am Dan Moore. I was born in a cane-field. The hands of Jesus touched me. I am come to a sick world to heal it. Only the other day, a dope fiend brushed against me—Dont

---

1. Expensive theater seats usually located along a side wall, box seats were considered the best seats in the theater. They were above stage level, and the closest were within arms' reach of the stage.
2. Throughout this story, a colon following the name of Dan or Muriel indicates that the thoughts, not the spoken words, of the character will follow.
3. The name given by newspapers to an unidentified individual in nineteenth-century London, England, who killed and mutilated several prostitutes.

laugh, you mighty, juicy, meat-hook men. Give me your fingers and I will peel them as if they were ripe bananas."

Some one might think he is trying to break in. He'd better knock. His knuckles are raw bone against the thick glass door. He waits. No one comes. Perhaps they havent heard him. He raps again. This time, harder. He waits. No one comes. Some one is surely in. He fancies that he sees their shadows on the glass. Shadows of gorillas. Perhaps they saw him coming and dont want to let him in. He knocks. The tension of his arms makes the glass rattle. Hurried steps come towards him. The door opens.

"Please, you might break the glass—the bell—oh, Mr. Moore! I thought it must be some stranger. How do you do? Come in, wont you? Muriel? Yes. I'll call her. Take your things off, wont you? And have a seat in the parlor. Muriel will be right down. Muriel! Oh Muriel! Mr. Moore to see you. She'll be right down. You'll pardon me, wont you? So glad to see you."

Her eyes are weak. They are bluish and watery from reading newspapers. The blue is steel. It gimlets Dan while her mouth flaps amiably to him.

Dan: Nothing for you to see, old mussel-head. Dare I show you? If I did, delirium would furnish you headlines for a month. Now look here. Thats enough. Go long, woman. Say some nasty thing and I'll kill you. Huh. Better damned sight not. Ta-ta, Mrs. Pribby.

Mrs. Pribby retreats to the rear of the house. She takes up a newspaper. There is a sharp click as she fits into her chair and draws it to the table. The click is metallic like the sound of a bolt being shot into place. Dan's eyes sting. Sinking into a soft couch, he closes them. The house contracts about him. It is a sharp-edged, massed, metallic house. Bolted. About Mrs. Pribby. Bolted to the endless rows of metal houses. Mrs. Pribby's house. The rows of houses belong to other Mrs. Pribbys. No wonder he couldn't sing to them.

Dan: What's Muriel doing here? God, what a place for her. Whats she doing? Putting her stockings on? In the bathroom. Come out of there, Dan Moore. People must have their privacy, Peeping-toms. I'll never peep. I'll listen. I like to listen.

Dan goes to the wall and places his ear against it. A passing street car and something vibrant from the earth sends a rumble to him. That rumble comes from the earth's deep core. It is the mutter of powerful underground races. Dan has a picture of all the people rushing to put their ears against walls, to listen to it. The next world-savior is coming up that way. Coming up. A continent sinks down. The new-world Christ will need consummate skill to walk upon the waters where huge bubbles burst . . . Thuds of Muriel coming down. Dan turns to the piano and glances through a stack of jazz music sheets. Ji-ji-bo, JI-JI-BO! . . .

"Hello, Dan, stranger, what brought you here?"

Muriel comes in, shakes hands, and then clicks into a high-armed seat under the orange glow of a floor-lamp. Her face is fleshy. It would tend to coarseness but for the fresh fragrant something which is the life of it. Her hair like an Indian's. But more curly and bushed and vagrant. Her nostrils flare. The flushed ginger of her cheeks is touched orange by the shower of color from the lamp.

"Well, you havent told me, you havent answered my question, stranger. What brought you here?"

Dan feels the pressure of the house, of the rear room, of the rows of houses, shift to Muriel. He is light. He loves her. He is doubly heavy.

"Dont know, Muriel—wanted to see you—wanted to talk to you—to see you and tell you that I know what you've been through—what pain the last few months must have been—"

"Lets dont mention that."

"But why not, Muriel? I—"

"Please."

"But Muriel, life is full of things like that. One grows strong and beautiful in facing them. What else is life?"

"I dont know, Dan. And I dont believe I care. Whats the use? Lets talk about something else. I hear there's a good show at the Lincoln this week."

"Yes, so Harry was telling me. Going?"

"To-night."

Dan starts to rise.

"I didnt know. I dont want to keep you."

"Its all right. You dont have to go till Bernice comes. And she wont be here till eight. I'm all dressed. I'll let you know."

"Thanks."

Silence. The rustle of a newspaper being turned comes from the rear room.

Muriel: Shame about Dan. Something awfully good and fine about him. But he dont fit in. In where? Me? Dan, I could love you if I tried. I dont have to try. I do. O Dan, dont you know I do? Timid lover, brave talker that you are. Whats the good of all you know if you dont know that? I wont let myself. I? Mrs. Pribby who reads newspapers all night wont. What has she got to do with me? She *is* me, somehow. No she's not. Yes she is. She is the town, and the town wont let me love you, Dan. Dont you know? You could make it let me if you would. Why wont you? Youre selfish. I'm not strong enough to buck it. Youre too selfish to buck it, for me. I wish you'd go. You irritate me. Dan, please go.

"What are you doing now, Dan?"

"Same old thing, Muriel. Nothing, as the world would have it. Living, as I look at things. Living as much as I can without—"

"But you cant live without money, Dan. Why dont you get a good job and settle down?"

Dan: Same old line. Shoot it at me, sister. Hell of a note, this loving business. For ten minutes of it youve got to stand the torture of an intolerable heaviness and a hundred platitudes. Well, damit, shoot on.

"To what? my dear. Rustling newspapers?"

"You mustnt say that, Dan. It isnt right. Mrs. Pribby has been awfully good to me."

"Dare say she has. Whats that got to do with it?"

"Oh, Dan, youre so unconsiderate and selfish. All you think of is yourself."

"I think of you."

"Too much—I mean, you ought to work more and think less. Thats the best way to get along."

"Mussel-heads get along, Muriel. There is more to you than that—"

"Sometimes I think there is, Dan. But I dont know. I've tried. I've tried to do something with myself. Something real and beautiful, I mean. But whats the good of trying? I've tried to make people, every one I come in contact with, happy—"

Dan looks at her, directly. Her animalism, still unconquered by zoo-restrictions and keeper-taboos, stirs him. Passion tilts upward, bringing with it the elements of an old desire. Muriel's lips become the flesh-notes of a futile, plaintive longing. Dan's impulse to direct her is its fresh life.

"Happy, Muriel? No, not happy. Your aim is wrong. There is no such thing as happiness. Life bends joy and pain, beauty and ugliness, in such a way that no one may isolate them. No one should want to. Perfect joy, or perfect pain, with no contrasting element to define them, would mean a monotony of consciousness, would mean death. Not happy, Muriel. Say that you have tried to make them create. Say that you have used your own capacity for life to cradle them. To start them upward-flowing. Or if you cant say that you have, then say that you will. My talking to you will make you aware of your power to do so. Say that you will love, that you will give yourself in love—"

"To you, Dan?"

Dan's consciousness crudely swerves into his passions. They flare up in his eyes. They set up quivers in his abdomen. He is suddenly over-tense and nervous.

"Muriel—"

The newspaper rustles in the rear room.

"Muriel—"

Dan rises. His arms stretch towards her. His fingers and his palms, pink in the lamplight, are glowing irons. Muriel's chair is close and stiff about her. The house, the rows of houses locked about her chair. Dan's fingers and arms are fire to melt and bars to wrench and force and pry. Her arms hang loose. Her hands are hot and moist. Dan takes them. He slips to his knees before her.

"Dan, you mustnt."

"Muriel—"

"Dan, really you mustnt. No, Dan. No."

"Oh, come, Muriel. Must I—"

"Shhh. Dan, please get up. Please. Mrs. Pribby is right in the next room. She'll hear you. She may come in. Dont, Dan. She'll see you—"

"Well then, lets go out."

"I cant. Let go, Dan. Oh, wont you please let go."

Muriel tries to pull her hands away. Dan tightens his grip. He feels the strength of his fingers. His muscles are tight and strong. He stands up. Thrusts out his chest. Muriel shrinks from him. Dan becomes aware of his crude absurdity. His lips curl. His passion chills. He has an obstinate desire to possess her.

"Muriel, I love you. I want you, whatever the world of Pribby says. Damn your Pribby. Who is she to dictate my love? I've stood enough of her. Enough of you. Come here."

Muriel's mouth works in and out. Her eyes flash and waggle. She wrenches her hands loose and forces them against his breast to keep him off. Dan grabs her wrists. Wedges in between her arms. Her face is close to him. It is hot and blue and moist. Ugly.

"Come here now."

"Dont, Dan. Oh, dont. What are you killing?"

"Whats weak in both of us and a whole litter of Pribbys. For once in your life youre going to face whats real, by God—"

A sharp rap on the newspaper in the rear room cuts between them. The rap is like cool thick glass between them. Dan is hot on one side. Muriel, hot on the other. They straighten. Gaze fearfully at one another. Neither moves. A clock in the rear room, in the rear room, the rear room, strikes eight. Eight slow, cool sounds. Bernice. Muriel fastens on her image. She smooths her dress. She adjusts her skirt. She becomes prim and cool. Rising, she skirts Dan as if to keep the glass between them. Dan, gyrating nervously above the easy swing of his limbs, follows her to the parlor door. Muriel retreats before him till she reaches the landing of the steps that lead upstairs. She smiles at him. Dan sees his face in the hall mirror. He runs his fingers through his hair. Reaches for his hat and coat and puts them on. He moves towards Muriel. Muriel steps backward up one step. Dan's jaw shoots out. Muriel jerks her arm in warning of Mrs. Pribby. She

gasps and turns and starts to run. Noise of a chair scraping as Mrs.
Pribby rises from it, ratchets down the hall. Dan stops. He makes a
wry face, wheels round, goes out, and slams the door.


2

   People come in slowly . . . mutter, laughs, flutter, whishadwash,
"I've changed my work-clothes—" . . . and fill vacant seats of Lincoln Theater. Muriel, leading Bernice who is a cross between a
washerwoman and a blue-blood lady, a washer-blue, a washer-lady,
wanders down the right aisle to the lower front box. Muriel has on
an orange dress. Its color would clash with the crimson box-draperies,
its color would contradict the sweet rose smile her face is bathed in,
should she take her coat off. She'll keep it on. Pale purple shadows
rest on the planes of her cheeks. Deep purple comes from her thick-
shocked hair. Orange of the dress goes well with these. Muriel
presses her coat down from around her shoulders. Teachers are not
supposed to have bobbed hair. She'll keep her hat on. She takes the
first chair, and indicates that Bernice is to take the one directly
behind her. Seated thus, her eyes are level with, and near to, the
face of an imaginary man upon the stage. To speak to Berny she
must turn. When she does, the audience is square upon her.
   People come in slowly . . . "—for my Sunday-go-to-meeting dress.
O glory God! O shout Amen!" . . . and fill vacant seats of Lincoln
Theater. Each one is a bolt that shoots into a slot, and is locked
there. Suppose the Lord should ask, where was Moses when the
light went out? Suppose Gabriel should blow his trumpet! The seats
are slots. The seats are bolted houses. The mass grows denser. Its
weight at first is impalpable upon the box. Then Muriel begins to
feel it. She props her arm against the brass box-rail, to ward it off.
Silly. These people are friends of hers: a parent of a child she
teaches, an old school friend. She smiles at them. They return her
courtesy, and she is free to chat with Berny. Berny's tongue, started,
runs on, and on. O washer-blue! O washer-lady!
   Muriel: Never see Dan again. He makes me feel queer. Starts
things he doesnt finish. Upsets me. I am not upset. I am perfectly
calm. I am going to enjoy the show. Good show. I've had some show!
This damn tame thing. O Dan. Wont see Dan again. Not alone.
Have Mrs. Pribby come in. She *was* in. Keep Dan out. If I love him,
can I keep him out? Well then, I dont love him. Now he's out. Who
is that coming in? Blind as a bat. Ding-bat. Looks like Dan. He
mustnt see me. Silly. He cant reach me. He wont dare come in here.
He'd put his head down like a goring bull and charge me. He'd
trample them. He'd gore. He'd rape! Berny! He wont dare come in
here.

"Berny, who was that who just came in? I havent my glasses."

"A friend of yours, a *good* friend so I hear. Mr. Daniel Moore, Lord."

"Oh. He's no friend of mine."

"No? I hear he is."

"Well, he isnt."

Dan is ushered down the aisle. He has to squeeze past the knees of seated people to reach his own seat. He treads on a man's corns. The man grumbles, and shoves him off. He shrivels close beside a portly Negress whose huge rolls of flesh meet about the bones of seat-arms. A soil-soaked fragrance comes from her. Through the cement floor her strong roots sink down. They spread under the asphalt streets. Dreaming, the streets roll over on their bellies, and suck their glossy health from them. Her strong roots sink down and spread under the river and disappear in blood-lines that waver south. Her foots shoot down. Dan's hands follow them. Roots throb. Dan's heart beats violently. He places his palms upon the earth to cool them. Earth throbs. Dan's heart beats violently. He sees all the people in the house rush to the walls to listen to the rumble. A new-world Christ is coming up. Dan comes up. He is startled. The eyes of the woman dont belong to her. They look at him unpleasantly. From either aisle, bolted masses press in. He doesnt fit. The mass grows agitant. For an instant, Dan's and Muriel's eyes meet. His weight there slides the weight on her. She braces an arm against the brass rail, and turns her head away.

Muriel: Damn fool; dear Dan, what did you want to follow me here for? Oh cant you ever do anything right? Must you always pain me, and make me hate you? I do hate you. I wish some one would come in with a horse-whip and lash you out. I wish some one would drag you up a back alley and brain you with the whip-butt.

Muriel glances at her wrist-watch.

"Quarter of nine. Berny, what time have you?"

"Eight-forty. Time to begin. Oh, look Muriel, that woman with the plume; doesnt she look good! They say she's going with, oh, whats his name. You know. Too much powder. I can see it from here. Here's the orchestra now. O fine! Jim Clem at the piano!"

The men fill the pit. Instruments run the scale and tune. The saxophone moans and throws a fit. Jim Clem, poised over the piano, is ready to begin. His head nods forward. Opening crash. The house snaps dark. The curtain recedes upward from the blush of the footlights. Jazz overture is over. The first act is on.

Dan: Old stuff. Muriel—bored. Must be. But she'll smile and she'll clap. Do what youre bid, you she-slave. Look at her. Sweet, tame woman in a brass box seat. Clap, smile, fawn, clap. Do what youre bid. Drag me in with you. Dirty me. Prop me in your brass box seat. I'm there, am I not? because of you. He-slave. Slave of a woman who is a slave. I'm a damned sight worse than you are. I sing your praises, Beauty! I exalt thee, O Muriel! A slave, thou art greater than all Freedom because I love thee.

Dan fidgets, and disturbs his neighbors. His neighbors glare at him. He glares back without seeing them. The man whose corns have been trod upon speaks to him.

"Keep quiet, cant you, mister. Other people have paid their money besides yourself to see the show."

The man's face is a blur about two sullen liquid things that are his eyes. The eyes dissolve in the surrounding vagueness. Dan suddenly feels that the man is an enemy whom he has long been looking for.

Dan bristles. Glares furiously at the man.

"All right. All right then. Look at the show. I'm not stopping you."

"Shhh," from some one in the rear.

Dan turns around.

"Its that man there who started everything. I didnt say a thing to him until he tried to start something. What have I got to do with whether he has paid his money or not? Thats the manager's business. Do I look like the manager?"

"Shhhh. Youre right. Shhhh."

"Dont tell me to shhh. Tell him. That man there. He started everything. If what he wanted was to start a fight, why didnt he say so?"

The man leans forward.

"Better be quiet, sonny. I aint said a thing about fight, yet."

"Its a good thing you havent."

"Shhhh."

Dan grips himself. Another act is on. Dwarfs, dressed like prize-fighters, foreheads bulging like boxing gloves, are led upon the stage. They are going to fight for the heavyweight championship. Gruesome. Dan glances at Muriel. He imagines that she shudders. His mind curves back into himself, and picks up tail-ends of experiences. His eyes are open, mechanically. The dwarfs pound and bruise and bleed each other, on his eyeballs.

Dan: Ah, but she was some baby! And not vulgar either. Funny how some women can do those things. Muriel dancing like that! Hell. She rolled and wabbled. Her buttocks rocked. She pulled up her dress and showed her pink drawers. Baby! And then she caught my eyes. Dont know what my eyes had in them. Yes I do. God, dont I though! Sometimes I think, Dan Moore, that your eyes could burn clean . . . burn clean . . . BURN CLEAN! . . .

The gong rings. The dwarfs set to. They spar grotesquely, playfully, until one lands a stiff blow. This makes the other sore. He commences slugging. A real scrap is on. Time! The dwarfs go to

their corners and are sponged and fanned off. Gloves bulge from
their wrists. Their wrists are necks for the tight-faced gloves. The
fellow to the right lets his eyes roam over the audience. He sights
Muriel. He grins.

Dan: Those silly women arguing feminism. Here's what I should
have said to them. "It should be clear to you women, that the proposition must be stated thus:

> Me, horizontally above her.
> Action: perfect strokes downward oblique.
> Hence, man dominates because of limitation.
> Or, so it shall be until women learn their stuff.

So framed, the proposition is a mental-filler, Dentist, I want gold
teeth. It should become cherished of the technical intellect. I
hereby offer it to posterity as one of the important machine-age
designs. P. S. It should be noted, that because it *is* an achievement
of this age, its growth and hence its causes, up to the point of maturity, antedate machinery. Ery . . ."

The gong rings. No fooling this time. The dwarfs set to. They
clinch. The referee parts them. One swings a cruel upper-cut and
knocks the other down. A huge head hits the floor. Pop! The house
roars. The fighter, groggy, scrambles up. The referee whispers to the
contenders not to fight so hard. They ignore him. They charge. Their
heads jab like boxing-gloves. They kick and spit and bite. They
pound each other furiously. Muriel pounds. The house pounds. Cut
lips. Bloody noses. The referee asks for the gong. Time! The house
roars. The dwarfs bow, are made to bow. The house wants more.
The dwarfs are led from the stage.

Dan: Strange I never really noticed him before. Been sitting there
for years. Born a slave. Slavery not so long ago. He'll die in his chair.
Swing low, sweet chariot.[4] Jesus will come and roll him down the
river Jordan. Oh, come along, Moses, you'll get lost; stretch out your
rod and come across. LET MY PEOPLE GO! Old man. Knows
everyone who passes the corners. Saw the first horse-cars. The first
Oldsmobile. And he was born in slavery. I did see his eyes. Never
miss eyes. But they were bloodshot and watery. It hurt to look at
them. It hurts to look in most people's eyes. He saw Grant and Lincoln. He saw Walt—old man, did you see Walt Whitman?[5] Did you
see Walt Whitman! Strange force that drew me to him. And I went
up to see. The woman thought I saw crazy. I told him to look into the

---

4. In Dan's description of the slave who has lived long enough to see the first automobiles,
   Toomer alludes to African American spirituals expressing hope for freedom on earth
   and freedom in heaven: "Swing Low, Sweet Chariot," "Roll, Jordan, Roll," "Let My
   People Go."
5. Walt Whitman (1819–1892), American poet.

heavens. He did, and smiled. I asked him if he knew what that rumbling is that comes up from the ground. Christ, what a stroke that
was. And the jabbering idiots crowding around. And the crossing-
cop leaving his job to come over and wheel him away . . .

The house applauds. The house wants more. The dwarfs are led
back. But no encore. Must give the house something. The attendant comes out and announces that Mr. Barry, the champion, will
sing one of his own songs, "for your approval." Mr. Barry grins at
Muriel as he wabbles from the wing. He holds a fresh white rose,
and a small mirror. He wipes blood from his nose. He signals Jim
Clem. The orchestra starts. A sentimental love song, Mr. Barry
sings, first to one girl, and then another in the audience. He holds
the mirror in such a way that it flashes in the face of each one he
sings to. The light swings around.

Dan: I am going to reach up and grab the girders of this building
and pull them down. The crash will be a signal. Hid by the smoke
and dust Dan Moore will arise. In his right hand will be a dynamo.
In his left, a god's face that will flash white light from ebony. I'll grab
a girder and swing it like a walking-stick. Lightning will flash. I'll
grab its black knob and swing it like a crippled cane. Lightning . . .
Some one's flashing . . . some one's flashing . . . Who in hell is flashing that mirror? Take it off me, godam you.

Dan's eyes are half blinded. He moves his head. The light follows.
He hears the audience laugh. He hears the orchestra. A man with a
high-pitched, sentimental voice is singing. Dan sees the dwarf. Along
the mirror flash the song comes. Dan ducks his head. The audience
roars. The light swings around to Muriel. Dan looks. Muriel is too
close. Mr. Barry covers his mirror. He sings to her. She shrinks
away. Nausea. She clutches the brass box-rail. She moves to face
away. The audience is square upon her. Its eyes smile. Its hands itch
to clap. Muriel turns to the dwarf and forces a smile at him. With a
showy blare of orchestration, the song comes to its close. Mr. Barry
bows. He offers Muriel the rose, first having kissed it. Blood of his
battered lips is a vivid stain upon its petals. Mr. Barry offers Muriel
the rose. The house applauds. Muriel flinches back. The dwarf
steps forward, diffident; threatening. Hate pops from his eyes and
crackles like a brittle heat about the box. The thick hide of his face
is drawn in tortured wrinkles. Above his eyes, the bulging, tight-
skinned brow. Dan looks at it. It grows calm and massive. It grows
profound. It is a thing of wisdom and tenderness, of suffering and
beauty. Dan looks down. The eyes are calm and luminous. Words
come from them . . . Arms of the audience reach out, grab Muriel,
and hold her there. Claps are steel fingers that manacle her wrists
and move them forward to acceptance. Berny leans forward and
whispers:

"Its all right. Go on—take it."

Words form in the eyes of the dwarf:

> Do not shrink. Do not be afraid of me.
> *Jesus*
> See how my eyes look at you.
> *the Son of God*
> I too was made in His image.
> *was once—*
> I give you the rose.

Muriel, tight in her revulsion, sees black, and daintily reaches for the offering. As her hand touches it, Dan springs up in his seat and shouts:

"JESUS WAS ONCE A LEPER!"

Dan steps down.

He is as cool as a green stem that has just shed its flower.

Rows of gaping faces strain towards him. They are distant, beneath him, impalpable. Squeezing out, Dan again treads upon the corn-foot man. The man shoves him.

"Watch where youre going, mister. Crazy or no, you aint going to walk over me. Watch where youre going there."

Dan turns, and serenely tweaks the fellow's nose. The man jumps up. Dan is jammed against a seat-back. A slight swift anger flicks him. His fist hooks the other's jaw.

"Now you have started something. Aint no man living can hit me and get away with it. Come on on the outside."

The house, tumultuously stirring, grabs its wraps and follows the men.

The man leads Dan up a black alley. The alley-air is thick and moist with smells of garbage and wet trash. In the morning, singing niggers will drive by and ring their gongs . . . Heavy with the scent of rancid flowers and with the scent of fight. The crowd, pressing forward, is a hollow roar. Eyes of houses, soft girl-eyes, glow reticently upon the hubbub and blink out. The man stops. Takes off his hat and coat. Dan, having forgotten him, keeps going on.

# Prayer

My body is opaque to the soul.
Driven of the spirit, long have I sought to temper it unto the
　　spirit's longing,
But my mind, too, is opaque to the soul.
A closed lid is my soul's flesh-eye.
O Spirits of whom my soul is but a little finger,
Direct it to the lid of its flesh-eye.
I am weak with much giving.
I am weak with the desire to give more.
(How strong a thing is the little finger!)
So weak that I have confused the body with the soul,
And the body with its little finger.
(How frail is the little finger.)
My voice could not carry to you did you dwell in stars,
O Spirits of whom my soul is but a little finger . . .

# Harvest Song[1]

I am a reaper whose muscles set at sundown. All my oats are cradled.
But I am too chilled, and too fatigued to bind them. And I hunger.

I crack a grain between my teeth. I do not taste it.
I have been in the fields all day. My throat is dry. I hunger.

My eyes are caked with dust of oatfields at harvest-time.
I am a blind man who stares across the hills, seeking stack'd fields
    of other harvesters.

It would be good to see them . . . crook'd, split, and iron-ring'd
    handles of the scythes. It would be good to see them,
    dust-caked and blind. I hunger.

(Dusk is a strange fear'd sheath their blades are dull'd in.)
My throat is dry. And should I call, a cracked grain like the
    oats . . . eoho—

I fear to call. What should they hear me, and offer me their grain,
    oats, or wheat, or corn? I have been in the fields all day. I
    fear I could not taste it. I fear knowledge of my hunger.

My ears are caked with dust of oatfields at harvest-time.
I am a deaf man who strains to hear the calls of other harvesters
    whose throats are also dry.

It would be good to hear their songs . . . reapers of the sweet-stalk'd
    cane, cutters of the corn . . . even though their throats
    cracked and the strangeness of their voices deafened me.

I hunger. My throat is dry. Now that the sun has set and I am
    chilled, I fear to call. (Eoho, my brothers!)

I am a reaper. (Eoho!) All my oats are cradled. But I am too
    fatigued to bind them. And I hunger. I crack a grain. It has
    no taste to it. My throat is dry . . .

O my brothers, I beat my palms, still soft, against the stubble of
    my harvesting. (You beat your soft palms, too.) My pain is
    sweet. Sweeter than the oats or wheat or corn. It will not
    bring me knowledge of my hunger.

1. First published in *Double Dealer* 4 (December 1922): 258.

# Bona and Paul[1]

I

On the school gymnasium floor, young men and women are drilling. They are going to be teachers, and go out into the world . . . thud, thud . . . and give precision to the movements of sick people who all their lives have been drilling. One man is out of step. In step. The teacher glares at him. A girl in bloomers, seated on a mat in the corner because she has told the director that she is sick, sees that the footfalls of the men are rhythmical and syncopated. The dance of his blue-trousered limbs thrills her.

Bona: He is a candle that dances in a grove swung with pale balloons.

Columns of the drillers thud towards her. He is in the front row. He is in no row at all. Bona can look close at him. His red-brown face—

Bona: He is a harvest moon. He is an autumn leaf. He is a nigger. Bona! But dont all the dorm girls say so? And dont you, when you are sane, say so? Thats why I love—Oh, nonsense. You have never loved a man who didnt first love you. Besides—

Columns thud away from her. Come to a halt in line formation. Rigid. The period bell rings, and the teacher dismisses them.

A group collects around Paul. They are choosing sides for basketball. Girls against boys. Paul has his. He is limbering up beneath the basket. Bona runs to the girl captain and asks to be chosen. The girls fuss. The director comes to quiet them. He hears what Bona wants.

"But, Miss Hale, you were excused—"

"So I was, Mr. Boynton, but—"

"—you can play basket-ball, but you are too sick to drill."

"If you wish to put it that way."

She swings away from him to the girl captain.

"Helen, I want to play, and you must let me. This is the first time I've asked and I dont see why—"

"Thats just it, Bona. We have our team."

"Well, team or no team, I want to play and thats all there is to it."

She snatches the ball from Helen's hands, and charges down the floor.

Helen shrugs. One of the weaker girls says that she'll drop out. Helen accepts this. The team is formed. The whistle blows. The game starts. Bona, in center, is jumping against Paul. He plays with her. Out-jumps her, makes a quick pass, gets a quick return, and

---

1. Composed in 1918, "Bona and Paul" is the first story Toomer wrote. It is based upon his experience as a student in 1916 at the American College of Physical Training in Chicago, Illinois.

shoots a goal from the middle of the floor. Bona burns crimson. She fights, and tries to guard him. One of her team-mates advises her not to play so hard. Paul shoots his second goal.

Bona begins to feel a little dizzy and all in. She drives on. Almost hugs Paul to guard him. Near the basket, he attempts to shoot, and Bona lunges into his body and tries to beat his arms. His elbow, going up, gives her a sharp crack on the jaw. She whirls. He catches her. Her body stiffens. Then becomes strangely vibrant, and bursts to a swift life within her anger. He is about to give way before her hatred when a new passion flares at him and makes his stomach fall. Bona squeezes him. He suddenly feels stifled, and wonders why in hell the ring of silly gaping faces that's caked about him doesnt make way and give him air. He has a swift illusion that it is himself who has been struck. He looks at Bona. Whir. Whir. They seem to be human distortions spinning tensely in a fog. Spinning . . . dizzy . . . spinning . . . Bona jerks herself free, flushes a startling crimson, breaks through the bewildered teams, and rushes from the hall.

2

Paul is in his room of two windows.
Outside, the South-Side L track cuts them in two.[2]
Bona is one window. One window, Paul.
Hurtling Loop-jammed[3] L trains throw them in swift shadow.
Paul goes to his. Gray slanting roofs of houses are tinted lavender in the setting sun. Paul follows the sun, over the stock-yards where a fresh stench is just arising, across wheat lands that are still waving above their stubble, into the sun. Paul follows the sun to a pine-matted hillock in Georgia. He sees the slanting roofs of gray unpainted cabins tinted lavender. A Negress chants a lullaby beneath the mate-eyes of a southern planter. Her breasts are ample for the suckling of a song. She weans it, and sends it, curiously weaving, among lush melodies of cane and corn. Paul follows the sun into himself in Chicago.
He is at Bona's window.
With his own glow he looks through a dark pane.

Paul's room-mate comes in.
"Say, Paul, I've got a date for you. Come on. Shake a leg, will you?"
His blond hair is combed slick. His vest is snug about him.
He is like the electric light which he snaps on.

2. The elevated train that runs through the South Side of Chicago.
3. The Loop: a downtown area of Chicago that once was the center of the shopping district; so-called because the elevated train ("L") tracks make a loop around the area. *Loop-jammed*: crowded with passengers coming from the Loop.

"Whatdoysay, Paul? Get a wiggle on. Come on. We havent got much time by the time we eat and dress and everything."

His bustling concentrates on the brushing of his hair.

Art: What in hell's getting into Paul of late, anyway? Christ, but he's getting moony. Its his blood. Dark blood: moony. Doesnt get anywhere unless you boost it. You've got to keep it going—

"Say, Paul!"

—or it'll go to sleep on you. Dark blood; nigger? Thats what those jealous she-hens say. Not Bona though, or she . . . from the South . . . wouldnt want me to fix a date for him and her. Hell of a thing, that Paul's dark: youve got to always be answering questions.

"Say, Paul, for Christ's sake leave that window, cant you?"

"Whats it, Art?"

"Hell, I've told you about fifty times. Got a date for you. Come on."

"With who?"

Art: He didnt use to ask; now he does. Getting up in the air. Getting funny.

"Heres your hat. Want a smoke? Paul! Here. I've got a match. Now come on and I'll tell you all about it on the way to supper."

Paul: He's going to Life this time. No doubt of that. Quit your kidding. Some day, dear Art, I'm going to kick the living slats out of you, and you wont know what I've done it for. And your slats will bring forth Life . . . beautiful woman . . .

*Pure Food Restaurant.*

"Bring me some soup with a lot of crackers, understand? And then a roast-beef dinner. Same for you, eh, Paul? Now as I was saying, you've got a swell chance with her. And she's game. Best proof: she dont give a damn what the dorm girls say about you and her in the gym, or about the funny looks that Boynton gives her, or about what they say about, well, hell, you know, Paul. And say, Paul, she's a sweetheart. Tall, not puffy and pretty, more serious and deep—the kind you like these days. And they say she's got a car. And say, she's on fire. But you know all about that. She got Helen to fix it up with me. The four of us—remember the last party? Crimson Gardens! Boy!"

Paul's eyes take on a light that Art can settle in.

### 3

Art has on his patent-leather pumps and fancy vest. A loose fall coat is swung across his arm. His face has been massaged, and over a close shave, powdered. It is a healthy pink the blue of evening tints a purple pallor. Art is happy and confident in the good looks that his mirror gave him. Bubbling over with a joy he must spend now if the night is to contain it all. His bubbles, too, are curiously tinted purple as Paul watches them. Paul, contrary to what he had thought he would be like, is cool like the dusk, and like the dusk, detached. His dark face is a floating shade in evening's shadow. He sees Art, curiously. Art is a purple fluid, carbon-charged, that effervesces beside him. He loves Art. But is it not queer, this pale purple facsimile of a red-blooded Norwegian friend of his? Perhaps for some reason, white skins are not supposed to live at night. Surely, enough nights would transform them fantastically, or kill them. And their red passion? Night paled that too, and made it moony. Moony. Thats what Art thought of him. Bona didnt, even in the daytime. Bona, would she be pale? Impossible. Not that red glow. But the conviction did not set his emotion flowing.

"Come right in, wont you? The young ladies will be right down. Oh, Mr. Carlstrom, do play something for us while you are waiting. We just love to listen to your music. You play so well."

Houses, and dorm sitting-rooms are places where white faces seclude themselves at night. There is a reason . . .

Art sat on the piano and simply tore it down. Jazz. The picture of Our Poets hung perilously.

Paul: I've got to get the kid to play that stuff for me in the daytime. Might be different. More himself. More nigger. Different? There is. Curious, though.

The girls come in. Art stops playing, and almost immediately takes up a petty quarrel, where he had last left it, with Helen.

Bona, black-hair curled staccato, sharply contrasting with Helen's puffy yellow, holds Paul's hand. She squeezes it. Her own emotion supplements the return pressure. And then, for no tangible reason, her spirits drop. Without them, she is nervous, and slightly afraid. She resents this. Paul's eyes are critical. She resents Paul. She flares at him. She flares to poise and security.

"Shall we be on our way?"

"Yes, Bona, certainly."

The Boulevard is sleek in asphalt, and, with arc-lights and limousines, aglow. Dry leaves scamper behind the whir of cars. The scent of exploded gasoline that mingles with them is faintly sweet. Mellow stone mansions overshadow clapboard homes which now resemble Negro shanties in some southern alley. Bona and Paul, and Art and Helen, move along an island-like, far-stretching strip of leaf-soft ground. Above them, worlds of shadow-planes and solids, silently moving. As if on one of these, Paul looks down on Bona. No doubt of it: her face is pale. She is talking. Her words have no feel to them. One sees them. They are pink petals that fall upon velvet cloth. Bona is soft, and pale, and beautiful.

"Paul, tell me something about yourself—or would you rather wait?"

"I'll tell you anything you'd like to know."

"Not what I want to know, Paul; what you want to tell me."

"You have the beauty of a gem fathoms under sea."

"I feel that, but I dont want to be. I want to be near you. Perhaps I will be if I tell you something. Paul, I love you."

The sea casts up its jewel into his hands, and burns them furiously. To tuck her arm under his and hold her hand will ease the burn.

"What can I say to you, brave dear woman—I cant talk love. Love is a dry grain in my mouth unless it is wet with kisses."

"You would dare? right here on the Boulevard? before Arthur and Helen?"

"Before myself? I dare."

"Here then."

Bona, in the slim shadow of a tree trunk, pulls Paul to her. Suddenly she stiffens. Stops.

"But you have not said you love me."

"I cant—yet—Bona."

"Ach, you never will. Youre cold. Cold."

Bona: Colored; cold. Wrong somewhere.

She hurries and catches up with Art and Helen.

### 4

Crimson Gardens. Hurrah! So one feels. People . . . University of Chicago students, members of the stock exchange, a large Negro in crimson uniform who guards the door . . . had watched them enter. Had leaned towards each other over ash-smeared tablecloths and highballs and whispered: What is he, a Spaniard, an Indian, an Italian, a Mexican, a Hindu, or a Japanese? Art had at first fidgeted under their stares . . . what are *you* looking at, you godam pack of owl-eyed hyenas? . . . but soon settled into his fuss with Helen, and forgot them. A strange thing happened to Paul. Suddenly he knew that he was apart from the people around him. Apart from the pain which they had unconsciously caused. Suddenly he knew that people saw, not attractiveness in his dark skin, but difference. Their stares, giving him to himself, filled something long empty within him, and were like green blades sprouting in his consciousness. There was fullness, and strength and peace about it all. He saw himself, cloudy, but real. He saw the faces of the people at the tables round him. White lights, or as now, the pink lights of the Crimson Gardens gave a glow and immediacy to white faces. The pleasure of it, equal to that of love or dream, of seeing this. Art and Bona and Helen? He'd look.

They were wonderfully flushed and beautiful. Not for himself; because they were. Distantly. Who were they, anyway? God, if he knew them. He'd come in with them. Of that he was sure. Come where? Into life? Yes. No. Into the Crimson Gardens. A part of life. A carbon bubble. Would it look purple if he went out into the night and looked at it? His sudden starting to rise almost upset the table.

"What in hell—pardon—whats the matter, Paul?"

"I forgot my cigarettes—"

"Youre smoking one."

"So I am. Pardon me."

The waiter straightens them out. Takes their order.

Art: What in hell's eating Paul? Moony aint the word for it. From bad to worse. And those godam people staring so. Paul's a queer fish. Doesnt seem to mind . . . He's my pal, let me tell you, you horn-rimmed owl-eyed hyena at that table, and a lot better than you whoever you are . . . Queer about him. I could stick up for him if he'd only come out, one way or the other, and tell a feller. Besides, a room-mate has a right to know. Thinks I wont understand. Said so. He's got a swell head when it comes to brains, all right. God, he's a good straight feller, though. Only, moony. Nut. Nuttish. Nuttery. Nutmeg . . . "What'd you say, Helen?"

"I was talking to Bona, thank you."

"Well, its nothing to get spiffy about."

"What? Oh, of course not. Please lets dont start some silly argument all over again."

"Well."

"Well."

"Now thats enough. Say, waiter, whats the matter with our order? Make it snappy, will you?"

Crimson Gardens. Hurrah! So one feels. The drinks come. Four highballs. Art passes cigarettes. A girl dressed like a bare-back rider in flaming pink, makes her way through tables to the dance floor. All lights are dimmed till they seem a lush afterglow of crimson. Spotlights the girl. She sings. "Liza, Little Liza Jane."

Paul is rosy before his window.

He moves, slightly, towards Bona.

With his own glow, he seeks to penetrate a dark pane.

Paul: From the South. What does that mean, precisely, except that you'll love or hate a nigger? Thats a lot. What does it mean except that in Chicago you'll have the courage to neither love or hate. A priori. But it would seem that you have. Queer words, arent these, for a man who wears blue pants on a gym floor in the day-time. Well, never matter. You matter. I'd like to know you whom I look at. Know, not love. Not that knowing is a greater pleasure; but that I have just found the joy of it. You came just a month too late.

Even this afternoon I dreamed. To-night, along the Boulevard, you found me cold. Paul Johnson, cold! Thats a good one, eh, Art, you fine old stupid fellow, you! But I feel good! The color and the music and the song . . . A Negress chants a lullaby beneath the mate-eyes of a southern planter. O song . . . And those flushed faces. Eager brilliant eyes. Hard to imagine them as unawakened. Your own. Oh, they're awake all right. "And you know it too, dont you Bona?"

"What, Paul?"

"The truth of what I was thinking."

"I'd like to know I know—something of you."

"You will—before the evening's over. I promise it."

Crimson Gardens. Hurrah! So one feels. The bare-back rider balances agilely on the applause which is the tail of her song. Orchestral instruments warm up for jazz. The flute is a cat that ripples its fur against the deep-purring saxophone. The drum throws sticks. The cat jumps on the piano keyboard. Hi diddle, hi diddle, the cat and the fiddle. Crimson Gardens . . . hurrah! . . . jumps over the moon. Crimson Gardens! Helen . . . O Eliza . . . rabbit-eyes sparkling, plays up to, and tries to placate what she considers to be Paul's contempt. She always does that . . . Little Liza Jane . . . Once home, she burns with the thought of what she's done. She says all manner of snidy things about him, and swears that she'll never go out again when he is along. She tries to get Art to break with him, saying, that if Paul, whom the whole dormitory calls a nigger, is more to him than she is, well, she's through. She does not break with Art. She goes out as often as she can with Art and Paul. She explains this to herself by a piece of information which a friend of hers had given her: men like him (Paul) can fascinate. One is not responsible for fascination. Not one girl had really loved Paul; he fascinated them. Bona didnt; only thought she did. Time would tell. And of course, *she* didn't. Liza . . . She plays up to, and tries to placate, Paul.

"Paul is so deep these days, and I'm so glad he's found some one to interest him."

"I dont believe I do."

The thought escapes from Bona just a moment before her anger at having said it.

Bona: You little puffy cat, I do. I do!

Dont I, Paul? her eyes ask.

Her answer is a crash of jazz from the palm-hidden orchestra. Crimson Gardens is a body whose blood flows to a clot upon the dance floor. Art and Helen clot. Soon, Bona and Paul. Paul finds her a little stiff, and his mind, wandering to Helen (silly little kid who wants every highball spoon her hands touch, for a souvenir), supple, perfect little dancer, wishes for the next dance when he and Art will exchange.

Bona knows that she must win him to herself.

"Since when have men like you grown cold?"

"The first philosopher."

"I thought you were a poet—or a gym director."

"Hence, your failure to make love."

Bona's eyes flare. Water. Grow red about the rims. She would like to tear away from him and dash across the clotted floor.

"What do you mean?"

"Mental concepts rule you. If they were flush with mine—good. I dont believe they are."

"How do you know, Mr. Philosopher?"

"Mostly a priori."

"You talk well for a gym director."

"And you—"

"I hate you. Ou!"

She presses away. Paul, conscious of the convention in it, pulls her to him. Her body close. Her head still strains away. He nearly crushes her. She tries to pinch him. Then sees people staring, and lets her arms fall. Their eyes meet. Both, contemptuous. The dance takes blood from their minds and packs it, tingling, in the torsos of their swaying bodies. Passionate blood leaps back into their eyes. They are a dizzy blood clot on a gyrating floor. They know that the pink-faced people have no part in what they feel. Their instinct leads them away from Art and Helen, and towards the big uniformed black man who opens and closes the gilded exit door. The cloak-room girl is tolerant of their impatience over such trivial things as wraps. And slightly superior. As the black man swings the door for them, his eyes are knowing. Too many couples have passed out, flushed and fidgety, for him not to know. The chill air is a shock to Paul. A strange thing happens. He sees the Gardens purple, as if he were way off. And a spot is in the purple. The spot comes furiously towards him. Face of the black man. It leers. It smiles sweetly like a child's. Paul leaves Bona and darts back so quickly that he doesnt give the door-man a chance to open. He swings in. Stops. Before the huge bulk of the Negro.

"Youre wrong."

"Yassur."

"Brother, youre wrong.

"I came back to tell you, to shake your hand, and tell you that you are wrong. That something beautiful is going to happen. That the Gardens are purple like a bed of roses would be at dusk. That I came into the Gardens, into life in the Gardens with one whom I did not know. That I danced with her, and did not know her. That I felt passion, contempt and passion for her whom I did not know. That I thought of her. That my thoughts were matches thrown into a dark window. And all the while the Gardens were purple like a bed of roses would be at dusk. I came back to tell you, brother, that white faces are petals of roses. That dark faces are petals of dusk. That I am going out and gather petals. That I am going out and know her whom I brought here with me to these Gardens which are purple like a bed of roses would be at dusk."

Paul and the black man shook hands.

When he reached the spot where they had been standing, Bona was gone.

to Waldo Frank.[1]

---

1. Waldo Frank (1889–1967), American author. A friend and mentor to Toomer, Frank
   was instrumental in the publication of *Cane*, for which he wrote a foreword to the 1923
   edition.

# Kabnis[1]

I

Ralph Kabnis, propped in his bed, tries to read. To read himself to sleep. An oil lamp on a chair near his elbow burns unsteadily. The cabin room is spaced fantastically about it. Whitewashed hearth and chimney, black with sooty saw-teeth. Ceiling, patterned by the fringed globe of the lamp. The walls, unpainted, are seasoned a rosin yellow. And cracks between the boards are black. These cracks are the lips the night winds use for whispering. Night winds in Georgia are vagrant poets, whispering. Kabnis, against his will, lets his book slip down, and listens to them. The warm whiteness of his bed, the lamp-light, do not protect him from the weird chill of their song:

> White-man's land.
> Niggers, sing.
> Burn, bear black children
> Till poor rivers bring
> Rest, and sweet glory
> In Camp Ground.

Kabnis' thin hair is streaked on the pillow. His hand strokes the slim silk of his mustache. His thumb, pressed under his chin, seems to be trying to give squareness and projection to it. Brown eyes stare from a lemon face. Moisture gathers beneath his armpits. He slides down beneath the cover, seeking release.

Kabnis: Near me. Now. Whoever you are, my warm glowing sweetheart, do not think that the face that rests beside you is the real Kabnis. Ralph Kabnis is a dream. And dreams are faces with large eyes and weak chins and broad brows that get smashed by the fists of square faces. The body of the world is bull-necked. A dream is a soft face that fits uncertainly upon it . . . God, if I could develop that in words. Give what I know a bull-neck and a heaving body, all would go well with me, wouldnt it, sweetheart? If I could feel that I came to the South to face it. If I, the dream (not what is weak and afraid in me) could become the face of the South. How my lips would sing for it, my songs being the lips of its soul. Soul. Soul hell. There aint no such thing. What in hell was that?

---

1. At one time, Toomer prepared this work as a drama with the hope that it would be produced on stage. Apparently it was once considered for production in a small playhouse, but there is no evidence that it was staged. The famous American director-producer Kenneth Macgowan rejected it because, he stated, it lacked a strong plot. Selections from the version of "Kabnis" that appears in *Cane* were first published in two parts in *Broom* 5 (August and September 1923): 12–16, 83–94. In August, *Broom* published section 1 of "Kabnis" under that title (pp. 12–16). In September, it published section 5 (pp. 83–94) under the same title.

A rat had run across the thin boards of the ceiling. Kabnis thrusts his head out from the covers. Through the cracks, a powdery faded red dust sprays down on him. Dust of slavefields, dried, scattered . . . No use to read. Christ, if he only could drink himself to sleep. Something as sure as fate was going to happen. He couldnt stand this thing much longer. A hen, perched on a shelf in the adjoining room begins to tread. Her nails scrape the soft wood. Her feathers ruffle.

"Get out of that, you egg-laying bitch."

Kabnis hurls a slipper against the wall. The hen flies from her perch and cackles as if a skunk were after her.

"Now cut out that racket or I'll wring your neck for you."

Answering cackles arise in the chicken yard.

"Why in Christ's hell cant you leave me alone? Damn it, I wish your cackle would choke you. Choke every mother's son of them in this God-forsaken hole. Go away. By God I'll wring your neck for you if you dont. Hell of a mess I've got in: even the poultry is hostile. Go way. Go way. By God, I'll . . ."

Kabnis jumps from his bed. His eyes are wild. He makes for the door. Bursts through it. The hen, driving blindly at the windowpane, screams. Then flies and flops around trying to elude him. Kabnis catches her.

"Got you now, you she-bitch."

With his fingers about her neck, he thrusts open the outside door and steps out into the serene loveliness of Georgian autumn moonlight. Some distance off, down in the valley, a band of pine-smoke, silvered gauze, drifts steadily. The half-moon is a white child that sleeps upon the tree-tops of the forest. White winds croon its sleepsong:

> rock a-by baby . . .
> Black mother sways, holding a white child on her bosom.
> when the bough bends . . .
> Her breath hums through pine-cones.
> cradle will fall . . .
> Teat moon-children at your breasts,
> down will come baby . . .
> Black mother.

Kabnis whirls the chicken by its neck, and throws the head away. Picks up the hopping body, warm, sticky, and hides it in a clump of bushes. He wipes blood from his hands onto the coarse scant grass.

Kabnis: Thats done. Old Chromo in the big house there will wonder whats become of her pet hen. Well, it'll teach her a lesson: not to make a hen-coop of my quarters. Quarters. Hell of a fine quarters, I've got. Five years ago; look at me now. Earth's child. The earth my mother. God is a profligate red-nosed man about town. Bastardy; me. A bastard son has got a right to curse his maker. God . . .

Kabnis is about to shake his fists heavenward. He looks up, and the night's beauty strikes him dumb. He falls to his knees. Sharp stones cut through his thin pajamas. The shock sends a shiver over him. He quivers. Tears mist his eyes. He writhes.

"God Almighty, dear God, dear Jesus, do not torture me with beauty. Take it away. Give me an ugly world. Ha, ugly. Stinking like unwashed niggers. Dear Jesus, do not chain me to myself and set these hills and valleys, heaving with folk-songs, so close to me that I cannot reach them. There is a radiant beauty in the night that touches and . . . tortures me. Ugh. Hell. Get up, you damn fool. Look around. Whats beautiful there? Hog pens and chicken yards. Dirty red mud. Stinking outhouse. Whats beauty anyway but ugliness if it hurts you? God, he doesnt exist, but nevertheless He is ugly. Hence, what comes from Him is ugly. Lynchers and business men, and that cockroach Hanby, especially. How come that he gets to be principal of a school? Of the school I'm driven to teach in? God's handiwork, doubtless. God and Hanby, they belong together. Two godam moral-spouters. Oh, no, I wont let that emotion come up in me. Stay down. Stay down, I tell you. O Jesus, Thou art beautiful . . . Come, Ralph, pull yourself together. Curses and adoration dont come from what is sane. This loneliness, dumbness, awful, intangible oppression is enough to drive a man insane. Miles from nowhere. A speck on a Georgia hillside. Jesus, can you imagine it—an atom of dust in agony on a hillside? Thats a spectacle for you. Come, Ralph, old man, pull yourself together."

Kabnis has stiffened. He is conscious now of the night wind, and of how it chills him. He rises. He totters as a man would who for the first time uses artificial limbs. As a completely artificial man would. The large frame house, squatting on brick pillars, where the principal of the school, his wife, and the boarding girls sleep, seems a curious shadow of his mind. He tries, but cannot convince himself of its reality. His gaze drifts down into the vale, across the swamp, up over the solid dusk bank of pines, and rests, bewildered-like, on the court-house tower. It is dull silver in the moonlight. White child that sleeps upon the top of pines. Kabnis' mind clears. He sees himself yanked beneath that tower. He sees white minds, with indolent assumption, juggle justice and a nigger . . . Somewhere, far off in the straight line of his sight, is Augusta. Christ, how cut off from everything he is. And hours, hours north, why not say a lifetime north? Washington sleeps. Its still, peaceful streets, how desirable they are. Its people whom he had always halfway despised. New York? Impossible. It was a fiction. He had dreamed it. An impotent nostalgia grips him. It becomes intolerable. He forces himself to narrow to a cabin silhouetted on a knoll about a mile away. Peace. Negroes within it are content. They farm. They sing. They love. They sleep. Kabnis wonders if perhaps they can feel him. If perhaps he gives them bad dreams. Things are so immediate in Georgia.

Thinking that now he can go to sleep, he re-enters his room. He builds a fire in the open hearth. The room dances to the tongues of flames, and sings to the crackling and spurting of the logs. Wind comes up between the floor boards, through the black cracks of the walls.

Kabnis: Cant sleep. Light a cigarette. If that old bastard comes over here and smells smoke, I'm done for. Hell of a note, cant even smoke. The stillness of it: where they burn and hang men, you cant smoke. Cant take a swig of licker.[2] What do they think this is, anyway, some sort of temperance school? How did I ever land in such a hole? Ugh. One might just as well be in his grave. Still as a grave. Jesus, how still everything is. Does the world know how still it is? People make noise. They are afraid of silence. Of what lives, and God, of what dies in silence. There must be many dead things moving in silence. They come here to touch me. I swear I feel their fingers . . . Come, Ralph, pull yourself together. What in hell was that? Only the rustle of leaves, I guess. You know, Ralph, old man, it wouldnt surprise me at all to see a ghost. People dont think there are such things. They rationalize their fear, and call their cowardice science. Fine bunch, they are. Damit, that was a noise. And not the wind either. A chicken maybe. Hell, chickens dont wander around this time of night. What in hell is it?

A scraping sound, like a piece of wood dragging over the ground, is coming near.

"Ha, ha. The ghosts down this way havent got any chains to rattle, so they drag trees along with them. Thats a good one. But no joke, something is outside this house, as sure as hell. Whatever it is, it can get a good look at me and I cant see it. Jesus Christ!"

Kabnis pours water on the flames and blows his lamp out. He picks up a poker and stealthily approaches the outside door. Swings it open, and lurches into the night. A calf, carrying a yoke of wood, bolts away from him and scampers down the road.

"Well, I'm damned. This godam place is sure getting the best of me. Come, Ralph, old man, pull yourself together. Nights cant last forever. Thank God for that. Its Sunday already. First time in my life I've ever wanted Sunday to come. Hell of a day. And down here there's no such thing as ducking church. Well, I'll see Halsey and Layman, and get a good square meal. Thats something. And Halsey's a damn good feller. Cant talk to him, though. Who in Christ's world

2. Liquor.

can I talk to? A hen. God. Myself . . . I'm going bats, no doubt of that. Come now, Ralph, go in and make yourself go to sleep. Come now . . . in the door . . . thats right. Put the poker down. There. All right. Slip under the sheets. Close your eyes. Think nothing . . . a long time . . . nothing, nothing. Dont even think nothing. Blank. Not even blank. Count. No, mustnt count. Nothing . . . blank . . . nothing . . . blank . . . space without stars in it. No, nothing . . . nothing . . .

Kabnis sleeps. The winds, like soft-voiced vagrant poets sing:

> White-man's land.
> Niggers, sing.
> Burn, bear black children
> Till poor rivers bring
> Rest, and sweet glory
> In Camp Ground.

2

The parlor of Fred Halsey's home. There is a seediness about it. It seems as though the fittings have given a frugal service to at least seven generations of middle-class shop-owners. An open grate burns cheerily in contrast to the gray cold changed autumn weather. An old-fashioned mantelpiece supports a family clock (not running), a figure or two in imitation bronze, and two small group pictures. Directly above it, in a heavy oak frame, the portrait of a bearded man. Black hair, thick and curly, intensifies the pallor of the high forehead. The eyes are daring. The nose, sharp and regular. The poise suggests a tendency to adventure checked by the necessities of absolute command. The portrait is that of an English gentleman who has retained much of his culture, in that money has enabled him to escape being drawn through a land-grubbing pioneer life. His nature and features, modified by marriage and circumstances, have been transmitted to his great-grandson, Fred. To the left of this picture, spaced on the wall, is a smaller portrait of the great-grandmother. That here there is a Negro strain, no one would doubt. But it is difficult to say in precisely what feature it lies. On close inspection, her mouth is seen to be wistfully twisted. The expression of her face seems to shift before one's gaze—now ugly, repulsive; now sad, and somehow beautiful in its pain. A tin wood-box rests on the floor below. To the right of the great-grandfather's portrait hangs a family group: the father, mother, two brothers, and one sister of Fred. It includes himself some thirty years ago when his face was an olive white, and his hair luxuriant and dark and wavy. The father is a rich brown. The mother, practically white. Of the children, the girl, quite young, is like Fred; the two brothers, darker.

The walls of the room are plastered and painted green. An old upright piano is tucked into the corner near the window. The window looks out on a forlorn, box-like, whitewashed frame church. Negroes are gathering, on foot, driving questionable gray and brown mules, and in an occasional Ford, for afternoon service. Beyond, Georgia hills roll off into the distance, their dreary aspect heightened by the gray spots of unpainted one- and two-room shanties. Clumps of pine trees here and there are the dark points the whole landscape is approaching. The church bell tolls. Above its squat tower, a great spiral of buzzards reaches far into the heavens. An ironic comment upon the path that leads into the Christian land . . . Three rocking chairs are grouped around the grate. Sunday papers scattered on the floor indicate a recent usage. Halsey, a well-built, stocky fellow, hair cropped close, enters the room. His Sunday clothes smell of wood and glue, for it is his habit to potter around his wagon-shop even on the Lord's day. He is followed by Professor Layman, tall, heavy, loose-jointed Georgia Negro, by turns teacher and preacher, who has traveled in almost every nook and corner of the state and hence knows more than would be good for anyone other than a silent man. Kabnis, trying to force through a gathering heaviness, trails in behind them. They slip into chairs before the fire.

Layman: Sholy[3] fine, Mr. Halsey, sholy fine. This town's right good at feedin folks, better'n most towns in th state, even for preachers, but I ken[4] say this beats um all. Yassur. Now aint that right, Professor[5] Kabnis?

Kabnis: Yes sir, this beats them all, all right—best I've had, and thats a fact, though my comparison doesnt carry far, y'know.

Layman: Hows that, Professor?

Kabnis: Well, this is my first time out—

Layman: For a fact. Aint seed you round so much. Whats th trouble? Dont like our folks down this away?

Halsey: Aint that, Layman. He aint like most northern niggers that way. Aint a thing stuck-up about him. He likes us, you an me, maybe all—its that red[6] mud over yonder—gets stuck in it an cant get out. (Laughs.) An then he loves th fire so, warm as its been. Coldest Yankee I've ever seen. But I'm goin t get him out now in a jiffy, eh, Kabnis?

Kabnis: Sure, I should say so, sure. Dont think its because I dont like folks down this way. Just the opposite, in fact. Theres more hospitality and everything. Its diff—that is, theres lots of northern exaggeration about the South. Its not half the terror they picture it.

3. "Surely."
4. "Can."
5. Also used to refer to preachers, pianists, or other educated or talented individuals.
6. The typical color of soil in parts of Georgia.

Things are not half bad, as one could easily figure out for himself without ever crossing the Mason and Dixie[7] line: all these people wouldnt stay down here, especially the rich, the ones that could easily leave, if conditions were so mighty bad. And then too, sometime back, my family were southerners y'know. From Georgia, in fact—

Layman: Nothin t feel proud about, Professor. Neither your folks nor mine.

Halsey (in a mock religious tone): Amen t that, brother Layman. Amen (turning to Kabnis, half playful, yet somehow dead in earnest). An Mr. Kabnis, kindly remember youre in th land of cotton—hell of a land. Th white folks get th boll; th niggers get th stalk. An dont you dare touch th boll, or even look at it. They'll swing y sho. (Laughs.)

Kabnis: But they wouldnt touch a gentleman—fellows, men like us three here—

Layman: Nigger's a nigger down this away, Professor. An only two dividins: good an bad. An even they aint permanent categories. They sometimes mixes um up when it comes t lynchin. I've seen um do it.

Halsey: Dont let th fear int y, though, Kabnis. This county's a good un. Aint been a stringin up I can remember. (Laughs.)

Layman: This is a good town an a good county. But theres some that makes up fer it.

Kabnis: Things are better now though since that stir about those peonage cases,[8] arent they?

Layman: Ever hear tell of a single shot killin moren one rabbit, Professor?

Kabnis: No, of course not, that is, but then—

Halsey: Now I know you werent born yesterday, sprung up so rapid like you aint heard of th brick thrown in th hornets' nest. (Laughs.)

Kabnis: Hardly, hardly, I know—

Halsey: Course y do. (To Layman) See, northern niggers aint as dumb as they make out t be.

Kabnis (overlooking the remark): Just stirs them up to sting.

Halsey: T perfection. An put just like a professor should put it.

Kabnis: Thats what actually did happen?

---

7. Originally commissioned by the Penn family of Pennsylvania and the Calvert family of Maryland to establish the border between those colonies. The Mason-Dixon Line is named after Charles Mason and Jeremiah Dixon, who completed the survey in the 1740s. It is also regarded as the divider between the Northern and Southern states during the American Civil War (1861–65).

8. In some Southern states, prisoners—especially black prisoners—were leased to work, without pay, for white landowners.

Layman: Well, if it aint sos only because th stingers already movin jes as fast as they ken go. An been goin ever since I ken remember, an then some mo. Though I dont usually make mention of it.

Halsey: Damn sight better not. Say, Layman, you come from where theyre always swarmin, dont y?

Layman: Yassur. I do that, sho. Dont want t mention it, but its a fact. I've seed th time when there werent no use t even stretch out flat upon th ground. Seen um shoot an cut a man t pieces who had died th night befo. Yassur. An they didnt stop when they found out he was dead—jes went on ahackin at him anyway.

Kabnis: What did you do? What did you say to them, Professor?

Layman: Thems th things you neither does a thing or talks about if y want t stay around this away, Professor.

Halsey: Listen t what he's tellin y, Kabnis. May come in handy some day.

Kabnis: Cant something be done? But of course not. This preacher-ridden race. Pray and shout. Theyre in the preacher's hands. Thats what it is. And the preacher's hands are in the white man's pockets.

Halsey: Present company always excepted.

Kabnis: The Professor knows I wasnt referring to him.

Layman: Preacher's a preacher anywheres you turn. No use exceptin.

Kabnis: Well, of course, if you look at it that way. I didnt mean— But cant something be done?

Layman: Sho. Yassur. An done first rate an well. Jes like Sam Raymon done it.

Kabnis: Hows that? What did he do?

Layman: Th white folks (reckon I oughtnt tell it) had jes knocked two others like you kill a cow—brained um with an ax, when they caught Sam Raymon by a stream. They was about t do fer him when he up an says, "White folks, I gotter die, I knows that. But wont y let me die in my own way?" Some was fer gettin after him, but th boss held um back an says, "Jes so longs th nigger dies—" An Sam fell down ont his knees an prayed, "O Lord, Ise comin to y," and he up an jumps int th stream.

Singing from the church becomes audible. Above it, rising and falling in a plaintive moan, a woman's voice swells to shouting. Kabnis hears it. His face gives way to an expression of mingled fear, contempt, and pity. Layman takes no notice of it. Halsey grins at Kabnis. He feels like having a little sport with him.

Halsey: Lets go t church, eh, Kabnis?

Kabnis (seeking control): All right—no sir, not by a damn sight. Once a days enough for me. Christ, but that stuff gets to me. Meaning no reflection on you, Professor.

Halsey: Course not. Say, Kabnis, noticed y this morning. What'd y get up for an go out?

Kabnis: Couldnt stand the shouting, and thats a fact. We dont have that sort of thing up North. We do, but, that is, some one should see to it that they are stopped or put out when they get so bad the preacher has to stop his sermon for them.

Halsey: Is that th way youall sit on sisters up North?

Kabnis: In the church I used to go to no one ever shouted—

Halsey: Lungs weak?

Kabnis: Hardly, that is—

Halsey: Yankees are right up t th minute in tellin folk how t turn a trick. They always were good at talkin.

Kabnis: Well, anyway, they should be stopped.

Layman: Thats right. Thats true. An its th worst ones in th community that comes int th church t shout. I've sort a made a study of it. You take a man what drinks, th biggest licker-head around will come int th church an yell th loudest. An th sister whats done wrong, an is always doin wrong, will sit down in th Amen corner[9] an swing her arms an shout her head off. Seems as if they cant control themselves out in th world; they cant control themselves in church. Now dont that sound logical, Professor?

Halsey: Reckon its as good as any. But I heard that queer cuss over yonder—y know him, dont y, Kabnis? Well, y ought t. He had a run-in with your boss th other day—same as you'll have if you dont walk th chalk-line. An th quicker th better. I hate that Hanby. Ornery bastard. I'll mash his mouth in one of these days. Well, as I was sayin, that feller, Lewis's name, I heard him sayin somethin about a stream whats dammed has got t cut loose somewheres. An that sounds good. I know th feelin myself. He strikes me as knowin a bucketful bout most things, that feller does. Seems like he doesnt want t talk, an does, sometimes, like Layman here. Damn queer feller, him.

Layman: Cant make heads or tails of him, an I've seen lots o queer possums in my day. Everybody's wonderin about him. White folks too. He'll have t leave here soon, thats sho. Always askin questions. An I aint seed his lips move once. Pokin round an notin somethin. Noted what I said th other day, an that werent fer notin down.

Kabnis: What was that?

Layman: Oh, a lynchin that took place bout a year ago. Th worst I know of round these parts.

Halsey: Bill Burnam?

9. A front area of the church, generally occupied by older female members of the congregation; so called because of their practice of shouting "amen" as approval and exhortation of the preacher.

Layman:  Na. Mame Lamkins.

Halsey grunts, but says nothing.

The preacher's voice rolls from the church in an insistent chanting monotone. At regular intervals it rises to a crescendo note. The sister begins to shout. Her voice, high-pitched and hysterical, is almost perfectly attuned to the nervous key of Kabnis. Halsey notices his distress, and is amused by it. Layman's face is expressionless. Kabnis wants to hear the story of Mame Lamkins. He does not want to hear it. It can be no worse than the shouting.

Kabnis (his chair rocking faster): What about Mame Lamkins?

Halsey:  Tell him, Layman.

The preacher momentarily stops. The choir, together with the entire congregation, sings an old spiritual. The music seems to quiet the shouter. Her heavy breathing has the sound of evening winds that blow through pinecones. Layman's voice is uniformly low and soothing. A canebrake, murmuring the tale to its neighbor-road would be more passionate.

Layman:  White folks know that niggers talk, an they dont mind jes so long as nothing comes of it, so here goes. She was in th family-way, Mame Lamkins was. They killed her in th street, an some white man seein th risin in her stomach as she lay there soppy in her blood like any cow, took an ripped her belly open, an th kid fell out. It was living; but a nigger baby aint supposed t live. So he jabbed his knife in it an stuck it t a tree. An then they all went away.[1]

Kabnis:  Christ no! What had she done?

Layman:  Tried t hide her husband when they was after him.

A shriek pierces the room. The bronze pieces on the mantel hum. The sister cries frantically: "Jesus, Jesus, I've found Jesus. O Lord, glory t God, one mo sinner is acomin home." At the height of this, a stone, wrapped round with paper, crashes through the window. Kabnis springs to his feet, terror-stricken. Layman is worried. Halsey picks up the stone. Takes off the wrapper, smooths it out, and reads: "You northern nigger, its time fer y t leave. Git along now." Kabnis knows that the command is meant for him. Fear squeezes him. Caves him in. As a violent external pressure would. Fear flows inside him. It fills him up. He bloats. He saves himself from bursting by dashing wildly from the room. Halsey and Layman stare stupidly at each other. The stone, the crumpled paper are things, huge things that weight them. Their thoughts are vaguely concerned with the texture of the stone, with the color of the paper. Then they remember the words, and begin to shift them about in sentences. Layman even

---

1. This is a fictionalized treatment of the lynching of Mary Turner, which took place in Valdosta, Georgia, in 1915.

construes them grammatically. Suddenly the sense of them comes back to Halsey. He grips Layman by the arm and they both follow after Kabnis.

A false dusk has come early. The countryside is ashen, chill. Cabins and roads and canebrakes whisper. The church choir, dipping into a long silence, sings:

> My Lord, what a mourning,
> My Lord, what a mourning,
> My Lord, what a mourning,
> When the stars begin to fall.

Softly luminous over the hills and valleys, the faint spray of a scattered star . . .

### 3

A splotchy figure drives forward along the cane- and corn-stalk hemmed-in road. A scarecrow replica of Kabnis, awkwardly animate. Fantastically plastered with red Georgia mud. It skirts the big house whose windows shine like mellow lanterns in the dusk. Its shoulder jogs against a sweet-gum tree. The figure caroms off against the cabin door, and lunges in. It slams the door as if to prevent some one entering after it.

"God Almighty, theyre here. After me. On me. All along the road I saw their eyes flaring from the cane. Hounds. Shouts. What in God's name did I run here for? A mud-hole trap. I stumbled on a rope. O God, a rope. Their clammy hands were like the love of death playing up and down my spine. Trying to trip my legs. To trip my spine. Up and down my spine. My spine . . . My legs . . . Why in hell didnt they catch me?"

Kabnis wheels around, half defiant, half numbed with a more immediate fear.

"Wanted to trap me here. Get out o there. I see you."

He grabs a broom from beside the chimney and violently pokes it under the bed. The broom strikes a tin wash-tub. The noise bewilders. He recovers.

"Not there. In the closet."

He throws the broom aside and grips the poker. Starts towards the closet door, towards somewhere in the perfect blackness behind the chimney.

"I'll brain you."

He stops short. The barks of hounds, evidently in pursuit, reach him. A voice, liquid in distance, yells, "Hi! Hi!"

"O God, theyre after me. Holy Father, Mother of Christ—hell, this aint no time for prayer—"

Voices, just outside the door:

"Reckon he's here."

"Dont see no light though."

The door is flung open.

Kabnis: Get back or I'll kill you.

He braces himself, brandishing the poker.

Halsey (coming in): Aint as bad as all that. Put that thing down.

Layman: Its only us, Professor. Nobody else after y.

Kabnis: Halsey. Layman. Close that door. Dont light that light.
For godsake get away from there.

Halsey: Nobody's after y, Kabnis, I'm tellin y. Put that thing
down an get yourself together.

Kabnis: I tell you they are. I saw them. I heard the hounds.

Halsey: These aint th days of hounds an Uncle Tom's Cabin,[2]
feller. White folks aint in fer all them theatrics these days. Theys
more direct than that. If what they wanted was t get y, theyd have
just marched right in an took y where y sat. Somebodys down by th
branch chasin rabbits an atreein possums.

A shot is heard.

Halsey: Got him, I reckon. Saw Tom goin out with his gun. Tom's
pretty lucky most times.

He goes to the bureau and lights the lamp. The circular fringe is
patterned on the ceiling. The moving shadows of the men are huge
against the bare wall boards. Halsey walks up to Kabnis, takes the
poker from his grip, and without more ado pushes him into a chair
before the dark hearth.

Halsey: Youre a mess. Here, Layman. Get some trash an start a
fire.

Layman fumbles around, finds some newspapers and old bags,
puts them in the hearth, arranges the wood, and kindles the fire.
Halsey sets a black iron kettle where it soon will be boiling. Then
takes from his hip-pocket a bottle of corn licker which he passes to
Kabnis.

Halsey: Here. This'll straighten y out a bit.

Kabnis nervously draws the cork and gulps the licker down.

Kabnis: Ha. Good stuff. Thanks. Thank y, Halsey.

Halsey: Good stuff! Youre damn right. Hanby there dont think
so. Wonder he doesnt come over t find out whos burnin his oil.
Miserly bastard, him. Th boys what made this stuff—are y listenin

2. In the South—and probably in other sections of the country—bloodhounds have been
used to track escaping prisoners and slaves. Harriet Beecher Stowe wrote the novel
*Uncle Tom's Cabin* (1852) to show the horrors of slavery and to persuade readers to
abolish it. One of the most dramatic incidents in the novel, and in the many stage
adaptations of it, occurs when bloodhounds pursue a fleeing slave mother and her
infant child who are trying to cross the frozen Ohio River to find freedom.

t me, Kabnis? th boys what made this stuff have got th art down like I heard you say youd like t be with words. Eh? Have some, Layman?

Layman: Dont think I care for none, thank y jes th same, Mr. Halsey.

Halsey: Care hell. Course y care. Everybody cares around these parts. Preachers an school teachers an everybody. Here. Here, take it. Dont try that line on me.

Layman limbers up a little, but he cannot quite forget that he is on school ground.

Layman: Thats right. Thats true, sho. Shinin[3] is th only business what pays in these hard times.

He takes a nip, and passes the bottle to Kabnis. Kabnis is in the middle of a long swig when a rap sounds on the door. He almost spills the bottle, but manages to pass it to Halsey just as the door swings open and Hanby enters. He is a well-dressed, smooth, rich, black-skinned Negro who thinks there is no one quite so suave and polished as himself. To members of his own race, he affects the manners of a wealthy white planter. Or, when he is up North, he lets it be known that his ideas are those of the best New England tradition. To white men he bows, without ever completely humbling himself. Tradesmen in the town tolerate him because he spends his money with them. He delivers his words with a full consciousness of his moral superiority.

Hanby: Hum. Erer, Professor Kabnis, to come straight to the point: the progress of the Negro race is jeopardized whenever the personal habits and examples set by its guides and mentors fall below the acknowledged and hard-won standard of its average member. This institution, of which I am the humble president,[4] was founded, and has been maintained at a cost of great labor and untold sacrifice. Its purpose is to teach our youth to live better, cleaner, more noble lives. To prove to the world that the Negro race can be just like any other race. It hopes to attain this aim partly by the salutary examples set by its instructors. I cannot hinder the progress of a race simply to indulge a single member. I have thought the matter out beforehand, I can assure you. Therefore, if I find your resignation on my desk by to-morrow morning, Mr. Kabnis, I shall not feel obliged to call in the sheriff. Otherwise . . ."

Kabnis: A fellow can take a drink in his own room if he wants to, in the privacy of his own room.

Hanby: His room, but not the institution's room, Mr. Kabnis.

---

3. Moonshining: the practice of making and selling liquor illegally (without paying tax to the government).
4. Principal.

Kabnis:  This is my room while I'm in it.

Hanby:  Mr. Clayborn (the sheriff) can inform you as to that.

Kabnis:  Oh, well, what do I care—glad to get out of this mud-hole.

Hanby:  I should think so from your looks.

Kabnis:  You neednt get sarcastic about it.

Hanby:  No, that is true. And I neednt wait for your resignation either, Mr. Kabnis.

Kabnis:  Oh, you'll get that all right. Dont worry.

Hanby:  And I should like to have the room thoroughly aired and cleaned and ready for your successor by to-morrow noon, Professor.

Kabnis (trying to rise):  You can have your godam room right away. I dont want it.

Hanby:  But I wont have your cursing.

Halsey pushes Kabnis back into his chair.

Halsey:  Sit down, Kabnis, till I wash y.

Hanby (to Halsey):  I would rather not have drinking men on the premises, Mr. Halsey. You will oblige me—

Halsey:  I'll oblige you by stayin right on this spot, this spot, get me? till I get damned ready t leave.

He approaches Hanby. Hanby retreats, but manages to hold his dignity.

Halsey:  Let me get you told right now, Mr. Samuel Hanby. Now listen t me. I aint no slick an span[5] slave youve hired, an dont y think it for a minute. Youve bullied enough about this town. An besides, wheres that bill youve been owin me? Listen t me. If I dont get it paid in by tmorrer noon, Mr. Hanby (he mockingly assumes Hanby's tone and manner), I shall feel obliged t call th sheriff. An that sheriff'll be myself who'll catch y in th road an pull y out your buggy an lightly attend t y. You heard me. Now leave him alone. I'm takin him home with me. I got it fixed. Before you came in. He's goin t work with me. Shapin shafts and buildin wagons'll make a man of him what nobody, y get me? what nobody can take advantage of. Thats all . . .

Halsey burrs off into vague and incoherent comment.

Pause. Disagreeable.

Layman's eyes are glazed on the spurting fire.

Kabnis wants to rise and put both Halsey and Hanby in their places. He vaguely knows that he must do this, else the power of direction will completely slip from him to those outside. The conviction is just strong enough to torture him. To bring a feverish, quick-passing flare into his eyes. To mutter words soggy in hot saliva. To jerk his arms upward in futile protest. Halsey, noticing his gestures,

5. Possibly "spic and span," i.e., spotlessly clean.

thinks it is water that he desires. He brings a glass to him. Kabnis slings it to the floor. Heat of the conviction dies. His arms crumple. His upper lip, his mustache, quiver. Rap! rap, on the door. The sounds slap Kabnis. They bring a hectic color to his cheeks. Like huge cold finger tips they touch his skin and goose-flesh it. Hanby strikes a commanding pose. He moves toward Layman. Layman's face is innocently immobile.

Halsey: Whos there?

Voice: Lewis.

Halsey: Come in, Lewis. Come on in.

Lewis enters. He is the queer fellow who has been referred to. A tall wiry copper-colored man, thirty perhaps. His mouth and eyes suggest purpose guided by an adequate intelligence. He is what a stronger Kabnis might have been, and in an odd faint way resembles him. As he steps towards the others, he seems to be issuing sharply from a vivid dream. Lewis shakes hands with Halsey. Nods perfunctorily to Hanby, who has stiffened to meet him. Smiles rapidly at Layman, and settles with real interest on Kabnis.

Lewis: Kabnis passed me on the road. Had a piece of business of my own, and couldnt get here any sooner. Thought I might be able to help in some way or other.

Halsey: A good baths bout all he needs now. An somethin t put his mind t rest.

Lewis: I think I can give him that. That note was meant for me. Some Negroes have grown uncomfortable at my being here—

Kabnis: You mean, Mr. Lewis, some colored folks threw it? Christ Almighty!

Halsey: Thats what he means. An just as I told y. White folks more direct than that.

Kabnis: What are they after you for?

Lewis: Its a long story, Kabnis. Too long for now. And it might involve present company. (He laughs pleasantly and gestures vaguely in the direction of Hanby.) Tell you about it later on perhaps.

Kabnis: Youre not going?

Lewis: Not till my month's up.

Halsey: Hows that?

Lewis: I'm on a sort of contract with myself. (Is about to leave.) Well, glad its nothing serious—

Halsey: Come round t th shop sometime why dont y, Lewis? I've asked y enough. I'd like t have a talk with y. I aint as dumb as I look. Kabnis an me'll be in most any time. Not much work these days. Wish t hell there was. This burg[6] gets to me when there aint.

6. Town.

(In answer to Lewis' question.) He's goin t work with me. Ya. Night air this side th branch aint good fer him. (Looks at Hanby. Laughs.)

Lewis: I see . . .

His eyes turn to Kabnis. In the instant of their shifting, a vision of the life they are to meet. Kabnis, a promise of a soil-soaked beauty; uprooted, thinning out. Suspended a few feet above the soil whose touch would resurrect him. Arm's length removed from him whose will to help . . . There is a swift intuitive interchange of consciousness. Kabnis has a sudden need to rush into the arms of this man. His eyes call, "Brother." And then a savage, cynical twist-about within him mocks his impulse and strengthens him to repulse Lewis. His lips curl cruelly. His eyes laugh. They are glittering needles, stitching. With a throbbing ache they draw Lewis to. Lewis brusquely wheels on Hanby.

Lewis: I'd like to see you, sir, a moment, if you dont mind.

Hanby's tight collar and vest effectively preserve him.

Hanby: Yes, erer, Mr. Lewis. Right away.

Lewis: See you later, Halsey.

Halsey: So long—thanks—sho hope so, Lewis.

As he opens the door and Hanby passes out, a woman, miles down the valley, begins to sing. Her song is a spark that travels swiftly to the near-by cabins. Like purple tallow flames, songs jet up. They spread a ruddy haze over the heavens. The haze swings low. Now the whole countryside is a soft chorus. Lord. O Lord . . . Lewis closes the door behind him. A flame jets out . . .

The kettle is boiling. Halsey notices it. He pulls the wash-tub from beneath the bed. He arranges for the bath before the fire.

Halsey: Told y them theatrics didnt fit a white man. Th niggers, just like I told y. An after him. Aint surprisin though. He aint bowed t none of them. Nassur. T nairy a one of them nairy an inch nairy a time. An only mixed when he was good an ready—

Kabnis: That song, Halsey, do you hear it?

Halsey: Thats a man. Hear me, Kabnis? A man—

Kabnis: Jesus, do you hear it.

Halsey: Hear it? Hear what? Course I hear it. Listen t what I'm tellin y. A man, get me? They'll get him yet if he dont watch out.

Kabnis is jolted into his fear.

Kabnis: Get him? What do you mean? How? Not lynch him?

Halsey: Na. Take a shotgun an shoot his eyes clear out. Well, anyway, it wasnt fer you, just like I told y. You'll stay over at th house an work with me, eh, boy? Good t get away from his nobs, eh? Damn big stiff though, him. An youre not th first an I can tell y. (Laughs.)

He bustles and fusses about Kabnis as if he were a child. Kabnis submits, wearily. He has no will to resist him.

Layman (his voice is like a deep hollow echo): Thats right. Thats true, sho. Everybody's been expectin that th bust up was comin. Surprised um all y held on as long as y did. Teachin in th South aint th thing fer y. Nassur. You ought t be way back up North where sometimes I wish I was. But I've hung on down this away so long—

Halsey: An there'll never be no leavin time fer y.


4

A month has passed.

Halsey's work-shop. It is an old building just off the main street of Sempter. The walls to within a few feet of the ground are of an age-worn cement mixture. On the outside they are considerably crumbled and peppered with what looks like musket-shot. Inside, the plaster has fallen away in great chunks, leaving the laths, grayed and cobwebbed, exposed. A sort of loft above the shop proper serves as a break-water for the rain and sunshine which otherwise would have free entry to the main floor. The shop is filled with old wheels and parts of wheels, broken shafts, and wooden litter. A double door, midway the street wall. To the left of this, a work-bench that holds a vise and a variety of wood-work tools. A window with as many panes broken as whole, throws light on the bench. Opposite, in the rear wall, a second window looks out upon the back yard. In the left wall, a rickety smoke-blackened chimney, and hearth with fire blazing. Smooth-worn chairs grouped about the hearth suggest the village meeting-place. Several large wooden blocks, chipped and cut and sawed on their upper surfaces are in the middle of the floor. They are the supports used in almost any sort of wagon-work. Their idleness means that Halsey has no worth-while job on foot. To the right of the central door is a junk heap, and directly behind this, stairs that lead down into the cellar. The cellar is known as "The Hole." Besides being the home of a very old man, it is used by Halsey on those occasions when he spices up the life of the small town.

Halsey, wonderfully himself in his work overalls, stands in the doorway and gazes up the street, expectantly. Then his eyes grow listless. He slouches against the smooth-rubbed frame. He lights a cigarette. Shifts his position. Braces an arm against the door. Kabnis passes the window and stoops to get in under Halsey's arm. He is awkward and ludicrous, like a schoolboy in his big brother's new overalls. He skirts the large blocks on the floor, and drops into a chair before the fire. Halsey saunters towards him.

Kabnis: Time f lunch.

Halsey: Ya.

He stands by the hearth, rocking backward and forward. He stretches his hands out to the fire. He washes them in the warm glow of the flames. They never get cold, but he warms them.

Kabnis: Saw Lewis up th street. Said he'd be down.

Halsey's eyes brighten. He looks at Kabnis. Turns away. Says nothing. Kabnis fidgets. Twists his thin blue cloth-covered[7] limbs. Pulls closer to the fire till the heat stings his shins. Pushes back. Pokes the burned logs. Puts on several fresh ones. Fidgets. The town bell strikes twelve.

Kabnis: Fix it up f tnight?

Halsey: Leave it t me.

Kabnis: Get Lewis in?

Halsey: Tryin t.

The air is heavy with the smell of pine and resin. Green logs spurt and sizzle. Sap trickles from an old pine-knot into the flames. Layman enters. He carries a lunch-pail. Kabnis, for the moment, thinks that he is a day laborer.

Layman: Evenin, gen'lemun.

Both: Whats say, Layman.

Layman squares a chair to the fire and droops into it. Several town fellows, silent unfathomable men for the most part, saunter in. Overalls. Thick tan shoes. Felt hats marvelously shaped and twisted. One asks Halsey for a cigarette. He gets it. The blacksmith, a tremendous black man, comes in from the forge. Not even a nod from him. He picks up an axle and goes out. Lewis enters. The town men look curiously at him. Suspicion and an open liking contest for possession of their faces. They are uncomfortable. One by one they drift into the street.

Layman: Heard y was leavin, Mr. Lewis.

Kabnis: Months up, eh? Hell of a month I've got.

Halsey: Sorry y goin, Lewis. Just gettin acquainted like.

Lewis: Sorry myself, Halsey, in a way—

Layman: Gettin t like our town, Mr. Lewis?

Lewis: I'm afraid its on a different basis, Professor.

Halsey: An I've yet t hear about that basis. Been waitin long enough, God knows. Seems t me like youd take pity on a feller if nothin more.

Kabnis: Somethin that old black cockroach over yonder doesnt like, whatever it is.

Layman: Thats right. Thats right, sho.

Halsey: A feller dropped in here tother day an said he knew what you was about. Said you had queer opinions. Well, I could have told him you was a queer one, myself. But not th way he was driftin.

7. Overalls.

Didnt mean anything by it, but just let drop he thought you was a little wrong up here—crazy; y'know. (Laughs.)

Kabnis: Y mean old Blodson? Hell, he's bats himself.

Lewis: I remember him. We had a talk. But what he found queer, I think, was not my opinions, but my lack of them. In half an hour he had settled everything: boll weevils, God, the World War. Weevils and wars are the pests that God sends against the sinful. People are too weak to correct themselves: the Redeemer is coming back. Get ready, ye sinners, for the advent of Our Lord. Interesting, eh, Kabnis? but not exactly what we want.

Halsey: Y could have come t me. I've sho been after y enough. Most every time I've seen y.

Kabnis (sarcastically): Hows it y never came t us professors?

Lewis: I did—to one.

Kabnis: Y mean t say y got somethin from that celluloid-collar-eraser-cleaned old codger over in th mud hole?

Halsey: Rough on th old boy, aint he? (Laughs.)

Lewis: Something, yes. Layman here could have given me quite a deal, but the incentive to his keeping quiet is so much greater than anything I could have offered him to open up, that I crossed him off my mind. And you—

Kabnis: What about me?

Halsey: Tell him, Lewis, for godsake tell him. I've told him. But its somethin else he wants so bad I've heard him downstairs mumblin with th old man.

Lewis: The old man?

Kabnis: What about me? Come on now, you know so much.

Halsey: Tell him, Lewis. Tell it t him.

Lewis: Life has already told him more than he is capable of knowing. It has given him in excess of what he can receive. I have been offered. Stuff in his stomach curdled, and he vomited me.

Kabnis' face twitches. His body writhes.

Kabnis: You know a lot, you do. How about Halsey?

Lewis: Yes . . . Halsey? Fits here. Belongs here. An artist in your way, arent you, Halsey?

Halsey: Reckon I am, Lewis. Give me th work and fair pay an I aint askin nothin better. Went over-seas an saw France; an I come back. Been up North; an I come back. Went t school; but there aint no books whats got th feel t them of them there tools. Nassur. An I'm atellin y.

A shriveled, bony white man passes the window and enters the shop. He carries a broken hatchet-handle and the severed head. He speaks with a flat, drawn voice to Halsey, who comes forward to meet him.

Mr. Ramsay: Can y fix this fer me, Halsey?

Halsey (looking it over): Reckon so, Mr. Ramsay. Here, Kabnis. A little practice fer y.

Halsey directs Kabnis, showing him how to place the handle in the vise, and cut it down. The knife hangs. Kabnis thinks that it must be dull. He jerks it hard. The tool goes deep and shaves too much off. Mr. Ramsay smiles brokenly at him.

Mr. Ramsay (to Halsey): Still breakin in the new hand, eh, Halsey? Seems like a likely enough faller once he gets th hang of it.

He gives a tight laugh at his own good humor. Kabnis burns red. The back of his neck stings him beneath his collar. He feels stifled. Through Ramsay, the whole white South weighs down upon him. The pressure is terrific. He sweats under the arms. Chill beads run down his body. His brows concentrate upon the handle as though his own life was staked upon the perfect shaving of it. He begins to out and out botch the job. Halsey smiles.

Halsey: He'll make a good un some of these days, Mr. Ramsay.

Mr. Ramsay: Y ought t know. Yer daddy was a good un before y. Runs in th family, seems like t me.

Halsey: Thats right, Mr. Ramsay.

Kabnis is hopeless. Halsey takes the handle from him. With a few deft strokes he shaves it. Fits it. Gives it to Ramsay.

Mr. Ramsay: How much on this?

Halsey: No charge, Mr. Ramsay.

Mr. Ramsay (going out): All right, Halsey. Come down an take it out in trade. Shoe-strings or something.

Halsey: Yassur, Mr. Ramsay.

Halsey rejoins Lewis and Layman. Kabnis, hangdog-fashion, follows him.

Halsey: They like y if y work fer them.

Layman: Thats right, Mr. Halsey. Thats right, sho.

The group is about to resume its talk when Hanby enters. He is all energy, bustle, and business. He goes direct to Kabnis.

Hanby: An axle is out in the buggy which I would like to have shaped into a crow-bar. You will see that it is fixed for me.

Without waiting for an answer, and knowing that Kabnis will follow, he passes out. Kabnis, scowling, silent, trudges after him.

Hanby (from the outside): Have that ready for me by three o'clock, young man. I shall call for it.

Kabnis (under his breath as he comes in): Th hell you say, you old black swamp-gut.

He slings the axle on the floor.

Halsey: Wheeee!

Layman, lunch finished long ago, rises, heavily. He shakes hands with Lewis.

Layman: Might not see y again befo y leave, Mr. Lewis. I enjoys t hear y talk. Y might have been a preacher. Maybe a bishop some day. Sho do hope t see y back this away again sometime, Mr. Lewis.

Lewis: Thanks, Professor. Hope I'll see you.

Layman waves a long arm loosely to the others, and leaves. Kabnis goes to the door. His eyes, sullen, gaze up the street.

Kabnis: Carrie K.'s comin with th lunch. Bout time.

She passes the window. Her red girl's-cap, catching the sun, flashes vividly. With a stiff, awkward little movement she crosses the doorsill and gives Kabnis one of the two baskets which she is carrying. There is a slight stoop to her shoulders. The curves of her body blend with this to a soft rounded charm. Her gestures are stiffly variant. Black bangs curl over the forehead of her oval-olive face. Her expression is dazed, but on provocation it can melt into a wistful smile. Adolescent. She is easily the sister of Fred Halsey.

Carrie K.: Mother says excuse her, brother Fred an Ralph, fer bein late.

Kabnis: Everythings all right an O.K., Carrie Kate. O.K. an all right.

The two men settle on their lunch. Carrie, with hardly a glance in the direction of the hearth, as is her habit, is about to take the second basket down to the old man, when Lewis rises. In doing so he draws her unwitting attention. Their meeting is a swift sun-burst. Lewis impulsively moves towards her. His mind flashes images of her life in the southern town. He sees the nascent woman, her flesh already stiffening to cartilage, drying to bone. Her spirit-bloom, even now touched sullen, bitter. Her rich beauty fading . . . He wants to—He stretches forth his hands to hers. He takes them. They feel like warm cheeks against his palms. The sun-burst from her eyes floods up and haloes him. Christ-eyes, his eyes look to her. Fearlessly she loves into them. And then something happens. Her face blanches. Awkwardly she draws away. The sin-bogies of respectable southern colored folks clamor at her: "Look out! Be a *good* girl. A *good* girl. Look out!" She gropes for her basket that has fallen to the floor. Finds it, and marches with a rigid gravity to her task of feeding the old man. Like the glowing white ash of burned paper, Lewis' eyelids, wavering, settle down. He stirs in the direction of the rear window. From the back yard, mules tethered to odd trees and posts blink dumbly at him. They too seem burdened with an impotent pain. Kabnis and Halsey are still busy with their lunch. They havent noticed him. After a while he turns to them.

Lewis: Your sister, Halsey, whats to become of her? What are you going to do for her?

Halsey: Who? What? What am I goin t do? . . .

Lewis: What I mean is, what does she do down there?

Halsey: Oh. Feeds th old man. Had lunch, Lewis?

Lewis: Thanks, yes. You have never felt her, have you, Halsey? Well, no, I guess not. I dont suppose you can. Nor can she . . . Old man? Halsey, some one lives down there? I've never heard of him. Tell me—

Kabnis takes time from his meal to answer with some emphasis:

Kabnis: Theres lots of things you aint heard of.

Lewis: Dare say. I'd like to see him.

Kabnis: You'll get all th chance you want tnight.

Halsey: Fixin a little somethin up fer tnight, Lewis. Th three of us an some girls. Come round bout ten-thirty.

Lewis: Glad to. But what under the sun does he do down there?

Halsey: Ask Kabnis. He blows off t him every chance he gets.

Kabnis gives a grunting laugh. His mouth twists. Carrie returns from the cellar. Avoiding Lewis, she speaks to her brother.

Carrie K.: Brother Fred, father hasnt eaten now goin on th second week, but mumbles an talks funny, or tries t talk when I put his hands ont th food. He frightens me, an I dunno what t do. An oh, I came near fergettin, brother, but Mr. Marmon—he was eatin lunch when I saw him—told me t tell y that th lumber wagon busted down an he wanted y t fix it fer him. Said he reckoned he could get it t y after he ate.

Halsey chucks a half-eaten sandwich in the fire. Gets up. Arranges his blocks. Goes to the door and looks anxiously up the street. The wind whirls a small spiral in the gray dust road.

Halsey: Why didnt y tell me sooner, little sister?

Carrie K.: I fergot t, an just remembered it now, brother.

Her soft rolled words are fresh pain to Lewis. He wants to take her North with him What for? He wonders what Kabnis could do for her. What she could do for him. Mother him. Carrie gathers the lunch things, silently, and in her pinched manner, curtsies, and departs. Kabnis lights his after-lunch cigarette. Lewis, who has sensed a change, becomes aware that he is not included in it. He starts to ask again about the old man. Decides not to. Rises to go.

Lewis: Think I'll run along, Halsey.

Halsey: Sure. Glad t see y any time.

Kabnis: Dont forget tnight.

Lewis: Dont worry. I wont. So long.

Kabnis: So long. We'll be expectin y.

Lewis passes Halsey at the door. Halsey's cheeks form a vacant smile. His eyes are wide awake, watching for the wagon to turn from Broad Street into his road.

Halsey: So long.

His words reach Lewis halfway to the corner.

5

Night, soft belly of a pregnant Negress, throbs evenly against the
torso of the South. Night throbs a womb-song to the South. Cane-
and cotton-fields, pine forests, cypress swamps, sawmills, and factories are fecund at her touch. Night's womb-song sets them singing.
Night winds are the breathing of the unborn child whose calm
throbbing in the belly of a Negress sets them somnolently singing.
Hear their song.

> White-man's land.
> Niggers, sing.
> Burn, bear black children
> Till poor rivers bring
> Rest, and sweet glory
> In Camp Ground.

Sempter's streets are vacant and still. White paint on the wealth-
ier houses has the chill blue glitter of distant stars. Negro cabins
are a purple blur. Broad Street is deserted. Winds stir beneath the
corrugated iron canopies and dangle odd bits of rope tied to horse-
and mule-gnawed hitching-posts. One store window has a light in
it. Chesterfield cigarette and Chero-Cola cardboard advertisements
are stacked in it. From a side door two men come out. Pause, for a
last word and then say good night. Soon they melt in shadows
thicker than they. Way off down the street four figures sway beneath
iron awnings which form a sort of corridor that imperfectly echoes
and jumbles what they say. A fifth form joins them. They turn into
the road that leads to Halsey's workshop. The old building is phosphorescent above deep shade. The figures pass through the double
door. Night winds whisper in the eaves. Sing weirdly in the ceiling
cracks. Stir curls of shavings on the floor. Halsey lights a candle. A
good-sized lumber wagon, wheels off, rests upon the blocks. Kabnis
makes a face at it. An unearthly hush is upon the place. No one
seems to want to talk. To move, lest the scraping of their feet . . .

Halsey: Come on down this way, folks.

He leads the way. Stella follows. And close after her, Cora, Lewis,
and Kabnis. They descend into the Hole. It seems huge, limitless in
the candle light. The walls are of stone, wonderfully fitted. They
have no openings save a small iron-barred window toward the top of
each. They are dry and warm. The ground slopes away to the rear
of the building and thus leaves the south wall exposed to the sun.
The blacksmith's shop is plumb against the right wall. The floor is

clay. Shavings have at odd times been matted into it. In the right-
hand corner, under the stairs, two good-sized pine mattresses, resting on cardboard, are on either side of a wooden table. On this are
several half-burned candles and an oil lamp. Behind the table, an
irregular piece of mirror hangs on the wall. A loose something that
looks to be a gaudy ball costume dangles from a near-by hook. To
the front, a second table holds a lamp and several whiskey glasses.
Six rickety chairs are near this table. Two old wagon wheels rest on
the floor. To the left, sitting in a high-backed chair which stands
upon a low platform, the old man. He is like a bust in black walnut.
Gray-bearded. Gray-haired. Prophetic. Immobile. Lewis' eyes are
sunk in him. The others, unconcerned, are about to pass on to the
front table when Lewis grips Halsey and so turns him that the
candle flame shines obliquely on the old man's features.

Lewis:  And he rules over—

Kabnis:  Th smoke an fire of th forge.

Lewis:  Black Vulcan?[8] I wouldnt say so. That forehead. Great
woolly beard. Those eyes. A mute John the Baptist of a new religion—
or a tongue-tied shadow of an old.

Kabnis:  His tongue is tied all right, an I can vouch f that.

Lewis:  Has he never talked to you?

Halsey:  Kabnis wont give him a chance.

He laughs. The girls laugh. Kabnis winces.

Lewis:  What do you call him?

Halsey:  Father.

Lewis:  Good. Father what?

Kabnis:  Father of hell.

Halsey:  Father's th only name we have fer him. Come on. Lets
sit down an get t th pleasure of the evenin.

Lewis:  Father John it is from now on . . .

Slave boy whom some Christian mistress taught to read the
Bible. Black man who saw Jesus in the ricefields, and began preach-
ing to his people. Moses- and Christ-words used for songs. Dead
blind father of a muted folk who feel their way upward to a life that
crushes or absorbs them. (Speak, Father!) Suppose your eyes could
see, old man. (The years hold hands. O Sing!) Suppose your lips . . .

Halsey, does he never talk?

Halsey:  Na. But sometimes. Only seldom. Mumbles. Sis says he
talks—

Kabnis:  I've heard him talk.

Halsey:  First I've ever heard of it. You dont give him a chance. Sis
says she's made out several words, mostly one—an like as not cause
it was "sin."

8. In Roman mythology, the blacksmith god; also the god of the hearth.

Cora laughs in a loose sort of way. She is a tall, thin, mulatto woman. Her eyes are deep-set behind a pointed nose. Her hair is coarse and bushy. Seeing that Stella also is restless, she takes her arm and the two women move towards the table. They slip into chairs. Halsey follows and lights the lamp. He lays out a pack of cards. Stella sorts them as if telling fortunes. She is a beautifully proportioned, large-eyed, brown-skin girl. Except for the twisted line of her mouth when she smiles or laughs, there is about her no suggestion of the life she's been through. Kabnis, with great mock-solemnity, goes to the corner, takes down the robe, and dons it. He is a curious spectacle, acting a part, yet very real. He joins the others at the table. They are used to him. Lewis is surprised. He laughs. Kabnis shrinks and then glares at him with a furtive hatred. Halsey, bringing out a bottle of corn licker, pours drinks.

Halsey: Come on, Lewis. Come on, you fellers. Heres lookin at y.

Then, as if suddenly recalling something, he jerks away from the table and starts towards the steps.

Kabnis: Where y goin, Halsey?

Halsey: Where? Where y think? That oak beam in th wagon—

Kabnis: Come ere. Come ere. Sit down. What in hell's wrong with you fellers? You with your wagon. Lewis with his Father John. This aint th time fer foolin with wagons. Daytime's bad enough f that. Ere, sit down. Ere, Lewis, you too sit down. Have a drink. Thats right. Drink corn licker, love th girls, an listen t th old man mumblin sin.

There seems to be no good-time spirit to the party. Something in the air is too tense and deep for that. Lewis, seated now so that his eyes rest upon the old man, merges with his source and lets the pain and beauty of the South meet him there. White faces, pain-pollen, settle downward through a cane-sweet mist and touch the ovaries of yellow flowers. Cotton-bolls bloom, droop. Black roots twist in a parched red soil beneath a blazing sky. Magnolias, fragrant, a trifle futile, lovely, far off . . . His eyelids close. A force begins to heave and rise . . . Stella is serious, reminiscent.

Stella: Usall is brought up t hate sin worse than death—

Kabnis: An then before you have y eyes half open, youre made t love it if y want t live.

Stella: Us never—

Kabnis: Oh, I know your story: that old prim bastard over yonder, an then old Calvert's office—

Stella: It wasnt them—

Kabnis: I know. They put y out of church, an then I guess th preacher came around an asked f some. But thats your body. Now me—

Halsey (passing him the bottle): All right, kid, we believe y. Here, take another. Wheres Clover, Stel?

Stella: You know how Jim is when he's just out th swamp. Done up in shine[9] an wouldnt let her come. Said he'd bust her head open if she went out.

Kabnis: Dont see why he doesnt stay over with Laura, where he belongs.

Stella: Ask him, an I reckon he'll tell y. More than you want.

Halsey: Th nigger hates th sight of a black woman worse than death. Sorry t mix y up this way, Lewis. But y see how tis.

Lewis' skin is tight and glowing over the fine bones of his face. His lips tremble. His nostrils quiver. The others notice this and smile knowingly at each other. Drinks and smokes are passed around. They pay no neverminds to him. A real party is being worked up. Then Lewis opens his eyes and looks at them. Their smiles disperse in hot-cold tremors. Kabnis chokes his laugh. It sputters, gurgles. His eyes flicker and turn away. He tries to pass the thing off by taking a long drink which he makes considerable fuss over. He is drawn back to Lewis. Seeing Lewis' gaze still upon him, he scowls.

Kabnis: Whatsha lookin at me for? Y want t know who I am? Well, I'm Ralph Kabnis—lot of good its goin t do y. Well? Whatsha keep lookin for? I'm Ralph Kabnis. Aint that enough f y? Want th whole family history? Its none of your godam business, anyway. Keep off me. Do y hear? Keep off me. Look at Cora. Aint she pretty enough t look at? Look at Halsey, or Stella. Clover ought t be here an you could look at her. An love her. Thats what you need. I know—

Lewis: Ralph Kabnis gets satisfied that way?

Kabnis: Satisfied? Say, quit your kiddin. Here, look at that old man there. See him? He's satisfied. Do I look like him? When I'm dead I dont expect t be satisfied. Is that enough f y, with your godam nosin, or do you want more? Well, y wont get it, understand?

Lewis: The old man as symbol, flesh, and spirit of the past, what do you think he would say if he could see you? You look at him, Kabnis.

Kabnis: Just like any done-up preacher is what he looks t me. Jam some false teeth in his mouth and crank him, an youd have God Almighty spit in torrents all around th floor. Oh, hell, an he reminds me of that black cockroach over yonder. An besides, he aint my past. My ancestors were Southern blue-bloods—

Lewis: And black.

Kabnis: Aint much difference between blue an black.

Lewis: Enough to draw a denial from you. Cant hold them, can you? Master; slave. Soil; and the overarching heavens. Dusk; dawn. They fight and bastardize you. The sun tint of your cheeks, flame of

9. Intoxicated, drunk.

the great season's multi-colored leaves, tarnished, burned. Split, shredded: easily burned. No use . . .

His gaze shifts to Stella. Stella's face draws back, her breasts come towards him.

Stella: I aint got nothin f y, mister. Taint no use t look at me.

Halsey: Youre a queer feller, Lewis, I swear y are. Told y so, didnt I, girls? Just take him easy though, an he'll be ridin just th same as any Georgia mule, eh, Lewis? (Laughs.)

Stella: I'm goin t tell y somethin, mister. It aint t you, t th Mister Lewis what noses about. Its t somethin different, I dunno what. That old man there—maybe its him—is like m father used t look. He used t sing. An when he could sing no mo, they'd allus come f him an carry him t church an there he'd sit, befo th pulpit, aswayin an aleadin every song. A white man took m mother an it broke th old man's heart. He died; an then I didnt care what become of me, an I dont now. I dont care now. Dont get it in y head I'm some sentimental Susie askin for yo sop.[1] Nassur. But theres somethin t yo th others aint got. Boars an kids an fools—thats all I've known. Boars when their fever's up. When their fever's up they come t me. Halsey asks me over when he's off th job. Kabnis—it ud be a sin t play with him. He takes it out in talk.

Halsey knows that he has trifled with her. At odd things he has been inwardly penitent before her tasking him. But now he wants to hurt her. He turns to Lewis.

Halsey: Lewis, I got a little licker in me, an thats true. True's what I said. True. But th stuff just seems t wake me up an make my mind a man of me. Listen. You know a lot, queer as hell as y are, an I want t ask y some questions. Theyre too high fer them, Stella an Cora an Kabnis, so we'll just excuse em. A chat between ourselves. (Turns to the others.) You-all cant listen in on this. Twont interest y. So just leave th table t this gen'lemun an myself. Go long now.

Kabnis gets up, pompous in his robe, grotesquely so, and makes as if to go through a grand march with Stella. She shoves him off, roughly, and in a mood swings her body to the steps. Kabnis grabs Cora and parades around, passing the old man, to whom he bows in mock-curtsy. He sweeps by the table, snatches the licker bottle, and then he and Cora sprawl on the mattresses. She meets his weak approaches after the manner she thinks Stella would use.

Halsey contemptuously watches them until he is sure that they are settled.

Halsey: This aint th sort o thing f me, Lewis, when I got work upstairs. Nassur. You an me has got things t do. Wastin time on

---

1. Food produced by sopping bread in gravy; here, the meaning seems to be "charity" or "pity."

common low-down women—say, Lewis, look at her now—Stella—
aint she a picture? Common wench—na she aint, Lewis. You know
she aint. I'm only tryin t fool y. I used t love that girl. Yassur. An
sometimes when th moon is thick an I hear dogs up th valley barkin
an some old woman fetches out her song, an th winds seem like th
Lord made them fer t fetch an carry th smell o pine an cane, an
there aint no big job on foot, I sometimes get t thinkin that I still do.
But I want t talk t y, Lewis, queer as y are. Y know, Lewis, I went t
school once. Ya. In Augusta. But it wasnt a regular school. Na. It was
a pussy Sunday-school masqueradin under a regular name. Some
goody-goody teachers from th North had come down t teach th niggers. If you was nearly white, they liked y. If you was black, they
didnt. But it wasnt that—I was all right, y see. I couldnt stand em
messin an pawin over m business like I was a child. So I cussed em
out an left. Kabnis there ought t have cussed out th old duck over
yonder an left. He'd a been a better man tday. But as I was sayin, I
couldnt stand their ways. So I left an came here an worked with my
father. An been here ever since. He died. I set in f myself. An its
always been; give me a good job an sure pay an I aint far from being
satisfied, so far as satisfaction goes. Prejudice is everywheres about
this country. An a nigger aint in much standin anywheres. But when
it comes t pottin round in doin nothin, with nothin bigger'n an ax-
handle t hold a feller down, like it was a while back befo I got this
job—that beam ought t be—but tmorrow mornin early's time
enough f that. As I was sayin, I gets t thinkin. Play dumb naturally t
white folks. I gets t thinkin. I used to subscribe t th *Literary Digest*[2]
an that helped along a bit. But there werent nothing I could sink m
teeth int. Theres lots I want t ask y, Lewis. Been askin y t come
around. Couldnt get y. Cant get in much tnight. (He glances at the
others. His mind fastens on Kabnis.) Say, tell me this, whats on your
mind t say on that feller there? Kabnis' name. One queer bird ought
t know another, seems like t me.

Licker has released conflicts in Kabnis and set them flowing. He
pricks his ears, intuitively feels that the talk is about him, leaves
Cora, and approaches the table. His eyes are watery, heavy with passion. He stoops. He is a ridiculous pathetic figure in his showy robe.

Kabnis: Talkin bout me. I know. I'm th topic of conversation
everywhere theres talk about this town. Girls an fellers. White folks
as well. An if its me youre talkin bout, guess I got a right t listen in.
Whats sayin? Whats sayin bout his royal guts, the Duke? Whats
sayin, eh?

Halsey (to Lewis): We'll take it up another time.

---

2. A literary magazine published from 1890 to 1938.

Kabnis: No nother time bout it. Now. I'm here now an talkin's just begun. I was born an bred in a family of orators, thats what I was.

Halsey: Preachers.

Kabnis: Na. Preachers hell. I didnt say wind-busters. Y misapprehended me. Y understand what that means, dont y? All right then, y misapprehended me. I didnt say preachers. I said orators. O R A T O R S. Born one an I'll die one. You understand me, Lewis. (He turns to Halsey and begins shaking his finger in his face.) An as f you, youre all right f choppin things from blocks of wood. I was good at that th day I ducked th cradle. An since then, I've been shapin words after a design that branded here. Know whats here? M soul. Ever heard o that? Th hell y have. Been shapin words t fit m soul. Never told y that before, did I? Thought I couldnt talk. I'll tell y. I've been shapin words; ah, but sometimes theyre beautiful an golden an have a taste that makes them fine t roll over with y tongue. Your tongue aint fit f nothin but t roll an lick hog-meat.

Stella and Cora come up to the table.

Halsey: Give him a shove there, will y, Stel?

Stella jams Kabnis in a chair. Kabnis springs up.

Kabnis: Cant keep a good man down. Those words I was tellin y about, they wont fit int th mold thats branded on m soul. Rhyme, y see? Poet, too. Bad rhyme. Bad poet. Somethin else youve learned tnight. Lewis dont know it all, an I'm atellin y. Ugh. Th form thats burned int my soul is some twisted awful thing that crept in from a dream, a godam nightmare, an wont stay still unless I feed it. An it lives on words. Not beautiful words. God Almighty no. Misshapen, split-gut, tortured, twisted words. Layman was feedin it back there that day you thought I ran out fearin things. White folks feed it cause their looks are words. Niggers, black niggers feed it cause theyre evil an their looks are words. Yallar niggers feed it. This whole damn bloated purple country feeds it cause its goin down t hell in a holy avalanche of words. I want t feed th soul—I know what that is; th preachers dont—but I've got t feed it. I wish t God some lynchin white man ud stick his knife through it an pin it to a tree. An pin it to a tree. You hear me? Thats a wish f y, you little snot-nosed pups who've been makin fun of me, an fakin that I'm weak. Me, Ralph Kabnis weak. Ha.

Halsey: Thats right, old man. There, there. Here, so much exertion merits a fittin reward. Help him t be seated, Cora.

Halsey gives him a swig of shine. Cora glides up, seats him, and then plumps herself down on his lap, squeezing his head into her breasts. Kabnis mutters. Tries to break loose. Curses. Cora almost stifles him. He goes limp and gives up. Cora toys with him. Ruffles his hair. Braids it. Parts it in the middle. Stella smiles contemptuously.

And then a sudden anger sweeps her. She would like to lash Cora from the place. She'd like to take Kabnis to some distant pine grove and nurse and mother him. Her eyes flash. A quick tensioning throws her breasts and neck into a poised strain. She starts towards them. Halsey grabs her arm and pulls her to him. She struggles. Halsey pins her arms and kisses her. She settles, spurting like a pine-knot afire.

Lewis finds himself completely cut out. The glowing within him subsides. It is followed by a dead chill. Kabnis, Carrie, Stella, Halsey, Cora, the old man, the cellar, and the work-shop, the southern town descend upon him. Their pain is too intense. He cannot stand it. He bolts from the table. Leaps up the stairs. Plunges through the work-shop and out into the night.

6

The cellar swims in a pale phosphorescence. The table, the chairs, the figure of the old man are amœba-like shadows which move about and float in it. In the corner under the steps, close to the floor, a solid blackness. A sound comes from it. A forcible yawn. Part of the blackness detaches itself so that it may be seen against the grayness of the wall. It moves forward and then seems to be clothing itself in odd dangling bits of shadow. The voice of Halsey, vibrant and deepened, calls.

Halsey: Kabnis. Cora. Stella.

He gets no response. He wants to get them up, to get on the job. He is intolerant of their sleepiness.

Halsey: Kabnis! Stella! Cora!

Gutturals, jerky and impeded, tell that he is shaking them.

Halsey: Come now, up with you.

Kabnis (sleepily and still more or less intoxicated): Whats th big idea? What in hell—

Halsey: Work. But never you mind about that. Up with you.

Cora: Oooooo! Look here, mister, I aint used t bein thrown int th street befo day.

Stella: Any bunk whats worked is worth in wages moren this. But come on. Taint no use t arger.

Kabnis: I'll arger. Its preposterous—

The girls interrupt him with none too pleasant laughs.

Kabnis: Thats what I said. Know what it means, dont y? All right, then. I said its preposterous t root an artist out o bed at this ungodly hour, when there aint no use t it. You can start your damned old work. Nobody's stoppin y. But what we got t get up for? Fraid somebody'll see th girls leavin? Some sport, you are. I hand it t y.

Halsey: Up you get, all th same.

Kabnis: Oh, th hell you say.

Halsey: Well, son, seeing that I'm th kindhearted father, I'll give y chance t open your eyes. But up y get when I come down.

He mounts the steps to the work-shop and starts a fire in the hearth. In the yard he finds some chunks of coal which he brings in and throws on the fire. He puts a kettle on to boil. The wagon draws him. He lifts an oak-beam, fingers it, and becomes abstracted. Then comes to himself and places the beam upon the work-bench. He looks over some newly cut wooden spokes. He goes to the fire and pokes it. The coals are red-hot. With a pair of long prongs he picks them up and places them in a thick iron bucket. This he carries downstairs. Outside, darkness has given way to the impalpable grayness of dawn. This early morning light, seeping through the four barred cellar windows, is the color of the stony walls. It seems to be an emanation from them. Halsey's coals throw out a rich warm glow. He sets them on the floor, a safe distance from the beds.

Halsey: No foolin now. Come. Up with you.

Other than a soft rustling, there is no sound as the girls slip into their clothes. Kabnis still lies in bed.

Stella (to Halsey): Reckon y could spare us a light?

Halsey strikes a match, lights a cigarette, and then bends over and touches flame to the two candles on the table between the beds. Kabnis asks for a cigarette. Halsey hands him his and takes a fresh one for himself. The girls, before the mirror, are doing up their hair. It is bushy hair that has gone through some straightening process. Character, however, has not all been ironed out. As they kneel there, heavy-eyed and dusky, and throwing grotesque moving shadows on the wall, they are two princesses in Africa going through the early-morning ablutions of their pagan prayers. Finished, they come forward to stretch their hands and warm them over the glowing coals. Red dusk of a Georgia sunset, their heavy, coal-lit faces . . . Kabnis suddenly recalls something.

Kabnis: Th old man talked last night.

Stella: And so did you.

Halsey: In your dreams.

Kabnis: I tell y, he did. I know what I'm talkin about. I'll tell y what he said. Wait now, lemme see.

Halsey: Look out, brother, th old man'll be getting int you by way o dreams. Come, Stel, ready? Cora? Coffee an eggs f both of you.

Halsey goes upstairs.

Stella: Gettin generous, aint he?

She blows the candles out. Says nothing to Kabnis. Then she and Cora follow after Halsey. Kabnis, left to himself, tries to rise. He has slept in his robe. His robe trips him. Finally, he manages to stand up. He starts across the floor. Half-way to the old man, he falls and lies quite still. Perhaps an hour passes. Light of a new sun is about to filter through the windows. Kabnis slowly rises to support upon his elbows. He looks hard, and internally gathers himself together. The side face of Father John is in the direct line of his eyes. He scowls at him. No one is around. Words gush from Kabnis.

Kabnis: You sit there like a black hound spiked to an ivory pedestal. An all night long I heard you murmurin that devilish word. They thought I didnt hear y, but I did. Mumblin, feedin that ornery thing thats livin on my insides. Father John. Father of Satan, more likely. What does it mean t you? Youre dead already. Death. What does it mean t you? To you who died way back there in th 'sixties. What are y throwin it in my throat for? Whats it goin t get y? A good smashin in th mouth, thats what. My fist'll sink int y black mush face clear t y guts—if y got any. Dont believe y have. Never seen signs of none. Death. Death. Sin an Death. All night long y mumbled death. (He forgets the old man as his mind begins to play with the word and its associations.) Death . . . these clammy floors . . . just like th place they used t stow away th worn-out, no-count niggers in th days of slavery . . . that was long ago; not so long ago . . . no windows (he rises higher on his elbows to verify this assertion. He looks around, and, seeing no one but the old man, calls.) Halsey! Halsey! Gone an left me. Just like a nigger. I thought he was a nigger all th time. Now I know it. Ditch y when it comes right down t it. Damn him anyway. Godam him. (He looks and re-sees the old man.) Eh, you? T hell with you too. What do I care whether you can see or hear? You know what hell is cause youve been there. Its a feelin an its ragin in my soul in a way that'll pop out of me an run you through, an scorch y, an burn an rip your soul. Your soul. Ha. Nigger soul. A gin soul that gets drunk on a preacher's words. An screams. An shouts. God Almighty, how I hate that shoutin. Where's th beauty in that? Gives a buzzard a windpipe an I'll bet a dollar t a dime th buzzard ud beat y to it. Aint surprisin th white folks hate y so. When you had eyes, did you ever see th beauty of th world? Tell me that. Th hell y did. Now dont tell me. I know y didnt. You couldnt have. Oh, I'm drunk an just as good as dead, but no eyes that have seen beauty ever lose their sight. You aint got no sight. If you had, drunk as I am, I hope Christ will kill me if I couldnt see it. Your eyes are dull and watery, like fish eyes. Fish eyes are dead eyes. Youre an old man, a dead fish man, an black at that. Theyve put y here t die, damn fool y are not t know it. Do y know how many feet youre under ground? I'll tell y. Twenty. An do y think you'll ever see th light of day again, even if you wasnt blind? Do y think youre out of slavery? Huh? Youre where they used t throw th worked-out, no-count slaves. On a damp clammy floor of a dark scum-hole. An they called that an infirmary. Th sons-a. . . . Why I can already see you toppled off that stool an stretched out on th floor beside me—not beside me, damn you, by yourself, with th flies buzzin an lickin God knows what they'd find on a dirty, black, foul-breathed mouth like yours . . .

Some one is coming down the stairs. Carrie, bringing food for the old man. She is lovely in her fresh energy of the morning, in the calm untested confidence and nascent maternity which rise from the purpose of her present mission. She walks to within a few paces of Kabnis.

Carrie K.: Brother says come up now, brother Ralph.

Kabnis: Brother doesnt know what he's talkin bout.

Carrie K.: Yes he does, Ralph. He needs you on th wagon.

Kabnis: He wants me on th wagon, eh? Does he think some wooden thing can lift me up? Ask him that.

Carrie K.: He told me t help y.

Kabnis: An how would you help me, child, dear sweet little sister?

She moves forward as if to aid him.

Carrie K.: I'm not a child, as I've more than once told you, brother Ralph, an as I'll show you now.

Kabnis: Wait, Carrie. No, thats right. Youre not a child. But twont do t lift me bodily. You dont understand. But its th soul of me that needs th risin.

Carrie K.: Youre a bad brother an just wont listen t me when I'm tellin y t go t church.

Kabnis doesnt hear her. He breaks down and talks to himself.

Kabnis: Great God Almighty, a soul like mine cant pin itself onto a wagon wheel an satisfy itself in spinnin round. Iron prongs an hickory sticks, an God knows what all . . . all right for Halsey . . . use him. Me? I get my life down in this scum-hole. Th old man an me—

Carrie K.: Has he been talkin?

Kabnis: Huh? Who? Him? No. Dont need to. I talk. An when I really talk, it pays th best of them t listen. Th old man is a good listener. He's deaf; but he's a good listener. An I can talk t him. Tell him anything.

Carrie K.: He's deaf an blind, but I reckon he hears, an sees too, from th things I've heard.

Kabnis: No. Cant. Cant I tell you. How's he do it?

Carrie K.: Dunno, except I've heard that th souls of old folks have a way of seein things.

Kabnis: An I've heard them call that superstition.

The old man begins to shake his head slowly. Carrie and Kabnis watch him, anxiously. He mumbles. With a grave motion his head nods up and down. And then, on one of the down-swings—

Father John (remarkably clear and with great conviction): Sin.

He repeats this word several times, always on the downward nodding. Surprised, indignant, Kabnis forgets that Carrie is with him.

Kabnis: Sin! Shut up. What do you know about sin, you old black bastard. Shut up, an stop that swayin an noddin your head.

Father John: Sin.

Kabnis tries to get up.

Kabnis: Didnt I tell y t shut up?

Carrie steps forward to help him. Kabnis is violently shocked at her touch. He springs back.

Kabnis: Carrie! What . . . how . . . Baby, you shouldnt be down here. Ralph says things. Doesnt mean to. But Carrie, he doesnt know what he's talkin about. Couldnt know. It was only a preacher's sin they knew in those old days, an that wasnt sin at all. Mind me, th only sin is whats done against th soul. Th whole world is a conspiracy t sin, especially in America, an against me. I'm th victim of their sin. I'm what sin is. Does he look like me? Have you ever heard him say th things youve heard me say? He couldnt if he had th Holy Ghost t help him. Dont look shocked, little sweetheart, you hurt me.

Father John: Sin.

Kabnis: Aw, shut up, old man.

Carrie K.: Leave him be. He wants t say somethin. (She turns to the old man.) What is it, Father?

Kabnis: Whatsha talkin t that old deaf man for? Come away from him.

Carrie K.: What is it, Father?

The old man's lips begin to work. Words are formed incoherently. Finally, he manages to articulate—

Father John: Th sin whats fixed . . . (Hesitates.)

Carrie K. (restraining a comment from Kabnis): Go on, Father.

Father John: . . . upon th white folks—

Kabnis: Suppose youre talkin about that bastard race thats roamin round th country. It looks like sin, if thats what y mean. Give us somethin new an up t date.

Father John:—f tellin Jesus—lies. O th sin th white folks 'mitted when they made th Bible lie.

Boom. Boom. BOOM! Thuds on the floor above. The old man sinks back into his stony silence. Carrie is wet-eyed. Kabnis, contemptuous.

Kabnis: So thats your sin. All these years t tell us that th white folks made th Bible lie. Well, I'll be damned. Lewis ought t have been here. You old black fakir—

Carrie K.: Brother Ralph, is that your best Amen?

She turns him to her and takes his hot cheeks in her firm cool hands. Her palms draw the fever out. With its passing, Kabnis crumples. He sinks to his knees before her, ashamed, exhausted. His eyes squeeze tight. Carrie presses his face tenderly against her. The suffocation of her fresh starched dress feels good to him. Carrie is about to lift her hands in prayer, when Halsey, at the head of the stairs, calls down.

Halsey: Well, well. Whats up? Aint you ever comin? Come on. Whats up down there? Take you all mornin t sleep off a pint? Youre weakenin, man, youre weakenin. Th axle an th beam's all ready waitin f y. Come on.

Kabnis rises and is going doggedly towards the steps. Carrie notices his robe. She catches up to him, points to it, and helps him take it off. He hangs it, with an exaggerated ceremony, on its nail in the corner. He looks down on the tousled beds. His lips curl bitterly. Turning, he stumbles over the bucket of dead coals. He savagely jerks it from the floor. And then, seeing Carrie's eyes upon him, he swings the pail carelessly and with eyes downcast and swollen, trudges upstairs to the work-shop. Carrie's gaze follows him till he is gone. Then she goes to the old man and slips to her knees before him. Her lips murmur, "Jesus, come."

Light streaks through the iron-barred cellar window. Within its soft circle, the figures of Carrie and Father John.

Outside, the sun arises from its cradle in the tree-tops of the forest. Shadows of pines are dreams the sun shakes from its eyes. The sun arises. Gold-glowing child, it steps into the sky and sends a birth-song slanting down gray dust streets and sleepy windows of the southern town.

**THE END**

# WALDO FRANK

## Foreword to the 1923 Edition of *Cane*†

Reading this book, I had the vision of a land, heretofore sunk in the mists of muteness, suddenly rising up into the eminence of song. Innumerable books have been written about the South; some good books have been written in the South. This book *is* the South. I do not mean that *Cane* covers the South or is the South's full voice. Merely this: a poet has arisen among our American youth who has known how to turn the essences and materials of his Southland into the essences and materials of literature. A poet has arisen in that land who writes, not as a Southerner, not as a rebel against Southerners, not as a Negro, not as apologist or priest or critic: who writes as a *poet*. The fashioning of beauty is ever foremost in his inspiration: not forcedly but simply, and because these ultimate aspects of his world are to him more real than all its specific problems. He has made songs and lovely stories of his land . . . not of its yesterday, but of its immediate life. And that has been enough.

How rare this is will be clear to those who have followed with concern the struggle of the South toward literary expression, and the particular trial of that portion of its folk whose skin is dark. The gifted Negro has been too often thwarted from becoming a poet because his world was forever forcing him to recollect that he was a Negro. The artist must lose such lesser identities in the great well of life. The English poet is not forever protesting and recalling that he is English. It is so natural and easy for him to be English that he can sing as a man. The French novelist is not forever noting: "This is French." It is so atmospheric for him to be French, that he can devote himself to saying: "This is human." This is an imperative condition for the creating of deep art. The whole will and mind of the creator must go below the surfaces of race. And this has been an almost impossible condition for the American Negro to achieve, forced every moment of his life into a specific and superficial plane of consciousness.

The first negative significance of *Cane* is that this so natural and restrictive state of mind is completely lacking. For Toomer, the Southland is not a problem to be solved; it is a field of loveliness to be sung: the Georgia Negro is not a downtrodden soul to be uplifted; he is material for gorgeous painting: the segregated self-conscious brown belt of Washington is not a topic to be discussed and exposed;

---

† From *Cane* by Jean Toomer (New York: Liveright Publishers, 1923). Copyright 1923 by Boni & Liveright, renewed 1950 by Jean Toomer. Used by permission of Liveright Publishing Corporation.

it is a subject of beauty and of drama, worthy of creation in literary form.

It seems to me, therefore, that this is a first book in more ways than one. It is a harbinger of the South's literary maturity: of its emergence from the obsession put upon its minds by the unending racial crisis—an obsession from which writers have made their indirect escape through sentimentalism, exoticism, polemic, "problem" fiction, and moral melodrama. It marks the dawn of direct and unafraid creation. And, as the initial work of a man of twenty-seven, it is the harbinger of a literary force of whose incalculable future I believe no reader of this book will be in doubt.

How typical is *Cane* of the South's still virgin soil and of its pressing seeds! and the book's chaos of verse, tale, drama, its rhythmic rolling shift from lyrism to narrative, from mystery to intimate pathos! But read the book through and you will see a complex and significant form take substance from its chaos. Part One is the primitive and evanescent black world of Georgia. Part Two is the threshing and suffering brown world of Washington, lifted by opportunity and contact into the anguish of self-conscious struggle. Part Three is Georgia again . . . the invasion into this black womb of the ferment seed: the neurotic, educated, spiritually stirring Negro. As a broad form this is superb, and the very looseness and unexpected waves of the book's parts make *Cane* still more *South*, still more of an æsthetic equivalent of the land.

What a land it is! What an Aeschylean beauty to its fateful problem! Those of you who love our South will find here some of your love. Those of you who know it not will perhaps begin to understand what a warm splendor is at last at dawn.

> A feast of moon and men and barking hounds,
> An orgy for some genius of the South
> With bloodshot eyes and cane-lipped scented mouth
> Surprised in making folk-songs. . . .

So, in his still sometimes clumsy stride (for Toomer is finally a poet in prose) the author gives you an inkling of his revelation. An individual force, wise enough to drink humbly at this great spring of his land . . . such is the first impression of Jean Toomer. But beyond this wisdom and this power (which shows itself perhaps most splendidly in his complete freedom from the sense of persecution), there rises a figure more significant: the artist, hard, self-immolating, the artist who is not interested in races, whose domain is Life. The book's final Part is no longer "promise"; it is achievement. It is no mere dawn: it is a bit of the full morning. These materials . . . the ancient black man, mute, inaccessible, and yet so mystically close to the new tumultuous members of his race, the simple slave Past, the shredding

Negro Present, the iridescent passionate dream of the To-morrow . . .
are made and measured by a craftsman into an unforgettable music.
The notes of his counter-point are particular, the themes are of intimate connection with us Americans. But the result is that abstract
and absolute thing called Art.

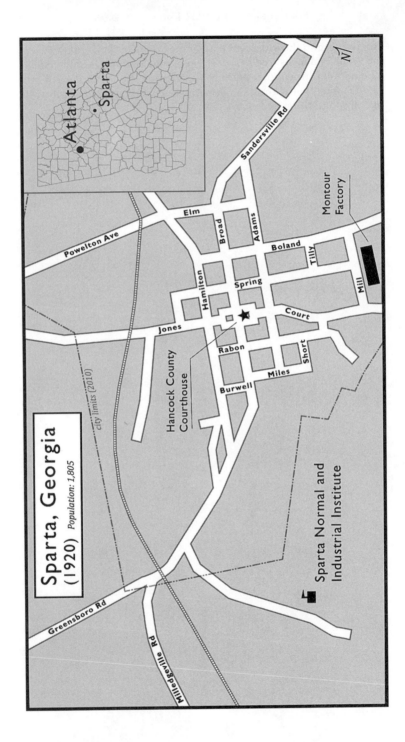

Sparta, Georgia
(1920) *Population: 1,805*

Atlanta

Sparta

*N*

Montour Factory

Hancock County Courthouse

Sparta Normal and Industrial Institute

*city limits (2010)*

Greensboro Rd

Milledgeville Rd

Powelton Ave

Elm

Broad

Adams

Boland

Tilly

Spring

Mill

Hamilton

Court

Jones

Rabon

Short

Miles

Burwell

Sandersville Rd

# BACKGROUNDS
# AND
# SOURCES

# Background Texts

## JEAN TOOMER

### The *Cane* Years[†]

I was in the house with two old people whom, despite the continual struggle with grandfather—he never gave up completely; he was a game fighting cock to the end—I loved. And they were dying. No, they weren't dying. Grandfather gradually declined—a tragic sight—and, one day he broke. After that, he was a doddering old man, not dying, not living, yet hanging on. He might hang on for years and years. But I had to take over whatever of his affairs needed attention. And I ran the house, even cooking meals and sweeping and cleaning. In a way, it was a good thing for them that I had returned. Neither Walter nor Bismarck was much in evidence. Bis came over rather regularly a couple of evenings a week. But he had his work to do, and could not have been of any help during the day. Walter dropped in now and again, but he showed a certain coolness, a certain resentment against his father. He had cause enough to. His life had not turned out well. He was grandfather's favorite son. His almost brusque manner pained the old gentleman more than anything else.

Grandmother, however, was showing forth one of the miracles of life. Each day her body was growing more feeble. You could almost see it thinning away. For weeks at a stretch she would have to be in bed. And, though grandfather worried and feared about his near-poverty, it was she who really felt conditions most acutely. Yet she bore up. Not a whimper from her. She was glad to have me there. As far as I could I shared my life with her, and she began living in my life. She would say every now and again that she only lived for me. But this was the miracle—as her body failed her, her spirit began taking on a more and more vivid life. Her mind became sharper—and also her tongue. She showed a vein of humor and satire that was the delight and amazement of all who came in.

† From *The Wayward and the Seeking: A Collection of Writings by Jean Toomer,* ed. Darwin T. Turner (Washington, D.C.: Howard University Press, 1980). Copyright © 1980 by Darwin T. Turner and Marjorie Content Toomer. Reprinted by permission of Howard University Press.

Most of grandfather's political friends had either died or deserted him. Very seldom did any of the men come in—and when they did, the picture of his decline was so painful to them that they left as soon as they could. But grandmother had several old and staunch women friends. They too were getting feeble, and they couldn't get around so well. But grandmother hardly went out at all. They had to come; and come they did. It was a tonic to them to hear her. Sometimes she would forget how weak her body was, and she'd begin planning to do this and that. And her criticisms of people, of life and manners, were penetrating to the degree of the uncomfortable. Yet, she usually gave everything a humorous turn which would take the sting out.

My days were divided between attention to the house and my grandparents, and my own work. At all possible times I was either writing or reading. I read all of Waldo Frank, most of Dostoevsky, much of Tolstoy, Flaubert, Baudelaire, Sinclair Lewis, Dreiser, most all of the American poets, Coleridge, Blake, Pater, in fine, a good portion of the modern writers of all western countries. In addition—Freud, and the psychoanalysts, and a miscellany of scientific and philosophical works. And I began reading the magazines: the *Dial*, *Poetry*, the *Liberator*, the *Nation*, *New Republic*, etc.

In my writing I was working, at various times, on all the main forms. Essays, articles, poems, short stories, reviews, and a long piece somewhere between a novel and a play. Before I had even so much as glimpsed the possibility of writing *Cane*, I had written a trunk full of manuscripts. The phrase "trunk full" is often used loosely. I mean it literally and exactly. But what difficulties I had! I had in me so much experience so twisted up that not a thing would come out until by sheer force I had dragged it forth. Only now and again did I experience spontaneous writing. Most of it was will and sweat. And nothing satisfied me. Not a thing had I done which I thought merited publication—or even sending to a magazine. I wrote and wrote and put each thing aside, regarding it as simply one of the exercises of my apprenticeship. Often I would be depressed and almost despair over the written thing. But, on the other hand, I became more and more convinced that I had the real stuff in me. And slowly but surely I began getting the "feeling" of my medium, a sense of form, of words, of sentences, rhythms, cadences, and rhythmic patterns. And then, after several years work, suddenly, it was as if a door opened and I knew without doubt that I was *inside, I knew literature*! And what was my joy!

But many things happened before that time came!

People round about wondered what I was doing. They said things. I was sufficiently individualized to hold and go my own way without stopping even to confound them. Once or twice I let fly. I got the reputation of being a very queer fellow. Those, even those who once upon a time had said what a fine dancer and what a sweet lover I was, gave me a sufficiently wide berth.

Vic had long since married someone and gone away. I never saw her after. Not till this day.

Phyllis was there but married. And, in any case, she no longer meant much to me. But somewhere in my heart I reserved—and still do—an affectionate place for her. But it was as though she and all the other people existed in another world. They could not enter mine. I did not want to enter theirs.

Kennedy alone was with me. I stretched him quite a bit, but he always came back for more. I wanted him to try writing. He had a life that, as I have suggested, read like Dostoevsky.[1] But I could not get him to. He was working now and again, and thinking a lot. But I was afraid that sex and drink would get him. He was burning all over, intense emotions, active brain, sexing and drinking and shooting pool—burning the candle at all three ends. He said I was the only person in life he trusted or gave a damn about. By now, his physical features were quite defined, set in the mould and with the expressions he would have for the rest of his life. A long slim body with long tapering fingers. He had the sensitivity of an artist, the lips of a sensualist, the eyes of a fanatic. He was tied up in a family complex—mother and sisters and brother whom he hated. He would not leave home and take a room by himself. He kept picking and flaring at them. He liked to walk the streets at night. I have never known anyone to feel the beauty of tree-shaded evening streets as he did. He liked to go to the zoo and watch the polar bears. He liked to talk with me. He'd read some of the things I'd written. "That's the stuff!" he'd exclaim. But he himself would not try to write a page. I worked very hard on him. Kennedy was the first one to enforce upon me the realization of how difficult it is to change human beings.

Two or three other people of my own age came in to see me.

As for my past life—the life of Chicago and New York, I seemed to have left it completely behind. I seldom wrote to or heard from my former friends in those cities.

Bismarck got very sick. I took over the running of his house also, and each day I went over and massaged him. He was over a month recovering. This took it out of me.

I met a sculptress, and she did a bust of me. But, of more importance to myself, two things happened. One, I suddenly found myself with a faculty for seeing into people. People had always interested me, and, through my experiences with so many and such different kinds, I had acquired some understanding of them, some ability to

---

1. Toomer attempted a novel based on Kennedy; but, as far as can be determined, he did not complete it.

read them. But this was like the sudden functioning of an entirely new function. I would see and understand that hidden and complex thing called motivation. As if a veil had been taken from my eyes I began seeing into the lives of grandmother, grandfather, my uncles, Kennedy, Phyllis, this sculptress, in short, everyone, as never before. And, I felt a marked increase of power to do things with and for people. Being able to see what and why they were as they were, I was enabled to see what they needed.

I met a girl several years younger than myself.[2] She was pretty and talented in music, but very bitter against life. I saw what she was, and, by questioning and reasoning—this was psychological reasoning—I learned how she had come to be that way. In her case I was more successful than with Kennedy. I actually squared her with life and enabled her to make a fresh start.

Meanwhile, conditions in the house were demanding more and draining more from me. But I was still keeping up all right.

I came in contact with an entirely new body of ideas. Buddhist philosophy, the Eastern teachings, occultism, theosophy. Much of the writing itself seemed to me to be poorly done; and I was certain that the majority of the authors of these books had only third or fourth-rate minds, or less. But I extracted the ideas from their settings, and they seemed to me among the most extraordinary I had ever heard. It is natural to me to put my whole heart into anything that really interests me—as long as I am interested. For the time being, only that thing exists in the world. These ideas challenged and stimulated me. Despite my literary purpose, I was compelled to know something more about them. So, for a time, I turned my back on literature and plunged into this kind of reading. I read far and wide, for more than eight months. Then, I became dissatisfied with just reading. I wanted to do some of the things they suggested. I wanted to see some of the things with my own eyes. I myself wanted a personal all-around experience of the world these books seemed to open. I tried several of the exercises; but then, abruptly stopped them. I concluded they were not for me. In general, I concluded that all of that was not for me. I was in this physical, tangible, earthly world, and I knew little enough of it. It was the part of wisdom to learn more and to be able to do more in this, before I began exploring and adventuring into other worlds. So I came back to earth and to literature. But I had profited in many ways by my excursion. The Eastern World, the ancient scriptures had been brought to my notice. Also, our own Christian Bible. I had read it as if it were a new book. Just simply as a work of literature I was convinced that we had nothing to equal it. Not even Shakespeare—my old God—wrote language

2. Probably Mae Wright, an African American.

of such grand perfection. And my religious nature, given a cruel blow by Clarence Darrow and naturalism and atheism, but not, as I found, destroyed by them—my religious nature which had been sleeping was vigorously aroused.

One other thing happened. From this reading, but not so much from it as from the ponderings and gatherings-up of impressions and experiences which it stimulated, there swung to the fore my picture and ideal of Man, of a complete and whole individual who was able to function physically, emotionally, and intellectually. This ideal was much fuller, with more substance and detail than that formed by my reading of Goethe, but it was in the same line and order of desirable and valuable human life.

But both my religious feelings and this ideal were gradually lost to my consciousness as I again got immersed in the difficulties and problems of learning the craft and art of writing. Literature, and particularly the craftsman's aspect of it, again became my entire world, and I lived in it as never before.

And now again I was reading only literary works. This was the period when I was so strongly influenced, first, by the Americans who were dealing with local materials in a poetic way. Robert Frost's New England poems strongly appealed to me. Sherwood Anderson's *Winesburg, Ohio* opened my eyes to entirely new possibilities. I thought it was one of the finest books I'd ever read. And, second, the poems and program of the Imagists. Their insistence on fresh vision and on the perfect clean economical line was just what I had been looking for. I began feeling that I had in my hands the tools for my own creation.

Once during this period I read many books on the matter of race and the race problem in America. Rarely had I encountered the nonsense contained in most of these books. It was evident to me, who had seen both the white and the colored worlds, and both from the inside, that the authors of these writings had little or no experience of the matters they were dealing with. Their pages showed very little more than strings of words expressive of personal prejudices and preferences. I felt that I should write on this matter. I did write several fragments of essays. And I did a lot of thinking. Among other things, I again worked over my own position, and formulated it with more fullness and exactitude. I wrote a poem called, "The First American," the idea of which was, that here in America we are in process of forming a new race, that I was one of the first conscious members of this race. . . .

*I had lived among white people. I had lived among colored people. I had lived among Jews. I had met and known people of the various* nationalistic groups. I had come in contact with my fellow country-men from the bottom to the top of the American scene.

I had seen the divisions, the separatisms and antagonisms. I had observed that, if the issue came up, very few of these United States citizens were aware of being Americans. On the contrary, they were aware of, and put value upon, their hearsay descents, their groupistic affiliations.

True, they were conscious of being anything but Americans. Yet, underlying what they were aware of, underlying all of the divisions, I had observed what seemed to me to be authentic—namely, that a new type of man was arising in this country—not European, not African, not Asiatic—but American. And in this American I saw the divisions mended, the differences reconciled—saw that (1) we would in truth be a united people existing in the United States, saw that (2) we would in truth be once again members of a united human race.

Now all of this, needless to say, did not get into the poem. Years were to pass before that could happen, before the germ of "The First American" could grow and ripen and be embodied in "The Blue Meridian." But into "The First American" I did put something of my actuality, something of my vision of America—though it needed explaining.

Soon after I had written it I read it to a friend of that time, a colored fellow of more than ordinary mental grasp. I considered him a sort of prodigy. I read the poem, and he looked blank. I explained it, and he looked puzzled. So I plunged in and gave him my position and my experiences at some length. At the end he said three words, "You're white."

"What are you?" I asked.

"Colored."

I threw up my hands. "After all I've said you still don't get the point. I am not talking about whites or blacks, I am talking about Americans. I am an American. You are an American. Everyone is an American. Don't you see what I mean?"

He shook his head then, he shook it ever afterwards. My reality was but words to him, words quite unrelated to what was real for him.

Never before had I realized the extent to which a consciousness of being colored had become fixed in members of that group. But there it was, fixed unshakably in a man of unusual intelligence. Never before had I known what a thorough job had been done in the matter of racial conditioning. But there it was, having gone down from his head and emotions to become lodged in the behavior patterns of his body. And a similar kind of fixing and conditioning had doubtless occurred also in members of the white group at large. . . .

Who was I to attempt to unfix all this? As I was neither a propa-gandist nor a reformer I concluded that it was not my business and I had best let it alone. Which is just what I did. The whole thing had

*started as an individual position; so then, in the future, I'd restrict it*
*to myself and to those who, because of their relations with me, were*
*individually concerned.*

["On Being an American"]

All of the above had taken place between the summer of 1920
and the spring of 1922.

It was during this spring that I began feeling dangerously drained
of energy. I had used so much in my own work. So much had been
used on my grandparents and uncles. I seldom went out. I seldom
could go out. Sometimes for weeks my grandmother would be laid
up in bed, and by now my grandfather was almost helpless. The
apartment seemed to suck my very life. And this is no figure of
speech. Everyone has had the experience of being with some person, of leaving this person and feeling bled. He is bled. This person
has taken stuff out of him. Just so, only for a protracted period, had
my grandfather taken energy from me. He was still taking it; and I
began to see the situation as a struggle for life between him and
myself. It was a question of who would die first.

There was nothing the matter with me organically, though I had
contracted a severe case of almost chronic nervous indigestion.
Mainly, it was a matter of energy. I felt utterly exhausted. Each
morning I was up before nine. I'd try to work, and just simply
couldn't. The little force I had gathered during sleep was soon
spent, and I'd be in a wretched state. But neither could I rest. To do
nothing was even worse than trying to squeeze something out of
myself. I drank what whiskey I could get. But when its effects wore
off, I was more drained than ever. I didn't know what on earth I was
going to do. I had no money even for a short vacation. And even if I
had had, I couldn't have left my grandparents alone. A nurse was
out of the question.

But, when the heat of summer came on, I got desperate. I felt I
would die or murder someone if I stayed in that house another day.
Somehow I managed to get enough money for a week's trip to
Harpers Ferry. And, luckily, I was able to make arrangements with
an old woman to be in the apartment for that time. Grandmother,
sensing my state, was glad I was going to have a slight breathing
spell. Grandfather, understanding very little other than his own
infirmities, was petulant. But I left.

I returned with a small store of force which was soon spent; and
I found myself in the same condition as before. The situation was
slowly but steadily growing worse. Never in my life before . . . [had
I felt] so utterly caught and trapped. It was as if life were a huge
snake that had coiled about me—and now it had me at almost my
last breath.

Just at this time a man, the head of an industrial and agricultural school for Negroes in Georgia, came to town. He was going to Boston in search of funds and wanted someone to act as principal during his absence. He was sent to me.

My situation was so desperate that any means of getting out of it appeared as a God-send. I accepted his offer. Besides, I had always wanted to see the heart of the South. Here was my chance.

I had grandfather sent to a hospital. I hired a woman to come and stay with grandmother. And off I went.

I arrived in Sparta and took up my duties. I still felt terribly drained, but the shock of the South kept me going.

The school was several miles from the village. All the teachers lived there. I had a little shack off to one side.

The setting was crude in a way, but strangely rich and beautiful. I began feeling its effects despite my state, or, perhaps, just because of it. There was a valley, the valley of "Cane," with smoke-wreaths during the day and mist at night. A family of back-country Negroes had only recently moved into a shack not too far away. They sang. And this was the first time I'd ever heard the folk-songs and spirituals. They were very rich and sad and joyous and beautiful. But I learned that the Negroes of the town objected to them. They called them "shouting." They had victrolas and player-pianos. So, I realized with deep regret, that the spirituals, meeting ridicule, would be certain to die out. With Negroes also the trend was towards the small town and then towards the city—and industry and commerce and machines. The folk-spirit was walking in to die on the modern desert. That spirit was so beautiful. Its death was so tragic. Just this seemed to sum life for me. And this was the feeling I put into *Cane*. *Cane* was a swan-song. It was a song of an end. And why no one has seen and felt that, why people have expected me to write a second and a third and a fourth book like *Cane,* is one of the queer misunderstandings of my life.

I left Georgia in late November of that year, after having been there three months. On the train coming north I began to write the things that later on appeared in that book.

Once again in Washington I had my grandfather brought back from the hospital. His condition there was too pitiable for me to bear. He touched my heart so strongly that I resolved to care for him till the very end. And this I did.

He sank very rapidly. All during December I nursed him; and, at the same time, I wrote the materials of *Cane*. In these last days he seemed to know just what I meant to him. I knew and realized all he had done for me. Our almost life-long struggle and contest was finished, and all my love and gratitude for the once so forceful and dominant but now so broken and tragic man came to the fore. He died the day after I had finished the first draft of "Kabnis," the long semi-dramatic closing-piece of *Cane*.

Walter and I took his body to New Orleans and interred it in the family vault, beside the remains of my mother.

Grandmother bore up remarkably well; and she and I continued living in the apartment. . . .

[The remainder of the autobiographical selections have been taken from "On Being an American" except where indicated.]

I resumed writing.

Some of the pieces were impure and formless. But some, I knew, were really written. These authentic ones I began sending out. The *Double Dealer* of New Orleans was the first to accept. Then the *Liberator* and, later, *Broom*. In these literary magazines I made my mark. Beyond them was Waldo Frank and the possibility of a book.

Now I felt warranted in sending something to Waldo Frank. I sent a batch of the best—and waited his response as if my whole life were at stake.

His words to me fed me as nothing else had done and confirmed my belief.

He too talked about a book. Now I wanted a book published as I wanted nothing else. I wanted it because it would be a substantial testament of my achievement, and also because I felt that it would lead me from the cramped conditions of Washington which I had outgrown, into the world of writers and literature. I saw it as my passport to this world.

But I had not enough for a book. I had at most a hundred typed pages. These were about Georgia. It seemed that I had said all I had to say about it. So what, then? I'd fill out. The middle section of *Cane* was thus manufactured.

I sent the manuscript to Frank. He took it to Horace Liveright. Liveright accepted it, but wanted a foreword written by Frank.

Frank himself had a book to write, based on Negro life.[3] It was arranged that he come to Washington and then both of us would go South.

Frank came. He stayed at the apartment with us. I took this opportunity to convey to him my position in America. I read to him "The First American." I explained my actuality and my ideas to the point where I felt sure he understood them. I did this because I wanted that we understand each other on this point too, and also because he was going to write the foreword to my book and I wanted

---

3. *Holiday* (1923). It is important to observe that Toomer states that he had completed *Cane* before Frank completed *Holiday*.

this introduction of myself to the literary world to be accurate and right.

We went South. We came back. Frank returned to New York. In several of his letters he referred to what he called my "vision," and seemed to feel that it "protected" me. Perhaps it did. But because of the way he used this word "protected," I was mainly concerned with whether or not he understood that it was not a vision, but an actuality. Once or twice I suspected that he, like my colored friend, felt it was words, fine words to be sure, but unrelated to reality. But I argued myself out of the suspicion by reminding myself that Waldo Frank was the author of *Our America.*

One day in the mail his preface to my book came. I read it and had as many mixed feelings as I have ever had. On the one hand, it was a tribute and a send-off as only Waldo Frank could have written it, and my gratitude for his having gotten the book accepted rose to the surface and increased my gratitude for the present piece of work in so far as it affirmed me as a literary artist of great promise. On the other hand, in so far as the racial thing went, it was evasive, or, in any case, indefinite. According to the reader he would have thought I was white or black, or again he may have thought nothing of it. But in any case he certainly would not *know* what I was.

Well, I asked myself, why should the reader know? Why should any such thing be incorporated in a foreword to *this* book? Why should Waldo Frank or any other be my spokesman in this matter? All of this was true enough, and I was more or less reconciled to letting the preface stand as it was, inasmuch as it was so splendid that I could not take issue with it on this, after all, minor point, inasmuch as my need to have the book published was so great, but my suspicions as to Waldo Frank's lack of understanding of, or failure to accept, my actuality became active again.

As I found out later from several sources, my doubts were warranted. I have been told that Frank, after seeing me and my family, after hearing my statement, not of words or visions but of facts, returned to New York and told people of the writer who was emerging into the world of American literature. In any event, it was thus through Frank's agency that an erroneous picture of me was put in the minds of certain people in New York before my book came out. Thus was started a misunderstanding in the very world, namely the literary art world, in which I expected to be really understood. I knew none of this at the time. . . .[4]

---

4. In this part of his autobiography, Toomer asserts that he should not have been identified as "Negro."

*I saw that it was important for me to be in New York. Grandmother also saw this. Walter had again married. He and his wife had taken a house. Grandmother went to live with them and I took a train for New York [in early summer, 1923]. And thus ended the three-year period of death and birth in Washington.*

*In New York, I stepped into the literary world. Frank, Gorham Munson, Kenneth Burke, Hart Crane, Matthew Josephson, Malcolm Cowley, Paul Rosenfeld, Van Wyck Brooks, Robert Littell—Broom, the Dial the New Republic and many more. I lived on Gay Street and entered into the swing of it. It was an extraordinary summer.*

*I wrote reviews, especially for Broom. I worked on the outline of a large complex novel that was to essentialize my experiences with America. I entered the aesthetic-machine-beauty program as sponsored by Munson in Secession and Josephson in Broom. I met and talked with Alfred Stieglitz and saw his photographs. I was invited here and there.*

*I went up to visit Frank at Darien, Connecticut. And here I met Margaret Naumburg and felt the whole world revolve . . .*

*. . . My birth, and it was truly a birth, came from my experiences with Margaret Naumburg. I do not wish to put these in outline. It is enough here to say that the very deepest centre of my being awoke to consciousness giving me a sense of myself, an awareness of the world and of values, which transcended even my dreams of high experience. All that I had been, all that I had ever done, were as if left behind me in another world. All the past would have seemed valueless had I not known that it was just this past which had prepared me for these experiences.*

["Outline of an Autobiography"]

. . . It was very exciting life and work, giving me a taste and an experience of the literary life such as I had never known before and have never experienced since. There was an excitement in the air. Writing was a living thing. We had programs and aims, and we were all caught up in a ferment. These were the last days of *Secession* and *Broom*. But the *Dial* and the *Little Review* were still going, and what was not yet an actuality we had as a glowing potentiality in our minds.

Sometimes I wondered what if anything Frank had said to these other fellows about my race. But it didn't matter much, one way or the other. What they thought of my race was of no more consequence than what I thought of theirs. The life was the thing—and we were having that life.

The first jolt I got was when I received a letter from Horace Liveright asking, in effect, that I feature myself as a Negro for some publicity he was getting out in connection with *Cain* [*sic*].[5] Now I had seen, talked, lunched with Liveright. Once he had said to me that he had run into prejudice in college, and he asked if I had. I said, "No." That was that. Otherwise, the question of race had not come up even in a vague way. Looking back on it, I can blame myself for not having opened the subject with him. However this may be, I received the request I have just mentioned.

I answered to the effect that, as I was not a Negro. I could not feature myself as one. His reply to this did nothing else than pull my cork. He said he didn't see why I should deny my race. This made me mad, and I was all for going to his office and telling him what was what in no uncertain terms, even at the risk of losing him as my publisher. Friends dissuaded me, and I let the matter drop, but not without having explained to them the facts of my racial actuality.

*Cain* [*sic*] came out. The reviews were splendid. It didn't sell well, but it made its literary mark—that was all I asked.

Meanwhile, since I was a human being as well as a writer, since I was living in this modern world of multiple experience as well as in the world of words and books, some extra-literary things had happened to me. Of these happenings, the only line that I will follow briefly is that which led me into the Gurdjieff work.


# JEAN TOOMER

## Why I Entered the Gurdjieff Work[†]

One day I was told that an English editor and writer named Orage had arrived in New York to prepare for the arrival of a man named Gurdjieff. Neither name meant a thing to me, but I asked questions. Gurdjieff, I learned, was the founder of an institute for the harmonious development of man. He had once been Ouspensky's teacher. The institute was located in France. Now he was on his way to America with a number of his pupils. I had read Ouspensky's *Tertium Organum*. Gurdjieff, Ouspensky's teacher, coming to New York? I became interested at once.

Shortly after hearing this news there came into my hands a pamphlet entitled: *G. Gurdjieff's Institute for the Harmonious Development of Man*. I began reading it. The first words made me feel that I was close to what I sought. I read with eagerness. I read with glow. I gave cries of joy as I came upon statement after statement that

5. We cannot explain the reason for this interesting spelling error in the typed manuscript. The reference obviously is to *Cane*.
† From Jean Toomer, *Selected Essays and Literary Criticism*, ed. Robert B. Jones (Knot-
   ville: The University of Tennessee Press, 1996). Reprinted by permission.

said what I wanted to hear said. Here it was. This was it. At last I had come upon something that "spoke to my condition." At last I had found a knowledge of man that spoke, I felt, not to my condition alone but to the condition of all people who had any psychological understanding of themselves and any realization of the need to be helped by those possessing a greater understanding. I talked of nothing else. I dreamed of nothing else, save to become a member of the Institute and begin actual work.

Gurdjieff and his pupils arrived. Public demonstrations were given of varied aspects of the Institute's program of training. To my mind they were amazing events that satisfied and exceeded anything that I could have asked for. I was in the audience but I saw and felt what went on as if I were already one of the participants. The performances began at theater time and continued on and on as though the pupils were capable of endless endurance. By twelve o'clock most of the onlookers had left. The demonstrations continued. I stayed to the very last, for I was endlessly fascinated and would have been happy had the program gone on through the night, every night.

There were demonstrations of gymnastic exercises. In past years I had practiced both Swedish and German gymnastics. More recently I had learned some of the exercises worked out by F. Matthias Alexander for the conscious control of the individual. Not anywhere at any time had I come upon exercises that, to my way of thinking and feeling, were comparable to these shown by Gurdjieff's pupils. These seemed to take hold of the body and literally re-create it. To see them being done made me want to do them. Nor was their appeal limited to the physical. To me they were strangely beautiful, and, in a way I could not explain, profound. No mere manual motions, these. They involved the whole man, I felt sure, and were means in the service of an essentially religious aim.

There were dances and sacred dances. From time to time I had seen a number of the individual dancers, and the groups and ballets that came to New York. Never had I witnessed dancing like this. It seemed of a different category, of another world. One dance in particular, a dance called "The Initiation of a Priestess," impressed me as being simply marvelous. It was pure religion. I felt I would want to become a member of the Institute if for no other reason than to learn and take part in this dance.

There was music. It was a powerful, dynamic, deeply moving music that touched chords of my being and seemed to awaken an ancient memory of a music I had once known, a life I had once lived, a world that had been mine and that I had left and forgotten. It made me feel as a wayfarer who was being recalled to his rightful way and destiny. It made me feel that all of us were as wayfarers who had gone astray and become lost, and I felt sorrow, pity, yearning, and then I was gathered into an irresistible march. It was a majestic march. It was a march of men. It was a march of resurrected people aware of their worth and dignity and the part they played in the noble procession of the universe.

Orage gave expositions of the ideas. Gurdjieff's total body of knowledge began to unfold. It was a most extraordinary body. Man and the world were gradually revealed in a light not to be found in modern science, not to be found in the sacred books of the East, not to be anywhere, so far as I knew, other than in this Gurdjieff work. Here was food for those vitally concerned to understand the answers to such questions as these. What is the world? Are there cosmic laws? Are there laws which apply to the psychological as well as to the physical universe? What is man's relation to the world? What is man? What are the chief components of the total human being? What is the human norm? What are we basically up against? What can man do? What are our possible attainments? How can we do what it is possible for us to do? What preliminary understandings, what initial methods of training, are indispensable if we would make a real beginning of the work of man?

I met Orage and had several talks with him. From certain things he said I was pretty sure that he knew and practiced methods in addition to those shown to the general public at these demonstrations. I will always remember the light that suddenly came from him when, after discussing the sufficiently terrible plight of man, he ended with these words—"Yes, but there is a way out." That was just what I wanted to hear, in just so many words, from him. I myself was intuitively certain there was a way out; but I wanted it said by someone who impressed me as having found it.

I watched Gurdjieff. Said I to myself—There is a man, if ever I have seen one. He seemed to have everything that could be asked of a developed human being, a teacher, a master. Knowledge, integration, many-sidedness, power—in fact he had a bit too much power for my comfort.

In addition to all the rest, there was an over-all impression. Each thing that was done was part of a whole. The exercises, the dances, the music, the ideas, each in their different ways said essentially the same thing. Each, through different approaches, impressed the same message on the heart. All together they evoked a life and a world that seemed utterly native to me. Here, without doubt, was a religion of training. Here was discipline, an invitation to conscious experiment, a flexible and complete system, a life and a way to which I felt I could dedicate my whole mind and heart and body and strength.

One would think, then, that I was quite set to ask to become a member of the Institute without further delay. Strange as it may seem, I did no such thing. I held back. Gurdjieff's power disturbed me. I was not sure of it, and I wanted to be sure before I placed myself wholly in his hands. This, at any rate, was how I explained it to myself. Then there were other reasons which we need not go into. It is enough to say that I did something that surprised everyone except the one person who knew the intimate facts of my personal life. I left New York. While the demonstrations were still going on I left New York and went to another part of the country. There some further things happened, and I was completely made ready.

The plain truth, I realized later, was this. Despite what I had been through, despite the understandings that had come to me, there was still lodged in my psyche a deep-seated unwillingness to put my life under the direction of anyone other than myself, and a stubborn belief that I could make my way on my own, aided by such help as I would receive in the course of ordinary life. So-called independence, so-called self-reliance and belief in myself, were this strong, still. By leaving New York, by breaking the connections that had begun to be formed between myself and the Institute, I gave myself another, and, as it proved, a final try at making an extraordinary grade without having extraordinary help.

Now what would I do? Circumstances supplied a partial answer. Certain things I had to do and wanted to do. By digging into myself I supplied the rest of the answer. An idea expressed in one of my notes came back to me. One's highest gift should be utilized until one has attained a faculty that is higher than it. It seemed to me that if I possessed any gift at all it was that of psychological thinking and understanding, and so I proposed to exercise it, now, intensively, hoping that I might thereby develop the "new and particular 'inertias'" referred to in the prospectus of the Institute.

# Correspondence†

## To Alain Locke
## November 11, 1919

1341 You St., N.W.,
Washington, D.C.

Dear Mr. Locke,

Will it be convenient for me to come around this Thursday, Nov. 13?

Jean Toomer.
Phone North 4321—J

## To Georgia Douglas Johnson
## December 1919

8 East 9th Street,
N.Y. City

A full Xmas to you and those you love.
Most of my energies have gone in work, work at the shipyards.[1]
Now, I know their life, so I've quit.
I'll have more time to write.

Jean Toomer

---

† The majority of the letters reprinted in this section appear in Mark Whalan's *The Letters of Jean Toomer 1919–1924* (Knoxville: The University of Tennessee Press, 2006). Toomer's letter to James Weldon Johnson appears in Frederick L. Rusch's *A Jean Toomer Reader: Selected and Unpublished Writings* (New York: Oxford University Press, 1993). Waldo Frank's letter to Jean Toomer of April 25, 1922, is reprinted courtesy of the Waldo Frank Papers, Special Collections, Van Pelt Library, University of Pennsylvania. All other letters reprinted courtesy of the Jean Toomer Papers, James Weldon Johnson Collection, Beinecke Rare Book and Manuscript Library.

1. Toomer undertook ten days of work in the New Jersey shipyards in late 1919.

## To Georgia Douglas Johnson
## January 7, 1920

8 East 9th St.,
New York, N.Y.

Dear G.D.J.,

Yesterday I called up Dr. Dubois.[1] At first he didn't remember me, even after mentioning the fact that you and he had talked of me. In fact, it wasn't until I chanced to mention my hike up here, that the light burst—or rather filtered through—it wasn't a very strong light—he ended by saying that if I would send some of my stuff to the office he would be glad to look it over.

How I really had expected something more. Any editor would have said as much as that. Anyone with two ounces of curiosity (literary or otherwise) in his make up would rather like to look over new material. I had thought he wanted to get in touch with me, even possibly to know me. Does he expect to do so by looking at my writings? If I were mature he could expect to see the man in the writer. But of an immature youngster—why no more than a chick can truly express himself within his shell. No, it will be some years before Jean Toomer the thinker, the feeler, the man in love with life in toto, passions, vices, sorrows, despairs—all of life, will be able to put half what is in him on the cool surface of a white sheet of paper. That is art. And as yet I am far from the finished artist. But even now I have opinions, ideas, ideals which I'll tell, straight from the shoulder, to anyone who asks for them. Woe be unto the timid whose curiosity has led them beyond the bounds of discretion!

I said I'd send the Doctor some of my writings. And so I shall. But not now. I'm not sending them to any publication. Thus my mood is now. Perhaps next week, next month, next year, I'll change.

But I'm going to send you some. Not this time though. I've been working so hard and long that I really haven't had time for any completed work, though I've got a bunch of sentences and phrases stacked away for use. And many many new experiences and thoughts. They're all collecting in my mind. Next letter ought to bring you one.

I shall write M.B. shortly.[2] Her book is at the house. I had intended coming down for New Year's, but it wouldn't work. I'll have my friend Cecil take it to her.[3]

---

1. W. E. B. Du Bois, who at the time was editor of the *Crisis*, the organ of the National Association for the Advancement of Colored People (NAACP).
2. Possibly Mary Burrill.
3. It has not been possible to identify several of the people Toomer mentions in this letter. A letter from "Cecil," who is obviously a friend from Washington, exists in the Beinecke archive, however; see Cecil to Toomer, September 29, 1923, Jean Toomer Papers, box 9, folder 286.

And I'll write Adella. That is, I'll soon have something to write her. I'm the last person to write and say nothing.

I would like your song. And I would also like those things from you that are poetry.

I'm off to a lecture.

Jean.

## To Georgia Douglas Johnson[1]
## February 20, 1920

8 East 9th St.,<br>New York, N.Y.

Dear G.D.J.,

The farther I go, the more I develop, every rung of the ladder that I leave behind seems to have clinging to it some person I used to feel in close sympathy with. Not that they have gone back but that my life values seem to be developing at a different ratio from theirs. In spite of the fact that since I came here I've met most modern poets and writers (of N.Y. and not including either Max Eastman or F.D.)[2] and several other interesting people, not one in this city can I call a true friend, that is, one who truly understands me, and I him. And of them all, only two are prospects of anything better. [letter torn here]

. . . one of them, and really expect things from that meeting.

I am not lonesome. There are quite a few who in their good way are friends, but every time I meet and leave them, I feel something lacking. It is distressing. And so I don't see them very often.

These past few months have easily been the biggest of my life. I can't, in a letter, tell the evolutions. I couldn't even if I knew them all. I'm coming down to Washington before so very long, and perhaps I can hint at them then.

I've been expecting that song of yours. And I thought you would send a few lines with your last letter. Won't you?

I enclose a few lines with this. I haven't had time to work them over.

---

1. This letter is very badly damaged. However, what remains gives an interesting insight into Toomer's state of mind in New York at this time.
2. Max Eastman (1883–1969), editor and socialist, had edited the *Masses* from 1912 to its demise due to government suppression in 1917, when he and coeditor Floyd Dell (the "F.D." whom Toomer mentions here) stood trial for offences against the Espionage Act.

142

## To Alain Locke
## December 24, 1920

1341 You St., N.W.,
Washington D.C.

Dear Mr. Locke,

Will you be in town next week? If so, I'd like to drop around and have a chat. I'm free every evening with the exception of Tuesday. So any other you name will suit me.

Best Christmas wishes to you and your mother.

—Jean Toomer.


## To Alain Locke
## January 26, 1921

1341 You St., N.W.,
Washington, D.C.

Dear A.L.L.,

I have managed to hold two meetings of a group (Mary Burrill, Georgia Johnson, Miss Scott (of Howard), Mary Croft, E.C. Williams, Henry Kennedy, and myself) whose central purpose is an historical study of slavery and the Negro, emphasising the great economic and cultural forces which have largely determined them.[1] The aim is twofold, first, to arrive at a sound and just criticism of the actual place and condition of the mixed-blood group in this country, and, second, to formulate an ideal that will be both workable and inclusive.

We need something to cement us. And that something can only spring out of a knowledge, out of certain fundamental facts which we have in common. It is to a lack of such a basis that I largely attribute our failure to get together in the past. The meetings should at least provide material for conversation other than the commonplace and trivial. As a natural outgrowth of them should come the reading of original efforts.

The first group came together a week ago Wednesday. I outlined the purpose of the meetings, and tried my best to throw a little fire in their hearts. Also gave out a few books for study and report. Last night, Miss Scott had prepared "An Historical Sketch of Slavery" by T. R. R. Cobb, while Henry Kennedy covered, and really in a fine

1. Georgia Douglas Johnson; and probably Clarissa Scott [later Scott Delaney], poet, educator and social worker (1901–1927). Edward Christopher Williams (1871–1929) was an educator, translator, dramatist, fiction writer, head librarian at Howard from 1916 on, and author of the recently rediscovered novel *When Washington Was in Vogue* (New York: Amistad, 2003). The novel was originally titled *The Letters of Davy Carr* and appeared serially—and anonymously—in the *Messenger* between January 1925 and June 1926. Williams was also principal of the Dunbar High School when Toomer was a student there. Henry S. Kennedy was a friend of Toomer's from high school, and Toomer would often refer to him as "Ken."

way, the same subject, dug mostly out of Wells.[2] This coming Wednesday I shall take up "Twenty Years of an African Slaver."[3] The subjects may be a trifle elementary for you, but now that we seem to be underway, I certainly would like to have you join us—whenever the time will permit. And if she would enjoy it, bring Mrs. L. by all means. I am trying to begin by eight.

Jean T.

Grandma was with us all last evening.


## To Alain Locke
## November 8, 1921

Box 85,<br>Sparta, Ga.,[1]

Dear A.L.L.,

There is poetry here—and drama, but the atmosphere for one in my position is almost prohibitory. However, I have something on tap that will surprise most people, if not yourself.

I have found, among other things, something that I have long suspected—I am a natural born teacher, take to it in fact with the inevitability of a Kentucky Blue-Grass to the racetrack. Of course I'm clearing hurdles altogether too high here, but I cant help it. I leap, and then look back to see the bewildered expression on my pupils' faces. It is quite interesting, though. Imagine the reaction of these Old Testament (ill) taught children running tangent to ideas of polytheism and diety [sic] evolution in their ancient history lessons! I'd give much to see the real inside workings, and to find out what name they have for me. I pray sometimes, at morning assembly, and I guess that reassures them.

I've learned a lot. Especially from an economic, sociological standpoint. 99% of the people who write and talk about the Negro hardly know his name. Artistically, the field is virgin. I think, however, that for its real exploitation, one would have to come into it under different circumstances.

Any interesting or probable material at Howard?

What things have you on?

My best wishes to Mrs. Locke.

Jean T.

2. *An Inquiry into the Law of Negro Slavery in the United States of America, to Which Is Prefixed, an Historical Sketch of Slavery,* by Thomas R. R. Cobb, appeared in 1858. Toomer probably refers here to H. G. Wells, whose popular *Outline of History* appeared in 1920 (New York: Macmillan).

3. Mayer Brontz (1809–1879) published *Captain Canot; or, Twenty Years of an African Slaver* in 1854 (London: Routledge).

1. In September 1921 Toomer look up a temporary position as the substitute principal of the all-black Sparta Agricultural and Industrial Institute in Sparta, Georgia. He stayed for two months, and Sparta becomes fictionalized as Sempter in *Cane,* providing much of the setting for the southern sections of the collection.

## To Alain Leroy Locke
## November 24, 1921

Box 85,
Atlanta, Ga.,

Dear A.L.L.,

I leave here Friday, both in the interest of the school (raising funds) and for purposes of my own.

Will be in Washington a week or so I think, and then will doubtless push on for New York. There, I am supposed to have several informal lectures arranged for me.

And of course I have material.

Want to see you.

Jean T.

## To Waldo Frank
## March 24, 1922

1341 You Street, N.W.
Washington, D.C.

Dear Waldo Frank,

I have just finished Rahab.[1] I get this far, and it is difficult for me to proceed. Fanny Luve is heroic, more so than any contemporary figure that I know. A spiritual heroism that makes mere physical bravado seem puny and childlike. A sort of ultimate heroism, one that rejects substitutes and narcotics, one that elevates essential Meaning above pain, that volitionally suffers to know Why . . . I do not know a single beautiful woman who would sacrifice her physical loveliness for an attempt to satisfy life as it relates to a fundamental inner need. (There is something fatalistic about Fanny.) Fanny Luve therefore seems to me to be ideal, really ideal, ideal in the sense that she calls forth aspiration.

Rahab is made "of the common stuff of everyday American life." Yes. But how you have spiritualized it! I get a sense of mass movement; a sense of something that is inevitable and permanent. You give horizons; a consciousness of life not simply of the present, but of the past and future, not merely of life as confined and limited by town or race or country, but of life as related to the universe.

Some of your scenes are so vivid that I have carried them with me into those states that just precede dreams. Page 58 and immediately following especially. "O my God how the world veers and plunges . . . what fools not to hold each other." I thank you for: "Her thoughts, her feelings, her pain were petal and stamen and pistil of the full

1. Frank's novel of 1922 (New York: Boni & Liveright).

flower of her realness." "We are no longer prophets . . . save in our lives. Live, Fanny." "And in the anger and the pain, I have understood why the world injures the world." And many others.

Our mental life is composed largely of unuttered thoughts, our emotional life of feelings never expressed. It seems to me that you have done a very wonderful thing in using them as you have done.

I am not quite clear about Samson Brenner. Will you tell me?[2]

In your Our America I missed your not including the Negro.[3] I have often wondered about it. My own life has been about equally divided between the two racial groups. My grandfather, owing to his emphasis upon a fraction of Negro blood in his veins, attained prominence in Reconstruction politics. And the family, for the most part, ever since, has lived between the two worlds, now dipping into the Negro, now into the white. Some few are definitely white: others definitely colored. I alone have stood for a synthesis in the matters of the mind and spirit analogous, perhaps, to the actual fact of at least six blood minglings. The history, traditions, and culture of five of these are available in some approximation to the truth. Of the Negro, what facts are known have too often been perverted for the purposes of propaganda, one way or the other. It has been necessary, therefore, that I spend a disproportionate time in Negro study. Recently, facts and possibilities discovered have lead to an interest mainly artistic and interpretive. Thus a special interest in Lucy and Fanny as she relates to her. No picture of a southern person is complete without its bit of Negro-determined psychology. Your inclusion is true.

As I finished the book, these words came into my mind: I have expressed myself.

If you have thought of me, I guess it has been to wonder in terms of mere survival. Music has gone under, that is, so far as becoming a creative musician is concerned. I simply did not have the money. But phrases and melodies still surge up, not as frequent or as powerful as two years ago. This, perhaps, because I have thrown my energies into writing. I have written any number of poems, several sketches in play form, and one long piece which I call a Play in Three Acts. The poems are largely impersonal, and have no relation to any definite segment of life. The sketches are attempts at an artistic record of Negro and mixed-blood America. Whatever their merits, this much is certain: they reveal an impulse to self-expression that is maturing, growing. Despite the inhibitions of Washington, despite my absolute lack of anything like creative friendship it is growing. Almost the first, and surely the last real talk was the one I had with you in Central

2. Fanny Luve and Samson Brenner are both characters in *Rahab*.
3. Frank's book of cultural criticism, 1919. In the chapter titled "The Land of Buried Cultures," he noted that there was a need to study "the cultures of the German, the Latin, the Celt, the Slav, the Anglo-Saxon and the African on the American continent: [to] plot their reactions one upon the other, and their disappearance as integral worlds in the vast puddling of our pioneering life. I have no space and no knowledge for so huge a picture." *Our America* (New York: Boni and Liveright, 1919), 97.

Park.[4] Such spiritual asceticism develops a strength whose reverse face is marked with sterility. I am reaching out. I have to. I wonder if you wouldnt like to read a few of my things?

Jean Toomer

## Waldo Frank to Jean Toomer
## April 25, 1922

Dear Jean,

### Natalie Mann

My first impression is that the central drama of Natalie, Merilh, Mertis, Law, etc is smothered by the form of the other stuff . . . the teaparties, the talk of the incidental. Then it occurs to me that the trouble is not with the density and amount of this milieu but with the deadness of the texture. If all this were living, the drama would live in it in its correct relation. The thing, therefore, needs rewriting rather than reconstructing. The life is not permeated into the whole thing. In individual scenes, there is a very beautiful colorful glow of life . . . as the lovescene of Natalie and Merilh, the two cabaret scenes . . . the gorgeous symbolism of the dance with Etty, and the lovely poem that M recites in N Y.

What is clear is: that you have a vision . . mothered and fathered of true temperament, pass on, intellectually well-midwifed . . . the start of a true Form, but that the Form is not yet there. Hence the texture drops out of your conception, becomes weak discussive talk. Your whole aim is so new, that the work of formulation must needs be absolutely independent: and to create Form out of chaos, as must all true american artists, takes time time time. Dont lose heart. You are one of the very very, pathetically rare, *real*.

### Kabnis

Here the texture is superb, but there is a sacrifice in the bone-structure. You have not yet the strength of pervasion of your own inspiration to give birth to a large form in which bone and stuff stand one and whole. Any bit of this thing is glowing and real, but as a whole it droops and loses its taut sustainedness. I wonder if you would not have done better in a freer form of narrative, in which your dialog, which has no kinship with the theatric, might have

---

4. Toomer refers here to his first meeting with Frank, in 1920. After seeing him at a party at Lola Ridge's, Toomer met him accidentally the next week in Central Park, when they became acquainted. See Scruggs and VanDemarr, *Jean Toomer and the Terrors of American History*, 61–62, and Cynthia Earl Kerman and Richard Eldridge, *The lives of Jean Toomer: A Hunger for Wholeness* (Baton Rouge: Louisiana State UP, 1987), 72–73.

thrived more successfully. I felt that the speech of the Ancient at the end was a sudden drop into particulars failing to take along and light with itself the general atmosphere you had built about his relationship with Kabnis. And Kabnis in the only partly formulated organism of the whole never altogether transcends inorganic life . . . But here too I feel that there is no true saying for you, save work and fidelity to the wondrously pure vision in you, and the *knowing* that if you nourish it with the best of yourself, like the mystery of all life, you will achieve your form. You have already left far behind you the imitative stage, the stage of acceptance of even the best near to you. You are already on your *own*. You are in that stage most difficult to navigate through when, being ahead of yourself you are temporarily in chaos . . . have left home planets and not reached your individual star. In this stage, only the deeply intuitive person can sense where your true form is hardening out of the mists. You have left behind the monkey crowd who, thinking they can appreciate literature, really love only its stinking afterbirths . . . and you have not quite reached that ultimate where you know you are wholly articulately organically yourself. Kabnis has in it the embryon of an expression which America has not had even the faintest inkling of, and which America demands if it is to become a real part of the human adventure. Color, spiritual penetration, counter-point of human wills, the intuition that they are harmmonics of a Unit, the power to convey line and volume in words, intellectual cleansing-capacity . . . all here, but not yet fused into the final art. By which I mean that the thing lies in the retrospective mind in its parts, in its details and that in the reading the mind does not catch on to a uniformly moving Life that conveys it whole to the end, but rather steps from piece to piece as if adventuring through the pieces of a still unorganized mosaic. Kabnis is however very near to its state of fusing. It makes me believe that you are extremely close to your true beginning in this deeply individual genre. Natalie, a more complex organism is a bit farther off.

### Poems

Naturally there are more perfect things among these shorter less organic creations. But although you are a poet, I dont think you'll find your final satisfaction in the mere direct lyric. Something in the way of a free woven narrative that includes the song of Nathan Merilh and gives the texture of the world he springs from will include you all.

Some of the poems are quite perfect. Seventh Street, Becky, Avey, (Daniel less so), Carma are lovely transcripts of a world old in America but new in American expression. The poems Cockswain, Beehive, Evening Song. Marble Faces are another depth . . . more metaphysical and yet well pictorialized here. Some of the things are

mere statement, not fleshed not living . . . like The First American.
Some, like Kivalt, are notes for yourself in a rich sensuous garb but
still notes that are true in their potential rather than in their
kinetic energy.

ON THE WHOLE, my dear Jean Toomer, I am enormously
inpressed by the power and fulness and fineness of your Say. . . . A
man whose spirit is like yours so high and straight a flame does not
need to be told that he has enormous gift, and that this means a
responsibility beyond the ken and the rules of the masses . . . nor
does he need anything one who feels himself his brother and knows
that such things need no direct articulation, can send him in a letter. Yet, corroboration from anybody helps. You must go on. You
must by whatever ruthless means which will not hurt your spirit,
preserve for yourself the freedom, the quiet and the peace in which
the spirit may turmoil and seethe and ecstacy to birth.

O if there is one thing I have learned, living in America, knowing
my own life and knowing the lives of the many many about me, it is
that the artist must have the greater wisdom of fighting for himself,
of knowing that only so can the time come when the American
world will be a place in which he can live. Today, every rhythm,
every will sent through the weave of America is fatal to creation . . .
and so often not alone economic pressure but the subly insidious
Myth of 'the duties of manhood, the need of making ones own way'
plunges the delicate artist tissues into a corrodent poisonous bath
of American 'reality' which eats them up. Dont think that you will
be helping yourself or America in a newspaper office or an advertising agency. If you can keep away, do! Keep to the streets, keep to
the quiet of your room . . . let that flame burn up clear. And remember that the world which will swallow you, annihilate you today if
you take its word and its thought in that very act will be rebuking
you who should know not only yourself better, but it better also . . .
who should know that you must as a part of it prevail against it and
so function for it.

When I look about me at the marketplace, I feel that so stinking
has become the rottenness, so prostrate are all the organs whereby
man has stood up proudly through the ages, that we are doubtless
very close to the new spring and the new seedlings. The so-called
literary and artistic milieus are indeed strewn with excrement and
decay . . . but so are the fallow fields.

Keep yourself warm underneath, in the soil, where the throb is . . .
and use every decent means in your reach to protect yourself from a
too early pushing to the surface.

your friend and brother

W. W. Frank

# To Waldo Frank
## April 26, 1922

1341 You Street, N.W.,
Washington D.C.

Dear Waldo Frank,

I am ahead of myself. That sums it up. "Natalie Mann" is three dramas, Natalie and Nathan, Mertis and Law, and Mary Carson.[1] I know them. My need of expressing them jumbled them into one, and my immaturity passed muster on them. Merilh, of course, is mostly myself. Natalie, except for an actual physical and potential spiritual basis, (in 1915 I loved a Natalie; she has dissipated herself) is imaginative.[2] Therman Law is the reflection of a man whose tragic life I have only vaguely foreshadowed. Likewise Mertis. The Mary Carson of actual life is easily the most compelling of them all. She has done a bust of me (I'll enclose a picture if I can find one).[3] Nothing short of maturity on my part will do her justice . . . To serve Natalie and Merilh I had to emasculate the others. And I was somewhat conscious of my process. No wonder much of the texture lacks life! On my next strongly creative impulse I think I'll tackle Mertis and Law. From the scenes you like I get this criticism for myself: whenever I strongly feel, when I feel that I, Jean Toomer, am creating this, I tend to achieve organic life. I felt that love scene. The cabarets were dominated by myself. The dance with Etty was Me. Yes, I feel that my form is slowly crystallizing. I know that it will take time. I am patient (two years without a let-up in Washington!) but I do get restless, and a little weary sometimes when I am not writing. Washington supplies me crude material, better perhaps than any other city could—in other ways my thirst for life is literally starved. Yet starving itself yields its residue of fortitude and strength. I believe that a true artist can compel from any environment sufficient life to keep him going. I have mastered Washington at least to that extent.

Kabnis sprang up almost in a day, it now seems to me. It is the direct result of a trip I made down into Georgia this past fall. That trip (my actual experience down there will interest you. I barely avoided a serious time) by the way, is more or less responsible for most of my stuff that you like. There, for the first time I really saw the Negro, not as a pseudo-urbanized and vulgarized, a semi-Americanized product, but the Negro peasant, strong with the tang of fields and

1. *Natalie Mann* was first published in *The Wayward and the Seeking: A Collection of Writings by Jean Toomer,* ed. Darwin T. Turner (Washington, DC: Howard UP, 1980), 243–325.
2. Possibly Phyllis Terrell. See Kerman and Eldridge, 64.
3. This bust was by May Howard Johnson, a Philadelphia-born sculptor who later taught at Howard.

soil. It was there that I first heard the folk-songs rolling up the valley at twilight, heard them as spontaneous and native utterances. They filled me with gold, and tints of an eternal purple. Love? Man they gave birth to a whole new life . . . I am certain that I would get more inner satisfaction from a free narrative form. That doubtless would have been my form but for the fact that certain scenes, as I visualized them on the stage, just simply would not be denied. When I say, "Kabnis," nothing inside of me says "complete, finished." By this I know that I shall go over it . . . Those Ancients have a peculiar attraction for me. I am very apt to let them say too much.

Almost a month ago I sent the Dial "Becky." It is the first thing I have sent them in quite a while (Marble Faces, about a year ago).[4] They are usually pretty prompt in returns; they are considering it. The Liberator has had Carma for two months. I would say that it was accepted were it not for the fact that last year I sent them a review of Eunice Tietjen's "Jake" which they kept for over a month, and rejected. I shall send something to Broom.[5] I do not know it; I do know the calibre of Lola Ridge.

What shall I say to you, dear friend? You have definitely linked me to the purpose and vision of what is best in creative America. You have touched me, you have held me; you have released me to myself. You have brought solidarity and comradeship within handshake, within love, of the eternal solitude . . .

I have a great desire that you know me, first hand, in relation to this environment. My own immediate background is crumbling rapidly. Grandfather died this past December. Grandmother is 76, and, while her spirit seems glowing brighter than ever, I do not think that her body will hold out so very long.[6] With her passing will go direct contact with America, with New Orleans, before the Civil War, during it, and during Reconstruction. Particularly, the link that holds me to the family will have snapped. Of the environment generally, the old families that rose to prominence after the Civil War are passing. Others, commercialized and socially climbing, are taking their place. The actual Mary Carson is fading. I would like you to get a glimpse at least before it all fades out. Washington, despite its stupidity, is lovely at this time of year. Like a fresh young girl, it is a physical loveliness. Restful, soothing. Could

---

4. No record of this poem exists. The Dial rejected "Becky" on May 8, 1922.
5. Broom (November 1921–January 1924) was created by Harold Loeb, with Alfred Kreymbourg as editor: it had editorial offices in Rome, where the cheapness of production allowed its lavish and beautiful design, and also its cover price of fifty cents an issue. It later moved to Berlin, and then to New York under the editorship of Matthew Josephson. It was distinguished by an international scope, and it often published artwork by European avant-garde painters as well as work by writers such as Jean Cocteau and Luigi Pirandello; the majority of its content remained American, however, and featured Amy Lowell, Ezra Pound, Robert Frost, Malcolm Cowley, Gertrude Stein, Hart Crane, Gorham Munson, Jean Toomer, Lola Ridge, William Carlos Williams, E. E. Cummings, and John Dos Passos.
6. She would die in 1928.

you come down? for a few days? Three of us (one of my uncles is with us) live here in a five room apartment. There is an extra room with a small bed—not particularly inviting, somewhat stuffy, but serviceable. Meals are irregular, but the food is good: I am chief cook! My uncle is out most of the time, and grandma sits in her front room. There are no customs or traditions to interfere with one's habits or one's solitude. As we are "camping out" and have been doing so for some years past, I shall not take it amiss if, after the first night's lodging you without more ado remove yourself to the nearest hotel. But as I get along fairly well, I imagine that you can stand it,—for a while at least. If you can spare the time away from New York, I think that you will find the excursion worth your while. As there are no preparations to be made, come any time. For me— well, you know just at this time what it would mean to me.

The MS came this morning,

Jean

I have enclosed a picture. What she has included and what she has omitted are very characteristic.

## To Waldo Frank
## August 21, 1922

1341 You Street, N.W.
Washington, D.C.

Dear Waldo,

dear brother, I have a phrase: You've got the stuff. It means everything *real* thats desirable. Well, you've got it.

All right, I'll take the advance.[1] That paper hasnt come from New Orleans as yet. But two nights ago I met an old friend of my grand-fathers, a man with a bit of influence in New Orleans. I told him the position that we are in. He has promised to do all he can as soon as he arrives in that city (which should be this coming Wednesday). The copy ought to be in our hands a week from Wed. But even this wont give the Commissioner of Pension time to pass on the case by Sept. 1st. But as soon as the money comes in, grandma will let me have it, and I'll forward it directly to you.

We should be able to get away the day after you arrive. I've writ-ten a man in South Carolina who indirectly knows of me.[2] Also there is a dentist here (away for a few days now on his vacation) who comes from a small town outside of Columbia, S.C.[3] Between the

1. Frank had offered to loan Toomer the money to cover the expenses of their trip south. See Frank to Toomer, n.d., Jean Toomer Papers, box 3, folder 83.
2. Toomer references R. S. Wilkerson, president of the Colored Normal Industrial Agri-cultural and Mechanical College of South Carolina at Orangeburg.
3. Possibly Moses Ehrlich.

two of them, I should locate a desirable place. But if they fail me, we'll just strike out. I don't see how we can miss it.

We'll be together. I'll explain conditions when you arrive.

Have you ever been in a Negro church? Not the white-washed article of respectable colored folks; but the shanty of the peasant Negro. God, but they *feel* the thing. Sometimes too violently for sensitive nerves; always sincerely, powerfully, deeply. And when they overflow in song, there is no singing that has so touched me. Their theology is a farce (Christ is so immediate): their religious emotion, elemental, and for that reason, very near the sublime.

love<br>Jean

Will you have a copy of City Block when you come?

## To John McClure
## July 22, 1922

1341 You Street, N.W.,<br>Washington, D.C.

Dear John McClure

that was a fine letter from you. Very fine. It sets one more solid pillar beneath me. I managed to get away to Harpers Ferry for two weeks. Most of my mail was forwarded. Yours, however, I just received a day or so ago.

I am sending a batch of Mss, and hope that a few at least will meet your needs. I have more on hand, of course, but those sent are among the ones which I will include in my book. If things go well it should come out sometime this coming Spring. I think that I shall call it CANE. Having as sub-heads Cane Stalks and Chorouses [sic] (Karintha, Fern etc. and two longer pieces) Leaves (poems), and Leaf Traciers [sic] in Washington, under which I shall group such things as "For M.W.," and other sharp, brief vignettes of which I have any number. I do not wish to force myself, and havent. But I feel that a precipitant is urgently needed just at this time. The concentrated force of a volume will do a great deal more than isolated pieces possibly could. And then, of course, more than anything else, I have the *impulse* to its creation. After all, whatever my mind says, I can only go things when I have a deep "feel" for them.

I do conceive of literature as an art. It is innate in me. The other sort of stuff I cannot write, as easy as many of my friends think it should be for me. They are a world apart, like the third is to the second dimension. I want to live the greater measure of the strictly human passions. When I use words I wish to create those things which can only come to life in them. I am violated to think of literature as nothing more than a vicarious experience of what one should be strong enough to wring from the social life. A simple rustic lyric has the power to touch me; but I do not confuse it with art. Life, human life, we must use, but its use must be accompanied by a dimensional transformation. I do not think it good, though, for an artist to aestheticize too much. To do so leads to sterility and absurdity. Of my writer friends (other than those you already know) only one has possibilities in the way you speak of. And she manifests them more in an appreciation of my stuff than in anything she has done. She has an undoubted instinct for good words and lines. I am certain that in her best moments she experiences a very genuine aesthetic emotion. But her faculty of expression is not up to her sensibilities. Nor is she sufficiently conscious. I do not think she ever will be. The inhibitions and taboos and life-limitations she labors under make even her modest achievement remarkable. I speak of Georgia Douglas Johnson of this city. I hear most of her best things. If at any time she attains your standard, I shall suggest that she send it to you. And I shall be increasingly awake for other efforts.

Thanks for the July number.

I too feel, in a very sincere way, that the Double Dealer cannot afford to hazard its existence for any single contributor. Whatever the momentary disappointment, any genuine artist in the long run will profit by your policy.[1]

Fraternally, Jean Toomer.

## To Claude McKay
## July 23, 1922

1341 You Street, N.W.,
Washington, D.C.

Dear Brother,

after the strange manner of such things, your book; forwarded to the Ferry, reached there the very evening that I left.[1] I had hoped that I might read it there . . . I notice that The Easter Flower is the first poem. It is quite perfect. Something wonderfully strong and beautiful burns within you. The sweet freshness, the fragrance of Spanish Needle. The power and surge of Enslaved. And the words you use as if you had just discovered them! But I must work deeper before I am betrayed into the commonplaces of appreciation.

1. Toomer refers here to McClure's fear that his subscription list would react harshly to some of the racial politics in Toomer's manuscript were he to print them in the *Double Dealer*.
1. McKay's book of poems *Harlem Shadows* (New York: Harcourt, Brace & Co., 1922), which contains the works Toomer mentions in this letter.

You did place me in high company. I love them in season and out, and so, felt perfectly at home.[2]

Yesterday I sent a bunch of Mss direct to the Liberator office. I hope that you will like them and be able to use one or two at least.

I want to see you. Perhaps I shall be able to make it before you get away. Russia must be very stimulating just about now.[3] But somehow I do not envy you your trip. The Experiment here in America has an almost complete hold upon my interests and imagination. Were it not that I am broadly curious and sympathetic I should be in danger of falling into provincialism. The strange turns of life even here in Washington (which is usually rated as an unspeakably dull place), the tragic consequences of spiritual abortion, the complacency, the warmth and color and waywardness—I love them all. I love this southland of my ancestors. In New York I have been nostalgic for the streets and faces of Washington. In Paris or Moscow I think that I would be the same. And my work, I guess, is progressing as good as it could in any other place. Besides, while at the Ferry I fell in love . . .

That is a great place, that Ferry. Its hill and rivers were the scenes of two youthful love affairs. This time, as night came on, its dusk blended with a face whose eyes held more love than any I have ever seen. I'll tell you, brother, the South means love. It has always happened so. Its lies and prejudices are dirty. Well, I'll eat the dirt provided that the life be sufficiently sweet.

Come down, if you can, before you go away.

Jean.

## To the Editors of the *Liberator*
## August 19, 1922

1341 You Street, N.W.,
Washington, D.C.

Dear Friends,

Whenever the desire to know something about myself comes from a sincere source, I am always glad to meet it. For in telling other folks I invariably tell my own self something. My family is from the South. My mother's father, P. B. S. Pinchback, born in Macon, Georgia, left home as a boy and worked on the Mississippi River steamers. At the beginning of the Civil War he organized and

2. McKay, confused by Toomer's first name, had thought him to be a woman. See McKay to Toomer, July 11, 1922, Jean Toomer Papers, box 4, folder 145.
3. McKay spent a year in Russia and spoke at the Fourth Congress of the Communist International. He became a minor celebrity there as a figurehead for oppressed African peoples—as he said, he was treated like a "black ikon in the flesh" ("The Magic Pilgrimage," in *A Long Way from Home* (London: Pluto P, 1985), 168). "The Magic Pilgrimage" contains his account of this experience.

was commissioned captain of a Negro company in New Orleans. Later, in the days of Reconstruction, he utilized the Negro's vote and won offices for himself, the highest being that of lieutenant, and then acting governor of Louisiana. When his heyday was over, he left the old hunting grounds and came to Washington. Here, I was born. My own father likewise came from Middle Georgia. Racially, I seem to have (who knows for sure) seven blood mixtures: French, Dutch, Welsh, Negro, German, Jewish, and Indian. Because of these, my position in America has been a curious one. I have lived equally amid the two race groups. Now white, now colored. From my own point of view I am naturally and inevitably an American. I have striven for a spiritual fusion analogous to the fact of racial intermingling. Without denying a single element in me, with no desire to subdue, one to the other, I have sought to let them function as complements. I have tried to let them live in Harmony. Within the last two or three years, however, my growing need for artistic expression has pulled me deeper and deeper into the Negro group. And as my powers of receptivity increased, I found myself loving it in a way that I could never love the other. It has stimulated and fertilized whatever creative talent I may contain within me. A visit to Georgia last fall was the starting point of almost everything of worth that I have done. I heard folk-songs come from the lips of Negro peasants. I saw the rich dusk beauty that I had heard many false accents about, and of which, till then, I was somewhat skeptical. And a deep part of my nature, a part that I had repressed, sprang suddenly to life and responded to them. Now, I can not conceive of myself as aloof and separated. My point of view has not changed; it has deepened, it has widened. Personally, my life has been torturous and dispersed. The comparative wealth which my family once had, has how dwindled away to almost nothing. We, or rather, they, are in the unhappy position of the lowered middle-class. There seem to have been no shopkeepers or shysters among us. I have lived by turn in Washington, New York, Chicago, Sparta, Georgia, and several smaller towns. I have worked, it seems to me at everything: selling papers, delivery boy, soda clerk, salesman, ship-yard worker, librarian-assistant, physical director, school teacher, grocery clerk, and God knows what all. Neither the universities of Wisconsin or New York gave me what I wanted, so I quit them. Just how I finally found my stride in writing, is difficult to lay hold of. It has been pushing through for the past four years. For two years, now, I have been in solitude here in Washington. It may be begging hunger to say that I am staking my living on my work. So be it. The mould is cast, and I cannot turn back even if I would.

If this brief sketch leaves unsaid anything that you are especially interested in, tell me, and I'll give you all I know.

Its all right about the pay. If the Liberator can keep going, that fact will compensate me.

Glad you liked those two pieces, and are going to use them. What about "Georgia Dusk"? Didnt I send it in with the large batch? I thought I did. And "Becky" and "Tell Me"? Those two I remember sending separately, and later. If you have them, and are considering them—all right. I just want to know.

Best wishes, always.

Jean Toomer

## To Alain Locke
## October 1, 1922

1341 You Street, N.W.
Washington, D.C.

Dear A L

I've got to get to New York for a season. My stuff is hanging. I havent done a thing since Spring. I have no money, so I must raise it; from five hundred to a thousand. Payment is uncertain, though I should be able to meet the notes in from three to five years. I've been thinking of Mrs Elbert.[1] You know her. What do you think of my writing her? Mrs Elbert occurs to me because the proposition would hardly appeal to one from a purely business point of view. Vision, and a literary interest are necessary. She fits the bill better than any other I can call to mind.

I'm working at the Howard now; assistant manager. And my hours are long. From 10AM to 11PM. But if you can find a moment or two, I'll manage to come around to see you.

Have you seen the DOUBLE DEALER and the LIBERATOR for Sept? Both have two pieces of mine.

## To Gorham B. Munson
## October 31, 1922

1341 You Street, N.W.,
Washington, D.C.,
31 Oct 1922

Dear Gorham B Munson,

Your letter came this morning. It stimulates. It contains just what I want: criticism that rubs me against myself; opinions, appreciations, interests, whose inherent fuel sets me going; thoughts that I value to the extent that I must test myself against them; and a general tone which makes me desire that my creations be intelligible to

1. I have been unable to find any biographical information on Ella H. Elbert. [Whalan's note]

other people. (My position here has been such that I unconsciously discount or ignore the reader.)

Theatre [sic] sprang to life a few weeks back when I was helping to manage the Howard. For a week or so my job kept me from writing it. The minute I was released, I brought it out. The piece was written in a single day. When the last word was down, something within me said FINIS, so I knew that any rewriting or elaboration would have to come at a later day. I was conscious, however, of a questionable brevity, a possibility of misunderstanding, and of Waldo Frank. But I wanted to touch you, so I sent it on.

I cannot *will* out of Waldo. With the exception of Sherwood Anderson some years ago (and to a less extent, Frost and Sandburg) Waldo is the only modern writer who has immediately influenced me. He is so powerful and close, he has so many elements that I need, that I would be afraid of downright imitation if I were not so sure of myself. But I know my own rhythm (it has come out fairly pure in a formative way, in some of my southern sketches. It is when I attempt a more essentialized and complex pattern that Waldo comes in.) and I feel with you that I will "eventually make a successful amalgamation with (my) own special contribution." I must *grow* out of him.

The general design of Theatre [sic] you certainly get. (I have made that clear.) And you see and [sic] John and Dorris until "the theatre flings off into chaos." Perhaps you still follow them as I meant that you should, perhaps I have failed to make my meaning clear. Perhaps I dont [sic] quite get your criticism. I dont [sic] know. I'll tell you what I'm driving at: there is a barrier between John and Dorris (from her point of view) not of race, but of respectability. Stage-folk are not respectable; audiences are. Dorris' pride and passion break through the stage attitude (which is voiced by Mame) and she uses the only art at her command: dancing, to win him. John's mind discounts Dorris, first, because he knows that she cannot satisfy him, second, for the reason that he is aware of the way in which this particular set of show girls look upon him: that he is dictie (respectable) and stuck up, and will have nothing to do with them. Dorris' dancing, however, pulls his passion from him to it. Dorris and John unite in a sort of incorporeal animalistic ecstasy. Dorris feels this union, and naturally expects John to be moved to action by it, to clap, to come up on the stage, to make love to her, at least to make a date with her. Instead, John rebounds from the actuality of Dorris, from the reality of his own passion, into a dream. (The part inclosed in * * * [Toomer's asterisks] is dream.) In this, he gives her an impossible beauty, and achieves an impossible contact. He is startled from his fancy by the bumper chord which is the actual end of Dorris' dancing. It is evident that he will never do more than dream of her. Dorris, on her part, failing to find in John's face the desire she had calculated on, and being incapable of seeing him except in terms of the two alternatives, concludes that what Mame said was right.

The humiliation of having failed, drives her into her dressing-room. The implication of the story is that of a dual separation: one, false and altogether arbitrary, the other, inherent in the nature of the two beings. This coincides loosely with a conception I have of the theatre, and of art in general, in its relation to life. (One side of the conception only, of course.)

In terms of this outline, would you say that Dorris experiences the crescendo? She does, of course, physically. But John's curve starts with intellection, swings down to passion in Dorris, and sweeps upward into dream. Except for physical motion, Dorris is largely inarticulate. This motion should be felt as an undercurrent all through the dream. As I reread my work, I see that I have failed in this. I have interposed some stuff that not only disolves [sic] her [im?]pulses, but throws the reader off the track. Dorris dances (I can say no more about her for her mind is simply a lush glow) John dreams. They both come to themselves at the same time. By statement in Dorris' case, by implication in John's, they both know their separateness. Because of his consciousness, and because of the actual range of his experience, John seems to me to be the logical one to emphasize. If you still see it in terms of Dorris, please tell me, for your thoughts will greatly help.

I'm particularly glad you liked "Stage-lights, soft, etc." and the autumn leaves figure, for in these I experienced immediate satisfaction. The sort of thing that accompanies image, that accompanies *expression*.

Your sentence that begins "I would urge crystallizing and crystallizing" strikes me as an usually [sic] fine piece of thinking. Mystery cannot help but accompany a deep, clear-cut image. Conscious mystery, like conscious profundity, is false and cheap. The great elements in literature are inherent in its designs, and cannot be willed or tacked on. In my reflective moments I desire the profound image saturated in its own lyricism. When I write, my imperfections have a way of closing the eyes of my ideal.

I am trying to get to New York. But the people to whom I have written asking for an advance of money have no precedent along this line—it is a slow business. Things have usually come my way, however, and I guess I'll be up that way before so very long. I want to talk to you. Your clarity, your horizons, your interest, will do much for me. And for my own part, I shall not come to you with empty hands.

John McClure wrote for something for Nov Double Dealer. As I have not heard from him, I'm expecting something to come out.

Thanks for SECESSION. And I'll send in the first piece I write which I think measures up to you.

# To Sherwood Anderson
## December 18, 1922

*1341 You Street, N.W.,*
*Washington, D.C.,*
*18 Dec 1922*

Dear Sherwood Anderson,

Just before I went down to Georgia I read Winesburg, Ohio. And while there, living in a cabin whose floorboards permitted the soil to come up between them, listening to the old folk melodies that Negro women sang at sun-down, The Triumph of the Egg came to me. The beauty, and the full sense of life that these books contain are natural elements, like the rain and sunshine, of my own sprouting. My seed was planted in the cane- and cotton-fields, and in the souls of black and white people in the small southern town. My seed was planted in *myself* down there. Roots have grown and strengthened. They have extended out. I spring up in Washington. Winesburg, Ohio, and The Triumph of the Egg are elements of my growing. It is hard to think of myself as maturing without them.

Ther [sic] is a golden strength about your art that can come from nothing less than a creative elevation of experience, however bitter or abortive the experience may have been. Your images are clean, glowing, healthy, vibrant: sunlight on forks of trees, on mellow piles of pine boards. Your acute sense of the separateness of life could easily have led to a lean pessimism in a less abundant soul. Your Yea! to life is one of the clear fine tones in our medley of harsh discordant founds. Life is measured by your own glowing, and you find life, you find its possibilities deeply hopeful and beautiful. It seems to me that art in our day, other than in its purely aesthetic phase, has a sort of religious function. It is a religion, a spiritualization of the immediate. And ever since I first touched you, I have thought of you in this connection. I let a friend of mine, a young fellow with no literary training but who is sensitive and has had a deep experience of life, read Out of Nowhere into Nothing when it first appeared in Dial. After having finished it he came back to me with face glowing, and said, "When any man can write like that, something wonderful is going to happen." I think that there is. I think that you touch most people that way. And when my own stuff wins a response from you, I feel a linking together within me, a deep joy, and an outward flowing.

Yesterday a letter came from John McClure in which he told me of your stopping past the Double Dealer office, of your reading the things of mine he had on hand. McClure was the real thing, at the *right* time. The impetus I received from him, and from the Double Dealer, has been wonderfully helpful to me. Dec Double Dealer has just come. It features Harvest Song. Good!

Naturally, my impulse was to write you when I first received your note. But at that time I was re-typing my stuff, writing three new pieces, and putting Cane (my book) together. I felt too dry to write. Now, the sap has again started flowing . . . [sic]

I am following Many Marriages with deep interest.

Wont [sic] you write and tell me more in detail how my stuff strikes you? And at first opportunity I would certainly like to have a talk with you.

## To Sherwood Anderson
## December 29, 1922

1341 You Street, N.W.,
Washington, D.C.

Dear Sherwood Anderson,

In your work I have felt you reaching for the beauty that the Negro has in him. As you say, you wanted to write not of the Negro but out of him. "Well I wasnt one. The thing I felt couldnt be truly done."[1] I guess you're right. But this much is certain: an emotional element, a richness from him, from yourself, you have artistically woven into your own material. Notably, in Out of Nowhere into Nothing. Here your Negro, from the stand point of superficial reality, of averages, of surface plausibility, is unreal. My friends who are interested in the "progress" of the Negro would take violent exception to such a statement as, "By educating himself he had cut himself off from his own people."[2] And from a strictly social point of view, much that they would say would be true enough. But in these pages you have evoked an emotion, a sense of beauty that is easily more Negro than almost anything I have seen. And I am glad to admit my own indebtedness to you in this connection.

The Negro's curious position in this western civilization invariably forces him into one or the other of two extremes: either he denies Negro entirely (as much as he can) and seeks approximation to an Anglo-Saxon (white) ideal, or, as in the case of your London acquaintance, he overemphasizes what is Negro. Both of these attitudes have their source in a feeling of (a desire not to feel) inferiority. I refer here, of course, to those whose consciousness and condition make them keenly aware of white dominance. The mass of Negroes, the peasants, like the mass of Russians or Jews or Irish or what not, are too instinctive to be anything but themselves. Here and there one finds a high type Negro who shares this virtue with his more primitive brothers. As you can imagine, the resistance against my stuff is marked, excessive. But I feel that in time, in its

---

1. Toomer quotes from Anderson's December 22 letter here. Jean Toomer Papers, box 1, folder 5.
2. Toomer quotes from "Out of Nowhere into Nothing" here.

social phase, my art will aid in giving the Negro to himself. In this connection, I have thought of a magazine. A magazine, American, but concentrating on the significant contributions, or possible contributions of the Negro to the western world. A magazine that would consciously hoist, and perhaps at first a trifle over emphasize a negroid ideal. A magazine that would function organically for what I feel to be the budding of the Negro's consciousness. The need is great. People within the race cannot see it. In fact, they are likely to prove to be directly hostile. But with the youth of the race, unguided or misguided as they now are, there is a tragic need. Talent dissipates itself for want of creative channels of expression, and encouragement. My own means are slim, almost nothing. I have had and am still having a hard pull of it. But as I write these lines there are two young people whom I am barely keeping above surface by the faith and love I have for them. I would deeply appreciate your thoughts in relation [to] this matter.

My book. Here's how the matter stands. Waldo Frank, whom I met three years ago in New York, has already taken it to Horace Liveright. Liveright has not as yet passed on it. And Waldo is writing the introduction. But as soon as I have definite information, I'll let you know. And I shall always treasure your offer of service at this time.[3]

Do you ever come down this way? For Negro life, its varying shades, its varying phases of consciousness and development there is no better place. I would be glad to share with you whatever I possess.

## To Waldo Frank[1]
## December 1922

My brother,
What does Liveright say?[2] Spring is the *right* time. I feel that it is. And all my calculations tell me so. Since last writing you, I've written a new piece, and have rewritten Theatre. Only one sketch more, and Cane will be ready. The design for this is clear in my mind. Another week like the two just past will see it finished. If pushed, there's no reason why Cane cant be sent to you by the first of next week. All I have to do is to double type certain of the things. And then, when Box Seat (thats the title of the piece I have still to write) is ready, I can send it on, for you to insert where I indicate. Of course I'd rather send the thing complete, but if there's need of rush . . .

3. On learning that Toomer was preparing a book, Anderson had offered to write an introduction and also to help him find a publisher.
1. This letter is dated from Toomer having received his first letter from Sherwood Anderson. Anderson's letter to Toomer was undated, but in Toomer's first response—December 18—he apologizes for not replying immediately. See Jean Toomer Papers, box 1, folder 5.
2. In *Jean Toomer and the Terrors of American History* (107), Scruggs and VanDemarr suggest that Frank had discussed the possibility of publishing *Cane* with Horace Liveright, the editor of Boni and Liveright—who had published most of Frank's books to date—in November or December of 1922. *Cane* was accepted after Christmas of that year.

I sent Kabnis to Lola Ridge. Except to tell me that my name is on the advanced ad for January, I havent heard from her. Wonder what she thinks . . .

Got a note from Sherwood Anderson. Says Nora hit a note he's long been wanting to hear. "More power to your elbow," says he. Yea. Yea!

I can manage another season in Washington. In fact I'm going good. All I want (and by God this is necessary) is that I don't have to spend the summer here. God, last summer! . . .

Word at last from Mrs. Elbert.[3] "Business is depressed." Father of Commerce, all powerful, unto thee we offer up our prayers. Amen. Amen, church members!

Finished Unwelcome Man: Spiritually formative in that it hasnt got the glow of you. In that your soul is beneath your mind, beneath your hurt. In that the fullness of you does not transfigure it. Life too mathematical. Analysis too sharp and brilliant: absorbs emotion. Mentally gripped, sustained, stronger as it goes on. Gives a wonderful consciousness. You are there—submerged. Here and there direct creation: pages 52–54, 299–301, 361–369. Julia Deering. Quincy in his relation to the House, to New York. Quincy at Christmas. Quincy especially towards the end.

It was a little slow going at first. I guess you were too mature and too close to your maturity to take a creative interest in childhood. Or something like that. But a deeply dimensioned world springs in to being with the first budding of Quincy's consciousness. The end held me. New Year's Eve, especially. Quincy's struggle, his strength and weakness, his inability to give himself, are real.

More later . . .

The essay comes along, but I've got to get Cane planted, and sink deep into you before it can come off.

love . . .
Jean.

## To Waldo Frank
## December 12, 1922

Washington DC

My brother!

CANE is on its way to you!

For two weeks I have worked steadily at it. The book is done. From three angles, CANE's design is a circle. Aesthetically, from simple forms to complex ones, and back to simple forms. Regionally, from the South up into the North, and back into the South again. Or, from the North down into the South, and then a return North. From the point of view of the spiritual entity behind the work, the curve really

3. Ella H. Elbert had sent Toomer her reply November 24. See Elbert to Toomer, Jean Toomer Papers, box 3, folder 76.

starts with Bona and Paul (awakening), plunges into Kabnis, emerges in Karintha etc. swings upward into Theatre and Box Seat, and ends (pauses) in Harvest Song.

Whew!

•  •  •

You will understand the inscriptions, brother mine: the book to grandma; Kabnis, the spirit and the soil, to you.

I believe that before the work comes out, Little Review, Dial, and Secession will have accepted certain of its pieces. The ones I mention are the certain ones.

Between each of the three sections, a curve. These, to vaguely indicate the design.

I'm wide open to you for criticism and suggestion.

Just these few lines now . . .

love

HOLIDAY?

## To Alain Locke[1]
## January 2, 1923

Dear AL,

Your card here today.

And just after it, a telegram from Waldo Frank saying that Boni and Liveright have accepted my book, CANE.

The year is surely starting good.

Heres to you!

Jean

The coming issue of Little Review will contain "Fern." The winter number of Modern Review will print "Esther" and a group of poems. Jan Broom will have "Karintha." Besides, they have "Beehive" and quite a long piece. Well, so things go.

J

## To Waldo Frank[1]
## Early January 1923

Brother,

Three times I've started that paper on you, each time with a new view point.[2] And as yet I havent hit the one that satisfies me: that

1. This letter is dated from Frank's telegram informing Toomer of *Cane*'s acceptance on January 2.
1. This letter was obviously written between Frank's telegram on January 2 and Toomer's signing and sending the contract for *Cane*'s publication to Horace Liveright on January 8.
2. This was part of Toomer's never-completed study of Frank.

includes you. If I could cut myself out altogether, see you unrelated to my own present problems, the job wouldnt be so hard. But in whatever I write it seems as though I must cock a sly eye at myself. To narrow you to my own immediate concerns would be to violate both of us. To meet you (and myself) above them, as I must, is curiously difficult. There is challenge in this. I accept the challenge.

I am going over the Dark Mother. I remember telling you that I thought it consciously over brilliant and obscure. I dont think so now. It has a wonderful earnestness, depth, power, and organization. And the deep impulse is easily one of revelation. Of course, looking back from City Block some of those negative elements still remain. But it, in itself, contains almost none of them. I was not ready for it at my first reading.

Sherwood Anderson and I have exchanged a few letters. I dont think we will go very far. He limits me to Negro. As an approach, as a constant element (part of a larger whole) of interest, Negro is good. But to try to tie me to one of my parts is surely to loose [sic] me. My own letters have taken Negro as a point, and from there have circled out. Sherwood, for the most part, ignores the circles. In direct contact I am certain that I would like him. His notes have a full-hearted warmth and ease about them. But I need something more.

In one of my letters I mentioned my book. He immediately offered to take it to a publisher for me, to write an introduction. I told him of you. Here's what he says, "And of course Waldo Frank is the ideal man to introduce you. He wrote the first understanding article about my own work and you may absolutely depend on him for understanding and sympathy toward any real effort."[3] There is some natural law that brings things to the man they're fitted for. My stuff has been true in direction. Not Sherwood Anderson (other than Negro, a sense of life, a sense of the tragic separateness, the tragic sterility of people, I dont think he would know what my writing is about); you. No one in this country (which means the world so far as CANE is concerned) but you my brother.

Grandma is in love with you. You are the first of my friends she has wholly approved of. And let me tell you, in her own way she is pretty sharp and critical. And she gets at the depth of things by way of her intuition. One by one, she sizes people up, and crosses them off. The book's acceptance, and more than this, your constant love and work and friendship mean a great deal to her. She fears the thought of me in the world after she is gone. My knowing you will make the going easier. She is a real woman, remarkable even, and one of the few whom I fundamentally respect and admire.

And oh brother I have any number of personal things to tell you. Girls . . . Mae (pain through her more than from any girl whom I

3. Anderson here refers to Waldo Frank's early review of his work, particularly his novel *Windy MacPherson's Son*, in *Seven Arts*. See "Emerging Greatness," *Seven Arts* 1 (November 1916): 73–78. Reprinted in *The Achievement of Sherwood Anderson*, ed. Ray Lewis White (Chapel Hill: U of North Carolina P, 1966), 20–24.

have known. The complete tragedy of color), and a new one, talented, strikingly of mixed color, emotional, intellectually understanding and curious, loveable, not yet set, still immature. But promising! Just the suggestion now. Significant details saved for those good old talks we are going to have.

Say, it'll be great to have HOLIDAY and CANE come out at the same time. But I wonder if our friends the people and the critics will be able to stand them. So much the worse for them if they cant.

Full speed ahead to you!

I'll look for the contract.

Love
Jean

## To Waldo Frank[1]
## Early to mid-January 1923

Brother,

Even before last fall I am certain that you saw race and color as surfaces. Perhaps your mind still retained a few inhibiting wraiths. But the fact is, that you were *ready* for the miracle to happen. For myself, I could sense no dissonance or qualification whatsoever. I dont look for these things. I dont have to. If they're there, I simply *know* it. Nothing could have been more natural and real than our experience in Spartanburg. And the difficulties were extreme. All along, your consciousness of life was been [*sic*] too deep and strong a thing to suffer restrictions and distortions. I felt this (in a vague way, of course) during the hour we had in Central Park. Our America sharpened the impression. After I had read Rahab and the Dark Mother, I then seemed to know. Without this knowing I doubt if I would ever have sent those mss. Or if I had sent them, they would have been in the nature of a test. My sending them to you was a natural step in their *expression*. And so it is with CANE. There is not another man in the world that I would let touch it. Any more than I would let someone write Karintha or Kabnis for me. You not only understand CANE; you are *in* it, specifically here and there, mystically because of the spiritual bond there is between us. When you write, you will express me, and in a very true way you will express yourself. This combination I believe to produce the only worthwhile Introduction.[2]

Sherwood Anderson has doubtless had a very deep and beautiful emotion by way of the Negro. Here and there he has succeeded in expressing this. But he is not satisfied. He wants more. He is hungry

1. This letter seems to follow from his discussion of Sherwood Anderson in the previous letter, and he seems not to have yet read *Holiday*, which Frank sent in mid-January.
2. Frank had asked, in an undated letter, "would you rather I didn't write the intro? I have so many enemies, brother mine, that perhaps you'd be better off without my open sponsorship. In that case, be frank. Don't misunderstand. I want to do it, but I don't want this pleasure that wd be mine to stand in your way." Frank to Toomer, n.d., Jean Toomer Papers, box 3, folder 83.

for it. I come along. I express it. It is natural for him to see me in terms
of this expression. I see myself that way. But also I see myself expressing *myself*, expressing *Life*. I expect artists to recognize the circle of
expression. When they dont, I'm not disappointed; I simply know that
in this respect they are second-rate. That in this respect they differ
but little from the mass which must narrow and caricature if it is to
grasp the thing at all. Sherwood's notes are very deep and sincere.
Hence I attribute his attitude to a natural limitation. This limitation,
extended, is noticeable in the bulk of his work. The range of his sensitivity, curiosity, and intelligence is not very wide. One's admiration
suffers, but one's personal liking need not be affected by this.

There is one thing about the Negro in America which most
thoughtful persons seem to ignore: the Negro is in solution, in the
process of solution. As an entity, the race is loosing [*sic*] its body, and
its soul is approaching a common soul. If one holds his eyes to individuals and sections, race is starkly evident, and racial continuity
seems assured. One is even led to believe that the thing we call
Negro beauty will always be attributable to a clearly defined physical
source. But the fact is, that if anything comes up now, pure Negro, it
will be a swan-song. Dont let us fool ourselves, brother: the Negro of
the folk-song has all but passed away: the Negro of the emotional
church is fading. A hundred years from now these Negroes, if they
exist at all will live in art. And I believe that a vague sense of this fact
is the driving force behind the art movements directed towards them
today. (Likewise the Indian). America needs these elements. They
are passing. Let us grab and hold them while there still is time. Segregation and laws may retard this solution. But in the end, segregation will either give way, or it will kill. Natural preservations do not
come from unnatural laws. The supreme fact of mechanical civilization is that you become a part of it, or get sloughed off (under).
Negroes have no culture to resist it with (and if they had, their position would be identical to that of the Indians), hence industrialism
the more readily transforms them. A few generations from now, the
Negro will still be dark, and a portion of his psychology will spring
from this fact, but in all else he will be a conformist to the general
outlines of American civilization, or of American chaos. In my own
stuff, in those pieces that come nearest to the old Negro, to the spirit
saturate[d] with folk-song: Karintha and Fern, the dominant emotion
is a sadness derived from a sense of fading, from a knowledge of my
futility to check solution. There is nothing about these pieces of the
buoyant expression of a new race. The folk-songs themselves are of
the same order. The deepest of them. "I aint got long to stay here."
Religiously: "I (am going) to cross over into camp ground."[3] Socially:
"my position here is transient. I'm going to die, or be absorbed."

3.  Lyric from the African American spiritual "Deep River," which Toomer returned to in
    "Kabnis."

When I come up to Seventh Street and Theatre, a wholly new life confronts me. A life, I am afraid, that Sherwood Anderson would not get his beauty from. For it is jazzed, strident, modern. Seventh Street is the song of crude new life. Of a new people. Negro? Only in the *boldness* of its expression. In its healthy freedom. American. For the shows that please Seventh Street make their fortunes on Broadway. And both Theatre and Box-Seat, of course, spring from a complex civilization, and are directed to it. And Kabnis is *Me*. Holiday? Brother, you are weaving yourself into the truth of the South in a most remarkable way. You need it to complete your own spiritual experience. Because of your need, a beauty that is in solution will continue to live.

Jean

## To Waldo Frank[1]
## Early January 1923

Brother mine

you certainly are the engineer and locomotive in this landing of CANE. And by god but you have a steady pull and a sharp clear eye going up grade. I wave my arms and cheer you!

The check and the contract came yesterday. I put the check in bank [*sic*]. I have signed the contract. I said that you were there when he dictated it.[2] So I knew it must be all right. I'll tell him of the alteration that you suggest.[3] Not mentioning you.

Sure, feature Negro.[4]

Here's to the success of the first series!

I'm anxious for HOLIDAY. And I'm in a fine condition to read it. The paper on you progresses, at present, mostly in my mind. Its coming into being is quite like most of my creative work. Once it is really clear, I'll see its form, and the actual writing will then be but a question of a few swift days.

My feelings about CANE are curious. I seem never to *hope*. I seem always to be *certain*. I didnt really hope for its acceptance. I felt

1. This letter is dated by Toomer's having signed and returned the contract for *Cane* on January 11.
2. Horace Liveright.
3. Frank had suggested that Liveright get no movie rights on subsequent books of Toomer's.
4. Toomer refers here to Frank's plans to organize the speaking engagement for Toomer, along with Alfred Kreymbourg, in New York. Frank had written that he had "told K. I was sure you could do your Negro stuff. It will of course be necessary, in case you are used, to feature something special like that, as by yourself you arent a drawing card,—AS YET." Frank to Toomer, n.d., Jean Toomer Papers, box 3, folder 84. Toomer's booking was conditional on good attendance in a first series of talks, which were given by Carl Sandburg, Amy Lowell, Gilbert Cannan, Eva Gauthier, Ratan Devi, and Frank. As the first series of recitals went badly, with few people attending except for the talk by Amy Lowell, Toomer was not needed at all. See Frank to Toomer, n.d., Jean Toomer Papers, box 3, folder 84.

fatally certain that it would be, or would not be. I should not have been very downcast had it been rejected. Now that it is accepted, the acceptance seems the most natural thing in the world. My joy comes not so much from the fulfilling of a hope as from what its acceptance actually means to me. I think my attitude towards sales is somewhat similar. Curious?

The violent swing away from Anderson is doubtless the extreme of the reaction.[5] Two years from now, and I think that the most cerebral element in the Secession group will have admitted this, will have recognized his positive qualities.

A good note from Munson. He hasnt read my mss (B-b Moon, box Seat, Theatre) yet. He says that he has just returned the page proofs of his study. "I know no one from whom I await word on that study more eagerly than I do from you . . ."

Also a note and a check from Lola Ridge. Says that she's been sick. That she's resigned from Broom. Do you know anything about this resignation that you can tell me? Lola thinks Kabnis beautiful, but in need of work. She has promised to write me more at length about it.

Mae.[6] Came down for the Thanksgiving holidays. I took her to the Howard-Lincoln football game. Surrounded by friends of mine—near-whites. As prejudiced as 'real' whites. Mae's loveliness didn't get a chance to show. Only her skin. She really seemed insignificant,—and black. And my friends didnt fail to take her (or rather, not take her) in terms of her color and in terms of what she seemed. New York couldnt have supplied a more cutting setting. I'll have to talk the rest . . .

Address: Box 224, Ashburnham, Mass.

Ken.[7] Same old boy. Joyed at my strides. More hopeful. Still following impulses and disciplines all his own.

Grandma says that youre an ANGEL.

love
Jean

## To Horace Liveright
## January 11, 1923

1341 You Street, N.W.,
Washington D.C.

Dear Mr. Liveright,

I deeply thank you for the acceptance, for the check (but it comes in good!), and for the contract.[1] I have signed it, and am returning it to you.

---

5. Toomer here refers to *Secession*'s bitter criticisms of Sherwood Anderson.
6. Mae Wright.
7. Probably Toomer's friend Henry Kennedy.
1. Toomer's advance was $150.

One point is not quite clear. Do we "share equally in the sale of . . . dramatic and motion picture rights" of my next two books, should you accept them? Or is this sharing restricted to CANE? If possible, I should like to have the sharing so restricted.[2]

I am glad to be in the fold. There is no other like it. The American group with Waldo Frank, Gorham B Munson, TS Eliot—well, it simply cant be beaten.[3]

Cordially,

## To Horace Liveright
## February 27, 1923

1341 You Street, N.W.,
Washington, D.C.

Dear Mr. Liveright,
Under separate cover I'm sending CANE.
Waldo's Foreword is included.
The book is done.
I look at its complacency and wonder where on earth all my groans and grunts and damns have gone.
It doesnt seem to contain them.
And when I look for the power and beauty I thought I'd caught, they too seem to thin out and elude me.
Next time, perhaps . . .

Cordially,
Jean Toomer

## To Horace Liveright
## March 9, 1923

1341 You Street, N.W.,
Washington, D.C.

Dear Mr. Liveright,
Your enthusiasm for CANE gives me a deep pleasure. And it also gives me an energy which I shall try to put to good purpose in the shaping of my next book. I have on hand here the crude material of two pieces that approximate Kabnis in length and scope. I have another long story forming in my mind. With these three I'm thinking to make my second volume. The milieu is constantly that of Washington. The characters are dynamic, lyric, complex. I am not

2. Liveright would respond, "I'm sorry to disappoint you, but you've sold your birthright, or half of it anyhow, on the dramatic and motion picture rights on your next two books as well as on the first." See Liveright to Toomer, January 12, 1922. Jean Toomer Papers, box 1, folder 16.
3. Boni and Liveright brought out Eliot's *The Waste Land* in 1922.

quite ready for a novel, but one is forming. As I vaguely glimpse and feel it, it seems tremendous: this whole black and brown world heaving upward against, here and there mixing with the white. The mixture, however, is insufficient to absorb the heaving, hence it but accelerates and fires it. This upward heaving is to be symbolic of the proletariat or world upheaval. And it is likewise to be symbolic of the subconscious penetration of the conscious mind. Doubtless, before it is finished, several smaller dramas will have been written. At any rate, the horizon for the next three years seems packed and crowded.

I have had Munson's Study of Waldo sent me by S4N for review. When the thing is done, I'll send you a copy. I have read the book through once. I think it an outstanding piece of critical writing.

The editor of the Modern Review, Fiswoode Tarleton, has promised to boost CANE up his way.[1] He has written to know if he can get a copy for review in his July number. What shall I tell him?

I am planning to come to NY sometime this Spring. I look forward, anxiously, to seeing and having a talk with you.

And of course I'm waiting for the proofs of CANE.[2]

Cordially,

## To Horace Liveright
## September 5, 1923

Box 651,
Ellenville, NY

Dear Mr. Liveright,

Your letter of Aug 29th on hand. First, I want to make a general statement from which detailed statements will follow. My racial composition and my position in the world are realities which I alone may determine.[1] Just what these are, I sketched in for you the day I had lunch with you. As a unit in the social milieu, I expect and demand acceptance of myself on their basis. I do not expect to be told what I should consider myself to be. Nor do I expect you as my publisher, and I hope, as my friend, to either directly or indirectly state that this basis contains any element of dodging. In fact, if my

1. See Tarleton to Toomer, March 2, 1923, Jean Toomer Papers, box 5, folder 179.
2. Liveright sent out the proofs of Cane on May 18, 1923; the publication date was set at September 1.
1. Liveright's August 29 letter had discussed a short biographical sketch that Toomer had prepared to assist with the publicity drive surrounding Cane. Liveright had asked Toomer to revise it, advising him to make it shorter and also stating that "I feel that right at the start there should be a definite note sounded about your colored blood." See Liveright to Toomer, August 29, Jean Toomer Papers, box 1, folder 16. For a discussion of the relationship between Toomer and Boni and Liveright, see Michael Soto's "Jean Toomer and Horace Liveright; or, A New Negro Gets 'Into the Swing of It,'" Jean Toomer and the Harlem Renaissance, ed. Geneviève Fabre and Michel Feith (New Brunswick, NJ: Rutgers UP, 2001), 162–87.

relationship with you is to be what I'd like it to be, I must insist that you never use such word, such a thought, again. As a B and L author, I make the distinction between my fundamental position and the position which your publicity department may wish to establish for me in order that *Cane* reach as large a public as possible,—in this connection I have told you, I have told Messrs Tobey and Schneider to make use of whatever racial factors you wish.[2] Feature Negro if you wish, but do not expect me to feature it in advertisements for you. For myself, I have sufficiently featured Negro in *Cane*. Whatever statements I give will inevitably come from a synthetic human and art point of view; not from a racial one. As regards my sketch-life—it was not my intention or promise to give a completed statement of my life. It was my intention to give briefly those facts which I consider to be of importance, and then to allow your publicity department or the writers on the various papers and magazines to build up whatever copy seemed most suited to their purposes. I expect, therefore, that you so use it. With this reservation: that in any copy not used for specific advertising purposes the essentials of my sketch be adhered to. I mean, for instance, that in copies of *Cane* sent out to reviewers (these are not advertisements)—that any pamphlets included in these copies should follow the essential lines of my sketch. All of this may seem over-subtle and over-refined to you, but I assure you that it isnt.

I shall go over the sketch and revise it as near as possible in accordance with your wishes.

And I'd be glad to have dinner with you at New Rochelle.

ever,
Toomer

## To Countee Cullen
## October 1, 1923

Box 651,
Ellenville NY

Dear Contee P Cullen [*sic*],

Thanks for your good words on *Cane*. I particularly liked the line: "a classical portrayal of things as they are" for in this I find you sensitive to my purposes.[1] If *Cane* is an achievement, then, on the side of content, it is a segment of contemporary (at least) reality,

2. B. G. Tobey and G. Schneider were members of the Boni and Liveright publicity department. Schneider had corresponded with Toomer about the sketch and had advised him that it was being sent in its entirety to the Associated Negro Press. Schneider to Toomer, August 28, 1923, Jean Toomer Papers, box 1, folder 16.
1. Cullen had written Toomer that he had "bought the first copy of *Cane* sold." As well as the praise Toomer quotes in this letter, Cullen had called it a "real race contribution." Cullen to Toomer, September 29, 1923, Jean Toomer Papers, box 1, folder 38

and, in its esthetic phase, it is prose and poetry adequate to the expression of this reality.

And I am also glad that you find my personality incompletely caught. A writer still in his twenties should have more stuff in him.

I believe the Oct Broom is to run a review of *Cane*.[2] Might be of interest.

I'll not forget you.

ever,
Jean Toomer

## To Georgia O'Keeffe
## January 13, 1924

Dear O'Keeffe,

Yours was no simple invitation to call; you opened the way and initiated a spiritual form. There were four of us, but the clear mobility of that evening did not come from the lowest common denominator (as it almost always does, whatever the group); it issued from the highest. This is achieved only in rituals when religions are young.

Have you come to the story "Bona and Paul" in *Cane?* Impure and imperfect as it is, I feel that you and Stieglitz will catch its essential design as no others can. Most people cannot see this story because of the inhibitory baggage they bring with them. When I say "white," they see a certain white man, when I say "black," they see a certain Negro. Just as they miss Stieglitz's intentions, achievements! because they see "clouds."[1] So that at the end, when Paul resolves these contrasts to a unity, my intelligent commentors [sic] wonder what its all about. Someday perhaps, with a greater purity and a more perfect art, I'll do the thing. And meanwhile the gentlemen with intellect will haggle over the question as to whether or not I have expressed the "South."

~

Before so very long, I'd like another evening with you.

Jean

2. See Matthew Josephson's "Great American Novels," *Broom* 5 (1923): 178–80.
1. Stieglitz's *Equivalents*, a series of photographs that he began in 1922 of clouds and sky. There were more than four hundred by 1931. Stieglitz originally called these photographs *Music* and *Songs of the Sky* but would come to prefer the title *Equivalents*. See Daniell Cornell, *Alfred Stieglitz and the Equivalent: Reinventing the Nature of Photography* (New Haven: Yale University Art Gallery, 1999).

# To James Weldon Johnson
## July 11, 1930

*1447 North Dearborn St*
*Chicago Ill*
*July 11 30*

Dear Mr Johnson,

My view of this country sees it composed of people who primarily are Americans, who secondarily are of various stocks or mixed stocks. The matter of descent, and of divisions presumably based on descents, has been given, in my opinion, due emphasis, indeed over-emphasis. I aim to stress the fact that we all are Americans. I do not see things in terms of Negro, Anglo-Saxon, Jewish, and so on. As for me personally, I see myself an American, simply an American.

As regards art I particularly hold this view. I see our art and literature as primarily American art and literature. I do not see it as Negro, Anglo-Saxon, and so on.

Accordingly, I must withdraw from all things which emphasize or tend to emphasize racial or cultural divisions. I must align myself with things which stress the experiences, forms, and spirit we have in common.

This does not mean that I am necessarily opposed to the various established racial or sociological groupings. Certainly it does not mean that I am opposed to the efforts and forces which are trying to make these groups creative. On the contrary, I affirm these efforts. I recognize, for example, that the Negro art movement has had some valuable results. It is, however, for those who have and who will benefit by it. It is not for me. My poems are not Negro poems, nor are they Anglo-Saxon or white or English poems. My prose, likewise. They are, first, mine. And, second, in so far as general race or stock is concerned, they spring from the result of racial blendings here in America which have produced a new race or stock. We may call this stock the American stock or race. My main energies are devoted and directed towards the building of a life which will include all creative people of corresponding type.

I take this opportunity of noting these things in order to clear up a misunderstanding of my position which has existed to some extent ever since the publishing of CANE. I am stating the same things whenever opportunity allows to everyone concerned. I feel that just now the time is ripe to give a definite expression of these views.

My best wishes for your anthology; and my warm regards to you and Mrs Johnson.

Sincerely,
Jean Toomer

# CRITICISM

# Contemporary Reviews

## MONTGOMERY GREGORY

### A Review of *Cane*†

The recent publication of "Cane" marks a distinct departure in southern literature and at the same time introduces a writer of extraordinary power in the person of Jean Toomer. Few books of recent years have greater significance for American letters than this "first" work of a young Negro, the nephew of an acting reconstruction governor of Louisiana. Fate has played another of its freakish pranks in decreeing that southern life should be given its most notable artistic expression by the pen of a native son of Negro descent.

It is a notorious fact that the United States south of the Mason and Dixon line has been, in the words of Mr. Mencken, a "Cultural Sahara." First torn and rent by the ravages of one of the most destructive civil strifes in all history, the states of the former confederacy have either used up their creative powers in mending the wreckage or have consumed them in the blighting fires of race hatred. The white South, with few exceptions, has sacrificed art for propaganda. Great art, like great deeds, cannot flourish in a land of bigotry and oppression. The great exception to this general indictment of the white South, Joel Chandler Harris, drew his material and his inspiration for his "Uncle Remus" stories from the unembittered and kindly lips of a former slave.

The Negro, altho immersed in the miasma of southern prejudice, because of his natural gentleness of soul and kindness of heart, suffers less from its pestilential influence than his white brother. Behold Paul Laurence Dunbar singing the plaintive songs of his people in immortal verse before the smoke of battle had cleared from the fields of Gettysburg and the Wilderness. Yet the Negro has been too conscious of his wrongs, too sensitive to oppression to be able to express the beauty of his racial life or to glorify his native soil. He

† From *Opportunity* 1 (December 1923): 374–75. Reprinted by permission of The National Urban League.

has likewise resented the use of his folk-life for artistic purposes. It has been conceded that the varied life of the Negro in America, especially his folk-life, offers almost unparalleled opportunities for the brush of the artist and the pen of the poet. Max Rheinhardt [*sic*], the world's premier dramatic director, during his recent visit to this country, stated that the chief contribution of America to the drama of tomorrow would be its development of Negro folk-drama. But what has been the attitude of the Negro himself? Unqualified opposition to the utilization of his mass life in fiction, in music, or in drama.

What has this attitude meant? It has robbed the race of its birth-right for a mess of pottage. It has damned the possibilities of true artistic expression at its very source. It has enabled the white artist to exploit the Negro race for personal recognition or commercial gain. Instead of a faithful and sympathetic portrayal of our race-life by our own artists, we have been the victims of this alien exploita-tion, with the result that caricatures of the race have been accepted as bona fide portraits.

Art is *self-expression.* The artist can only truly express his own soul or the race-soul. Not until Rene Maran, a Negro, had pic-tured the native life of Africa in "Batouala," did the dark conti-nent find a true exponent of its wrongs and of its resentment against a cruel bondage. The white missionary or itinerant visitor had always described the natives in the light of his own precon-ceived prejudices.

America has waited for its own counterpart of Maran—for that native son who would avoid the pitfalls of propaganda and moral-izing on the one hand and the snares of a false and hollow race pride on the other hand. One whose soul mirrored the soul of his people, yet whose vision was universal.

Jean Toomer, the author of "Cane," is in a remarkable manner the answer to this call. Sprung from the tangy soil of the South, he combines the inheritance of the old Negro and the spirit of the new Negro. His grandfather, P. B. S. Pinchback, was acting governor of Louisiana and later settled in Washington where his grandson, Jean Toomer, was born in 1894. Thus his childhood was spent in a home where dramatic incidents of slavery, of the Civil War and of Reconstruction, were household traditions. The "Song of the Son," one of the several exquisite lyrics that appear in "Cane," shows the deep affection which young Toomer has for the old South:

> "An everlasting song, a singing tree,
> Caroling softly souls of slavery,
> What they were, and what they are to me.
> Caroling softly souls of slavery."

A youth rich in wide human experience and marked by a natural love for solitude followed. Later came an opportunity to teach at a small school in Georgia, where he secured the contacts with life in the South which were to give him his final inspirations for the book which is the subject of this criticism. "I felt strange, as I always do in Georgia, particularly at dusk. I felt that things unseen to men were tangibly immediate. It would not have surprised me had I had a vision. . . . When one is on the soil of one's ancestors, most anything can come to one."

"Cane" is not to be classified in terms of the ordinary literary types, for the genius of creation is evident in its form. Verse, fiction, and drama are fused into a spiritual unity, an "aesthetic equivalent" of the Southland. It is not a book to be intellectually understood; it must be emotionally, aesthetically felt. One must approach it with all of his five senses keenly alive if appreciation and enjoyment are to result. No previous writer has been able in any such degree to catch the sensuous beauty of the land or of its people or to fathom the deeper spiritual stirrings of the mass-life of the Negro. "Cane" is not OF the South, it is not OF the Negro; it IS the South, it IS the Negro—as Jean Toomer has experienced them. It may be added that the pictures do not pretend to be the only possible ones in such a vast panorama of life. "The Emperor Jones" was a study of one Negro as Eugene O'Neill saw him. That only. So with "Cane." It cannot be justly criticized because it does not harmonize with your personal conceptions, Mr. Reader!

"Cane" has three main divisions. The first division is laid in the land of cane, cotton and sawdust piles—Georgia. The second part deals with the more sophisticated life of the Negro "world within a world" in Washington. The third section is an intense drama of all the complicated elements of southern life, with its setting also in Georgia.

The writer will be pardoned for expressing his decided preference for the sketches, stories, and poems which comprise part one. Here the matchless beauty of the folk-life of the southern Negro is presented with intriguing charm. It is realism—not of the reportorial type found in "Main Street" writing—but the higher realism of the emotions. Here we have that mysterious, subtle and incomprehensible appeal of the South made all the more interesting because of the discordant and chaotic human elements submerged there. Of course, one is conscious of the protest of those who confuse superficial and transitory political and economic conditions with the underlying eternal elements. Those with an eye for beauty, an ear for music, and a heart for emotion, while abhorring the temporary victimizing of the South by unscrupulous demagogues, must still appreciate the fundamental Beauty which is revealed in "Cane."

The power of portraiture is unmistakable. No effort is made to create ideal characters or to make them conform to any particular standard. Here we have the method of Maran and all great artists. The characters appear in all of their lovable human qualities. We love them and yet pity them for human weaknesses for which not they but their ignorance and environment are largely responsible. It is not a question of morality but of life.

Toomer appreciates as an artist the surpassing beauty, both physical and spiritual, of the Negro woman and he has unusual facility of language in describing it. There is "Karintha at twenty, carrying beauty, perfect as the dusk as the sun goes down." A wayward child of nature whose tragedy was that "the soul of her was a growing thing ripened too soon." Of "Carma" it is said, "She does not sing; her body is a song." I prefer "Fern" to all the other portraits because the author has succeeded in conveying exquisite physical charm coupled with an almost divine quality of inarticulate spirituality. Sufficient tribute has never been paid to the beauty of the Negro woman's eyes. Visitors from foreign lands have frequently pointed out this unique glory of our women. Is it any wonder? For do not their eyes express from mysterious depths the majesty of lost empires, the pathos of a woman's lot in slavery, and the spirit of a resurgent race? Fern's eyes. "Face flowed into eyes. Flowed in soft cream foam and plaintive ripples, in such a way that wherever your glance may momentarily have rested, it immediately thereafter wavered in the direction of her eyes. . . . If you have ever heard a Jewish cantor sing, if he has touched you and made your own sorrow seem trivial when compared with his, you know my feeling when I followed the curves of her profile, the mobile rivers, to their common delta." But her eyes were not of ordinary beauty. "They were strange eyes. In this, that they sought nothing—that is nothing that was obvious or tangible or that one could see. . . . Her eyes, unusually weird and open, held me. Held God. He flowed in as I have seen the countryside."

Mention must also be made of "Blood Burning Moon," a short story which closes this first section. Its splendid technique and striking theme are attested by the fact that O'Brien has included it in his collection of the best short stories of 1923.

A series of impressionistic views of Negro life in Washington, D.C., follows in the middle section of "Cane." Again one must be cautioned that the beauty of the work must be captured thru the senses. Seventh Street is a "crude boned, soft-skinned wedge of nigger life breathing its loafer air, jazz songs and love, thrusting unconscious rhythms, black reddish blood into the white and white-washed wood of Washington." Thickly scattered thru these pages are unforgettable "purple patches" which reveal the animate and inanimate life of You Street thru the sensitive emotional reactions of a poet. It must also be said that the style is more labored and sometimes puzzling. One feels at times as if the writer's emotions had out-run his expression. Is it that Mr. Toomer's highest inspiration is to be found in the folk-life of his beloved Southland and that his unmistakable distaste for the cramped and strictly conventionalized life of the city Negro restricts his power of clear and forceful language? There is not the same easy rhythmic cadence of expression here as in the first division. There are also a few apparent irrelevancies (for the reader) in the text which add nothing to the total effect and detract from the artistic value of the whole. "Box Seat" which reaches high points of excellence in the portraiture of "Muriel," "Dan," and "Mrs. Pribby," and in its dramatic narrative style, limps at times with obscure writing. The thoughts attributed to "Dan," on page 124, are a case in point and strain the demand of art to the breaking point. The remaining narratives in this division are of great merit but on the whole are not of the same excellence as his chapters of Georgia life.

The drama of "Ralph Kabnis" closes the book and marks a return to Georgia. This is no ordinary drama. It can only be likened to the grimly powerful work of the Russian dramatists. Only Eugene O'Neill in America has written anything to measure up to its colossal conception. One competent critic has stated that only the Moscow Art Theatre could do justice to such a drama. It is to be hoped that a Negro Theatre will immediately arise capable of producing "Kabnis" and other plays sure to follow from Toomer.

"Kabnis" is the fitting climax to a remarkable book. Here are placed upon the stage the outstanding factors in the inner circle of Negro life. The traditional Negro is there—the Negro of the past—mute, blind, motionless, yet a figure of sphinx-like mystery and fascination. There is a type of young Negro, attractive, frivolous, and thoughtless. Then there is Kabnis himself, the talented, highly emotional, educated Negro who goes south to elevate his people but who lacks the strength of mind and character to withstand the pressure of the white South or the temptations within his own group. Finally, there is Lewis. "He is what a stronger Kabnis might have been. . . . His mouth and eyes suggest purpose guided by an adequate intelligence." Yet he does not understand these black people of the South and they do not understand him. In the end he flees from the situation without in any way helping his people who needed his help.

Evidently the author's implication is that there must be a welding into one personality of Kabnis and Lewis: the great emotionalism of the race guided and directed by a great purpose and a super-intelligence.

"Cane" leaves this final message with me. In the South we have a "powerful underground" race with a marvelous emotional power which like Niagara before it was harnessed is wasting itself. Release it into proper channels, direct its course intelligently, and you have possibilities for future achievements that challenge the imagination. The hope of the race is in the great blind forces of the masses properly utilized by capable leaders.

"Dan goes to the wall and places his ear against it. That rumble comes from the earth's core. It is the mutter of powerful and underground races. . . . The next world savior is coming up that way."

# ROBERT LITTELL

## A Review of *Cane*[†]

"Reading this book," says Mr. Waldo Frank in his introduction, "I had the vision of a land, heretofore sunk in the mists of muteness, suddenly rising up into the eminence of song. . . . This book *is* the South." Not the South of the chivalrous gentleman, the fair lady, the friendly, decaying mansion, of mammies, cotton and pickaninnies. Nor yet the South of lynchings and hatreds, of the bitter, rebellious young Negro, and of his emigration to the North. Cane does not remotely resemble any of the familiar, superficial views of the South on which we have been brought up. On the contrary, Mr. Toomer's view is unfamiliar and bafflingly subterranean, the vision of a poet far more than the account of things seen by a novelist— lyric, symbolic, oblique, seldom actual.

In many respects, Mr. Toomer recalls Waldo Frank. They seem curiously to coincide at their weakest points. Such sentences as these might have been written by either of them: "Dark swaying forms of Negroes are street-songs that woo virginal houses . . . Dan Moore walks southward on Thirteenth Street . . . girl eyes within him widen upward to promised faces . . . Negroes open gates and go indoors, perfectly." Such phrases mean either almost nothing, or a great deal too much. In the case of Mr. Frank they seem to contain, bottled up within them, the very essence of what he wants to say; in the case Mr. Toomer, they are occasional, accidental, and could be brushed off without damage to the whole. While Mr. Toomer often tries for puzzling and profound effects, he accomplishes fairly well what he sets out to do, and Cane is not seething, like nearly all Mr. Frank's books, with great inexpressible things bursting to be said,

† From the *New Republic* 37 (December 26, 1923): 126.

and only occasionally arriving, like little bubbles to the surface of a sea of molten tar.

Cane is sharply divided into two parts. The first is a series of sketches, almost poetic in form and feeling, revolving about a character which emerges with very different degrees of clarity. The second half is a longish short story, Kabnis, quite distinct from the sketches, and peculiarly interesting. In this Mr. Toomer shows a genuine gift for character portrayal and dialogue. In the sketches, the poet is uppermost. Many of them begin with three or four lines of verse, and end with the same lines, slightly changed. The construction here is musical, too often a little artificially so. The body of the sketch tends to poetry, and to a pattern which begins to lose its effectiveness as soon as one guesses how it is coming out. The following, which is about a third of one of the sketches, is a fair sample of Mr. Toomer writing at his best:

> Her soul is like a little thrust-tailed dog that follows her, whimpering. She is large enough, I know, to find a warm spot for it. But each night when she comes home and closes the big outside storm door, the little dog is left in the vestibule, filled with chills till morning. Some one . . . eoho Jesus . . . soft as a cotton ball brushed against the milk-pod cheek of Christ, will steal in and cover it that it need not shiver, and carry it to her where she sleeps upon clean hay cut in her dreams.

It isn't necessary, to know exactly what this means in order to find pleasure in reading it. Which is one way of defining poetry. And once we begin to regard Mr. Toomer's shorter sketches as poetry, many objections to the obscurer symbolism and obliqueness of them disappear. There remains, however, a strong objection to their staccato beat. The sentences fall like small shot from a high tower. They pass from poetry into prose, and from there into Western Union.

Kabnis, the longest piece in the book, is far the most direct and most living, perhaps because it seems to have grown so much more than been consciously made. There is no pattern in it, and very little effort at poetry. And Mr. Toomer makes his Negroes talk like very real people, almost, in spots, as if he had taken down their words as they came. A strange contrast to the lyric expressionism of the shorter pieces. A real peek into the mind of the South, which, like nearly all such genuinely intimate glimpses, leaves one puzzled, and—fortunately—unable to generalize.

Cane is an interesting, occasionally beautiful and often queer book of exploration into old country and new ways of writing.

184

# W. E. B. DU BOIS AND ALAIN LOCKE

## The Younger Literary Movement†

There have been times when we writers of the older set have been afraid that the procession of those who seek to express the life of the American Negro was thinning and that none were coming forward to fill the footsteps of the fathers. Dunbar is dead; Chesnutt is silent; and Kelly Miller is mooning after false gods while Brawley and Woodson are writing history rather than literature. But even as we ask "Where are the young Negro artists to mold and weld this mighty material about us?"—even as we ask, they come.

There are two books before me, which, if I mistake not, will mark an epoch: a novel by Jessie Fauset and a book of stories and poems by Jean Toomer. There are besides these, five poets writing: Langston Hughes, Countée Cullen, Georgia Johnson, Gwendolyn Bennett and Claude McKay. Finally, Negro men are appearing as essayists and reviewers, like Walter White and Eric Walrond. (And even as I write comes the news that a novel by Mr. White has just found a publisher.) Here then is promise sufficient to attract us. . . .

The world of black folk will some day arise and point to Jean Toomer as a writer who first dared to emancipate the colored world from the conventions of sex. It is quite impossible for most Americans to realize how straight-laced and conventional thought is within the Negro World, despite the very unconventional acts of the group. Yet this contradiction is true. And Jean Toomer is the first of our writers to hurl his pen across the very face of our sex conventionality. In "Cane" one has only to take his women characters *seriatim* to realize this: Here is Karintha, an innocent prostitute; Becky, a fallen white woman; Carma, a tender Amazon of unbridled desire; Fern, an unconscious wanton; Esther, a woman who looks age and bastardy in the face and flees in despair; Louise [*sic*], with a white and a black lover; Avey, unfeeling and unmoral; and Doris [*sic*], the cheap chorus girl. These are his women, painted with a frankness that is going to make his black readers shrink and criticize; and yet they are done with a certain splendid, careless truth.

Toomer does not impress me as one who knows his Georgia but he does know human beings; and, from the background which he has seen slightly and heard of all his life through the lips of others, he paints things that are true, not with Dutch exactness, but rather with an impressionist's sweep of color. He is an artist with words but a conscious artist who offends often by his apparently

† From the *Crisis* 27 (February 1924): 161–62. Reprinted by permission of The National Urban Leauge.

undue striving for effect. On the other hand his powerful book is filled with felicitous phrases—Karintha, "carrying beauty perfect as the dusk when the sun goes down,"—

> "Hair—
> Silver-grey
> Like streams of stars"

Or again, "face flowed into her eyes—flower in soft creamy foam and plaintive ripples." His emotion is for the most part entirely objective. One does not feel that he feels much and yet the fervor of his descriptions shows that he has felt or knows what feeling is. His art carries much that is difficult or even impossible to understand. The artist, of course, has a right deliberately to make his art a puzzle to the interpreter (the whole world is a puzzle) but on the other hand I am myself unduly irritated by this sort of thing. I cannot, for the life of me, for instance see why Toomer could not have made the tragedy of Carma something that I could understand instead of vaguely guess at; "Box Seat" muddles me to the last degree and I am not sure that I know what "Kabnis" is about. All of these essays and stories, even when I do not understand them, have their strange flashes of power, their numerous messages and numberless reasons for being. But still for me they are partially spoiled. Toomer strikes me as a man who has written a powerful book but who is still watching for the fullness of his strength and for that calm certainty of his art which will undoubtedly come with years.

# GORHAM B. MUNSON

## The Significance of Jean Toomer†

There can be no question of Jean Toomer's skill as a literary craftsman. A writer who can combine vowels and liquids to form a cadence like "she was as innocently lovely as a November cotton flower" has a subtle command of word-music. And a writer who can break the boundaries of the sentences, interrupt the placement of a fact with a lyrical cry, and yet hold both his fact and his exclamation to a single welded meaning as in the expression: "A single room held down to earth . . . O fly away to Jesus . . . by a leaning chimney . . . ," is assuredly at home in the language and therefore is assuredly free to experiment and invent. Toomer has found his own speech, now swift and clipped for violent narrative action, now languorous

† From *Opportunity* 3 (September 1925): 262–63. Reprinted by permission of The National Urban Leauge.

and dragging for specific characterizing purposes, and now lean and sinuous for the exposition of ideas, but always cadenced to accord with an unusually sensitive ear.

It is interesting to know that Toomer, before he began to write, thought of becoming a composer. One might have guessed it from the fact that the early sketches in *Cane* (1923) depend fully as much upon a musical unity as upon a literary unity. *Karintha*, for example, opens with a song, presents a theme, breaks into song, develops the theme, sings again, drops back into prose, and dies away in a song. But in it certain narrative functions—one might mention that lying back of the bald statement, "This interest of the male, who wishes to ripen a growing thing too soon, could mean no good to her"—are left undeveloped. Were it not for the songs, the piece could scarcely exist.

But electing to write, Toomer was too canny to try to carry literature further into music than this. *Cane* is, from one point of view, the record of his search for suitable literary forms. We can see him seeking guidance and in several of the stories, notably *Fern* and *Avey*, it is the hand of Sherwood Anderson that he takes hold. But Anderson leads toward formlessness and Toomer shakes him off for Waldo Frank in such pieces as *Theatre* where the design becomes clear and the parts are held in a vital esthetic union. Finally, he breaks through in a free dramatic form of his own, the play *Kabnis* which still awaits production by an American theatre that cries for good native drama and yet lacks the wit to perceive the talent of Toomer.

The form of *Kabnis* is a steep slope downward. In the first scene Ralph Kabnis, a neurotic educated Negro who has returned to Georgia from the North, stands on the top of the slope and delivers a monologue, which reveals his character as that of a frustrated lyricist. In Scene Two he begins to fall in the direction of his weaknesses, in Scene Three there occurs an opportunity to check his descent, but his momentum carries him straight past it, and in the remaining scenes he lands in a cellar of debauchery. The action of the play then is linear, but what Kabnis falls through is a rich milieu composed of a symbolic ancient Negro who has experienced slavery, an honest craft-loving wheelwright, a bourgeois school supervisor, a clear-headed forceful radical black, a couple of prostitutes, a church audience, a minister, and little Carrie K., fresh symbol of a possible future. Toomer's formal achievement is just this: to utilize a milieu and a character, the first as a dense living slope, the second as a swiftly descending point tracing out a line of action upon the first.

It is necessary and important that an artist should be in command of his tools, but if we feel that craftsmanship is only a means to an end, we must proceed to inquire what end Toomer's skill was designed to suit.

*Cane* is the projection of a vivid personality. What the fundamental motives were that impelled this projection we cannot say, but we can pick out a few probably subsidiary motives that will perhaps indicate Toomer's status at the moment he completed *Cane*. Clearly, he desired to make contact with his hereditary roots in the Southland. One of the poems in *Cane* is an unmistakable recognition of this desire.

> "O land and soil, red soil and sweet-gum tree,
> So scant of grass, so profligate of pines,
> Now just before an epoch's sun declines
> Thy son, in time, I have returned to thee,
> Thy son, I have in time returned to thee."

From this one infers a preceding period of shifting and drifting without settled harborage. Weary of homeless waters, he turns back to the ancestral soil, opens himself to its folk-art and its folk-ways, tries to find his roots, his origins. It is a step toward the definition of himself.

What can we add to this purpose? We can say that Toomer makes a very full response to life, a response that is both robust and sensitive, and we can say, to use the conventional phrase, that he "accepts life." It is plain that he has strong instincts, welling and deep and delicate emotions, and a discriminating and analytical intellect (more fully revealed in his critical work); and these are all keenly aware of life. This life that floods in upon his equipment Toomer finds to be potent and sweet, colorful and singing, interesting and puzzling, pathetic and worthy of respect; he is able to accept it,—perhaps because his survey of it shows it to be beautiful and mysterious. As any rate, the only fully adumbrated attitude in *Cane* is that of the spectatorial artist. But that raises the question, under what circumstances can the artist be a spectator?

To be a spectator one must have a firm and fixed point of vantage. Where can such a point be found today? Our social framework is admittedly unsettled, but it is less generally perceived that culturally we are being blown into chaos. Our heritage came from Judea, Greece and Rome, and to that heritage we have added science. Today, it needs but a glance at the vitality of the early Christians and at the legalism and stupor of the modern church to realize that something basic and essential has passed away from Christianity. From the testimony of the humanists themselves we are entitled to conclude that humanism is in decay. And science, upon which the nineteenth century depended, has turned to inner conflict, uncertainty and groping. In short, the Occidental world now has no one body of common experience, no ancestral faith, no *concensus omnium bonorum*, no principle of unification, put it how you will, to which men everywhere may make appeal and upon which the spectatorial artist might situate himself. The great movement of the last few centuries has been romanticism which has glorified personal uniqueness and universal flux and has driven us all away from any possible center of human experience. Born into such circumstances, what is the artist to do? He must choose to work either toward integration or toward disintegration.

Nietzsche, it should be recalled, looked upon artists as casters of glamor over progression and retrogression alike. That is, by virtue of their magic they could glorify either, they could be their saviors or betrayers. An artist who does not care where the lure and grace that he sheds over the objects led his entranced followers naturally will not inquire very deeply into his purpose for creation. He creates beauty and lets truth and goodness go hang. But an artist who feels that his gifts entail a grave responsibility, who wishes to fight on the side of life abundant rather than for life deficient, must pause and seek the answers to certain questions. What is the function of man? What are the potentials of man and what may he become? What is experience and what is knowledge? What is the world?

The significance of Jean Toomer lies in his strenuous attempt to answer these questions. Shortly after writing *Cane*, he formed two convictions. One was that the modern world is a veritable chaos and the other was that in a disrupted age the first duty of the artist is to unify himself. Having achieved personal wholeness, then perhaps he would possess an attitude that would not be merely a reaction to the circumstances of modernity, merely a reflection of the life about him, but would be an attitude that could act upon modernity, dissolve away the remainder of an old slope of consciousness, and plant the seeds for a new slope.

So he turned to an intensive study of his own psychology. He sifted psychoanalysis for what minute grains of truth it might supply, he underwent the training for "conscious control of the body" prescribed by F. Matthias Alexander, he spent a summer at the Gurdjieff Institute, Fontainebleau, France, where he obtained what he regards as the best method for his quest. We should note that his search is distinguished from that of many other American artists (Sherwood Anderson may be cited as typical) by its positive scientific character. These others work from a disgust or a negation. They cut loose from something they abhor and, unprovided with any method, drift aimlessly in search of a leaven which somewhere, somehow, will heal.

Toomer has a method and an aim, and he devoted his whole time and energy to them. In his own words, this is what he is doing: "I am. What I am and what I may become I am trying to find out."

He is a dynamic symbol of what all artists of our time should be doing, if they are to command our trust. He has mastered his craft. Now he seeks a purpose that will convince him that his craft is nobly employed. Obviously, to his search there is no end, but in his search there is bound to occur a fusion of his experience, and it is this fused experience that will give profundity to his later work. His way is not the way of the minor art master, but the way of the major master of art. And that is why his potential literary significance outweighs the actualized literary significance of so many of his contemporaries.

## PAUL ROSENFELD

### Jean Toomer[†]

Momentarily the prose of *Cane* is artificially exalted, hooked to the Frankian pitch as to a nail high up in the wall. And night is the soft belly of a pregnant negress, and "her mind" a pink mesh bag filled with baby toes. But quickly the inflations subside. The happy normal swing resumes, the easy rhythm of a strainless human frame.

Not all the narratives intend the quality of legendary song. Certain give the fragmentated moods of the contemporary psychic conflict, and throb with hysterical starts and tearing dissonance. Yet saving the few derailing exaltations, the swing and balance of the limber body walking a road is ever-present. The musical state of soul seems primary in Jean Toomer. The pattern generates the tale. He tunes his fiddle like a tavern minstrel, and out of the little rocking or running design there rises the protagonist, solidifying from rhythm as heroes once solidified from mist: crouched white-woman Becky who had two negro sons; Carma in overalls and strong as any man; Kabnis with his jangling nerves and flooding nostalgic lyricism. The rhythm forms the figures most. The words are but flecks of light gleaming on the surface of bronze.

He has his hand lightly, relaxedly, upon substances. The words transmit the easy sensations. They come warm and fuzzy and rich not with the heat and density of bodies crowded in tenements, but with the level beat of a blood promenaded in resinous forests amid blotches of June sun on needles and cones. It is the "sawdust glow of night" and the "velvet pine-smoke air." "The sun which has been

†   From *Men Seen: Twenty-four Modern Authors* (New York: The Dial Press, 1925), 227–33.

slanting over her shoulder, shoots primitive rockets into her mangrove-gloomed, yellow flower face." He assembles words as a painter negligently rubbing pastels; leaving where he touches warm singing blobs of brown and red.

There are no rings laming this imagination, most the time: and binding it in on his proper person. Toomer's protagonists, symbols and situations are not of the nature of prearrangements: objects glued together on a mental plane and revealing through wooden joints and inner dislocation the artificial synthesis. His creative power offers to bring this young poet-novelist high in the ranks of living American letters. Characters and narratives move, and move in unpremeditated, unpredictable curves. Yet in their sudden tangential departures and radical developments they remain logical with a logic profounder than the intellect's. Not all the personages and situations of the stories, it is true, are submitted to extended composition and developed. The majority remain exposed in a single scene and through a single view. Yet in the nouvelle *Kabnis* Toomer has produced an extended composition. The focal character is moved through several episodes, and with each episode the scope of the story deepens. Characters and situations are satisfying both as symbol and as fact; and toward the conclusion both are transposed without violence to a level of reality deeper than that upon which they were launched. Possibly the upper conscious level of mind alone could have produced the earlier scenes; they may be semi-autobiographical, and felt with the aid of Sherwood Anderson and *The Portrait of the Artist as a Young Man*. But not the fantastic scene in the cellar, with its opposition of the torn differentiating negroids and the figure of the ancient African slave mumbling in his corner. Some inner substance in the author moved while writing this tale. He was no longer the same man who began it, when writing the end. He had stepped on a level of pure invention.

Toomer's free gift has given him the vision of a parting soul, and lifted his voice in salutation to the folk-spirit of the negro South. He comes like a son returned in bare time to take a living full farewell of a dying parent; and all of him loves and wants to commemorate that perishing naïveté, only beautiful one America has had, before universal ugly sophistication cover it also. Those simple singing people who have joy and have pain, and voice them frankly, largely, utterly have come to hold for him a great earthly beauty and tragedy. Their sheer animal litheness and pathos has become savage and satisfying to his breast:

> A feast of moon and men and barking hounds
> An orgy for some genius of the South
> With blood-hot eyes and cane lipped scented mouth—

He follows the elasticity, resiliency of young rubber, into the brown belt of Washington: feels it in its conflict with the sophistication and mechanization of white America; watches it weakened and threatened and torn in the bodies of self-conscious, half-educated people, girls become self-centered and men playing the piano in vaudeville theatres and going dreaming of Walt Whitman under the lamps of Seventh Street. And here he perceives, like new strange harmonies sounding through the subtle dissonances of life, promises of an inner healing for these splintered souls, a new strength, swiftness and singleness of motive. A new soul calls. The negroid poet of the story pulled from his base by the wilfulness of a passionate white girl, half lets his amorous opportunity pass in a proud gesture of balladry. Through the woof of *Kabnis* there go the figures of Lewis and Carrie; and Lewis is a man who has become fearless and self-confident and fine; and Carrie is a girl in whom has persisted flowerlike a beauty of instinct.

But these figures are prophetic not only for men of negro blood. They throw forward much in America; for they are symbols of some future America of which Jean Toomer by virtue of the music in him is a portion. He looks two ways. Through this recognition of the beauty of a doomed simplicity some simplicity, sensuosity, passionateness not of the South or of the past asserts, cries out, comes conscious of itself: some America beyond the newspapers, regimented feelings, edgeless language—timid, uncertain, young—in streaming music nevertheless drawing more imminent.

Both Anderson and Frank have helped rouse the impulse of Toomer. Yet it was the imagists with their perfect precision of feeling that fevered him most for work. Some clarity in himself must have responded to the clearness of these poets. That his definiteness remains as yet less intense than theirs is plain. Perhaps because his gift is warmer and more turbulent, it is also less white and clear. Whatever the cause, the Frankian inflations, and the wobbling of the focus between Kabnis and Lewis in the finale of the novelette, leave the indecision a little plainer than we would have it. Large as is the heralding which comes through him, Toomer remains as yet much of the artist trying out his colors, the writer experimenting with a style. And still, these movements of prose are genuine and new. Again a creative power has arrived for American literature: for fiction, perhaps for criticism; in any case, for prose. Other writers have tried, with less happiness, to handle the material of the South. They have had axes to grind; sadisms to exhaust in whipping up passion for the whites; masochisms to release in waking resentment for the blacks. But Toomer comes to unlimber a soul, and give of its dance and music.

# Critical Interpretations

## STERLING A. BROWN

### Jean Toomer†

Jean Toomer is best as a poet in the beautiful prose of *Cane* (1923). His few poems in the same volume, however, are original and striking. Jean Toomer has written that Georgia opened him up; "Reapers" and "Cotton Song," show this awaking to folk material. In "Georgia Dusk" there is a sense of the ominous mystery of the Southland:

> The sawmill blows its whistle, buzz-saws stop,
> And silence breaks the bud of knoll and hill. . . .
> Smoke from the pyramidal sawdust pile
> Curls up, blue ghosts of trees. . . .
> . . . . the chorus of the cane
> Is caroling a vesper to the stars. . . .

With a mastery of the best rhythmical devices of Negro folk-music, "Song of the Son" expresses the return of the younger Negro to a consciousness of identity with his own, a return to folk sources, to the "caroling softly souls of slavery"—

> O land and soil, red soil and sweet-gum tree,
> So scant of grass, so profligate of pines,
> Now just before an epoch's sun declines,
> Thy son, in time, I have returned to thee,
> Thy son, I have in time returned to thee.
> In time, for though the sun is setting on
> A song-lit race of slaves, it has not set. . . .

In spite of the small number of his poems, Toomer remains one of the finest and most influential of Negro poets. His long silence has been broken with the publication of "Blue Meridian," a rather long

† From *Negro Poetry and Drama and The Negro in American Fiction* (New York: Atheneum, 1969). Reprinted with the permission of Scribner, a Division of Simon & Schuster, Inc., from *Negro Poetry and Drama* by Sterling A. Brown. Copyright © 1937 by The Associates in Negro Folk Education. Copyright renewed © 1969 by Atheneum Publishers. All rights reserved.

poem calling for a "new America, to be spiritualized by each new American." In it there are only occasional references to Negro life:

> The great African races sent a single wave
> And singing riplets to sorrow in red fields
> Sing a swan song, to break rocks
> And immortalize a hiding water-boy. . . .

# LANGSTON HUGHES

## Gurdjieff in Harlem[†]

One of the most talented of the Negro writers, Jean Toomer, went to Paris to become a follower and disciple of Gurdjieff's at Fontainebleau, where Katherine Mansfield died. He returned to Harlem, having achieved awareness, to impart his precepts to the literati. Wallace Thurman and Dorothy Peterson, Aaron Douglas, and Nella Larsen, not to speak of a number of lesser known Harlemites of the literary and social world, became ardent neophytes of the word brought from Fontainebleau by this handsome young olive-skinned bearer of Gurdjieff's message to upper Manhattan.

But the trouble with such a life-pattern in Harlem was that practically everybody had to work all day to make a living, and the cult of Gurdjieff demanded not only study and application, but a large amount of inner observation and silent concentration as well. So while some of Mr. Toomer's best disciples were sitting long hours concentrating, unaware of time, unfortunately they lost their jobs, and could no longer pay the handsome young teacher for his instructions. Others had so little time to concentrate, if they wanted to live and eat, that their advance toward cosmic consciousness was slow and their hope of achieving awareness distant indeed. So Jean Toomer shortly left his Harlem group and went downtown to drop the seeds of Gurdjieff in less dark and poverty-stricken fields.

They liked him downtown because he was better-looking than Krishnamurti, some said. He had an evolved soul, and that soul made him feel that nothing else mattered, not even writing. From downtown New York, Toomer carried Gurdjieff to Chicago's Gold Coast—and the Negroes lost one of the most talented of all their writers—the author of the beautiful book of prose and verse, *Cane*.

The next thing Harlem heard of Jean Toomer was that he had married Margery Latimer, a talented white novelist, and maintained to the newspapers that he was no more colored than white—as certainly his complexion indicated. When the late James Weldon John-

† From *The Big Sea* (New York: Alfred A. Knopf, 1940). Reprinted by permission of Farrar, Straus and Giroux and Harold Ober Associates Incorporated.

son wrote him for permission to use some of his poems in the *Book of American Negro Poetry*, Mr. Johnson reported that the poet, who, a few years before, was "caroling softly souls of slavery" now refused to permit his poems to appear in an anthology of *Negro* verse—which put all the critics, white and colored, in a great dilemma. How should they class the author of *Cane* in their lists and summaries? With Dubose Heyward and Julia Peterkin? Or with Claude McKay and Countee Cullen? Nobody knew exactly, it being a case of black blood and white blood having met and the individual deciding, after Paris and Gurdjieff, to be merely American.

One can't blame him for that. Certainly nobody in Harlem could afford to pay for Gurdjieff. And very few there have evolved souls.

Now Mr. Toomer is married to a lady of means—his second wife—of New York and Santa Fe, and is never seen on Lenox Avenue any more. Harlem is sorry he stopped writing. He was a fine American writer. But when we get as democratic in America as we pretend we are on days when we wish to shame Hitler, nobody will bother much about anybody else's race anyway. Why should Mr. Toomer live in Harlem if he doesn't care to? Democracy is democracy, isn't it?

# ROBERT BONE

## [Jean Toomer's *Cane*][†]

The writers of the Lost Generation, as John Aldridge has observed, "were engaged in a revolution designed to purge language of the old restraints of the previous century and to fit it to the demands of a younger, more realistic time."[1] Stein and Hemingway in prose, Pound and Eliot in poetry, were threshing and winnowing, testing and experimenting with words, stretching them and refocusing them, until they became the pliant instruments of a new idiom. The only Negro writer of the 1920's who participated on equal terms in the creation of the modern idiom was a young poet-novelist named Jean Toomer.

Jean Toomer's *Cane* (1923) is an important American novel. By far the most impressive product of the Negro Renaissance, it ranks with Richard Wright's *Native Son* and Ralph Ellison's *Invisible Man* as a measure of the Negro novelist's highest achievement. Jean Toomer belongs to that first rank of writers who use words almost as a plastic medium, shaping new meanings from an original and highly personal style. Since stylistic innovation requires great technical dexterity, Toomer displays a concern for technique which is fully two

---

† From *The Negro Novel in America* (New Haven. Yale University Press, 1958). Reprinted permission.
1. *After the Lost Generation*, New York and London, McGraw–Hill, 1951, p. 88.

decades in advance of the period. While his contemporaries of the Harlem School were still experimenting with a crude literary realism, Toomer had progressed beyond the naturalistic novel to "the higher realism of the emotions," to symbol, and to myth.

Jean Toomer (1894–) was born in Washington, D.C., where his parents, who were cultivated Negroes of Creole stock, had moved in order to educate their children. Toomer's maternal grandfather, P. B. S. Pinchback, had been acting governor of Louisiana during Reconstruction days, so that tales of slavery and Reconstruction were a household tradition. Toomer was educated for the law at the University of Wisconsin and at the City College of New York, but literature soon became his first love. An avant-garde poet and short-story writer, he contributed regularly to such little magazines as *Broom, Secession, Double Dealer, Dial,* and *Little Review.* After a brief literary apprenticeship in cosmopolitan New York, he visited rural Georgia as a country schoolteacher—an experience which directly inspired the production of *Cane.*

During his formative period Toomer was a member of a semi-mystical literary group which included Hart Crane, Waldo Frank, Gorham Munson, and Kenneth Burke. Influenced philosophically by Ouspensky's *Tertium Organum,* they formed a bloc called Art as Vision—some of their catchwords being "the new slope of con-sciousness," "the superior logic of metaphor," and "noumenal knowledge." The group eventually split over the writings of Gurd-jieff, the Russian mystic. So far did Toomer succumb to Gurdjieff's spell that he spent the summer of 1926 at the Gurdjieff Institute in Fontainebleau, France, returning to America to proselytize actively for his mystical philosophy.

In spite of his wide and perhaps primary association with white intellectuals, as an artist Toomer never underestimated the impor-tance of his Negro identity. He attained a universal vision not by ignoring race as a local truth, but by coming face to face with his particular tradition. His pilgrimage to Georgia was a conscious attempt to make contact with his hereditary roots in the Southland. Of Georgia, Toomer wrote: "There one finds soil in the sense that the Russians know it—the soil every art and literature that is to live must be embedded in."[2] This sense of soil is central to *Cane* and to Toomer's artistic vision. "When one is on the soil of one's ancestors," his narrator remarks, "most anything can come to one."

What comes to Toomer, in the first section of *Cane,* is a vision of the parting soul of slavery:

> . . . for though the sun is setting on
> A song-lit race of slaves, it has not set;

2. Quoted in Alain Locke, "Negro Youth Speaks," *The New Negro* (New York, Boni, 1925), p. 51.

Though late, O soil, it is not too late yet
To catch thy plaintive soul, leaving, soon gone.

The soul of slavery persists in the "supper-getting-ready songs" of the black women who live on the Dixie Pike—a road which "has grown from a goat path in Africa." It persists in "the soft, listless cadence of Georgia's South," in the hovering spirit of a comforting Jesus, and in the sudden violence of the Georgia moon. It persists above all in the people, white and black, who have become Andersonian "grotesques" by virtue of their slave inheritance. Part I of *Cane* is in fact a kind of Southern *Winesburg, Ohio*. It consists of the portraits of six women—all primitives—in which an Andersonian narrator mediates between the reader and the author's vision of life on the Dixie Pike.

There is Karintha, "she who carries beauty" like a pregnancy, until her perfect beauty and the impatience of young men beget a fatherless child. Burying her child in a sawdust pile, she takes her revenge by becoming a prostitute; "the soul of her was a growing thing ripened too soon."

In "Becky" Toomer dramatizes the South's conspiracy to ignore miscegenation. Becky is a white woman with two Negro sons. After the birth of the first, she symbolically disappears from sight into a cabin constructed by community guilt. After the birth of the second, she is simply regarded as dead, and no one is surprised when the chimney of her cabin falls in and buries her. Toward Becky there is no charity from white or black, but only furtive attempts to conceal her existence.

Carma's tale, "which is the crudest melodrama," hinges not so much on marital infidelity as on a childish deception. Accused by her husband of having other men ("No one blames her for that") she becomes hysterical, and running into a canebrake, pretends to shoot herself. "Twice deceived, and the one deception proved the other." Her husband goes berserk, slashes a neighbor, and is sent to the chain gang. The tone of the episode is set by the ironic contrast between Carma's apparent strength ("strong as any man") and her childish behavior.

Fern, whose full name is Fernie May Rosen, combines the suffering of her Jewish father and her Negro mother: "at first sight of her I felt as if I heard a Jewish cantor sing. . . . As if his singing rose above the unheard chorus of a folksong." Unable to find fulfillment, left vacant by the bestowal of men's bodies, Fern sits listlessly on her porch near the Dixie Pike. Her eyes desire nothing that man can give her; the Georgia countryside flows into them, along with something that Toomer's narrator calls God.

"Esther" is a study in sexual repression. The protagonist is a near-white girl whose father is the richest colored man in town. Deprived of normal outlets by her social position, she develops a neurotic life of fantasy which centers upon a virile, black-skinned, itinerant preacher named King Barlo. At sixteen she imagines herself the mother of his immaculately conceived child. At twenty-seven she tries to translate fantasy into reality by offering herself to Barlo. Rebuffed and humiliated, she retreats into lassitude and frigidity.

Louisa, of "Blood-Burning Moon," has two lovers, one white and the other colored. Inflamed by a sexual rivalry deeper than race, they quarrel. One is slashed and the other is lynched. Unlike most Negro writers who have grappled with the subject of lynching, Toomer achieves both form and perspective. He is not primarily concerned with antilynching propaganda, but in capturing a certain atavistic quality in Southern life which defies the restraints of civilized society.

Part II of *Cane* is counterpoint. The scene shifts to Washington, where Seventh Street thrusts a wedge of vitality, brilliance, and movement into the stale, soggy, whitewashed wood of the city. This contrast is an aspect of Toomer's primitivism. The blacks, in his color scheme, represent a full life; the whites, a denial of it. Washington's Negroes have preserved their vitality because of their roots in the rural South, yet whiteness presses in on them from all sides. The "dickty" Negro, and especially the near-white, who are most nearly assimilated to white civilization, bear the brunt of repression and denial, vacillating constantly between two identities. Out of this general frame of reference grow the central symbols of the novel.

Toomer's symbols reflect the profound humanism which forms the base of his philosophical position. Man's essential goodness, he would contend, his sense of brotherhood, and his creative instincts have been crushed and buried by modern industrial society. Toomer's positive values, therefore, are associated with the soil, the cane, and the harvest; with Christian charity, and with giving oneself in love. On the other side of the equation is a series of burial or confinement symbols (houses, alleys, machines, theaters, nightclubs, newspapers) which limit man's growth and act as barriers to his soul. Words are useless in piercing this barrier; Toomer's intellectualizing males are tragic figures because they value talking above feeling. Songs, dreams, dancing, and love itself (being instinctive in nature) may afford access to "the simple beauty of another's soul." The eyes, in particular, are avenues through which we can discover "the truth that people bury in their hearts."

In the second section of *Cane,* Toomer weaves these symbols into a magnificent design, so that his meaning, elusive in any particular episode, emerges with great impact from the whole. "Rhobert" is an attack on the crucial bourgeois value of home ownership: "Rhobert wears a house, like a monstrous diver's helmet, on his head." Like Thoreau's farmer, who traveled through life pushing a barn and a hundred acres before him, Rhobert is a victim of his own property instinct. As he struggles with the weight of the house, he sinks deeper and deeper into the mud:

> Brother, Rhobert is sinking
> Let's open our throats, brother
> Let's sing Deep River when he goes down.

The basic metaphor in "Avey" compares a young girl to the trees planted in boxes along V Street, "the young trees that whinnied like colts impatient to be free." Avey's family wants her to become a school teacher, but her bovine nature causes her to prefer a somewhat older profession. Yet, ironically, it is not she but the narrator who is a failure, who is utterly inadequate in the face of Avey's womanhood.

In "Theatre" Toomer develops his "dickty" theme, through an incident involving a chorus girl and a theater-manager's brother. As John watches a rehearsal, he is impressed by Dorris' spontaneity, in contrast to the contrived movements of the other girls. He momentarily contemplates an affair, but reservations born of social distance prevent him from consummating his desire, except in a dream. Dorris, who hopes fleetingly for home and children from such a man, is left at the end of the episode with only the sordid reality of the theater.

"Calling Jesus" plays a more important role than its length would indicate in unifying the symbolism of the novel. It concerns a woman, urbanized and spiritually intimidated, whose "soul is like a little thrust-tailed dog that follows her, whimpering." At night, when she goes to sleep in her big house, the little dog is left to shiver in the vestibule. "Some one ... eoho Jesus ... soft as the bare feet of Christ moving across bales of Southern cotton, will steal in and cover it that it need not shiver, and carry it to her where she sleeps, cradled in dream-fluted cane."

In "Box Seat" Toomer comes closest to realizing his central theme. The episode opens with an invocation: "Houses are shy girls whose eyes shine reticently upon the dusk body of the street. Upon the gleaming limbs and asphalt torso of a dreaming nigger. Shake your curled wool-blossoms, nigger. Open your liver-lips to the lean white spring. Stir the root-life of a withered people. Call them from their houses and teach them to dream."

The thought is that of a young man, whose symbolic role is developed at once: "I am Dan Moore. I was born in a canefield. The hands of Jesus touched me. I am come to a sick world to heal it." Dan, moreover, comes as a representative of "powerful underground races": "The next world-savior is coming up that way. Coming up. A continent sinks down. The new-world Christ will need consummate skill to walk upon the waters where huge bubbles burst." The redemption motif is echoed in Dan's communion with the old slave: "I asked him if he knew what that rumbling is that comes up from the ground." It is picked up again through the portly Negro woman who sits beside Dan in the theater: "A soil-soaked fragrance comes from her. Through the cement floor her strong roots sink down . . . and disappear in blood-lines that waver south."

The feminine lead is played by Muriel, a school teacher inclined toward conventionality. Her landlady, Mrs. Pribby, is constantly with her, being in essence a projection of Muriel's social fears. The box seat which she occupies at the theater, where her every movement is under observation, renders her relationship to society perfectly. Her values are revealed in her query to Dan, "Why don't you get a good job and settle down?" On these terms only can she love him; meanwhile she avoids his company by going to a vaudeville performance with a girl friend.

Dan, a slave to "her still unconquered animalism," follows and watches her from the audience. The main attraction consists of a prize fight between two dwarfs for the "heavy-weight championship"; it symbolizes the ultimate degradation of which a false and shoddy culture is capable. Sparring grotesquely, pounding and bruising each other, the dwarfs suggest the traditional clown symbol of modern art. At the climax of the episode the winner presents a blood-spattered rose to Muriel, who recoils, hesitates, and finally submits. The dwarf's eyes are pleading: "Do not shrink. Do not be afraid of me." Overcome with disgust for Muriel's hypocrisy, Dan completes the dwarf's thought from the audience, rising to shout: "JESUS WAS ONCE A LEPER!" Rushing from the theater, he is free at last of his love for Muriel—free, but at the same time sterile: "He is as cool as a green stem that has just shed its flower."

Coming as an anticlimax after "Box Seat," "Bona and Paul" describes an abortive love affair between two Southern students at the University of Chicago—a white girl and a mulatto boy who is "passing." The main tension, reminiscent of Gertrude Stein's *Melanctha,* is between knowing and loving, set in the framework of Paul's double identity. It is not his race consciousness which terminates the relationship, as one critic has suggested, but precisely his "whiteness," his desire for knowledge, his philosophical bent. If he had been able to assert his Negro self—that which attracted Bona to him in the first place—he might have held her love.

In "Kabnis" rural Georgia once more provides a setting. This is the long episode which comprises the concluding section of *Cane.* By now the symbolic values of Toomer's main characters can be

readily assessed. Ralph Kabnis, the protagonist, is a school teacher
from the North who cringes in the face of his tradition. A spiritual
coward, he cannot contain "the pain and beauty of the South"; cannot embrace the suffering of the past, symbolized by slavery; cannot come to terms with his own bastardy; cannot master his
pathological fear of being lynched. Consumed with self-hatred and
cut off from any organic connection with the past, he resembles
nothing so much as a scarecrow: "Kabnis, a promise of soil-soaked
beauty; uprooted, thinning out. Suspended a few feet above the soil
whose touch would resurrect him."

Lewis, by way of contrast, is a Christ figure, an extension of Dan
Moore. Almost a T. S. Eliot creation ("I'm on a sort of contract with
myself"), his function is to shock others into moral awareness. It is
Lewis who confronts Kabnis with his moral cowardice: "Can't hold
them, can you? Master; slave. Soil; and the overarching heavens.
Dusk; dawn. They fight and bastardize you. The sun tint of your
cheeks, flame of the great season's multicolored leaves, tarnished,
burned. Split, shredded, easily burned" (p. 218).

Halsey, unlike Kabnis, has not been crushed by Southern life, but
absorbed into it. Nevertheless, his spiritual degradation is equally
thorough. An artisan and small shopkeeper like his father before him,
he "belongs" in a sense that Kabnis does not. Yet in order to maintain his place in the community, he must submit to the indignities of
Negro life in the South. Like Booker T. Washington, whose point of
view he represents, Halsey has settled for something less than manhood. Restless, groping tentatively toward Lewis, he escapes from
himself through his craft, and through an occasional debauch with
the town prostitute, whom he loved as a youth.

Father John, the old man who lives beneath Halsey's shop, represents a link with the Negro's ancestral past. Concealed by the present generation as an unpleasant memory, the old man is thrust into
a cellar which resembles the hold of a slave ship. There he sits, "A
mute John the Baptist of a new religion, or a tongue-tied shadow of
an old." When he finally speaks, it is to rebuke the white folks for
the sin of slavery. The contrast between Lewis and Kabnis is sharpened by their respective reactions to Father John. Through the old
slave, Lewis is able to "merge with his source," but Kabnis can only
deny: "An' besides, he aint my past. My ancestors were Southern
blue-bloods."

In terms of its dramatic movement "Kabnis" is a steep slope downward,[4] approximating the progressive deterioration of the protagonist. Early in the episode Kabnis is reduced to a scarecrow replica
of himself by his irrational fears. His failure to stand up to Hanby,

4. See Gorham B. Munson, *Destinations* (New York, 1928), pp. 178–96.

an authoritarian school principal, marks a decisive loss in his power of self-direction. Gradually he slips into a childlike dependence, first on Halsey, then on the two prostitutes, and finally on Halsey's little sister, Carrie Kate. In the course of the drunken debauch with which the novel ends, Kabnis becomes a clown, without dignity or manhood, wallowing in the mire of his own self-hatred. The stark tragedy of "Kabnis" is relieved only by the figure of Carrie Kate, the unspoiled child of a new generation, who may yet be redeemed through her ties with Father John.

A critical analysis of *Cane* is a frustrating task, for Toomer's art, in which "outlines are reduced to essences," is largely destroyed in the process of restoration. No paraphrase can properly convey the aesthetic pleasure derived from a sensitive reading of *Cane*. Yet in spite of Toomer's successful experiment with the modern idiom—or perhaps because of it—*Cane* met with a cold reception from the public, hardly selling 500 copies during its first year. This poor showing must have been a great disappointment to Toomer, and undoubtedly it was a chief cause of his virtual retirement from literature. Perhaps in his heart of hearts Jean Toomer found it singularly appropriate that the modern world should bury *Cane*. Let us in any event delay the exhumation no longer.

# DARWIN T. TURNER

## The Failure of a Playwright†

In 1922 Sherwood Anderson wrote to a twenty-seven-year old poet and short story writer, "You are the only Negro I've seen who seems really to have consciously the artist's impulse."[1] One might quibble that Mr. Anderson revealed his ignorance of or disdain for Paul Laurence Dunbar and Charles Chesnut but his tribute only faintly echoed the praise lavished on Jean Toomer in the early 1920's by Waldo Frank, Gorham Munson, W. S. Braithwaite, Allen Tate, and Robert Littell, literary figures whose pronouncements commanded respect. For the general reader, Toomer's reputation rests upon *Cane* (1923), a collection of stories, sketches, and poems of such high quality that historians of literature by American Negroes mourn his failure to produce more books. Almost unknown, however, is his struggle to

---

† This essay is based on research made possible by a study grant from the American Council of Learned Societies. Reprinted by permission.
1. Letter from Anderson to Toomer, undated, c. 1923. All letters and unpublished manuscripts referred to in this essay are housed in the Jean Toomer Collection at Fisk University, Nashville, Tennessee.

succeed as a dramatist. For more than a decade Jean Toomer experimented with dramatic form and technique in order to blend social satire with lyric expression of modern man's quest for spiritual self-realization. It was, as Waldo Frank wrote, an aim so new that it required a new form.[2]

The 1920's were so marked by experimentation in the American theater that pioneering playwrights and set-designers seem to have conspired to revolt against the form, language, and staging of conventional drama, which purported to imitate or represent the actualities of life. But when Toomer completed his first plays in the spring of 1922, the "revolution" was little more than sniper-fire. The Provincetown players had produced Eugene O'Neill's *The Emperor Jones* (1920) and *The Hairy Ape* (1922). Elmer Rice's expressionistic *The Adding Machine* and John Howard Lawson's *Roger Bloomer* would not be produced until 1923. Two to seven years away were other experimental dramas by O'Neill and Lawson, by George Kaufman and Marc Connelly, by John Dos Passos, E. E. Cummings, Sophie Treadwell, and Channing Pollock. Toomer, therefore, did not imitate a literary fad; he was sufficiently far ahead of his time that success would have assured him an important place in the annals of American drama.

Unlike Rice, Kaufman and Connelly, and some of the other dramatists, he did not exploit the novelty of dramatic techniques which had been popularized in other countries. He sought to perfect a technique by which he might most effectively use his artistic talent to objectify mankind's spiritual struggle and to ridicule the society which chains man with false moral standards and false values. Toomer's unique talent, as he later demonstrated in *Cane*, was a lyric impressionism which demanded language more flexible than the patter imitating actual conversations. He needed intensity to express the powerful emotions of his protagonists; but he also needed stylized artificiality to reflect the dullness and superficiality of the guardians of middle-class morals. The emotional impact of the scenes often depends not on the words but on the tone created by the words. Because he was concerned with mankind rather than with private men, he imitated the German Expressionistic playwrights who posited each character for a human type. And he elevated dance from its customary functions of spectacle and mood; literally and symbolically, it is the rhythmic means by which characters release themselves from inhibiting forces. To achieve these effects, he needed the flexibility of nonrepresentational technique and form. His, therefore, was no deliberate rebellion against the dramatic

2. Letter from Frank to Toomer, April 25, 1922.

conventions of his time; those forms simply were inadequate to express his intention.

In his first drama, *Natalie Mann* (1922), Toomer argued for the freedom of the young, middle-class Negro women. Nathan Merilh, a Christ-like representation of Jean Toomer, seeks to free Natalie from middle-class morés and from her dependence upon him. After defying convention by living with him in New York, she achieves total self-realization when, after he has collapsed at the climax of a dance ritual evolving individual personality from national and social origins, she comprehends his divinity and the meaning of his sacrifice of himself.

Natale's success is contrasted with the failure of Mertis, product of the same society. Having failed to choke the life force by teaching, engaging in social work, and fighting for Negroes' rights, she timidly enters a self-developing relationship with Law, Nathan's friend. Her search begins too weakly and too late; she dies from chill.

Lyric intensity characterizes the lovers and the soul-releasing dances of Nathan and Etta, a primitivistic Negro, who has discovered an ethic untainted by her fathers' repressive morality or the destructive lusts of white men. Contrasted with this lyric freedom are scenes of dullness, seeping from artificial banal, self-appointed guardians of public morality, who plan to destroy any Negroes unwilling to obey their code. Having dedicated themselves to reshaping their race to fit the mold sanctioned by white society, they deplore the rowdy habits of some Negroes, extol the moral superiority of Negro women and condemn spirituals and other reminders of the Negro's past. Convinced that natural expression of emotion is improper, they reflect their sterility in painfully self-conscious phraseology larded with allusions to the best writers and philosophers.

Toomer, however, does not attribute the repression to the racial characteristics of the Negro, but to his desire to be accepted in American society. For three hundred years, Nathan Merilh says, "An unsympathetic and unscientific white posture has gestured with scorn and condemnation at what it calls the benighted moral looseness of the Negro."[3] Lacking the self-assurance of the French, who have ridiculed the moral pretensions of the Anglo-Saxon,

> the Negro, cursed by his ignorance of moral evolution, of moral relativity, and lack of any sense of autonomous development, has not been so fortunate. He has knuckled to. . . . What should be the most colorful and robust of our racial segments is approaching a sterile and denuded hypocrisy. . . . [4]

3. From a manuscript copy of *Natalie Mann*.
4. *Ibid.*

The Negro woman, Toomer argues, has been restricted even more severely than the male. She is limited to marriage or prostitution, for white society blocks artistic, industrial, or political careers of all except the few Negro geniuses insensitive to pain.

Not surprisingly, faint echoes of George Bernard Shaw haunt the play: the style and thought of Shaw's plays had inspired Toomer's first serious considerations of a literary career.[5] Toomer's experiments with symbolic uses of character and of dance are more original. Except in *The Hairy Ape* and *The Emperor Jones*, symbolic uses of characters were uncommon in American drama in 1922, although they constituted a major characteristic of the Expressionistic drama which Georg Kaiser and Ernst Toller were writing in Germany. Toomer's concept of characterization, however, probably did not derive from a specific literary source but from his inclination to abstract meaning from particulars. In the set for Nathan Merilh's room, for instance, he symbolized Nathan's harmonious blending of facial elements by a portrait which is an idealized composite of a picture of Tolstoy and a picture of a powerful African. The dance, for Toomer, symbolized the rhythmic freedom of the emotion through which self-realization must be achieved. Although symbolic uses of dance are common in ballet, American dramatists of the Twenties generally overlooked such possibilities. The nearest approximations to Toomer's device are less imaginative uses of jazz in John Howard Lawson's *Processional* (1925) and John Dos Passos' *The Moon is a Gong* (1926). Lawson marched striking workers to jazz cadences; Dos Passos symbolized the relationship of characters by their dances. Both later dramatists made dance a vivid accessory; Toomer used it to express meaning.

Despite his imaginative techniques, Toomer did not fully realize his intention. After examining a draft of the play, Waldo Frank advised Toomer that the texture of the "teaparties, the talk of the incidental" was dead.[6] The obtuseness of Frank's criticism reveals the cardinal weakness of the drama. If Frank, sophisticated in literary symbolism, failed to comprehend the tonal implications of the contrived artificiality, keener judgment could not be expected from theater-goers habituated to the realistic, the comic, and the melodramatic. Toomer apparently abandoned the play when he could not improve the form for there is no record that he attempted to publish it or to have it produced.

He evidenced more faith in a second play, *Kabnis*, which a companion piece to *Natalie Mann*, had been written before April, 1922.

---

5. Toomer gave Shaw this credit in an unpublished journal written about 1936.
6. Letter from Frank to Toomer, April 25, 1922.

Published in revised form in *Cane, Kabnis* negates the possibility that an intellectual Negro can achieve self-realization in the South.

Ralph Kabnis, a Northern Negro who has been teaching in a Southern school, is discharged when his principal sees him intoxicated. Choosing to remain in the South despite the fears which motivate his drinking, he becomes a handyman and an apprentice in a blacksmith shop. Although he has hoped to root himself in that section of the country which he posits for the ancestral soil of his race, he cannot imitate the natives. Uneducated Negroes reject him because they know that he is different. Unlike Principal Hanby, Kabnis cannot compensate for his lost self-respect by abusing less powerful Negroes Trained to a middle-class respect for education and humiliated to a fear of white Southerners, he cannot pattern after Blacksmith Halsey, who, contemptuous of formal education, enjoys manual labor, and, secure in his self-esteem, loses no dignity when he greets his white customers deferentially. Poetically sensitive and easily shocked, Kabnis cannot imitate Layman, a jackleg preacher, who preserves his own life by mutely observing the abuse, the injustice, and the violence inflicted upon Negroes while he safeguards his income by offering them relief through the fervor of a primitive religion which he knows to be impotent. Insufficiently sensual to control Stella, who has been born of the lust of white men and victimized by the lust of leaders of the Negro community, Kabnis must content himself physically with Cora, whose sensuality is imitative, and spiritually with Carrie K, a youthful, pure, mother-image. Debauched, impotent himself, cognizant of the impotence of education and religion, he awaits inspiration and guidance to come from the message of Father John, an incoherent babbler from the Negro's past. But when Father John finally mumbles something which can be understood, it is merely the banal. "The white people sinned when they made the Bible lie." As the play ends, Kabnis, carrying a bucket of dead coals to his workshop, trudges upward from the basement where Father John is dying in the arms of Carrie K.

The only scintillating ray in this morbid allegory of Negro impotence is Lewis, who, like Nathan Merilh, is both an ectype of Jean Toomer and a Christ-figure. Reared in the North, educated, sensitive but not poetically ineffectual, he can control his actions by will and reason, or can respond naturally to emotional impulse, the life-force, which orders the spiritual and physical union of male with female. Having contracted with himself to remain among his people for a month, he observes them compassionately and communicates satisfactorily with all of them. Sympathetic but emotionally detached, he offers help but is forced to leave when they seek instead the anodynes of drink and sex.

Lacking *Natalie Mann's* lyric language, exciting dances, and patirical social commentary, *Kabnis* has the somber tone of a medieval morality play, written in the style of twentieth-century Expressionism. For Toomer the play proved a disappointment. For two years he tried unsuccessfully to arrange a staging, but producers' reactions can be defined by the rejection by Kenneth Macgowan, one of the most daring experimental producers of his generation:

> It won't do as it stands. The dialogue is good dialogue, the characters are exceedingly good. The incidents are most of them very interesting. But I feel that the play lacks the one thing a play can't lack—a general dramatic design.[7]

Unfortunately for Toomer, he and Macgowan preceded the Theater of the Absurd. Macgowan could not see beyond Eugene O'Neill, who experimented with plot construction, language, setting, and sound, but who worked within a clearly defined plot which had both beginning and end. Toomer's efforts anticipated the dramas of Samuel Beckett and Ionesco. Like *Waiting for Godot, Kabnis* is a spectacle of futility and impotence. Like Ionesco's *The Chairs,* it suspensefully prepares for a trenchant summation of life, which will give meaning to the play and to life itself; but the expected explosion is muted in both plays to the wet-sack whisper of a banal restatement of the obvious. Judged by the standards of 1922, *Kabnis* is a pale form of the Expressionism which had not yet become familiar in America; judged by the standards of 1956 it is good Theater of the Absurd.

In 1923, when Alain Locke asked for a work to be included in *Plays of Negro Life,* Toomer sent him the already completed "Balo," which is the least comprehensible of all his dramas. Non-dramatic and plotless, "Balo" seems to be an experiment with dialogue rather than a completed play.

Using dialect for the first time, Toomer pictured the morning and the evening of a Negro family in Georgia. Idled by lack of work, the father—a preacher and a farmer—spends the morning reading theology. In the evening the family entertain relatives.

*Balo* suggests the essences of daily living and of the Negro folk: the friendliness and the co-operation of the interrelation ships among neighbors, the pleasantness of a meal shared with relatives, the emotional enthusiasm of a spiritual, the saintliness of Uncle Ned (a healthier, more articulate Father John and the religious fervor of Balo, a young son in the family. Lacking dramatic or emotional tension, however, *Balo* seems an experiment to achieve greater flexibility

---

7. Letter from Macgowan to Toomer, dated September 22, 1923.

and freedom for prose forms rather than a work intended for the stage. Ironically, however, *Balo*, unlike Toomer's other dramas, has been produced on the stage.

His early efforts exhausted and his plays apparently unwanted, Toomer abandoned drama for a few years. By the time he wrote *The Sacred Factory* (1927), Expressionism had become so familiar to American critics and audiences that the term was freely used to describe almost any experimentation with nonrepresentational techniques. In starkly simple Expressionism comparable to that of Ernst Toller's *Man and the Masses*, Toomer found form for his most artistically successful drama, which reveals the dull existences of the working classes and the frustrated, repressed lives of the middle class.

For the first time, Toomer used a nonrepresentational stage set. Pillars divide the state into three chambers not separated by walls. The domed central chamber resembles a religious structure, dominated by blue lighting. The adjacent chambers represent the homes of the workers and the cultured people.

After a choral incantation, the workers pantomime their lives. Having completed the stiff, awkward ritual dance of marriage, the man leaves for work, the woman moves in circles, the man returns; they eat, become sleepy, go to bed, arise; the man goes to work, the woman circles. Children are born; after circling briefly with their mother, they leave. The man dies, the woman mourns, the woman dies. Like robots, they have lived and died without interest, desire, hope, or possibility.

In the chamber of the middle class, John and Mary, awakening to life, are joined by a child who wonders where she is. The mother's imaginative explanation that they are on "a little speck of dust on a great vast elephant full of stars" elicits ridicule from the chorus. When the child poses additional questions about life and about God, the physician-husband, interrupting, lowers the tone from metaphysical to mundane by arguing with the wife. Accusing the wife of being a perfectionist who seeks ideal existence with a new husband, he charges that she sublimated her emotional needs in intellectual activities at the age of eighteen instead of satisfying them by marrying. Education, philosophy, morality, he continues, are drugs destroying mankind.

Having responded by chant and dance to each accusation made by the husband, the chorus now sings its worship of the drugstore which dispenses art, science, and religion. Its appeal to religion and God is ignored, however, by the scientist-husband and by the saint who has separated herself from the chorus.

Estranged from her husband, the wife regrets their failure to become a single blend of her faith and his knowledge. Separated from him spiritually, she remains with him physically because she will not desert her child.

The mood of the final act is established by the chorus's acclaiming the joy and the horror of war. Looking back to the early years of the marriage, the husband asserts that their first estrangement developed from the conflict between his intellect and her emotion. After the conflict became apparent, he dedicated himself to pleasure, which mankind calls "God." Having risen to protest the scientist's allegation that men seek only pleasure, the chorus kneels and chants its worship of the Madonna. When Being enters the room, John refuses to die because he has not lived. Confused, the child enters the central chamber and seats herself.

Despite the abstractness and despite the ambiguous conclusion, it is somewhat surprising that Toomer failed to find a producer for *The Sacred Factory*. The play certainly is as artistic as some of the pseudo-Expressionism shown to New York audiences in 1927. Perhaps, however, producers feared the absence of a conventional protagonist with whom the audience might sympathize. Mary, a symbol of emotion and of Woman, compels more sympathy than any other individual figure, but she is too obviously designed merely to be the target for John's tirades. Mankind is the actual, pathetic protagonist but a protagonist abstracted from abstractions evokes intellectual rather than emotional response. And intellectual appeal alone does not form lines at ticket windows.

When publishers rejected *The Gallonwerps*, a satirical novel. Toomer rewrote it as a play for gigantic marionettes. Earlier in the century, designer-director Gordon Craig had proposed using gigantic marionettes as actors to transcend the limitations of human actors. Toomer, however, conceived of the marionettes as a dramatic, visual emphasis of his thesis that the world is a puppet-show manipulated by a master puppeteer.

In *The Gallonwerps* (1928), the master is enigmatic, mystical, cultured, worldly Prince Klondike of Oldrope, an expert "diker" or practitioner of the art of tricking people in such a way that they enjoy being tricked. The drama itself is the tale of a necessary "dike."

Under the pretext of helping Wimepime Gallonwerp assemble an audience to listen to the philosophical ideas of Wistwold, her husband, Prince Klondike plans to steal Little Gasstar from the watchful nurse Elginbora. Assisted by the confusion attending one of the many arguments of the guests, Klondike succeeds with his plan. Later, having hidden Little Gasstar, he returns to the Gallonwerp home to take Wimepime and Wistwold with him.

A dramatization of the ego's rescue of the id from the superego, *The Gallonwerps* depends too heavily upon satiric caricatures and

quips. Some of the character-types are interesting. The prince, more
Mephistophelean than Nathan Merilh or Lewis, is the familiar
extension of Jean Toomer. Wimepime, a world-famous beauty of
Billboa of Baaleria (Chicago of America), has her prototype in
Natalie Mann, the female who must be awakened to self-realization.
Wistwold, an idealist and a dreamer, hopes to save the world by
appealing to reason. Wimepime and Wistwold thus symbolize the
awakened emotion and the intellect which, Toomer believed, must
be merged within a fully realized individual.

Some character types earn recognition from the prince: Limph
Krok, a sensitive pedant who is sickened by contact with the world
of sweating bodies and mundane thoughts; Breastbuck Coleeb, a
sarcastic but genial naturalist who, perhaps, has his prototype in
Clarence Darrow; and Boldkire Kigore, a masterbuilder, a leader
of men, almost worthy to be a rival of the prince. Those whom the
prince condemns are the female leader who, with chains of Approval,
binds society to her fixed and shallow ideas; the poseur who pretends originality for the philosophic ideas which he has gathered
from books; the artificially sophisticated world traveler; the mindless
woman who repeats her lover's ideas; the tasteless nouveau-riche
being roomed for her sale into European nobility; the prim and offi-
cious busybody; the effeminate artist; and the man who assumes
authority on every subject.

Successful drama, however, must offer audiences more than interesting stereotypes. As Gorham Munson warned, Toomer had failed
to assume the possibility of a disinterested reader or spectator.[8] Actually, Toomer had been misguided by the effusive praises he had
received from friends. Circulated in manuscript form among them,
*The Gallonwerps* had been pronounced a success by those who recognized themselves among Toomer's caricatures and by some who
respected him as a published author and worshipped him as their
spiritual leader. Exalted by these, Toomer was unprepared for the
uninformed reader who would neither laugh at the intimate joke nor
comprehend the philosophical and psychological doctrines. Although
he tried to rewrite *The Gallonwerps* during the early Thirties, publishers and producers who had feared to introduce it during the
booming Twenties scarcely considered it during the Depression.

After an abortive attempt at more realistic drama, *A Drama of the
Southwest* (1935), based on his experiences in New Mexico, Toomer
abandoned efforts to write drama for stage production but continued to write dialogue. In 1937 and again in 1941, he published
Socratic dialogues in the *New Mexico Literary Sentinel*. As late as
1947, he attempted magazine sale of a brief satirical drama of modern man, who, deserted by a wife pre-occupied with meetings, sol-

8. Letter from Munson to Toomer, dated March 19, 1928.

aces himself with the sympathetic companionship of the robot who serves as a maid. Rejection of this drama ended Toomer's unsuccessful flirtation with drama.

Despite imaginative techniques, occasionally striking characterizations, and frequently brilliant dialogue, Toomer failed to sell his nonrepresentational drama to producers of his generation. Accustomed to looking for a plot in even the most abstract Expressionistic drama they knew, they were irritated to find only a lecture by Jean Toomer, masked as Christ or Mephistopheles. At least two of the plays—*Kabnis* and *The Sacred Factory*—merit, however, a sympathetic reading by a contemporary producer of off-Broadway theater. Conditioned by Beckett, Ionesco, Genet, and Albee to the intellectual excitement of spending a few hours puzzling out the meaning of a play, audiences of the Sixties are sufficiently sophisticated to appreciate Jean Toomer's expression of the futility and the frustration of man's existence.


# ARNA BONTEMPS

## Introduction to the 1969 Edition of *Cane*†

Looking back on the Harlem Renaissance of the 1920's, the distinguished scholar and sociologist, Charles S. Johnson, observed that "A brief ten years have developed more confident self-expression, more widespread efforts in the direction of art than the long, dreary two centuries before." Recalling the sunburst of Jean Toomer's first appearance, he added, "Here was triumphantly the Negro artist, detached from propaganda, sensitive only to beauty. Where [Paul Laurence] Dunbar gave to the unnamed Negro peasant a reassuring touch of humanity, Toomer gave to the peasant a passionate charm. . . . More than artist, he was an experimentalist, and this last quality has carried him away from what was, perhaps, the most astonishingly brilliant beginning of any Negro writer of this generation."

*Cane*, the book that provoked this comment, was published in 1923 after portions of it had appeared earlier in *Broom, The Crisis, Double Dealer, Liberator, Little Review, Modern Review, Nomad, Prairie* and *S 4 N.* But *Cane* and its author, let it be said at once,

† From *Cane*. Perennial Classic Edition (Liveright Publishers, 1923), vii–x, xii–xvi. Copyright © 1969 by Arna Bontemps, from *Cane* by Jean Toomer. Used by permission of Liveright Publishing Corporation.

    Several paragraphs of this essay originally appeared, in a slightly different form, in "The Negro Renaissance: Jean Toomer and the Harlem Writers of the 1920's," by Arna Bontemps, in *Anger, and Beyond: The Negro Writer in the United States*, edited with an Introduction by Herbert Hill (New York: Harper & Row, Publishers, 1966).

presented an enigma from the start—an enigma which has, in many ways, deepened in the years since its publication. Given such a problem, perhaps one may be excused for not wishing to separate completely the man from his work.

During the summer of 1922 Toomer had sent a batch of unpublished manuscripts to the editors of the *Liberator*, Max Eastman and his assistant Claude McKay. They accepted some of the pieces enthusiastically and requested biographical material from the author. Toomer responded with the following:

> Whenever the desire to know something about myself comes from a sincere source, I am always glad to meet it. For in telling folks I invariably tell my own self something. My family is from the South. My mother's father, P. B. S. Pinchback, born in Macon, Georgia, left home as a boy and worked on the Mississippi River steamers. At the beginning of the Civil War he organized and was commissioned captain of a Negro company in New Orleans. Later, in the days of Reconstruction, he utilized the Negro's vote and won offices for himself, the highest being that of lieutenant, and then acting governor of Louisiana. When his heyday was over, he left the old hunting grounds and came to Washington. Here I was born. My own father likewise came from Middle Georgia. Racially, I seem to have (who knows for sure) seven blood mixtures: French, Dutch, Welsh, Negro, German, Jewish, and Indian. Because of these, my position in America has been a curious one. I have lived equally amid the two race groups. Now white, now colored. From my own point of view I am naturally and inevitably an American. I have strived for a spiritual fusion analagous to the fact of racial intermingling. Without denying a single element in me, with no desire to subdue one to the other, I have sought to let them function as complements. I have tried to let them live in harmony. Within the last two or three years, however, my growing need for artistic expression has pulled me deeper and deeper into the Negro group. And as my powers of receptivity increased, I found myself loving it in a way that I could never love the other. It has stimulated and fertilized whatever creative talent I may contain within me. A visit to Georgia last fall was the starting point of almost everything of worth that I have done. I heard folk-songs come from the lips of Negro peasants. I saw the rich dusk beauty that I had heard many false accents about, and of which till then, I was somewhat skeptical. And a deep part of my nature, a part that I had repressed, sprang suddenly to life and responded to them. Now, I cannot conceive of myself as aloof and separated. My point of view has not changed; it has deepened, it has widened. Personally, my life has been torturous and dispersed. The comparative wealth

which my family once had, has now dwindled away to almost nothing. We, or rather, they, are in the unhappy position of the lowered middle-class. There seems to have been no shop-keepers or shysters among us. I have lived by turn in Washington, New York, Chicago, Sparta, Georgia, and several smaller towns. I have worked, it seems to me, at everything: selling papers, delivery boy, soda clerk, salesman, shipyard worker, librarian-assistant, physical director, school teacher, grocery clerk, and God knows what all. Neither the universities of Wisconsin or New York gave me what I wanted, so I quit them. Just how I finally found my stride in writing, is difficult to lay hold of. It has been pushing through for the past four years. For two years, now, I have been in solitude here in Washington. It may be begging hunger to say that I am staking my living on my work. So be it. The mould is cast, and I cannot turn back even if I would.

Neither the editors of the *Liberator* nor the lonely youth taking care of his decrepit grandparents in Washington, watching them slowly deteriorate after having led exciting and eventful lives, could have realized that this sudden outpouring was itself a strange harbinger. *Cane* was published the following year. While a few sensitive and perceptive people went quietly mad, as the saying goes, about this wholly extraordinary book, they seemed unable to enlarge its audience. Only two small printings were issued, and these vanished quickly. However, among the most affected was practically an entire generation of young Negro writers then just beginning to emerge; their reaction to Toomer's *Cane* marked an awakening that soon thereafter began to be called a Negro Renaissance. . . .

If such a first work as *Cane* was betokened by the biography he sent to his friends at the *Liberator* on August 19, 1922, it was also a harbinger of a very different sort. It foreshadowed a wild search for identity that was to drive Toomer through all the years that followed till his death in 1967 and, eventually, even to preempt his talent.

Some of Toomer's admirers, putting *Cane* beside the early work of such contemporaries as William Faulkner and Ernest Hemingway, have wondered why he appears to have stopped short and deliberately turned his back on greatness. If this was indeed what happened, a few clues as to the reasons might be cited.

As a youngster Toomer had been fascinated by the idea of self-improvement by body-building and he had enrolled in correspondence courses. His efforts had been remarkably successful, and the beautiful child of Nina Pinchback, daughter of a controversial celebrity, had grown into a personable and athletic youth. By the time of *Cane's* publication in 1923, he had turned to an intensive study of his own psychology, and in the same year encountered the ideas of Georges Ivanovitch Gurdjieff, a system or teaching by which one sought to attain through instruction and discipline new levels of experience, beginning with the difficult first step to self-consciousness and progressing to world- and possibly cosmic-consciousness. A year later he spent the summer at the Gurdjieff Institute at Fontainebleau, France, explaining to his friends, "I am. What I am and what I may become I am trying to find out."

Half a dozen years passed and he had still not resolved this problem when in 1931 he undertook a psychological experiment with a group of friends living in a cottage in Portage, Wisconsin. Not too much is known about this, and one can only assume it was in line with the Gurdjieff aims. The townsfolk, probably fearing that the "experiment" was a disguise for some sort of free love adventure, were horrified, though they pressed no accusations. A year later, Toomer married Marjory Latimer, a descendant of the early New England poet, Anne Bradstreet, and a renowned New England clergyman, John Cotton. She had been a member of the group of men and women associated with Toomer in the experiment, and her friendship with him had been an outgrowth. She was also known as one of the most promising young novelists in the United States. Marjory Latimer Toomer died the following year giving birth to their only child.

A sojourn in the Southwest, sometimes troubled, always questing, followed. During this time he appears to have made some prominent converts to the Gurdjieff system; Langston Hughes' poem "A House in Taos" was believed by some to have been inspired by Toomer's experiences there. In 1934, however, Toomer contracted an equally surprising second marriage. It was his destiny, apparently, to be closely linked with *Marjories*. With Marjorie Content, daughter of Harry Content, a member of the New York Stock Exchange, he appeared to vanish from literature among the tolerant Quakers of Bucks County, Pennsylvania. When next heard from, he was writing for the *Friends Intelligencer*, sometimes calling himself by his father's first name, lecturing piously to Friends' meetings, and occasionally making vague references to the racial blend in him.

An inquiry by a young Quaker friend of mine elicited a frank though guarded response from a General Secretary of the Philadelphia Yearly Meeting of the Religious Society of Friends. At a time when the committee that was running the George School would not permit the faculty to accept Negro applicants, someone volunteered that there was already a so-called Negro in attendance. The finger was pointed at Toomer and the child by his first wife, but Toomer parried the questions and no action was taken.

Within his own heart and mind, however, the fundamental issue was too big to be disposed of so lightly. "All of this," wrote the General Secretary, "is possibly a basis for Jean's present condition. I have recited it because of Arna Bontemps' request for biographical information for the last twenty years. He may know most of it and more, but it is during the last twenty to thirty years that I have known Jean. . . . This information was given me by Jean at my request. He did not indicate that it was confidential but it is certainly personal and should be handled in that spirit."

As this sequence occurred, Toomer made notes for an autobiography in which he proposed to cope with the problems raised by his situation. It was never developed fully, but his outlines suggest that he remembered vividly the ordeal of muscle-building in which he had engaged as a boy, his restoration after an exhausting "spell of sex," his growing disgust with "most of the life" around him in Washington, his painful vigil while watching "Pinchback's break-up," and the decline of their once well-to-do family into poverty, and eventually the grueling confrontation with himself on setting out for the University of Wisconsin. "I would again be entering a white world; and, though I personally had experienced no prejudice or exclusion either from the whites or the colored people, I had seen enough to know that America viewed life as if it were divided into white and black. Having lived with colored people for the past five years, at Wisconsin the question might come up. What was I? I thought about it independently, and, on the basis of fact, concluded I was neither white nor black, but simply an American. I held this view and decided to live according to it. I would tell others if the occasion demanded it."

On November 7, 1923, Allen Tate, then a member of the Fugitives and one of the editors of *The Fugitive*, wrote to Jean Toomer at the suggestion of their mutual friend Hart Crane. Tate wrote him again in May 1924. Both times it was connected with a train stopover in Washington which he thought would provide an opportunity for them to meet face to face. But it never happened. Tate appears to have been reaching toward Toomer, tentatively and vaguely, on behalf of the Fugitive enclave. Had they met, perhaps some good might have resulted, both to them and to him.

Between these two attempts to meet Toomer, Tate reviewed *Cane* for the Nashville *Tennessean*, saying that parts of it "challenge some of the best modern writing," and that he judged it "highly important for literature." It was a perceptive and prophetic reading of a timeless book.

# JOHN M. REILLY

## The Search for Black Redemption: Jean Toomer's *Cane*[†]

The migration of Southern black people to Northern cities that began at the time of the First World War represents a psychological as well as geographical movement. Leaving the conditions of peasantry black people moved from the highly controlled society of traditional caste relationships to circumstances where imprecise racial restrictions and changed conditions of employment and living impel individuals to become self-conscious and, within the limits of the ghetto, self-determining. The consequence of the mass migration and the internal transformation of hundreds of thousands of dark-skinned Americans has been a strong racial awareness emerging in the 1920's in the nationalism of Marcus Garvey's United Negro Improvement Association with its black business ventures, a program for an independent state in Africa, and the aim of uniting 400,000,000 colored people in the search for a single destiny.

The counterpart of Garvey's urban nationalism was the cultural movement that came to be known as the Negro Renaissance. It evidenced racial pride in the feeling expressed by writers that they had to create without regard for stereotypical audience expectations if they were to understand the special experience of black America. As Langston Hughes put it in a manifesto of the 1920's: "We younger Negro artists who create now intend to express our individual dark-skinned selves without fear or shame. If white people are pleased, we are glad. If they are not, it doesn't matter. . . . If colored people are pleased, we are glad. If they are not, their displeasure doesn't matter either."[1]

Despite their social class and political differences, Garveyites and artists agreed in their devotion to self-discovery. However their programs might differ, first priority for all was enunciation of the inherent meaning of being black. In that respect, of course, the movement begun in the 1920's remains vital in the 1970's, for the dislocation of the black diaspora and the need to come to terms with the effects of a slave past have created a necessity for questions of identity to remain at the core of black literature.

A monument of the early period of self-discovery is Jean Toomer's book *Cane* (1923). Informed by a desire for reclamation of the racial

---

† Originally published in *Studies in the Novel* 2.3 (Fall 1970): 312–13. Reprinted by permission.
1. Quoted in Langston Hughes, "The Twenties: Harlem and Its Negritude," *African Forum*, I (Spring 1966), 20.

past, *Cane* asserts some of the major values of the Negro Renaissance, so that as the problem of identity remains central to black literature, all attempts to resolve the problem demand our attention.

*Cane,* however, is a problematic book itself, not the sort to generate direct imitation, nor to be read widely without critical discussion. "There are many odd and provocative things about *Cane,*" writes Arna Bontemps, "and not the least is its form. Reviewers who read it in in a kind of frappé. Realism was mixed with what they called mysticism, and the result seemed to many of them confusing."[2] Readers of our time may be less confused, but the form of *Cane* still is not patent. In fact it is easy to support the impression that *Cane* is a collection of fragments coincidentally unified by a common binding. For example, there is this external evidence. Toomer published separately some of the sketches he eventually grouped in *Cane;* thus, portions appeared in *Broom, Liberator, Modern Review* and other magazines, while Alain Locke published two sketches from *Cane* in his famous anthology *The New Negro* (1925). Moreover, fragmentary effect is suggested internally by Toomer's use of a large cast of characters appearing individually in different pieces and by the presence in the one volume of two-page sketches and a long short story, impressionistic prose and semi-dramatic narrative. Full appreciation of the book, therefore, depends upon our finding in the apparent "miscellany . . . of fictional portraits and poems of life in the villages of Georgia and Washington, D.C."[3] the basis of unity.

The means of unity may be briefly described. In *Cane* Toomer has dropped from his narrative the conventional dependence upon causal sequence, continuous presence of leading characters, and chronological progression. In their place he has adopted the compressed statement of images linked by their intrinsic associations, and he has represented those imagistic statements becoming synthesized either in the mind of a narrator, in the consciousness and unconsciousness of a character, or in the ambience of locale. Toomer, thus, links his various sketches and lyrics into a poetically structured record of a search for the route to self-expression and consequent redemption for the artist and his race.

Analysis of Toomer's method must begin with two of the poems that appear early in the text. Toomer uses lyrics as epigraphs for his prose pieces and scatters snatches of verse throughout the text as refrains of the characters. Quite often commentary is direct as, for example, in "November Cotton Flower," which follows the

2. "The Negro Renaissance: Jean Toomer and the Harlem Writers of the 1920's," *Anger, and Beyond: The Negro Writer in the United States,* ed. Herbert Hill (New York, 1966), p. 25.
3. James A. Emmanuel and Theodore L. Gross, eds. *Dark Symphony: Negro Literature in America* (New York, 1968), p. 97.

prose sketch of Karintha who is described "as innocently lovely as a November cotton flower." Karintha, who happens to be the subject of the first sketch in *Cane*, is also characterized in a poetic epigraph by "skin like dusk on the eastern horizon." This image then is extensively developed in one of the two thematically determining poems: "Georgia Dusk" and "Song of the Son"[4] (pp. 21–23) [16–17].

The seven stanzas of "Georgia Dusk" set a rural scene with metonymic images of working life—a saw mill with its smoking sawdust pile, plowed and seeded cotton lands. The richness of the setting is said to offer "An orgy for some genius of the South. . . . Surprised in making folk-songs from soul sounds." The soul is obviously that of the men in a later stanza with "race memories of king and caravan, who go singing through the footpaths of the swamp." These blacks carrying their African identity in their unconscious being sing till the "pine trees are guitars," and the "chorus of the cane. Is caroling a vesper to the stars." Thus, according to Toomer's imagery, the spirit of the workmen animates nature and, at the same time, establishes the metaphor of folk-songs as the expression of fundamental self and an outlet for black soul. Moreover, spontaneous outpouring of soul in folk music is potentially a means of salvation, for the final stanza of "Georgia Dusk" images the songs with power to "give virgin lips to cornfield concubines," and to "Bring dreams of Christ to dusky cane-lipped throngs."

Paired with his lyric celebration of the redemption of the folk through spontaneous expression of their inner selves is Toomer's announcement in "Song of the Son" of a means of redemption for a black poet. The parting souls of the formerly enslaved black people carol softly in folk song bringing their historical era to a close, and "just before an epoch's sun declines," says the poet, as "Thy son . . . I have returned to thee." Though it is late, there is still time "To catch thy plaintive soul. . . ." In a striking image of fulfillment and rebirth Toomer likens the ex-slaves to "purple ripened plums." One plum saved for him provides a seed that becomes an "everlasting song, a singing tree, / Caroling softly souls of slavery, / What they were, and what they are to me." In image and sensibility the poet is represented in this poem as achieving a unity with his black ancestors, finding inspiration for his song, and glimpsing a place for himself in the spiritual fulfillment of the race.

The operative themes of "Georgia Dusk" and "Song of the Son"— acceptance of the racial past and spontaneous expression—represent

4. Since the first edition published by Boni and Liveright in 1923, *Cane* has been reprinted twice. The first reprint was by University Place Press (New York, 1951), and most recently *Cane* has been reissued in a Harper and Row Perennial Classic paperback edition (New York, 1969). Citations in the text refer to the [1969] edition. [Page numbers in square brackets refer to this Norton Critical Edition.]

the goals of the search for identity throughout *Cane*. The poetic manner of the lyrics is also present, and highly appropriate, throughout *Cane* for two reasons. First is the fact that most of the characters can neither conceptualize nor articulate the goals because they are folk characters, but the second and most important reason is that Toomer conceives of self-discovery as an intuitive experience which must be described or, rather, transmitted in a way that will preserve the content of feeling. The prose in *Cane*, therefore, is impressionistic and non-discursive.

The first discrete section of the book contains six sketches. Each is set in rural Georgia and focuses on a woman's relationship to her instinctual sexual being. The first tells of Karintha. From childhood she is pursued by men in lust, until in time she drops a fatherless child from her womb. Having been forced to ripen too soon, she indulges the men who buy her body but stays spiritually aloof from them "carrying beauty, perfect as dusk when the sun goes down."

Becky of the second sketch is a white woman with two mulatto sons. As a result of her violation of caste prohibitions, Becky must live isolated in an old cabin with her sullen boys until one day she is killed when it collapses on top of her. The narrator and his companion ride by, and to them the scene appears to be a mysterious vindication, but of what they don't know. In confusion they ride frantically into town where folks wait to hear their story. But the story is over. It is all implication.

To impatient male lust and caste taboos Toomer adds jealousy to complicate sexual expression in his third sketch, "Carma." This sketch also amplifies the portrayal of the instinctual woman with imagery that relates her to forces greater than her individual person. In opening the piece the narrator describes the sight of Carma in overalls driving a "Georgia chariot" down the Dixie Pike, which he recognizes "has grown from a goat path in Africa." The scene is heavily sensual. Pine-needles glow like mazda, sawmill smoke curls in the air, and a sad song is heard in the distance, while "the smell of farmyards" is said to be "the fragrance of the woman." Her body is a song, dancing, it seems, in a forest momentarily African. In these circumstances, replete with imagery of the folk soul and the expressive self, the narrator recounts an episode of the "crudest melodrama." In response to her husband's accusation that she has had other men, Carma runs into the cane and pretends to shoot herself. When he discovers the deceit, her husband in frustration slashes one of his fellows and ends up in the chain gang. This melodrama provides the overt action of the sketch, but the chief effect, as in the other sketches, is conveyed by the imagery relating to feeling and expression.

The significance of the instinctual females climaxes in Toomer's sketch of Fern. Dominating her portrait are her eyes, eyes that attract men, eyes into which the rest of Fern's face and then the whole countryside seem to flow. Like Karintha, Fern by her beauty compels men to desire, but unlike Karintha she carries their attentions to the point where they are deeply devoted to doing things for her. Nothing they do, however, is sufficient to her beauty or notable enough for her to acknowledge. Fern evidently symbolizes natural beauty becoming transformed into spirit. Part black and part Jewish, her appearance affects the narrator as does the sorrowful song of a cantor. Walking up the Dixie Pike almost any time of day one is likely to see her sitting on the railing of her porch, her head tilted slightly forward because of a nail in the post which she won't take the trouble to pull out. If the suggestion of spiritual power seems strained by the possibility that that detail alludes to the Cross of Jesus, it may be enforced more clearly by the narrator's saying that Fern, though she had many men's bodies, "became a virgin." (It will be recalled that the cornfield concubines in "Georgia Dusk" receive virgin lips through the power of folk soul.) As a type of a blessed virgin Fern offers to the narrator salvation through the sensations of mystical unification with his past and people. Walking out with Fern on an evening the narrator felt, as always in Georgia dusk, "that things unseen to men were tangibly immediate." He half expected a vision, for "when one is on the soil of one's ancestors, most anything can come to one." Not he but Fern has the vision. It brings her to her knees crying convulsively about Christ Jesus. Though she speaks unintelligibly through it, Fern's vision gives meaning to the narrator. Passing her house again, this time on a train returning North, he sees Fern's face and eyes with "something that I call God flowing into them . . ." (p. 33) [21].

For the narrator it appears that redemption is achieved by that insight; yet the cumulative effect of the sketches suggests that spiritual redemption must be continually sought. Even in sensory experience many do not reach a state of soulful expression. For example, the male sexual partners of the women in the sketches of rural Georgia seem not to share spiritual feeling with them. Perhaps they are too sensual, entrapped by lust. Toomer doesn't say, but it is clear that while the way to redemption lies through expression of the spontaneous feeling latent in black people, there are so many obstacles to the way that it must continually be repeated.

The final two sketches in the first part of *Cane* represent two such destructive obstacles to spontaneous feeling. In "Esther" the narrator tells of a near-white middle-class storekeeper's daughter who conceives a love for the black King Barlo upon the occasion when Barlo is possessed of a vision of slave history and subsequent salvation. An old black woman was so inspired by the effect of Barlo's vision of a future redemption of black people that she drew a black Madonna on the courthouse wall. A portrait was also traced in Esther's young mind. In her adolescence it leads her to dream of having a child. "How had she come by it? She thinks of it immaculately" (p. 40) [26]. Immaculate conception is not a positive image however, for it omits the sensory experience necessary to black redemption in *Cane*. When Esther is twenty-seven years old, still unmarried and virgin, she hears that Barlo has returned to town, and she goes to claim her fancied love. Apprehensively she enters at midnight into the lowlife joint where he consorts with ordinary people. Almost immediately she is embarrassed by the lower-class women and laughed at by Barlo. To save her pride and the repressive structures in her mind, Esther's consciousness tells her that sex with a drunken man must be sinful. As "jeers and hoots pelter bluntly upon her back," she goes out into the void of her life where "there is no air, no street, and the town has completely disappeared" (p. 48) [28]. By negation, therefore, Toomer makes clear that redemption can only come "naturally."

The final sketch in part one, "Blood-Burning Moon," is an explicit treatment of racial caste mores. Here two men, of different race, desire the same black woman. Their jealous rivalry ends in the death of both men, the white by knifing, the black by lynching. The passionate conflict, and the deaths, occur because the white man presumes that his race gives him special claim to a black girl and exempts him from having to consider her feelings and her lover's. But it is important to see that the social protest also supports Toomer's theme of natural expression by showing that the spontaneous feeling of the characters is diverted by the artificial creations of society, the caste system.

Throughout *Cane* the dynamic force of irrational feeling is the leading motive of action. When it is instinctual, as in sex, the feeling is conveyed by imagery alluding to spiritual redemption and in a representation of environment assimilated to person. The "cane" of the title, like the pine and the soil, thereby derives meaning from the people who work in it and conveys in concrete form the complex of feeling and experience that is the soul of the Georgia blacks. On the other hand, irrational feeling is not always redemptive, for a person can be socially conditioned to repress instinct or to exploit it in others. In these cases Toomer describes motive in images of life-destruction and exploitation. For example, in "Blood-Burning Moon" the burning of Tom Burwell occurs in an antebellum cotton factory.

The second discrete part of *Cane* follows the trail of history to portray characters who have migrated from the rural South to

Washington, D.C. The whole section displays considerable stylistic experimentation beyond the methods of narration established in Part One and, therefore, also deserves close attention.

The section opens with a highly impressionistic account of a black neighborhood in Washington, D.C. The area is the bastard of Prohibition and the war: "A crude-boned, soft-skinned wedge of nigger life breathing its loafer air, jazz songs and love, thrusting unconscious rhythms, black reddish blood into the white and white-washed wood of Washington" (p. 71) [41]. The first character intro-duced, in a separate sketch, is Rhobert, the bourgeoisie who "wears a house, like a monstrous diver's helmet, on his head." With Rhobert's appearance in the narrative it is evident that spontaneous black life is threatened in the city by people's increasingly individualistic social ambition. In the succeeding sketch of "Avey" an analytic cast of mind, a correlative of urban self-consciousness, proves to be the obstacle to the flow of feeling.

Avey is described as a sort of Karintha in the North, who goes through life oblivious of the respectable conventions regarding sex and uninterested in bettering her social position in the schoolteach-er's job for which she has been educated. Finally, however, it is the articulate, self-conscious narrator who is the complete failure. He longs for Avey but cannot take her. In time he rises above her in social position and then rationalizes his continuing desire for her with the idea that they are destined for an artistic life together. Attempting to tell Avey about his plans for them he puts her to sleep.

A similar point is made by the following sketch, "Theater." This one represents John, the theater manager's brother, fantasizing his desire for Dorris, one of the dancers. Dorris's spontaneous dance expresses her physical and emotional desires in a visible and avail-able way. The entire stage crew and cast are drawn into the orbit of her movement. John is too, until he proceeds to a dream of Dorris where he has the satisfaction of an abstracted and controlled con-ception of her but of course lacks the sensory gratification that would make fantasy unnecessary. Frustratedly, Dorris rushes from stage crying bitterly, leaving John sitting immobile.

The theme of the first part of *Cane* is reinforced by the impres-sionistic style of narration that conveys the sensations of instinc-tual life as the narrator comes to feel them. With the second part of *Cane* that style is no longer functional for Toomer, because he believes the urban environment, in contrast to the world of cane and soil and pine, and the changing social experience cuts people off from the sources of feeling and vitiates their spirit. Toomer, therefore, needs a style in the second part of *Cane* that conveys the disintegration of collective and of spontaneous life, and for that reason he introduces, in "Theater," a variety of expressionistic writing that projects subjective states of mind without the intervention of a first person narrator. In this style he uses name tags, as in a playscript, to introduce his characters' thoughts, while their appearances and actions are stated with emphasis on physical appearance and without the evident presence of anyone's consciousness. The thoughts of the characters in this way are opened to the reader, but they are nevertheless the thoughts of people who feel themselves to be, and are in fact, isolated to an extent that cripples them.

"Box Seat" carries the objectification of subjective states to a climax and links the second part of the book to the first by examination of the motif of spiritual redemption in the environment of individualistic urban society. Dan Moore, the leading male, is a redeemer figure much like King Barlo. The hands of Jesus have touched him, he feels, and he can hear through the walls of houses and beneath the asphalt streets the sound of underground races and a world savior struggling to arise. In this society, though, people aren't going to let anything rise from the underground/unconscious. They are pictured as living in metallic, sharp-edged houses keeping cold walls between each other, and when they go to the theater, the site of artistic expression supposedly, they are described sliding like bolts into metal slots that keep them rigidly upright. Dan struggles to bring passion into a relationship with Muriel, to make her yield to feeling, but Muriel gives her attention to a struggle to direct her life by a code of respectability. What she has not yet internalized of its repressive nature is supplied by her landlady, a surrogate mother whose presence intrudes a "cool, thick glass" between Dan and Muriel. Aside from Dan, only an elderly black woman he sits beside in the theater retains the vitality of Southern rural life. Her strong roots appear to sink down beneath the ear disappearing in "bloodlines that waver south." Briefly Dan feels that he can follow those roots with his hands and sense the earth throb against his heart, but only briefly, because others in the theater audience object to Dan's unruly behavior and break his mood of communion. To climax this tale of the redeemer in the city, Toomer brings onto the stage of the Lincoln Theater a pair of dwarfs who delight the audience with a boxing match, followed by a serenade in which one of the fighters offers a rose, bedewed with his blood, to Muriel. Trapped in indecision, Muriel cannot freely accept the debased emblem of love as social pressure demands, nor can she express the revulsion she feels. Reluctantly, she at last reaches for the flower just as Dan rushes from the theater crying scornfully at Muriel's confusion: "Jesus was once a leper!" Failed in his efforts at redemption,

Dan walks away, oblivious of a man seeking to pick a fight with him for disturbing the theater audience with his unpredictable behavior.

"Bona and Paul," the final sketch in Part Two of *Cane*, reviews the conflict between spontaneous feeling and reflective thought in an episode between a mulatto boy and a Southern-born white girl. Bona is drawn to Paul by an attraction that overwhelms her caste conditioning. Paul, on the other hand, is reluctant with Bona, as in all his personal relationships, because of his uncertainty about his racial status. When Paul is at last ready to love, he insists upon talking about it to a doorman, assuring him that it is a genuine love. When he turns from this self-conscious apology, Bona is gone.

Lyrics carrying themes from the sketches intersperse the second section as the first. Two are notable. "Her Lips are Copper Wires" (p. 101) [55] has the poet ask in imagery of a city lighting system for an electrifying love. "Harvest Song" (pp. 132–33) [69], anticipating the story of Kabnis in the final section of the book, is the song of a reaper who hungers for some indefinite satisfaction; but rather than seek his hunger's object, he prefers to beat his hands against the stubble, painfully obliterating desire. Contrasting with the lyrics of fulfillment in Part One, these poems emphasize the conversion of the urge for life into a retreat from its sensations.

"Kabnis," the long story making up the third part of *Cane*, returns to rural Georgia for setting and once more concerns a Northerner seeking to relate to the life of black Southerners. This time, however, Toomer objectifies the story with the dramatic tags and descriptions he introduced in the section on Washington. Six scenes move the leading character from an initial mood of anguish in which he inexplicably rejects the beauty of the Georgia night, through an intensified period of guilt marked by a fear of bodily harm, and finally bring him to a condition of self-hate where he despairs of either a personal or a social redemption.

At the opening of the story Ralph Kabnis, who has come South to teach school, finds himself being fired by his pompous principal for somehow setting a bad example to the students. He is inadequate to withstand this change of fortune, because he is already consumed by bitterness that leads him to pray to God to give him "an ugly world. . . . Stinking like unwashed niggers." Do not chain him, he prays, to the hills and valleys "heaving with folk-songs." Then in the twisted logic of his despair Kabnis argues to himself that God "doesn't exist, but nevertheless he is ugly. Hence, what comes from him is ugly" (p. 162) [83]. What outrage has turned Kabnis to rejection of the spirit embodied in the Georgia countryside is not clear at first, though gradually his despair becomes concentrated on thoughts of violence and lynching.

Unintentional encouragment in this line of thinking is provided to Kabnis by Halsey, a local blacksmith, and Layman, "by turns teacher and preacher, who has traveled in almost every nook and corner of the state and hence knows more than would be good for anyone other than a silent man" (p. 169) [86]. The two of them provide Kabnis knowledge of Southern ways and try to reassure him when he becomes terrified with the thought that he may become a lynch victim. They don't deny violence, but they are matter of fact about the ways it occurs. The gap between their view of lynching and Kabnis' unreasoning terror cannot be bridged, and neither response is finally satisfactory. Without doubt the white society is vicious and shockingly anti-life. This is made clear in the account Layman gives of white folks killing a pregnant woman and then tearing the baby from her belly and pinning it to a tree. On the other hand, Kabnis takes the threat of violence into himself and converts anticipation into a guilt so overwhelming that he is deracinated, becoming, in the imagery of the story, a scarecrow replica of himself.

A stranger named Lewis brings the theme of redemption into Kabnis' story. When Kabnis meets Lewis there is a brief moment of possible union for their intuitive selves before Kabnis rejects the advance. In the description of that moment Toomer reiterates themes that run throughout *Cane*. "His eyes turn to Kabnis. In the instant of their shifting, a vision of the life they are to meet. Kabnis, a promise of soil-soaked beauty; uprooted, thinning out. Suspended a few feet above the soil whose touch would ressurect him. Arm's length removed from him whose will to help. . . . There is a swift intuitive interchange of consciousness. Kabnis has a sudden need to rush into the arms of this man. His eyes call 'Brother.' And then a savage, cynical twist-about within him mocks his impulse and strengthens him to repulse Lewis" (pp. 191–92) [96]. Like Muriel and others in the world of *Cane*, Kabnis out of fear blocks the flow of spontaneous feeling.

Kabnis' story, thus, is a climax to the volume. In the first section of *Cane* Toomer establishes the need for and the conditions of redemption. The second part of the book, the stories of Washington, D.C., represents increased inhibition of spontaneous life. Now the characters become more *self*-repressing because of the mentality they have developed in the city. Where the narrator could respond to a redeemer in the person of Fern in the first part, the characters in the second part reject the means of redemption. Then in "Kabnis" Toomer describes a man who has fully internalized the repressive forces of the environment. In "Blood-Burning Moon" violence came from without. In Kabnis' story the threat is projected from within. Though Kabnis is in the South, which appears to be animated with soul through imagery of song and light, he deliberately closes his senses. Just as deliberately he rejects Lewis, who would stimulate his feeling for the soil and collective humanity.

The final two scenes of "Kabnis" occur in a basement hole beneath Halsey's workshop. Within this hole is an old man "like a bust in black walnut" whom Lewis calls Father John and Kabnis calls Father of Hell. He is a mute presence evidently signifying the slave ancestry, kept hidden from the present but appropriately an inhabitant of the room in which Halsey, Kabnis, and the others put aside constraints to drink and consort with whores. A visit to the room of Father John becomes, therefore, an excursion into the past, an opportunity for sensual release and, for the blacks variously compromising with their social environment, an encounter with the terms of their underlying identity.

Significantly, in this underground/unconscious setting Lewis communes with Father John, wordlessly sensing the vital force present in the soil and its fruit: "Cotton bolls bloom, droop. Black roots twist in a parched red soil beneath a blazing sky. Magnolias, fragrant, a trifle futile, lovely, far off. . . . His eyelids close. A force begins to heave and rise" (pp. 214–15) [105]. When Lewis opens his eyes after this momentary communion, his appearance infuriates Kabnis. The old man, Kabnis is driven to say, looks like a black cockroach. "An besides, he aint my past. My ancestors were Southern blue-bloods" (p. 217) [106]. Prodded and contradicted by Lewis, Kabnis then raves until he is revealing that a nightmarish form eats into his soul, feeding on the words others speak and driving him to wish, in an image reminiscent of the lynching story he had heard from Layman, that "some lynchin white man ud stick his knife through it an pin it to a tree' (pp. 224–25) [109].

In the context of *Cane*, Ralph Kabnis, so fearful of life, is complementary to characters such as the "I" narrator of Part One who sense the possibility of spontaneous life, for Toomer's book is about life in *black* America. In that realm, violence has always been present as the chief instrument of social control, so that an expedition into the zones of black identity inevitably describes the effect that the threat of violence must have upon personality.

In the final scene of the story the mark of violent oppression is fully revealed as Ralph Kabnis speaks of his death wish directly to Father John. First he taunts and reviles Father John for his impassivity and his ugliness, but the tone of speech makes clear that Kabnis is expressing self-hate. Then Father John speaks. First he says the word "sin," and then the statement that the white folks sinned when they made the Bible lie in a justification of slavery. This too Kabnis reviles, while saying much the same thing in his own words. The only sin is what is done against the soul, Kabnis says, and the world is conspiring to sin against him. "I'm the victim of their sin.

I'm what sin is" (p. 226) [141]. In this formula Kabnis reveals his condition. He is the victim of racial oppression—a sin—and the consequence is that he has become like the crime, a foe of life.

The bleakness of "Kabnis" is raised briefly by the character of Carrie Kate, Halsey's sister. She too is moved by the appeal of Lewis to feel the possibility of intuitive union. In her case the "sin-bogies of respectable southern colored folks clamor at her" to watch out and she draws back. But in the final scene when Kabnis has been reduced to a groveling wretch, Carrie offers him succor. She draws the fever from his head and comforts him. Then, kneeling before Father John, she murmurs "Jesus, come," while outside the sun "arises from its cradle" and shines down upon the town sending "a birthsong slanting down gray dust streets" to coalesce with Carrie in an image of the continued possibility of spiritual redemption.

In description of his source of artistic inspiration, Jean Toomer wrote: "Georgia opened me. . . . There one finds soil, soil in the sense the Russians know it,—the soil every art and literature that is to live must be imbedded in."[5] The statement suggests how deeply he felt the importance of *Cane*. Toomer himself after all was a man of Southern heritage who went from the city to teach school in Sparta, Georgia. Of course, the personal experience must have contributed greatly to the conception that unites his sketches and lyrics in *Cane*, and in that respect the book is a symbolic record of the sensitive author's attempt to relate to his personal past.

Finally, however, *Cane* is most important to its readers because of its place in Afro-American literary tradition. The point can be made simply by observation of the relationship between *Cane* and that classic of black literature, *The Souls of Black Folk* (1903). Du Bois' book is also a collection of independent pieces recording a Northern observer's understanding of Southern black life. In anticipation of the techniques of *Cane*, Du Bois the social scientist humanized his research findings by a use of narrative style that invites the reader to tour the rural areas, the linking of essays with songs as epigraphs, and animation of the entire book with repeated use of a thematic metaphor—the veil. For his part, Toomer could not have failed to realize that his book repeated the symbolic return to ancestral scenes that grounded *The Souls of Black Folk*, developed Du Bois' theme of a reconciliation between the "Talented Tenth" and the black masses, and imaginatively extended the meanings latent in the image of black folks' souls.

In its own decade *Cane* epitomized the desire among black artists to deal with folk experience in sophisticated literature. Today, when the problem of its form no longer seems so baffling, the relevance

5. Quoted in *The New Negro*, ed. Alain Locke (New York, 1925), p. 51.

of *Cane* has, if anything, been increased, because in its exploration of identity as a process of liberating the spontaneous self in an
often oppressive environment we can see how *Cane* established the
major terms of the twentieth century black writer's chief theme—
the redemption of personality.

# BERNARD BELL

## A Key to the Poems in *Cane*†

In the wake of the rising tide of interest in Afro-American literature and the acquisition of the Jean Toomer manuscripts by Fisk
University in 1963, critics began digging into their libraries to take
a closer look at *Cane* (1923)—the book that launched the Harlem
Renaissance. But insofar as the poems in the book are concerned,
the rediscovery of *Cane* seems to have generated more heat than
light. Critics either, like Robert Bone, completely ignore them or,
like Darwin Turner and Todd Lieber, fail to explore their full implications to the integrity of the thematic and structural concerns of
the work.[1] This paper attempts to explicate the meaning of these
poems and to outline briefly how they are interwoven into one of
the most innovative novels of the twentieth century.

On one level *Cane* is a deeply religious quest—a book whose
search for the truth about man, God, and America takes its nameless narrator on a circular journey of self-discovery. At the time he
was writing *Cane*, Toomer was on the road to becoming an essentialist. "I am not a romanticist," he declared in his autobiography.
"I am not a classicist or a realist, in the usual sense of these terms.
I am an essentialist. Or, to put it in other words, I am a spiritualizer,
a poetic realist."[2] Basically this means two things. First, it reveals
Toomer's belief in the idea that metaphysical essences, especially
the soul, really subsist and are intuitively accessible. After the publication of *Cane*, Toomer became deeply involved with the teaching
of Gurdjieff, but he continued to express in writing his conviction
"that in each human being there is an undying essence or soul that
survives the death of the perishable body, and persists ultimately to
fulfill God's purpose."[3] Secondly, it means that as a writer, he tried,

---

† From *CLA Journal* 14 (March 1971): 251–58. Reprinted by permission.
1. See Bone, *The Negro Novel in America*, rev. ed. (New Haven: Yale University Press,
   1965); Turner, "Jean Toomer's *Cane*," *Negro Digest*, XVIII (January, 1969), 54–61; and
   Lieber, "Design and Movement in *Cane*," *CLA Journal* (September, 1969), 35–50.
2. Jean Toomer, "Earth-Being" (Fisk University Library: Unpubl. MS, n. d.), p. 18.
3. See Jean Toomer, *The Flavor of Man* (Philadelphia, 1949), p. 18. See also the philosophical works: *Essentials* (Chicago: Lakeside Press, 1931); the novels. "The Gallonwerps" (Uupubl. MS, ca. 1927), "Caromb" (Unpubl. MS, ca. 1932), and "Eight-Day

in his own words, "to lift facts, things, happenings to the planes of rhythm, feeling, and significance . . . to clothe and give body to potentialities."[4]

*Cane* is an intricately structured, incantational book. Divided into three major parts, it progresses from a highly poetic to a heavily dramatic form. "Karintha," the opening sketch of Part One, is barely five pages in length and depends on the refrains of a song for its haunting effects, while 'Blood-Burning Moon," the sixteen page concluding sketch of the same section, finds its unity and force in its narrative structure. Similarly, the striking metaphorical style of the brief first sketch in Part Two, "Seventh Street," culminates in the symbolism and dramatic internal monologue of "Bona and Paul." "Kabnis," the single sketch that comprises the whole of Part Three, is cast in the form of an allegorical play.

The structure of the book also reveals the influence of Toomer's reading in psychology and philosophy. Its three major divisions might be compared to the Freudian theory of personality, an Hegelian construct, or the Gurdjieffian triad. As I argue elsewhere,[5] Toomer anticipates the mystical theory of Gurdjieff in that he too believed that man was composed of three nearly independent forces: the intellect, emotions, and body.[6] Toomer further believed that it was imperative for man to synthesize or harmonize these apparently disparate elements. Thus, Part One of *Cane*, with its focus on the slave past and the libido presents the rural thesis, while Part Two with its emphasis on the modern world and the super-ego offers the urban antithesis. Part Three then becomes a synthesis of the earlier sections, with Kabnis representing the black writer whose difficulty in reconciling himself to the dilemma of being a black American prevents him from tapping the creative powers of his soul. Unlike the appeal to logic of an Hegelian construct, however, Toomer attempts to overwhelm the reader with the truth of his mystical theory of life through images and symbols whose appeal is more to the senses than to the intellect.

Contrary to Professor Turner's observation, none of the fifteen poems in Parts One and Two are "exquisite only in the sharpness and suggestiveness of their imagery."[7] They are all functional, serving to elucidate or to set the stage or to provide a transition between the sketches. "Reaper" and "November Cotton Flower," for example,

World" (Unpubl. MS, ca. 1933); and the short stories: "Love on a Train," "Drackman," "Fronts," "New Beach," "Pure Pleasure," and "Winter on Earth" in Toomer MSS at Fisk University Library.
4. Toomer, "Earth-Being," p. 18.
5. Bernard Bell, "*Cane*: A Portrait of the Black Artist as High Priest of Soul," Unpubl. MS (1969).
6. Jean Toomer, "On Being American" (Fisk University Library: Unpubl. MS. n. d.), p. 48.
7. Turner, "Jean Toomer's *Cane*," p. 60.

are companion poems to the first sketch. They reinforce the haunting appeal and religious core of "Karintha." In the first, Toomer depicts "Black reapers" and "Black horses" cutting down "weeds" and "a field rat." In addition to its emblematic representation of death as a timeless source of tension in life, this image of harvest alludes to the cyclical rhythm of Nature. "November Cotton Flower" continues to develop this pastoral image of the tension between life and death, while at the same time clarifying the relationship between Karintha and the cotton flower. Neither the "boll-weevil's coming" nor "the winter's cold" nor the scarcity of cotton nor the "drouth" prevents this delicate, ephemeral flower from blooming:

> Old folks were startled, and it soon assumed
> Significance. Superstition saw
> Something it had never seen before;
> Brown eyes that loved without a trace of fear.
> Beauty so sudden for that time of year.[8]

On the one hand, these lines reinforce the mysterious power of Karintha's beauty by comparing it to that of the cotton flower that blooms in a hostile environment; on the other, they suggest by the contrast between the reaction of the old folks to the flower and that of the men to Karintha that those who stand in awe of Nature possess not only a lust for life but a greater capacity for love.

The poems "Face" and "Cotton Song" extend the religious symbolism of "Becky." Portraying the "channeled muscles of a woman's face as "cluster grapes of sorrow / purple in the evening sun / nearly ripe for worms" (p. 14) [12], "Face" draws on the traditional typology of the suffering and sacrifice of Christ. "Cotton Song" complements this image of the Crucifixion with a subtle reference to the Resurrection as black stevedores call for strength to roll a bale of cotton aboard ship. The obvious Biblical analogue here is the huge boulder that was miraculously rolled away from the tomb of Christ. In the refrains "Come, brother, roll roll!" and "We aint agwine to wait until the Judgment Day" the exhortative mood of the poem reaches a crescendo.

The next two poems, "Song of the Son" and "Georgia Dusk," expand on the regional imagery and metaphysical meaning of "Carma." The opening stanza of "Song of the Son" picks up the "sad strong song" of the singing girl in "Carma":

> Pour O pour that parting soul in song,
> O pour it in the sawdust glow of night,

8. Jean Toomer, *Cane* (New York: Harper and Row, 1969), p. 7 [8]. Subsequent references to this work will be found in the text. [Page numbers in square brackets refer to this Norton Critical Edition.]

> Into the velvet pine-smoke air to-night,
> And let the valley carry it along.
> And let the valley carry it along. (p. 21) [16]

In the plaintive cry of these lines we discover Toomer, the poet-novelist, turning to his folk heritage and slave past for spiritual inspiration:

> O land and soil, red soil and sweet-gum tree,
> So scant of grass, so profligate of pines,
> Now just before an epoch's sun declines
> Thy son, in time, I have returned to thee,
> Thy son, I have in time returned to thee. (p. 21) [16]

The desolation of the red soil "scant of grass" contrasts with the abundance of pines, and the decline of "an epoch's sun" points up the nostalgic return of the black artist to his roots.

The key to the irony and yoking together of disparate elements in the poem is found in the play on the word "son" in the last two lines of the stanza. The pun is a subtle allusion to the Son of God, which in the context of the rapid association of ideas in the poem, stresses the Christian paradox that in death there is life. This is particularly true of the slaves and their songs:

> O Negro slaves, dark purple ripened plums,
> Squeezed, and bursting in the pine-wood air,
> Passing, before they stripped the old tree bare
> One plum was saved for me, one seed becomes

> An everlasting son, a singing tree,
> Caroling softly souls of slavery,
> What they were, and what they are to me,
> Caroling softly souls of slavery. (p. 21) [16]

More than anything else, these lines celebrate the slave spirituals as sorrowful and joyous songs. Spirituals, Toomer seems to say, are the "one seed" of the past that enabled the slaves to transcend the grim hardships of their bondage. Moreover, since these songs embody the spirit of the many thousand gone, they, like the mythical tree of life, possess the power to arouse the eternal soul of man.

Toomer looked on his experiences as a school administrator in Georgia, the home state of his grandfather, P. B. S. Pinchback, as a return to his folk past. A lyrical expression of this feeling is found in "Georgia Dusk," which deals with the tradition of Afro-American spirituals and folk songs. In the opening two stanzas of

the poem, the similarity between a Southern barbecue and a Bac-
chanalian feast is clear:

> The sky, lazily disdaining to pursue
>> The setting sun, too indolent to hold
>> A lengthened tournament for flashing gold,
> Passively darkens for night's barbecue,
>
> A feast of moon and men and barking hounds,
>> An orgy for some genius of the South
>> With blood-hot eyes and cane-lipped scented mouth,
> Surprised in making folk-songs from soul sounds. (p. 22) [17]

The word that stands out in these two stanzas is "genius." Stirred by
the ritual of the feast, the first black genius of the South wove the
sights and sounds of his African past and his bitter-sweet slave
experience into soulful music.

The imagery of the final three stanzas of "Georgia Dusk" are
equally striking in their archetypal ethnic allusions:

> Meanwhile, the men, with vestiges of pomp,
>> Race memories of king and caravan,
>> High-priests, an ostrich, and a juju-man,
> Go singing through the footpaths of the swamp.
>
> Their voices rise . . . the pine trees are guitars,
>> Strumming, pine-needles fall like sheets of rain . . .
>> Their voices rise . . . the chorus of the cane
> In caroling a vesper to the stars . . .
>
> O singers, resinous and soft your songs
>> Above the sacred whisper of the pines,
>> Give virgin lips to cornfield concubines,
> Bring dreams of Christ to dusky cane-lipped throngs.
>>>>>>>           (pp. 22–23) [17]

Like the magical powers attributed to pre-colonial African rituals,
the voices of the men blend with the rhythmic sounds of the New
World and become mystical agents of transformation.

Two cryptic nature poems follow "Fern." "Nullo" gives an aura of
wonder and mystery to the common, everyday phenomenon of "A
spray of pine-needles, / Dipped in western gold" falling in the quiet
forest. "Rabbits knew not of their falling, / Nor did the forest catch
aflame" (p. 34) [22]. In "Evening Song" the metaphysical forces of
life are represented by the image of a pastoral character "curled like
the sleepy waters where the moon waves start," dreaming with her
"Lips pressed against my heart" (p. 35) [23]. In its waxing and waning
the moon is the traditional symbol of the cyclical pattern of life its

changing phases influencing the cycle of fertility in humans and Nature alike.

Like the other poems in the novel, "Conversion" and "Portrait in Georgia" are closely related to the themes and imagery of the sketches they connect. "Conversion" heightens the meaning of the parable in Barlo's sermon by exposing the Christian deception of substituting "a white-faced sardonic god" for the "African Guardian of Souls." The grim image of a woman in "Portrait in Georgia" forcefully establishes the sexual link between the Southern ritual of lynching and the myths of white purity and black bestiality.

In contrast to the ten poems in Part One, there are only five in Part Two. However, they are characterized by the same dramatic tensions between either the body, emotions and intellect or man and modern social conventions. In an extended cosmic metaphor, "Beehive" depicts man's failure to develop his intellectual and spiritual potential by associating the mechanical activity of human life with that of bees. "Storm Ending" captures the insensitivity of man to the awesome beauty of Nature, while "Her Lips are Copper Wire" focuses on the lips, the breath, and the tongue as transmitters of the electrical current of the soul. "Prayer" continues this theme with the plea: "O Spirits of who my soul is but a little finger, / Direct it to the lid of its flesh-eye" (p. 131) [68]. In "Harvest Song," the last of the poems, the image of a reaper overpowering the knowledge of his hunger by beating the film of his hand against a stubble of grain communicates the delicate balance that exists between the mind, emotions and dy. Indeed, the primary focus of Part Two is on the corruption of the mind when it is enslaved by the genteel mores of society as well as the mind when it has rid itself of that form of oppression. Properly used, mind, emotions, and body can be one. Spirituals, folk songs, jazz and poetry are vehicles for the attainment of this end.

Finally, Part Three is "Kabnis," the most symbolical part of the book. Its six subsections are more dramatic than poetic and bring the quest of Kabnis, the poet-narrator, full circle. His journey carried him through the Edenic Garden of the South, then on to the Cities of Babylon in the North and finally back to the fertile soil of his father's father, Georgia. Throughout his odyssey Kabnis seeks to know the mystery of life, to contain within himself the beauty and the pain of his Afro-American heritage, and to capture all this in the magic of the word. However, despite his contacts with others, especially Father John, the indomitable spirit of the black American's past, and Carrie Kate, the fragile hope of the future of the race, Kabnis remains at the close of the book only "a promise of soil-soaked beauty; uprooted, thinning out. Suspended a few feet above the soil whose touch would resurrect him" (p. 191) [96]. As

for the poems in the earlier sections, they communicate the spiritual core of *Cane* and suggest the metaphysical forces necessary to
bring the crass materialism of American society and the sensuality
of man's nature into harmony.

# CATHERINE L. INNES

## The Unity of Jean Toomer's *Cane*†

When *Cane* was first published in 1923 it met with a variety of
critical responses ranging from enthusiasm to bewilderment and
caution. Waldo Frank, in his introduction to the book praised
Toomer as a true poet and saw *Cane* as marking the "dawn of direct
and unafraid creation."[1] William Stanley Braithwaite was also enthusiastic, claiming that Jean Toomer was the first Negro writer to
refuse to compromise artistic vision in writing about race, and the
first to be truly "objective"[2]—a seemingly inappropriate description
which is also used later by David Littlejohn who informs us that
Toomer views Negro life with "chilling objectivity," and then immediately adds that *Cane* is a book where "common things are seen as
if through a strangely neurotic vision."[3] Although Littlejohn begins
his two page discussion of *Cane* by admitting it is an "esoteric work,
difficult to grasp, define and assess,"[4] he ends by dismissing it as
"too insubstantial to be remembered."[5]

Since 1930, *Cane* (except for one or two of its poems) has been
largely ignored or dismissed as a seeming "hodge-podge of verse,
songs, stories, and plays."[6] In the past decade, however, a few critics
have begun to take a second look, and Robert Bone has hailed it "as
a measure of the Negro novelist's highest achievement," ranking
with *Native Son* and *Invisible Man*.[7] Despite Bone's rather cursory
study and a helpful article by Todd Lieber, "Design and Movement
in *Cane*,"[8] the book remains an intriguing and enigmatic work
whose full meaning and artistic significance await detailed exploration. As Arna Bontemps has pointed out, when *Cane* was first published "the 'new criticism,' as we have come to recognize it, had

† From *CLA Journal* 15 (March 1972): 306–322. Reprinted by permission.
1. Quoted by Arna Bontemps, "The Negro Renaissance: Jean Toomer and the Harlem
   Writers of the 1920's," *Anger and Beyond*, ed. Herbert Hill (New York Harper and Row,
   1966), pp. 25–26.
2. *Ibid.*, p. 23.
3. *Black on White* (New York: Grossman, 1966), p. 59.
4. *Ibid.*, p. 58.
5. *Ibid.*, p. 60.
6. Edward Margolies, *Native Sons* (Philadelphia: J. B. Lippincott Company, 1968), p. 39.
7. *The Negro Novel in America*, rev. ed. (New Haven: Yale University Press, 1965), p. 81.
8. *CLA Journal*, XIII (September, 1969), 35–50.

scarcely been heard from then, and apparently it still has not discovered Toomer, but the chances are it may yet find him challenging."[9]

My aim in this paper is to try and take up that challenge, exploring *Cane* with the aid of P. D. Ouspensky's *Tertium Organum* and the "new" critical methods, concentrating on some of the recurring images and symbols in the book and tracing their relation to one another and to the theme and structure of the work as a whole. Limitations of time and space will permit me to point to only a few of the dominant *leitmotifs* in a work whose construction is more reminiscent of a musical composition such as Mussorgsky's *Pictures at an Exhibition* or Berlioz' *Symphonie Fantastique* than the conventional novel.[1]

The symbol which introduces the book and which dominates the whole of Part I is that of the dusk:

> Her skin is like dusk on the eastern horizon,
> O cant you see it, O cant you see it,
> Her skin is like dusk on the eastern horizon
> . . . When the sun goes down[2]

Many of the complex associations which surround this symbol are suggested in this first section: Karintha "carries *beauty*, perfect as the dusk when the sun goes down," and throughout the work there will be recurring references to the beauty of dusky skins. Dusk is associated also with ripeness, with "Purple of the dusk / Deep-rooted cane," with "Negro slaves, dark purple ripened plums," and with autumn and harvest time, "for the soul of her was a growing thing ripened too soon." Dusk also refers to the last glow of the setting sun, "just before an epoch's sun declines," that moment when the sun's glow is poignantly beautiful because it is fast disappearing. Finally, and perhaps most importantly, dusk represents a moment of fusion of dark and light, of past and future; a mingling of colors—the moment when it is neither day or night but both, a moment which is matched by and reminds one of the dawn. It is the moment of intuitive apprehension rather than logical distinction: "I felt strange, as I always do in Georgia, particularly at dusk. I felt that things unseen to men were tangibly immediate" (31) [21].

The significance of dusk as a central symbol of fusion, a time when the invisible world and the aesthetic realm a most strongly felt

9. *Anger and Beyond*, p. 29.
1. Gorham B. Munson, in "The Significance of Jean Toomer," *Destinations* (New York: J. H. Sears and Company, 1928), does analyze the musical structure of "Karintha" and points out that Toomer had wanted to be a composer. I suspect that a detailed analysis of the whole book might show a very close analogy with late Nineteenth Century symphonic structure.
2. Jean Toomer, *Cane* (New York: Harper and Row, 1969), p. 1. Hereafter all page references to this edition will be included in the text. [Page numbers in square brackets refer to this Norton Critical Edition.]

(a connection expressed in "Georgia Dusk" is, I believe, closely tied to Jean Toomer's study of the theories of P. D. Ouspensky, author of *Tertium Organum*, a book which also influenced Hart Crane, Kenneth Burke, Waldo Frank and Gorham Munson, a group of writers with whom Toomer associated in the Twenties.[3]

Ouspensky considered his work a successor to Aristotle *Organon* and Francis Bacon's *Novum Organum*, replacing the laws of scientific observation and deduction with the "third Canon of Thought," or the logic of intuition. Whereas the scientists, exploring observable phenomena and the world of appearances, insist on distinctions between things ("Everything is either A or not-A"), Ouspensky insisted on the superior reality of the "noumenal" or subjectively felt world long ago explored by Eastern sages and early Christian mystics, a world where "Everything is *both* A and Not-A."[4] The *Tertium Organum* urges the development of a new group of supermen capable of "cosmic consciousness," which involves the idea and sensation of a living universe in which the hidden meaning of all things will be realized and felt, and the unity of all things understood. Such an understanding must come through the blending of emotional and intellectual modes of apprehension.

> Cosmic consciousness may develop in purely emotional soil . . . and is also possible of attainment through the emotion attendant upon creation—in painters, musicians and poets. Art in its highest manifestations is a path to cosmic consciousness.
> For the manifestation of cosmic consciousness it is necessary that the center of gravity of *everything* shall lie for man in the inner world, in self-consciousness, and not in the outer world at all.[5]

While Part I of *Cane* is suffused in the subjective, lyrical vision and is an implicit presentation of intuitive, non-logical consciousness, the striving for a fusion of opposites, along with the consequences of failure to achieve it, is expressed most explicitly by Lewis in Part III:

> Kabnis: Aint much difference between blue and black.
> Lewis: Enough to draw a denial from you. Cant hold them, can you? Master; slave. Soil; and the overarching heavens. Dusk; dawn. They fight and bastardize you. The sun tint of your cheeks, name of the great season's multi-colored leaves, tarnished, burned. isn't, shredded: easily burned. No use . . . (218) [106–07]

3. Bone, p. 81.
4. *Tertium Organum* (New York: Alfred A. Knopf, 1922), pp. 262–265.
5. *Ibid.*, pp. 330–331.

A year before *Cane* was published, Jean Toomer wrote:

> Racially, I seem to have (who knows for sure) seven blood mix-
> tures: French, Dutch, Welsh, Negro, German, Jewish and
> Indian. . . . I have strived for a spiritual fusion analogous to
> the fact of racial intermingling. Without denying a single ele-
> ment in me, with no desire to subdue one to the other, I have
> sought to let them function as complements. I have tried to let
> them live in harmony.[6]

The symbolism of racial fusion associated with striving for cosmic
consciousness, though suggested in "Karintha," "Song of the Sun"
and "Georgia Dusk," is most clearly developed in "Fern," an impression of Fernie May Rosen who unites Jewish and Negro, canticle
and folk-song, and into whose eyes flowed "her face, the countryside and something that I call God . . ." (33) [21]. She suggests the
state in which "the center of gravity of *everything* lies in the inner
world of self-consciousness." Fern is the passively receptive consciousness, responding to and becoming one with her world, which
includes the anguished past of Jewish and African peoples—an
anguish from which the narrator is unable to redeem her because
he is unable to understand. His consciousness of himself as a separate entity prevents him from giving himself up wholly to Fern,
from flowing into her, and so he remains perplexed, knowing only
that the material, sensual things he might offer are inadequate.

The theme of the striving for racial fusion symbolizing spiritual
harmony and of the failure of the passive female and active male
to unite is taken up with some variations in "Esther," the story or a
repressed girl who once catches a glimpse of the cosmic vision
through the trance of King Barlo whose image then becomes "the
starting point of the only living patterns that her mind was to know"
(40) [25]. Toomer stresses the contrast between Esther and Barlo.
Her face "chalk-white," and later becomes the "color of the gray
during that dances with dead cotton leaves" (43) [27]. Barlo, on the
other hand, is "black. Magnetically so. . . . A clean-muscle magnificent, black-skinned Negro" who in his trance "assume the outlines
of his visioned African."

Esther's dream of union with Barlo not only emphasizes the
theme of fusion of opposites, but also introduces another major
*motif* which will be sounded more clearly and triumphantly at the
end of the work—that of redemption—which is linked also with the
imagery of dusk and dawn, and the connotations of a fading beauty
and a new promise. Barlo speaks of his vision of past glory:

6. Quoted by Bontemps in his "Introduction" to *Cane* (New York: Harper and Row, 1969,
p. viii.

> ". . . I saw a man arise, an he was big an black an
> powerful—" . . .
>     "—but his head was caught up in th clouds. An while he was
> agazin at th heavens, heart filled up with th Lord, some little
> white-ant biddies came an tied his feet to chains." (38) [25]

Toomer reminds that dusk is "rapidly falling." Then comes the
prophecy of dawn:

> Barlo rises to his full height. He is immense, to the people he
> assumes the outlines of his visioned African. In a mighty voice
> he bellows:
>     "Brothers an sisters, turn your faces t th sweet face of the
> Lord, an fill your hearts with glory. Open your eyes an see th
> dawnin of th mornin light. Open your ears—" (39) [25].

Inspired by this vision, a black woman drew a portrait in charcoal
of a black madonna on the courthouse wall. Esther dreams of
becoming that madonna, building fantasies of a child recued from
fire, claimed as her own. "She thinks of it immaculately."

The story of Esther also emphasizes the repression and prudish-
ness which destroy her dream and finally make Barlo hideous to
her—a theme which will receive full treatment in Part II.

Two poems dealing with the perversion of religion and of sensual
beauty lead into the grim story which ends Part I, the story of the
fatal competition between white Bob Stone and black Tom Burwell
(whose name echoes Barlo), opposites between whom Louisa is forced
to try and choose. For Louisa, Burwell's "black balanced, and pulled
against the white of stone when she thought of them" (52) [31]. It is
significant, I think, that this episode takes place *after* dusk, in the
false and ominous light of the "blood-burning moon," in a factory
town, and that Tom is dragged into a factory to be killed. His head
in the flames is compared to blackened stone. The lynching of Tom
Burwell by "white men like ants upon a forage" not only recalls the
vision of Barlo ("Some little white-ant biddies came an tied his feet
to chains"), but also looks forward to the migration North and to
Toomer's depiction of the psychic destruction of black people, the
conquest of subjective consciousness by white pragmatism and materialism, in the industrial urban environment, the "factory town," to
be portrayed in Part II of *Cane*. And, of course, "Blood-Burning
Moon" is a fearful depiction of how whites had instigated a reign of
terror in the South in an attempt to destroy black men physically
and psychologically—a reign of terror which distorts the lives of
those who are portrayed in Part III.

Part II begins with an invocation of the contrast between "the
white and whitewashed wood of Washington" and black inhabited

Seventh Street, a wedge "thrusting unconscious rhythms, black reddish blood" into the "stale and soggy wood of Washington." "Seventh Street" serves as a transition between Part I and Part II, moving the reader from South to North, from black Georgia soil and purple dusk to Washington's night life and hustling pace of the Prohibition era.

The next sketch, "Rhobert" (robot?), is a structural parallel to "Karintha," introducing the dominant theme and symbol for Part II. Like "Karintha" it is also faintly elegiac in tone, but whereas the mode of "Karintha" is more purely lyrical echoing the folk ballad, "Rhobert," like the whole of Part II is much more sardonic and intellectualized, and closer to the urban blues in tone.

Bone has discussed the importance of this section as "an attack on the crucial bourgeois value of home ownership."[7] The recurring house imagery implies this and much more acquiring the complexity and thematic significance of the dusk imagery in Part I. The house which Rhobert wears on his head and which slowly crushes him is a symbol not only of materialism but also of positivistic thinking, the dualistic logic the separation of mind and body, soul and spirit described by Ouspensky as characterizing the Third and inferior Form of Consciousness. Just as Becky in Part I was crushed by the cabin built by the community to hide her and her "sin," so the house becomes in Part II a symbol of repression and Puritanism, preventing the fusion of sense, emotion and intellect, and representing a barrier to the open receptivity which is the concern of Part I. It is significant that nearly all the scenes in Part I take place outside, in the light of the setting sun, imbued with the sounds and smells of the "whispering pines," the "rustling cane," the fragrance of fermenting syrup, the strain of folk songs, the sense of "soil and overarching heavens." In contrast, all the scenes in Part II, with the important exception of "Avey," take place inside buildings, in houses, in theatres, in rooms, where the lighting is artificial or distorted.

As "Rhobert" forms a structural parallel and thematic contrast to "Karintha," "Avey" recalls and contrasts with "Fern." Both these sketches feature the first person narrator and his attempt to understand and come to terms with an enigmatic woman. As Fernie May Rosen is a symbol of racial/spiritual fusion and of emotional kinship between soil, land and Negro people of the South, so Avey represents her people transplanted to the urban environment of V Street (she *is a* V Street), where "the young trees had not outgrown their boxes then. V Street was lined with them. When our legs grew cramped and stiff from the cold of stone, we'd stand around a box and whittle it" (76) [44].

7. *The Negro Novel in America*, p. 84.

Like Fern, Avey remains indifferent to the narrator who, gradually adopting the competitive spirit of the North, begins to condemn Avey for "her downright laziness. Sloppy indolence. . . .
Among those energetic Swedes, or whatever they are, I decided to
forget her" (82–83) [46]. But the narrator's attempt to forget and
condemn his racial heritage as symbolized by Avey is futile. Once
again we hear echoes of the opening *motif* in "Karintha": "One
evening in early June, met at the time when the dusk is most lovely
on the eastern horizon, I saw Avey, indolent as ever, leaning on the
arm of a man, strolling under the recently lit arc-lights of U Street"
(84) [47].

Despite the winds from the South, despite his ardent talk sketched
with wonderful self-irony by Toomer, the narrator cannot arouse
Avey:

> I described her own nature and temperament. Told how they
> needed a larger life for their expression. How incapable Wash-
> ington was of understanding that need. How it could not meet
> it. I pointed out that in lieu of proper channels, her emotions
> had overflowed into paths that dissipated them. I talked, beau-
> tifully, I thought, about an art that would be born, an art that
> would open the way for women the likes of her. I asked her to
> hope, and build up an innerlife against the coming of that day.
> I recited some of my own things to her (86–87) [48].

The ending of "Avey" indicates that the narrator's hope for a new
dawning, a new union with his blood heritage, has been a false
one, for his dream, his "song" is not "sun-lit" but is based on an
artificial and idealized conception of Avey, a purely cerebral "plot-
ting of destiny" (to borrow a phrase from the next section), cut off
from its Southern roots. Avey remains an "orphan-woman," her face
pale and lacking the "gray crimson-splashed beauty of the dawn"
(88) [48].

Two poems, "Beehive" and "Storm Ending," emphasize the contrast between the dreamed, artificial "silver honey" spun by "silver
bees intently buzzing," and the rich refreshing "rain like golden
honey" dripped from flowers "bitten by the sun." "Theater" takes up
this contrast, modulating the silver dream and golden nature *motifs*
in the figures of John and Dorris John's mind and body function
separately: "And as if his own body were the mass-heart of a black
audience listening to them singing, he wants to stomp his feet and
shout. His mind, contained above desires of his body, singles the
girls out and tries to trace origins and plot destinies" (92) [51].

Dorris, depicted in the lemon, crimson and purple colors of dusk,
recalls the soul of her people as her dance transcends the mechanical, planned movements of the other chorus girls:

Dorris dances. She forgets her tricks. She dances.
Glorious songs are the muscles of her limbs.
And her singing is of cane brake loves and mangrove feast-
ings. (98) [53–54]

But John's passion is "diluted" by his inability to merge mind and
body; his dream, like the narrator's in "Avey," an artificial thing
composed of treeless streets where satin slippers tread dead autumn
leaves, a dream bathed in melancho Dorris sees that her dance has
become "a dead thing in the shadow which is his dream." She is left
staring at the white-washed ceiling of her drab dressing room.

Separation of soul from body is also the theme of "Calling Jesus,"
where the soul is imaged as a whimpering dog shut out of the "big
house," able to steal in only at night "Cradled in dream-fluted cane"
(103) [56].

"Box Seat," placed almost in the middle of the book, presents in
surreal, often grotesque terms the central conflict of the whole work.
Dan Moore, who recalls Barlo and prefigures Lewis, is a precursor of
the new redeemer: "Look into my eyes. I am Dan Moore. I was born
in a canefield. The hands of Jesus touched me. I come to a sick world
to heal it" (105–106) [57]. He is able to feel the cosmic forces,
vibrant rumbles from the earth's deep core, "the mutter of powerful
underground races" (108) [58]. He is able to commune with the old
slave, to feel the strong roots of the portly Negress, to penetrate the
physical phenomenal world and pass beyond the dualistic thinking
of his fellows. As he tells Muriel, "Life bends joy and pain, beauty
and ugliness, in such a way that no one may isolate them. No one
should want to. Perfect joy, or perfect pain, with no contrasting element to define them would mean a monotony of consciousness,
would mean death. Not happy, Muriel. Say that you have tried to
make them create. Say that you have used your own capacity for life
to cradle them. To start them upward-flowing" (112) [60].

But Dan, a representative of the Southern heritage portrayed in
Part I, is unable to break down the walls, the bolts, the glass windows
that imprison Muriel, who remains a "she-slave" shackled by the
Northern mode of thought and morality. Mrs. Pribby with her steel
blue eyes represents Muriel's super-ego and remains constantly alert:

Muriel: . . . Dan, I could love you if I tried. . . . I wont let
myself. I? Mrs. Pribby who reads newspapers all night wont.
What has she got to do with me? She *is* me, somehow. No she's
not. Yes she is. She is the town, and the town wont let me love
you, Dan. (110) [59]

Whereas Muriel's Mrs. Pribby represents "the submission to the
group consciousness of the family, of the clan, of the tribe, etc.,"

Dan, who won't "fit in," outraging Muriel and the theater audience by his behavior, looks forward to the return of the "law inside oneself."

Dan's manifestation of the new consciousness is followed by an even more explicit statement of Ouspensky's doctrine in the poem, "Prayer," where the image of the "little finger" echoes these lines from the *Tertium Organum*:

> But we do not realize, do not discern the presence of ratio-nality in the phenomena and laws of nature. This happens because we study always not the whole but the part, and we do not divine the whole which we wish to study—by studying the little finger of man we cannot discover his reason. It is the same way in our relation to nature: we study always the little finger of nature. When we come to realize this and shall under-stand that *every life is the manifestation of a part of some whole*, then only the possibility of knowledge of that whole opens to us.[8]

The final section of Part II, "Bona and Paul," associates the protago-nist with Paul's Epistle to the Corinthians and the famous chapter on the supreme importance of charity. Paul is described as looking through a "dark pane," cool and detached, and contemptuous of Bona and his companions. Paul's vision of love and unity between black and white comes too late: Bona has left him.

"Kabnis," the Third Part of Toomer's work, is a brilliant portrayal of the modern fragmented consciousness, uprooted from the tradi-tions of the past and unable to find a place in which to grow natu-rally. As Lewis perceives him, Kabnis is "a promise of soil-soaked beauty; uprooted, thinning out. Suspended a few feet above the soil whose touch would resurrence him" (191) [96]. Tormented by the fear of the white Southern contemptuous of the Negroes who have remained in the Southern and the culture they have developed, denying his racial king with them, he can only turn to cynicism, self-contempt, alco and self-conscious debauchery to conceal his pain.

A product of the Northern experience, Kabnis is unable return to that emotional consciousness of Part I which bathes Georgia in the rich after-glow of the setting sun. Project his own self-division, fear and contempt upon his environment Kabnis perceives it as opposed to him ("Hell of a mess I've got in: even the poultry is hostile." p. 159) [82] The pines "whispering to Jesus" are supplanted by the mocking songs of the night winds:

> White-man's land.
> Niggers, sing.
> Burn, bear black children

8. *Tertium Organum*, p. 215.

Till poor rivers bring
Rest, and sweet glory
In Camp Ground, (pp. 157, 167, and 209) [81, 85, 103]

God has become an ugly, external force, "a profligate, red nosed man about town" (161) [83], who so torments him with the opposition between the ugliness (of white lynchers, cackling hens and hogpens) and the beautiful serenity of the night that his bitterness erupts in the violent beheading of the cackling hen. The rich, mellow harvest time of Part I has become "Gray, cold changed autumn weather" (167) [85]. "Georgia hills roll off into the distance, their dreary aspect heightened by gray spots of unpainted one—and two-room shanties" (169) [86]. The church described as a "forlorn, box-like, whitewashed frame church," recalls the imagery which dominates Part II. Here the "hysteria" of the spirituals echoes Kabnis' own hysteria and replaces the rich, elegaic outpourings of the songs in Part I. As Kabnis scuttles back to his cabin, "a scarecrow replica of a man," sure that the Southerners are about to run him out, the dusk imagery of Part I reappears in new form: "a false dusk has come early. The countryside is ashen and chill" (180) [91].

After the cynicism and torment of Kabnis, we are offered a series of alternative reactions to the problem of existing in the white-controlled South. There is the school principal, Hanby, who represents in many ways the Booker T. Washington approach of "proving" to white folks that the Negro race is acceptable—on their terms. Asserting his power over black people while bowing to white men "without ever completely humbling himself," Hanby is the prototype of the college principal in Ellison's *Invisible Man* (as Father John is in some ways a precursor of the grandfather). Fred Halsey represents second and more worthy alternative, a dignified artisan who takes pride in his work and refuses to be humbled by Hanby. Lewis, asked to describe Halsey, responds, "Fits here. Belongs here. An artist in your way, arent you, Halsey" (200) [99]. But while Halsey is, as Sterling Brown points out, both "courageous and dignified,"[9] he is not capable of evolving into the man of cosmic consciousness. He can admire and appreciate Lewis, but cannot become like him.

Lewis, "a tall wiry copper-colored man, thirty perhaps," is the real alternative to Kabnis. "He is what a stronger Kabnis might have been, and in an odd faint way resembles him" (189) [95]. Described on several occasions as Christ-like, Lewis is an extension of Barlo and Dan Moore, a man capable of the cosmic vision, of penetrating the world of appearances, and of fusing together past and present, anguish and joy, "soil and the overarching heavens. Dusk; dawn."

9. *The Negro in American Fiction*, p. 153.

Along with Lewis, the possibility of a new dawning is offered by Carrie K., whose name echoes that first woman, Karintha, and whose soul is also in danger of ripening too soon ("Her spirit-bloom, even now touched sullen, bitter. Her rich fading . . ." p. 205) [101]. She can be saved by Lewis, but like Muriel and Esther is frustrated by the community mores; as she remembers "the sin-bogies of respect-able of respectable southern colored folks," "her face blanches" and she steps back from Lewis.

Yet it is Carrie K. who feeds the old man in the cellar, who is con-cerned about his welfare and who tries to communicate with him. To Kabnis this old man "like a bust in black walnut" is merely a "tongue-tied shadow of the old," a symbol of the hell he wants to forget and disown. To Lewis he is "a mute John the Baptist of a new religion," "the symbol, flesh and spirit of the past" (211–217) [104–06].

Although Kabnis remains till the end contemptuous of Father John and unwilling to hear him; although Lewis, no longer above to bear the anguish of his people in the South, leaves for the North, Toomer's final tableau suggests hope that a new consciousness will grow out of the African and Southern heritage of Black people, that the new dawning envisaged by Barlo will emerge for (and from) his "song-lit" race:

> . . . Carrie's gaze follows him [Kabnis] till he is gone. Then she goes to the old man and slips to her knees before him. Her lìmurmur, "Jesus come."
>
> Light streaks through the iron-barred cellar window. Within it soft circle, the figures of Carrie and Father John.
>
> Outside, the sun arises from its cradle in the tree-tops of the forest. Shadows of pines are dreams the sun shakes from its eyes. The sun arises. Gold-glowing child, it steps into the sky and sends a birth-song slanting down gray dust streets and sleepy windows of the southern town. (239) [115]

This closing tableau also unites another pair of opposites whose struggle to achieve a harmonious and complementary relationship has been a central theme throughout the work: the male and female principles. The conflict is introduced in the "Karintha" section, where the male is depicted as impatient for Karintha's dusky beauty: "This interest of the male, who wishes to ripen a growing thing too soon, could mean no good to her" (1) [5].

As *Cane* develops, it accumulates associations of the male prin-ciple with reaping, harvesting, cane-cutting, cotton-picking, work-ing in the saw-mills—images which in turn link with the autumn/dusk *motif*. Thus the male relates to will, conscious purpose, action and becoming (sense of past and future and power of prophecy), whereas woman connotes receptivity, passive ripening, emotion and being in the present. Parts I and II depict a series of encounters in which the impatient male is unable to respond at the right time or in the right way to the questions raised in "Fern": What is the role of the male in regard to the passively receptive consciousness Fern symbolizes? What is that "something" he should do for her? What is the relation between emotion and intellect? The narrator's lack of understanding prevents him from helping her to evolve to a higher consciousness, and her anguish can only become more intense, remaining trapped and inarticulate. His impatience with Avey leaves her uprooted and orphaned without the soil needed to grow beautiful, and she remains sleepily unconscious of the need to change. Dorris' present being, her "soul" dance, is lost in John's intellectualized dream of the future. And Bona flees from the cool intellectual detachment of Paul who learns too late the meaning of *caritas*. In "Harvest Song," we hear the anquished cry of the male harvester hungering for emotional sympathy, for the nourishment of the female, a cry echoed by Paul when he tells Bona, "I cant talk love. Love is a dry grain in my mouth unless it is wet with kisses" (144) [74].

One of Ouspensky's main concerns was to stress that *both* the emotions and the intellect are organs of knowledge, and that the highest form of consciousness must include the fusion of both. He defined "spirituality" as a fusion of the intellect with the higher emotions: "The intellect is spiritualized from the emotions; the emotions are spiritualized from the intellect."[1] In order for cosmic consciousness to evolve, he claimed, the seed must be present, but it must be cultivated by a conscious effort of the will and intellect:

> A new order of receptivity grows in the soil of the intellect and higher emotions, but it is not created by them. A tree grows in the earth, but it is not created by the earth. A seed is necessary. This seed may be in the soul or absent from it. When it is there it can be cultivated or choked; when it is not there it is impossible to replace it with anything else.[2]

This imagery of soil, seed and tree is taken up by Toomer in the "Song of the Son," which, as Todd Lieber points out,[3] is a central statement of *Cane's* purpose:

> Though late, O soil, it is not too late yet
> To catch thy plaintive soul, leaving, soon gone,
> Leaving, to catch thy plaintive soul soon gone.

1. *Tertium Organum*, p. 218.
2. *Ibid*. p. 219.
3. "Design and Movement in *Cane*," *CLA Journal*, XIII (September, 1969), 87.

> O Negro slaves, dark purple ripened plums,
> Squeezed, and bursting in the pine-wood air,
> Passing, before they stripped the old tree bare
> One plum was saved for me, one seed becomes
>
> An everlasting song, a singing tree,
> Caroling softly souls of slavery,
> What they were, and what they are to me,
> Caroling softly souls of slavery.   (21) [16]

While "Song of the Son," with its play on song/sun/son and on soul/soil, focusses on the development of art, "a singing tree," the poem which immediately follows, "Georgia Dusk," emphasizes the development of religion, past and present, linked with art:

> Meanwhile, the men, with vestiges of pomp,
>     Race memories of king and caravan,
>     High-priests, an ostrich, and a ju-ju man,
> Go singing through the footpaths of the swamp.
>
>                    . . . .
>
> O singers, resinous and soft your songs
>     Above the sacred whisper of the pines,
>     Give virgin lips to cornfield concubines,
> Bring dreams of Christ to dusky cane-lipped throngs.
>                              (22–23) [17]

These two poems in particular and the constant references to religious experience and to folk song throughout Part I relate to Ouspensky's claim that religion and art grow out of and are the organized forms of emotional knowledge.[4] Both Parts I and II also depict the degeneration of emotional consciousness and the perversion of religion and art when they are deprived of the conscious effort to cultivate and grow toward a higher form. Thus religion, which was a mystical unity with God and the universe for Fern, for Muriel has become a series of taboos and restrictions which prevent her from reaching Dan and the higher consciousness he represents. As mentioned earlier, Becky is buried by these same taboos, symbolized by the cabin built to hide and separate her from the community, a perversion of religion represented by the Bible leaves flapping idly on her mound, and recalled when Father John finally speaks his "truth" that "white folks made the Bible lie." Similarly the rich folk songs and lyrical outpourings which suffuse Part I gradually dissipate into the mechanical routines and "tricks" of the chorus girls in "Theater," the grotesque boxing match and serenade

---

4. *Tertium Organum*, pp. 230–231.

staged by the dwarf in "Box Seat," and the Walpurgis-like caperings of Kabnis in Part III.

So also the intellect deprived of emotion degenerates into the fragmented consciousness, cynicism and egocentricity represented by Kabnis (and, to a certain extent, Hanby). In contrast to Part I where the focus is on women, on the lyric consciousness, with the form appropriately lyrical, permeated with feeling and sympathy, Part III is peopled and dominated almost entirely by men, portraying their attempts to "make it" in the South and their contemptuous treatment of women such as Stella and Cora. The semi-dramatic form of Part III and most of Part II is also appropriate to their emphasis on conflict, activity and becoming. Only at the end, with the tableau of Carrie K. and Father John, is a moment of stasis achieved, a moment which unites religion and art, past seed and future promise.

My discussion of *Cane* has been limited to the metaphysical and symbolic level and has ignored other equally important and effective aspects of the book, such as fiction and characterization, the richly interwoven imagery, the word music and musical "texture" of Toomer's writing, the carefully wrought architecture. Part of the incredible achievement of Toomer's work is that it works brilliantly and subtly on *all* levels, so that the characters are both psychologically convincing and symbolic, the scenes depicted in prose and poetry are at the same time brilliantly painted landscapes and subjective projections, the words and sounds are sensuously heard, echoing and modulating other sounds and phrases without becoming more sound. All these aspects deserve detailed study—which would, I believe, lead to the conclusion that *Cane* is one of the most brilliantly executed and richly complex works to have been written in America.

## CHARLES T. DAVIS

### Jean Toomer and the South: Region and Race as Elements within a Literary Imagination†

If we are to take the word and trust the memories of those who participated in the Negro Renaissance in the 1920s, the most exciting single work produced by the movement was *Cane* by Jean Toomer.[1]

† From *Black Is the Color of the Cosmos: Essays on Afro-American Literature and Culture, 1942–1981*, ed. Henry Louis Gates, Jr. (Washington, D.C.: Howard University Press, 1989). Reproduced by permission.
1. For example, Countee Cullen wrote: "I bought the first copy of *Cane* which was sold, and I've read every word of it. . . . It's a real race contribution, a classical portrayal of things as they are." Letter to Jean Toomer, September 29, 1923, in Jean Toomer Collection, Fisk University Archives, Nashville, Tenn., Box 1, Folder 12, No. 386. Charles S. Johnson, editor in 1923 of *Opportunity: A Journal of Negro Life*, recalled in later years

*Cane* appeared in 1923,[2] the work of an author not entirely unknown. Portions of *Cane* had appeared in *The Crisis* and in an impressive number of little magazines, known for their commitment to revolutionary ideas and experimental writing. The list reads like the index of the study by Hoffman, Allen, and Ulrich, *The Little Magazine: Broom, Double Dealer, Liberator, Little Review, Nomad, Prairie,* and *S4N*. It suggests that Toomer was a part of a lively intellectual world that considered with great seriousness the cultural situation of America at the time.[3] And it suggests too that the publication of *Cane* was an event of national consequence, not a local or provincial phenomenon or simply a racial one, the case, indeed, if Toomer's achievement were simply the satisfaction of being another Negro who had managed to publish a book. After all, just a year before, T.S. Eliot had published *The Waste Land* in another of these little magazines, *The Dial,* and we have just barely recovered from that event. Toomer arrived with a bang, with a set of qualifications that could hardly be more impressive.

Though Toomer's achievement is not limited, finally, by reference to either region or race, it exploits in an unusual way both of these elements. Technically, Toomer was not a Southerner. Or to put it better, his connection with the South was not direct; it resembles Frost's association with New England. Robert Lee Frost was born in San Francisco, of parents originally from New England; Nathan Eugene Toomer, later called Jean, whose parents were originally from the South, with family ties to the state of Georgia, was born in Washington, D.C. For both writers the connection with the region was a form of recovery of a lost heritage. Gorham Munson, who wrote a book about Frost as well as participating vigorously in the organization and the direction of little magazines concerned about the future of modern machine culture, put the point plainly when he said in a review of *Cane* that Toomer "desired to make contact with his hereditary roots in the Southland."[4] For both writers, then, the return was a passionate involvement with countercultural implications; that is to say, Frost and Toomer deliberately turned their

---

his reaction to the emergence of Jean Toomer: "Here was triumphantly the Negro artist, detached from propaganda, sensitive only to beauty." Arna Bontemps, "The Awakening: A Memoir" in *The Harlem Renaissance Remembered*, ed. A. Bontemps (New York: Dodd, Mead and Co., 1972). p. 9.

2. Published by Boni and Liveright, Inc. The edition cited throughout this study is a Perennial Classic paperback edition published by Harper and Row (New York, 1969). Subsequent references to *Cane* will appear parenthetically in the text of my essay. [Page numbers in square brackets refer to this Norton Critical Edition.]

3. Sherwood Anderson's interest in *Cane* is to be measured by this generous offer: "I hoped to write something about Cane for Freeman but it had been given to some one else. It your publisher knows of any place I can write of it I'll be mighty glad to do it. My admiration for it holds." Letter to Jean Toomer, January 14, 1924, in Toomer Collection, Box 1, Folder 1, No. 51.

4. "The Significance of Jean Toomer," *Opportunity*, 3 (September 1925). 262.

backs upon contemporary urban culture to seek a more satisfying reality in rural surroundings. In a loose sense their attitudes can be called pastoral. Munson sketches the typical background for the pastoral quest, probably without an intimate knowledge of Toomer's early life: ". . . one infers a preceding period of shifting and drifting without settled harborage. Weary of homeless waters he turns back to ancestral soil. . . ."[5]

"Shifting" does accurately describe much of what we know of Toomer's early career, which displays an excessive movement from place to place and a rapid change from one intellectual commitment to another. After graduation from Dunbar High School in Washington, D.C., Toomer enrolled in 1914 at the University of Wisconsin, moved to the Massachusetts College of Agriculture in 1915, and stopped for a while in Chicago in 1916. Later there were brief sojourns in Milwaukee and New York. Always in between there was a return to Washington. Not until 1920 did his movement about the country stop, when Toomer settled in Washington, convinced then that he should devote his time and energy fully to reading and writing.

The outline of Jean Toomer's autobiography,[6] a work projected but never apparently completed, reveals an active and wide-ranging mind. The attraction to agriculture and physical culture seemed to be uppermost at Madison, Wisconsin; the exposure to socialist and materialist thought occurred in Chicago, and to the writings of Bernard Shaw in Milwaukee. Working as a clerk in New York City and later as a general manager for Acker and Company in 1919 in Ossining made possible the cultivation of a whole range of new interests, music among them. But meeting new people was just as important to him as the authors whom he read, Goethe, Whitman, Ibsen, and again Shaw, or the lectures that he attended. Though Toomer met at this time Lola Ridge, the American editor of *Broom*, E.A. Robinson, Witter Bynner, Scofield Thayer, and other literary figures prominent in the New York scene, no one had a greater impact upon him than did Waldo Frank, whose *Our America* he had read with care. It is the New York adventure that seemed to be decisive in turning Toomer's attention to art. When the inevitable return to Washington came in 1920, Toomer was prepared to commit himself to more systematic reading, addressing not only all of the works of Waldo Frank, but books by Tolstoy, Flaubert, Baudelaire, Dostoyevsky, Sinclair Lewis, Dreiser, Sherwood Anderson, Frost, and Freud. He read the little magazines too, absorbing from Frank and others a critical attitude toward an American society which had become warped by the demands of modern technology and unchecked urbanization.

5. Ibid.
6. Toomer Collection, Box 14, Folder 1.

Toomer was ripe for a sweeping commitment of some kind in 1920, one that would affirm man's basic emotional life rather than his intellectual achievement, one, as Frank put it graphically later, that would protect him from the stink of the marketplace and keep him "warm underneath, in the soil, where the throb is."[7]

The specific form of Toomer's commitment was determined by a factor beyond his control, by his ancestry, which involved intimately both region and race, both the recognition of the South as home and the affirmation of an allegiance to the black race. Jean was the grandson of P. B. S. Pinchback, who was at one time during Reconstruction days Lieutenant-Governor, then Acting Governor of the state of Louisiana. He was the son of Pinchback's daughter Nina, who had married briefly Nathan Toomer, a union that actually terminated in 1895 after a year of marriage and was formally dissolved in 1899. Jean was especially close to his grandparents, with whom he lived after Nina's death in 1909. The strong emotions that swept through Toomer's consciousness while he was writing *Cane* were deeply intertwined with his concern for his grandfather's declining health. Indeed, Toomer recalled in the notes for an autobiography that Pinchback died the day after he had finished the first draft of "Kabnis." The suggestion of the end of an era, so strong in *Cane*, may owe something to the feelings and the sympathies of the young artist as he observed the last moments of a man, once so powerful and vigorous, reduced to a broken and pathetic figure.[8] The journey to New Orleans to place Pinchback's body in the vault already occupied by Toomer's mother must have reenforced the intimation of an imminent conclusion, aroused the echoes in his ears of a "swan-song"[9] that was personal as well as cultural.

The event that provoked Toomer's emergence as an artist had preceded Pinchback's death; it had, no doubt, psychic reverberations of great consequence. This was the period of three months in 1921 which Toomer spent in Georgia. He had accepted an offer to replace a principal of a school in Sparta who had gone North to raise funds for the school, a necessity familiar to the administrators of many Southern black educational institutions at the time. For Toomer, going to Georgia was a return. Both grandfather Pinchback and father Nathan Toomer had come from Georgia. Jean recalls the impression that the new Georgia scene made upon him: "The setting was crude in a way, but strangely rich and beautiful. . . . There was a valley, the valley of *Cane*, with smoke-wreaths during the day and mist at night. . . ."[1]

7. Letter to Jean Toomer, April 25, 1922, in Toomer Collection.
8. Toomer Collection, Box 14, Folder I, No. 59.
9. Ibid.
1. Ibid.

The discovery of the physical characteristics of the region was only a part of Toomer's total response. Another part had more to do with what was heard than with what was seen. The artist was moved by the spirituals sung by the blacks in Georgia. He was touched not merely by their beauty but by the sense that they represented a dying folk-spirit, a creative impulse doomed to be destroyed by the small town and then the city, by the inevitable encroachment of industry, commerce, and the machine. What occurred, of course, was the coalescence of two quite divergent drives in Toomer. One certainly, as Munson suspected, was the desire to stop the drift in his life, to find a home, even though a temporary one. The second was the expected reaction of a talented but disciplined student well trained in the curriculum promoted by Waldo Frank and Sherwood Anderson. In discovering his heritage Toomer rejected contemporary culture with its emphasis upon urbanization and a machine technology.

The touchy point about Toomer's return is race or, rather, allegiance to a race. The problem is more complicated than it appears to be. In Georgia, Toomer identified with the life of blacks and he acquired in this way a deep appreciation for the richness and strength that came from the intimate connection existing there between man and soil. Arna Bontemps, in his "Introduction" to a reissue of *Cane*, quotes from a letter written by Toomer to the editors of *The Liberator* magazine in the summer of 1922 which offers matter that has a direct bearing on this point. In it Toomer describes his racial background: ". . . I seem to have (who knows for sure) seven blood mixtures: French, Dutch, Welsh, Negro, German, Jewish, and Indian." Then he adds, in what must have seemed at the time an amazing piece of heresy: "Because of these, my position in America has been a curious one. I have lived equally amid the two race groups. Now white, now colored." American society in 1920, perhaps less so now, was pathologically sensitive to racial attachments. It was bad enough for Faulkner, early in the next decade, to create a character in *Light in August* who was a Negro by sociological definition alone,[2] but here from young Toomer, in life, not in art, we have the assertion that he could choose his racial identity. He adds in the letter to *The Liberator*: "Within the last two or three years, however, my growing need for artistic expression has pulled me deeper and deeper into the Negro group. And as my powers of receptivity increased, I found myself loving it in a way that I could never love the other. It has stimulated and fertilized whatever creative talent I may contain within me. A visit to Georgia last fall was the starting point of almost everything of worth that I have done."[3]

2. Joe Christmas in *Light in August* (New York: Random House, 1932).
3. Letter to the *Liberator*, 1922, quoted by Arna Bontemps in his "Introduction" to *Cane*, pp. [212–13].

Toomer chose to be black. His stance was artistically useful because he allowed himself maximum freedom in defining his heritage. It was not something that he had to accept because he was trapped, as many Americans were, by history or family or caste or race. It was something that he discovered, or, since the discovery was essentially a matter of consciousness, something that he made. Toomer brought rare objectivity and sensitivity to his task, and in his time perhaps only he was equipped to create his form of the South, preeminently a black South, one just as strongly projected as the old forms, but more beautiful in the description of the land, more complicated in revealing the tangled, half-articulated emotions of its people, and more deeply human.

Making something new demands a rejection of what is at hand. As a black American in 1920 Toomer had available to him at least three forms of the South, none of which he accepted.

There was the world created by the Plantation Tradition, especially by the dialect poems of Paul Laurence Dunbar, which had appeared originally in the late nineteenth and early twentieth centuries and had been reprinted, subsequently, in special editions, sometimes lavishly illustrated.[4] This was a black South full of memories of good times on the old plantation, demonstrations of the efficacy of Christian piety, and antics of collapsible, indestructible comedians in black face. What is referred to here is the popular impression of Dunbar's verse, reinforced by faithful and frequent recitation by blacks and whites all over America. A study of the whole Dunbar canon reveals a troubled poet deeply sensitive especially to the materialist and mechanistic thought at the turn of the century. But Dunbar's South, for most Americans, was not to be distinguished from that projected by the minstrel stage and created nostalgically in sentimental fiction. By 1920 blacks had ceased to take it seriously, if they ever had, except for those enterprising artists who sought to extract from it profitable theatrical or musical formulas.

A second South was linked to the name of Booker Washington, who offered it to the world in the pages of *Up From Slavery*.[5] These presented a picture of improving relations involving blacks and whites and an improving economic status for blacks. Patience, Christian virtue, and hard work would result in prosperity soon; but civil rights, the vote, and full citizenship would take longer. Survival demanded the compromise of manhood, perhaps, but Washington

---

4. Dunbar's poems appeared originally in six volumes during his lifetime: *Oak and Ivy* (1893), *Majors and Minors* (1895), *Lyrics of Lowly Life* (1896). *Lyrics of the Hearthside* (1899), *Lyrics of Love and Laughter* (1903), *Lyrics of Sunshine and Shadow* (1905). In addition there were special editions like *Poems of Cabin and Field* (New York: Dodd, Mead and Co., 1899), with photographs by the Hampton Institute Camera Club and Decorations by Alice Morse.

5. Doubleday, 1901.

had the Social Darwinist's faith that all good things would come in time to those best equipped to have them. Washington's South was real enough, but by 1920 it had lost credibility with most black intellectuals. His reality seemed to be restricted to those oases in the South that tended to justify his convictions. Meanwhile, the masses of blacks in the South lived poor, desperate lives unleavened by the force of Booker's rhetoric.

The design of the South that inspired greatest conviction among intellectual blacks was that sketched by W.E.B. Du Bois in *The Souls of Black Folk, The Crisis* magazine, *Darkwater*, and elsewhere.[6] Certain salient features stand out. Du Bois claimed that a condition of naked oppression existed in the South, which was not improving as a place for blacks to live and to work. The people who seemed to be most oppressed lived in rural areas where law and sharp business practices combined to exploit them. Du Bois asserted that Washington's optimistic predictions about economic progress for blacks in the South were empty, if not absurd, when blacks lacked the basic rights of citizenship to protect their property. The hope for an improved life rested with the leadership of the Talented Tenth, the educated members of the black middle class to be found largely in the towns and the black schools. At issue for Du Bois always was manhood, which could not be sustained by anything other than a broad and liberal education (rather than industrial training) and could not survive the daily humiliations imposed by a segregated society.

The South that Toomer made succeeded in reversing nearly all of Du Bois's conclusions, without echoing Dunbar's pious sentiments or referring to the necessity for a pragmatic accommodation with whites in Southern communities. What supported the new view was not facts, as Du Bois would define them, not statistical surveys coming out of Atlanta University, but an emotional response, a young man's impression of the black heritage he had returned to discover.

Toomer saw a beautiful land of pine trees, mist, and red soil (not the red clay that Du Bois despised so thoroughly that he refused to bury his infant son in it),[7] a land in which fertility was finally stronger than terror, though moved by a threat of violence that seemed all-pervasive. He admired the black "peasants," the strong people who lived close to the soil and reflected in their preoccupation with sex and mystical religious experience the fertility of the land. "Peasants"[8] is Toomer's term, with a meaning far removed from the "peasants" of Faulkner's *The Hamlet*, descriptive there of farmers who had been

6. *The Souls of Black Folk* (Chicago: A. C. McClurg and Co., 1903); *Darkwater: Voices from Within the Veil* (New York: Harcourt, 1920).
7. In "Of the Passing of the First-Born," *The Souls of Black Folk* (New York: Fawcett. 1961). p. 155.
8. Letter to *The Liberator*, p. 155.

exploited and humiliated by ruthless predators. The weak people in
Toomer's South (Esther is one of them) were the shopkeepers, the
light-skinned Negroes of the middle class, the potential members
of the group that Du Bois had labelled the Talented Tenth. They
lived in the towns and they were both attracted and repelled by the
crude black energy they saw in the peasants. Life was the issue here,
and middle-class conventions and aspirations denied life and, inci-
dentally, love. Black manhood survived in the South as a response,
in part, to a more powerful force. But only in part. Fred Halsey, a
pillar of strength in the dramatic narrative "Kabnis," has other
sources of power: pride in his profession as a master craftsman and
an owner of a wagon-shop, and delight in using his mind in debating
with the professors, Lewis and Kabnis. The signs of degeneration
are present everywhere—in the lack of coordination of body and
spirit, in sexual excess, and in mystical hysteria. They are external
as well as internal, with the menace of physical violence, with death
by lynching always close. The forces of degradation may kill the
body but not destroy the integrity and the spirit of the truly strong:
Barlo, the black preacher; Tom Burwell, Louisa's black lover in
"Blood Burning Moon"; Fred Halsey. Toomer's Southern exposure
produced a wholly new way of looking at Southern life, one that is
related clearly to the position of the Nashville Fugitives, as Bontemps notes in his "Introduction,"[9] but one quite different, finally,
because the controlling point of view is black, not white.

The invaluable documentation of Toomer's approach to the South
found in his letters and in his notes toward an autobiography throws
light upon the poem, "Song of the Son," which functions really as a
form of preface to the whole of *Cane*. We are introduced to the consciousness of a poet-speaker who imposes unity upon the verses,
sketches, narratives, and symbolic signs that make up the body of the
work.

"Song of the Son" describes a return to a scene from which the
poet has been long separated. The initial lines suggest an amount
of detachment. In much the way that Whitman often did, in "Crossing Brooklyn Ferry," for example, the poet requests the landscape
to arrange itself for his pleasure:

> Pour O pour that parting soul in song,
> O pour it in the sawdust glow of night,
> Into the velvet pine-smoke air to-night,
> And let the valley carry it along,
> And let the valley carry it along, (p. 21) [16]

---

9. Bontemps, "Introduction," *Cane*, p. xvi [211].

What is at stake is not merely the desire for physical delight, though this is strong; the poet realizes that he is responding to "that parting soul," the spirit in the land. The reference to "parting" introduces the problem of time. The poet has returned "just before an epoch's sun declines," at that moment when the land is losing a value that it has long possessed. This is one that the speaker was either not aware of or not appreciative of when he was present at this scene before. The value itself is the culture of "A song-lit race of slaves," a culture that was unique and rich. For one thing, it was intimately tied to the land, so deeply intertwined that the slaves can be referred to as organic growths—"dark purple ripened plums." For another, the culture is sad, "plaintive," because the slaves are under pressure, suffering, indeed, from oppression and because, further, it is disappearing, dying. The two characteristics form the basis for song, for the spirituals sung by the slaves and other forms of artistic expression that flow naturally from a unified existence. What is being lost, as the poet looks and ruminates, is song, along with other vestiges of the slave culture, not simply the music itself but the ability to make music. We are not told what the hostile forces are that oppose song, though we are led inevitably to speculate about them—perhaps, freedom from suffering, or the city, or education, or modern society. The poet has returned in time to secure possession of one vestige of the old culture, one "plum" providing the seed that would enable him to reconstruct the earlier civilization. This is important to do because of the ancient beauty that becomes now available to him and because the new awareness forms a basis for new songs, to be created, no doubt by the poet. The double emphasis cannot be missed: "What they [souls of slavery] were, and what they are to me" (p. 21) [16]. The conclusion of the poem resembles the dramatic end of "Out of the Cradle Endlessly Rocking," when Whitman says, after at least a partial reconciliation with death, symbolized by the sea: "The sea whisper'd me."[1]

   "Song of the Son" presents the consciousness that stands behind the varied verbal structures in *Cane*. In the poem it is a sophisticated intelligence yearning for completion and adequate expression and finding the means for achieving these ends in contact with the South and with a newly discovered black culture. It plays multiple roles elsewhere in *Cane*. It is responsible for the sympathy and understanding expressed by the narrator of "Karintha" and "Carma," for that need to explain the actions of the characters in the stories, to place their behavior within an appropriate intellectual context. On occasion the consciousness becomes embodied in characters, in the curious "I" figures in "Becky" and "Fern" who seek to penetrate the deeper mysteries and contradictions of Southern life. Always one

---

1. *Leaves of Grass*, ed. H. W. Blodgett and Sculley Bradley (New York: Norton, 1968). p. 253.

of the important functions of the brooding intelligence which invests *Cane* is projection, as significant characters, despite differences in race and station in society, share the desire for a fuller life, one in which their half-understood and half-articulated impulses may have a place.

The preoccupation with the problems of consciousness is responsible for the design in *Cane*. Toomer is not content simply to explore the situations in which an alien Northern intelligence confronts Southern realities; he is as much concerned with analyzing the factors that have shaped the Northern mind. He sees the necessity for regional connection, for the Northern black to acquire the emotional strengths that black Southerners still possess, though they may be rapidly losing them. What haunts Toomer's mind is a circle based upon regional relationships, or, more accurately, a broken circle, since the author does not reach the point in *Cane* of successful prefiguration, the anticipation of the full existence for man, what would be called later the "all around development of man," involving the "constructive functioning" of body, emotions, and mind.[2]

Toomer's own comments on the structure for *Cane* are invaluable and offer a beginning for any discussion of the organization of the whole work. In December 1922, Waldo Frank received a letter from Toomer announcing the completion of *Cane* and defining the principles which were intended to give unity to his achievement:

> From three angles, *Cane*'s design is a circle. Aesthetically, from simple forms to complex ones, and back to simple forms. Regionally, from the South up to the North, and back into the South again. Or, from the North down into the South, and then a return North. From the point of view of the spiritual entity behind the work, the curve really starts with Bona and Paul (awakening), plunges into Kabnis, emerges in Karintha, etc., swings upward into Theater and Box Seat, and ends (pauses) in Harvest Song.[3]

Toomer's first comment on form is plain enough and requires little explanation. The Georgia tales and "Kabnis" are reasonably straightforward narratives, with intensities that are either lyric or dramatic. They are without the symbolic complexity of the middle section of *Cane*, the one devoted to the North. We find here the experimental sketches "Seventh Street," "Rhobert," and "Calling Jesus," presenting a level of abstraction not discovered elsewhere. Moreover, in the narratives "Theater" and "Box Seat" symbolic devices and distortion are employed with subtlety and effectiveness.

---

2. Outline for an autobiography, Toomer Collection, Box 14, Folder 1, pp. 63–64.
3. Letter to Waldo Frank, December 12, 1922, Toomer Collection, Box 3, Folder 6, No. 800. Toomer supplies no punctuation for the titles.

The dance in "Theater" represents the ideal of a fulfilled relationship between Dorris and John, who come from different classes in the highly stratified black society of Washington, D.C. In "Box Seat" the seats in the Lincoln Theater are "slots," "bolted houses" (p. 117) [62], cutting Muriel off from rewarding connection with anyone else, especially from her desperate, would-be lover Dan. In both stories the emphasis is placed upon what the characters think rather than upon what they do. "Box Seat" relies more heavily upon distortion than does "Theater," a fact particularly evident with the use of the dwarf to stand for the revulsion which the conventional Muriel feels toward any life existing outside of her cherished middle-class patterns. There is a deliberate correspondence between the complexity of Toomer's literary technique and the complexity of the Northern urban environment. What is magnified, thereby, is the struggle of the human spirit, bound by dehumanizing conventions and mechanical restrictions, to achieve freedom and satisfaction.

The more puzzling part of Toomer's statement of intention involves the reference to regions. We have an apparent contradiction: we begin *Cane* either in the South or in the North, and we conclude the work either in the South or in the North. What seems to be apparent nonsense becomes rewardingly clear only when the element of consciousness is considered, what Toomer calls "the spiritual entity behind the work."[4] The external order for *Cane*, recorded simply as it appears, establishes the first background in Georgia, the second in Washington and Chicago, and the third again in Georgia. It is South, North, South.

But if the action is viewed organically, we take our cue from the form of the consciousness as defined by "Song of the Son." Toomer suggests that we begin with "Bona and Paul," a story in which Paul discovers that he is not like Bona. The racial difference, felt deeply first in the Crimson Gardens, a nightclub in Chicago, is the basis for Paul's rejection by Bona; at the same time Paul experiences something less painful and equally important, the need to explain his attraction for Bona to the huge black man who opens and shuts the door of the nightclub. Frustration, then, is accompanied by the intimation of a new connection, "awakening,"[5] Toomer called it. "Kabnis," looked at this way, is the direct confrontation with what it means to be black in the South. The trial for the Northern Kabnis is disturbing, humiliating, and apparently futile, with only infrequent suggestions of black strength. The affirmation of difference and the tribute to black emotional power are to be found in the Georgia stories, especially in the portraits of sensual black women. The progress

4. Ibid.
5. Ibid.

of consciousness moves next to the North where city realities are weighed against Southern black strength. Dorris's dance and Dan's plea to the prim Muriel grow from the same impulse that moves Karintha and Carma. This is stated most explicitly in "Box Seat," when Dan sits beside a portly black lady in the Lincoln Theater. Her fragrance arouses racial memories in Dan: "Her strong roots sink down and spread under the river and disappear in blood-lines that waver South. Her roots shoot down. Dan's hands follow them. Roots throb. Dan's heart beats violently. He places his palms upon the earth to cool them. Earth throbs" (p. 119) [63]. The center of the resistance to the frigid and mechanical North is located in racial memories that linger, shards and vestiges of an old black culture.

"Harvest Song" in this context is the conclusion of *Cane*. It is a poem that denies its title, since it is not the celebration of work done well and the grain collected. What is missing is enjoyment, the ability of the poet to taste and to receive nourishment from the product that has demanded so much sweat and toil:

> I am a reaper whose muscles set at sundown. All my oats are cradled.
> But I am too chilled, and too fatigued to bind them. And I hunger. (p. 132) [69]

Nourishment and enjoyment demand friendship with others, a sense of brotherhood and community. The poet, though he is reluctant and too timid to attempt the unexpected, moves to a point that he cries out to his fellow laborers:

> O my brothers, I beat my palms, still soft, against the stubble of my harvesting. (You beat your soft palms, too.) My pain is sweet. Sweeter than the oats or wheat or corn. It will not bring me knowledge of my hunger. (p. 133) [69]

There is no sign that the cry is responded to, as it is, say, in another harvest poem, Frost's "The Tuft of Flowers."[6] And without response there is not satisfaction for hunger, not even the knowledge of what hunger is. "Harvest Song" offers a strong plea for human values, for the virtues of emotional connection, one that relates immediately to Toomer's description of Northern society, in which mind, work, and propriety have crushed soul.

The central movement of *Cane*, interpreted in terms of a developing consciousness, is then North, South, North. The curve ends, Toomer writes, in "Harvest Song," but the term that he uses as a substitute for "ends," that is to say, "pauses," is a better one.[7] The

6. Robert Frost, *Complete Poems* (New York: Holt, Rinehart and Winston, 1949), pp. 31–32. The terminal lines are: "'Men work together,' I told him from the heart,' / 'Whether they work together or apart.'"
7. Letter to Frank, December 12, 1922.

poet stands poised at the end of "Harvest Song," waiting for the responding cry that does not come. The progress of the curve stops, short of completion, the fulfillment of a design that might be viewed as a rounded circle. Toomer is not prepared to explore completion or to celebrate a triumphant ending—nor was this his intention— because completion would mean nothing less than the promise of a redeemed America, a fusion of North and South, a region that for him is emotional and black.

Curveship has another meaning for the structure of *Cane*. In the same letter to Frank in which he suggested various ways of reading his newly completed work, Toomer wrote: "Between each of the three sections, a curve. These, to vaguely indicate the design."[8] It is useful to consider what this means when we look at the relationships between the sections. What may be promised is a substantial connection in materials and problems. We discover with close examination that that kind of correspondence does exist in fact, with significant differences separating the sections resting, rather, in the way the familiar questions are resolved.

The first two sections, one devoted to the Georgia scenes and the other to urban episodes, connect in this fashion, and, indeed, seem to balance each other. The same problems thread their way through both divisions of the book. Karintha and Avey suffer from excessive, undirected, almost unconscious sexuality. But there is a difference: men are still awed by Karintha's mysterious beauty, but some cynics, not the narrator, consider Avey to be a common whore. "Fern" and "Calling Jesus" are comments on the attempted invasion of the body by the soul, with vastly different consequences. Fern welcomes the descent of the spirit that startles her more worldly city-admirer. On the other hand, the unnamed girl of "Calling Jesus" rejects the possibility of a larger and more deeply mystical experience because she is content with her "large house" and absorbed in shallow dreams. Only Jesus can bring a change. Esther in the story given her name and Dan in "Box Seat" share a common urge for freedom and love and are reduced to near madness by the insensitivity and lack of understanding in their love objects. Esther's pathetic proposal to Barlo seems ridiculous and absurd to those who frequent Nat Bowle's place because the pattern of her sterile existence is far removed from that of ordinary black people. Dan's cry causes disruption in the Lincoln Theater partly because he sees accurately, as others do, that Muriel's impulse to reject the gift of the dwarf performer is based upon a conventional distaste for what is considered in life crude, deformed, and black. "Blood-Burning Moon" and "Bona and Paul" present interracial affairs that end in failure, but with a difference. White Bob Stone, despite his family tradition and his inherited

8. Ibid.

contempt for blacks, makes a total commitment to his love for the black Louisa to the point of willing his own death. The black Paul loses the white Bona as a consequence of a moment of distraction. The fine words which state Paul's passion reveal also a lack of integration in his personality and his inability to give himself wholly to love in the way that Stone or his black rival, Tom Burwell, do. In Toomer's world the pulse of life beats more slowly in Chicago.

"Kabnis," in one sense, is a fitting conclusion for *Cane* because it gives expression to nearly all of the themes developed in the two earlier sections. We find the intense resentment of middle-class restraints, the undirected sexuality, the attempt to achieve a mystical knowledge of some kind, and the awesome gap between the races. "Kabnis" is also an effective demonstration of the inconclusiveness of *Cane*, offering a most thorough exploration of the unhappy disjunction between mind and emotion that has haunted the black characters of the urban section. But "Kabnis," as Toomer suggested, falls earlier within the development of the central consciousness informing the whole book, at some point before the discovery of the energy of black folk to be found in "Karintha" and "Carma." There are suggestions of that power in Kabnis's futile effort to extract wisdom from Father John, the old black man who is a vestige of the slave civilization. Viewed within the perspective of the organic cycle, "Harvest Song" offers a more appropriate termination. Frustration is not localized. There the long lines of free verse and the repetitive elements recall Whitman's poems of celebration, but the American harvest is sterile. Unhappiness, pain, fear, and hunger are incongruously present with the sources of the good life immediately at hand. And all paths in *Cane*, whether in the North or South or whether pursued by blacks or whites, lead to this disturbing end.

*Cane* owes everything to the symbolic representation of region and race. Toomer discovered his blackness in Georgia, and armed with this revelation he was able to construct a pattern of life which contrasted with what he had seen about him in the cities of the North. Neither pattern was to be satisfying finally. The writing of *Cane* occurred at a very special moment in Toomer's life. This time came when his awareness of his own heritage was heightened by the impending death of grandfather Pinchback, when his sense of the corruption of modern urban society was keen as a result of a close intellectual association with Waldo Frank and Sherwood Anderson, and when the exposure to black rural life in Georgia resolved momentarily his own ambivalent and uncertain feelings about racial identity. This moment was enough to link him to other writers of the Harlem Renaissance, who were at the time struggling to conquer feelings of uncertainty and inadequacy of a different kind in an effort to achieve an expression of that which was most authentic in their lives.

Toomer was correct when he commented in retrospect that *Cane* was a "swan-song."[9] It was the end not only of a way of Southern black life, as he saw it, but of his own commitment to place that life in art. Even during the year of *Cane*'s publication, 1923, Toomer's attention turned to problems that he considered to be more fundamental than the challenge of producing another work modelled on *Cane*. When he looked at his friends and acquaintances, many of whom were committed in some way to the world of art, he was compelled to say: "Most of the men and women were growing into lopsided specialists of one kind or another; or, they were almost hopelessly entangled in emotional snarls and conflicts. And neither literature nor art did anything for them. In short, my attention had been turned from the books and paintings to the people who produced them; and I saw that these people were in a sorry state. What did it really matter that they were able by talent to turn out things that got reviews?"[1] Toomer continued to write, but he was not destined to produce anything that matched *Cane*'s power. His primary concern became experimentation in life rather than in art, an endeavor to be heavily influenced by contact with Gurdjieff's ideas, occurring for the first time in 1923. Before we deplore the loss to art as a consequence of this decision, we should recall that it was the aftermath of another experiment in life, Toomer's brief period of existence as a black in Georgia, that brought us *Cane*.

*1974*

# ALICE WALKER

## The Divided Life of Jean Toomer[†]

In 1923, when he was twenty-nine years old, Jean Toomer published *Cane*, a book that sang naturally and effortlessly of the beauty, passion, and vulnerability of black, mostly Southern, life. In form it was unique: there were stories interspersed with poems, a novelette constructed like a play, and delicate line drawings that casually accented pages throughout. Some critics called the book a novel, some called it a prose poem, some did not know what to call it; but all agreed that *Cane* was original, and a welcome change from earlier fiction that took a didactic or hortatory position on black and interracial American life.

9. Outline for an autobiography, Toomer Collection, Box 14, Folder 1, p. 59.
1. Ibid., p. 63.
† From *The New York Times*, © [July 13, 1980] *The New York Times*. All rights reserved. Reprinted by permission of *The New York Times* and the author.

It was an immediate hit among those writers who would eventually make the Harlem Renaissance—including Langston Hughes and Zora Neale Hurston—who, apparently without knowing much about its author, accepted *Cane* as a work of genius and were influenced by it. Hughes was moved to explore the dramatic possibilities of interracial, intrafamilial relationships in the South in his plays and poems. Hurston was encouraged to portray the culture of rural black Southerners as generative, vibrant, and destined for a useful, if vastly changed, future in the modern world, though Toomer himself had considered *Cane* the "swan song" of that culture.

Not much was known about Toomer in black literary circles, because he never belonged to any; and shortly after *Cane* was published he no longer appeared even in white ones. By the time the Harlem Renaissance was in full swing, in the mid- and late 1920s, the book was out of print, largely forgotten, and its author an infrequently discussed mystery.

Toomer was still a mystery over forty years later, in 1969, when, at the height of the black studies movement, *Cane* was reissued and again captured the imagination of readers with its poetic complexity and sensitive treatment of black men and especially black women. By this time, the late Arna Bontemps, poet, novelist, and Curator of Special Collections at Fisk University, had access to Toomer's autobiographical writings: Toomer had died in 1967. Bontemps wrote sympathetically, albeit guardedly, of Toomer's long isolation in a Washington, D.C. brownstone, watching his grandparents decline, of the brief, three-month trip to Sparta, Georgia, that was the inspiration for *Cane*, and of the "crisis" about his racial identity. Some of the mystery surrounding Toomer's personality began to be dispelled.

This present collection of Toomer's writings, *The Wayward and the Seeking* (apparently there is much more), edited and shaped by Darwin T. Turner, also does much to clarify the Jean Toomer mystery. There is a large section of autobiographical fragments, three short stories, and many poems, including "The Blue Meridian," Toomer's definitive statement of his vision of America. Also included are two interesting and often provocative plays that illustrate both Toomer's sensitivity to women and his ultimate condescension toward them, as well as a selection of maxims and aphorisms commenting on nature and humanity from Toomer's previously published booklet *Essentials*.

Feminists will be intrigued by what Toomer writes about his mother and grandmother. His mother was an intelligent woman, utterly dominated by her father, whom she spent her whole, relatively short life trying to defy. She died when Toomer was fifteen, after the second of two mysterious at-home operations that, as described here, read like abortions. His grandmother was also dominated by her husband, until his health began to decline in old age. Then she, old and ill herself, blossomed magnificently from a sweet, silent shadow of her husband into a woman of high humor, memorable tales, satiric jibes at anything and everything. She is reported to have had "some dark blood."

It will no doubt be hard, if not impossible, for lovers of *Cane* to read *The Wayward and the Seeking* (the title is from one of Toomer's poems) without feelings of disappointment and loss. Disappointment because the man who wrote so piercingly of "Negro" life in *Cane* chose to live his own life as a white man, while Hughes, Hurston, Du Bois, and other black writers were celebrating the blackness in themselves as well as in their work. Loss because it appears this choice undermined Toomer's moral judgment: there were things in American life and in his own that he simply refused to see.

Toomer's refusal to acknowledge the racism around him is especially lamentable. He lived in Washington with his grandparents for nearly the first twenty years of his life, and when he left to attend the University of Wisconsin, he decided he would say nothing of his racial identity unless asked. If asked, he would say, basically, that he was an American. The subject "never came up," he writes, and within two weeks he was "taking this white world as a matter of course, forgetting that I had been in a colored group." He does not find it odd that when his schoolmates mistake him for an Indian they brutalize him so severely on the football field that he is forced to call time out for good. "If others had race prejudice that was their affair," he wrote, "as long as it did not manifest itself against me." Given this deliberate blindness, it is no wonder that the fiction he wrote after *Cane* depicts primarily white people and never documents their racism in any way; it is as if Toomer believed an absence of black people assured the absence of racism itself.

To many who read this collection Toomer will appear to be, as he saw himself, a visionary in his assumption that he was "naturally and inevitably" an American—a "prototype" of the new race now evolving on the American continent, "neither white nor black." They will note that it was not Toomer who ordained that a single drop of black blood makes one black. Toomer, looking more white than black, could as easily argue the opposite point: that several obvious drops of white blood make one white. They will think it heroic of Toomer to fling off racial labels and to insist on being simply "of the American race." They will not be bothered by the thought that, during Toomer's lifetime, only white people were treated simply as Americans.

Other readers will no doubt consider Toomer a racial opportunist, like his grandfather, P. B. S. Pinchback, Governor of Louisiana during Reconstruction, who, according to Toomer, settled in New Orleans before the Civil War and commanded a regiment of federal troops during the war. After "the war ended and the black man [was] freed and enfranchised," Pinchback saw his "opportunity in the political arena. He claimed he had Negro blood, linked himself with the Negro cause, and rose to power." Once having obtained power Pinchback did nothing of substance for the masses of black men who voted for him. He and his family lived richly among upper-class whites until his money began to dwindle from playing the horses too much. He then moved among "colored" people who were so nearly white that "they had never run up against the color line." It was among these white and near-white neighbors that Toomer grew up.

Like his grandfather, Toomer apparently used his "connection" to black people only once, when it was to his advantage to do so. When he was attempting to publish excerpts from *Cane*, he sent some stories to the *Liberator*, one of whose editors was black writer Claude McKay. He explained that though he was of French, Welsh, Negro, German, and Jewish and Indian ancestry, his "growing need for artistic expression" pulled him "deeper and deeper into the Negro group. And as my powers of receptivity increased, I found myself loving it in a way that I could never love the other. It has stimulated and fertilized whatever creative talent I may contain within me. A visit to Georgia last fall was the starting point of almost everything of worth that I have done. I heard folk-songs come from the lips of Negro peasants. I saw the rich dusk beauty that I had heard many false accents about, and of which till then, I was somewhat skeptical. And a deep part of my nature, a part that I had repressed, sprang suddenly to life and responded to them. Now I cannot conceive of myself as aloof and separated."

Once *Cane* was published, however, Toomer told a different story. When his publisher asked him to "feature" himself as a Negro for *Cane*'s publicity, Toomer replied that as he was not a Negro, he could not feature himself as one. He dropped out of literary circles, joined a Gurdjieffian commune intent on self-realization, met the well-connected white novelist Margery Latimer and married her. She died a year later in childbirth. His second wife, the affluent Marjorie Content Toomer, also white, settled down with him on a farm among the "tolerant Quakers" of Bucks County, Pennsylvania, where, after seventy-three years of living as "an American," Toomer died in a nursing home.

A few of us will realize that *Cane* was not only his finest work but that it is also in part based on the essence of stories told to Toomer by his grandmother, she of the "dark blood" to whom the book is dedicated, and that many of the women in *Cane* are modeled on the tragic indecisiveness and weakness of his mother's life. *Cane* was for Toomer a double "swan song." He meant it to memorialize a culture he thought was dying, whose folk spirit he considered beautiful, but he was also saying good-bye to the "Negro" he felt dying in himself. *Cane* then is a parting gift, and no less precious because of that. I think Jean Toomer would want us to keep its beauty, but let him go.

1980

# DAVID BRADLEY

## Looking Behind *Cane*†

### I

I was introduced to Jean Toomer in the spring of 1970 when I was a student at the University of Pennsylvania, taking a course in "Black Literature." I had enrolled in the course under duress; 1970 was a year of tension in the black consciousness movement, and American blacks everywhere—especially those on college campuses— were under pressure from their peers, black and white as well, to, as Roberta Flack sings, "Be Real Black For Me." One of the things you were supposed to do—along with drinking sweet wine, listening to cool jazz, and attending boring discussion sessions—was to take courses which were "relevant to the struggle" and/or which "explored Black Culture." I preferred beer and classical music, and refused to attend meetings; I was under some pressure to conform to the fourth norm.

I had, however, enrolled in the Black Literature course for deeper reasons, although I doubt I could have articulated them at the time. I was an English major then, reading a lot of books, and was constantly plagued by a mild irritation at the way black people were presented in literature, even—or perhaps I should say, especially— "modern" and "contemporary" literature. Few characters—the only truly notable exceptions were Twain's Jim and Faulkner's Lucas Beauchamp—seemed to have any real humanity. I suspected that black authors would write about black people with a little more empathy than most white writers apparently could—or would.

I had no real proof to support that suspicion, which was another reason I enrolled in the course. It was bad enough, although easily explainable, that I had gotten to college without ever having read a book-length work of literature which I knew to have been written by a black person; but I considered it robbery—although again, easily explainable (if you happen to be cynical)—that I had gotten through two years as an English major without having to read such a book

† From the *Southern Review* 21.3 (Summer 1985): 682–94. Reprinted by permission.

either. The simple, sad fact was that writing by blacks was mostly unrepresented in basic literature courses, and if I wanted to study it—not just read it, but study it with the same sort of professional guidance I got when I confronted Faulkner or Hemingway—then I had to do it in a special course segregated for black literature.

Those were my stated reasons for taking the course. But there was something clandestine going on, too. I was calling myself an English major and even making noises about graduate school, but the truth was I meant to be a writer, and I needed to know if black people wrote—or ought to write—any differently from white people, not only about black characters, but about everything. The dogma of the times insisted that there was a "black aesthetic," that blacks had different artistic problems and different ways of solving them. In liberal circles, the alleged difference was assumed to be an unrelievedly positive thing. The trouble was that when I compared my writing to that of the authors I most admired, the only difference I saw was that they knew what they were doing and I did not. But perhaps, I reasoned, I was being too hard on myself. Perhaps I wasn't bad at all; I was just measuring myself by the wrong standards. Maybe the harder I worked to measure up to those standards, the farther I would get from what I should really be trying to be.

And so I came to English 289, Readings in Black Literature, in search of literature that would help me define myself in a number of ways. I did not expect to love the whole of "Black Literature" anymore than I loved the whole of "Seventeenth-Century Literature." I was hoping merely to stumble on one author in whose work I could immediately and instinctively recognize a paradigm for my own.

The less said about the course, the better. It was as good as any course can be when the subject material is selected with reckless disregard for genre, period and social context; no critic in his right mind would design a seminar that considered the poetry of Anne Bradstreet, the novels of Upton Sinclair and the drama of David Rabe, yet this course combined the poetry of Phillis Wheatley, the novels of Richard Wright and the drama of Amiri Baraka. By the third week of the course I realized that the instructor was every bit as much a victim of political pressure as I was; by the fourth week I knew that that exhilarating moment when you look at the material and perceive the pattern that ties it all together would, in this course, never come. But along about the ninth week I read a recent reprint of a book first published forty years before. It was called *Cane*, by someone named Jean Toomer.

In some ways, *Cane* made about as much sense as the course. It was a hodge-podge of genres—poems, sketches, a novella, a short play. It lacked, in many instances, the kind of polish and unified intention that I had come to admire in and expect from great literature. Some of the characters were barely developed, and the plots . . . well, even the narrator admitted that one tale was "crudest melodrama." And that narrator! I had learned by then that the defining of narration was one of the basic concerns in modern criticism, but *Cane*'s narrative voice was impossible to define in critical terms, like "restriction," "point of view" or "ironic distance." In a lot of ways, *Cane* was not only a hodge-podge, but an amateurish one.

But God, it was beautiful! It dealt with passions and people, not mindless emotion and stereotypes, as did most books that purported to speak of black people (and by now I realized that a lot of "Black Literature" fit into that scruffy category). There was sensuality, religious ecstasy, rage, humor—vibrant expressions not of "blackness" but of the humanity of people who were black. I appreciated that, sometimes, it was wanting in terms of technique. But the strength of the emotion made me realize for the first time what technique was *for*. And Toomer, as author, was frankly and joyously connected, not with some abstract "Black History" but with the earthy realities of a Black past. Toomer didn't explore it, he *believed* in it. *Lived* it. *Loved* it. And I loved him.

*Cane* inspired me; I wanted to talk about it. Unfortunately I tried to open discussion with a young lady in the class whose "black consciousness" was in a highly advanced state. At the mention of Toomer, she glared. "*You* would like him," she snapped. "He denied his blackness." This was, in 1970, a capital offense. As she stalked angrily away I realized that once again I was responding to the wrong standards. I began to wonder if there was any hope for me.

For more than a decade I lived with the confusion occasioned by that exchange. How, I wondered, could a writer accept so completely in his work what he repudiated in his life? At last I decided to look into the matter—to look behind *Cane*.

II

Nineteen seventy was a critical year—the year when the backlash response to the social upheaval of the sixties had become as visible as a distinct and powerful ideology. While back in 1968 the doves may have forced Lyndon Johnson to give up the Presidency, the electorate had given a warm response to George Wallace and had elected Richard Nixon. The liberals may have passed the 1968 Civil Rights Act, but the conservatives had tacked on the "Rap Brown" Amendment, making it a federal crime to cross state lines with intent to incite a riot.

This backlash, although later defined in nonradical, almost Cromwellian terms, as "hardhat" response to "longhaired" radicalism, was in large measure racist. George Wallace's 1963 vow, "Segregation

now! Segregation tomorrow! Segregation forever!" had been a sub-
liminal hum behind the buzzwords of his 1968 campaign, and
Nixon's "Law and Order" was an easily decoded slogan endorsing
brutalization of blacks by urban police forces. By 1970 there was a
growing sense of bewilderment and beleaguerment among liberals,
white and, especially, black, who saw the battles fought and won in
the sixties rejoined, refought and this time lost. The danger on the
right seemed to justify extreme measures: the injection of essentially
political concerns into the study of American culture—i.e., Black
Studies courses; the use, and at times misuse, of the facts of history
to support liberal views.

Ironically, the publishing industry, traditionally conservative but
notoriously ponderous, was only then beginning to respond to the
liberal impulses that had gathered momentum in the first two-thirds
of the decade. While as late as 1966 most of the various manifestos,
statements and declarations of liberal or radical groups, many of
which enjoyed a great popularity with the liberal intelligentsia and
would therefore have been highly profitable for commercial publishers, were being issued by small, occasionally *ad hoc,* often non-
commercial presses; in that year Glad Day Press published Stokely
Carmichael's *Toward Black Liberation* and the perennial avant-garde
Grove Press issued *The Autobiography of Malcolm X.* But by the late
sixties, while most of America seemed to be leaning right, some of
the most reputable and, in some cases, conservative houses were taking over the publication of radical statements. The venerable Dial
Press published Julius Lester's *Look Out Whitey! Black Power's Gon'
Get Your Mama* in 1968, followed by a book by H. Rap Brown in
1969. Random House, at that time a subsidiary of blue-chip RCA,
took Carmichael from Glad Day, issuing *Black Power* (co-authored
with Charles Hamilton) in 1967 and *Stokely Speaks* in 1971, giving
him Bobby Seale (*Seize the Time,* 1970), Amiri Baraka (*Raise, Race,
Rays, Raze,* 1971) and Huey Newton (*To Die for the People,* 1972) as
stablemates.

Nor were the publishers limiting the product to polemics; fiction
writing was affected as well. While it had been the fashion for some
time to publish novels about blacks written, usually in paternalistic
idiom, by whites, often southerners—*To Kill A Mockingbird,* Harper
Lee's sentimental rehash of Faulkner's *Intruder in the Dust: The
Liberation of Lord Byron Jones,* Tennessean Jesse Hill Ford's tale of
a southern black undertaker who dares file for divorce; *The Confessions of Nat Turner,* Virginian William Styron's perversion of history,
in which the black leader of one of the most significant rebellions
in American history is supposedly motivated by love of a white girl—
the late sixties saw an upsurge of novels about blacks written by
blacks, many of them first novels: Ishmael Reed's *The Free Lance*

*Pallbearers* (1967); John Edgar Wideman's *A Glance Away* (1968); Toni Morrison's *The Bluest Eye* (1970); Alice Walker's *The Third Life of Grange Copeland* (1970). At the same time the publishers began to search their vaults—and anybody else's—in search of old books by black authors which, whatever their intrinsic merit, might have enough historical significance to be adopted by black studies courses. One of these re-publications was *Cane*.

In many ways the conditions that surrounded *Cane*'s second publication were reminiscent of those that surrounded its first. Nineteen twenty-three was a crucial year in an increasingly conservative era that followed a time of relative liberality. The social sentiments that gave rise to Wilsonian Progressivism, the "New Freedom," and female suffrage came to an end in 1919 when Attorney General A. Mitchell Palmer, formerly a Wilsonian Progressive, launched a series of raids on the increasingly violent radical groups. The "Red Scare" climate was evidenced by events like the arrest of more than six thousand persons, the two indictments of John Reed, the trial of Sacco and Vanzetti, the deportation of 250 to Russia, the three-year incarceration of Eugene V. Debs, the expulsion of five duly elected Socialists from the New York State Legislature, and the decision of the United States Supreme Court in 1924, in *Gitlow vs. New York*, that it was within the powers of the State to suppress revolutionary utterances regardless of their actual effect, since "a single revolutionary spark may kindle a fire that, smouldering for a time, may burst into a sweeping conflagration. It cannot be said that the State is acting arbitrarily or unreasonably when it . . . seeks to extinguish the spark without waiting until it has enkindled the flame. . . ."

As was the case in 1970, the conservatism of the twenties was essentially racist, although the twenties-brand racism was so laughably extreme as to be virtually subtle. Madison Grant had articulated its terms in 1916, when he declared in *The Passing of the Great Race in America* that the inferior "races" represented by Jews and even Mediterranean and Alpine Europeans were attenuating the moral and cultural superiority of Nordic stock. This philosophy was reiterated and popularized by Kenneth Roberts who, in 1922, wrote a series of articles for the *Saturday Evening Post*. By the year of *Cane*'s initial publication, the Ku Klux Klan had reached the height of its resurgence and was claiming 2.5 million members, and crowds of five and six hundred were reported to be watching lynchings. Nineteen twenty-four saw the legal confirmation of this broadly racist tendency: the passage of the Johnson-Reed Act, an immigration law designed to "purify" the racial preponderance of the basic strain by basing immigration quotas on the population not as it existed, but as it *had* existed a third of a century—and four censuses—previous.

Publishing, too, followed a pattern similar to that which it would follow in the sixties, issuing books, especially novels, about blacks written by whites, notably Waldo Frank's *Holiday* (1923) and Carl Van Vechten's *Nigger Heaven* (1926), then by the end of the decade moving to books about blacks by blacks (many of them first novels), notably Rudolph Fisher's *The Walls of Jericho* (1928), and Wallace Thurman's *The Blacker the Berry* (1929)—books which years later would be linked to the so-called "Harlem Renaissance." But at least one publisher had been ready to make this move earlier: in 1923 Boni & Liveright had published a book which it publicized as "a book about negroes by a negro," despite the author's bald assertion that he was not a Negro at all—that book was *Cane*.

### III

"Dear Mr. Toomer:
For some time we, and by we I mean a group of three friends, the other two of whom are literary men, one colored and one white, have wondered who and what you are. . . ."

Thus began a letter to Jean Toomer, written in 1923 by one Claude Barnett, a black newspaper editor. The question—blunt, almost impolite—expresses a dichotomously dichromic way of thinking that has for six decades tainted public perception of Toomer and of *Cane*. For what Claude Barnett was asking Toomer was not in any way philosophical; all he wanted to know was, was Toomer black. "There have been several arguments," Barnett wrote, "the literary men contending that your style and finish are not negroid, while I . . . felt certain that you were—for how else could you interpret 'us' as you do . . . ?" This was an expression of the assumptions basic to the time, namely that blacks were pretty much incapable of artistic expression (hence the newsworthy nature of the "Harlem Renaissance") and the notion that blacks—almost like Orientals—were so mysterious that no one who was not a black could truly understand them, although they could and did portray them—to great profit in the cases of Eugene O'Neill (*The Emperor Jones, All God's Chillun Got Wings*), Marc Connelly (*Green Pastures*), and DuBose Heyward (*Porgy*). The latter assumption—despite fame, profits and prizes to the contrary—was at the basis of the Toomer revival of the sixties; ironically blacks, who had become aware of white America's tendency to stereotype for political and economic purposes, accepted the twenties' stereotype of Toomer, in part because it confirmed the ideology of the sixties. What the sixties wanted were stories of blacks who had been held back by racism, making them heroes if they overcame it, victims if they did not. Toomer's story, vaguely known as it was, seemed to be such a moral tale. What was glossed over whenever possible was Toomer's apparent repudiation of blackness, the accusation that, as one white critic, David Littlejohn, put it, Toomer "suddenly declared himself white." The twenties, for reasons equally political, were not minded to ignore the matter. Identifying him as a Negro, as Liveright did, threw up a challenge to the popular notion that blacks were barely literate, as Barnett's letter implies. Moreover, the intellectual community was still a little embarrassed over the case of Charles Chesnutt, whose stories about "simple blacks" seen through the eyes of a white assumed a far more ironic meaning when it was belatedly learned that the author was black.

*Cane's* publication resulted in the same kind of "misunderstanding." Bruno Lasker graced his joint review of Frank's *Holiday* and Toomer's *Cane* with the assertion that the men were one and the same when referring to *Cane*: "In this medley of poems, sketches, and short stories, Frank—for is not 'Jean Toomer' a polite fiction?" The chagrin Lasker must have felt was made explicit by John Bennett, a founder of the Poetry Society of South Carolina, who discovered that a nonresident member of the Society named Jean Toomer was publishing a book called *Cane* that the Society was about to announce as a book by a member, and that was being advertised in items "running all over the *Times*" (meaning the *New York Times Book Review*) as "a book about negroes by a negro." Wrote Bennett: "It is to laugh! Eh? Or not to laugh?"

The Poetry Society decided to ignore Toomer and made no announcement of books by members that year. *Time* magazine did not ignore him, unfortunately, even nearly a decade after *Cane* was published, running an article on him in March of 1932. The occasion for such renewed attention was the surfacing of a rumor that the new husband of the novelist Margery Bodine Latimer, a gentleman who had been identified by the local press as "Nathan Jean Toomer," author of *Essentials: Definitions and Aphorisms*, was none other than Jean Toomer, who had been identified by the *New York Times Book Review* as the author of *Cane*, a "book about negroes by a negro." This was of interest to *Time* because Miss Latimer, a reputed descendant of the New England poetess Anne Bradstreet, was not a Negro. Responding to the crushing significance of the event, *Time* sent a reporter to the couple's home in Carmel, California.

The story that resulted was a marvel of journalistic objectivity. "No Negro," it began, "can legally marry a white woman in any Southern State. But Wisconsin does not mind, nor California." Toomer was described as a "Negro philosopher," Latimer as a "Novelist." The piece was titled "Just Americans," an irreverent reference to Toomer's assertion that America was spawning a new race of people who "will achieve tremendous works of art, literature and music. They will not be white, black or yellow—just Americans."

Toomer thus, wittingly or unwittingly, articulated the antithesis to Madison Grant's and Kenneth Roberts' thesis of degenerate mongrelization.

The *Time* article had its most immediate effect not on Toomer's career, but on Latimer's—the sales of her novels declined. Toomer felt compelled to write a pamphlet, "A Fact and Some Fictions," which he had printed and circulated to his friends, an interesting course of action, since if *Time* was so fascinated, one wonders why another magazine would not have published Toomer's response. Or perhaps, given Toomer's ideas, it is not curious. In any event, the pamphlet represents the strongest evidence that Toomer did, in fact, "declare himself white," for in it Toomer wrote of his grandfather, P. B. S. Pinchback: "Whereas others would have thought it to their disadvantage to claim Negro blood, Pinchback thought it to his advantage. So he claimed it. . . . Thus it happened that he and his family became associated with the Negro. . . . With me, however, there is neither reason nor motive for claiming to have Negro blood. So I do not claim it. . . . Others have, however, occasionally seen fit to claim it for me. . . . I have neither claimed to have or disclaimed having Negro blood. . . . As for being a Negro, this of course I am not—neither biologically nor socially."

Thus, in 1932, Toomer seemed to contradict the assertion made in a letter to Claude McKay (who, like Barnett, was interested in Toomer's biography), written in 1923: "Racially, I seem to have (who knows for sure) seven blood mixtures: French, Dutch, Welsh, Negro, German, Jewish, and Indian," and through this contradiction, to have testified to his own guilt of the charge Littlejohn would later make.

Nor was this the only action of Toomer's that could be—and has been—interpreted as declaring himself white, or, as Horace Liveright apparently put it, trying to "deny his race." He did, apparently, change his name on the application for his marriage to Latimer—although he was born with the name Nathan Eugene Toomer—and had obviously changed the Eugene to Jean previously and publicly. He may have failed to mention his authorship of *Cane* to the local press—although that may have been a ruse to avoid the kind of publicity that eventuated. His own writings do attest that he was irritated with Horace Liveright's determination to advertise *Cane* as being written by a Negro, and that he told Liveright that, "as I was not a Negro, I could not feature myself as one." It is also true that, in 1932, he wrote, "Since the publication of 'Cane' there have unfortunately arisen certain misunderstandings. . . . Though I am interested in and deeply value the Negro, I am not a Negro." And it is certain that, by the time he was rediscovered by the sixties, he had committed three other sins that implied he was denying his blackness; he had sent his child to a private school that would not accept blacks, he had failed to identify himself with any of the movements for Civil Rights, and he had married a white woman—had done it twice, in fact. Thus was Toomer tried and convicted in two eras in which the issue of race was of great importance.

Was Jean Toomer a Negro? For if he was not, then he could hardly be accused of trying to pass for white. If, as Toomer claimed and as appears to be the case, the black blood he possessed came from his grandfather, who bore such meager resemblance to a black that blacks were impressed that he claimed to be black, it is unlikely that Toomer himself was more than one-eighth black, possibly only one-sixteenth. Even during the antebellum era, this would not have made Toomer legally black. No state had, at that time, adopted the doctrine that a single drop of black blood made one black. Virginia, in 1849, established the color line at one fourth. South Carolina's Court of Appeals went so far as to rule that there had to be a "visible mixture," and that social factors should be considered: "It may appear that a man of worth . . . should have the rank of a white man," using the same combination of criteria that Toomer did in "A Fact and Some Fictions." Of course by the time *Cane* was published, antebellum practicality had been replaced by rabid irrationality. South Carolina, in the late nineteenth century, changed the definition to "one-eighth Negro blood" and, in the twentieth century, to "any ascertainable trace." Nevertheless, the answer to the question of whether Toomer was black would have been answered differently in different times. Clearly, at some times and places he would have been white. Clearly, too, he had as much right as anybody to define himself that way if he chose. But in fact, he never did.

Toomer's actions and statements reveal a curious pattern for one intent on declaring himself white. In his various autobiographical writings, including portions of the pamphlet, Toomer claimed that he did not know how much black blood, if any, had flowed in his grandfather's veins. This is not the same as saying there wasn't any. In fact, Toomer speculated that "Pinchback's mother possibly had some dark blood. It might have been Negro or Indian or Spanish or Moorish or some other." He characterized his mother's complexion as "Italian-olive" and his father's as that "of an Englishman who has spent time in the tropics," surely not exaggerating their darkness, but certainly not hiding it. Nor did he hide his own, as when he wrote to Waldo Frank of the necessary procedures for a planned journey south: "At whatever town we stay, I'll have to be known as a Negro. First, only because by experiencing white pressure can the venture bear its fullest fruit. Second, because the color of my skin (it is nearly black from the sun) at the present time makes such a course a physical necessity." Moreover, he associated himself for some years with publications that had a decidedly black orientation,

submitting an essay to Alain Locke for *The New Negro*, allowing
Locke to use his drama *Balo* in *Plays of Negro Life* (1927), and allowing himself to be listed in the 1927 edition of *Who's Who in Colored America*. And he wrote to McKay, at a time when he was
virtually an unknown quantity, that he had, possibly, some Negro
blood, shortly thereafter responding to Barnett, a journalist who
could hardly be counted on to keep the matter confidential, that "In
so far as the old folk songs, syncopated rhythms, the rich sweet taste
of dark-skinned life, in so far as these are Negro, then I am body and
soul, Negroid. . . ."

Jean Toomer was not denying his race; that is clear. And in the
grammatical precision of his response to Barnett, the clear distinction between adjective forms is clear indication of what Toomer
was doing: resisting the all-encompassing and expectation-laden
label Negro, something no era apparently has been able to accept or
comprehend.

In the twenties Toomer was a "Negro writer"; he was never allowed
by commentators, black and white, to be anything else—although
the labels surely changed with the times. In 1932, *Time*'s "Negro
philosopher" was also described as the product of "cultured Negroes
of old Creole stock" by Eugene Holmes. In 1948, Hugh M. Gloster
made him a "colored writer," and a decade later Robert F. Bone made
him "the only Negro writer of the 1920's who participated on equal
terms in the creation of the modern idiom." In 1966, Toomer, in the
hands of Arna Bontemps, "faded completely into white obscurity." By
1971, he was "the first Negro writer" to be dedicated to "writing as an
art, not a Negro art," according to Frank Durham. By 1980, according to Brian Benson and Mabel Dillard, Toomer had had "no desire
to perpetuate the traditions common to black authors"—whatever
they were. What is tragic about this rather bizarre preoccupation
with labeling Toomer as black—an effort that is doomed, as Toomer
noted ("They can pile up records and labels a mile high, and in the
end they will find, pinned under that pile, not me but their own
intelligence.")—is that it has interfered with the process of understanding "who and what" Toomer really was.

Toomer, for example, has often been presented as the leading
edge of the Harlem Renaissance, despite the fact that he apparently
spent little time in Harlem and did not mention the place in his
autobiographical writings, instead characterizing his New York
experience: "In New York, I stepped into the literary world. Waldo
Frank, Gorham Munson, Kenneth Burke, Hart Crane, Matthew
Johnson, Malcolm Cowley, Paul Rosenfeld, Van Wyck Brooks, Robert Littell—*Broom*, the *Dial*, the *New Republic*. . . . I lived on Gay
Street. . . ." And, moreover, he disclaimed artistic connection with
the "New Negro" in an essay that Alain Locke, in his book on the

"New Negro," refused to publish—while nevertheless publishing sections of *Cane*.

But the worse effect of this obsession with Toomer's blackness, or lack of it, has been to conceal what he was trying to achieve—a different, but equally important kind of unity. "I have strived," he wrote McKay, "for a spiritual fusion analogous to the fact of racial intermingling. Without denying a single element in me, with no desire to subdue one to the other, I have sought to let them function in harmony." This striving found expression, in the twenties, in poetry: "My style, my aesthetic, is nothing more nor less than my attempt to fashion my substance into works of art," he wrote to Barnett in 1923. "My poems," he wrote to James Weldon Johnson seven years later, "are not Negro poems, nor are they Anglo-Saxon or white or English poems. My prose likewise. They are, first, mine. And second . . . they spring from the result of racial blending here in America." To read *Cane* as the expression of a black consciousness is therefore, inevitably, to misread it. But it has been so read. This has lost us some understanding.

The fact that *Cane* was so misread in the twenties lost us more than that; it lost us Toomer. For, though *Cane* is flawed and the man who wrote it had a lot to learn about craft, he clearly possessed instincts and sensitivities and intelligence that would have brought him to the forefront of American letters. But Toomer became frustrated with the insistence that he be one race or the other. He has been accused of denying his blackness; in fact, he was guilty of refusing to deny everything else.

Toomer understood that there was a certain self-protectiveness in the insistence of some that he was black, for he wrote to Frank: "Sherwood Anderson has doubtless a very deep and beautiful emotion by way of the Negro. Here and there he has succeeded in expressing this. But he is not satisfied. He wants more. He is hungry for it. I come along. I express it. It is natural for him to see me in terms of this expression." But understanding did not lead to acceptance: "He limits me to Negro. As an approach, as a constant element (part of a larger whole) of interest Negro is good. But to tie me to one of my parts is to lose me."

Not everyone lost him. Waldo Frank seemed to understand what Toomer was about before Toomer did, for he wrote in his preface to the first edition, "A poet has arisen in the land who writes, not as a Southerner, not as a rebel against Southerners, not as a negro, not as an apologist or priest or critic: who writes as a poet," and, in varying his parallel construction, indicated that he shared Toomer's belief in a "non-racial" future: "The simple slave Past, the shredding Negro Present, the irridescent passionate dream of the Tomorrow. . . ." And Paul Rosenfeld, in *Men Seen, Twenty-four Modern Authors* (1925), wrote that the characters of *Cane* "are prophetic not only for men of negro blood. They throw forward much in America; for they are symbols of some future America of which Jean Toomer by virtue of the music in him is a portion. He looks two ways. Through this recognition of the beauty of a doomed simplicity, sensuosity, passionateness not of the South or of the past asserts, cries out, comes conscious of itself: some America beyond the newspapers, regimented feelings, edgeless language . . . drawing more imminent."

But most did lose Toomer. The Establishment determined to make him a Negro expert on Negroes ignored his essays on race. His 1925 "The Negro Emergent" went unpublished. His "Race Problems in Modern Society," published in 1928, apparently attracted little attention. Frustrated, Toomer wrote: "My writing . . . the very thing that should have made me understood was being so presented and interpreted that I was not much more misunderstood in this respect than at any other time in my life."

By 1932, Toomer had decided to adopt a new tactic and so declined to participate in the preparation of a volume on race in America and refused to have his work included in *The Book of American Negro Poetry,* or to have a copy of his privately published *Essentials* (1931) placed in the Schomberg Collection at the New York Public Library (all actions that later were used to support the "passing" accusation). "In order to establish my view," he wrote, "I have had—for a time—to swing into a rather extreme position which has not allowed me to be associated with any race other than what we call the American race."

It is hard to say what Toomer thought was going to happen after "a time." Perhaps he thought that sanity would assert itself. In this he was sadly wrong. For this tactical decision, made out of anger or frustration or perhaps real calculation, was nothing less than a turning away from the source of his art. "Within the last two or three years, however," he had written to McKay in 1922, "my growing need for artistic expression has pulled me deeper into the Negro group. And as my powers of receptivity increased I found myself loving it in a way I could never love the other. It has stimulated and fertilized whatever creative talent I may contain within me. Now I cannot conceive of myself as aloof, and separated. My point of view has not changed; it has deepened, it has widened."

And so, in the end, this is the tragedy of Jean Toomer—a tale of oppression that the "liberal" sixties not only ignored, but perpetuated. Some have said Toomer denied his self and turned away from greatness. In fact he was driven away from the source of that greatness. And the saddest thing, perhaps, is that he knew it. "We are," wrote finally the man who had once so joyously celebrated his connection with the Negro past, "split men, disconnected from our own resources, almost severed from our *Selves*, and therefore out of contact with reality."

# CHARLES SCRUGGS

## Textuality and Vision in Jean Toomer's *Cane*†

The triptych as an artistic form is the perfect vehicle for an Aristotelian plot; its tripartite structure has a beginning, middle, and end. Yet in the experimental atmosphere of the 1920s, American author Jean Toomer used the triptych in *Cane* (1923) to combine short stories whose movement would be both linear (Aristotelian) and nonlinear. In discovering the possibilities of the triptych, Toomer was indebted to Sherwood Anderson's *Winesburg, Ohio* (1919) and Waldo Frank's *City Block* (1922), two short story cycles that he had read with considerable care and admiration and whose authors he knew personally. It was Frank's stories, however, that finally had the greater impact upon Toomer, because Frank's notion of "spherical form" suited Toomer's conception of the spiritual center of *Cane*.

Gorham Munson may have been the critic who caused Toomer to look closely at the aesthetic form of *City Block*. In 1923, he had written a book on Frank describing the form of *City Block* as "spherical," insisting that the stories "fit into an inevitable circle," and that there was "a curve cementing them together and giving the Whole a dynamic propulsion forward" Toomer reviewed Munson's book for the little magazine *S4N*, and the words quoted above are not Munson's but his.[1] It is problematical whether Toomer saw Munson's book early enough to have it influence *Cane,* but a letter to Munson in 1923 hints that Toomer had already done some thinking about aesthetic form before he read Munson's *Waldo Frank: A Study* (1923). Toomer wrote Munson

> . . . from this study [on Frank], perhaps more than from any single source, I see the importance of form. The tree as a symbol comes to mind. A tree in summer. Trunk, branches: structure. Leaves: the fillers out, one might almost say the padding. The sap is carried in the trunk etc. From it the leaves get their sustenance, and *from their arrangement comes their meaning* (italics mine) . . . This symbol is wanting, of course, because a

---

† From *Journal of the Short Story in English* 10 (Spring 1988): 93–114. Reprinted by permission.

1. Jean Toomer, "The Critic of Waldo Frank: Criticism, An Art Form," *S4N*, No. 30 (January, 1924), no pagination. Toomer is quite accurate; Munson had noted to the "spherical form of *City Block*, arguing that the stories "take their positions on a circle." See Gorham B. Munson, *Waldo Frank: A Study* (New York: Boni and Liveright, 1923), pp. 50, 51.

tree is stationary, because it has no progressions, no dynamic movements. A machine has these, but a machine is all form, it has no leaves. Its very abstraction is now the death of it. Perhaps it is the purpose of our age to fecundate it. But its flower, unlike growing things, will bud within the human spirit.[2]

In his book on Frank, Munson has said that the "spacing" of the stories of *City Block* was crucial to understanding the total entity,[3] and Toomer is obviously referring to this point by his emphasis on the "arrangement" of the leaves on the tree. Yet to understand completely Toomer's use of the metaphor, we also need to look at another emphasis beside that of order. The "sap" that runs through the trunk of the tree is the energy that causes the branches to grow and the leaves to blossom, and Toomer suggests that if the machine were humanized, its energy could be harnessed and transformed. The result would be a form no longer abstract but organic (a flower).

I stress this last point because the urban metaphor is integral to the total aesthetic form of *Cane*. Critics of Toomer's book have ignored Toomer's complex use of this metaphor, or they have argued that the city and the machine are linked in an unholy alliance in *Cane* and that all the literary elements in the text focus upon the contrast between sterile city and fecund country, a contrast especially revealed in the book's second section.[4] This dichotomy is much too neat, for although Toomer does expose the materialistic side of the modern city in *Cane* (in "Rhobert," for instance), he also associates the city with energy, as expressed by the metaphor of electricity in the poem, "Her Lips are Copper Wires." Indeed, the theme of energy and power is endemic to all of Toomer's writing, and he often used the metaphor of the machine to express it, as shown by this passage from the Whitmanesque "Blue Meridian," a long poem (1936) that celebrates the visionary city as a symbol of renewal and rebirth:

> The eagle you should know, American,
> Is a sublime and bloody bird,

---

2. Jean Toomer to Gorham Munson, March 19, 1923, Toomer Papers, Fisk University Library—hereafter referred to as TP.
3. *Waldo Frank: A Study*, p. 50.
4. See Robert Bone, *The Negro Novel in America* (Rev. Ed.) (New Haven: Yale University Press, 1965), p. 84; Todd Lieber, "Design and Movement in *Cane*," *CLA Journal*, 13 (September, 1969), 54; Brian Joseph Benson and Mabel Mayle Dillard, *Jean Toomer* (Boston: Twayne, 1980), p. 69; Nellie McKay, *Jean Toomer: Artist* (Chapel Hill: University of North Carolina Press, 1984), p. 88; Odette C. Martin, "*Cane*: Method and Myth," *Obsidian* 2 (Spring, 1976), 12; Cynthia Earl Kerman and Richard Eldridge, *The Lives of Jean Toomer: A Hunger for Wholeness*. (Baton Rouge: Louisiana State University Press, 1987), p. 103. And this by no means exhausts the list. Indeed, the anti-urban bias is pervasive in the criticism of the Harlem Renaissance itself; Robert Bone has recently argued that it is the driving force in the "short fiction" of the period. See his *Down Home: A History of Afro-American Short Fiction from Its Beginnings to the End of the Harlem Renaissance* (New York: Putnam, 1975).

A living dynamo
Capable of spiritualizing and sensualizing.[5]

We notice immediately Toomer's refusal to shy away from the Romantic paradox that the spiritual is wedded to an energy that is both vital and destructive ("bloody"). Toomer believed with Dylan Thomas that without "the force that through the green fuse drives the flower," there is no flower, only the dead semblance of one. More specifically, in 1922 he had read in manuscript Hart Crane's "For the Marriage of Faustus and Helen."[6] In that poem, Helen is the inchoate city, and Faustus is the poet who must wed her if he is to create the visionary city within himself. As the "eternal gun-man" who slaughters those who enter her citadels unaware of her complexity, Helen is the symbol of the chaos and speed of the modern technological city; paradoxically, she is also the "Capped arbiter of beauty in this street." The poet must reconcile her opposites in a higher vision before she, the earthly Helen, will shed her mortality for the "mounted, yielding cities of the air,"[7] a line Toomer would echo in his essay on Alfred Stieglitz.[8] In other words, Crane's point is that by embracing the earthly city in all her ugliness (the "gunman"), the poet frees her from being Helen the whore and transfigures her into the Helen that made Troy immortal.[9]

The theme of the transformed city is also central to Waldo Frank's early fiction, especially to *The Dark Mother* (1920), *Rahab* (1922), and *City Block* (1922), as well as to *Our America* (1919), a non-fictional exploration of America that Toomer also read and esteemed. In *City Block*, the city is both protagonist and central unifying symbol—not the earthly city but the palimpsest city that lies beneath its chaos. In the separate stories, Frank documents the varying degrees of success or failure of the characters to bring this palimpsest city to the surface, a city that would replace the earthly city of abstract, linear laws with one based upon St. Paul's caritas. The force in the earthly city that is capable of generating this change is Eros, in W. H. Auden's phrase, the "builder of cities."

---

5. Jean Toomer, "Blue Meridian," *The New American Caravan*, ed. Alfred Kreymborg, et al (New York: Mcauley, 1936); reprinted in *The Wayward and The Seeking: A Collection of Writings By Jean Toomer*, ed. Darwin T. Turner (Washington, D.C.: Howard University Press, 1980), p. 219.
6. Hart Crane to Jean Turner, undated letter (circa 1922), TP: ". . . here is the carbon of Faustus and Helen that I promised."
7. Hart Crane, "For the Marriage of Faustus and Helen," in *The Complete Poems and Selected Letters of Hart Crane*, ed. Brom Weber (London: Oxford University Press, 1968), p. 32.
8. See Jean Toomer, "The Hill," in *America and Alfred Stieglitz*, ed. Waldo Frank, et al (New York: Doubleday, Doran, 1934), p. 297. Toomer claims that Stieglitz cannot be confined to any one place, to either the country or city: ". . . he is rooted in himself . . . not rooted to earth; rooted to air."
9. See Philip R. Yannella, "Inventive Dust," in *Hart Crane: A Collection of Critical Essays*, ed. Alan Trachtenberg (Englewood Cliffs: N.J.: Prentice Hall, 1982, 182–86).

Energy that resulted in a metaphysical transformation was also a theme that appealed to Toomer. In an "Open Letter to Gorham B. Munson," then co-editor of *Secession* with Kenneth Burke, Toomer complained that Munson's little magazine was becoming only a "toy model of a machine," all form and no power: "Power, friend, power! . . . if *Secession* doesn't watch itself, there's where it is going to fall down. Not in criticism, but in imaginative writing." For Toomer, it is power that generates form, and hence he delighted in making the outrageous statement that "There is not a statue in Washington with the living beauty of line and balance of certain Pierce Arrow cars."[1] That Toomer links the beauty of "imaginative writing" with that of an automobile is connected to his belief, via Plato's *Symposium,* that all forms of beauty ultimately spring from the same source: Eros. Thus in discussing his own work, such as "Theatre" and "Box Seat," he talked about the protagonist of each story as a "central dynamic figure propelled by inherent energy."[2] In other words, it was energy, not conflict, that drove the story forward, and it was dynamic form, not resolution, that gave the story meaning.

Kenneth Burke's elaboration upon Aristotle helps to explain Toomer's point. Toomer had been reading Kenneth Burke's literary reviews in 1921–22 in *The Dial,* reviews that contained the seeds of Burke's future studies of literary form.[3] As early as 1921, Burke was considering notions of form that would expand Aristotle, arguing that a true conception of form works from the inside out, from emotion to logic, from idea to expression. Also—and this would prove to be important for Toomer's use of the short story—Burke argued that the aesthetic movement of a work of art need not always be in a straight line toward an obvious clarity. In 1921, he noted that Frank's "characters are meant to be like pebbles dropped into a pool: he tries to draw ever-widening circles around them. His plots are conceived in the same non-temporal, not-spatial tone."[4] Indeed, Burke would structure his own collection of short stories, *The White Oxen* (1924), in a non-spatial direction, beginning his book with realistic stories and ending it with stories that were "rhetorical" and abstract.[5] According to Burke in *A Grammar of Motives* (1945), Aristotle's *entelechy*

1. Jean Toomer, "Open Letter to Gorham B. Munson," *S4N,* No. 25 (March, 1923), no pagination.
2. Jean Toomer to Gorham Munson, March 23, 1923, TP. The connection between the Dionysian spark and transcendent art is also reflected in "Banking Coal, a poem published in Dubois' *Crisis* in 1922: I'd like to tell those folks that one grand flare / Transferred to memory tissues of the air / Is Worth . . . All money ever saved by banking coal."
3. Toomer may have been introduced to Burke at the office of *The Dial* when he met Mumford there in 1920 (Unpublished Autobiography, TP). Or he may have met him through Munson, for Toomer's letters to Munson around this time suggest that all three of them—Toomer, Munson and Burke—were intimately acquainted.
4. Kenneth Burke, "Enlarging the Narrow House," *The Dial,* 73 (September, 1922), p. 347.
5. See Burke's "Author's Note" to *The White Oxen and Other Stories* (New York: Albert and Charles Boni, 1924).

puts the emphasis where it belongs, not upon a plot composed of causally-related events but upon a plot that actualizes a potential within itself. As early as 1922, he was already expressing the germ of this point of view in *The Dial*: "Form in literature must always have its beginnings in idea. In fact, our word for idea comes from a Greek word whose first meaning is 'form.'"[6]

One sees Burke's influence upon Toomer in another letter that Toomer wrote to Munson; in this instance the student attempts to teach the teachers. He observed to Munson that "Garden Party," a short story published by the two co-editors of *Secession*, was marred by a conventional denouement. The author, said Toomer, "has simply brought an intellectual, a cerebral quality to bear on" the story, and hence its ending, "in lieu of arresting form," is nothing more than what "humor and clarity can give."[7] This observation brings to mind his use of the tree as a metaphor for form. As an acorn becomes an oak, it has actualized its potential, but its limitation as an "arresting form" is that it is stationary ("no progressions, no dynamic movements"). In searching for the perfect aesthetic form for *Cane*, Toomer wanted a vehicle empowered by a life force that spiritualized and transformed experience.

Toomer's discovery of *Cane*'s final form was no easy process. According to his most recent biographers, "by April of 1922," he had "completed" most of the diversified building blocks—short stories, sketches, poems, and even a play—that he would eventually put together as *Cane*.[8] Yet it was not until December 12, 1922 that Toomer wrote Waldo Frank—by this time, both a mentor and friend—that the book was "done" and that its "design is a circle."[9] In the eight months between April and December, Toomer immersed himself in the subject of literary form, a preoccupation reflected in the letters and literary reviews that he wrote around this time. He was helped in his search by his association with certain American intellectuals in the early 1920s who were engaged in reconstructing the form of American culture. Although these intellectuals were too

---

6. Kenneth Burke, "Heaven's First Law," *The Dial*, 72 (February, 1922), 200. Also, see Kenneth Burke, *Grammar of Motives* (New York: Prentice Hall, 1945), pp. 261, 62. I am indebted to Robert L. Heath for this connection between the Burke of the 1920s and the later Burke. See his informative *Realism and Relativism: A Perspective on Kenneth Burke* (Macon, Georgia: Mercer University Press, 1986).

7. Jean Toomer to Gorham Munson, March 23, 1923, TP. In this letter, it is clear that Toomer associates Burke with ideas about aesthetic form: "hence the whole question really narrows down to one of form . . . Burke appears to me to be a crystal. He has the crystal's brillance, clarity of outline and hardness." Yet Toomer also saw faults in Burke's intelligence: "And he shares with the crystal its resistence to shapes other than its own, its fixation, its fulfilled potentials, its incapacity for growth." Not surprisingly, Toomer gave a mixed review of *The White Oxen*. See "Oxen Cart and Warfare," *Little Review*, 10 (Autumn-Winter, 1924–25), 44–48.

8. Cynthia Earl Kerman and Richard Eldridge, *The Lives of Jean Toomer*, p. 86.

9. Jean Toomer to Waldo Frank, December 12, 1922, TP.

mercurial to be called a specific movement—Ernest Boyd tried to
satirize some of them under the category "Aesthete: Model 1920"—
they all in their different ways revolted against various expressions of
what Lewis Mumford called the "Pragmatic Acquiescence."[1] Mumford might focus his wrath upon the rectangularly laid out American
city, Kenneth Burke upon the well-made play. Yet if people as different as Burke, Waldo Frank, Mumford can be lumped together, it is
due to their antagonism to a mindless pragmatism in American life.
In other words, they revolted against a life without intelligent form.

As early as 1920, Toomer began to establish friendships with many
of them. In that year, he met Lewis Mumford, Van Wyck Brooks, and
Waldo Frank, and in the months to come, he would also establish a
warm literary correspondence with Hart Crane and Sherwood Anderson. He would confess to Anderson that both "*Winesburg, Ohio*, and
the *Triumph of the Egg* are elements of my growing. It is hard to think
of my maturing without them."[2] Not only did both books serve to
shape Toomer's conception of the short story, but *The Triumph of the
Egg* (1921) could not fail to impress Toomer because of its unusual
form. Anderson had assembled a potpourri of disparate materials—
prose, poems, short stories, even photographs of sculpture—into a
unified whole, giving Toomer the idea that the right aesthetic form
could transform even a sow's ear into a silk purse.

Yet he would choose Frank over Anderson as a model because
Frank's pursuit of spiritual wholeness, embodied in what Toomer
called Frank's "mystical realism" was closer to what Toomer believed
art should strive to achieve.[3] Moreover, the image of the circle—
Frank's "spherical form"—solved a problem for Toomer.[4] Since a
circle ends where it begins, it allowed him to create a narrative structure that would have a "dynamic propulsion forward" at the same
time that it turned back upon itself. As we shall see, Toomer wanted
to end *Cane* in a state of innocence, albeit an informed innocence,
and this was to echo the lyricism of his opening sketch, "Karintha."
Moreover, the geographical pattern of the book's three sections
moves from South (first section) to North (second section) to South
(third section), but this circular pattern is pushed forward by the
narrator's urban perspective.

What Toomer will do is to use Sherwood Anderson's influence
upon him to construct a persona in the book's first section that

1. The phrase is the title of Mumford's fourth chapter in *The Golden Day: A Study in
American Experience and Culture* (New York: Boni and Liveright, 1926). For Boyd's
amusing essay, "Aesthete: Model 1924," *American Mercury*, 1 (January, 1924), 51–56.
2. Jean Toomer to Sherwood Anderson, December 18, 1922, TP.
3. Jean Toomer, "The Critic of Waldo Frank: Criticism, An Art Form," SN4, No. 30 (January, 1924), no pagination.
4. Also, see Robert Perry, *The Shared Vision of Waldo Frank and Hart Crane* (Lincoln:
University of Nebraska Press, 1966), especially the last chapter, "Mystical Geometry."

mirrors one aspect of his relationship to the South. That is, Toomer takes what he conceives to be Anderson's limitations and makes use of them within a larger conception of literary form than the individual short story. Thus the stories of *Winesburg, Ohio* and *The Triumph of the Egg* play a part in section one of *Cane*, just as the visionaries of *City Block* influence section two; the twin worlds of Frank and Anderson come together in section three. At the heart of *Cane* is not the pastoral world per se, but a pastoral world that is filtered through an urban consciousness; this consciousness is sometimes confused, sometimes enlightened, but by no means is it defined by the arbitrary boundaries of space and time. In this paper, I intend to focus on the triptych composed of "Fern," "Avey," and "Kabnis," three stories that taken together are a microcosm of the macrocosm. Each story appears in one of *Cane*'s three sections, and the pattern that develops from these combined stories reflect the aesthetic form of *Cane* itself.

II

In a brilliant article on *Winesburg, Ohio*, Walter Rideout discusses a triptych—"Nobody Knows," "An Awakening," and "Sophistication"—within the short story cycle.[5] The progression of the three stories, argues Rideout, reflects the growing maturation of the ubiquitous George Willard. Willard begins a vain, callow and insensitive youth ("Nobody Knows"), suffers an initiation into the world of experience ("An Awakening") and ends by realizing that silence often conveys more meaning than words. Appropriately, *Winesburg*'s last story is called "Departure" in which a mature Willard leaves the small midwestern town for the great world.

There is no doubt that Anderson's Willard influenced Toomer's conception of his own naive narrator in *Cane*. Moreover, the implied theme that Willard would leave Winesburg, only to return to it in memory, also had its appeal, and yet *Winesburg* had a finality of form and a theme of human futility that bothered Toomer. One thing that had impressed Toomer about *City Block* is that the triptych did not lead in one direction; stories in *City Block* were protean: they formed and reformed to make new triptychs.

Thus though Toomer was profoundly influenced by Anderson's courage—that his characters rebelled against the restrictions that stifled their lives—Toomer began to notice certain deficiencies in Anderson the writer. The linear movement of *Winesburg*, in Toomer's eyes, reflected a larger limitation of vision, and in 1922 Toomer expressed certain reservations about Anderson to Waldo Frank.

---

5. Walter B. Rideout, "The Simplicity of Winesburg, Ohio," *Shenandoah*, 13 (Spring, 1962), 20–31.

The trouble with Anderson, said Toomer, is that his work never rises above the immediate and the tangible. Although his "sweet narrative gift swings along like a carriage dog nosing the dust and flowers of a mid-western roadside," his perception of reality is limited to those things that exist along the road, and like a carriage dog he is always moving in a straight line. He may notice "the tragedy of unpainted clapboards and closed doors" of passing farmhouses, but he never opens the "closed doors" to perceive the fourth dimensional world beyond them. In this respect, Anderson's greatest virtue—his sharp, sensuous response to reality—also indicates a spiritual nearsightedness.[6]

Toomer's reading of the Bible, the *Bhagavad-Gita,* and the English Romantics, especially Blake, around this time caused him to take a dim view of the American "realists," and he unjustly began to put Anderson in their camp.[7] But there was also another thing that bothered him about Anderson. In Anderson's appraisal of Toomer's own work, Toomer complained to Frank, Anderson "limits me to Negro," and he also reduced Toomer's themes to those of his own, to "a sense of the tragic separateness, the tragic sterility of people."[8] Moreover, Anderson had the naive idea that black people should always be placed in a pastoral world or defined by a pastoral ideal. In "Seventh Street" and "Theatre"—two prose pieces solidly set in an urban environment—"a wholly new life confronts me. A life, I'm afraid, Sherwood Anderson would not get his beauty from."[9] That Toomer balked against a conception of black life confined to the pastoral should be warning to those who have tried to squeeze him into this category.[1]

In truth, Toomer sought a fusion of country and city in *Cane,* just as in his own life he sought "a spiritual fusion" of the different bloodlines of his own biological inheritance.[2] This fusion would result in a whole that was greater than the sum of its parts. As he was to tell Gorham Munson, "the problem of art is to make 2 plus 2 equal 5 [and] . . . Waldo Frank at his best is 5."[3] And for Toomer, *City Block* was Frank "at his best." Toomer was so impressed with this book of short stories that when Frank published it himself in a limited edition in 1922, Toomer acted as his agent, helping him to sell it. On

6. Jean Toomer to Waldo Frank, undated (circa summer, 1923), TP.
7. See *The Wayward and the Seeking,* pp. 117, 120. In a section of the unpublished autobiography not included in *The Wayward and the Seeking,* Toomer said that Mumford introduced him to the *Bhagavad-Gita,* having recognized "a certain mystic strain in me."
8. Jean Toomer to Waldo Frank, undated (circa summer, 1923), TP.
9. Jean Toomer to Waldo Frank, undated (circa summer, 1923), TP.
1. I include myself here. See Charles Scruggs, "The Mark of Cain and the Redemption of Art: A Study in Theme and Structure of Jean Toomer's *Cane,*" *American Literature,* 44 (May, 1972), 278.
2. See Cynthia Earl Kerman and Richard Eldridge, *The Lives of Jean Toomer,* p. 96.
3. Jean Toomer to Gorham Munson, undated (circa 1922), TP. This was high praise, in the same letter, Kenneth Burke got only a "4."

July 31, 1922, as the book was being published, Toomer wrote to philanthropist J. E. Moorland, urging him to buy a copy, saying, "I believe CITY BLOCK to be one of the most significant contributions of our age to what is best and most enduring in American letters."[4] In another letter to Moorland later that year, he was more precise in describing Frank's "aim" in the work: "it is this: to establish the spiritual reality which is ever at the center of outward forms, to wring a measure of eternal beauty from the world's suffering."[5] That last statement explains why Toomer finally chose Frank over Sherwood Anderson as a model, for he believed that the "spiritual reality" revealed in *City Block* was tied to the book's "spherical form."

III

Dedicated to Waldo Frank, "Kabnis" is the lynchpin upon which the aesthetic form of *Cane* depends, for *Cane* was not fully formed as an idea in Toomer's mind until he found a way to end it with "Kabnis." Yet Toomer had originally written "Kabnis" as a play, and he had sent it off to be considered by Kenneth Macgowan of the Provincetown Players. A remark in Macgowan's letter of rejection to Toomer has an interesting implication for *Cane*. Macgowan complained that "Kabnis" had no "general, dramatic design," and though Toomer bitterly responded that Macgowan was wrong, it may be that Toomer anticipated Macgowan's criticism before he ever received his letter.[6] By the time of the rejection, *Cane* had already been published with "Kabnis" in it, and it was strictly speaking no longer a play, but a long story. Toomer may have believed that if Kabnis remained the central figure of a play, the dramatic movement could only go in one direction: descent. For Kabnis is an intellectual manqué, and without another perspective, the play's conclusion is hardly optimistic. Yet if Toomer himself added a narrator's perspective at the end, one that would transform the play to a new form, then not only would its meaning change but this transformed play could serve as the final piece to complete the puzzle of *Cane*'s structure.

In the well-known letter that Toomer wrote to Frank in December 12, 1922, saying the book was "done," he included "Kabnis" within an aesthetic form that was protean:

> From three angles, *Cane*'s design is a circle. Aesthetically, from simple forms to complex ones, and back to simple forms. Regionally, from the South up into the North, and back into the South again. Or from the North down into the South and then a

---

4. Jean Toomer to J. E. Moorland, July 31, 1922, the Moorland-Spingarn Research Center, Howard University Library—hereafter referred to as M/S Center.
5. Jean Toomer to J. E. Moorland, December 7, 1922, M/S Center.
6. Jean Toomer to Margery Latimer, Toomer's future wife, September 24, 1923, TP. Toomer told Latimer of Macgowan's letter of rejection and his response.

return North. From the point of view of the spiritual entity
behind the work, the curve really starts with Bona and Paul
(awakening), plunges into Kabnis, emerges in Karintha etc.
swings upward into Theatre and Box Seat, and ends (pauses) in
Harvest Song . . . Between each of the three sections, a curve.
These, to vaguely indicate the design.

Leaving aside the problem of where the individual pieces fit upon
the graph of the circle, let us look closely at Toomer's statement
regarding "Kabnis." He implies that on the circle's chart "Kabnis"
symbolizes the nadir of spiritual descent. Certainly the scene in
Halsey's cellar, echoing, as it does, Dostoevski's *Notes From The
Underground* and Joyce's *Ulysses* (the Nighttown section), would
seem to substantiate this view. Yet this view can only be taken if we
isolate certain features of the story and neglect others. As Toomer's
remarks on region imply, all the stories and poems in *Cane* can shift
their places on the circle, because Toomer, like Frank in *City Block,*
is trying to escape the notion of empirical reality implied by a literal
minded interpretation of the Aristotelian plot. Turn the circle upside
down, and "Kabnis," like Frank's last story in *City Block* called
"Beginning," can be the origin and not the end of the cycle.

Let us look more closely at the two sentences involving region.
Why, for instance, does Toomer say that the movement is from South
to North to South, and then immediately reverse the pattern? The
question can be answered if we consider Toomer's first sentence to be
concerned with literal geography; the second, with moral geography.
For though the first sentence outlines the actual settings of the
book's three sections (South, North, South), the second sentence
describes the spiritual reality of those settings (North, South, North).
Toomer begins with an urbanized narrator who cannot make sense
of what he sees in the South because he has been uprooted from the
soil (first section); then Toomer places him and his various personas
in Washington and Chicago where the South continues to exert its
spiritual influence upon the city (second section); finally, Toomer
returns him to the South where in "Kabnis" (third section) he is
reborn as the narrator of *Cane.* So in the last section, Toomer implies
that the North is metaphorically present in the South. The book's
central paradox is that like Emerson's worm who must pass through
"all the spires of form" before he becomes a man,[7] so Toomer must be
reborn in the city before he can be reborn in the South as an author.

Seen symbolically, then, a region's reality is fluid not fixed, circular not linear; the South can be both brutish and beautiful, both
soul-stifling and soul-fulfilling. And the city possesses the same
mysterious nature: it is both the home of the dynamo that confines

---

7. See the poem that serves as the epigraph to Emerson's famous essay on "Nature."

people to a spiritual prison and of the god Dionysius that energizes them into poets and visionaries. The city is the home of two Cains: the man bearing the mark of servitude and the craftsman, the maker of poems and heroic cities.

One can also detect other hints of strategy surfacing in Toomer's letters around this time. Consider, for instance, a remark that Toomer made to Munson about "Fern": "I agree with you in all you say about Fern. Too much Anderson. Too much waste. I could work it over, but I don't think it important enough to spend time on. I'm through with that phase. Next!"[8] But clearly "that phase" could be put to use if it were embodied in a more comprehensive phase; that is, Toomer could place "Fern" within a larger structure where Anderson's theme of human futility would serve to propel the narrative movement forward to a more satisfying conclusion to human endeavor. After reliving the frustrations of the narrator of "Fern" in the character of Kabnis, the narrator of "Kabnis" emerges with a new vision, one that encompasses even "Fern." The perspective from "Kabnis" allows the reader to see that not everything in "Fern" illustrates "the tragic separateness . . . of people."

The story's real protagonist is not Fern but Toomer—or rather Toomer's narrator. That is, "too much Anderson" refers to both the personality of the narrator and his failed attempt to penetrate who and what Fern is. Like George Willard of *Winesburg*, he's a talker, a failed detective, and an ingenue. An outsider from the North, he has a reputation among the locals for "nosing around."[9] He knows of Fern's reputation through gossip, that she is something of a mystery in the local town: a woman given to visions, a woman inaccessible to males though they once possessed her body. So confused are the men by her indifference to them that they translate her into something sacred—"She became a virgin"—and they set out like Medieval knights to "do some fine thing for her (p. 14) [18]."

The narrator finds himself attracted to her mystery, and she begins to assume a metaphysical significance for him: "the whole countryside seemed to flow into her eyes (p. 15) [19]." He thinks that he can succeed where the locals have failed, that he has the wit that they lack to penetrate her essence, but Toomer finally exposes him as a city slicker: "What could I do for her? Talk, of course (p. 16) [20]." Although he seems to recognize the inappropriateness of "talk" ("To what purpose? and what for?"), the world of talk is the world he is trapped in. "Damn if I knew how to begin" is his initial response to Fern, and he babbles on about crops, the weather, and so on. Like Willard in "An

8. Jean Toomer to Gorham Munson, undated (circa 1922), TP.
9. Jean Toomer, *Cane*, ed. Darwin T. Turner (1923; reprint. New York: Liveright, 1975), p. 15. All references to Cane are from this edition and appear in the text. [Page numbers in square brackets refer to this Norton Critical Edition.]

Awakening," he is mesmerized by his own rhetoric—and confused by it, hence all the sentences that end in question marks in "Fern." Language is that which has deceived him into thinking he knows more than others, but though his rhetoric flits around Fern like a chicken-hawk around a chicken, he knows no more about her at the end than the boy in Anderson's "The Egg" knew about either the chicken or the egg. Indeed, the irony of the story is that he becomes precisely like the other frustrated males: "Nothing ever came to Fern, not even I. Something I would do for her. Some fine unnamed thing (p. 17) [21]." The final comedy is that he passes on the burden of pursuing Fern's mystery to someone else ("And, friend, you?"), mentioning her name for the first time in the story's last sentence as though it were an incantation, as though the magical power of the words could pinpoint her essence: "Her name, against the chance that you might happen down that way is Fernie May Rosen (p. 17) [21]."

But the name of the rose conjures up no ultimate reality in this story, and perhaps the very Jewishness of her name points to the mysterious gods that seem to govern the South. In any event, it is a mistake to read the narrator's "words" for Toomer's, for the story quite clearly shows the powerlessness of words by themselves. Thus when Toomer's narrator argues that Fern would not be happier in the North either as a "solitary girl sitting at a tenement window looking down upon the indifferent throngs of Harlem," or as a prostitute or doctor's wife in Chicago (pp. 15, 16) [19, 20], we should not take this as an expression of Toomer's primitivism or his anti-urbanism. It reflects, rather, the narrator's frustration, his inability to place Fern anywhere. Later, in "Avey," the second story in Toomer's triptych, he will show us a woman who does become a prostitute in the North, and though she does not sing like "a Jewish cantor (p. 14) [18]"—Toomer's metaphor for Fern's compelling presence—she is also self-contained. The difference this time will be that Toomer's narrator begins to penetrate the meaning of her unsung song, and this will metamorphose the world of "talk" into a world transformed by the Word.

Throughout *Cane*'s first section, the South remains out of focus for Toomer and his various personas. In this respect, the confusion of Fern's narrator—the futility of his effort to pierce the veil of existence—is characteristic of most of the pieces in the first section of *Cane*. We can only read "Song of the Son," a poignant poem in the first section, in an ironic light if we look closely at the kind of illumination (son = sun) Toomer's returned artist brings to bear on the tales he narrates, the poems he sings. As a singing tree, he sings eloquently of the "tragic separateness" of human beings and the natural beauty of the South, but when he attempts to understand their relationship, he croaks like a frog. And this is no artistic flaw on Toomer's part—he intends the irony, as I have shown in my analysis of "Fern." What he wishes finally to do, however, is to subsume the misunderstandings of the first section within a larger illumination provided by the structure of the whole book. Like Toomer's various personas, we as readers move from the perspective of confusion, to that of partial vision, to that of total vision, one that allows us to return to the first section with new eyes.

Appropriately, the protagonists of three important stories in *Cane*'s second section have names associated with prophets who have apocalyptic visions: John, Daniel, and Paul. In the urban setting of the second section of *Cane*, two forces are in conflict: law, associated with St. Paul's spirit-killing "Letter," and the primeval energy of the poet who can breath life into the earthly city. Yet all three visionaries in "Theatre," "Box Seat," and "Bona and Paul" fail to resurrect the Heavenly City, for their visions are shortcircuited by defects of character. John's vision dissipates into dream; Dan's, into anger; and Paul betrays his vision by the very language he hoped would serve as its midwife. Only "Avey" suggests a way to change words into the Word, and it is significant that in treating the theme of the renewed city in this story, Toomer keeps his narrator nameless, as he did in "Fern" It is as if Toomer is saying that the name only arrives with the fully realized vision, just as his name in the book called *Cane* will only appear as the author of its fully realized aesthetic form.

"Avey" focuses upon a young man's continuing relationship with a woman whose mystery he cannot penetrate; his awakening to her reality comes at the precise moment that he understands the city into which she was born. In the manner of Sherwood Anderson, Toomer uses a first-person narrator to underscore the perceptual obtuseness of his observer, an obtuseness that appears in the very first line of "Avey": "For a long while she was nothing more to me than one of those skirted beings whom boys at a certain age disdain to play with (p. 42) [44]." The irony here is that the narrator implies that Avey will soon become more than a "skirted" being to him, yet what we find in the story is that as their relationship progresses, he keeps putting her in different categories of confinement. The "skirted" being is first desirable as a sexual object, then reduced to the object of Ned's "smutty wisdom (p. 42) [44]." Later, as the college-educated narrator becomes puffed up with his own wisdom, she appears to him as "no better than a cow (p. 44) [46]." And even later, he acknowledges Ned's judgment: "She was no better than a whore (p. 45) [47]."

In one sense the story documents Avey's slow descent into prostitution, and the story might have been an example of literary naturalism, if it had remained on that level. For instance, Avey is associated with an image of a boxed tree; yet as the story develops, the reader suspects that the image symbolizes the narrator's myopic vision more than it does Avey's situation. This image is perhaps Toomer's most direct allusion to *City Block*, for the narrator accepts his city block's circumscribed attitude toward Avey. Moreover, he is an incessant talker like George Willard (*Winesburg*) and John Dawson (*City Block*). Frustrated by what he considers to be Avey's perverse desire to treat him as a child and not as a lover, he says: "I talked. I knew damned well that I could beat her at that (44) [45]." It is partially the "talk" of course that keeps him from understanding his "real relation to her (p. 45) [47]." What that relationship is he discovers on a hill overlooking the city, a hill upon which the hospital Soldier's Home is located. This is a place where lovers go to be alone, but the narrator deceives himself into believing that he goes there to look into the "simple beauty of another's soul," this time Avey's. It is here that he indulges in his romantic fantasies about women, an indulgence that is no different from the sexual reasons for which others visit the hill. As he works himself up into a rhetorical lather that will move Avey to accept him as a lover, he is suddenly confounded by a sense of Avey's mortality and his own.

At this point in the story Toomer's indebtedness to Sherwood Anderson is apparent. In "Sophistication" (*Winesburg*), Anderson has a similar scene in which human connectedness becomes more important than lust, in which George Willard and Helen Barnes have fleeting glimpses of each other's inner selves in the welter of the world's confusion. The power of the story lies in Anderson's reticence at developing any symbolic possibilities beyond the momentary revelations of the two people. Toomer's ending is more ambitious. Frustrated by Avey's lack of response to him, the narrator resorts to the only thing he knows how to do: talk. The comedy of the situation arises from the contrast between his talk—confident, presumptuous, self-aggrandizing—and the silent, unknown woman to whom his talk is addressed. And yet vanity fades into a moment of vision as he sees her with her eyes closed, his talk having put her to sleep. He senses that Avey's hesitation to accept him as a lover may have been out of a real affection for him. For she tacitly understands that friendship is a more enduring affection than sex, and that in keeping their relationship on a certain level of reality, the narrator sees that she has been the sensitive one, not him. He sees too that what he took for laziness is exhaustion; it is not so much his talk that has put her to sleep as it is life that has drained her, and he perceives her in repose as though she is wearing a death mask. "My passion died," he said, and what replaces it is compassion. In a sense, it is Marguerite he weeps for—his own lost innocence, as well as hers. If Toomer had ended the story here, it would have been an acceptable imitation of an Anderson short story. But as he protects the sleeping Avey, he sees "the dawn steal over Washington," and the city is transformed in his mind from the Washington of the black bourgeoisie, who has played an ignoble part in shaping Avey's life, to the symbolic polis of the Republic:

> The Capitol dome looked like a gray ghost ship drifting in from sea. Avey's face was pale, and her eyes were heavy. She did not have the gray crimson-splashed beauty of the dawn. I hated to wake her. Orphan-woman . . . (p. 47) [48]

The combination of colors explains why Anderson saw *Cane* as "a painting story,"[1] but this is symbolic portraiture, the kind that Toomer admired in Frank.

The "gray crimson-splashed" dawn is the natural backdrop for a symbolic clash between the "pale" Avey and the world of human artifice, the "gray ghost ship" of the dome. The "dome" recalls *City Block*, specifically, "Under the Dome: Tau" and "Under the Dome: Aleph," and like Frank, Toomer sees the symbolism in mythical terms. If the "dome" reminds the Jewish immigrants in "Under the Dome: Aleph" and "Under the Dome: Tau" that they are still Wandering Jews in the earthly city, so Toomer's dome provides an ironic commentary upon the fate of black people in the New World.

For the Capitol dome, with its statue of liberty on top, is a symbol of the rational principles that govern the Republic and its symbolic city. As architecture, the dome reflects the enlightenment's revolt against the Gothic cathedral with its spire's emphasis upon mystery rather than understanding. Just as Christopher Wren, after the Great Fire, rebuilt the old Gothic cathedral of St. Paul's upon the principle of the dome, thus illustrating the harmonious laws of nature so recently discovered by that great architect of the universe, Sir Isaac Newton, so the several architects of the Capitol constructed their dome upon a similar metaphysical foundation. The Republic was to be a nation founded upon law, not upon a king's caprice, and thus the circular dome symbolizes a perfect but comprehensible universe, for from within the dome, one can perceive the symmetry of the entire structure.

Moreover, the Capitol's setting within the city was also to be symbolic, "the city's most dominating monument." And although Pierre L'Enfant's geometrical plans for the city were never precisely followed, the Capitol's placement within this urban scheme was realized: "a gridiron arrangement of streets cut by diagonal avenues radiating from the capitol and white house. . . ."[2] In other words, the Capitol and the white house were to be at the center of the circle; the white house, a symbol of the practical seat of government; the

---

1. Sherwood Anderson to Jean Toomer, January 3, 1924, TP: "I've often wondered—do you paint? God what a painting story your people have got."
2. *Columbia Encyclopedia* (New York: Columbia University Press, 1963) (3rd ed.), pp 338, 2291.

Capitol, a symbol of its theoretical center: a world of law that guided the ship of state.

Toomer's brilliant juxtaposition of the "pale" Avey and the "ghost ship" makes this story powerful. Just as Blake in "London" sets in opposition the "chartered" city and the diseased prostitute who places a curse upon it, so Toomer contrasts with the white city, the city of idealism that has become in "Seventh Avenue" a soggy white (or, in echoing the Bible, "a whited sepulcher")[3] and yet both white and gray are colors associated with unreality: ghosts. The failure of the country's ideals—indeed their failure being seen in its corrupt laws, especially regarding slavery and segregation—has turned the dome gray and Avey "pale." Like the prostitute in Blake's poem, she is the "orphan" that the polis claims no responsibility for, and yet her very presence is a curse upon it and a reminder of its failures to live up to the ideal, rational principles it has set for itself. Or put another way, the myth of Cain (the pun in Toomer's title) presupposes that the city is founded by a fratricide, an assumption made by St. Augustine when he identified the earthly city as Rome (Romulus kills Remus). So too Washington as a symbol of an America founded by slavery turns Avey pale as death. The Capitol dome looks like a "ghost ship" because it is a reminder of a slave ship, not of the sacred principles of liberty upon which the country is supposedly founded. In black folklore, the mark upon Cain is his white skin, having turned this color in horror at what he had done,[4] and in Washington the taint of slavery, in all its forms, turns the city and its victims into a ghastly white.

In empathizing with Avey's suffering, Toomer's narrator escapes the categories the city creates for her. In this sense, he becomes like the figure of Christ who refuses to judge the woman taken in adultery. Tony Tanner's observations upon the city in relationship to this Biblical story shed considerable light on the meaning of "Avey." The judgment upon the adulteress by the Pharisees represents the voice of the city, a world that "By defining itself as a city . . . immediately creates nonsocial space outside it." According to the city, the nonsocial space outside its walls is the world of anarchy and barbarism; whereas the social space circumscribed by the city is made visible by its laws. Yet Christ's voice—his refusal to "participate in [a] purely secular attitude to the woman and to discuss her as a category"— implies that the city's judgment is not absolute, that there is a higher court to which one can appeal than the court of the city's laws. Christ's judgment in the Temple—"He that is without sin among you, let him cast the first stone at her"—reminds the city that there

3. Matthew 23:27.
4. See James Baldwin, *The Fire Next Time* (New York: Dial, 1963), p. 55.

is a "sacred space" between city (law) and field (anarchy) that is "a silent realm for which society gradually withdraws and where language itself finally gives back the deed to the doer of the deed, restoring to it that opacity and that problematic privacy that the Mosaic law sought to deny."[5]

I would argue that Tanner's "sacred place" is a second city and that the temple where Christ renders his judgment upon both the Pharisees and adulteress is its symbolic center. That invisible city stands in opposition to the visible one, which has turned "gray" as it has turned black people "pale." (Compare Blake's "London": "How the Chimney-sweeper's cry / Every black'ning church appalls; and the hapless Soldier's sigh / Runs in blood down Palace walls"). That invisible city is the city of vision, vision that has its roots in empathy. This then would imply the symbolic meaning of Avey's name, as Paule Marshall notes when she calls her own protagonist in *Praisesong for the Widow* (1983) "Avey, short for Avatara."[6] For in recognizing the incarnated god within the prostitute, the narrator is blessed or "haled" (Ave = Avey) at the story's end. And like Mrs. Luve in *Rahab* and *City Block*, Avey is a Mary Magdalen figure who is responsible for bringing out the Christ in others and for making realizable the "sacred space" of the temple within the alternative city.

All of Toomer's heroes are projections of himself, but Toomer was insistent, and surprisingly candid, in admitting that Kabnis was "me."[7] Throughout much of his story, Kabnis is no hero but a spineless parody of an artist, and like the narrators of "Fern" and "Avey," he is a talker. He also embodies elements of Dan, John, and Paul, but snivels and whines in ways that even in their weakest moments they never do. Yet, finally, he is a better candidate for the poet's purple robes than any of Toomer's previous personas, for he transcends their intellectuality by returning to a spiritual innocence that is only shared by the narrator of "Avey." It is for this reason that "Fern," "Avey," and "Kabnis" make up a triptych within the whole of *Cane*; Kabnis must pass through the narrators of "Fern" and "Avey" before he evolves into the narrator of *Cane* at his story's end. In this, he is like Coleridge's Ancient Mariner who changes from subject to story-teller, uttering a moral so precise in its simplicity that it puts philosophy to shame. It is here that we begin to understand Toomer's remark to Frank that *Cane* progresses from "simple forms to complex ones, and back to simple forms." For Kabnis' verbal intellectuality dissolves finally into the eloquent silence of a painting. Having reached this point on the circle, Toomer can then return to his book's beginning, to the

5. Tony Tanner, *Adultery and the Novel: Contract and Transgression* (Baltimore: Johns Hopkins University Press, 1979), pp. 19, 21, 22.
6. Paule Marshall, *Praisesong for the Widow* (New York: E. P. Dutton, 1984), p. 251.
7. Jean Toomer to Waldo Frank, undated (circa summer, 1923), TP.

simplicity of the portraits of Karintha and Fern in which all
contraries—suffering/beauty; youth/mortality; male/female—are
resolved within the context of aesthetic form. This "eternal return"—
the phrase belongs to Mircea Eliade—is in keeping with Toomer's
remark to Anderson "that art in our day . . . has a sort of religious
function."[8] In 1923, writing *Cane* was a mode of transcendence for
Toomer akin to a religious experience; it was only after *Cane*, when
he became interested in religious mystics like Gurdjieff, that he
came to believe that "I would far rather form a man than form a
book."[9]

The ending of "Kabnis" is also the beginning of *Cane*. When Kabnis scoffs at Father John's oracular utterance—that "white folks . . .
made the Bible lie"—Carrie K rebukes him: "Brother Ralph, is that
your best Amen?" (pp. 115, 16) [114]." The rebuke is justified, for
Kabnis bears the burden of the white folks' lie. Fleeing his own self-
loathing, he believes the myth that black people bear the mark of
Cain and for that reason are inferior and deserve to be enslaved.[1]
His transformation begins when he is humbled by the innocent Carrie K: he "sinks to his knees before her, ashamed, exhausted," and
they embrace (p. 116).

What follows is a second symbolic gesture. The room empty except
for Carrie K and the old man, Carrie K then kneels (as Kabnis did to
her) and embraces him, murmuring "'Jesus, come.'" The lines after
these probably ended the original play, for they serve as stage directions: "Light streaks through the iron-barred cellar window. Within
its soft circle, the figures of Carrie and Father John." But the very
last lines of the published story in *Cane* are clearly added by a narrator who has himself been transformed from Kabnis to Toomer:

> Outside, the sun arises from its cradle in the tree-tops of the
> forest. Shadows of pines are dreams the sun shakes from its
> eyes. The sun arises. Gold-glowing child, it steps into the sky
> and sends a birth-song slanting down gray dust streets and
> sleepy windows of the southern town. (p. 116) [115]

The transition from the aura emanating from the two figures inside
(the "soft circle") to the circle of the sun's "cradle" outside is like an
editing technique from *Citizen Kane*, and it serves to emphasize the
link between Toomer and the religious significance of the embracing
couple. As a reborn Kabnis, Toomer has thrown off his previously
sophisticated personas of John, Daniel, and Paul to become the innocent Christ. That is, he has Christ's informed innocence: "Truly, I
say to you, whoever does not receive the kingdom of God like a

8. Jean Toomer to Sherwood Anderson, December 18, 1922, TP.
9. *The Wayward and the Seeking*, p. 19.
1. See Winthrop Jordan, *White Over Black: American Attitudes toward the Negro 1550–
   1812* (Baltimore: Johns Hopkins University Press, 1969), pp. 242, 416.

child shall not enter it."[2] In reaction to Carrie K's rebuke, Kabnis becomes "ashamed" like a child, and the sun itself is a "gold-glowing child." Carrie K's embracing of Kabnis suggests a sacred connection between artist (Kabnis) and innocence (Carrie). So too when Carrie embraces Father John, youth embraces age, the present the past, and the special aura in which they are encircled suggests a resolution of the conflicts that have beset the previous characters in *Cane*. The resolution is not rational but religious, as if Toomer is saying that there is a peace that passes understanding, one that can resolve the anguish felt by the singer of "Harvest Song." In more common-place terms, one might say that the final scene depicts the triumph of hope over despair, for the problems that beset Afro-Americans—conflicts between generations, between classes, between country and city—are transient and even trivial compared with the hope that like a seed springs eternal. Youth will continue to blossom like the spring; age will find its tongue and keep inherited wisdom alive, and black writers will continue to write books like *Cane* that celebrate the life force over adversity.

The artist's final vision of Carrie K and Father John is like a religious painting, and the world outside the window, to the artist's eye, participates in the revelatory moment. Ultimately, the perspective, as I have said, is urban—not "urban" as urbanity but as St. Augustine defines it: an awareness of a shared, spiritual community. Indeed, perhaps the dramatic movement of St. Augustine's *Confessions* sheds light on the urban vision in *Cane*. As Kenneth Burke has noted, St. Augustine moves up the graded stages of spiritual awareness as though he were traveling to the Heavenly City on an elevator that began on the ground floor: "First, there is the 'Upward Way' from 'lower terms' to a unitary transcendent term." Secondly, however, there is a reverse movement downward whereby the elevator travels by the same floors as it did going up, but now they are seen in a new light. From this perspective, they are now "modified by the unitary principle . . . of the 'transcendent' term."[3] Rereading *Cane* from the perspective of the "transcendent term" (the ending of "Kabnis"), the reader understands why Toomer needed the book's second section. Before he could truly see those resources that bonded black people together into a whole, he needed to experience isolation, frustration, and disharmony in the earthly city. He needed to shed its accumulated vanities—its masculine orientation, its intellectual pretenses—like so much excess clothing. Having experienced defeat in Cain's city, he could then return to the South as the beaten Kabnis, a man who contained, nonetheless, a potential for humility that would

---

2. Luke 18:17. Also, see *The Wayward and the Seeking*, p. 52. The association of the child with the days of wonder is an important theme in his unpublished autobiography.
3. Kenneth Burke, *The Rhetoric of Religion: Studies in Logology* (Boston: Beacon Press, 1961), p. 37.

transform Augustine's negative image—Cain as the founder of the earthly city—into a positive one. For Cain means "smith," and Toomer at the book's end is transformed into a word-smith; the city founded by this Cain is one, like Hart Crane's, built in the air. As a visionary city, this "city of words," to use Tanner's phrase, recasts the earthly city into new terms, for Toomer calls "Bona and Paul" the "awakening," as if Paul's prophetic vision yet awaits the black artist who will bring the Heavenly City to down earth.

## GAYL JONES

### Blues Ballad: Jean Toomer's "Karintha"†

Not all stories affected by oral tradition are written in dialect or folk-speech, though most of these stories have what E. M. Forster calls "a connection with voice," a connection which extends to "characters . . . plot and comments on life . . . fantasies . . . views of the universe."[1] In this sense the narration, dramatic structure, and presentation of character in Jean Toomer's short story "Karintha"[2] reveal the effects of orality and the motives of oral tradition.

"Karintha" is the first story in a magnificent collection of prose fiction, poetry, and drama published in 1923 by Jean Toomer, a forerunner of the Harlem Renaissance period. His seminal volume *Cane* continues to influence contemporary African American writers concerned with nontraditional forms and the connection between linguistic innovation, psychological reality, and social-historical context. Here is Robert A. Bone's famous quote from the jacket of the 1969 Harper and Row edition: "Stein and Hemingway in prose, Pound and Eliot in poetry, were threshing and winnowing, testing and experimenting with words, stretching them and refocusing them, until they became the pliant instruments of a new idiom. The only Negro writer of the 1920's who participated on equal terms in the creation of the modern idiom was a young poet-novelist named Jean Toomer." Bone goes on to classify *Cane* as "an important American novel." It is often classified as a novel because of its architectonic structure—the recurring themes, metaphors, images; the bridges between histories, personalities, geographical and dramatic spaces and scenes; and because the whole book attempts to answer a question posed by the first story which speaks

---

† From *Liberating Voices: Oral Tradition in African American Literature* (Cambridge: Harvard University Press, 1991). Reprinted by permission of the publisher, Harvard University Press. Copyright © 1991 by Gayl Jones.

1. E. M. Forster, *Aspects of the Novel* (New York: Harcourt, Brace, 1927), pp. 64–66.
2. Jean Toomer, "Karintha," *Cane* (1923, rpt. New York: Harper and Row, 1969), p. 1. all quotations from *Cane* are taken from this edition.

mysteriously of "sins against the soul." Toomer's "creation of the modern idiom," like that of Langston Hughes (whom Bone fails to acknowledge in his critical vista), is influenced by the pliant instruments of oral tradition: the blues and ballad.

### "Karintha" as Blues

Although "Karintha" is not written in dialect, it nevertheless has the resonance of oral tradition. One not only *reads* Toomer, one *hears* him; his words live beyond the page, full of rhythm and metaphor, sight and sound, lyrical drama. His work has the dynamics, the spring and seasoning of speech and music.

Blues repetition weaves the sentences and amplifies the texture of the story. In fact, "Karintha" is introduced by a verse:

> Her skin is like dusk on the eastern horizon,
> O cant you see it, O cant you see it,
> Her skin is like dusk on the eastern horizon
> . . . When the sun goes down.

The lines sing through repetition, but we puzzle at their meaning and we wait to discover it, and to discover the woman, to hear her blues. And when we complete Karintha's story the same verse is repeated at the end, the chorus is magnified, gains new dimension, once the whole ritual blues story is told. If the introductory verse raises a question, the repeated last verse does not answer it completely, but makes the question more complex in light of the whole experience. In her article "Blues Roots of Poetry," Sherley A. Williams speaks of this internal strategy of the blues: "Unlike sacred music, the blues deals with a world where the inability to solve a problem does not necessarily mean that one can, or ought to, transcend it. The internal strategy of the blues is action, rather than contemplation."[3] "Karintha" is such an open-ended blues, and Karintha the character is as double-edged and contradictory as any blues.

Karintha's story begins, like a blues song, with a lyrical summary of her circumstances, which provides the background for her dilemma, motives, actions, and values: "Men had always wanted her, this Karintha, even as a child, Karintha carrying beauty, perfect as dusk when the sun goes down. Old men rode her hobbyhorse upon their knees. Young men danced with her at frolics when they should have been dancing with their grownup girls. God grant us youth, secretly prayed the old men. The young fellows counted the time to pass before she would be old enough to mate with them.

---

3. Sherley A. Williams, "The Blues Roots of Contemporary Afro-American Poetry," *Chant of Saints*, Michael S. Harper and Robert B. Steptoe, eds. (Urbana: University of Illinois Press, 1979), p. 125.

This interest of the male, who wishes to ripen a growing thing too soon, could mean no good to her." Men want to hurry her along to womanhood while she is still a girl. Perhaps she too is trying to be a woman. Karintha is action, full of cruelty and beauty, paradoxes of repetition and variation that link her childhood to her womanhood. "She stoned the cows, and beat her dog, and fought the other children . . . Even the preacher, who caught her at mischief, told himself she was as innocently lovely as a November cotton flower. But Karintha is a woman, and she has had a child. A child fell out of her womb onto a bed of pine-needles in the forest. Pine-needles are smooth and sweet. They are elastic to the feet of rabbits . . . A sawmill was nearby. Its pyramidal sawdust pile smouldered. It is a year before one completely burns. Meanwhile, the smoke curls up and hangs in odd wraiths about the trees, curls up, and spreads itself out over the valley . . . Weeks after Karintha returned home the smoke was so heavy you tasted it in water." Toomer does not tell us directly here what cruelty Karintha has done to her child, but the elisions and the juxtapositions tell us. Her full humanity resides in the contradictions of her character; her adult behavior springs from a deeper, more complex cruelty, but it parallels and grows out of her childhood behavior. Her character fits George Kent's assertion regarding the blues: "While I admire a good deal of the blues tradition, it seems to me to contain a good deal of instability and disorder." Blues form also "might enable people to deal with formlessness." Like Karintha's character, it is a mixture of limitations and possibilities. But, according to Kent, blues contains "a whole lot of precariousness."[4] Karintha, then, in this nonromanticized definition of the blues, is a blues person. However, the blues form, which penetrates the prose, also orders her precarious experience.

Repetition, as part of the thematic and verbal architecture of the story, sets off the lyrical beginning (the problem introduced), middle (its complications and consequences), and end/beginning (the open end of blues ritual). The experiences of sexual dilemma and tyranny, plus Karintha's own involvement in acts of cruelty, reinforce the blues theme. "Karintha is a woman" is part of the internal repetitive structure and always moves the reader to the next level of character recognition: "Karintha is a woman. She who carries beauty, perfect as dusk when the sun goes down. She has been married many times. Old men remind her that a few years back they rode her hobby-horse upon their knees. Karintha smiles, and indulges them when she is in the mood for it. She has con-

4. George Kent, interviewed by Roseann P. Bell in *Sturdy Black Bridges*, Rosean P. Bell, Bettye J. Parker, and Beverly Guy-Sheftall, eds. (New York: Anchor, 1979), p. 220.

tempt for them. Karintha is a woman. Young men go to the big cities and run on the road. Young men go away to college. They all want to bring her money. These are the young men who thought that all they had to do was to count time. Karintha is a woman. Men do not know that the soul of her was a growing thing ripened too soon."

The repetition in traditional blues often has a similar function. Repetition in this tradition does not mean stasis, but change/new recognition; a turning point or carrying forward of experience follows each repeated line. In "Dink's Blues,"[5] for instance, each stanza crystallizes the next level of experience and meaning. Poetry in the blues tradition also suggests this active repetition. Thus in the Peruvian poet Cesar Vallejo's "The anger that breaks the man into children," each "the anger of the poor" resolves one stanza and pushes it into the next:

> The anger that breaks the man into children,
> that breaks the child, into equal birds,
> and the bird, afterwards, into little eggs;
> the anger of the poor
> has one oil against two vinegars.
>
> The anger that breaks the tree into leaves,
> the leaf into unequal buds
> and the bud, into telescopic grooves;
> the anger of the poor
> has two rivers against many seas.
>
> The anger that breaks the good into doubts,
> the doubt, into three similar arcs
> and the arc, later on, into unforeseeable tombs;
> the anger of the poor
> has one steel against two daggers.
>
> The anger that breaks the soul into bodies,
> the body into dissimilar organs
> and the organ, into octave thoughts;
> the anger of the poor
> has one central fire against two craters.[6]

Native American writer N. Scott Momaday's *Angel of Geese and Other Poem* (1974) also demonstrates the power of this incremental

5. Langston Hughes and Arna Bontemps, eds., *Book of Negro Folklore* (New York: Dodd, Mead, 1958), pp. 392–94.
6. César Vallejo, "The anger that breaks the man into children," *Giant Talk: An Anthology of Third World Writings*, Quincy Troupe and Rainer Schulte, eds. (New York: Vintage, 1975), p. 3.

repetition, which contains energy and sustains movement; and which enlarges the parameters of experience and implication.

There are many kinds of dynamic repetitions in "Karintha." The line repetitions and parallelisms discussed above match internal repetition and variation of internal rhyme: see, feet, sweet, mischief, past, flashes, thought, fought, caught; of consonance: few, feet, front, dart, bit, black, bird, dusk, during, supper, songs, stop, stoned; of assonance: smoke, over, hugged, sudden, running, dust, dusk, hush, bit, vivid. Many of these examples—internal rhyme/assonance/consonance—occur simultaneously. This also contributes to the lyricism and lyrical transformations of the story and its connection with voice and song.

Finally, and most importantly, blues repetition enhances the moral recognition of the story: "Karintha is a woman. Men do not know that the soul of her was a growing thing ripened too soon." This is the initial metaphor that will be reiterated and modified throughout, providing further accounts of moral dilemma and character transformation.

### "Karintha" as Ballad

The repetitive rhythms and elements of blues structure also characterize the ballad, and it is often the rhythmical clues—the rhyme, repetition, and variation—that, like the blues and blues vocabulary, link the personality described with the strategies of remembrance as oral transmission. The first stanza of the John Henry ballad is an example of this:

> Some say he's from Georgia
> Some say he's from Alabam
> But it is wrote on the rock at the Big Ten Tunnel,
> John Henry's a East Virginia Man,
> John Henry's a East Virginia Man.[7]

In the ballad tradition it is the line that concludes the stanza rather than the one that introduces it which is repeated; it is the key to character and what Gertrude Stein has called "the rhythm of personality." The repetitive structure of the ballad connects it with the blues, but its perspective distinguishes it from the blues tradition, and it is the perspective of "Karintha" linked with the blues experience that propels it into the ballad tradition. Another modern example is Gertrude Stein's "Melanctha" and *Portraits and Prayers*, suggesting the possibility of a complex link between her inventions and the inventions of African American idiom in making words and

---

7. Hughes and Bontemps, *Book of Negro Folklore*, p. 345.

describing events.[8] As the West Indian poet and dramatist Derek Walcott has said, "the tone of the language in America was Black,"[9] perhaps hearing it with greater clarity than any American could. Here is how Stein's language shows an improvisational attitude and "sense of dynamism and change"[1] that one finds in African American linguistic innovations inspired by oral tradition:

> Juan Gris is a Spaniard. He says that his pictures remind him of the school of Fontainebleau. The school of Fontainebleau is a nice school Diana and others. In this he makes no mistake but he never does make a mistake. He might and he is he is and he might, he is right and he might be right, he is a perfect painter and he might be right. He is a perfect painter, all right he might be right.
>
> Juan Gris is a Spaniard. He says that his last pictures he says that they are as alike as the school of Fontainebleau he says that they are like the pictures of the school of Fontainebleau if he can be like, if he can be like, if he can be like the school of Fontainebleau and not alike. And as not alike.
>
> Juan Gris is a Spaniard.
>
> Juan Gris is a Spaniard and his pictures.[2]

This excerpt and variant of stream-of-consciousness is certainly influenced by the cubists—Gris himself, Braque, Picasso, and others (she also did a cubist word portrait of Picasso)—in the fragmentations and juxtapositions, but one wonders again whether there might not also be the incremental repetition and syntactical details of blues balladry, and in the fragmentations and juxtapositions the effect of African American jazz as well. Surely there is some of it in her fictional prose portrait of the black woman Mclanctha. If this interpretation is correct, it would point to an important aspect of the evolution of the American voice in literature—and what critics have called Stein's "echoes of Midwestern talk"[3] may also be patterned on echoes of Black America. In turn, Stein's cadences influenced the native styles of both Hemingway and Fitzgerald, especially the intricate repetitions in Hemingway's style.

Janheinz Jahn makes a distinction between the techniques of blues and those of the ballad. He notes the blues' references to social background, its double meanings. But more important is that the blues offer "subjective testimony,"[4] whereas the ballad describes

8. Michael S. Harper, interviewed by James Randall, *Ploughshares,* 7:1 (1981), p. 19.
9. Quoted by Harper, ibid., p. 27.
1. Ibid., p. 19.
2. Gertrude Stein, *Portraits and Prayers* (New York: Random House, 1934), p. 46.
3. Robert E. Spiller, Willard Thorp, Thomas H. Johnson, Henry Seidel Canby, Richard M. Ludwig, eds., *Literary History of the United States* (New York: Macmillan, 1963).
4. Janheinz Jahn, Neo-African Literature: A History of Black Writing (New York: Grove Press, 1968), p. 173.

a third-person experience.[5] In Toomer's story we are fascinated with
the rhythms of Karintha's personality, her reported experiences, the
tension and suspense in the repetition, but we never move into the
interior landscape of the woman—her personal ironies, frustrations, contradictions. We stay on the outside of her personality.
"Karintha is a woman," we know, and we know what she does, but
we don't know the conscience and consciousness of that from inside
her. The narrative reports actions, physical descriptions, imagery.
The ballad, Jahn says, is "not . . . a first person song, has no justification or confrontation."[6] (This is certainly "Karintha.") Jahn is
examining a specific ballad, which has repetitive lines of blues and
blues experiences and metaphors, but is never a part of the subjective territory of the blues:

> Old man Ben, he's so bent 'n' lame;
> Old man Ben, he's so bent 'n' lame,
> He loves his baby 'n' he ain't got a job to his name.
>
> She's got a head like a monkey, feet like a bear,
> Mouth full of tobacco, squirting it everywhere,
> But she's his baby, he loves her just the same;
> She's his Garbo 'n' he's her big he-man.[7]

Of course, this is not to say that the method is a shortcoming in
Toomer's writing; it is simply to establish that the first story in *Cane*,
rendered lyrically rather than dramatically, is blues/ballad rather
than either blues singly or ballad alone. "Karintha" introduces both
the metaphorical and concrete substances of the stories that follow in *Cane*, from the blues ballad of "Becky" "who had two Negro
sons," through the tensions of personality and conflict in "Carma,"
to John in "Theater," who seeks to rid his mind of passion, to the
dilemma of identity in the final story, "Kabnis." The main aspects of
this blues balladry are repeated, but later in the book we move from
third person to enter the true territory of the blues' interior conflicts
of conscience and consciousness, through the "I"-witnessed stories
and stream-of-consciousness, shifting dramatic focus. In "Kabnis"
we are in the blues mode from the beginning, as we explore Kabnis's
interior landscape and personality through snatches of speech and
rumination:

> Near me. Now. Whoever you are, my warm glowing sweetheart,
> do not think that the face that rests beside you is the real Kab-
> nis. Ralph Kabnis is a dream. And dreams are faces with large
> eyes and weak chins and broad brows that get smashed by the

5. Ibid., p. 174.
6. Ibid., p. 171.
7. Ibid.

fists of square faces. The body of the world is bull-necked. A dream is a soft face that fits uncertainly upon it . . . God, if I could develop that in words. Give what I know a bull-neck and a heaving body, all would go well with me, wouldn't it, sweetheart? If I could feel that I came to the South to face it. If I, the dream (not what is weak and afraid in me) could become the face of the South. How my lips would sing for it, my songs being the lips of its soul. Soul. Soul hell. There aint no such thing. What in hell was that?

Kabnis is talking to himself here, but he speaks of what his creator has done, is doing: singing, his stories like songs. He has returned South after the urbanization—a psychic consequence of the "great migration" of the central stories of the book, from "Seventh Street" to "Bona and Paul." Kabnis is one of the so-called "talented tenth" (Du Bois) in search of direction and wholeness—his self-conscious manhood complements the feminine portraits in the first cycle of the book. (Like Karintha he too is built of contradictions, but we see the inner life of his contradictory landscape as we saw the exterior consequences of hers.) In addition to these Kabnis is in search of the "spiritual emancipation" which Alain Locke called the Harlem Renaissance period itself. The inner life that we explore in "Kabnis" of course continues the important transition from the turn-of-the-century stories. For these our focus was always on descriptions of exterior reality rather than the possibilities of the psychological realm, whereas the movement of *Cane* reflects the movement inward that one sees in African American literary history—a movement that does not negate the social reality that influences the psychological reality. But it is Toomer that initiated for the African American writer the "conceptual voyage," the concern with "the forces existing in . . . human behavior."[8] Kabnis's return to the South parallels the author's return for the same essential purposes. Toomer spoke of the spiritual and artistic consequences of his return: "A visit to Georgia last fall was the starting point of almost everything of worth that I have done. I heard folk-songs come from the lips of Negro peasants. I saw the rich dusk beauty that I had heard many false accents about, and of which till then, I was somewhat skeptical. And a deep part of my nature, a part that I had repressed, sprang suddenly to life and responded to them. Now, I cannot conceive of myself as aloof and separated."[9] With regard to our earlier assertions concerning viewpoint, it is significant that such contact caused Toomer to deepen and widen as it "stimulated and fertilized" his creative talent.

8. *Giant Talk,* Troupe and Schulte, eds., p. xliii.
9. Toomer, *Cane,* quoted from Arna Bontemps's introduction.

Jean Toomer's "Karintha" suggests another direction for exploring how African American fiction writers have made use of oral
tradition in transitions of form and content. Though some of the
stories in *Cane* contain dialect and "ready" dialect, the oral traditional impulses lie mainly in the narrative motives and modes, the
orality and tonal atmosphere of the language; and the insistence of
overall structural imperatives from oral idiom. Toomer, too, presages
later African American "fictioneers" (Kostelanetz) who will wholly
redefine form from oral perception: Ishmael Reed, Henry Dumas,
Alexis Deveaux, Leon Forrest, Steve Cannon, Ntozake Shange, and
others. He uses the incremental repetitions that one finds in both
the blues and ballad traditions for structure, emphasis, character
progression, and intensified moments; he achieves the combined
force—when the whole book is viewed—of subjective and objective
territory. Assertions of identity and self-definition in the "I am" of
the blues represent the subjective territory, while the objective territory has its counterpart in the third person pronouns (s/he) of the
ballad tradition. Direct actions, as in the blues tradition, enable the
reader/listener to pay heed to what a character feels and does rather
than what is proper to feel and do. The ambivalence, ambiguities,
and contradictions of public and private behavior complicate character (the blues can often be "embarrassing" and criticize meaning
and values, balancing "strong contrasts . . . and opposing forms and
forces in significant unity,"[1] in this way clarifying how people actually think and feel and act in their adjustment to self and will to be
human).

Repetitions reveal situations and advance story interest, give a
flexible sense of time that may be contracted, stretched, bent in
successive changes. Blues repetition finally expands and broadens
meaning as it makes character visible by emphasis and recurring
presence. The last line of the story does not therefore merely repeat
the words of the beginning, but strengthens and reinforces sense of
character, context, and meaning:

> Her skin is like dusk on the eastern horizon,
> O cant you see it, O cant you see it,
> Her skin is like dusk on the eastern horizon
> . . . When the sun goes down.

> Goes down . . .

The oral dynamics of blues and ballad contribute, then, to Toomer's
creation of the modern idiom in a story that combines a concern with
song (literary technique connected to voice) and moral landscape.

---

1. Jean Toomer, *Essentials* (Chicago: Lakeside Press, 1923).

# GEORGE B. HUTCHINSON

## Jean Toomer and the
## "New Negroes" of Washington†

Up to now, scholars have neglected important evidence of the nature and extent of Jean Toomer's contact with black authors associated with the "New Negro" renaissance prior to and during the composition of *Cane*. Thus one of the chief students of his work has written recently that "he made no efforts to connect himself to a black tradition in letters, and his interactions with contemporary black artists were, at best, minimal and individualized. He acknowledged no black writers as having had an impact on him, and no one black read, criticized, or made suggestions about *Cane* while it was in progress."[1] Similarly, in their recent biography of Toomer, by far the most complete available, Cynthia Earl Kerman and Richard Eldridge suggest that only in 1922 (after his acquaintance with Waldo Frank) did Toomer become "an occasional visitor to the home of Alain Locke. . . . It was at Locke's home that Jean met some of the bright young [African-American] authors."[2] However, correspondence in the Alain Locke collection at the Moorland-Spingarn Research Center at Howard University proves that, in fact, Toomer knew Alain Locke at least as early as 1919, that he participated in the "literary evenings" (which were originally *Toomer's* idea) at Georgia Douglas Johnson's home between 1920 and 1922, and that, indeed, he attempted to sway the participants in her salon to his own views of the "American" race by leading a series of study sessions concerned with the topic. It appears that these sessions had an important impact on Georgia Douglas Johnson's own volume of 1922, *Bronze*. Moreover, it seems highly likely that, in fact, Toomer read portions of *Cane* before the group.

The correspondence that supports these contentions has thus far escaped the notice of Toomer scholars, who have not consulted the

† From *American Literature* 63.41 (December 1991). Copyright © 1991, Duke University Press. All rights reserved. Used by permission of the publisher.

1. Nellie McKay, "Jean Toomer in His Time: An Introduction," in *Jean Toomer: A Critical Evaluation* (Washington: Howard Univ. Press, 1988), p. 10. The research for this article was pursued as part of a larger project entitled "American Cultural Nationalism and the Harlem Renaissance," which was funded in 1989–90 by a National Endowment for the Humanities fellowship. I would like to thank Esme E. Bhan, Research Associate at the Moorland-Spingarn Research Center, for generously aiding my research.
2. *The Lives of Jean Toomer: A Hunger for Wholeness* (Baton Rouge: Louisiana State Univ. Press, 1987), pp. 91–92. Throughout their generally outstanding biography, Kerman and Eldridge make no reference to materials in the Alain Locke Papers at the Moorland-Spingarn Research Center of Howard University. Nellie Y. McKay's *Jean Toomer, Artist* (Chapel Hill: Univ. of Carolina Press, 1984) also neglects this source, as have the many other works on Toomer's life and art.

Alain Locke papers.[3] The first evidence of Toomer's connection with Locke is a simple note addressed to Locke, dated 11 November 1919, asking if it would be convenient for Toomer to visit the Howard University professor on the thirteenth. Clearly, Toomer had known Locke previously, although they were probably not on close terms. In another note of 24 December 1920 Toomer writes that he would like to stop by and "chat," and sends Christmas greetings to Locke's mother, which would indicate that the two men were by then rather well acquainted with each other.

Four months earlier, on 20 August 1920, Georgia Douglas Johnson, in writing to thank Locke for his "magnificent review" of her book *The Heart of a Woman and Other Poems* (1918), went on to mention that "Jean Toomer is here, could you bring your mother over Saturday evening to my home. I think Mary Burrill [a black playwright] will be there. Mr. Toomer wishes to show us his books also. He says that he has some very good finds." Clearly, Toomer was at least occasionally spending evenings at Johnson's home and sharing his reading during this period shortly following his first involvement with the New York intellectuals. Moreover, as the letter implies, he had been involved with the Washington group even before he met Lola Ridge, Waldo Frank, and company: "He has met some of the very delightful writers of New York and has improved immensely. Also I wish you would hear his two little gems." As this letter is dated over a year before Toomer would journey to Sparta, Georgia, his "gems" probably do not include pieces published in *Cane*, but one cannot dismiss the possibility out of hand. Certainly, the evidence proves that Toomer was sharing his writing with the chief circle of black writers in Washington three years before the publication of *Cane* and over a year and a half before he was in regular correspondence with Waldo Frank. It hints, further, at the possibility of a longstanding acquaintance for which evidence is slim probably for the simple reason that he had no reason to correspond with people living in his own city.

In the fall and winter of 1920–21, Toomer was meeting with the Washington group at Georgia Douglas Johnson's home and introducing them to his ideas, the books he had been reading, and some of the work he himself had written. Indeed, these evenings surely

3. A neglected but important article on the literary circle led by Georgia Douglas Johnson does make brief reference to this correspondence and connects Toomer with Johnson and Locke. See Ronald M. Johnson, "Those Who Stayed: Washington Black Writers of the 1920s," *Records of the Columbia Historical Society* 50 (1980), 484–99. Concerning the Washington group, see also Jeffrey C. Stewart, "Alain Locke and Georgia Douglas Johnson, Washington Patrons of Afro-American Modernism," *Washington Studies* 12 (July 1986), 37–44. Throughout my article, passages from the correspondence in the Alain Locke Papers are quoted with permission of the Moorland-Spingarn Research Center, Howard University. The correspondence from this collection, which has yet to be catalogued, will be identified within my text by date and the name of Locke's correspondent.

constitute the autobiographical basis for scenes in his posthumously published play, *Natalie Mann*, which involves—among other things—the conflict between one of Toomer's hero/prophets of the "new race" (Nathan Merilh) and a group of repressed, bourgeois "Negro" intellectuals.[4] Merilh and his lover, Mertis Newbolt, ultimately leave Washington and settle into an apartment in New York City, where they are involved with a multi-ethnic group of left-wing writers and intellectuals partially resembling the circle with which Toomer himself associated. None of the characters in either Washington or New York seems individually drawn from a person Toomer knew in those places, and the representation of the Washington circle makes it out to be more repressive and imitative of white culture than was Johnson's group. The characters in the play, for example, are ashamed of the spirituals. Nonetheless, the theme that African-American intellectuals must emerge from a double "crust" of American "Puritanism" and excessive racial self-defensiveness—which merely exacerbates their self-inhibitions—is one that appears in Toomer's manuscripts of the period and that he clearly considered applicable to the Washington intelligentsia.[5]

On 26 January 1921, some eight months before he would go to Sparta, Georgia, Toomer wrote Alain Locke that he had held two meetings at Johnson's home of a group "whose central purpose is an historical study of slavery and the Negro, emphasizing the great economic and cultural forces which have largely determined them. The aim is twofold, first, to arrive at a sound and just criticism of the actual place and condition of the mixed-blood group in this country, and, second, to formulate an ideal that will be both workable and inclusive."[6] In taking on the topic of "miscegenation," Toomer was going to the heart of one of the most taboo topics in American

---

4. *Natalie Mann*, in *The Wayward and the Seeking: A Collection of Writings by Jean Toomer*, ed. Darwin Turner (Washington: Howard Univ. Press, 1980), pp. 243–325.

5. See, in particular, "The Negro Emergent," box 51, folder 1114; untitled ms., box 48, folder 1010; and letter to Mac Wright, 4 August 1922, box 9, folder 283, all in the Jean Toomer Papers, Collection of American Literature, Beinecke Rare Book and Manuscript Library, Yale University, and quoted with permission of the Yale University Library. Of Georgia Douglas Johnson herself, Toomer wrote to John McClure, "Too much poetic jargon, too many inhibitions check the flow of what I think to be real (if slender) lyric gift." Letter of 6 October 1922, in Jean Toomer Papers, box 7, folder 22.

6. Alain Locke Papers. The members of this group included Mary Burrill (the black playwright), Georgia Douglas Johnson, a Miss Scott of Howard University, Mary Craft, E. C. Williams, and Henry Kennedy (Toomer's longtime friend). This may well have represented the beginning of the weekly "conversations" at Johnson's home that would take place regularly for a decade. Gloria T. Hull quotes Johnson as saying the evenings were Toomer's idea. However, because the first public mention of them does not appear until October 1926 (in Gwendolyn Bennett's "Ebony Flute" column for *Crisis* magazine), Hull implies that they began in the mid-twenties. At this point Toomer had been out of contact with the Washington artists and intellectuals for nearly three years. If the weekly conversations were Toomer's idea, they would surely have started between 1920 and 1922 when Toomer was in Washington and in regular contact with Johnson, Locke, and their friends. See Hull, *Color, Sex, and Poetry: Three Women Writers of the Harlem Renaissance* (Bloomington: Indiana Univ. Press, 1987), p. 165.

culture generally, apparently striving to help his friends break out of their "crust" to achieve an "inclusive" vision. The terms match those Nathan Merilh uses to describe his own philosophy in *Natalie Mann*. The phrasing leaves it unclear as to whether Toomer considers the "mixed-blood group" to *be* the Negro group or a group no longer identical with the Negro group. It is worth pointing out, however, that Johnson herself, like perhaps most of those who met at her home, was quite light-skinned and knew of considerable "miscegenation" in her family background. Moreover, both she and Toomer could remember a period in which racial definition in Washington society was less rigid, less distinctly bifurcated into "black" and "white" worlds, than it had become by 1920, the last year in which the "mulatto" designation was included in the U. S. census. A short generation or two earlier, the "mulatto elite" had not been so closely identified with the black masses as they were during the twenties, and liaisons between whites and "mulattoes," including marriage, were more prevalent and openly acknowledged than they would be by 1915.[7] One of the great ironies of Toomer's career is that he matured during the very period in which black as well as white Americans became most insistent upon maintaining "racial integrity."

Some evidence of the nature of the "ideals" to which Toomer attempted to lead the study-group members can be found in Georgia Douglas Johnson's own work of this period. Toomer mentions in his letter to Locke that "as a natural outgrowth" of the meetings "should come the reading of original efforts." Surely it was at this time that Johnson herself wrote the poems of the "new race" which constitute the central section, "Exaltation," in her volume of 1922, *Bronze* (Boston: B. J. Brimmer). "Cosmopolite" is worth quoting in full:

> Not wholly this or that,
> But wrought
> Of alien bloods am I,
> A product of the interplay
> Of traveled hearts.
> Estranged, yet not estranged, I stand
> All comprehending;
> From my estate
> I view earth's frail dilemma;
> Scion of fused strength am I,
> All understanding,
> Nor this nor that
> Contains me. (p. 59)

7. For a fascinating discussion of the gradual rigidification of the black/white racial dualism in the United States, see Joel Williamson, *New People: Miscegenation and Mulattoes in the United States* (New York: Free Press, 1980), pp. 61–139.

This poem conveys a very different concept of the "mulatto" than that of, say, Langston Hughes—whose "tragic mulatto" would be not a "fused" and all-comprehending child of "traveled hearts," "scion" of an "estate" transcending the color line, but rather a self-divided, disinherited, homeless soul conceived in heartless lust and identified as "neither white nor black" (as opposed to *both* white *and* black).[8]

Indeed, an integral biracial identity rarely appears as a viable possibility in American literature. According to Judith Berzon, the options open to fictional "mulattoes" are restricted to their becoming African-American race leaders, "'passing,' adopting a white middle-class image and value system, or succumbing to despair."[9] Even in African-American fiction since the Harlem Renaissance, typically the "mulatto" character either is destroyed (or spiritually diminished) by inner conflicts caused by his/her alienated condition in a racially bifurcated society, or he/she becomes "whole" by becoming wholly "black." The idea of biracial persons achieving healthy identities by embracing their multiple ancestry has been virtually unthinkable to both writers and critics; such persons are truly the invisible men and women of our racial ideology, and pose the most radical challenge to racialist discourse.[1] Toomer and Johnson offer rare retorts to conventional encodings of the "mulatto" (for whom we still have no generally accepted, non-pejorative name). Both confronted the challenge of arriving at tropes which would combat the negative and "tragic" imagery. In "Fusion," Johnson would use the "river" image that appealed to Toomer as a metaphor for the fact of racial intermingling:

> How deftly does the gardener blend
> This rose and that
> To bud a new creation,
> More gorgeous and more beautiful
> Than any parent portion,
> And so,
> I trace within my warring blood
> The tributary sources,
> They potently commingle
> And sweep
> With new-born forces! (*Bronze*, p. 60)

Although Johnson makes use of the traditional trope of "warring blood," she feels the internal conflict as the prelude to a potent synthesis. Her phrasing, moreover, directly contradicts the concept,

---

8. See especially Hughes's poems "Cross," in *The Weary Blues* (New York: Knopf, 1926), p. 52; and "Mulatto," in *Fine Clothes to the Jew* (New York: Knopf, 1927), pp. 71–72.
9. *Neither White Nor Black* (New York: New York Univ. Press, 1978), p. 14.
1. For a provocative discussion of this issue, see especially Werner Sollors, "'Never Was Born': The Mulatto, an American Tragedy?" *Massachusetts Review*, 27 (1986), 293–316.

once common in Southern white racial ideology, that "mulattoes" could not reproduce with each other beyond two or three generations. "Highly ephemeral persons," "effete . . . both biologically and, ultimately, culturally," according to a pervasive mythology, they were destined to disappear since they could reproduce only by "backcrossing" with blacks or whites.[2] This is hardly the view that Johnson conveys in what is arguably the climactic section of her carefully organized volume. In "Perspective" (also part of the "Exaltation" section of *Bronze*), the speaker takes comfort in the thought that she is "a dark forerunner of a race burgeoning" (p. 61); clearly this refers not to the great Negro race whose forerunners date back many centuries, but to a *new* "race."

Johnson seems, at least provisionally, to have adopted some of Toomer's views about the new American people. Indeed, from the early twenties on she would return to related themes throughout her life.[3] Later biracial writers would claim her as a "foremother": "The extent of her influence, of her philosophy of dawn-men born of the fused strength of tributary sources, deserves to be properly recognized. She was the first to give to peoples of mixed origin the pride in themselves that they so badly needed. She was the mother who nourished a whole generation of Eurasians and other 'mixed breeds' like myself," wrote Cedric Dover in 1952.[4] Her poems help support the idea that in his talks with the "New Negro" group that gathered at Johnson's house in the same year he went to Georgia, Toomer presented his developing racial ideology. It was no doubt one of this group who, when Toomer finished reading and explaining his poem "The First American" to him, shook his head and said, "You're white."[5]

Toomer kept up his contact with the Washington circle as he worked on *Cane*. Indeed, he wrote Locke from Sparta on 8 November 1921, stating that "There is poetry here—and drama, but the atmosphere for one in my position is almost prohibitory"—suggesting something of the autobiographical facts behind "Kabnis." Interestingly, in this letter Toomer expresses his sense that the life of the "Negro" of the South offers a "virgin" field to the writer, yet he does not believe that he can fully take advantage of it—"for its real exploitation, one would have to come into it under different circumstances"

2. Williamson, pp. 73, 95. See also Thomas F. Gossett, *Race: The History of an Idea in America* (Dallas: Southern Methodist Univ. Press, 1963); and George Stocking, *Race, Culture, and Evolution* (New York: Free Press, 1968), pp. 48–49. It is interesting to note that images such as these infuse much of the modern scholarship concerning the "disappearances" of Jean Toomer and Nella Larsen.

3. See Hull, pp. 155–211.

4. "The Importance of Georgia Douglas Johnson," *Crisis*, 59 (1952), 635.

5. Toomer, "On Being an American," Jean Toomer Papers, box 15, folder 2. This episode is discussed in Kerman and Eldridge, pp. 80–81. "The First American" was a poem, no longer extant, that conveyed Toomer's conception of the "new race" coming into being in the United States, a mixture of all the "older" races, and of which he considered himself the first conscious member. After considerable revision it became "Blue Meridian."

(presumably, not as a teacher). Less than three weeks later, he would write Locke again to say that he would soon be leaving, "both in the interest of the school (raising funds) and for purposes of my own"— evidence that he was expected to remain associated with the school beyond the two months he actually spent teaching there. He goes on to mention that he will be in Washington for several days before pushing on for New York, where "several informal lectures" were supposed to be arranged for him: "And of course I have material. Want to see you."[6] What this letter proves is that Toomer was sharing the material that went into *Cane* with Locke from early on, that he in fact turned to Locke as an advisor and supporter during the crucial period in which his book was taking shape.

Moreover, he continued to do so. On 1 August 1922 he wrote to express his appreciation for Locke's criticism of an unspecified piece which apparently went into *Cane*: "I liked your criticism. The cocoon *is* both tight and intense." This letter also indicates that Locke was putting him in touch with one of Locke's own closest friends and most trusted critics, C. Henry Dickerman: "Dickerman has not returned the Ms. but there is no hurry. Little Review has the original."[7] Locke (or "Lockus" as Dickerman addressed him) and "Dickus" were intimate friends from their years at Philadelphia's Central High School until Dickerman's early death in 1927.[8] Their letters show an astonishing range of knowledge about literature, from the Greek classics to the full gamut of pre-Raphaelites and early modernists of Europe. That Locke would pass on one of Toomer's sketches—probably "Fern"—to this trusted friend indicates the deep interest and confidence he had in Toomer's work.[9]

Toomer was clearly grateful for whatever advice Locke had to offer, and he asked Boni and Liveright to send this advisor a copy of *Cane* as soon as it came out, agreeing at the same time to give Locke "some sort of play" for a volume Locke was planning in August 1923.[1] Hence, just before the publication of *Cane*, Toomer seems to feel no conflict with Locke or ambivalence about being connected with his project—although we know that at this time Toomer was fully committed to his theory of the "American race" and that he did not consider himself a Negro. On the other hand, Locke certainly considered himself a mentor to Toomer. In an undated, private note

6. Toomer to Locke, 24 November 1921, in Alain Locke correspondence, Moorland-Spingarn Research Center, Howard University.
7. Toomer to Locke, 1 August 1922.
8. See letters from Dickerman in Alain Locke correspondence, Moorland-Spingarn Research Center, Howard University. Not only had Dickerman, who was white, gone to Harvard with Locke after high school, but both had been Rhodes Scholars together at Oxford. The two men shared intimate confidences about their sexual lives, the literature of homosexuality, and their own literary ambitions.
9. The reference to the *Little Review* suggests that the unnamed work was "Fern," the only Toomer piece of this period that was published in that magazine.
1. Toomer to Locke, 17 August 1923.

located amid the correspondence with Countee Cullen, he refers to Toomer as one of his "spiritual children," consoling himself that if some day he must plead guilty to "corrupting the youth" he can take pride in the artists he had nurtured: "Can a bad tree bring forth good fruit?"

With the publication and public reception of *Cane*, Toomer's connection with Locke—and apparently with the other members of the Washington group—came largely to an end. Yet he did not cut off all contact with "New Negroes" in Harlem. Ethel Ray Nance (Charles S. Johnson's assistant at *Opportunity* magazine) remembered his visiting the Harlem apartment she shared with Regina Anderson in 1924 or 1925, when prominent black writers often dropped by.[2] Moreover, well after *Cane* appeared, black friends such as Dorothy Peterson and Aaron Douglas continued to visit him at his home on East 10th Street, according to his second wife.[3] Toomer was not, then, avoiding contact with black artists at this time, although he did not count himself one of them. Neither was he "turning his back" on them; he apparently desired their company. At least for the time being, his actions in this respect remained consistent with those of the pre-*Cane* period. In fact, in 1925, he ran meetings in Harlem attempting to convert black intellectuals to the Gurdjieff system for the "harmonious development of man"—which entailed adopting Toomer's basic racial position.[4] Moreover, following up on an earlier commitment, Toomer would allow Locke to use the play *Balo* in an anthology of "Negro plays" (which he probably did not interpret to mean plays necessarily *by* Negroes, as indeed many Harlem Renaissance writers, including Locke, did not), and Locke would use pieces from *Cane* in *The New Negro* (without Toomer's permission); but in other respects their relationship ended. This is one more indication of the dismay Toomer apparently felt when he was identified as a "Negro writer" after the publication of his book. Perhaps he felt that Locke, along with other friends, had betrayed him in ignoring his long-held convictions concerning the "American race"—convictions he had openly shared with and explicitly articulated for the African-American intelligentsia of Washington, and which perhaps, as David Bradley and Alain Solard have argued, he believed essential to an adequate understanding of *Cane* itself.[5]

2. Ann Allen Shockley, transcript of interview with Mrs. Ethel Ray Nance, 18 November and 23 December 1970, Oral History Collection, Fisk University Library.
3. Ann Allen Shockley, taped interview with Marjorie Content Toomer, 24 October 1970, Oral History Collection, Fisk University Library.
4. Kerman and Eldridge, pp. 143–44.
5. Bradley, "Looking Behind *Cane,*" *Southern Review,* 21 (1985), 692–93: Solard, "The Impossible Unity: Jean Toomer's 'Kabnis,'" in *Myth and Ideology in American Culture,* ed. Regis Durand (Villeneuve d'Ascq: Univ. de Lille III, 1976), pp. 175–94.

# BARBARA FOLEY

# Jean Toomer's Washington and the Politics of Class: From "Blue Veins" to Seventh-street Rebels[†]

> Familiarity, in most people, indicates not a sentiment of comradeship, an emotion of brotherhood, but simply a lack of respect and reverence tempered by the unkindly . . . desire to level down whatever is above them, to assert their own puny egos at whatever damage to those fragile tissues of elevation which constitute the worthwhile meshes of our civilization.
>
> —Jean Toomer[1]

> It is generally established that the causes of race prejudice may primarily be found in the economic structure that compels one worker to compete against another and that furthermore renders it advantageous for the exploiting classes to inculcate, foster, and aggravate that competition.
>
> —Jean Toomer, "Reflections on the Race Riots"

It is a critical commonplace that Jean Toomer's *Cane* is a largely autobiographical work displaying its author's discovery of his profound identification with African Americans and their culture. This concern is signaled in Toomer's own often-quoted statements: the 1922 *Liberator* letter in which he remarked that "my growing need for artistic expression has pulled me deeper and deeper into the Negro group" and that, during his visit to Georgia the previous fall, "a deep part of my nature, a part I had repressed, sprang suddenly to life and responded" to the "rich dusk beauty" of "Negro peasants" with "folk-songs [at their] lips" (Rusch 16); the 1923 letter to Sherwood Anderson noting that "my seed was planted in the *Cane*—and cotton fields, . . . was planted in *myself* down there" (Rusch 17). But the tenuousness of Toomer's identification with his black ancestry— both before and after the composition of *Cane*—has also been noted: his 1914 registration at the University of Wisconsin as a person of "French Cosmopolitan" heritage (Krasny 42); his break with Waldo Frank over the latter's labeling *Cane* as the work of a "Negro writer" and his reluctance to have excerpts included in Alain Locke's *The New Negro* (1925); his subsequent statement to James Weldon Johnson that the "Negro Art movement . . . is for those who have and will benefit [*sic*] by it . . . [but] is not for me" (11 July 1930, TP, Box 4, Folder 119); his 1934 remark in the *Baltimore Afro-American* that "I have not lived as [a Negro], nor do I really know whether

---

† From *Modern Fiction Studies* 42.2 (1996): 289–321. © 1996 The Purdue Research Foundation. Reprinted with permission of The Johns Hopkins University Press.
1. This is taken from an undated memorandum book in the Toomer papers. All indications are that this book dates from 1921.

there is colored blood in me or not" (qtd. in Estes-Hicks 9). Critics differ in their assessments of Toomer's resolution to the dilemma of racial identification. Some view him as a perceptive commentator on the social construction of race who was—and continues to be— victimized by the pigeon-holing of a race-obsessed society (Bradley; Byrd; Hutchinson, "American Racial Discourse"). Others view him as an elitist and a coward—even a racist—who, while briefly energized by an acknowledgment of his blackness in the *Cane* period, could not come to terms with being black in the United States and ultimately fled over the color line (Margolies; Gibson; Miller). Most scholars situate him somewhere in between these psychological and ideological poles. It is widely agreed, however, that *Cane* is a complex and contradictory articulation of racial consciousness by a complex and contradictory human being.[2]

I have no disagreement with the proposition that racial consciousness is central to *Cane*. I shall stress here, however, an issue that is often obscured in discussions of Toomer's attitudes toward and conceptions of race—namely, the imprint left by his consciousness of class. Scholars and biographers have noted that Toomer's youth was spent in the financially comfortable and socially select environment provided in the home of his maternal grandfather, P. B. S. Pinchback, who had been Acting Governor of Louisiana during Reconstruction and subsequently became a prominent member of Washington's light-skinned black elite. But they have tended to underemphasize the complex admixture of snobbery and social activism shaping the outlook of the aristocracy of color among whom Toomer was raised. While commentators have, moreover, frequently noted in passing Toomer's youthful interest in socialist politics and working-class movements, they have routinely dismissed this interest as a brief and trivial phase, ending abruptly in 1919. I shall argue that we misread *Cane*—and other early 1920s Toomer texts—if we

2. The Toomer archive is replete with contradictory signals regarding Toomer's racial identity. Although he had stayed in Greenwich Village during a pre-*Cane* sojourn, when Toomer visited New York in 1923 he apparently considered staying at the Hotel Theresa in Harlem, to which he had inquiries about costs (TP, Box 3, Folder 97). Yet he turned down an invitation to contribute to Nancy Cunard's anthology *Negro* on the grounds that "although I am interested in and deeply value the Negro, I am not a Negro" (TP, Box 1, Folder 24). While Toomer's later statements about his racial identity appear to call into question whether or not he actually had any African heritage, his unpublished autobiography, on which he was working at the same time that he issued these denials, makes it clear that his grandfather Pinchback thought of himself as a black man. Describing the rationale behind the family's decision to send him to the black Garnet School rather than to the local white school, Toomer remarks, "For Pinckney Benton Stewart Pinchback to send his grandson to a white school, no, that will not do. It might look as if he were going back on his race and wanting me to be white" (TP, Box 19, Folder 500). It is, I think, best to view Toomer's later repudiations of black identity as a repudiation of racial designations as such. As he mused in his journal regarding a 1929 review of the French edition of *Cane* that dubbed its author a Negro, such occurrences pointed to "the real difficulties involved in managing this organism named Toomer" (TP, Box 61, Folder 1419).

ignore their author's continuing interest in a left-wing social analysis. In many readings of *Cane*, in other words, race is decoupled from class: Toomer's articulation of the problematic of racial identification is construed largely in isolation from considerations of economic power and social stratification. Even as they treat the patently social issues of race and racism, *Cane* critics often divest these questions of their full import, positing Toomer's "search for identity" primarily as an individual's subjective quest for reconciliation with his own mixed heritage, thus obscuring the historical and economic forces that render "race" such a profoundly ideological concept in the first place.

Recoupling race with class permits us to resituate in history the consciousness that produced *Cane*—which, as my two epigraphs indicate, was contradictory indeed. I have elsewhere shown that the first and third sections of *Cane* are much more fully engaged with the social realities of Hancock County, Georgia—its history of slave rebellion, its lynch violence, its oppressive religious and educational institutions—than is widely acknowledged. I argue here that Toomer's formative experiences among the capital's "blue-veined" aristocracy of color, as well as his engagement with socialist politics, had a profound impact upon the categories through which he perceived and articulated racial issues in his writings of the early 1920s—especially the Washington, D.C., portion of *Cane*.

In order to appreciate the complex attitudes toward class evinced in Toomer's writings, it is necessary first to outline the distinctive features of the world of Washington's Negro aristocracy. Willard Gatewood notes that the "black upper class" that rose to ascendancy in the post-Civil War period

> justified its claims to a privileged status on various grounds, including its record of achievement, status as antebellum free people of color, culture and education, and to a lesser degree, wealth. They viewed themselves as the products of a natural selection from which they had emerged as the strongest and fittest of the race. They stood in sharp contrast to those who belonged to the "submerged masses." (24)

While groupings of black aristocrats were present in cities throughout the South, the Midwest, and the East, "[f]rom the end of Reconstruction until at least World War I Washington was the center of the black aristocracy in the United States. . . . No other city possessed such a concentration of 'old families,' . . . whose emphasis on family background, good breeding, occupation, respectability, and color bound them into an exclusive, self-consciously elitist group" (Gatewood 39). Dubbed the "Negro Four Hundred" by the *Washington*

*Bee*, for several decades the capital's principal black newspaper, this elite numbered "not more than ninety to a hundred families" (C. Green 141) but exerted an influence far beyond its numbers.

Very few of the Negro aristocrats possessed wealth comparable to that owned by the white American ruling class; especially after the turn of the century, all were to one degree or another restricted by the increasing pressures of Jim Crow racism. Most of the wealthiest members of the "Negro Four Hundred" led lives entirely apart from their "cave-dwelling" white counterparts: white socialite Mrs. John Logan noted in 1901 that "no matter to what degree of affluence, education, or culture a colored man may rise, neither he nor his family will have any social relations with white people" (521). Some "white Negroes" who were light enough to be taken for Caucasian "quietly [took] their places in the ranks of white people exclusively" (F. Williams, "Perils" 421). But many light-skinned blacks able to "pass"—as well as the greater number of darker-shaded people— enjoyed both security and comfort in black high society. Significantly, it was not until 1920 that the category of "mulatto"—with the various privileges that this designation entailed—would disappear from the racial categories included in the U.S. Census (Hutchinson, "American Racial Discourse" 229). Some men among the Negro aristocracy worked in law and medicine; Paul Laurence Dunbar noted in 1900 that "there are so many engaged in [the professions] that it would keep one busy counting or attempting to count the dark-skinned lawyers and doctors one meets in a day" (32). Others worked in education or government—at times "passing" in the increasingly segregated workplaces of the nation's capital but living black lives after work. Some women presided over political and cultural salons; others involved themselves in the club movement, which aimed to mobilize "the few competent in behalf of the many incompetent" to work for "the social uplift of the negro race" (F. Williams, "The Club Movement" 101, 99). While occasionally, as Constance Green has pointed out, the "well-educated" daughters of such families, "barred from suitable occupations by an inflexible caste system, drift[ed] into the life of the *demi-monde*" (138), for the most part the offspring of the Negro aristocracy were models of bourgeois conduct, taking their cues from texts such as E. Azalia Hackley's *The Colored Girl Beautiful* (1916) and Edward S. Green's *National Capital Code of Etiquette* (1920). The families of the "Negro Four Hundred" favored resorts such as Harper's Ferry, Saratoga, Newport, and Cape May during the summer months. They educated their children at the M Street High School (after 1916 called Dunbar High School)—"the only example in our history of a separate black school that was able, somehow, to be equal," notes Kenneth Clark (qtd. in Anderson 104)—before sending them on to the Ivy League or the prestigious

black colleges. Many in the Negro aristocracy hoped that, by demonstrating their gentility, they would eventually earn full assimilation into white society; in the meanwhile, however, they lived lives
of refinement and ease.[3]

The aristocracy of color were, however, frequently castigated for
their separation from the black masses. Nowhere was this criticism
sharper than around the issue of "blue veinism"—a "reference to
skin light enough to reveal one's blue veins" (Gatewood 153). John
E. Bruce, a black columnist who wrote for many years under the
name "Bruce Grit," as early as 1877 published a withering satiric
commentary on "Washington's Colored Society" as

> a species of African humanity which is forever and ever
> informing the uninitiated what a narrow escape they had from
> being born white. They have small hands, aristocratic insteps
> and wear blue veins, they have auburn hair and finely chiselled
> features. . . . They are opposed to manual labor, their physical
> organization couldn't stand it, they prefer light work such as
> shuffling cards or dice. . . . Around the festive board, they are
> unequalled for their verbosity and especially for their aptness
> in tracing their ancestry. (qtd, in Frazier 300)

Calvin Chase, editor and publisher of the *Washington Bee*, characterized the Negro aristocracy as "would-be whites" and derided
their pretensions to culture, declaring that, in the Monday Night
Literary (later called the Mu-So-Litt), "there is more intelligence
excluded than [included]" (qtd. in Gatewood 161; C. Green 139;
Anonymous). He also lambasted the elite's "colorphobia": "There is
as much color prejudice among certain classes of colored people,"
he declared, "as there is among certain classes of white people"
(*Bee* 27 February 1915).

The years 1880–1920 were the heyday of Washington's black
aristocracy, but the capital's reputation for elitism and intraracial
color prejudice persisted well past World War I. Langston Hughes,
writing about his experiences in Washington in the mid-1920s,
commented upon the Negro aristocrats' propensity to boast about
their college degrees and possessions, their "well-ancestored" pedi-
grees, and their light skins. Recalling with distaste one young Wash-
ingtonian's proud claim that at his fraternity dance the women were
"nothing but pinks . . . —looki[ng] just like 'fay' women," Hughes
concluded that his associates' ideals "seemed most Nordic and un-
Negro. . . . [T]hey appeared to be moving away from the masses of

3. For more on Harper's Ferry, see Terrell and, especially, Mae Wright Peck's comments
   in O'Daniel, "Jean Toomer and Mae Wright." For more on the M Street (Dunbar)
   School, see Terrell; Anderson; Majors, 229; and Robinson. For more on the goal of
   assimilation, see Murray.

the race rather than holding an identity with them." The works of Jean Toomer and other Washington-based black writers, he learned, were unknown in "society" circles: "In supposedly intellectual gatherings I listened to conversations as arid as the sides of the Washington monument." Seventh Street, by contrast, was "always teemingly alive with dark working people who hadn't yet acquired 'culture' and the manners of stage ambassadors, and pinks and blacks and yellows were still friends without apologies" (Hughes, "Wonderful" 226–27). Seventh Street blacks, "folks with practically no family trees at all . . . who work hard for a living with their hands, . . . looked at the dome of the Capitol and laughed out loud" (Hughes, *Big Sea* 208–09). It was the migrants of Seventh Street, not the "pinks" of the capital's upper-class enclaves, who inspired Hughes's prolific poetic production during his 1920s Washington period (Rampersad 103). Melvin B. Tolson, writing to Locke as late as 1942, remarked on the same phenomenon, noting that to him Washington was "the copestone of Negro snobbery" (16 December 1942, LP, Box 164–90, Folder 11).

By the time of World War I, however, Washington's black aristocracy had entered a state of crisis. Much of its embattled situation can be traced to the increasing racism of the federal government, embodied in the segregation of government offices. Begun under the Republicans, office segregation became near universal in the Wilson administration, during which "piece by piece the world of colored Washington fell apart" (C. Green 171). A 1913 NAACP report noted that "those segregated are regarded as people apart, almost as lepers" (qtd. in C. Green 173). Booker T. Washington wrote in the same year that he had "never seen the colored people [of Washington] so discouraged and so bitter as they are at the present time" (qtd. in C. Green 177). Former Register of Deeds Henry Lincoln Johnson charged that, since Wilson's election, "the persistent aim of the Democratic Party has been to eliminate and humiliate the negro" (4). The *Bee* fulminated against the "race discrimination" extending from federal offices to churches and theaters, calling it "as great an outrage as was ever committed under the protecting eyes of the government since the times when fugitive slaves were restored to their so-called owners" (*Bee* 10 May 1913). Rigorous segregation spread to public facilities where light-skinned Negro aristocrats had previously slipped past: one theater "employed a black doorman to spot and bounce intruders whose racial origins were undetectable by whites" (C. Green 207).

The 1919 Washington race riot brought to the fore the desperation of the black masses and the Negro aristocracy's increasing cynicism about the prospects for racial progress. Sparked by salacious press reports of black male sexual assaults (Kerlin 76–79), the riot was begun at Seventh Street and Pennsylvania Avenue by several hundred white ex-servicemen who, joined by more than a thousand white civilians, "proceeded to take over the city from the Capitol to the White House" (L. Williams 26). "This Nation's Capital is in a disgrace," declared the *Bee*. "The great Capital of the Nation is in the hands of a mob, and innocent colored citizens are assaulted." In several pockets of the black community, the attackers were met with armed resistance. Guns were rushed into the city by blacks in nearby Baltimore, and in the southwest portion of the capital, the *Bee* boasted, "the colored population held its own" (*Bee* 26 July 1919). James Weldon Johnson declared that "[t]he Negroes saved them-selves and saved Washington by their decision not to run but to fight. . . . If the white mob had gone unchecked—and it was only the determined effort of black men that checked it—Washington would have been another and worse East St. Louis" (243). A woman writing to the *Crisis* anticipated the language of Claude McKay's "If We Must Die" in her comment that "[t]he Washington riot gave me the thrill that comes once in a lifetime. . . . At last our men had stood like men, struck back, were no longer dumb, driven cattle" (qtd. in L. Williams 56, 59). But although the violence, which seethed out of control for almost a week, had been initiated entirely by whites, "only eight or nine of the hundred-odd persons arrested were whites, and of these only one was convicted for carrying a con-cealed weapon" (C. Green 192). The *Bee* editorialized, "It is strange that every effort was made to disarm defenseless colored citizens and no effort made to disarm the whites" (*Bee* 26 July 1919). The NAACP's request that the *Washington Post* be indicted for its role in inciting the riots was ignored (*Bee* 2 August 1919). The govern-ment's principal response to the 1919 riot was to harden its segrega-tionist posture: when the Lincoln Memorial was dedicated in 1922, blacks in attendance—"blue veins" and masses alike—were seated in a roped-off Jim Crow section.

Part of Washington's Negro aristocracy responded to Wilsonian segregation and repression with increased activism and militancy. The perception that no dark-skinned individual would be exempt from Jim Crow led increasing numbers of the elite to the realization that "they could not remain detached from the lower-class black" (C. Green 177). Meetings of two thousand denounced segregation (*Bee* 21 November 1914). By 1916 the Washington, D.C., branch of the NAACP, with 1,164 members, was the largest in the country; the *Bee*, which had previously declared that "Negro leadership . . . is a sham and a mockery" and that "all this about the advancement of Colored People could be poured into a two ounce bottle" (*Bee* 27 February 1915), was now supporting the NAACP and calling for racial solidarity (Chase 173). As Onita Estes-Hicks has pointed out, one result of the imposition of Jim Crow upon the previously exempted Washington elite was the growth of a significant cultural nationalist movement that antedated the Harlem Renaissance. Du Bois's "Star of Ethiopia" pageant, which featured a "massive back-ground of an Egyptian temple . . . and a thousand actors," was per-formed in 1915 before audiences "aggregating fourteen thousand" (Du Bois, *Dusk* 272). M Street High School became a hotbed of debate over the relative merits of Booker T. Washington's and Du Bois's educational philosophies—debates in which the latter rou-tinely won, since a "group of exceptionally inspiring teachers" at M Street were recent NAACP recruits who were "pass[ing] the torch to their students" (C. Green 174).

While some members of the Negro aristocracy were clearly con-cerned about more than the niceties in Edward Green's book of etiquette, the Washington Four Hundred were severely buffeted during the postwar period. As a result of Wilsonian segregation, passing—as a mode of life, not simply a temporary convenience—became an increasingly common phenomenon among Washington's light-skinned black elite. This development "tended to disrupt the solidarity of the top level of Washington's colored world" (C. Green 208). Moreover, the Negro aristocracy was threatened by internal changes. Some of these, Gatewood explains, were generational: "The ranks of the old guard, who had displayed pride in family tra-dition and had been most insistent on drawing the line against what they considered the vulgar and uncouth, had been depleted by death." Gatewood concludes, "[t]he rising tide of racism and the fading of hopes for an integrated society, as well as the decline in the economic base of the old upper class, eroded the prestige and influence of a group that had nurtured ties with whites and advo-cated assimilation to the larger society" (335).

Toomer grew up among Washington's aristocrats of color. His grandfather Pinchback had been one of the wealthiest members of the black elite in New Orleans. Soon after the Pinchbacks' 1893 move to the upscale Bacon Street neighborhood in the capital city, the estimated value of Pinchback's fortune was some $90,000, and he enjoyed an income of $10,000 per year (Gatewood 44; Haskins 252).

> The "Governor" built a red brick thirteen-room house on Bacon Street near the Chinese embassy. Heated throughout by hot water radiators and lavishly furnished, the house contained two large parlors and a fine library. A succession of cooks and maids, in addition to a gardener known as Old Willis, a former slave, attended the house and spacious grounds. Present at their house-warming reception . . . was the "crème de la crème of Washington's colored society." (Gatewood 43)

Through Pinchback's inveterate gambling and several poor investments, the family fortunes declined dramatically after 1910, when
the family sold the Bacon Street house and moved to more modest
quarters in a middle-class black neighborhood. Nonetheless, it was
in this house that Jean Toomer spent his childhood. Jean Toomer
was a descendant of "the most exclusive and persistent mulatto
elite in America" (Williamson 147).

Like most other members of the aristocracy of color, Pinchback
exhibited contradictory attitudes toward the lower classes of blacks.
On the one hand, his commitment to racial uplift was evinced in
his decision to enter political life on behalf of his people. Indeed,
Pinchback—with his light complexion, Creole wife, and substantial
fortune—had the option to live his life as a white man; as W. E. B.
Du Bois noted, the New Orleans aristocrat "[t]o all intents and purposes . . . was an educated well-to-do congenial white man with but
a few drops of negro blood" (qtd. in Rankin 427). On the other
hand, Pinchback was not above categorizing the masses of blacks
in terms at times indistinguishable from those used by white rac-
ists. As he wrote in 1912 to a friend with reference to his disappointment at many blacks' continuing allegiance to Theodore
Roosevelt, "Lincoln made a mistake when he freed the mass of niggers" (qtd. in Gatewood 170). Toomer came from an environment
where "nigger" was not a term connoting relaxed familiarity but a
carrier of distinctly denigrating class and racial overtones.

Toomer's mature attitude toward the privilege of his early years
was ambivalent. Some of his comments exhibit a dispassionate
objectivity. His grandfather, he remarked in his autobiographical
writings of the 1930s, had possessed "ideals and aims for his children" that were "similar to those of most ruling-class Americans of
his time" (Turner 26). Toomer himself experienced "feeling [like] a
member of the upper class, the governing class, the aristocracy"
(TP, Box 19, Folder 501). Although the Bacon Street house was in a
white neighborhood and Toomer passed the first six or seven years
of his life "as a white boy" (TP, Box 19, Folder 500), families such as
the Francises and the Terrells, who occupied the top of the "blue
vein" pyramid, were "friends of the family" (TP, Box 19, Folder 498).
Passing his high school years in the relaxed and privileged atmosphere of M Street High School, with evening river cruises on the
Potomac and what he called "lyric interludes at Harper's Ferry and
Arundel" (Turner 88), Toomer enjoyed a comfortable life. His youthful teenage friends among Washington's black aristocracy "had
simply not been imprinted" with racial consciousness, Toomer concluded. "They lived within their own world, not on the antagonistic
periphery of it where clashes are most likely to occur. (Even with a
race riot going on, the deep centers of both groups can be quite

calm.). . . . They seldom or never came in contact with members of the white group in any way that would make them racially self-conscious" (Turner 86). Writing to Frank in 1922, Toomer viewed his family's decline as part of a broad sociological phenomenon: "[T]he old families that rose to prominence after the Civil War are passing [and] [o]thers, commercialized and social climbing, are taking their place" (Toomer to Frank, 26 April 1922, Frank Papers, Box 23, Part I).[4]

At times, however, a certain lingering pride in his elite origins emerges from Toomer's retrospective descriptions:

> In the Washington of those days—and those days have gone now—there was a flowering of a natural but transient aristocracy, thrown up by the, for them, creative conditions of the post-war period. These people, whose racial strains were mixed and for the most part unknown, happened to find themselves in the colored group. They had a personal refinement, a certain inward culture and beauty, a warmth of feeling such as I have seldom encountered elsewhere or again. . . .
>
> Those of my new friends who became my best friends were, in a racial sense, no different from the boys and girls I had known in white groups. They behaved as American youths of that age and class behave. . . . They were my kind, as much as the children of my early Washington years had been. (Turner 85)

Toomer's characterization of Washington's black elite as a aristocracy, possessing "personal refinement" and "inward culture and beauty," as well as his assertion that his peers from this group were "my kind," suggest that—as both experiencing youth and contemplative man—Toomer to a degree associated privilege with merit.

Toomer's struggles with the ambiguity of his own racial appearance—which many scholars see as formative of his complex attitudes toward race—are thus inseparable from his consciousness of his inherited class position. His adolescent decision to "say nothing [about his racial identity] unless the question was raised" produced "outraged . . . feelings" in the young Toomer. The reason for this outrage, however, was that he felt threatened that his "aristocracy might be invaded," as he confessed: "I might be called to question by louts, white, black or any other color" (Turner 93). What is noteworthy here is not so much Toomer's ambivalence about how he should define his racial identity—the point most commonly noted by biographers and critics—as the peculiar admixture of antiracism and snobbery on Toomer's part. Not only does he claim to belong to

---

4. It is not clear in Toomer's comment whether he means "passing" in the sense of going out of existence or of racial passing. In this context the two meanings overlap somewhat.

an "aristocracy"; he refers to "my aristocracy" almost as an intrinsic feature of his make-up.

That such elitist attitudes characterized not just the retrospective Toomer of the 1930s but also the Toomer of the *Cane* period is evidenced by the following comment in the memorandum book that Toomer apparently carried around with him in Georgia:

> Familiarity, in most people, indicates not a sentiment of comradeship, an emotion of brotherhood, but simply a lack of respect and reverence tempered by the unkindly . . . desire to level down whatever is above them, to assert their own puny egos at whatever damage to those fragile tissues of elevation which constitute the worthwhile meshes of our civilization. (n.d., Memorandum Book, TP, Box 60, Folder 1410)

It is the scion of Bacon Street who here bemoans the "level[ing]" threat posed by "familiarity" to the "fragile tissues of elevation" that presumably hold society together.[5]

It would be one-sided, however, to view Toomer's only legacy from Washington's black elite as a nostalgia tinged with snobbery. For the Negro aristocracy's activist tradition was also part of his inheritance. While Toomer's autobiographical writings are, Estes-Hicks notes, silent on the heady atmosphere at M Street School, it is difficult to believe that during his high school years Toomer was not affected by the debate there over the relative merits of Du Bois's and Washington's approaches to education—especially since Pinchback was closely aligned with Washington and put him up regularly when the educator came to the capital city on business (71). That Toomer kept in touch with some of his M Street mentors, moreover, is demonstrated by his participation with various former and current M Street faculty—along with members of the Howard University community—in a study group that Toomer himself helped to organize in 1921. Refuting the commonly held notion that Toomer cut his artistic teeth among the white modernist crowd clustered in Greenwich Village, George Hutchinson has recently demonstrated that, during several months preceding the fall 1921 trip to Sparta that inspired most of *Cane*, as well as during several months after his return, Toomer's intellectual and political development was significantly shaped by his interaction with Alain Locke, Georgia Douglas Johnson, and other figures frequently associated with the "Harlem" Renaissance. Indeed, Hutchinson argues in "Jean Toomer and the 'New Negroes' of Washington," Toomer's theory that "Americans" were the products of racial admixtures and that the categories of

---

5. The memorandum book can be dated from the early *Cane* period because it contains fragments of some of the lyrics appearing in *Cane*. See below, Note 9.

"black" and "white" belie the nation's sociological complexity cannot be understood apart from the collective discourse over race in which this largely "blue-veined" study group engaged.[6]

Also noteworthy about the Washington writers group is that they engaged in a study of slavery and the economics of racism. As Toomer noted to Locke in January 1921, the group was hearing reports on T. R. R. Cobb's *Historical Sketch of Slavery*, "Twenty Years of an African Slaver" and "the same subject dug mostly out of Wells"— presumably H. G. Wells's *An Outline of History*, published in 1920 (26 January 1921, LP, Box 164–90, Folder 12). A number of texts produced by writers in the group addressed racial violence, featuring the 1919 race riots and various recent lynching incidents. Indeed, Toomer's fictional portrait of the grotesque lynching of Mary Turner (who is called Mame Lamkins in the "Kabnis" section of *Cane*) was predated by portraits of the Turner murder by Carrie Clifford and Angelina Grimké, both writers associated with the group (R. Johnson 489; Hull 129–31). Conventional as some of them may have been in their literary tastes and in their guiding conception of racial uplift, the members of the Washington writers group—particularly, it would seem, the women—insistently focused upon the oppression endured by the black masses. Toomer was to a degree biting that hand that had fed him when he complained in 1922 that his work was "growing . . . [d]espite the inhibitions of Washington, despite my absolute lack of anything like creative friendship" (Toomer to Frank, 24 March 1922, FP).[7]

6. In a January 1921 letter to Alain Locke, Toomer listed as the participants in the first two meetings of the group: poet Georgia Douglas Johnson (who was married to Henry Lincoln Johnson); Clarissa Scott (later Delany), daughter of Emmett Scott, Booker T. Washington biographer and Howard University administrator; Mary P. Burrill, playwright; E. C. Williams, former teacher at M Street School and head of Howard's Library School; Mary Craft, a descendant of the famous abolitionists and slave autobiographers William and Ellen Craft; and his friend of many years, Henry Kennedy. Angelina Grimké—also a former M Street English teacher—is not listed among the participants, but, given the tangency of her interests with those of Toomer, Johnson, and Clifford in the early 1920s, it is difficult to believe she did not attend at least some of the meetings. Jessie Redmon Fauset also is not listed among the participants. That she knew Toomer him quite well, however, is indicated by familiar references to Toomer in a later letter from Fauset to Johnson in 1924 (22 September 1924, Johnson Papers, Box 162-1, Folder 32). Johnson's informal Saturday Night salon, dubbed the "Saturday Nighters," which emerged as the focal point of the capital's black intellectual activity in the mid- to late twenties— involving such well-known figures as Fauset, Zora Neale Hurston, Marita Bonner, Hughes, and Bruce Nugent—clearly grew out of the early efforts of the 1920–22 discussion group that Toomer helped to found.
7. Toomer's letters to Georgia Douglas Johnson from New York in 1920 reveal a lonely young man writing to a mentor/mother figure whose support he greatly needs (especially 20 February 1920, 4 March 1920, and 4 June 1920, Johnson Papers, Box 162-2, Folder 9). He also generously praises her work in these letters: "I read your lines and I swear that as love lyrics aiming not at the rhythmic . . . virtuosities of the genius but at the true expression of emotion and feeling filtered thru the imagination they come nearer my heart than anything I've read. Send me more" (4 March 1920). Such comments contrast with his condescending comments to John McClure about Johnson's poetry two years later: "[Johnson's] faculty of expression is not up to her sensibilities.

While Toomer was clearly affected by the strains of progressivism among Washington's black elite, at least as important to his thinking about racial oppression and class stratification, I would contend, was his short-lived but deeply influential experience with the U.S. socialist movement. Toomer's biographers routinely treat his contact with left-wing ideas as a mere youthful flirtation, quickly ended by exposure to the "real" proletariat during his ten-day experience working among pipefitters in a New Jersey shipyard in 1919 (Kerman and Eldridge 71; McKay 45). But Toomer's biographers omit from their bibliographies of Toomer's works two articles published in 1919 in the *The New York Call*, organ of the Socialist Party in New York—even though these articles reveal a Toomer directing both lyrical and analytical powers toward the articulation of an unmistakably left-wing analysis of U. S. society.[8]

In the first, a June 1919 piece entitled "Ghouls," Toomer creates a grotesque parable in which "war profiteers," with "[full] cheeks" and "eyes glow[ing] with the light of conquest," sweep into coffers coins borne in by slaves—"coins of all shapes and sizes. . . . coins stained with the tears of children, wrung from the breasts of mothers . . . red and gory with the blood of men." The slaves, first driven from the room while the "masters . . . divide the spoil," finally "with a peculiar light in their eyes . . . stalk in and place upon the table a bundle." The tale ends on a note combining Gothicism with proletarian didacticism: "The profiteers, mindful only of the treat before them, ripped open the bag and grabbed at its contents. But they recoiled, afraid, for they had touched there the hearts of men" ("Ghouls" 3). That Toomer chose not to assign his slaves a particular racial designation implies an analysis here of slavery as wage-slavery; the only significant colors in the sketch are red and gold. While couched in the mythic idiom of parable, "Ghouls" offers a biting Marxist critique of the historically specific phenomenon of capitalist profiteering during World War I.

The second *New York Call* article, an August 1919 piece entitled "Reflections on the Race Riots," shows Toomer viewing the phenomenon of U. S. racism from an explicitly Marxist standpoint. Applaud-

---

Nor is she sufficiently conscious, I do not think she ever will be. The inhibitions and taboos and life-limitations she labors under make even her modest achievement remarkable" (22 July 1922, TP, Box 2, Folder 46). For a portrait of Johnson as the matron/intellectual center of the Washington New Negro movement, see Stewart. For more on this movement as a precursor to the Harlem Renaissance, see Moses. Carrie Clifford's tribute to Mary Turner is contained in her poem "Little Mother (Upon the Lynching of Mary Turner)." Grimké addressed the Turner murder four times: in "Blackness," "The Waitin'," "The Creaking," and "Goldie" (Hull 129–31; Grimké 218–51, 282–306). For abiding conservative elements in the discussion group, however, see Note 4, below. For more on Toomer's treatment of Turner, see Foley, "Georgia on My Mind."
8. For the bibliographical citation of the *New York Call* articles, I am indebted to Estes-Hicks's unpublished dissertation (134).

ing Washington's black population for its militancy in resisting racist violence, Toomer notes, "[i]t now confronts the nation, so voluble in acclamation of the democratic ideal, so reticent in applying what it professes, to either extend to the Negro (and other workers) the essentials of a democratic commonwealth or else exist from day to day never knowing when a clash may occur, in the light of which the Washington riot will diminish and pale. . . . This is essentially a time for action"(8). Clearly Toomer views black oppression as a form of proletarian oppression and sees the race riot as a possible presage of large-scale insurrectionary class violence. If only because it offers a view of Toomer's politics so different from what one has come to expect, the article's analysis of the material basis of racism is worth quoting at length:

> In the literature of the Socialist movement in this country there is to be found a rational explanation of the causes of race hatred, and in the light of these, a definite solution, striking at the very root of the evil, is proposed. It is generally established that the causes of race prejudice may primarily be found in the economic structure that compels one worker to compete against another and that furthermore renders it advantageous for the exploiting classes to inculcate, foster, and aggravate that competition. If this be true, then it follows that the nucleus of race co-operation lies in the substitution of a socialized community for a competitive one. To me, it appears that nothing less than just such an economic readjustment will ever bring concord to the two races; for, as long as there are governing classes and as long as these classes feel it to their gain to keep the masses in constant conflict, just so long will a controlled press and educational system incite and promote race hatred. Where there is advantage to be secured by racial antagonism, heaven and hell will be invoked to that purpose. Demagogues may storm and saints may plead; but America will remain a grotesque storm-center torn by passion and hatred until our democratic pretensions are replaced by a socialised reality. (8)

Toomer may not have become an active organizer for the working-class movement or continued writing for the *Call*. But clearly in 1919 he adhered to a class analysis of the structural underpinning of racism in the capitalist economy and advocated socialist revolution as the only plausible solution to the problems of racial oppression and working-class division.[9]

9. While Toomer came into contact with Socialists in Chicago in 1918, he may also have been influenced by the pro-socialist cast of Du Bois's thought at this time. Du Bois published several editorials quite favorable to socialism in the *Crisis* in 1920–21, and in his *Darkwater: Voices from Within the Veil* declared, "Whether known as Communism or Socialism or what not, these efforts are neither new nor strange nor terrible, but world-old and seeking an absolutely justifiable human ideal—the only ideal that can be sought: the direction of individual action in industry so as to secure the greatest good of

Toomer's interest in left-wing ideas did not perish when he abandoned the pipefitters; when he was writing and publishing *Cane* three years later, Toomer was still expressing unambiguously radical sentiments. He wrote to publisher Horace Liveright in 1923 that his next book would treat "this whole black and brown world heaving upward against, here and there mixing with the white. The mixture, however, is insufficient to absorb the heaving, hence it but accelerates and fires it. This upward heaving is to be symbolic of the proletariat or world upheaval. And it is likewise to be symbolic of the subconscious penetration of the conscious mind" (9 March 1923, TP, Box 1, Folder 16). In his *Cane*-period journal, Toomer predicted the tragedy that would result if black anger were to find a non-class-conscious outlet: "If the workers could bellow, 'We Want Power,' the walls of capitalism would collapse. They are as yet too weak for that. . . . If the Negro, consolidated on race rather than class interests, ever becomes strong enough to demand the exercise of Power, a race war will occur in America" (TP, Box 60, Folder 1411). At this time, moreover, Toomer saw his own writing as part of a project of class emancipation, for he somewhat apocalyptically noted that "[i]t is evidence of weakness that men like myself are not forced into the service of the governing class, or exiled, or murdered" (TP, Box 60, Folder 1411). While such comments exude a somewhat sophomoric idealism and hardly establish Toomer as a card-carrying leftist, they indicate that he, like many cultural radicals of the 1920s, saw no contradiction between psychic awakening, racial militancy, and class insurrection. The Toomer who wished to safeguard the "fragile tissues of elevation" was also drawn toward social and political movements that would abolish elevation altogether.[1]

---

all" (138). Du Bois's fable "The Princess of the Hither Isles," with its fairy-tale style and its apocalyptic imagery of hearts torn from the bodies of the oppressed, may also have been an influence on Toomer when he wrote "Ghouls" (75–80). ("The Princess of the Hither Isles" appeared in *Darkwater* in 1920 but was first published in the *Crisis* in 1913.) Angelina Grimké, through her association with the *Birth Control Review*, was also in close touch with both Socialists and Communists in the early 1920s (see Mary Knoblauch to Grimké, 25 May 1920, Grimké Papers, Box 38–1, Folder 10, and Gertrude Nafe to Grimké, 28 October 1920, Grimké Papers, Box 38–1, Folder 13).

1. Toomer's statements on politics are as contradictory as those on racial identity. Kerman and Eldridge and McKay base their contentions that Toomer rejected the left on the oft-quoted statement from his unpublished autobiography that his experience among the pipefitters led him to the realization that socialism "was for people like Shaw and Sidney Webb. . . . But as for working for a betterment in the lives of the proletariat, this was a pipe dream possible only to those who had never really experienced the proletariat" (Turner 111–12,). But this cynical assessment was countered by a continual acknowledgement of the grounding of racism in capitalist exploitation. That Toomer had a stronger focus on class in mind in early drafts of *Cane* than in the published version is suggested by the rough (and not completely legible) version of "Reapers" appearing in his *Cane*-period memorandum book:

> Black workmen with the sound of steel on stone
> Are sharpening scythes they swing them through the reeds
> Mules pulling a mowing machine fills [*sic*]?
> A rat with belly close to ground
> A ? machine. (TP, Box 60, Folder 1410)

Two of Toomer's early 1920s imaginative texts that are set in the
nation's capital are significantly illuminated when considered in
the context of the author's contradictory attitudes toward class. In
"Withered Skin of Berries," the central dilemma of the tale's light-
skinned government-worker protagonist, Vera, stems largely from
her inability to acknowledge the yearnings of both body and spirit:
like Esther of *Cane* and others among Toomer's "high yellow" characters, both female and male, she suffers from severe sexual repression and emotional alienation. Vera's struggle for racial and sexual
self-knowledge is mapped by her choice among three suitors—her
white coworker Carl, the dark-skinned Art, and the light-skinned
poet-rebel David Teyy (clearly an honorific portrait of Toomer himself). But the tale's construction of its protagonist's search for identity is located amidst the constrictions imposed upon Vera by racial
discrimination in a workplace where an admission of her racial
identity would entail dismissal or at least transfer to another work-
site. It is thus a tale quite specifically commenting on the impact of
Wilsonian segregation upon Washington's "blue veins." Read in
this context, the tale's continual reversion to the picturesque Lover's
Leap at Harper's Ferry—which Vera visits with each of her suitors—
takes on added significance. Vera's suicidal urge to plunge into the
Potomac and "cross over into camp ground" is countered by David's
plea that she envision the river as the still-flowing blood of John
Brown: the resolution to individual fear, urges David/Toomer, rests
in activist resistance to racism. Whether Vera will accede or comply

---

The published version of the poem makes no mention of a "machine" and substitutes
the words "reapers" for "workmen" and "Black horses" for "Mules." Elements of a class
analysis of racism persist into Toomer's later writings, both unpublished and published. In an undated journal entry apparently from the 1930s, Toomer mused, "Under
the cult of things—men must be treated as things. The upper class attitudes today
toward the workers. Any upper class man, who considers the workers as human beings,
is considered enemy to class, because he violates the code upon which it is founded"
(TP, Box 65, Folder 1484). In "Race Problems and Modern Society" (1928), Toomer
commented,

> There are no such things as innate racial antipathies. We are not born with them.
> Either we acquire them from our environment, or else we do not have them at
> all. . . . There is no need to present new facts to support the statement that race
> problems are closely associated with our economic and political systems. . . . It is
> well known that whenever two or more races (or nationalities) meet in conditions
> that are mainly determined by acquisitive interests, race problems arise as by prod-
> ucts [sic] of economic issues. The desire for land, the wish to exploit natural
> resources, the wish for cheap labor—wherever these motives have dominated a situ-
> ation involving different races, whether the races are set in rivalry, or with one
> dominant and the other dominated, race problems also have sprung up. (81–89)

In another undated essay, Toomer combined a spiritualist concern with the psychic
effects of racist "binding" with a materialist formulation of racism as a "force" acting
on black and white alike from without:

> Negro and white or whoever is so held, both feel that they are being held to their
> detriment. Both feel the damaging effects of the binding force. But neither, of
> course, understand [sic] that it is precisely a force that is holding them. Therefore
> they do not and indeed cannot truly get together to overcome their common enemy.
> No, each separatistically [sic] blames the other. . . . Oppose the force, not the man.
> (Rusch 111)

with the constraints of her world is thus signalled by her attitude toward Harper's Ferry: is it a leisured site for middle-class romantic dalliances or a historic reminder of the continuing necessity for struggle? If we do not keep in mind the status of Harper's Ferry as a vacation spot favored by the "Negro Four Hundred" of Washington, the tale's strategic use of setting is rendered opaque, indeed unreadable.[2]

In *Natalie Mann*, Toomer's play about the quest for liberation from the strictures of bourgeois black society undertaken by a number of young black intellectuals and artists, Toomer's portraiture of Washington's "blue veins" is sharp and satiric. Mary Carson—a figure based on the actual sculptor of the same name who participated in the meetings of the Washington artists' group (Toomer to Frank, 26 April 1922, FP, Box 23, Part I)—is the play's principal representative of the intellectual pretensions and moral shortcomings of the capital city's would-be intelligentsia. In response to Carson's contention that "we are an intelligent section [of the colored people]" whose duty it is to "combat materialism with our own God-given weapons," the intrepid Mervis Newbolt responds, "Thats all very nice, Mrs. Carson, but dont you think there are more immediate problems which we ought to clear up first. . . . Lynching and Jim-Crowism, for example?" (Turner 258). While some critics have contended that, through Carson and her associates, Toomer is offering a satirical representation of the study group to which he himself belonged (Hutchinson 685; Estes-Hicks 215), Jeffrey Stewart is correct, I think, to point out that the broader target of Toomer's lampoon is the "aggressively assimilationist bourgeois society of Washington" (39). The intellectuals featured in *Natalie Mann* bear a stronger resemblance to "blue vein" cultural groups such as the Mu-So-Litt derided by Chase than to Toomer's study-group companions. Moreover, most members of the self-consciously "cultured" group portrayed in *Natalie Mann* do not evince the awareness of past and present racial violence that appears to have set the tone for Toomer's discussions with his colleagues.

Toomer's ambivalent attitudes toward his position of class privilege emerge in his doubled portrayal of himself in *Natalie Mann*. He clearly projects himself in the play's rebellious middle-class hero, Nathan Merilh, who is, Toomer noted to Frank, "mostly myself" (Toomer to Frank, 26 April 1922, FP, Box 23, Part I). But he also projects a part of himself in the character of the working-class Tome Mangrow, who says of Nathan, "Aint he got dictie airs? . . . . Aint he had easy times and nose-bags always full? Aint he got clean sheets

2. Toomer wrote to Frank in July 1922 that, in his "last piece," he had "made partial use . . . of the opportunity for a vivid symbolism" in Harper's Ferry as a literary setting (Toomer to Frank, 19 July 1922, FP, Box 23, Part I). For more on racial discourse in this story, see Christensen and Hutchinson, "American Racial Discourse."

and a soft bed to tuck into tonight? Wher'd they all come from? And what is he going to do with them? Steal an rob, an pay the police to protect his stealing?" (279). Nathan's rejoinder projects his creator's divided estimate of his class inheritance. Unabashedly remarking that he has been "fortunate in wealth but still more fortunate in disposition, energy, and point of view," Nathan contends that his money has been "maliciously hostile" to his talents:

> I have had to fight through. Money would have made me like my father. Education would have made me believe as all the upper classes do. My sole obligation would have been to preserve, to increase, what an all-wise God in His unfailing charity and beneficence had given me. Those who didnt have, werent supposed to have. Else He'd have given it to them. (280)

Toomer's uncertain irony in characterizing Nathan renders his hero's proclamation somewhat disingenuous: Nathan's repudiation of his tainted patrimony is partial at best. Nonetheless, through Mertis, Nathan, and Tome, Toomer clearly offers a sharp critique of the elite's complacency—a complacency unambiguously based in their exploitative relation to the masses. Composed at the same time he was writing *Cane, Natalie Mann* reveals that Toomer was highly critical of his inherited social status as a scion of Bacon Street—even if he also found it hard to suppress a certain pride in the anguished self-awareness that this very class position had made possible for him.[3]

Above all, however, *Cane* takes on important new dimensions when read in the light of Toomer's conflicting class loyalties. Critics have frequently noted that the second part of *Cane*, which is set primarily in Washington, D.C., offers a sardonic commentary on a mechanized, commodified, and alienated urban setting. The portraiture of human possibility here is seen by some critics to contrast dramatically with the representation of an unalienated and sexually unrepressed—if materially oppressed—Georgia peasantry in the text's opening section (Reckley; Hollis; Schultz). Toomer himself described to Frank his intentions in the second part of *Cane* in the lyrical and organicist terms that characterize many of his statements about his own work: "I am trying to grasp Washington. Not as

---

3. Toomer, who was fond of playing games with names, may have chosen the name "Tome Mangrow" not only for the obvious valorization implied in the surname but also for the resemblance to his own surname in the character's given name. "Nathan" was, moreover, both the name of Toomer's father and Toomer's own first name at birth (his full birthname was Nathan Eugene Toomer). Raised in the Pinchback household where the name of Toomer's father was never mentioned, Toomer was called "Eugene Pinchback" as a child. He took the name "Jean Toomer" soon before writing *Cane* and started calling himself "Nathan Eugene Toomer" once again in middle age. To propose that Tome and Nathan are doubles obviously signifies on both textual and extratextual levels.

a cut and dried something to intellectualize, remember, and write about, but as a vital, living feature of my consciousness. I do not wish it to have the objective validity that smacks of the thin truth of most 'historical' novels. I want it to be something that comes to birth in me" (Toomer to Frank, 5 May 1922, FP, Box 23, Part I). Despite Toomer's stated antipathy to the "thin truth" of historical mimesis, however, his success in "grasp[ing] Washington" as a "vital, living feature of [his] consciousness" did to a significant degree derive from his creation of a portrait possessing "objective validity." Part Two of *Cane* cannot be fully understood without reference to its historically specific depiction of the heightening of both race and class contradictions in the world of Toomer's young manhood.

"Bona and Paul," for example, gains a crucial historical dimension when read as a commentary not simply on its light-skinned hero's dilemma of racial identification but also on the increasing segregation of public facilities in the world in which Toomer attained maturity. While this tale is *not* set in Washington—as are all the other Part II sketches—but in Chicago, it is plausible to assume that the job of the black doorman at the Crimson Gardens, like that of doormen in the nation's capital, entails spotting light-skinned blacks seeking entry into the club. "As he swings the door for [Bona and Paul]," after all, the doorman's eyes "are knowing" (78) [77].[4] Read in the context of the heightening of Jim Crow in the postwar period, "Bona and Paul" thus portrays a young man eager not only to validate his personal integrity, both racial and sexual, but also to defy segregation. "I came back to tell you, brother, that white faces are petals of roses. That dark faces are petals of dusk," remarks Paul to the doorman, "That I am going out and gather petals" (78) [77]. Paul's confession to the doorman—which costs him Bona—is perhaps less immature and gratuitous than is often supposed, for it will probably guarantee his future exclusion from the club his white friends like to frequent. Composed at a time when Washington's Negro aristocrats were smarting from the recent lash of Wilsonian segregation, "Bona and Paul" articulates not so much the young Toomer's ambivalent racial identification as his profound resentment of the increasingly oppressive social practices making such identification a necessity.[5]

In "Avey," too, the situation of the autobiographical narrator gains in significance when put in the context of Toomer's youthful experiences in black elite Washington. The nameless hero is first taken into Avey's arms during a Potomac river cruise similar to the excursions Toomer used to enjoy with his friends in the fashionable young

4. Page numbers in square brackets refer to this Norton Critical Edition.
5. "Bona and Paul" was the first piece written for *Cane*; it was probably composed in 1919 (Kerman and Eldridge 69).

set. The hero is next drawn to Avey at Harpers Ferry, where his family—again, like Toomer's—passes its summer vacation. The two characters' adolescent romance is thus enabled by their common class backgrounds. When five years later the narrator reencounters Avey and finds that she has become a prostitute, however, he is inclined to attribute Avey's choice of vocation to her indolent sensuality—even though it is more likely that her family was one of those on the fringes of black bourgeois society that could not keep their educated but unemployable daughters from drifting into the *demi-monde*. That he has himself been working in a shipyard and "hik[ing] and bumm[ing]" (45) [47] between New York and Washington—hardly activities of a youth of secure bourgeois status, though similar to those of the young wandering Toomer in 1919—simply evinces his blindness to the fact that Avey's declassing has just been gendered differently from his own. The narrator's smug approach to Avey is thus inseparable from a sense of class privilege that his gender has permitted him to retain:

> I have a spot in Solder's Home to which I always go when I want the simple beauty of another's soul. . . . I know the policeman who watches the place of nights . . . I tell him that I do not come there with a girl to do the thing he's paid to watch out for. I look deep in his eyes when I say these things, and he believes me. . . . (46) [47]

Where Paul feels obliged to explain himself to the doorman with the knowing eyes, the "Avey" narrator clearly has the servant classes under control.

Toomer's portrayal of the egocentric young male artist in "Avey" has an irreducible class component.

> I traced my development from the early days up to the present time, the phase in which I could understand her. I described her own nature and temperament. Told her how they needed a larger life for their expression. How incapable Washington was of understanding that need . . . I pointed out that in lieu of proper channels, her emotions had overflowed into paths that dissipated them. I talked, beautifully, I thought, about an art that would be born, an art that would open the way for women like her. (46) [48]

In commentaries on this passage critics have routinely focused on Toomer's satiric representation of the self-absorbed male who at once displaces his own sexual urges onto Avey's "nature and temperament" while reducing her to an object of aesthetic contemplation (Blake 203–204; Hollis; Doyle 99–100). Equally as important as the narrator's gendered portraiture, however, is his confident representation of himself as a self-appointed judge of "Washington's" incapacity to understand Avey's supposed need for fuller self-expression. For "Washington" here metonymically signifies not the metropolis itself, but that segment of its population that the narrator considers significant—namely, its culturally conservative elite. Toomer's early 1920s letters to Alain Locke and Waldo Frank contain similar references to the inhibiting and stultifying effect of "Washington" upon the artistic temperament. Treated, like Nathan Merilh of *Natalie Mann*, with an uncertain degree of irony, the narrator in "Avey" simultaneously criticizes the cultural shallowness and sexual repressiveness of his class and asserts his ambivalent identification with that class.[6]

More than any of the sketches in Part II of *Cane*, however, the prose poem "Seventh Street" requires a dramatic reinterpretation when read as a gloss on the racial demographics of the nation's capital. The area around Seventh Street—the center of working-class Washington and a magnet for newly migrated blacks from the South—is not a part of the city that Toomer is likely to have frequented as a child or youth. It was to Seventh Street, we will recall, that Hughes fled in order to escape the "blue veins." But when Toomer spoke of how his family's circle inhabited a "deep center" distant from the race riots, he was referring to more than the geographical or even the cultural distance between Seventh Street and the more secluded neighborhood further west and north where his family had lived. For Seventh Street had furnished the hub of the 1919 race riot about which Toomer had written in the *New York Call*. It was at the Knights of Columbus hut at the corner of Seventh Street and Pennsylvania Avenue that the ex-servicemen had started the riot; it was at the corner of Seventh and T Streets that the arms delivered from Baltimore to Washington's black community had been distributed (C. Green 191–94). Several of the sites designated in the *Bee* as flashpoints of racial violence had been along Seventh Street (*Bee* 26 July 1919), which the *New York Times* had in fact referred to as the riot's "bloodfield" (L. Williams 40).

"Seventh Street," as critics have frequently pointed out, is in part a modernist and primitivist celebration of working-class black culture—"a crude-boned, soft-skinned wedge of nigger life. . . . thrusting unconscious rhythms, black reddish blood into the white and whitewashed wood of Washington. Donald Petesch notes, "[The newly migrated blacks'] energy and vitality, their flowing blood, is placed in opposition to the white world of Washington, a fixed world

---

6. In an undated letter to Frank, Toomer, quoting Alain Locke, observed, "Washington is stagnation" (n.d., FP, Box 23, Part I). For an astute discussion of the relation of gender to class in another of Cane's urban sketches, see Flowers.

of place, of old structures and old possessions" (201; see also North). Toomer himself wrote to Frank that "[The life of Seventh Street and Theatre] is jazzed, strident, modern. Seventh Street is the song of crude new life. Of a new people" (n.d., TP, Box 3, Folder 83). But while the sketch articulates in part the popular modernist view of blacks as the irrepressible id of civilized society, it also assails the state-sponsored violence of the government and the impotence of the "blue veins." "Seventh Street" plays upon both literal and figurative associations of its central image of flowing blood: "Blood suckers of the war would spin in a frenzy of dizziness if they drank your blood. Prohibition would put a stop to it. Who set you flowing? White and whitewash disappear in blood. Who set you flowing? Flowing down the smooth asphalt of Seventh Street, in shanties, brick office buildings, theaters, drug stores, restaurants, and cabarets? Eddying on the corners?" (39) [41]. The prose expressionistically treats "black reddish blood" as the return of the repressed, countering the puritanism of Prohibition with the uninhibited energy of the culture of the Southern migrants. But the "black reddish blood" also is said to cause a fearful "dizziness" among the cannibalistic "blood suckers of the war" who imbibe it—a dramatic conceit that recalls the dominant trope of Toomer's 1919 portraiture of war profiteers in "Ghouls." Above all, however, the almost surrealistic imagery of blood flowing through the streets quite naturalistically refers to the blood that was indeed let in the "bloodfield" that was Seventh Street; significantly, the blood in Toomer's sketch flows in "eddies" not just around the sites of leisure— cabarets, restaurants, theaters—but also around those of work, commerce, and domicile—office buildings, drug stores, shanties. The commonplace critical reading of this image as an expression of primitivist *élan vital* misses the urgency of Toomer's historical mimesis. He is linking the war overseas with the war at home.

Furthermore, Toomer's pairing of "white" with "whitewash" invites the reader to view the marble white of the capital's buildings—the Lincoln Memorial dedicated before a segregated audience in 1922, the White House and Capitol between which racist mobs had rampaged in 1919—as symbolic of the nation's hypocritical refusal to extend democratic rights to all its citizens. Toomer had offered just such a judgment of governmental duplicity four years before in "Reflections on the Race Riots," when he lamented that a nation "so voluble in acclamation of the democratic ideal" was "so reticent in applying what it professes" (8). The pairing of "white" and "whitewash" further suggests, however, an ironic equation between the complacency of the Negro elite—whom Toomer referred to on at least one occasion as "whitewash"—and the callousness of the ruling-class whites whose mode of existence the Negro aristocrats so sedulously emulated. The term "whitewash" thus refers not only to governmental racism but also to the complicity of the "blue veined" elite who inhabit their "deep center" away from the heart of the race riot. Even though the celebration of "nigger life" in "Seventh Street" smacks of a certain patronizing romanticism, it is noteworthy that Toomer here repudiates his grandfather's denigrating use of the term "nigger" and announces his allegiance to the black proletarian masses who had undertaken the first major urban resistance to racial violence in the nation's history. "Seventh Street" announces a partisanship that is at once cultural and political.[7]

The omission of any serious consideration of class in most Toomer criticism has divested Toomer's work of a crucial social and historical dimension. In part the blame for this distortion can be laid upon Toomer himself, whose comments about his own writing tended to stress its mythic, lyrical, and transhistorical qualities—that is, those features that have subsequently come to be seen as definitive of high modernism. In part, however, the stripping away of history from Toomer's early texts—most crucially affecting *Cane*—has been carried out by critics approaching Toomer through the lens of a high modernist a priori. That is, seeking a representation largely untrammeled by specific historical reference, many Toomer critics have, not unsurprisingly, discovered such a representation. This high modernist a priori has frequently been compounded by an anti-Marxist a priori which posits that writers' left-wing commitments—unless codified and repeatedly articulated as explicit doctrine—should not be taken especially seriously. Such a premise conveniently prevents scholars from asking the questions that would enable them to uncover those primary texts that would refute the premise—in Toomer's case, the almost universally neglected 1919 writings published in the *New York Call*. The resurrection of these writings does not require us to conclude that Toomer "really was" a radical after all; as I have been suggesting, Toomer's class politics were as contradictory as his racial politics. But these writings—as well as the multiple references to social stratification throughout Toomer's

7. In a 1922 letter to Frank, Toomer contrasted the "shanty [church] of the peasant Negro," where the worshippers manifest a "religious emotion, elemental, very near the sublime," with the "whitewashed article of respectable colored folk" (Toomer to Frank, 21 August 1922, FP, Box 23, Part I). Toomer's running battle with the conservatism of "blue-veined" Washington is reflected in an exchange over "Seventh Street" between himself and Mary Burrill, a participant in the Toomer-initiated discussion group and member of one of the leading families in the "Negro 400." Burrill wrote Toomer a somewhat frosty note in which she faulted Toomer's grammar in the sketch and commented that it "remains wrong because of the premise from which you start. The place has changed only in *kind* not in degree. It has always been the rendez-vous of the shiftless Negro with his pockets full of ill-gotten gains." Toomer replied huffily, "You missed the change, the sudden influx of life into [Seventh Street] as a result of prohibition and the war. . . . If you were to experience the inner life of Seventh Street you would appreciate my contrast even more" (TP, Box 1, Folder 22).

portraiture of Washington society—require us to adjust the lenses through which we read his work.

The obfuscation of social and historical references in *Cane* and other early 1920s Toomer texts has also been enabled, moreover, by the dominant critical tendency to decouple race from class—or, in commentary acknowledging their interrelation, to assert that this relation is conjunctural rather than dialectical. Even analyses that reject essentialist notions of race and read Toomer as a racial deconstructionist *avant la lettre* ordinarily treat "race" itself as a largely autonomous—if highly mediated and socially constructed—phenomenon. What is revealed in Toomer's autobiographical, dramatic, journalistic, and fictional writings of the period beginning in 1919 and extending up to the 1930s, however, is that his conceptualization of American racial discourses and practices was profoundly shaped by his awareness of class—not only as a set of subject positions but also as a set of social relations and a basis for theorizing those social relations. We have recently been reminded that "race matters." Toomer, I believe, would have us remember that "class matters" as well—"matters," indeed, as the "matter" that makes "race" such a persistently agonizing and complex issue in U.S. society and in the texts wherein that society is represented.

### WORKS CITED

Anderson, Jervis. "A Very Special Monument." *New Yorker* 20 Mar. 1978: 93–94, 100–102, 104–108, 110–21.

Anonymous. "'Color Lines' among the Colored People." *Literary Digest* 72 (18 March 1922): 42, 44.

Blake, Susan L. "The Spectatorial Artist and the Structure of *Cane*." *CLA Journal* 17 (1974): 516–34.

Bradley, David. "Looking Behind *Cane*." *Southern Review* 21 (1985): 682–94.

Byrd, Rudolph. "Jean Toomer and the Afro-American Literary Tradition." *Callaloo* 8 (1985): 310–19.

Chase, Hal. "William C. Chase and the Washington Bee." *Negro History Bulletin* 36 (1973): 172–74.

Christensen, Peter. "Sexuality and Liberation in Jean Toomer's 'Withered Skin of Berries.'" *Callaloo* 11 (1988): 616–26.

Clifford, Carrie W. "Little Mother (Upon the Lynching of Mary Turner)." *The Widening Light*. Boston: Walter Reid, 1922. 19–20.

Doyle, Laura. *Bordering on the Body: The Racial Matrix of Modern Fiction and Culture*. New York: Oxford UP, 1994.

Du Bois, W. E. B. *Darkwater: Voices from within the Veil*. New York: Harcourt, Brace and Howe, 1920.

————. *Dusk of Dawn: Essay Toward an Autobiography of a Race Concept.* 1940; rpt. New York: Schocken, 1968.

Dunbar, Paul Laurence. "Negro Life in Washington." *Harper's Weekly* 13 Jan. 1900: 32.

Estes-Hicks, Onita. *Jean Toomer: A Biographical and Critical Study.* Diss. Columbia U, 1982.

Flowers, Sandra Hollin "Solving the Critical Connundrum of Jean Toomer's 'Box Seat.'" *Studies in American Fiction* 25 (1988): 301–305.

Foley, Barbara. "Georgia on My Mind: Economics and History in Jean Toomer's *Cane*." Unpublished Essay.

————. "Jean Toomer's Sparta." *American Literature* #67 (1995): 747–75.

Frank, Waldo. The Waldo Frank Papers. Van Pelt Library, U of Pennsylvania.

Frazier, E. Franklin. *The Negro Family in the United States.* Rev. ed. New York: Dryden, 1951.

Gatewood, Willard B. *Aristocrats of Color: The Black Elite 1880–1920.* Bloomington: Indiana UP, 1990.

Gibson, Donald B. *The Politics of Literary Expression: A Study of Major Black Writers.* Contributions in Afro-American and African Studies, No. 63. Westport, CT: Greenwood P, 1981.

Green, Constance McLaughlin. *The Secret City: A History of Race Relations in the Nation's Capital.* Princeton: Princeton UP, 1967.

Green, Edward S. *National Capital Code of Etiquette.* Washington: Austin Jenkins, 1920.

Grimké, Angelina Weld. *The Angelina Grimké Papers.* Moorland-Springarn Research Center. Howard University.

————. *Selected Works of Angelina Weld Grimké.* Ed. Carolivia Herron. New York: Oxford UP, 1991.

Hackley, E. Azalia, *The Colored Girl Beautiful.* Kansas City, MO: Burton, 1916.

Haskins, James. *Pinckney Benton Stewart Pinchback.* New York: Macmillan, 1973.

Hollis, Burney J. "Central Conflict Between Rural Thesis and Urban Antithesis in Jean Toomer's Avey." O'Daniel 277–86.

Hughes, Langston. *The Big Sea.* New York: Alfred A, Knopf, 1940.

————. "Our Wonderful Society," *Opportunity: Journal of Negro Life* 5 (1927): 226–27.

Hull, Gloria. *Color, Sex, and Poetry: Three Women Writers of the Harlem Renaissance.* Bloomington: Indiana UP, 1987.

Hutchinson, George B. "Jean Toomer and the 'New Negroes' of Washington." *American Literature* 63 (1991): 683–92.

————. "Jean Toomer and American Racial Discourse." *Texas Studies in Language and Literature* 35 (1993): 226–50.

Johnson, Georgia Douglas. *The Georgia Douglas Johnson Papers.* Moorland-Spingarn Research Center, Howard U.

Johnson, Henry Lincoln. *The Negro Under Wilson.* Washington: Republican National Committee, 1916.

Johnson, James Weldon. "The Riots: An NAACP Investigation." *Crisis* 18 (1919): 241–43.

Johnson, Ronald M. "Those Who Stayed: Washington Black Writers of the 1920s." *Records of the Columbia Historical Society* 50 (1980): 484–99.

Kerlin, Robert T. *The Voice of the Negro: 1919.* 1920. New York: Arno and The New York Times, 1968.

Kerman, Cynthia Earl, and Richard Eldridge. *The Lives of Jean Toomer: A Hunger for Wholeness.* Baton Rouge: Louisiana State UP, 1987.

Krasny, Michael J. "Jean Toomer's Life Prior to *Cane*: A Brief Sketch of the Emergence of a Black Writer." O'Daniel 41–46.

Locke, Alain. *The Alain Locke Papers.* Moorland-Spingarn Research Center, Howard U.

Logan, Mrs. John A. *Thirty Years in Washington: Or Life and Scenes in Our National Capital.* Hartford, CT: A. D. Worthington, 1901.

Majors, Gerri, with Doris E. Saunders. *Black Society.* Chicago: Johnson, 1976.

Margolies, Edward, *Native Sons: A Critical Study of Twentieth-Century Black American Writers.* Philadelphia: J. B. Lippincott, 1968.

McKay, Nellie Y. *Jean Toomer, Artist: A Study of His Literary Life and Work, 1894–1936.* Chapel Hill: University of North Carolina P, 1984.

Miller, R. Baxter. "Blacks in His Cellar: The Personal Tragedy of Jean Toomer." *Langston Hughes Review* 11 (1992): 36–40.

Moses, Wilson J. "The Lost World of the Negro, 1895–1919: Black Literary and Intellectual Life before the 'Renaissance.'" *Black American Literature Forum* 21 (1987): 61–84.

Murray, Daniel. "The Color Problem in the United States." *Colored American Magazine* December 1904: 719–24.

North, Michael. *The Dialect of Modernism: Race, Language, and Twentieth-Century Literature.* New York: Oxford UP, 1994.

O'Daniel, Therman B. *Jean Toomer: A Critical Evaluation.* Washington, D.C.: Howard UP, 1988.

———. "Jean Toomer and Mae Wright: An Interview with Mae Wright Peck." O'Daniel 25–40.

Petesch, Donald A. *A Spy in the Enemy's Country: The Emergence of Modern Black Literature.* Iowa City: U of Iowa P, 1989.

Rampersad, Arnold. *The Life of Langston Hughes: Volume I: 1902–1941: I, Too, Sing America.* New York: Oxford UP, 1986.

Rankin, David. "The Origins of Black Leadership in New Orleans During Reconstruction." *Journal of Southern History* 40 (1974): 417–36.

Reckley, Ralph, Sr. "The Vinculum Factor: 'Seventh Street' and 'Rhobert' in Jean Toomer's *Cane.*" *CLA Journal* 31 (1988): 484–89.

Robinson, Henry S. "The M Street High School, 1891–1916." *Records of the Columbia Historical Society of Washington, D.C.* 51 (1984): 119–42.

Rusch, Frederik L., ed. *A Jean Toomer Reader: Selected Unpublished Writings.* New York: Oxford UP, 1993.

Schultz, Elizabeth. "Jean Toomer's 'Box Seat': The Possibility for 'Constructive Crisises,'" O'Daniel 297–310.

Stewart, Jeffrey C. "Alain Locke and Georgia Douglas Johnson, Washington Patrons of Afro-American Modernism." *G. W. Washington Studies* 12 (1986): 37–44.

Terrell, Mary Church. *A Colored Woman in a White World.* Salem, NH: Ayer, 1986.

Toomer, Jean. *Cane.* 1923. New York: Liveright, 1969.

———. The Jean Toomer Papers. Beinecke Library, Yale U.

———. "Ghouls." *New York Call* 15 June 1919, Sunday Magazine Section 2: 3.

———. *Natalie Mann: A Play in Three Acts.* Turner 243–325.

———. "Race Problems and Modern Society." *Man and His World.* Ed. Baker Brownell. New York: D. Van Nostrand, 1928, 67–111.

———. "Reflections on the Race Riots." *New York Call* 2 August 1919: 8.

———. "Withered Skin of Berries." Turner 139–65.

Turner, Darwin T., ed. *The Wayward and the Seeking: A Collection of Writings by Jean Toomer.* Washington: Howard UP, 1980.

*Washington Bee.*

Williams, Fannie B. "The Club Movement Among Negro Women." *Voice of the Negro* March 1904: 99–107.

———. "Perils of the White Negro." *Colored American Magazine* December 1907: 421–23.

Williams, Lee E., III. *Post-War Riots in America 1919 and 1946: How the Pressures of War Exacerbated American Urban Tensions to the Breaking Point.* Lewiston: Edwin Mellen, 1991.

Williamson, Joel. *New People: Miscegenation and Mulattoes in the United States.* New York: New York UP, 1984.

# MEGAN ABBOTT

## "Dorris Dances . . . John Dreams": Free Indirect Discourse and Female Subjectivity in *Cane*†

Many of the chapters that comprise Jean Toomer's *Cane* share a common textual anxiety, which is rooted in the relation between the narrators and the female characters.[1] In *Cane*, women are often the sites onto which men project their judgements and desires, and many of the chapters explore, implicitly or explicitly, the effect this has on the women involved. But while the narrators in these chapters often emphasize the extent to which women are damaged by functioning primarily as vessels of others' meaning, they inevitably become part of the same dynamic—either covertly, as in "Karintha," or overtly, as in "Fern" and "Avey," where the narrators enter the stories as characters.

In "Fern," for example, the narrator empties Fern out with his rhetoric by claiming in part that her eyes "sought nothing" (16) [18][2] and by describing them as a tabula rasa on which everything else—the land, the South—is painted: "the whole countryside seemed to flow into her eyes. Flowed into them with the soft listless cadence of Georgia's South" (17) [19]. But at the same time, the narrator's ability to interpret Fern accurately is called into question. At first he expresses mere interpretive uncertainty: "Something inside of her got tired of [men], *I guess* . . ." (16, emphasis added) [18]. Later, he is unable to understand her "fit," which he does not know (or claims he does not know) if he has caused:

> I must have done something—what, I dont know, in the confusion of my emotion. She sprang up. Rushed some distance from me. Fell to her knees, and began swaying, swaying. Her body was tortured with something it could not let out. Like boiling sap it flooded arms and fingers till she shook them as if they burned her. (19) [21]

In this passage, the narrator seems to be withholding some action from us ("I must have done something"), but we never learn what it is. We can try to read Fern's response, but we only receive this response through the narrator, who claims not to understand it: The narrator seems to enter Fern's consciousness here (how else could he

---

† From *Soundings: An Interdisciplinary Journal* 80.4 (Winter 1997): 455–74. Reprinted by permission.
1. It is impossible to establish a universal narrator for *Cane*. The narrator of "Becky," for example, sounds like a native of the town (he is a member of the congregation and a friend of Barlo), while the narrator of "Fern" admits to being new—a Northerner.
2. Page numbers in square brackets refer to this Norton Critical Edition.

feel the sensation of "boiling sap" in her arms?), but he also says clearly that he is unable to enter her consciousness and that his attempts to understand her actions are hopeless. He describes her as "tortured with *something*," but he cannot tell us what it is. And when Fern begins speaking, he cannot understand her words and reports instead that she uttered "plaintive, convulsive sounds" (19) [21].

This episode embodies a central tension in *Cane*, which is generated by the male characters' efforts to interpret and project their desires onto women whose "true" consciousness is never revealed to them—or to the reader. This tension is evident at the narratalogical level as well. The narrators often fall into free indirect discourse with male characters in the stories, adopting their speech-patterns and locutions so that their consciousness seems to pervade the narrative.[3] For example, the narrator in "Blood-Burning Moon" slips into Tom's speech in the following passage:

> Tom felt funny. Away from the fight, away from the stove, chill got to him. He shivered. He shuddered when he saw the full moon rising towards the cloud-bank. He who didnt give a godam for the fears of old women . . . Bob Stone. Better not be. (32) [32–33]

And he slips into Bob's speech at times as well.

> His family had lost ground. Hell no, his family still owned the niggers, practically. Damned if they did; or he wouldnt have to duck around so . . . [Louisa] was lovely—in her way. Nigger way. What way was that? Damned if he knew. Must know. (33) [34]

But the narrator never slips into Louisa's speech, even though her role in the narrative is just as important as Tom's or Bob's. In fact, very few of the narrators ever merge with female characters in this way. The male characters and the narrators speculate about and act on women, but these women rarely take the foreground in their own narratives.

Seen in these terms, the narratological situation in *Cane* is not unlike the one that Henry Louis Gates, Jr., finds in Zora Neale

---

3. As a number of critics have pointed out, the term "free indirect discourse" is not without problems. Indeed there is substantial disagreement among scholars about its origin and meaning. For a useful summary of this controversy, see Gates 208–209. Among the best introductions to free indirect discourse are Stephen Ullman's *Style in the French Novel* and Brian McHale's "Free Indirect Discourse." Ullman refers to free indirect discourse (which he calls, alternately, free indirect "speech" and free indirect "style") as the third alternative "stand[ing] halfway between the two orthodox types"—these types being direct style, where "words are reproduced as they were uttered" and indirect style, where the words are "embedded in the narrative itself" (95). He goes on to note that free indirect style "agrees with direct speech in preserving various emotive elements which have to be sacrificed in indirect reporting: questions, exclamations, interjections; adverbs . . . which give the utterance a subjective colouring; colloquial, vulgar and slang terms which are expressive of the speaker's character and attitude" (97).

Hurston's *Their Eyes Were Watching God*. Gates argues that Hurston "introduced free indirect discourse into African American narration" by developing a narrative style that is halfway between direct discourse (rendered in dialect) and narrative commentary. In his words, "Hurston's innovation is to be found in the middle spaces between these two extremes of narration and discourse, in what we might think of as represented discourse, which as I am defining it includes both indirect and direct discourse" (191).

But while Gates's analysis of Hurston's use of free indirect discourse is persuasive, his comments about *Cane* are less compelling. He argues that *Cane* is split between standard English" narration and the "black oral voice" (178), and he maintains that the latter is "a different voice from the narrator's, as a repository of socially distinct, contrapuntal meanings and beliefs" (181). As a result, he suggests, Toomer was unable to synthesize the narrator's voice and the characters' as Hurston had done, and was left instead with "a tension between the two voices" (194).

The narrators in *Cane* are often hopelessly separated from the characters whose stories they tell, and that separation is heightened when class distinctions exist between the narrator and a character. But gender distinctions are far more persistent than class distinctions here: male characters of many classes (including Bob and Tom in "Blood-Burning Moon," Paul in "Bona and Paul," and Dan Moore in "Box Seat") do blend with their narrators, while female characters of any class rarely do. And when they do, the blending is always tenuous and fleeting.

## "Esther' "s Discourse: Flirting with Subjectivity

It is this tenuousness that makes "Esther" so disconcerting. Unlike Karintha, Becky, Carma, Fern, Avey, or Louisa, Esther is not merely a site onto which male narratives are projected.[4] She is actually permitted an intensely privileged relationship with the narrator of her story.[5] In the sections that begin "Sixteen," "Twenty-two" and "Esther is twenty-seven," Esther's consciousness pierces through the narrative, and the narrator and Esther seem to merge in what

4. W. Edward Farrison notes that—in contrast to the "simple recountings" that constitute the "Fern" and "Avey"—"Esther," "Blood-Burning Moon," "Box Seat," and "Theater" all offer a "blending of associationism and stream of consciousness" (301)—though he does not explore the specifics of the narrative approach, nor does he note the use of free indirect discourse.
5. Susan Blake argues that the "spectatorial artist" ("represented sometimes by a narrator, sometimes simply by the narrative voice" [516]) who controls *Cane*'s narrative "remains aloof from *both* the men and the women" (518, emphasis added), and that only in "Esther" and "Blood-Burning Moon" "does the creative voice attempt to enter into the into the conflict" (518). While I am arguing that gender plays a more problematic role in the narratorial dynamics, Blake's discussion of the "spectatorial artist" and his ambivalent relationship to the characters is most compelling.

appears to be free indirect discourse. Describing Esther's dream, for example, the narrator comments that "She alone is left to take the baby in her arms. But what a baby! Black, singed, woolly, tobacco-juice—ugly as sin" (24) [26]. And while reporting her ruminations about her life, he says, "[Esther] thinks about men. 'I don't appeal to them. I wonder why. . . . She thinks of Barlo. Barlo's image gives her a slightly stale thrill. She spices it by telling herself his glories. Black. Magnetically so" (24–25) [26]. These passages blur the distinction between Esther and the narrator, and they contain several of the standard markers of free indirect discourse, including exclamatory sentences ("But what a baby!") and an idiomatic, fragmented, speakerly style ("Black Magnetically so").[6]

At times, Esther's consciousness is foregrounded so intensely that it seems to permeate the narrative entirely.

> [The wind] is still blowing, but to her it is a steady, settled thing like the cold. She wants her mind to be like that. Solid, contained, and blank as a sheet of darkened ice. She will not permit herself to notice the peculiar phosphorescent glitter of the sweet-gum leaves. (26) [27–28]

While the narrator does step in with "*to her*, it is a steady, settled thing" (emphasis added), Esther's consciousness dominates the narrative here. Later, it becomes so dominant that if Esther misses something, so do we: "She is violently dizzy. Blackness rushes to her eyes. And then she finds that she is in a large room, Barlo is before her" (26) [28].

Still, the narrator's relation to Esther is more tentative, and more troubled, than other narrators' relations to male characters. At two crucial points in "Esther" the narrator suddenly reveals that he is no longer 'with' Esther, and, consequently, neither are we. The first is at the end of the long opening section, "Nine," following an account of Barlo's religious ecstasy. Because this account begins with Esther walking down the street, it seems to be told from her perspective, and we are encouraged to believe this by passages such as the following:

> She is about to turn in Broad from Maple Street. White and Black men loafing on the corner hold no interest for her. Then a strange thing happens. A clean-muscled, magnificent, black-skinned Negro, whom she had heard her father mention as King Barlo suddenly drops to his knees. (22) [24]

We seem to be with Esther here, but a page later, in the midst of the story of Barlo's fit, the narrator interrupts Barlo's words with a dash and says, "Years afterward Esther was told that at that very

---

6. For these and other indicators of free indirect discourse, see McHale 249–83.

moment a great, heavy, rumbling voice actually was heard" (23) [25]. Suddenly, the narrator treats the situation as if Esther were not there at all. When did Esther leave? Or did she? We do not know, and the narrator does not tell us.

Similarly, in the last paragraph of the story, we move suddenly out of Esther's consciousness into Barlo's and then back into Esther's: "Esther doesnt hear. *Barlo does. His faculties are jogged.* She sees a smile, ugly and repulsive to her . . ." (27, emphasis added) [00].

These two narrative shifts, slight as they are, undermine the connection between Esther and the narrator. And although the last line of the story ("There is no air, no street, and the town has completely disappeared" [27] [28]) presents an apparently unmediated transcription of Esther's perspective (there is no "*It seems* to Esther that . . . )", the reader is still left on unsteady ground, unsure whether the narrative voice embodies her consciousness or not.

The question of the narrative perspective in "Esther" is further complicated by the fact that we never hear Esther speak. This makes it difficult to be certain whether, or when, the narrative merges with her in free indirect discourse, since we have no way to trace the similarities between her speaking voice and the narrator's in such passages (though as McHale shows, there are other indicators of free indirect discourse, including exclamatory and idiomatic rhetoric).

The fact that we never hear Esther speak may suggest, on the one hand, that we never leave her consciousness, since the only way to hear her in conversation would be to enter a world outside her own mind. But on the other hand, it may suggest that we never enter her consciousness, that she is prevented from reaching us directly through either speech or interior monologue. This ambiguity further undermines the apparent closeness between Esther and the narrator, and leaves the reader uncertain whether the narrator is interpreting her accurately or projecting his own consciousness onto her.

### "Who Tells?": John and Narration in "Theater"

The narrative situation in "Theater" is almost the reverse of that in "Esther": the main female character, Dorris, speaks both in conversation and in interior monologues, but she is blocked from free indirect discourse for most of the text. In addition, the story explicitly foregrounds its own concerns with narrator-character relations, and thus provides what is, in effect, a commentary on *Cane*'s overall difficulty in approaching female consciousness.[7]

7. John M. Reilly argues that there is a shift in narrative style from the first section of *Cane* (in which "Esther" appears), where the "impressionistic style . . . conveys the sensations of instinctual life as the narrator comes to feel them," to Part 2 (in which "Theater" appears) where the "expressionistic writing . . . projects subjective states of

Unlike most of the women in the novel (with the prominent and problematic exception of Esther), Dorris is repeatedly foregrounded, as the narrative shifts to her voice, and unlike Karintha and Fern and Avey, who are seen and interpreted by male characters and their narrators, Dorris is permitted to "read" the primary male character in her story, John. But while John's consciousness is often so prominent that it seems to merge with the narrator's, Dorris's appears only at the close of the story. Moreover, while both John's and Dorris's viewpoints are explored, only John is permitted his own narrative, in his dream. And during this narrative, Dorris interprets him as shut off from her forever, hopelessly blind to her art and deaf to her voice.

The first lines of "Theater" serve both the set the scene and to highlight the subjective perspective from which the story is told. The narrator says,

> Life of nigger alleys, of pool rooms and restaurants and near-beer saloons soaks into the walls of Howard Theater and sets *them* throbbing jazz songs. Black-skinned, *they* dance and shout above the tick and trill of white-walled buildings. At night, *they* open doors to people who come in to stamp *their* feet and shout. (52, emphasis added) [51]

The rhythmic, stylized language in this passage creates such a strong sense of personality that one wonders *who* this narrator is—a question that becomes even more pressing when we meet John, whose speech is so similar to the narrator's that it makes these lines seem like an example of free indirect discourse. Equally important, this passage presents us with a narrator who explicitly sets himself apart from the "they" who dance and throb and shout.[8] Is this a class distance (or even a race distance)? If it is, the connection to John becomes even stronger, since his speech is informed by class distinctions as well.

After setting the scene, the narrative shifts abruptly: "Afternoons, the house is dark and the walls are sleeping singers until rehearsal begins. Or until John comes within them. Then they start

---

mind without the intervention of a first person narrator. In this style [Toomer] uses name tags, as in a playscript, to introduce his characters' thoughts, while their appearances and actions are stated with emphasis on physical appearance and without the evident presence of anyone's consciousness" (202). I would problematize the way Reilly reads the first section by noting "Esther"'s complicated narrative structure. I would also question Reilly's elision of a narrative consciousness in "Theater" and the other stories in the second part of *Cane*, since it seems to me that there is a narrator in "Theater," though not the explicit first-person narrator that appears in much of the first section of the book. And I will argue in my reading of "Theater" that we should attend to the differences between the narrative treatment of John and of Dorris as well.

8. I will refer to the narrator as "he" not just for the sake of convenience, but also because I believe there to be an implicitly male narrator who aligns himself primarily with John, or is aligned with John, due to their common view of Dorris' as the gendered other.

throbbing to a subtle syncopation. And the space-dark air grows softly luminous" (52) [51]. There seems to be little space between the narrator and John in this passage. If it read, "*To John*, the walls throb," or even "*It seemed that* the walls throbbed," the effect would be quite different. We would understand that the narrator is reporting John's view of the world to us. But as the text stands, with the walls that *start* throbbing and the air that *grows* luminous when John enters, John's subjectivity is greatly privileged. His perception is not even presented as such. His mere entrance into the theater, and the narrative, transforms his point of view into the narrative, the action. What John feels and perceives becomes the narrator's reality—and the reader's.

The movement here from the narrator's consciousness to John's also shows that neither point of view is superior to the other. Although the narration does shift to John's point of view, this perspective is not presented as more subjective and thus less "real" than the narrator's. After all, the narrator's comment that the "walls are sleeping singers" is a poetic *prosopopoeia,* a subjective, personal interpretation of the theater before the rehearsal begins. If the narrator's thought had ended with "the house is dark," the contrast between the narrator and John would have been more clear-cut—a case of objective reporting versus subjective impressionism. But as the passage stands, we experience one subjectivity followed by another. This sudden but easy shift from the narrator to John makes one wonder whether the narrator is interpreting John or assuming his perspective, and it suggests that the narrator and John are tightly intertwined.

The relationship between the narrator and John soon becomes even more complicated. The narrative does not, at this point, remain with John. As we enter the next paragraph, we move out of John and back into the narrator, who can see John. He presents us with "objective" facts: "John is the manager's brother. He is seated at the center of the theater, just before rehearsal. Light streaks down upon him from a window high above. One half his face is orange in it. One half his face is in shadow" (52) [51]. But the sentence that follows is more subjective: "The soft glow of the house rushes to, and compacts about, the shaft of light" (52) [51], and it is not entirely clear whose subjectivity is foregrounded. Is it the narrator's? Is it John's? Or both? The emphasis on the "soft" glow echoes the earlier description of the "space-dark air grow[ing] softly luminous," which occurs in the midst of a passage in which John and the narrator seem to be merging. The repetition reinforces the connection between John and the narrator, and as Gates says of *Their Eyes Are Watching God,* it makes it "extraordinarily difficult to distinguish the narrator's voice from the protagonist's" (191). But while for Gates the use of free indirect discourse signals the protagonist's approach to selfhood (191), it serves here as a sign of gender tensions. The narrator's connection to John is *not* balanced (as we will see) by a connection to Dorris—and that difference is significant.

The narrator then says, "Life of the house of the slowly awakening stage swirls to the body of John and thrills it" (52) [51]. This passage tells us about John's sensate experience, but it also implies that he is a passive object, an inanimate figure on whom these sensory stimuli converge. It is as though John himself occupies the conventional narratorial position: he is at the center of the action without participating in it. He can observe and even feel but at a safe distance. He is, after all, quite literally the *audience* here.

John's distance from the action is connected to what the narrator says is a split within him. This split was implied by the description of the shadow bisecting John's face, and it now becomes explicit: "John's body is separate from the thoughts that pack his mind" (52) [51]. The mind/body split is a persistent literary trope, of course, but here it serves very specific purposes in terms of class, gender, and narration—three terms that are inextricably bound in "Theater" and in other sections of *Cane*.

The narrator next offers a mysterious fragment: "Stage-lights, soft, as if they shine through clear pink fingers" (52) [51]. This impression seems to be the narrator's, but we cannot be sure that it is not John's. For the third time in as many paragraphs, the atmosphere of the theater is described as "soft," and as McHale notes, such repetition is a frequent indication of free indirect discourse. The viewing position has once again become problematized, and the sense of mystery deepens when we learn immediately afterward that beneath the lights, "hid by the shadow of a set," is Dorris (52) [51]. This is the first reference to Dorris, and it is significant that she is both visible (how else would the narrator know she's there?) and "hidden;" at least from John. As we will see, she is simultaneously visible and invisible for much of the text.

The narrator continues to merge in and out of John: "Other chorus girls drift in. John feels them in the mass. And as if his own body were the mass-heart of a black audience listening to them singing, he wants to stamp his feet and shout" (52) [51]. This passage brings us directly into John's emotions, and it also repeats the phrase "mass-heart," which the narrator used earlier to describe those who attend the nightly shows. The repetition again links John and the narrator—both discursively, through the insertion of the narrator's discourse into John's consciousness, and in terms of their class allegiances. Just as the narrator referred to the "mass-heart of black people" as "them," John is not part of the audience he watches so emotionally here. Instead, he responds "as if" he were part of this audience; he feels what he thinks they would feel, and his body acts as he imagines they would act.

John's distance from the action, and the separation between his mind and his body, are reinforced by the next sentence: "His mind, contained above desires of his body, singles the girls out, and tries to trace origins and plot destinies" (52) [51]. John is clearly not part of the action here, and his mind is described as quite separate from his desire-plagued body. In addition, John is described here as a kind of author who is trying to "write" the women he watches. This description connects him once again to the narrator, indeed to most of the narrators in *Cane*, many of whom are also concerned with tracing the "origins and plot destinies" of the women in their narratives.

A pianist then begins to play, the women begin to dance, and we enter a passage that embodies one of Toomer's many narrative experiments:

> John: Soon the director will herd you, my full-lipped, distant beauties, and tame you, and blunt your sharp thrusts in loosely suggestive movements, appropriate to Broadway. (O dance!) Soon the audience will paint your dusk faces white and call you beautiful. (O dance!) Soon I . . . (O dance!) I'd like. . . . (52–53) [51]

Because this passage is not in quotation marks, it does not appear to be direct discourse, and because it begins "John:" it does not appear to be mediated by the narrator. Instead, it seems to be an interior monologue, an unmediated transcription of John's thoughts. Similar passages recur throughout the text, and because they appear to give us direct access to John's thoughts we might expect them to help us to distinguish between John and the narrator. But this is not the case. Instead, as we shall see, the style and language of these passages often bleeds into those before and after them, making it even more difficult to determine where John and the narrator begin and end.[9]

At the most superficial level, this passage describes the way in which a director restrains and guides wild talent, and the way in which spectators transform what they see to suit their own desires. But because of the obvious parallels between a director and a writer or narrator, and between a spectator and a reader, the passage also provides an implicit description of the complicated interplay between writer, narrator, and reader in *Cane*.

---

9. George Kopf argues that the parenthetical "(O dance!)" moments in this passage embody an "interior monologue by way of third-person omniscience." He suggests that "The remainder of the story's action can be read as a quest for identification of [this] third voice which appears in John's monologue," and he asks, "Is John conscious of these words, or does he merely feel that somewhere below the point of recognition?" (500).

In addition since the passage ends with John apparently trying to articulate what he would like to do to or with the dancers, it suggests that he is or would like to be a director, writer, or narrator himself, further reinforcing the connection between John and the narrator of "Theater." And since the subjects of John's meditation here are women who dance but do not speak, the passage explicitly foregrounds a central dynamic in this story and many others in *Cane*—the efforts by men to interpret and control women without understanding them or, at times, even allowing them to speak.

The next paragraph does not begin "John:" so it presumably embodies the narrator's perspective, and it does offer a more objective description of the women dancing: "Girls laugh and shout. Sing discordant snatches of other jazz songs. Whirl with loose passion into the arms of passing show-men" (53) [51]. But this could be John's perspective as well. And although these sentences are punctuated by periods instead of ellipses, two are actually sentence fragments, similar to those at the end of John's interior monologue. Immediately following this description, in fact, we switch back to John's monologue, which is partly couched in sentence fragments as well: "John: Too thick. Too easy. Too monotonous. Her whom I'd love I'd leave before she knew that I was with her. Her? Which? (O dance!) I'd like to . . ." (53) [52]. Once again, the rhetorical similarities make it difficult to distinguish clearly between John and the narrator.

At the beginning of the next paragraph we are back in what is ostensibly the narrator's more objective perspective: "Girls dance and sing. Men clap" (53) [52]. But once again, this could be John's perspective as well, and by the end of the next three sentences the narrator's consciousness and John's have clearly merged. "The walls sing and press inward. They press the men and girls, they press John towards a center of physical ecstasy. Go to it, Baby!" (53) [52]. When we learn that the "walls sing," we are reminded of the narrator's comment in the first paragraph, "the walls are sleeping singers," which also preceded a switch to John's consciousness. In that passage there was a shift from the factual ("the house is dark") to the metaphoric; here there is a similar shift from factual declaration to narratorial *prosopopoeia*. Not surprisingly, the ensuing lines offer an impressionistic review of all John and the narrator see, hear, and feel:

> Fan yourself, and feed your papa! Put . . . nobody lied . . . and take . . . when they said I cried over you. No lie! The glitter and color of stacked scenes, the gilt and brass and crimson of the house, converge towards a center of physical ecstasy. John's feet and torso and his blood press in. He wills thought to rid his mind of passion. (53) [52]

The last two sentences here, which echo previous descriptions of the split between John's mind and his body, do seem to leave John's perspective, offering the narrator's interpretation of his experience. But they can also be read as embodying John's own interpretation of his experience. And it is perhaps most accurate to say that they highlight the ambiguous space between the narrator and John—a space that often blurs, raising the question of how distinct they really are.

### "Enter Dorris": A Voice from the Stage

Dorris enters the text a few paragraphs later: "Above the staleness, one dancer throws herself into it. Dorris" (53) [52]. It is unclear whether this introduction embodies the narrator's perspective or John's; which of them sees her as a spark of life in a stale routine? The narrator does tell us that "John sees her," suggesting that he is outside of John. But the ensuing description could once again be John's as well: "Her hair, crisp-curled, is bobbed. Bushy, black hair bobbing about her lemon-colored face. Her lips are curiously full, and very red. Her limbs in silk purple stockings are lovely" (53) [52]. What we have, in fact, is a three-tiered view: the narrator, John, and the reader are all looking at Dorris, and all are focused on her body. This triple perspective heightens Dorris's role as spectatorial object. She is not an agent but a site of desire, just as Karintha and Fern are.[1]

The next paragraph contains another of John's interior monologues:

> John: Stage-door johnny; chorus girl. No, that would be all right. Dictie, educated, stuck up; chorus girl. Yep. Her suspicion would be stronger than her passion. It wouldn't work. Keep her loveliness. Let her go. (53) [52]

This passage embodies a struggle between John's desire (his attraction to Dorris) and his mind (his decision to "Let her go"), and between his class ("dictie, educated") and Dorris's ("showgirl"). The mind/body split blends disturbingly with the class division, and with the gender division as well. Dorris is entirely physical here: John is at least half-cerebral. But Dorris's tempting, "low-class" sexuality brings out a physical response in him that he resists intellectually.

John does not present these views as his own, however; after all, he is *not* saying, "Show-girl, loose, no-good." Instead, he couches them as Dorris's view of him, and he assumes that her attitude

---

1. Janet Whyde writes, in her useful piece "Mediating Forms: Narrating the Body in Jean Toomer's *Cane*," that while Dorris' "body evokes the physical freedom of passion and desire, she remains a slave to John's interpretation of her" (48). This is certainly true at this point in the story, but as we will see Dorris does not remain completely bound by John's reading of her.

would cause their relationship to fail: "Her suspicion would be stronger than her passion. It wouldn't work." But he has no way of knowing any of this, since he and Dorris have not yet spoken. He reads and interprets her without any input from her at all, and he begins and ends their relationship without ever moving beyond the act of seeing her.

Dorris's lack of agency is reinforced by the continuing connection between John and the narrator—suggested here by his comment about her "loveliness," which echoes the description of her legs as "lovely" in the previous paragraph.[2] If John ignores her views entirely in his mini-narrative of their relationship, and if he is more and more entwined with the narrator, then where is Dorris to emerge, if at all? Is she doomed to be only read, never reading others or controlling how they read her?

At this moment, Dorris herself is foregrounded, but in a cryptic way. "Dorris sees John and knows that he is looking at her" (53) [52]. At last, Dorris's perspective is presented—even if by the narrator. But the next line complicates this apparent shift to Dorris: "Her own glowing is too rich a thing to let her feel the slimness of his diluted passion" (53) [52]. In this sentence we are narratorially in a place that cannot be Dorris's. We are looking *at* her again, at her "glowing," through the narration. The narrator is being extremely subjective here. He is making a judgment about what Dorris feels, and also categorizing both Dorris and John (the former "glowing" richly and the latter having "diluted passion"). But we have lost our brief connection to Dorris.

The narrative shifts again to Dorris's perspective:

> "Who's that?" she asks her dancing partner.
> "The manager's brother. Dictie. Nothin doin, hon"
> Dorris tosses her head and dances for him until she feels she has him. Then, withdrawing disdainfully, she flirts with the director. (53) [52]

But while the last paragraph here does embodies Dorris's point of view, the diction is still clearly the narrator's, our engagement with Dorris's consciousness is very brief, and what we learn about her is purely physical—she is focused entirely on performing for the male gaze.

In the following paragraph, however, we finally get Dorris's internal voice, presented as John's has been three times already.

---

2. As I argued above, that paragraph itself showed evidence of the merging of the narrator and John, but even if one reads it as presenting the narrator's views alone, the repetition here suggests the connection between them.

Dorris: Nothin doin? How come? Aint I as good as him? Couldnt I have got an education if I'd wanted one? Dont I know respectable folks, lots of them, in Philadelphia and New York and Chicago? Aint I had men as good as him? Better. Doctors an lawyers. Whats a manager's brother, anyhow? (53–54) [52]

Dorris's voice is idiomatic and slangy, very different from the narrator's or John's, or from their merged voice, and what she says reveals the extent of John's misreading. Instead of considering John "stuck-up," Dorris reveals anxiety about her own class status and insists that she is as good as he is. Here we have Dorris as we never have Karintha or Fern or Avey—who are all near-mute receptacles, puzzles read by men and left silent by a narration that circles but never enters their consciousnesses.

Over the next few paragraphs, Dorris and her dancing partner, Mame, grumble at the director, who tries to make them perform the routine his way. Mame tells him to "Go to hell, you black bastard," and Dorris asks, "Whats eatin at him, anyway?" (54) [53]. But the more they resist his strictures, his attempts to write their movements ("Now follow me in this, you girls"), the more he tries rhetorically to control them ("I told you to stay on the stage, didnt I?" [53]). [54] Once again, the director serves implicitly as a stand-in for the narrator, for any narrator or writer, and for John. In fact, the director's speech segues directly into John's at one point. The director shouts "and then you shimmy," and the narrative shifts to one of John's internal monologues, which begins "—and then you shimmy" (54) [53].

The director does finally let Dorris and the other women dance as they wish: "They forget set steps; they find their own. The director forgets to bawl them out. Dorris dances" (54) [53]. This dance is in many ways the high point of Dorris' appearance in the story, and the narrator clearly thinks it is a glorious thing. But he also describes it almost entirely in terms of the effect it has on John and the other male spectators.[3] As Dorris begins to dance, for example, the narrator tells us that "Odd ends of stage-men emerge from the wings, and stare and clap. A crap game in the alley suddenly ends. Black faces crowd the rear stage doors" (54) [53]. Similarly, in the midst of the dance, Dorris looks directly at John, but the narrator give us this gaze from John's perspective: "Dorris's eyes burn across the space of seats to him" (54) [53]. And when the dance momentarily unites John and Dorris and heals the split within John, the narrator

3. Dorris is given another interior monologue in the midst of her dance, which allows her to express some of her feelings about John ("I bet he can love. Hell, he can't love. He's too skinny.") and some of her own desires ("O will you love me? And give me kids; and a home, and everything?"). But it also paradoxically reinforces her role as an object of male attention, since it ends "Just watch me" (54) [00].

is once again with John, not Dorris, and his language echoes earlier passages of free indirect discourse in which he and John merged.

> Glorious songs are the muscles of her limbs.
> And her singing is of canebrake loves and mangrove feastings.
> The walls press in, singing. Flesh of a throbbing body, they press close to John and Dorris. They close them in. John's heart beats tensely against her dancing body. Walls press his mind within his heart. (55) [54]

At this point, in fact, the narrative shifts from what John is experiencing externally to what he is imagining—a shift that initially seems surprising but that makes more sense once we realize that the narrator has been with John all along: "And then, the shaft of light goes out the window high above him. John's mind sweeps up to follow it. Mind pulls him upward into dream. Dorris dances . . . John dreams" (55) [54]. For the next four paragraphs (all but two of the last six in the story), John's dream takes over the narrative, cutting off the reader's access to Dorris and to her dance.

John's dream does more than block our access to Dorris, however. It is a separate narrative that tells of his imagined courtship of Dorris. As a separate narrative, John's dream replaces the "real" Dorris of the story with an imaginary one, a point I will return to below. It also allows John to tell a story of his own, a power and privilege denied to Dorris. And it makes him the structural equivalent of the main narrator for this portion of the text. This privilege gives his perspective additional authority, since as Susan Sniader Lanser writes, "If the persona uttering a given stance is in a position of dominance in the narrative structure, then his or her ideology carries more authority than it would carry if expressed by a subordinate personage" (220).

The authority that accrues to John as a narrator here is reinforced by the similarities between his dream narrative and the other narratives in *Cane*. In the dream, for example, John tells us that as he walks toward the stage door to meet Dorris "his feet feel as though they step on autumn leaves" (55) [54], which echoes the moment in "Fern" when Fern and the narrator of her story sit down "where reddish leaves had damned the creek a little" (19). Similarly, John tells us that the scent of Dorris's perfume resembles "a southern canefield" (55) [54], which echoes the many references to canefields in "Carma," "Blood-Burning Moon," and "Fern." Indeed, *Cane* is virtually *written on* Dorris's body in John's narrative: "Her face is tinted like the autumn alley. Of old flowers, or of a southern canefield, her perfume" (55) [54]. And this passage itself echoes a similar moment in "Fern" when the narrator says of Fern that "the whole countryside seemed to flow into her eyes, Flowed into them with the soft listless cadence of Georgia's South" (17) [19].

Even more important for our purposes, however, are the similarities between John's dream narrative and the passages of free Indirect discourse in which he and the narrator of "Theater" merge. In John's dream, for example, Dorris wears "a loose black gown splashed with lemon ribbons" (55) [54], which echoes the earlier description of her "lemon-colored face" (53) [52]. And later in the dream, John finds himself with Dorris in a room that has "singing walls" and "Lights, soft, as if they shine through clear pink fingers" (55) [00], both of which echo the description of the theater in the opening pages of the story. These and other similarities further reinforce John's narrative authority, and they reveal once again that his consciousness and the narrator's are closely linked.

The connection between John and the narrator, and the importance of John's role as a narrator, are made even more clear in the last paragraph of his dream: "John reaches for a manuscript of his, and reads. Dorris, who has no eyes, has eyes to understand him. He comes to a dancing scene. The scene is Dorris. She dances. Glorious Dorris. Dorris whirls, whirls, dances . . ." (55) [54]. In this passage, John is doing explicitly what he and the narrator have been doing implicitly throughout the story: he is "writing" Dorris. It is his manuscript; he has written Dorris onto the page, into the text, in his own hand. And he therefore contains her, within his dream.[4] Once we leave the dream, it is clear that Dorris has been dancing all along, her own dance, not the dance inscribed for her in John's manuscript. But John has not been watching, and therefore neither have we.[5]

When we leave John's dream, however, we are fully with Dorris, We see things, including John, from her perspective; and for the first and only time in the story, she and the narrator merge. All of this is evident in the first few sentences of this passage: "Dorris, flushed, looks quick at John. His whole face is in shadow. She seeks for her dance in it. She finds it a dead thing in the shadow which is his dream" (56) [54]. Dorris reads John's dreaming state as a death

4. As Whyde writes of this moment, "What does he read [when he picks up the manuscript]? He reads the Dorris of his creation, the Dorris of his text" (49).
5. One could consider Dorris's failed attempt to elicit the response she wants from John as an example of what Barbara E. Bowen describes as the use of a call-and-response structure in Cane. Bowen cites "Theater" as one of the pieces in Cane—along with "Bona and Paul" and "Box Seat"—in which Toomer explores the "problematics of response" (200). As she writes, "Toomer's story of failed response begins in the middle of the book, and takes him back through all the narrators whose failure to consummate love is emblematic of their failure to hear a response" (201). Bowen uses this approach to Cane to argue that "The untroubled assumption of voice at the heart of the call-and-response pattern is no longer possible in a world altered by Romanticism," adding interestingly that this "clash of traditions" may be secondary to an even more stunning "confrontation" that is staged in Cane, a confrontation between "self-consciousness [and] nostalgia for untroubled voice" (201–202).

mask, her attempt to reach him through her dance as an utter failure. Crucially, the narrator shares Dorris's perspective here; he gives no hint that he knows what John is dreaming about, suggesting that both he and Dorris are cut off from John by his dream. And Dorris shares the narrator's perspective as well; her description of John's face "in shadow" echoes and extends the narrator's earlier comment that "One half [of John's] face is in shadow" (52) [51], and like this earlier description, it implies that there is a split between John's mind and his body.

The link between Dorris and the narrator continues for the rest of the paragraph.

> She rushes from the stage. Falls down the steps into the dressing room. Pulls her hair. Her eyes, over a floor of tears, stare at the whitewashed ceiling. (Smell of dry paste, and paint, and soiled cloth.) Her pal comes in. Dorris flings herself into the old safe arms, and cries bitterly. (56) [54]

This is Dorris at last. Her sensory experience (the smells hovering in her dressing room), her colloquial diction ("Her pal comes in"), and her personal history (Mame's "old, safe arms" hinting that this is not the first time Dorris has cried in them) all enter the narrative here, while John is gone entirely, presumably still lost in his reverie.

Taken as a whole, this paragraph is the purest expression of Dorris's perspective in "Theater." We no longer have just her direct discourse and her actions. We now have her consciousness merging with the narrator's, the two sensibilities temporarily intermingling, just as John's consciousness has merged with the narrator's throughout most of the rest of the story.

But while Dorris has achieved a narratological victory here, the story's last sentence renders it hollow. "'I told you nothin doin,' is what Mame says to comfort her" (56) [54]. In these words, the narrator takes control of the narrative and passes judgement on Dorris's situation. Mame's words are not comforting; they are an ironic "I told you so." They also serve to distance the narrator from Dorris, leaving him free from blame despite his closeness to John and his role in her degradation. The over-arching power of the narrator, of any narrator, has never been clearer.

Of course, reaching any definitive conclusion about *Cane*'s gender politics is neither practical nor appropriate. Many critics have wrestled with the complicated stances that the text takes towards women.[6]

6. Among these critics are Gates, McKay, and Blake. Blake comments about the first part of *Cane*. "Superficially the stories are about the women, but the real interest—the interest developed throughout the book—is in the men who labor to possess them. They are the active characters, artist figures with the will to limit, control, define experience. The women—silent, passive, elusive—represent the experience that the men are trying to grasp" (517).

But what has been less-often discussed is the relationship between *Cane*'s gender politics and its narrative structure. On the narrative level, as we have seen, Toomer replicates the text's thematic ambivalence toward female subjectivity in a variety of ways. Indeed, the audacious complexity of *Cane*'s justly-praised narrative structure multiplies the levels at which we must confront the text's startling slipperiness in relation to female consciousness—and its bold awareness of its own slipperiness. The narratological play reveals the text's ultimate reflexivity and self-consciousness about its thorny gender politics, and makes *Cane* its own most artful critic.

### WORKS CITED

Blake, Susan L. "The Spectatorial Artist and the Structure of *Cane*." *CLA Journal* 17 (June 1974): 516–34.

Bowen, Barbara E. "Untroubled voice: call and response in *Cane*." *Black Literature and Literary Theory*. Ed. Henry Louis Gates, Jr. NY: Routledge, 1990. 187–205.

Farrison, W. Edward. "Jean Toomer's *Cane* Again." *CLA Journal* 15 (March 1972): 295–302.

Gates, Jr., Henry Louis. *The Signifying Monkey: A Theory of African-American Literary Criticism*. NY: Oxford UP, 1988.

Kopf, George. "The tensions in Jean Toomer's 'Theater.'" *CLA Journal* 17.4 (June 1974): 498–503.

Lanser, Susan Sniader. *The Narrative Act: Point-of-View in Prose Fiction*. Princeton: Princeton UP, 1981.

McHale, Brian. "Free Indirect Discourse: A Survey of Recent Accounts," *PTL: A Journal for Descriptive Poetics and Theory of Literature* 3 (1978): 249–83.

McKay, Nellie Y. *Jean Toomer, Artist: A Study of His Literary Life and Work, 1894–1936*. Chapel Hill: U of North Carolina P. 1984.

Reilly, John M. "The Search for Black Redemption: Jean Toomer's *Cane*." *Studies in the Novel* 2 (Fall 1970): 312–24. Rpt. in *Cane: A Norton Critical Edition*, Ed. Darwin T. Turner. NY: W. W. Norton, 1988. 196–207.

Toomer, Jean. *Cane: A Norton Critical Edition*. Ed. Darwin T. Turner. NY: W. W. Norton, 1988.

Ullman, Stephen. *Style in the French Novel*. Cambridge: Cambridge UP, 1957.

Whyde, Janet M. "Mediating Forms: Narrating the Body in Jean Toomer's *Cane*." *The Southern Literary Journal* 26.1 (Fall 1993): 42–53.

# WERNER SOLLORS

## Jean Toomer's *Cane*:
## Modernism and Race in Interwar America[†]

*Time and space have no meaning in a canefield.*
Jean Toomer, *Cane*

*Cane* is a remarkable expression of the modernist movement in literature that swept the United States and Europe in the first half of the twentieth century. Published in 1923 (before Ernest Hemingway's and William Faulkner's first important books were to appear), *Cane* was a powerful contribution to the stream of modernism that had begun with Gertrude Stein's *Three Lives* and James Joyce's *Dubliners* and continued with Sherwood Anderson's *Winesburg, Ohio*, Waldo Frank's manifesto, *Our America*, Hart Crane's poem *The Bridge*, and Eugene O'Neill's plays, a movement that was amplified by Alfred Stieglitz's photographs, Georgia O'Keeffe's paintings, the montage technique of the silent film, and the modern sounds of the blues and of jazz. The cultural historian Henry F. May called the watershed between Theodore Roosevelt and O. Henry on the one side and Greenwich Village and T. S. Eliot on the other a "cultural revolution";[1] the "revolution" in literature was spread by a younger generation of writers who loved the adjective "new," who chose many modern themes and settings, and who often looked to the other arts for inspiration. *Cane* is on our side of this transformation toward aesthetic modernism, psychological scrutiny, bohemian self-searching, increasing ethnic expression, and engagement with new ideologies.[2]

The author with the enigmatically androgynous name Jean Toomer (1894–1967) took up, but never completed, studies in history, anthropology, agriculture, and physical training; he was early attracted to atheism and socialism, later to the mystical and introspective Gurdjieff movement, to the Quakers, and to an Indian guru, and he spent important years in such artists' colonies as Greenwich Village, Taos, New Mexico, and Carmel, California. He participated in an early experiment in group psychology in Portage, Wisconsin, that neighbors suspected was a free-love movement. He published poems, plays, and prose pieces on the pages of all the right small, experimental, and often radical literary magazines such

† From *Jean Toomer and the Harlem Renaissance*, ed. Geneviève Fabre and Michel Feith (New Brunswick, NJ: Rutgers University Press, 2001). © Werner Sollors. Reprinted by permission.
1. May, *American Innocence.*
2. For a full discussion of Toomer in the context of the American avant-garde. Lost Generation, and Harlem Renaissance, see Soto, "Literary History."

as *Broom*, *Liberator*, and *Modern Review*. Toomer submitted a play to O'Neill's Provincetown Playhouse, befriended Sherwood Anderson and Hart Crane, and was intimate with Georgia O'Keeffe; his second wife, Marjorie Content, had previously been married to the editor of *Broom*, who was caricatured as Robert Cohn in Hemingway's *The Sun Also Rises*.

Not very well known outside of the United States, Toomer was a searcher among the modernist intellectuals of his time. His writing, most excellently embodied by *Cane*, represents an attempt to answer his close friend Waldo Frank's demand that American writers "study the cultures of the German, the Latin, the Celt, the Slav, the Anglo-Saxon and the African on the American continent: plot their reactions one upon the other, and their disappearance as integral worlds,"[3]

Frank and Toomer spent some time together in Spartanburg, South Carolina. Inspired by this trip, Frank published his novel of perverted interracial lust and violence, *Holiday*. Toomer had previously worked as an acting principal in a black school in Sparta, Georgia, for two months—his first extended stay in the rural South—during which time the idea for *Cane* germinated. (He called Sparta "Sempter" In *Cane*.) He read the town newspaper, the *Sparta Ishmaelite*, and lived in an old cabin. This is the way Toomer remembered his emotional reaction to Sparta later on: "There was a valley, the valley of 'Cane,' with smoke-wreaths during the day and mist at night. A family of back-country Negroes had only recently moved into a shack not too far away. They sang. And this was the first time I'd ever heard the folk-songs and spirituals. They were very rich and sad and joyous and beautiful. But I learned that the Negroes of the town objected to them. They called them 'shouting.' They had victrolas and player-pianos. So, I realized with deep regret, that the spirituals, meeting ridicule, would be certain to die out. With Negroes also the trend was toward the small town and then toward the city—and industry and commerce and machines. The folk-spirit was walking in to die on the modern desert. That spirit was so beautiful. Its death was so tragic. Just this seemed the sum of life to me. And this was the feeling I put into *Cane*. *Cane* was a swan-song. It was a song of an end."[4]

Published the year before Horace Kallen coined the term "cultural pluralism," *Cane* was a meditation on what Toomer felt was

3. Frank, *Our America*, cited in the context of the Frank-Toomer correspondence by Terris, "Waldo Frank," 306.
4. From an autobiographical sketch cited to Darwin T. Turner in the Norton Critical Edition of *Cane* (New York, 1988), 141–42, from which I cite parenthetically in the text. Further references to other sources in this edition will be made as Turner, *Cane*. A larger excerpt appears in Darwin T. Turner. ed., *The Wayward and the Seeking*, 121; this collection will be referred to as Turner, *Wayward*. [Page numbers in square brackets refer to this Norton Critical Edition.]

the disappearing African culture on the American continent. It was also an aesthetic experiment of the first order.

> Oracular.
> Redolent of fermenting syrup,
> Purple of the dusk,
> Deep-rooted cane.

From the beginning to the ending of *Cane* the reader is drawn into a magical and mysterious world of pine needles and clay, of autumn leaves and dusk, of spiritual striving and human failing, of love and violence, but it also tells of the movement from country roads to city streets and from natural to industrial sounds.

Toomer achieves his effects by a carefully orchestrated system of verbal repetition and musical progression in a book whose very form resists classification. Is *Cane* a novel? A melange of experimental pieces of differing length? A synthesis of various forms of experimentation? A mosaic? Most of all, it is a book sui generis, a fusion of poetry, prose, and drama (in "Bona and Paul" and "Kabnis"), a text that appeals to all senses by presenting strong visual images and musical and rhythmic effects that evoke smells and powerful feelings of pain and suffering. Its very form is an attempt at finding a literary equivalent for the dislocations that modernity had wrought by moving people from soil to pavements, making them ashamed of their traditional folk culture or changing it into commercial entertainment, and radically altering the epic pace of sun and seasons, of sowing and reaping, into the accelerated and syncopated rhythm of trains and cars, the staccato of quickly shifting images and thoughts. Despite all the apparent variations in genres, the book has the effect of a long poem that is held together by recurring images. The book reflects on the country without idyllic nostalgia and on the city without teleological hope. Both are historically changing worlds of failed human understanding and of at times horrifyingly brutal encounters, since Toomer locates his work in the aftermath of World War I and in the white-black racial violence of the South and North. The modernist book *Cane* thus vies for the space of the spirit, of the human soul, that seems threatened under the rule of modernity— both in the country and the city. "We have two emblems, namely, the machine gun and the contraceptive," Toomer writes regretfully.[5] Can the lost soul of a fertile peasant past be found again in the elusively modernist form of a book that artistically, even artificially, reconstitutes life-asserting wholeness by resisting easy generalizations and a priori assumptions? *Cane* makes an attempt to do just

---

5. Toomer, *Essentials* (1931; reprint with an introduction by Rudolph P. Byrd. Athens: University of Georgia Press, 1991), xxxii.

that—even though Toomer articulated his keen awareness that there is no possibility of going back to a shared past.

> The modern world was uprooted, the modern world was break-ing down, *but we couldn't go back*. There was nothing to go back to. Besides, in our hasty leaps into the future we had burned our bridges. The soil, the earth was still there, even under city pavements and congested sky scrapers.
>     But such peasantry as America had had—and I sang one of its swan songs in *Cain* [sic]—was swiftly disappearing, swiftly being industrialized and urbanized by machines, motor cars, phonographs, movies. . . . "Back to nature," even if desirable, was no longer possible, because industry had taken nature unto itself. Even if he wanted to, a city person could not become a soil person by changing his locale and living on a farm in the woods.
>     So then, whether we wished to or not, we *had to go on*[6]

Toomer's answer to this problem could not lie in a return to tradi-tional values, be they monarchy, religion, or mere conservatism, for "those who sought to cure themselves by a return to more primitive conditions were either romantics or escapists." No, going on, going on to create, searching for aesthetic wholeness and a new vision in a fragmented modern world, that was the only viable answer. The critique of modernity impelled Toomer to move forward the project of modernism.

*Cane* makes its renders self-conscious in order to let them yearn for a fresher and fuller look at the world. This effort is captured in the book's repeated allusions to St. Paul's Epistle to the Corinthi-ans: "For now we see through a glass darkly; but then face to face; now I know in part; but then shall I know even as I am known"—a passage that Ralph Waldo Emerson and Nathaniel Hawthorne had also cherished and that Henry Roth and Ralph Ellison were to draw on later. Is it possible to have full knowledge and self-knowledge in the modern world? In pursuing this question in the United States, Toomer also searched for a more cosmic understanding of the wholeness of a polyvocal America as it was once sung by Walt Whit-man and now proclaimed by Waldo Frank. And as many visionaries before him, Toomer espoused the fragmentary as the necessary part of larger totalities.

The interrelatedness of fragmentation and quest for wholeness structures *Cane*. The book is divided into three parts that are marked by parentheses: (, ) and (). "Between each of the three sec-tions, a curve. These, to vaguely indicate the design," Toomer wrote

---

6. Turner, *Wayward*, 129. Kerman and Eldridge, *Lives*, 116, also call attention to this passage.

to Waldo Frank on December 12, 1922.[7] The two segments realign and aim for a circle without fully achieving its closure in the third part.

Part one is set in Georgia, the rural South. It is mostly focused on women, starting with Karintha, whose very name may represent a nod in the direction of Gertrude Stein's "Melanctha," or may allude to St. Paul's "Corinthians," ending with Louisa in "Blood-Burning Moon."

"Karintha" originally appeared in the context of the drama *Natalie Mann* (1922), in which Toomer's mouthpiece, Nathan Merilh, reads "Karintha" as evidence that historically grown, black sacred art remained a valid and important source of inspiration to the intellectual who found himself surrounded by modern Marxist and nationalist interrogators.[8] Yet Karintha is more of a modern Mary Magdalene than a conventional sacred figure. Men bring her money, and her imagistic constitution is that of a woman whose running is a "whir" and whose "skin is like dusk when the sun goes down"—a leitmotif of the story in the repetition of which Toomer visibly blurs the line between poetry and prose: it is typeset as a prose sentence and as a poem. In the play, Therman Law, a young man (who is also the friend of Nathan Merilh, who in turn is presented as the author of "Karintha") reflects:

> What should be the most colorful and robust of our racial segments is approaching a sterile and denuded hypocrisy as its goal. What has become of the almost obligatory heritage of folk-songs? Jazz on the one hand, and on the other, a respectability which is never so vigorous as when it denounces and rejects the true art of the race's past. They are ashamed of the past made permanent by the spirituals. My God, imagine the took on the face of Dvořák.[9]

The poems and the portraits of rural women that follow intensify the reader's sense of hearing Toomer's "swan song," of experiencing fragments of a passing rural world in which natural images, especially those of sunsets and autumn, and religious sentiments increasingly give way to such intrusions of modernity as railroad tracks and factories and to scenes of violence. Becky, introduced with a paradoxical subtitle reminiscent of Bertolt Brecht's dramatic strategies as "the white woman who had two Negro sons," lives on a "ground islandized between the road and railroad track" (18) [9].

---

7. Excerpted in Turner, *Cane*, 152.
8. The play was published in Turner, *Wayward*, 243–325. See also the discussions by McKay, *Toomer*, and Byrd, *Years*, as well as Terris, "Waldo Frank."
9. Turner, *Wayward*, 290.

Fern is presented as if narrator and reader were seeing her from a train thundering by:

> Besides, picture if you can, this cream-colored solitary girl sitting at a tenement window looking down on the indifferent throngs of Harlem. Better that she listen to folk-songs at dusk in Georgia, you would say, and so would I. Or, suppose she came up North and married. Even a doctor or a lawyer, say, one who would be sure to get along—that is, make money. You and I know, who have had experience in such things, that love is not a thing like prejudice which can be bettered by changes of town. Could men in Washington, Chicago, or New York, more than the men of Georgia, bring her something left vacant by the bestowal of their bodies?
>
> I ask you, friend, (it makes no difference If you sit in the Pullman or the Jim Crow as the train crosses her road), what thoughts would come to you . . . had you seen her in a quick flash, keen and intuitively, as she sat there on her porch when your train thundered by? Would you have got off at the next station and come back for her to take her where? Would you have completely forgotten her as soon as you reached Macon, Atlanta, Augusta, Pasadena, Madison, Chicago, Boston, or New Orleans? (18) [19–20]

Esther, who has come to sexual maturity, walks into a jeering crowd like a somnambulist, and the story ends like a Franz Kafka tale: "She steps out. There is no air, no street, and the town has completely disappeared" (27) [20]. The undercurrent of violence emerges with the blood-stained blade of the scythe that has cut a rat in the poem "Reapers" and erupts at the end of the first section as the factory town mob lynches Louisa's black lover, Tom Burwell, whose steel blade had slashed his white rival Bob Stone's throat.

In part two *Cane* takes us to cities, especially Washington and Chicago in the age of mass migration and urbanization. (In 1910 about a quarter of all African Americans lived in cities, in 1940, half of them.) The rhythm changes abruptly in this world that is characterized by postwar disillusionment, by a proliferating entertainment industry, and by the syncopations of jazz that Toomer incorporates into his prose in order to render a life that is "jagged, strident, modern. Seventh Street, located in black Washington, is the song of crude new life. Of a new people" (41) [167]. The surrealistic Rhobert, who wears his house like a diver's helmet, is an urban counterpart to Becky, as the narration again repeats prose sentences as poems. The image of the man who sinks is connected with the World War I experience that reduced God to "a Red Cross man with a dredge and a respiration-pump" and makes the singing of the traditional spiritual "Deep River" seem out of place:

Lets build a monument and set it in the ooze where he
goes down. A monument of hewn oak, carved in
nigger-heads. Lets open our throats, brother, and
sing "Deep River" when he goes down.

Brother, Rhobert is sinking.
Lets open our throats, brother,
Lets sing Deep River when he goes down.
(43) [42–43]

The self-conscious narrator of "Avey"[1] resembles that of "Fern."
Again, the wish for a performance of the spiritual "Deep River,"
this time by the Howard University Glee Club, marks the contrast
to rural religion, a contrast that shapes also the vignette of the
young woman on the street in "Calling Jesus." "Theater" continues
the jazz theme, and Toomer adopts some blues lines here: "Arms
of the girls, and their limbs, which . . . jazz, jazz . . . by lifting up
their tight street skirts they set free, jab the air and clog the floor in
rhythm to the music. (Lift your skirts, Baby, and talk t papa!)" (52)
[51]. In "Box Seat," Dan Moore reflects on a man who saw the first
Oldsmobile but was born a slave: "He saw Grant and Lincoln. He
saw Walt—old man, did, you see Walt Whitman?" The new urban
world is not even one lifetime removed from the Civil War and slavery; and this recent history also casts its shadow over the failed
interracial romance between Bona and Paul in the story that ends
the second part and corresponds most directly to "Blood-Burning
Moon": just as Bob Stone wanted Louisa because she was black and
he "went in as a master should and took her. Direct, honest, bold,"
so Bona in the new world of a Chicago gymnasium and the nightclub Crimson Gardens is attracted to Paul because she suspects he
is black: "That's why I love" (72) [70]. Bona's (and Toomer's) lyrical
labels "harvest moon" and "autumn leaf" cannot displace the racial
slur "nigger" that is, for Bona, a source of attraction. The weight of
such historical racial categories ("a priori" recurs here) impinges
upon the consciousness of the youths: "Bona is one window. One
window, Paul" (73) [71].

In part three, "Kabnis," the artist himself is *seen* rather than having merely a stronger or weaker presence as observer. Like Toomer,
Kabnis is a secular urban intellectual who goes to rural Georgia
to teach. Partly inspired by Joyce's *Portrait of the Artist as a Young
Man*, "Kabnis"—written as a play and submitted to O'Neill's associate Kenneth Macgowan—shows the development of a tortured

---

1. Jones, *Prison-House*, 42. suggests that "Avey" is reminiscent of Joyce's "Araby." He also
links the story's theme of the modern woman's indifference to men's sexual advances to
Eliot's *Waste Land*.

mind through encounters with nursery rhymes, religion, and various role models such as a teacher, preacher, cartwright, radical, and visionary. There are many things Kabnis has to face about society, history, and himself, but the core of what he must come to terms with is a legacy of violence. When drunk and self-critical, Kabnis attempts to articulate his aesthetic against the avalanche of words that makes the country go down: "I want t feed th soul—I know what that is; th preachers dont—but I've got t feed it" (111) [109]. When he adds, "I wish t God some lynchin white man ud stick his knife through it an pin it to a tree," he likens his concept of the soul to the brutal story of the pregnant Mame Lamkins that the preacher Layman had told him earlier: when she tried to hide her husband, who was wanted, she was killed, and the living baby was torn out of her stomach and stuck to a tree with a knife, as if it were a perverse new crucifixion (92) [90].[2] The ending of "Kabnis" is like a rebirth, and the book ends as a birth song with a sunrise.

The three parts of *Cane* confront the divisions of South and North, women and men, as well as black and white, whereas the structure of the book tends to bridge such divisions and strive toward unity. In a letter to Waldo Frank of December 12, 1922, Toomer suggested another sequence in which one might read the book: "*Cane's* design is a circle. Aesthetically, from simple forms to complex ones, and back to simple forms. Regionally, from the South up into the North, and back into the South again. Or, from the North down into the South, and then a return North. From the point of view of the spiritual entity behind the work, the curve really starts with Bona and Paul (awakening), plunges into Kabnis, emerges in Karintha etc. swings upward into Theatre and Box Seat, and ends (pauses) in Harvest Song. Whew!"[3]

The book may then be said to follow at least a double curve: one that goes from beginning to end and one that starts in the middle and ends with "Harvest Song." Yet *Cane* could also be read in many other sequences, since many parts resonate with many other parts because of the book's poetic structure. Toomer's method also resembles the

2. The tale may go back to an incident Walter White reported in his book *Rope and Faggot*. White writes: "In the ten years from January 1, 1918, through 1927, American mobs lynched 454 persons. Of these, 38 were white, and 416 were coloured. Eleven of the Negro victims were women, three of them at the time of lynching with child" (20–21). White gives a detailed account of the lynching of Mary Turner (the pregnant wife of Hayes Turner, who had been killed by a mob): "Securely they bound her ankles together and, by them, hanged her to a tree. Gasoline and motor oil were thrown upon her dangling clothes; a match wrapped her in sudden flames . . . The clothes burned from her crisply toasted body, in which, unfortunately, life still lingered, a man stepped towards the woman and, with his knife, ripped open the abdomen in a crude, Cæsarean operation. Out tumbled the prematurely born child. Two feeble cries it gave—and received for answer the heel of a stalwart man, as life was ground out of the tiny form" (28–29).
3. Excerpted in Turner, *Cane*, 152. This letter is also cited and perceptively discussed by McKay, Toomer, and Byrd, *Years*, among others.

film montage technique of Eisenstein as it juxtaposes sequences that the reader/viewer must put together, must "suture." Unity is achieved by various repetitions and leitmotifs that create a sense of thematic cohesion and rhythm and shape the design of the text.[4]

Toomer aims for a particular kind of lyrical specificity expressed in strong and often enigmatic images that recur in repeated words, phrases, and shorter or longer sentences throughout the book. Although the precise meaning of an instance on a given page may be hard to define, the very fact that words are repeated throughout the book gives the reader a sense of acoustic and visual familiarity, a phenomenon reminiscent of *Three Lives*. For example, *Cane* is a book of repeated "thuds," harsh knocking sounds that syncopate the reading from "Becky" (8) [9] to the end of "Kabnis" (117) [15]. In "Blood-Burning Moon" the thud is the sound of Bob's body falling and of the mob's action, giving a menacingly violent undercurrent of meaning to such later thuds as those in the gymnasium in "Bona and Paul." Similarly, there are trees throughout the book, but it is the tale of Mame Lamkins in "Kabnis" that gives them their precise sense of eeriness. *Cane* is a book full of sunset and dusk imagery that is virtually omnipresent in the poems and the prose, thus calling particular attention to the emphatic sunrise at the end. Karintha is described as a "November cotton flower"—the title of a poem appearing a few pages later.[5] The repetition of "pines whisper to Jesus" in "Becky" anticipates "Calling Jesus" and the whispering nightwind in "Kabnis." Read this way, the book is woven of recurring sounds and images in such words as sawmill, pine, cotton, dixie pike, street, smoke, wedge, window, moon, cloud, purple, cradle, sin, and, of course, cane. Robert Jones has stressed how Gertrude Stein's love for "-ing" forms also affected Toomer; he focused on "Seventh Street" with its reiterated "zooming cadillacs. Whizzing, whizzing down the street-car tracks," its "thrusting unconscious rhythm"—all coming to a climactic moment in "Black reddish blood. Pouring for crude-boned soft skinned life, who set you flowing?" And: "Flowing down the smooth asphalt of Seventh Street, in shanties, brick office buildings, theaters, drug stores, restaurants, and cabarets? Eddying on the corners? Swirling like a blood-red smoke up where the buzzards fly in heaven?"[6] (39) [41].

4. Bone, *Negro Novel*, McKay, *Toomer*, John M. Reilly, and Patricia Watkins (both in Turner, *Cane*) are among the critics who have developed aspects of the unity of *Cane*. As Turner suggests, names also recur from one section to another; John Stone in "Becky" is the father of Bob Stone in "Blood-Burning Moon," and David Georgia also appears in both of these tales; Barlo appears in "Becky" and "Esther," and the Dixie Pike in "Carma" and "Fern." For a concise statement of elements that contradict a unifying reading of *Cane* see Byrd, *Years*. 15ff.
5. John M. Reilly, in Turner, *Cane*, 198.
6. See Jones, *Prison-House*, 47. The question is repeated three more times and served as inspiration to Farah Griffin's study *"Who Set You Flowin'?"*

Additionally, many sections contain further patterns of repeated phrases and sentences within a single story or vignette. At times (as in "Becky" or "Calling Jesus") the phrasing with the central set of images appears at the beginning and the end, as prose or poetry. In stories like "Blood-Burning Moon" the internal repetition is remarkable; one can see how this works in Toomer's prose by looking at a few representative sentences:

> The full moon sank upward into the deep purple of the cloud-bank. An old woman brought a lighted lamp and hung it on the common well whose bulky shadow squatted in the middle of the road, opposite Tom and Louisa. The old woman lifted the well-lid, took hold the chain, and began drawing up the heavy bucket. As she did so, she sang. Figures shifted, restlesslike, between lamp and window in the front room of the shanties. Shadows of the figures fought each other on the gray dust of the road. Figures raised the windows and joined the old woman in song. Louisa and Tom, the whole street, singing:
>
> > Red nigger moon. Sinner!
> > Blood-burning moon. Sinner!
> > Come out that fact'ry door.
> > (33) [33–34]

Many sentences contain words that echo earlier sentences. By the time we read the sentence, "Its yell echoed against the skeleton stone walls and sounded like a hundred yells" (36), most of the nouns are themselves echoes. This makes for a musical and visual progression. By using such words as "yell" as subjects of short sentences, Toomer also gives an energetic, imagistic quality to his descriptions, as he seems focused on a telling detail. "Fern" opens with a sentence in which "face" is the subject and that makes grammatical sense, contains only familiar words, and evokes a strong image, yet is also quite mysterious: "Face flowed into her eyes" (16) [18].

Such a phrasing is reminiscent of Ezra Pound's "In a Station of the Metro." Toomer may, in fact, be consciously following R. S. Flint's and Ezra Pound's 1913 imagist maxims that exhorted poets to treat the "thing" directly, use absolutely no word that does not contribute to the presentation, compose in the sequence of a musical phrase, not the sequence of a metronome, and arrive at an image that presents an intellectual and emotional complex in an instant of time.[7] Toomer's images certainly are not ornaments; they *are* the speech.

---

7. Darwin T. Turner and Rudolph P. Byrd, among others, have briefly discussed imagist aspects of Toomer's work. Flint's and Pound's maxims are cited in William Pratt, ed., *The Imagist Poem* (New York: Dutton, 1963), 18.

The dialectic of the accustomed familiarity of given words that make physical things visible and vivid and the "oracular" strangeness of their precise meanings that surrounds the verbally constituted world with questions and ambiguity is given fullest play in Toomer's descriptions such as that of Louisa: "Her skin was the color of oak leaves on young trees in fall"[8] (30) [31]. This is a strongly visual image that makes the reader see things fresh, yet it would be hard to associate one specific color with such a description. It is no coincidence that for Toomer such lyricism also has the function of avoiding a label. Toomer shared with imagists such as T. E. Hulme a disdain for abstractions and a desire to let fresh metaphors make you continuously see a physical thing; thus Toomer does not call Karintha a "prostitute" (though reviewers like W. E. B. Du Bois did); the narrator only says that men bring her their money.[9] Yet Toomer brings to this program, again reminiscent of Stein's, a particular wish that goes beyond the aesthetic.

Louisa's skin color is an alternative to a racial label, a needling engagement with a reader's desire to know whether a character is black or white. Toomer's response is, "Her skin was the color of oak leaves on young trees in fall." We remember that Bona, too, saw Paul in the following way: "He is a harvest moon. He is an autumn leaf. He is a nigger." These are three grammatically parallel sentences, two of which offer lyrical perception and one of which is not just an abstraction and cliché, but the worst ethnic slur as a label (though for Bona this very abstraction is also a source of attraction). For Jean Toomer the worst aesthetic strategy was to employ a cliché—and he saw language as complicitous in racial domination.

> Damn labels if they enslave human beings—
> above race and nationality there is mankind.

*Cane* is a modernist work that has its specific milieu in the world of American race relations, polarized along the color line that divides black and white, whether in Sparta, Washington, or Chicago. Toomer's stylistic choices are an expression of his refusal to endorse this racial divide. To be sure, *Cane* was a book in which black life, rural and urban, was strongly thematized. But this was not all. His aesthetic was connected to a quest for unity, and one may say that Toomer was a spiritual searcher for all of his life. On May 16, 1923, Toomer wrote to DuBose Heyward: "Both black and white folk come into *Cane*'s pages. For me, this is artistically inevitable. But in no instance am I concerned primarily with race;

---

8. The description continues in drawing out tree imagery—which has a sinister undertone in view of the lynching that is coming and the Mame Lamkins story in "Kabnis."
9. T. E. Hulme cited in Pratt, *Imagist Poem*, 28. Du Bois review reprinted in Durham, *Merrill Studies*, 40–42; also excerpted in Turner, *Cane*, 170–71.

always, I drive straight for my own spiritual reality, and for the spiritual truth of the South."[1]

This quest for wholeness and Toomer's own "spiritual reality" is related to the book's racial and historical thematic. If America is fragmented, black and white, male and female, Southern and Northern, rural and urban, Toomer sees his own mission, by contrast, as providing a ground for spiritual unity. His quest for union, for wholeness, for the circle is achieved precisely by thematizing the divisions that the book's author felt were so destructive and virulent in the modern world: race, sex, class, region. Toomer saw himself as a visionary who would try to redirect renders toward a wholeness—however elusive it might be—that they had lost in their differentiations by category, In other words, Toomer's aesthetic modernism was connected to an attack on false perceptions, prejudices, a priori assumptions, and labels. He was attracted to Waldo Frank, James Joyce, Eugene O'Neill (he submitted "Kabnis" to the Provincetown Players and wrote a rave notice on "The Emperor Jones") and Gertrude Stein (through Alfred Stieglitz, who had published some early Stein; both Toomer and Stein contributed an homage to Stieglitz in a volume published in 1934). Toomer found that modernist forms helped to complicate facile notions about social life. Georgia O'Keeffe had painted *Birch and Pine Trees—Pink* (1925) as a modern version of a "portrait" of her friend Jean Toomer, to whom she wrote, "There is a painting I made from something of you the first time you were here." The "dancing" trees were thus a "surrogate portrait of her close friend."[2] This was, of course, also a way of deflecting from portraits as realistic representations (including typical ones) to portraits as purely formal expression. Toomer wrote to Georgia O'Keeffe on January 13, 1924:

> Have you come to the story "Bona and Paul" in *Cane!* Impure and imperfect as it is, I feel that you and Stieglitz will catch its essential design as no others can. Most people cannot see this story because of the inhibitory baggage they bring with them. When I say "white," they see a certain white man, when I say "black," they see a certain Negro. Just as they miss Stieglitz's intentions, achievements! Because they see "clouds." So that at the end, when Paul resolves these contrasts to a unity, my intelligent commentators wonder what its [*sic*] all about. Someday perhaps, with greater purity and a more perfect art, I'll do the thing. And meanwhile the gentlemen with intellect will

1. Cited in Kerman and Eldridge, *Lives*, 95.
2. Eldredge, *O'Keeffe*, 44. For a full analysis of Toomer's literary work in relationship to O'Keeffe's and Stieglitz's visual arts, see Nadell, "Experience."

haggle over the question as to whether or not I have expressed the "South."[3]

This is most dramatically apparent in Toomer's notions of racial identity, including his own. A philosophical spirit in a world of race antagonisms, Toomer was bent on any verbal strategy that would promote the transcendence rather than the hardening of racial categories, all the more so since Toomer had a modern, analytical understanding of the mechanisms of racial differentiation. Racial tension to him was not an ancient survival but a new creation. In his essay "Race Problems and Modern Society," published in 1929, he writes that

> the new Negro is much more Negro and much less American than was the old Negro of fifty years ago. From the point of view of sociological types, the types which are arising among Negroes, such as the business man, the politician, the college student, the writer, the propagandist, the movie enthusiast, the bootlegger, the taxi driver, etc.—these types among Negroes are more and more approaching the corresponding white types. But, just as certain as it is that this increasing correspondence of types makes the drawing of distinction supposedly based on skin color or blood composition appear more and more ridiculous, so it is true that the lines are being drawn with more force between the colored and white groups.[4]

In an unpublished essay entitled "The Americans" he views America as the place

> where mankind, long dismembered into separate usually repellant groupings, long scattered over the face of the earth, is being reassembled into one whole and undivided human race. America will include the earth.
>
> There is a new race here. For the present we may call it the American race. That, to date, not many are aware of its existence, that they do not realize that they themselves belong to it—this does not mean it does not exist; It simply means it does not yet exist for them because they, under the suggestion of hypnotic labels and false beliefs, are blind to it. Bur these labels and beliefs will die. They too must and will die. And the sight of people will be freed from them, and the people will become less blind and they will use their sight and see.

---

3. Rusch, *Reader*, 280–281.
4. Toomer, "Race Problems," 98–99. This essay, reprinted in *Theories of Ethnicity: A Classical Reader* (New York: New York University Press, 1996), 168–190, has not received much attention by Toomer scholars. See, however, Williams, "Eugenics," 1–12; and Lindberg, "Raising *Cane*."

> This new race is neither white nor black nor red nor brown. These are the old terms for old races, and they must be discarded. This is a new race; and though to some extent, to be sure, white and black and red and brown strains have entered into its formation, we should not view it as part white, part black, and so on. . . . Water, though composed of two parts of hydrogen and one part of oxygen, is not hydrogen and oxygen; it is *water*.[5]

The logic of segregationism was all the more absurd to Toomer since he perceived that the old African American culture was disappearing, whereas the new American culture was a shared crossover culture. He asked himself: "Was Seventh Street Negro?" and answers: "Only in the boldness of its expression. In its healthy freedom. American. For the shows that please Seventh Street make their fortunes on Broadway."[6] Black culture was, for Toomer, an intricate part and tastemaker of American culture, and yet the mental (and social) boundaries between black and white were being reinforced rather than blurred.

What could a writer do to fight such racial blindness and ridiculousness as was prominent, for example, in the Virginia legislature, which passed the *Act to Preserve Racial Purity* in 1924, defining any person "in whom there is ascertainable any Negro blood" a colored person? The U.S. census after 1920 also no longer provided a category for interracial or biracial Americans.[7] Toomer was convinced that a rethinking of the power of language in creating group divisions was in order, especially for writers. His aesthetics had to work against, and his theoretical pronouncements had to attack and transcend, facile labels. In the essay "The Americans" he stressed, after having made the analogy with water, in a very modern way the sociological (not biological) nature of racial distinctions:

> There is only one pure race—and this is the *human* race. We all belong to it—and this is the most and the least that can be said of any of us with accuracy. For the rest, it is mere talk, mere labelling, merely a manner of speaking, merely a sociological, not a biological, thing. I myself merely talk when I speak of the blending of the bloods of the white, black, red, and brown races giving rise to a new race, to a new unique blood, when I liken the combination of these strains to the combination of hydrogen and oxygen producing water. For the blood of all the

5. Rusch, *Reader.* 107–108.
6. Letter to Waldo Frank, late 1922 or early 1923, excerpted in Turner, *Cane,* 151. Toomer's view of black culture as prototypically American culture prefigures the thought of Albert Mummy in *The Omni-Americans* Ralph Ellison in *Shadow and Act.*
7. For an excellent discussion of Toomer in this context see Hutchinson, "Racial Discourse," 226–150.

races is *human* blood. There are no differences between the blood of a Caucasian and the blood of a Negro as there are between hydrogen and oxygen. In the mixing and blending of so-called races there are mixtures and blending of the same stuff.[8]

In his postimagist collection of aphorisms, *Essentials* (1931), he draws the consequences from such reflections and writes about himself:

> I am of no particular race. I am of the human race, a man at large in the human world, preparing a new race.
>
> I am of no specific region. I am of earth.
>
> I am of no particular class. I am of the human class, preparing a new class.
>
> I am neither male nor female nor in-between. I am of sex, with male differentiations.
>
> I am of no special field, I am of the field of being.[9]

The fourth of these "definitions" might explain the reason why in 1920 he chose the name "Jean" over his baptismal name Nathan Eugene for publication; this choice made Toomer part of a 1920s penchant among modernists for gender ambiguity.[1]

Yet it was particularly the first maxim that remained his greatest concern. Toomer would express similar sentiments in his Whitman-inspired poem "Blue Meridian" (1936) and in his autobiographical writings. Toomer, who was in this respect, too, an heir to Walt Whitman's utopian hopes for the New World, tended to see both "America" and the first person singular "I" as potentially all-inclusive. He writes in "On Being an American":

> I had lived among white people. I had lived among colored people. I had lived among Jews. I had met and known people of the various nationalistic groups. I had come into contact with my fellow countrymen from the bottom to the top of the American scene.
>
> I had seen the divisions, the separatisms and antagonisms. I had observed that, if the issue came up, very few of these United States citizens were aware of being *Americans*. On the

8. Rusch, *Reader*, 109.
9. Toomer, *Essentials*, xxiv.
1. One thinks, for example, of Man Ray's portrait of Marcel Duchamp as Rrose (1921) or of Anton Räderscheidt's doubling self-portrait (1928).

contrary, they were aware of, and put value upon, their hearsay descents, their groupistic affiliations.[2]

He therefore suggested to the editor of *Prairie* magazine: "It is stupid to call me anything other than an American."[3]

Toomer's identity choice was at odds, however, with the way in which race is defined in the United States. When Nathan Eugene Pinchback Toomer was born on December 26, 1894, he was born into a family with a long-standing tradition of racial ambiguity.[4] His father, Nathan Toomer, had been born in 1841 and may have been a slave or freeborn. He was the light-skinned son of a prosperous Georgia plantation owner of English, Dutch, and Spanish descent and a "woman of mixed blood, including Negro and Indian." Nathan Toomer lived on both sides of the color line: as a white man in the South, and as a Negro in Washington, D.C. He was a restless man and left Jean's mother, Nina Pinchback (1868–1909), a year after Jean's birth. Nina was the daughter of Pinckney Benton Stewart Pinchback (the son of a white father, Major William Pinchback, who also had a legal white wife and family on his Virginia plantation) and a Mulatto slave mother, Eliza Benton Stewart, who was, according to Toomer, "of English, Scotch, Welsh, German, African, and Indian stock." She bore William ten children, the first in 1829 at age fifteen or sixteen; after the sixth childbirth, William manumitted her and the surviving children. Pinckney was born in 1837 in Macon, Georgia, when the family was journeying west after the Jacksonian Indian removals. In 1846 P. B. S. Pinchback and his brother Napoleon were sent to Hiram S. Gilmore High School in Cincinnati, "a private academy catering to the offspring of just such unions as the Major and his mulatto helpmate" (Arna Bontemps). After Major William Pinchback's death, no money was forthcoming; Napoleon functioned as head of the family but went insane, and the family broke up. The twelve-year-old Pinckney was on his own and worked as steward on riverboats, became a gambler, and moved to New Orleans where, in 1860, he married Toomer's maternal grandmother, Emily Hethorne, an Anglo-French Creole woman who was light in appearance and about whose racial background there is conflicting information. Pinchback, too, was so lightskinned that his sister Adeline advised him in 1863 to pass for white. Pinchback became the first African American to serve as governor of a state when he was appointed in 1872 as acting governor of Louisiana. (At

2. Turner, *Wayward*, 121.
3. Toomer to Samuel Pessin, cited in Kerman and Eldridge, *Lives*, 99.
4. The biographical information is derived from Turner, *Cane*, from Bone, *Down Home*, from Onita Marie Estes-Hicks, "Jean Toomer: A Biographical and Critical Study (*Cane*)" (Ph.D. diss., Columbia University, 1982), and from conversations with the late Marjorie Content Toomer. See also Hicks, "National Identity," 22–44.

one point Toomer declared that Pinchback had only said he was black for the political motive of being appointed governor during Reconstruction.) In addition to their daughter, Nina, the Pinchbacks also had three sons, Pinckney, who was educated at Andover and the Philadelphia College of Pharmacy, Bismarck, a freethinker and lawyer, and Walter, who served in the Spanish-American War in Cuba and later became a doctor. Nina was sent to the private Riverside School in Massachusetts. After his parents' divorce in 1899 Jean Toomer lived with her and his grandparents in a black middle-class neighborhood in Washington, D.C.; his mother remarried in 1906. Her new husband, Archibald Combes (sometimes spelled Coombs), descended from the famous New Jersey Mulatto colony Gouldtown in Cumberland County, near Bridgeton (probably from Jacob Coombs, the son of William Coombs and Elizabeth Pierce Coombs, and Clara Gould Coombs, a direct descendant of the Gouldtown founders), yet both Nina and Combes were described as "white" on their marriage certificate. Toomer lived with his mother and stepfather in Brooklyn and in a white neighborhood in New Rochelle for three years when he was twelve to fourteen years old. After Nina Pinchback's death, Jean Toomer lived with his maternal grandparents in Washington, D.C., and graduated from the famous black Dunbar (then called M Street) High School.

Obviously, his mysterious father's Georgia background and the Georgia birth of his overpowering maternal grandfather made Toomer's teaching experience in Sparta a much deeper quest: "When one is on the soil of one's ancestors, anything can come to one," he writes in *Cane*; and in "Song of the Son" it is hard not to think of an autobiographic significance to the lines of the son who comes to the soil "to catch thy plaintive soul."

> Thy son, in time, I have returned to thee,
> Thy son, I have In time returned to thee.[5]

Toomer's project in *Cane* was thus an aesthetic experiment, a study of a vanishing rural folk culture, a quest for the meaning of modern "America" and his own Americanness, and the expression of a profoundly personal and deeply felt genealogical engagement. He described his own background in a famous letter to Max Eastman and Claude McKay, the editors of the radical *Liberator*, in 1922, in order to explain *Cane*:

> Racially, I seem to have (who knows for sure) seven blood mixtures: French, Dutch, Welsh, Negro, German, Jewish, and Indian. Because of these, my position in America has been a

5. W. Edward Farrison, in Turner, *Cane*, 179, argues, however, that "thy son" need not be Identified as Toomer.

curious one. I have lived equally amid the two race groups. Now white, now colored. From my own point of view I am naturally and inevitably an American ... Within the last two or three years, however, my growing need for artistic expression has pulled me deeper and deeper into the Negro group. And as my powers of receptivity increased, I found myself loving it in a way that I could never love the other. It has stimulated and fertilized whatever creative talent I may contain within me. A visit to Georgia last fall was the staring point of almost everything of worth that I have done. I heard the folksongs come from the lips of Negro peasants. I saw the rich dusk beauty that I had heard many false accents about, and of which till then, I was somewhat skeptical. And a deep part of my nature, a part I had repressed, sprang suddenly to life and responded to them. Now, I cannot conceive of myself as aloof and separated.[6]

"American" as an ideal self-description meant for Toomer an identification for people of all backgrounds who could acknowledge their shared and mixed characteristics—in opposition to the silent usurpation of the term "American" to stand for "white American." The United States as a reality, however, was characterized by an emphasis on "groupistic" descent, which drew Toomer both closer to a deeper experience of black life and to a more profound claim on his Americanness. Like many nineteenth-century New Orleans Creoles, Toomer lived—and responded intellectually and aesthetically to— the paradox of American racial construction that simply defined him as "black," all his other "ascertainable" ancestry notwithstanding. When he and the novelist Margery Latimer, a descendant of Anne Bradstreet, got married in March of 1931 (after the group psychology experiment at Portage, Wisconsin), he issued the following, familiar-sounding statement, entitled "A New Race In America":

There is a new race in America. I am a member of this new race. It is neither white nor black nor in-between. It is the American race, differing as much from white and black as white and black differ from each other. It is possible that there are Negro and Indian bloods in my descent along with English, Spanish, Welsh, Scotch, French, Dutch, and German. This is common in America, and it is from all these strains that the American race is being born. But the old divisions into white, black, brown, red are outworn in this country. They have had their day. Now is the time of the birth of a new order, a new

6. Cited in Arna Bontemps's introduction to Toomer, Cane [212–13 in this edition]. The latter part of this letter is included in Turner, Cane, 128–129, and cited in Kerman and Eldridge, Lives, 96.

vision, a new ideal of man. I proclaim this order. My marriage
to Margery Latimer is the marriage of two Americans.[7]

The *World Telegram* headline read "Negro Who Wed White Novelist Sees New Race." Whatever Toomer saw, the newspaper failed to
see—and the headline seems like a translation of one of Toomer's
*Essentials* into a journalistic cliché.[8]

Toomer would not only deplore such sensationalist and hostile
labeling at a time that interracial marriage was prohibited in the
majority of the United States; upon the completion of *Cane* he also
came to reject the label "Negro writer." He received largely favorable reviews and comments from black intellectuals: for example,
the authoritative Du Bois praised Toomer for daring to "hurl his
pen across the very face of our sex conventionality," noted that he
painted things "with an impressionist's sweep of color," and admired
the book's "strange flashes of power" even when it was difficult to
understand it; and the aesthete Alain Locke thought that *Cane*
was, with Wright's *Native Son* and Ellison's *Invisible Man*, one of the
three best works of the modern period and found that in Toomer's
text "the emotional essences of the Southland were hauntingly
evoked in an impressionistic poetic sort of realism."[9] Yet Toomer
questioned—as we saw in his letter to O'Keeffe—his role as a representative of "the South," and, more controversially, he did not
wish to be included in anthologies such as Nancy Cunard's *Negro*.[1]
He was also apprehensive of friendly writers who, like Sherwood
Anderson, saw him too exclusively as "Negro." He wrote to Waldo
Frank around March 1923: "Sherwood limits me to Negro. As an

7. Rusch, *Reader*. 105.
8. Lindberg, "Raising *Cane*," 73 n. 17, comments on this passage: "Toomer is not even a
   writer, but simply a Negro looking for a new race through (dread) miscegenation."
   North, *Dialect*, 163, describes the "almost hysterical" reaction of *Time* magazine to
   Toomer's marriage to Latimer: *Time* "quoted his idea about the new American race
   with scorn and affected alarm under the ironic title of 'Just Americans.' The article
   suggested that some states, like Wisconsin, where Toomer and Latimer were married,
   were insufficiently vigilant against marriages between the races," See Kerman and
   Eldridge, *Lives*, 202, for other responses.
9. Such other important black American writers as Countée Cullen, James Weldon Johnson, William Stanley Braithwaite, Jessie Fauset, and Claude McKay also responded
   enthusiastically to Toomer's *Cane*, as McKay, *Toomer*, 238, has shown. In addition,
   Rudolph P. Byrd cites a letter by Sterling A. Brown describing *Cane* as "one of the most
   beautiful and moving books of contemporary American literature" and discusses
   Toomer's influence on Langston Hughes, Michael Harper's "Cryptograms," Alice
   Walker's *Meridian*, Ernest J. Gaines's *The Autobiography of Miss Jane Pittman*, and
   Gloria Naylor's *The Women of Brewster Place* (Byrd, *Years*, 183–189).
1. See McKay, *Toomer*, 46–50; Byrd, *Years*, 97, cites the Toomer letter to Cunard of Feb-
   ruary 8, 1930: "Though I am interested in and deeply value the Negro, I am not a
   Negro. And though I have written about the Negro, and value the material and the art
   that is Negro, all my writings during the past seven years have been on other subjects.
   In America I am working for a vision of this country as composed of people who are
   Americans first, and only of certain descents as secondary matters." Toomer did, however, contribute to Sterling Brown's *Negro Caravan* (1941), perhaps because Brown had
   praised *Cane* as an *American* book.

approach, as a constant element (part of a larger whole) of interest, Negro is good. But try to tie me to one of my parts is surely to [lose] me. My own letters have taken Negro as a point, and from there have circled out. Sherwood, for the most part, ignores the circles."[2] Conversely, Toomer would also question Frank's failure to include the Negro more fully in *Our America*: "No picture of a southern person is complete without its bit of Negro-determined psychology."[3]

For Toomer, black and white were linked together like twins, like yin and yang; but racist labels, lazy thinking, and faith in clichés prevented this reality from finding universal creative expression. And it is here that Toomer perceived his own avant-garde position. In the ideal American world of racial reciprocity, Toomer conceived of his art as a spiritual sort of racial amalgamation, which he explained in his letter to McKay and Eastman: "I have strived for a spiritual fusion analogous to the fact of racial intermingling. Without denying a single element in me, with no desire to subdue one to the other, I have sought to let them function as complements. I have tried to let them live in harmony."[4] A few days earlier, he had similarly written to John McClure; "I alone, as far as I know, have striven for a spiritual fusion, analogous to the fact of racial intermingling. It has been rough riding. Nor am I through. Have just begun, in fact. This, however, has neither social nor political implications. My concern is solely with art. What am I? From my own point of view, naturally and inevitably an American."[5]

Toomer thought that *Cane* was only the beginning of a long road. Though, indeed, many projects and fragments, long manuscripts, a few literary publications, and published essays and aphorisms followed, no second Toomer book to equal the brilliance of *Cane* ever appeared. *Cane* united aesthetic experimentation, the contemplation of African American folk culture in modern America, the themes of genealogical origins, migration, and interracialism, while it challenged easy labels and insisted on the need for a new spiritual wholeness. It remains Toomer's outstanding contribution to modern literature.

2. Cited in Kerman and Eldridge, *Lives*, 97.
3. Toomer to Frank, April 26, 1922. Cited in Kerman and Eldridge, *Lives*, 87.
4. Cited in Arna Bontemps's introduction to Toomer, *Cane*, [212 in this edition]; Turner, *Cane*, 128; and Kerman and Eldridge, *Lives*, 96.
5. Toomer to McClure, July 22, 1922, cited in Kerman and Eldridge, *Lives*, 96.

# MARK WHALAN

## Jean Toomer and the Avant-Garde†

In 1923, amongst the many reviews of Jean Toomer's *Cane*, came two of very contrasting opinion. Disdaining "certain innovators who conceive language to be little more than a series of ejaculatory spasms," the *Minneapolis Journal* suggested "if the Negro (and the south) is to become really articulate its new writers must seek better models than those Mr Toomer follows."[1] In contrast, the African American critic Montgomery Gregory, writing in the first issue of *Opportunity*, soon to become the pre-eminent forum for the incipient New Negro Renaissance, waxed more lyrical:

> Fate has played another of its freakish pranks in decreeing that southern life should be given its most notable artistic expression by the pen of a native son of Negro descent . . . Verse, fiction and drama are fused into a spiritual unity, an "aesthetic equivalent" of the Southland . . . "Cane" is not OF the South, it is not OF the Negro; it IS the South, it IS the Negro—as Jean Toomer has experienced them.[2]

Despite their differences in opinion, these reviews nonetheless shared the evaluative criteria that characterized the reaction to *Cane*—and determined its importance—both in 1923 and in most of the subsequent (and voluminous) criticism devoted to it. Both were concerned with the effectiveness of the formal innovations and formal eclecticism of the work; with how well Jean Toomer had found either a voice or an "aesthetic equivalent" for the South; and to what degree Toomer was a "representative man," a figurehead and a model for subsequent African American writing. The reviews also suggest a critical terrain that would figure largely in the decade; the interest in "the folk," the politics of the observer—namely who had the authority to observe, and how one's situation affected what could be seen; and the political value of formal experimentalism. *Cane* was one of the first texts to pose these issues for the writers, periodicals, and audiences of the New Negro Renaissance, and it

† From *The Cambridge Companion to the Harlem Renaissance*, ed. George Hutchinson (Cambridge, England: Cambridge University Press, 2007). Permission is gratefully acknowledged [by the author] to reproduce manuscript material from the Jean Toomer Papers, James Weldon Johnson Collection, Beinecke Rare Book and Manuscript Library, Yale University. Reprinted with the permission of Cambridge University Press.
1. *Minneapolis Journal*, October 14, 1923. Review and publicity material in Jean Toomer Papers, Box 26 Folder 612, Jean Toomer Papers are hereafter abbreviated to JTP.
2. From *Opportunity* 1 (December 1923), 374–375. Reprinted in Jean Toomer, *Cane*, ed. Darwin T. Turner (New York: Norton, 1988), pp. 165–66. [See also pp. 177–179 in this volume. Page numbers in square brackets refer to this Norton Critical Edition.]

was widely admired by the new generation of African American
authors emerging in the 1920s. Unique and challenging, the
"spasms" of what proved to be Toomer's only major work were far
from the aesthetic dead-end predicted by the *Minneapolis Journal*.

Part of this uniqueness sprang from Jean Toomer's own social
position. As he wrote in 1928, "I have never lived within the 'color
line,' and my life has never been cut off from the general course and
conduct of American white life."[3] This liminality, and his refusal to
accept the ever-hardening application of the "one-drop rule" in
social conduct, meant that from at least his early twenties he "passed
from the one [racial group] to the other quite naturally, with no loss
of my own identity and integrity" (56). Although Toomer exaggerated this social mobility later in his career, his ability to mix with
disparate and diverse artistic and intellectual communities—
communities separated as much by aesthetic principle as by race—
undoubtedly formed the basis for *Cane*'s stunning formal complexity
and range. It also underpinned his complex meditation on racial
liminality in *Cane*, a facet which, as George Hutchinson notes,
"remained virtually invisible to critics for over half a century."[4]

A key part of that diverse social mixture was Toomer's childhood
in an environment steeped in the most contemporary debates and
ideas in African American culture and politics. Born in 1894 and
deserted by his father before he was a year old, Toomer spent most
of his youth in the home of his maternal grandfather, P. B. S.
Pinchback. Pinchback was a part of the "Negro Four Hundred," the
elite African American middle class of Washington, which Toomer
referred to as a "natural and transient aristocracy."[5] Pinchback had
been acting Governor of Louisiana during reconstruction, and this
background gave Toomer access to the African American intelligentsia of the city that congregated around Howard University and
the Dunbar High School. During the early 1920s, and after several
misadventures at various northern universities and colleges, Toomer
based himself back in Washington. Now committed to writing (he
had briefly considered becoming a musician), he sent drafts of
poetry and thoughts on issues of racial politics to his friends Alain
Locke and Georgia Douglas Johnson, and was a guest at their
houses. He attended reading groups on the history of slavery
attended by the poet Clarissa Scott, the author and Howard Librarian E. C. Williams, and the playwright and teacher Mary Burrill.

3. "The Crock of Problems," in *Jean Toomer: Selected Essays and Literary Criticism*, ed.
Robert B. Jones (Knoxville: University of Tennessee Press, 1996), pp. 55–59, at 56.
4. "Identity in Motion: Placing *Cane*," in Geneviève Fabre and Michel Feith, eds., *Jean
Toomer and the Harlem Renaissance* (New Brunswick, NJ: Rutgers University Press,
2001), pp. 38–56, at 53.
5. Jean Toomer, *The Wayward and the Seeking: A Collection of Writings by Jean Toomer*,
ed. Darwin T. Turner (Washington, DC: Howard University Press, 1982), p. 85.

He used these connections to get an (ultimately disappointing) introduction to W. E. B. Du Bois; it was also these contacts that led him to briefly consider editing a magazine devoted to African American culture. He also used these connections to land a temporary job as the substitute school principal for the all-black Sparta Agricultural and Industrial Institute in Georgia in 1921, a job which proved crucial in the genesis of *Cane* and which he romanticized in all his recollections of it. As he later remarked on his first sustained experience of the rural South:

> Here was red earth, here pine trees, and smoke or haze in the valley. Here was cane or cotton fields, here cabins. Here was the south, before cities. Here were Negroes, people of the earth, and their singing. Never before had I heard spirituals and work songs. Here I heard them in their native setting, and they were like a part of me. At times I identified with the whole scene so intensely that I lost my own identity.[6]

As *Cane* demonstrates, Toomer was fascinated by black preindustrial culture in the South, the work songs that set the tempo for field labour and the spirituals that testified to the emancipatory yearnings—both physical and metaphysical—of an enslaved people. Along with many other authors and anthropologists in the 1920s, he was attracted to how these forms relied on improvisation and interpretation, in contrast to the increasingly standardized and schematized consumer economy driving both the postwar economic boom and the great migration. *Cane*, in this respect, represented what he called a "swan-song," as "the folk-spirit was walking in to die on the modern desert" (*Wayward* 123). He was also attracted to the way these folk forms established community, both in the call-and-response dynamic of the work song and the field holler, and the ancestral community of slavery they established for all people of African descent in the USA. Accordingly, the field cry of "eoho" echoes across *Cane*, from "Cotton Song" to "Calling Jesus" and "Harvest Song"; under the guise of gathering in the cotton harvest the work song pattern of "Cotton Song" calls all African Americans to participate in the collective labour of establishing freedom. His interest contained elements of celebration, and elements of salvage. In "Song of the Son," for example, Toomer establishes himself as a cultural saviour; "just before an epoch's sun declines / Thy son, in time I have returned to thee, / Thy son, I have in time returned to thee" (*Cane* 14) [16]. In becoming the planter of a "singing tree / Caroling softly souls of slavery," he claims to preserve in poetry this oral heritage of the black South, and it was this sentiment that made

6. "On Being an American," JTP Box 20 Folder 513, p. 38.

"Song of the Son" a favourite amongst anthologists of Negro writing in the 1920s.

However, Toomer's collection was far from being an anti-modern, nostalgic lament for the concreting over of a rural, oral culture: accordingly, it is not the straightforward elegy for an organic and foundational "folk culture" that various African American cultural nationalists in the 1920s sometimes pretended it was. This is partly because, as Charles Scruggs and Lee VanDemarr have suggested, the "terrors of American history" are never far from the vivid landscapes and lyrical folksongs of Toomer's Georgia. The relation between the rural African Americans Toomer portrayed and the red Georgian soil was not one of nurture and organic connection, but one of enforced servitude and ambivalence; he later drew the distinction "between the wish to return to nature, and the desire to touch the soil. Nature . . . is a virginal tract of land. The soil is tilled land, saturate with the life of those who have worked it," and the subtext of *Cane* is the brutal and enslaved nature of that "saturation."[7] These terrors of history are often tacit, or signalled by ellipsis, such as the silence that surrounds the whereabouts of Karintha's baby in the first story of the collection. At other times they are shockingly explicit, such as the way that the ritualized burning of a black man in the act of lynching is inextricable from the discursive construction of white female beauty in the South in "Portrait in Georgia," whereby the woman's "slim body" is "white as the ash / of black flesh after flame" (*Cane* 29) [30].

Crucially, the most developed character in *Cane*, Ralph Kabnis, is paralyzed by his inability to relate to southern history in the form of Father John, the ex-slave who lives in the cellar of Fred Halsey's workshop. Indeed, Kabnis's inability to face this "father of hell" results in his "misshapen, split-gut, tortured, twisted words" (104, 110) [104, 109]. The threat of violence and the memory of violence— often an institutionalized violence—is a constant pressure in Toomer's South; as Kabnis thinks, "things are so immediate in Georgia" (86) [84]. Moreover, this violence does not run merely along racial lines, as many of the most evocative portraits of part one of *Cane* are of abused women. As Vera Kutzinski observes of the women in *Cane*, "that they are mysterious, elusive and sexually disturbing is a function not of their 'nature' but the male narrators' need carefully to filter out emotionally and ideologically troubling histories of sexual and economic abuse, along with obvious differences in social class, which would (and do) interfere with these figures' ability to represent cultural and spiritual purity and wholeness."[8] As many

7. JTP Box 60 Folder 1411.
8. "Unseasonal Flowers: Nature and History in Placido and Jean Toomer," *Yale Journal of Criticism* 3 (1990), 153–79, at 169.

critics have noted, this issue of the "spectatorial artist" and how the northern, male, middle-class observers of part one frame, interpret and desire these women makes thematically explicit the question of what type of "cultural work" occurred in the 1920s when working-class, rural black women enter literary representation.[9] As such, the position (and the selectivity) of the observer—a topic of interest which united contemporary anthropology and modernist aesthetics—becomes a troubling problem for Toomer, and a vital issue for considering how what Toomer's friend Waldo Frank called the "buried cultures" of America's racial minorities could be brought into the current of contemporary literature.

If Toomer drew heavily on black folk culture in *Cane*—both on its formal resources and on its figurations of suffering, oppression, and resistance—he also engaged in a more substantial way than any other figure of the New Negro Renaissance with the ideas of the white avant-garde. Imagism and futurism, Robert Frost's suggestive evocations of place in his understated language (along with his supple use of traditional verse forms), and Sherwood Anderson's lyric, open-ended short fiction and his ear for the rhythms of speech were all important influences on Toomer's style. So too were the psychological exteriorizations of the drama of Eugene O'Neill, and the lively imagery of Lola Ridge's poetry. Most significant, however, was the prose and cultural criticism of Waldo Frank. As Toomer admitted, "He is so powerful and close, he has so many elements that I need, that I would be afraid of downright imitation if I were not so sure of myself."[1] Toomer and Frank shared a fascination with the spiritual and political charge that inhered in the meeting of strangers from across social divides; in the importance of symbol to demonstrate how the metaphysical is anchored in the mundane; and in the importance of moulding prose to fit the contours of subjective experience—for as Frank said, "our standard of reality is an accumulating, gyrating and disappearing flux of subjective contributions."[2] Moreover, both shared a Whitmanesque sense of the prophetic and socially inclusive powers of the artist; as Frank exclaimed with typical grandeur and egotism, "the life of America is a stupendous symbol of the human chaos which such an artist

9. See Susan L. Blake, "The Spectatorial Artist and the Structure of *Cane*," *CLA Journal* 17 (June 1974), 516–34; reprinted in *Cane*, pp. 217–23; Laura Doyle, *Bordering on the Body: The Racial Matrix of Modern Fiction and Culture* (Oxford: Oxford University Press, 1994); and Nathan Grant, *Masculinist Impulses: Toomer, Hurston, Black Writing, and Modernity* (Columbia: University of Missouri Press, 2004).
1. *The Letters of Jean Toomer, 1919–1924*, ed. Mark Whalan (Knoxville: University of Tennessee Press, 2006), pp. 90–91.
2. Waldo Frank, "Note on the Novel," in *Salvos: An Informal Book about Books and Plays* (New York: Boni and Liveright, 1924), pp. 223–31, at 227.

beholds in all life ere the transfiguring magic of his unitary vision
has been worked upon it."[3]

Aspects of Frank's cultural criticism also appealed to Toomer. In
*Our America* (1919), Frank had followed Van Wyck Brooks's lead in
seeing the dominance of the "Pioneer" and the "Puritan" mentality
in American life as deeply detrimental to American collectivity in
privileging material gain above cultural and spiritual connection.
Moreover, Frank saw this legacy as inherently racialized, the result
of an Anglo-Saxon cultural hegemony. Consequently Frank, along
with several contemporary anthropologists such as Edward Sapir,
felt lessons could be learned from what they perceived to be more
culturally and spiritually rich and complex ways of life in North
America, particularly from the Native American tribes in the Southwest and their interactions with Spanish culture, which had been
"buried" by Anglo-Saxon cultural dominance.[4] Frank hoped these
"buried cultures" could help effect a revolution akin to those that had
occurred in Europe, wherein a "deep potential energy—religious,
aesthetic—which is simply the love of life and which, applied by
suffering and education to the level of practical demands, [became]
indefeasibly the kinetic energy of revolt."[5]

Toomer was attracted to this brand of lyrical revolution, which
built on his commitment to socialist ideas evident from his 1919
publications in the socialist paper *The Call*, and also on his attendance at the "worker's university," New York's Rand School, in
1918.[6] It also offered him a political application for what he had
experienced in Georgia. As Toomer told Frank in his first letter to
him in 1922, "In your Our America I missed your not including the
Negro," and he let his work speak for itself in suggesting how rural
African American culture might be exactly the type of "buried culture" that had so fascinated Frank in 1919. Accordingly, Frank was
soon planning a revised edition of *Our America* to include a section
on Negro culture, with Toomer graciously suggesting "What little I
know is freely open to you" (*Letters* 31, 49). As 1922 progressed, Frank
became Toomer's most important and intimate literary comrade;
they addressed each other as "brother" in their prolific correspondence, and read and edited each other's work. Toomer introduced
Frank to the African American culture of the rural South in their

3. Waldo Frank, "The Artist in Our Jungle," in *In the American Jungle*, 1925–36 (New York: Farrar and Rinehart, 1937), pp. 149–53, at 152.
4. See Edward Sapir, "Culture, Genuine and Spurious," 1924; reprinted in *Selected Writings of Edward Sapir in Language, Culture and Personality*, ed. David G. Mandelbaum (Berkeley: University of California Press, 1949), pp. 308–31; and Susan Hegeman, *Patterns for America: Modernism and the Concept of Culture* (Princeton, NJ: Princeton University Press, 1999).
5. Waldo Frank, *Our America* (New York: Boni and Liveright, 1919), p. 231.
6. See Charles Scruggs and Lee VanDemarr, *Jean Toomer and the Terrors of American History* (Philadelphia: Pennsylvania University Press, 1998), p. 48.

trip to South Carolina in the summer; Frank returned the favor by providing formal suggestions of how individual text-pieces could interrelate in his 1922 short story cycle *City Block*. He also introduced Toomer to the publishers Boni and Liveright, and provided several other contacts in the white avant-garde.

Perhaps the most significant of these was Gorham B. Munson, editor of the little magazine *Secession*. As Malcolm Cowley later recollected, the postwar "younger generation"—including writers who coalesced around *Secession* such as e.e. cummings, Kenneth Burke, Hart Crane, and Matthew Josephson—held "a new interest in form . . . one can forecast safely that our younger literature will be at least as composed as a good landscape."[7] In keeping with this new interest, Munson spoke of *Secession*'s attraction to the "cerebral" qualities of art, in particular "abstractness, the concomitant of form"—a preoccupation also evinced by his work on theorizing the process of reader-response—in contrast to the more "emotional, instinctive" properties of Frank.[8] Toomer was instructed by these distinctions, and was also interested in Munson's refusal to condemn industrialization and its production of mass culture, a rejection Frank had embarked upon fairly completely in *Our America*. In his largely laudatory critical study of Frank, Munson sided with the Dadaists connected with *Secession* in averring that Frank's groundwork for a lyrical revolution in American culture had overlooked a crucial resource, suggesting that mass culture and mechanical technologies such as the skyscraper, the movies, and electric light may well represent the "peculiar genius of the American people thrusting into a new age."[9] In an open letter to Munson, Toomer would sound almost like a Futurist in echoing that sentiment, describing Washington as "pregnant, warm, dynamic, tensioned, massed, jazzed, lovable . . . I had been in every powerhouse in the city before I dragged myself into the Corcoran Gallery."[1]

Consequently, Toomer began to become more interested in the fusion of cultures then forming the milieu of black urban life, a milieu that was growing rapidly and erratically owing to the Great Migration. In early 1922 he described black migrants to American cities as "a pseudo-urbanized and vulgarized, a semi-Americanized product," but by early 1923 he saw them as "jazzed, strident, modern. Seventh Street [a major black thoroughfare in Washington] is the song of crude new life. Of a new people. Negro? Only in the <u>boldness</u>

---

7. Malcolm Cowley, *Exile's Return* (New York: Viking Books, 1956), pp. 99–100.
8. Gorham Munson, *The Awakening Twenties: A Memoir-History of a Literary Period* (Baton Rouge: Louisiana University Press, 1985), p. 168.
9. Gorham Munson, *Waldo Frank: A Study* (Boni and Liveright: New York, 1923), p. 25.
1. "Open Letter to Gorham Munson," *S4N* 25 (March 1923), n.p.; reprinted in *Jean Toomer: Selected Essays and Literary Criticism*, pp. 19–20, at 19. See also Mark Whalan, "Jean Toomer, Technology, and Race," *Journal of American Studies* 36 (2002), 459–72.

of its expression. In its healthy freedom. American" (*Letters* 36, 116). This attitude was evident in the (sometimes violent) vibrancy and gaudiness of the middle section of *Cane*, set in Washington and Chicago. The "bootleggers in silken shirts" driving Cadillacs in "Seventh Street," the ethereal, jazzy Crimson Gardens nightclub in "Bona and Paul," the open play of fantasy, desire and a degree of performative identity in black theaters in "Theater" and "Box Seat," all indicated Toomer's belief that black urban life was a crude, inventive, vivid and revitalizing force for the future of American culture. As with his portrayal of the South, it is not an unbridled celebration; the black middle class's adherence to what he referred to as the "Anglo-Saxon ideal," an ideal which stressed both white supremacy and the primacy of materialism, comes in for severe criticism, as does the ability of urban geography and planning to stratify and segregate according to class and race in highly effective ways. These concerns are also evident in Toomer's minor work of the period, particularly his story "Withered Skin of Berries" and the drama "Natalie Mann." Despite these reservations, however, Toomer's interest and faith in this "New People"—what he would later call the "Negro Emergent"—would last long beyond his *Cane* years.

What would not, however, was his willingness to identify himself as a member of that group. Throughout 1922 and early 1923 he discussed his "Negro blood" with several correspondents, and wrote an essay identifying his "Negro descent."[2] But by the fall of 1913 he was responding hotly to his publisher Horace Liveright's accusation that he was "dodging" the facts of his racial identity, an accusation prompted by Toomer's reluctance to be labeled a Negro in *Cane*'s publicity material. "My racial composition and my position in the world are realities which I alone may determine," he informed Liveright, a statement that flew in the face of the ever more stringent legal codes then policing the color line (*Letters* 171). In later autobiographies Toomer would blame those he felt had sought to pin him to a Negro identity; the primary culprit here was Waldo Frank, who he charged with leaving a telling ambiguity over his racial identity in the preface to *Cane* (*Wayward* 126). By the early 1930s, Toomer was refusing to allow parts of *Cane* to be published in anthologies of Negro writing. A year later, in a statement accompanying his marriage to the white author Margery Latimer, he would affirm that "There is a new race in America. I am a member of this new race. It is neither white nor black nor in-between. It is the American race . . ."[3] This affirmation underpinned his finest late poem, "Blue

---

2. Jean Toomer, "The South in Literature," 1923; reprinted in *Jean Toomer: Selected Essays and Literary Criticism*, pp. 11–16, at 12.
3. "A New Race in America," 1931; reprinted in *A Jean Toomer Reader: Selected Unpublished Writings*, ed. Frederik L. Rusch (New York: Oxford University Press, 1993), p. 105.

Meridian" (1936), which prophesies the transcendence of racial categorizations and the arrival of "the man of blue or purple / Beyond the little tags and small marks" (*Wayward* 232). Yet the nationally syndicated newspaper coverage of his marriage—"Negro who wed white writer sees new race" was one headline—was a grimly ironic reminder of how far his position was from the laws and social conventions of the time.[4] This aspect of Toomer's life led to him being hailed as a pioneer in challenging racial essentialism by some, and as a person who had selfishly abandoned the fledgling New Negro Renaissance by others; and it formed one of the two important shifts his career took in late 1923 and 1924.[5]

The other was his embrace of the teachings of Georges I. Gurdjieff, an Armenian mystic whose theory for the "harmonious development of man" proposed that the instincts, intellect, and emotions must work in balance to allow a person to become whole and to undergo further—and higher—development. Gurdjieff's theories became highly popular in western avant-garde circles for individuals seeking spiritual—and effectively apolitical—solutions to the many social and cultural anxieties and conflicts that afflicted the 1920s. By the end of 1923 Toomer had become disaffected with the spiritual thinness of literary New York, weary of the vacuous debates and posturing he felt to be rife. Soon, however, a pamphlet outlining the work at Gurdjieff's institute at Fontainebleau, France, and a demonstration of "sacred dances" by a Gurdjieff group in New York supervised by Gurdjieff and A. R. Orage, seemed to provide answers. As he remembered, "Here was a work that indicated what must be done in order to achieve a balanced development. Here was a work whose scope was greater and more complete than anything I had dreamed of. Here, in fine, was truth" (*Wayward* 131).

By July of 1924 Toomer had sailed for France and Fontainebleau, and begun a life involved in the Gurdjieff work which lasted in a fully committed form until 1935, and which marked the entirety of the rest of his intellectual career. It also marked a change in his approach to writing, which became more didactic and denotational, As P. D. Ouspensky, one of Gurdjieff's disciples, explained, "In real art there is nothing accidental. It is mathematics . . . The artist knows and understands what he wants to convey and his work cannot produce one impression on one man and another impression on

4. See Cynthia Kerman and Richard Eldridge, *The Lives of Jean Toomer: A Hunger for Wholeness* (Baton Rouge: Louisiana State University Press, 1987), p. 202.
5. One admirer of Toomer's stance on this issue is Frederik L. Rusch; see his "The Blue Man: Jean Toomer's Solution to His Problems of Identity," *Obsidian* 6.3 (1980), 38–54. A critical reaction to Toomer's refusal of a black identity is Robert B. Jones, *Jean Toomer and the Prison House of Thought: A Phenomenology of the Spirit* (Amherst: University of Massachusetts Press, 1993).

another."[6] Although it is open to debate just how fully Toomer sub-scribed to this theory of "objective" art, after 1924 his work moved away from the fertile indeterminacy of his highly figurative style, and from the direct socio-economic concerns of the *Cane* period. Although Toomer continued to have poetry published in avant-garde magazines, and wrote several significant essays, publishers consistently rejected the novels he wrote after 1924. The only other book-length project that came to print was his privately issued collection of aphorisms, *Essentials*, which appeared in 1931.

However disappointing African American authors found Toomer's apostasy from the New Negro Movement, the contribution of *Cane* to the New Negro Renaissance from what Toomer called his time engaged in "Negro study" was a powerful one, effecting a manifold influence on the writing of the subsequent decade (*Letters* 31). W. E. B. Du Bois cautiously welcomed Toomer as "a writer who first desired to emancipate the colored world from the conventions of sex," and Toomer's frank treatment of sex and sexuality, particularly how they were intimately interrelated to the formation of racial and class identity, set the tone for much of the work that considered this topic in the Harlem Renaissance (*Cane* 171) [184]. In his seminal defence of the unique qualities of black American culture, Langston Hughes praised *Cane* for its "truly racial" contribution to American literature, by which he doubtless meant its sophisticated adaptation of black musical forms into literary usage—demonstrating how a modernist embrace of these forms could overcome the "racial mountain" of slavishness to Anglo-Saxon, bourgeois aesthetic taste.[7] Moreover, Toomer's use of the hidden, the secret, the indeterminate, and the overdetermined symbol in his work presented a model of political engagement and social critique which transcended the limitations of "protest fiction," for as James Baldwin would later famously write, *Cane* demonstrated that "only within [a] web of ambiguity, paradox, this hunger, danger, darkness, can we find at once ourselves and the power that will free us from ourselves."[8] *Cane*'s status as the product of a conjunction of avant-garde ideas and folk culture, as a cornerstone of any canon of American modernism and New Negro writing, and as an index to one of the most unusual biographies in contemporary American writing all participate in its ambiguity, paradox, danger, and darkness, its continuing ability to unsettle, astonish, and provoke.

6. P. D. Ouspensky, *In Search of the Miraculous* (London: Routledge and Kegan Paul, 1950), pp. 26–27.
7. Langston Hughes, "The Negro Artist and the Racial Mountain," 1926; reprinted in *The Norton Anthology of African American Literature*, ed. Henry Louis Gates Jr. and Nellie Y. McKay (New York: Norton, 1997), pp. 1267–71, at 1270.
8. James Baldwin, "Everybody's Protest Novel," 1949; reprinted in *Notes of a Native Son* (London: Penguin, 1995), pp. 19–28, at 21.

# GINO MICHAEL PELLEGRINI

## Jean Toomer and *Cane:*
## "Mixed-Blood" Impossibilities[†]

Even though Jean Toomer was black and white, his fascination with miscegenation in his hybrid short-story cycle *Cane* (1923) was puzzling and untimely. Joel Williamson writes that by 1915 the one-drop rule had been accepted by both blacks and whites in the North and South (109). Hence, mixed bloods with visible traces of blackness, including members of the former mulatto elite, would be judged as black by both blacks and whites. At best, they could be "in some way, satisfyingly black" (153). In this article, I put forward a reading of Toomer and *Cane* that explains his fascination with miscegenation in terms of his hope for what was possible in America. Specifically, his unique and solitary position vis-à-vis the New Negro in Black Washington and the Young American in White Manhattan provided him with the reasons, models, and ideals to believe that, in *Cane*, he could effectively voice and sketch out a mixed-race sensibility and community that would be grasped and appreciated by the American public. However, in the process of writing *Cane*, he came face to face with the rigid categories and limits of the black-white color line in the Jim Crow era, which rendered unintelligible and unsustainable in the culture at large the mixed-race sensibility and community he sought to express and develop. In other words, we see in *Cane* the ultimately futile clash of Toomer's Young American ideals with the socio-political realities of the black-white color line. *Cane* reveals the pain and frustration of this clash through muffled and ambivalent narrative voices, and through sketches of unacknowledged, crippled, misunderstood, and lost mixed race protagonists.

### Jean Toomer between 1918 and 1923:
### Contingency, Politics, and the Promise of Art

In their book *Jean Toomer and the Terrors of American History*, Charles Scruggs and Lee VanDemarr contend that the Toomer who wrote *Cane* should be read first and foremost as a political writer, although it is true that by end of 1924 he had embraced the spiritual teachings of George Gurdjieff to such an extent that he "could no longer identify with the material that had inspired [*Cane*]" (Larson 22), and would henceforth eschew black identity. Gurdjieff was an Eastern European mystic of mysterious origin who eventually

† From *Arizona Quarterly* 64.4 (Winter 2008): 1–20. Reprinted from *Arizona Quarterly* 64.4 (2008) by permission of the Regents of the University of Arizona.

settled in France. Toomer was so swayed by Gurdjieff's notion of spiritual wholeness that he actually became his disciple and traveled to France for advanced training (38). This significant turn of events in Toomer's life has led many critics to read *Cane* as a kind of spiritual autobiography in which Toomer utilizes modernist form and narrative techniques in an attempt to transcend the polarities of racial categorization and achieve spiritual wholeness. However, critics who read Toomer strictly as a modernist and/or spiritualist tend to overlook connections between *Cane* and his early political writings. His belief in socialism and support for Negro rights are evident in "Reflections on the Race Riots," an article about the Washington D.C. race riots of 1919, which Scruggs republished in the *Arizona Quarterly* alongside Toomer's other pre-*Cane* political writings that originally appeared in the socialist newspaper, *The New York Call*. In this article, Toomer defends the Negroes who rioted in reaction to Washington police brutality. He refers to them as "difficult to exploit," and attributes "race prejudice" to the "economic structure" and class exploitation. Added to this, he presents socialism both as a means to explain the plight of the Negro and as the one and only political system that can reform a racist nation (Scruggs 121). In 1919, *The Nation* also published two letters that Toomer wrote to the editor, one regarding socialism and the other regarding Negro rights (*Letters* 1–3).

His decision to voice his socialist and pro-Negro views in print was not without precedent either. He was intimately familiar with the political arena and with the role of being a public representative of the black masses and a defender of their civil rights inasmuch as he was raised by his grandfather, P. B. S. Pinchback, and his wife in their Washington D.C. home. Pinchback, who was also racially mixed but identified as a Negro, served as both the lieutenant governor and governor of Louisiana during the era of Reconstruction, and continued to be an influential political figure after moving his family to Washington in 1890 (Larson 169). In 1919, Toomer also associated himself with Alain Locke and his Washington social circle. At the time, Locke was a young professor at Howard University and a leading voice of the emergent New Negro movement. Toomer helped organize a study group with Locke, Georgia Johnson and others in Locke's circle that focused on historical and sociological aspects of Negro life in America. Toomer spent much of his time outside of Washington after 1921, but maintained a correspondence with Locke and Johnson through 1923 in which he shared much of the material about race, racism, and miscegenation that he had gathered down South in Georgia in preparation for writing the character sketches, poems, and short stories that would eventually compose *Cane* (268).

Toomer would come to view literature and art as the most effective means to uplift the minds of the masses and in so doing create cultural change in America. In New York, he participated in lectures at the radical Rand Institute and attended leftist social gatherings to meet like-minded thinkers and artists. In this way, he met Waldo Frank, who would later become his friend and mentor, give direction and form to the writings that would be included in *Cane*, and persuade his own publisher, Boni and Liveright, to accept *Cane* for publication. In 1920, Frank was an affluent and young Jewish intellectual who wrote modernist fiction and cultural criticism. He was also an established writer and well known within the literary and publishing circles of the New York Left. In 1916, he started his own cultural-literary magazine with two other young Jewish intellectuals—James Oppenheim and Paul Rosenfeld. *Seven Arts* was founded on and sought to promote the following ideals about art and culture: American culture should embrace rather than suppress the cultural histories and artistic expressions of the different American immigrant groups; the artist/writer has the right to reclaim his literary heritage; art and literature can regenerate America (Scruggs and VanDemarr 70). Van Wyck Brooks and Randolph Bourne, who were already established cultural critics, joined *Seven Arts* a short while after its inception. Their scholarship that critiqued the exclusionist ideology and practices of the dominant Anglophile groups in academia and in the American culture at large provided a systematic theoretical framework and program for *Seven Arts* which, in turn, led to the formation of Young America, a loosely tied literary group that would grow to include writers, artists, and intellectuals such as Sherwood Anderson, Hart Crane, Gorman Munson, Alfred Stieglitz, Georgia O'Keeffe, Lola Ridge, Lewis Mumford, Kenneth Burke, and Jean Toomer (84). Unfortunately, *Seven Arts* lost its funding and was forced to shut down for publishing Bourne's articles that criticized the role of the United States in WWI.

When Toomer met Frank for the first time in 1920 he had not read his controversial and popular new book, *Our America* (1919), nor was he familiar with Young America and with the history of *Seven Arts*. Frank, smarting from the shutting down of *Seven Arts*, wrote *Our America* in reaction to the growing tide of nativism, anti-Semitism, and censorship on the Left during and following WWI. He argued for a heterogeneous and hybrid America as a source of strength and promise. He explains in his preface, perhaps to avoid censorship and possible repercussions for his American publishers, that French publishers requested that he write a book that would describe to a French audience the history and cultures of America in relation to "conformist utterance" (Frank ix). Specifically, *Our*

*America* extends the program of Bourne, Brooks, and *Seven Arts* in order to critique Anglo-Saxon culture for attempting to "stamp out" from the time of the Puritans onward non-Anglo-American cultures and histories. In view of this aim, Frank discusses "buried cultures" such as those of the American Indians and Mexicans and states that Young America is about the discovery of these "adumbrated groups" (10). Furthermore, fusing the political and the literary, Frank contends that the artist/writer has the power to bring into existence a more pluralist, democratic, "trans-national" American culture by creating works that investigate, recover, and record the suppressed histories, utterances, and cultures—the "usable pasts"—of Jews, Italians, Russians, French, Slavs, Germans, and other non-Anglo-Americans. As an example, he invokes Walt Whitman as the American writer par excellence who records and celebrates in his poetry the cultures and histories of the different immigrant groups that populated New York at the turn of the twentieth century, "the multitude" that makes up the various "strains" of American culture. For this reason, Frank specifies that for Young America Whitman was far more than the father of free verse, social revolution, and cultural liberation (203). Frank concludes *Our America* with a chapter that presents the New York of his day as the model for a "trans-national" American culture yet to come, and he names and lauds the intellectuals, writers, and artists of Young America, announcing optimistically that their work will "lift America into self-knowledge" (5).

The program of Young America that Frank articulates and develops in *Our America* provided Toomer with the motivation and means to fuse his hybrid racial heritage with his socialist commitment and new literary aspirations. When Frank was attacked by novelist and suffragette Mary Austin in *The Nation* for promoting the interests of what she saw as the New York Jewish literary establishment in *Our America*, Toomer—perhaps seeing an opportunity to gain Frank's confidence—came to his defense by writing "Americans and Mary Austin" in which he explained Frank's ideas and argued that Austin's criticisms were based on nativist and anti-Semitic presumptions (Scruggs 122–26). Frank wrote Toomer a thank-you letter in October 1920 after reading his article in *The New York Call*. Toomer wrote him back more than a year later to tell him that what he found lacking in *Our America* was an account of the American Negro. In his letter, Toomer also described his mixed-race background so as to establish his credentials as a Negro, and he included poems and sketches that, in his words, were to be read as "attempts at an artistic record of Negro and mixed-blood America" (*Letters* 32). Frank responded to Toomer's writings with genuine enthusiasm. He saw Toomer's potential as a Negro writer, while he also would have seen him as forerunner of a utopian, hybrid, and "trans-national" America yet to come. That is, Frank saw that Toomer and other "new people," as Charles Chesnutt called them in *The House behind the Cedars* (1900), would be possible in the future.

In 1922, Frank came to consider Toomer a close friend and a new member of Young America. Toomer was elated about this development: "The euphoria Toomer felt over being associated with Waldo Frank and the group of intellectuals known during the Great War as Young America cannot be overestimated" (Scruggs and Van-Demarr 6). Frank provided Toomer with literary identification and legitimacy and connected him directly to Anderson, Crane, Munson, and indirectly to the work of the other writers, artists, and intellectuals of Young America. In addition, through Frank, Toomer gained prime access to the publishers of modernist and leftist literary magazines. In this way, he was able to publish in 1922 and 1923 many of the poems, character sketches, and stories that appeared later in *Cane*. Toomer would express his gratitude to Frank by dedicating "Kabnis" to him and by asking him to write the introduction to *Cane*. Moreover, he indicates to the reader that *Cane* should be read as a contribution to Frank's *Our America* project by placing curves before each of its three sections. The curves are emblematic of suppressed cultural "strains" and the hope of a "trans-national" American culture yet to come that would embrace such difference.

*Cane* then would not have been realized without the influence of Frank and the program of Young America. That is, Toomer came to believe after reading *Our America* that he had the right to investigate and recover his own literary heritage in its entirety; that the cultural and racial difference that he embodied could be an integrating force; and that an artistic record of this suppressed, heterogeneous culture and history (his hybrid ancestry) would be a catalyst for cultural change in America. In light of his appropriation of the ideals of Young America, an attempt "at an artistic record of Negro and mixed-blood America" seemed to his mind at the time both justified and within reach. Hence, in the months that passed from Frank's thank-you letter to his reply, Toomer devised and launched his own project modeled after *Our America*. In other words, he would start to investigate, recover, and record his hybrid literary heritage. The investigation of his literary heritage, like the sections of *Cane*, would be divided between the North and the South. For the writings in the Northern section, Toomer drew from his personal experiences and observations. After graduating from high school in Washington, Toomer, at his grandfather's expense, wandered back and forth from Washington to various Northern cities in search of his calling in life. He studied agriculture for one semester at the University of Wisconsin and another at the Massachusetts

College of Agriculture, and in 1916 he studied physical education for a year at the American College of Physical Training in Chicago (Larson 179). In stories and sketches such as "Bona and Paul," "Avey," "Theater", and "Box Seat", Toomer draws from and reflects upon his personal experiences and observations while living in Chicago, New York, and Washington. Toomer would have to travel down South to investigate that part of his heritage. Georgia was the place of origin for both sides of his family. The opportunity came in 1921 when he agreed to temporarily replace the principal of a Negro school in Sparta, Georgia, who had to travel up North to raise money for his school. Toomer used his three months in Sparta to investigate the local history of Negro and mixed-blood America and to gather materials for the stories, sketches, and poems that constitute the Southern section of *Cane*. On one level the final section of *Cane*, "Kabnis," is a fictional account of Toomer's attempt while living in Sparta to investigate, uncover, and record the "mixed-blood" part of his heritage, as well as the social, historical, and economic forces that led to its creation, suppression and displacement to the North.

When Toomer finally replied to Frank's thank-you letter he was clear on the purpose of his project, perhaps to the point where he would have continued to write even had Frank responded negatively to his writings. This did not happen. As a result, over the months in which he transformed his materials and writings from 1921 into the highly polished pieces that appear in *Cane*, he continued to "[draw] upon two different communities of thinking, roughly centered in black Washington and white Manhattan" (Hutchinson 43). Starting with Frank, Toomer attempted to communicate the full scope of his project to members of each community. Unfortunately, both communities claimed Toomer as a Negro and read his writings as predominantly representative of Negro America. In other words, the "mixed-blood America" aspect of his project fell on deaf ears. Frank came closest to understanding the full extent of Toomer's project, probably seeing his fascination with "mixed-blood America" in terms of a possible utopian future. Anderson and Crane reveal in their correspondence with Toomer that their understanding of his writings did not extend beyond common stereotypes and assumptions about Negroes and the black experience held by Anglo and European Americans at the time. In general, the Young Americans saw Toomer as a spokesperson for Negro America and a vehicle that could help them gain entry into that world. In view of this shared perception, Frank would ask Toomer to accompany him down South in 1922 and help him pass as black so that he could gather original and authentic material on Negro life and racism for his own planned novel, *Holiday* (1923). Furthermore, Frank probably peddled *Cane* to Boni and Liveright as a book about Negro life written by a Negro. In turn, Boni and Liveright marketed Toomer, despite his objections, as a Negro writer and *Cane* as a book with a "rhythmic beat" comparable to that produced by "the primitive tom-toms of the African jungle" (Soto 172).

Unlike the Young Americans, Locke and Johnson were intimately familiar with the complex history of miscegenation in the South. They would have therefore recognized that Toomer was a product of that history, though they might not have fully understood why in 1921 he wanted to investigate and recover his full literary heritage to create "an artistic record of mixed-blood America." Locke would have understood Toomer's project in its entirety as unrealistic and politically ineffective. Countee Cullen's comments about Toomer in a letter that he sent to Locke are generally representative of the manner in which Toomer and *Cane* were received in Black Washington amongst advocates of New Negro politics. Cullen criticized Toomer for failing in *Cane* to look "beyond the muck and mire of things" (Cullen qtd. in Scruggs and VanDemarr 219). In other words, the historical record of miscegenation that *Cane* portrays was not in line with the positive image of the Negro that Cullen, Locke, and other New Negro advocates wanted to present to White America in the 1920s. As a result, New Negro advocates, on the whole, recognized and applauded the positive and unambiguous aspects of Negro life portrayed in *Cane*, but the social and historical facts, costs, and complexities of miscegenation that Toomer foregrounds, "the muck and mire of things," had to be ignored at that time for the betterment of the race. This type of selective appropriation of his writings, most notably by Locke in his prominent anthology *The New Negro* (1925), aggravated Toomer and explains in part why he chose to distance himself from Locke and his other Black Washington friends. That is, even though he was a devout disciple of Gurdjieff by 1925, Toomer still deeply resented individuals and groups of people who limited him and his multifaceted work to the category of Negro.

In short, Toomer and his project as a whole were largely misunderstood, especially by the people he thought were closest to him and his work. However, he should not have been surprised or indignant about this outcome since he initially presented himself as a Negro to both White Manhattan and Black Washington. That is, much as his grandfather used his blackness to further his own political career, Toomer, always an opportunist, used his blackness and identified as a Negro to make himself socially and politically recognizable, understandable, and hence publishable. Nevertheless, it was also the case that in 1921 Toomer sincerely believed that, albeit under the influence of the ideals of Young America, he could be both a representative of Negro America and, at the same time, be recognized as a spokesperson for the suppressed cultural strain of mixed-blood America. In this way he could investigate and recover his full literary heritage and create a work of literature that when received by the masses would change American culture and help lift Americans into self-knowledge. Toomer, however, would come to realize *in medias res* that he had been mistaken. In the process of writing and revising the materials for *Cane*, he reached an impasse with the terrors of American history—the social, historical, political, and material reality of the black-white color line in the Jim Crow era. The ideals of Young America that in 1921 had temporarily allowed him to believe that it was possible for him to sidestep and look beyond this reality did not hold up under the weight of the dictates and limits of the black-white color line. In other words, Toomer would come to realize that the buried history of miscegenation in the South had produced a mixed-blood America of which he was a part that could not be sustained and was thus destined to dissolve and disappear within the rigid segments of White America and Negro America. He had therefore launched an idealistic investigation into his literary heritage that yielded, and could only have yielded, not answers, resolution, and recognition—"a usable past"— but more questions, uncertainties, silences, denials, and complications. In what was probably a draft of a letter to Frank in late 1923, Toomer remarked how painful the writing process had been for him practically every step of the way. He writes, "In truth, it was born in an agony of internal tightness, conflict, and chaos." More significantly, one can detect in the diction, narrative voices, characterization, ellipses and lacunas of *Cane* the impasse that Toomer reached in his project, as well as the feelings of pain, frustration, alienation, uncertainty, constraint, impotence, and dread that accompanied his failure.

### Rendering Mixed-Blood America: An Unusable Past and Unintelligible Present

The opening character sketch in *Cane*, "Karintha," implies the failure of Toomer's project, foreshadows the writings that follow, and represents the book as a whole. Karintha, who lives in a small Georgia town, is young, beautiful, and racially mixed with skin "like dusk on the eastern horizon" (3) [5].[1] Men, young and old, and the reader can infer, black and white, have wanted her since she was a little girl. The sympathetic narrator warns, however, that "this interest of the male, who wishes to ripen a growing thing too soon, could mean no good to her" (3) [5]. These men assume that her beauty is

---

1. Page numbers in brackets refer to this Norton Critical Edition.

the source of their sexual desire for her, but Toomer's diction implies that her beauty is relative to their gaze and to her exotic multiracial somatic features. That is, the narrator stresses that she is perceived as a "thing" or an object. For this reason, "men do not know that the soul of her was a growing thing ripened too soon" (4) [6], and it follows then that they would fail to recognize the visible signs of her pathology when she was a little girl: that she beat her dog, stoned the cows, and fought with other children (3) [5]. Even the preacher, so enamored by her physical beauty, excuses her troubling behavior as innocently lovely as a November cotton flower (3) [5]. Put another way, the development of her unique human potential, "the soul of her," is arrested and then redirected in relation to the racialized milieu that surrounds her. This milieu shapes and limits her development from adolescence to womanhood. Her transition into womanhood occurs once she recognizes that she can profit from her value in the community as a desired object or commodity: "they all want to bring her money" (6) [0]. The commodification and arrested development of Karintha exemplify how from Toomer's socialist perspective capitalism sustains the biracial system that both produces and suppresses the cultural strain of mixed blood America and entraps the mixed race protagonists that populate the pages of *Cane*.

A woman now, Karintha decides to abort her mixed-race baby. This image of infanticide in the opening pages of *Cane* is emblematic of the suppression of mixed-blood America and of the failure of Toomer's own project: "But Karintha is a woman, and she has had a child. A child fell out of her womb onto a bed of pine-needles in the forest. Pine-needles are smooth and sweet. They are elastic to the feet of rabbits . . ." (4) [6]. Toomer's use of ellipsis and antithesis here ("smooth and sweet" contrasted to horrific image of her murdered baby) signals the reader to think critically about the social significance of her act, and perhaps reach the conclusion that her act is as much socially prompted as individually chosen. That is, if she had grown up in a different milieu in a different time, she would not have been impelled to abort her baby. In this milieu, she does not belong to a family or to a community that would have cared that she was pregnant, that would have claimed her and her baby as its own, and that would have noticed her absence. So, she walks out of town nine months pregnant, and she bears and aborts her baby alone, its body left abandoned. These images of solitariness and abandonment are representative of a collective mixed race sensibility, yearning, and expression of which Karintha and her baby are a part. Furthermore, next to the pine needles there is a sawmill and a slowly burning sawdust mound, and one can infer that Karintha places the body of her baby there. Weeks after she returns home the smoke from the smoldering sawdust still hovers thick in sky above the valley for people to smell. The body of her baby, literally undetectable in the smoke, is breathed in by the townspeople. The irony here is that the baby would have been socially invisible to the townspeople anyway had it lived, much as they failed to see or understand the "soul" of its mixed race mother. In the biracial social system, the soul of Karintha, her mixed-race baby, and Toomer's project are buried alive before they have a chance to develop, influence others, bear fruit, and bring about cultural change in America. As Monica Michlin notes, Toomer's text "bleeds out of itself" and "goes down" from its very first page (Michlin 107).

The other sketches of mixed-race women and men in *Cane* also reveal how the American biracial system marks multiracial difference, and limits, blocks, and cripples the person who embodies such difference. For instance, much like Karintha, "Fern" and "Esther" are confronted by social-economic situations that prompt them to ripen too soon and develop in ways that are self-detrimental and that limit their potential. Fern finds herself objectified and entrapped by the eyes of others in the Georgia town where she lives. "We walked down the Pike with people on all the porches gaping at us. 'Doesn't it make you mad?' She meant the row of petty gossiping people. She meant the world" (*Cane* 19) [20–21]. However, the narrator warns that if she were to move up North to Washington, Chicago, or New York she would encounter a similar racialized milieu ("she meant the world") and thus would probably find herself at risk for being turned into a kept woman or into a prostitute. In reaction to her internalization of the limits and dictates of black-white color line, Fern drops to her knees, her body convulses, and she screams— "Her body was tortured with something it could not let out" (19) [21]. In a similar manner, the biracial system blocks and redirects the psychosocial and sexual development of Esther, the mixed race daughter of a grocery store owner in a small Georgia town. As a little girl, Esther thinks that she has fallen in love with King Barlo, a large, physically imposing, dark-skinned Negro who claims divine inspiration and passes from town to town in the South to preach and collect money. King Barlo returns to town when Esther is twenty-seven: "Her body is lean and beaten. She rests listlessly against the counter, too weary to sit down" (25) [27]. Perhaps driven by the need to alleviate her sense of weariness, solitude, and desperation, which are effects of the raciated climate that surrounds her, she decides that she must confront King Barlo and tell him how she feels. She finds him late at night in a house in the black part of town—there seems to be a party, she walks up the stairs, Barlow is drunk, and black men and women are gathered all around. He refers to her as a "lil milk-white gal," tells her "this aint th place fer y," and wants to know what she wants (27) [28]. Black women standing about the room laugh at her and shoo her away once they realize what she wants. She feels repulsed; he is not at all like she imagined him: "She draws away, frozen. Like a somnambulist she wheels around and walks stiffly to the stairs. Down them. Jeers and hoots pelter bluntly upon her back. She steps out. There is no air, no street, and the town has completely disappeared." The sketch ends with her outside of the house and alone. This conclusion reveals and confirms the solitary and marginal social position that she occupies. She belongs to neither the black or white community, and like Fern there is no place for her to go.

"Avey" grows up in Washington an orphan and racially mixed, and much like Karintha, men, young and old, have wanted her since she was a little girl. The narrator grew up with Avey in the same neighborhood and has always been enamored of her. A grown man, he returns home to Washington and looks for her. He sees her one evening walking along U Street with a male companion. She appears to be living the life of a kept woman. She wears expensive clothing, but looks worn out, listless, and somnolent. The narrator asks Avey to walk with him to Soldier's Home, the park where he goes to be alone with the soul of another. There he explains to her that "her emotions had overflowed into paths that dissipated them" because the "proper channels" for such emotions do not exist in society (48) [48]. He knows her situation, suppression, and depression because they are also his own. In other words, the narrator sees that the dictates and limits of the black-white color line have stymied the development of the soul and potential inside of her. He also thinks that he has a remedy for her situation. He believes that art, his art, will change her situation as well as the culture of black-white color line: "I talked beautifully I thought, about an art that would be born, an art that would open the way for women the likes of her. I asked her to hope, and build up an inner life against the coming of that day" (48) [48]. This passage communicates the aim of Toomer and of the other members of Young America to uplift the minds of the masses with their art/literature and thereby effect cultural change in America. Unfortunately, Avey has fallen asleep and does not hear the narrator talk: "Then I looked at Avey. Her heavy eyes were closed. Her breathing was as faint and regular as a child's in slumber. My passion died" (48) [48]. This pessimistic conclusion implies that Avey's arrested psychosocial development and her precarious and marginal position in society are unchangeable. This conclusion also implies that the rigid segments of the black-white color line have effectively blocked the communication channel between Toomer's intended audience and the purpose of his project. Hence, both the narrator's art and Toomer's project will in all probability fall short of being born.

The narrator of "Avey" and the other mixed race male narrative voices in *Cane* must navigate the same rigid segments of black-white color line that limit and damage the mixed-race women whom they describe. For this reason, these narrative voices, on the whole, are sympathetic, but also hesitant, ambivalent, and conflicted about their own social standing. They also shift in and out grammatically from first to third person, and they are continually on the move from place to place. Hence, the narrative voices in *Cane* might be thought of as trying to stave off the blocks, dictates, and categories of a society structured through the black-white color line long enough for an art to be born—theirs and Toomer's—that will change American culture and thereby liberate them and women like Avey, Esther, and Fern. The aim of their art is to recover through a meticulous piecing together of words, phrases, and lyrical rhythms the sensibility, yearnings, and embodied difference of the mixed-race women and men they portray, whose "souls" and potentialities have been stamped out and re-channeled in and through the biracial system in the service of the dominant Anglophile culture. At the same time, these narrative voices, cognizant of their own uncertain and marginal status within the biracial system, portray their mixed-race subjects as powerless to circumvent the dictates and limits that the biracial system thrusts upon them. Caught in this dilemma between the aim of their art and the historical-material reality of their situation, the male narrative voices of *Cane*—perhaps unintentionally on Toomer's part—also reveal and express their own feeling of dread and impotence.

Further, these narrative voices reveal themselves as powerless to change situations in which they are both participants and witnesses. This is clearly the case in "Becky"; "Becky was the white woman who had two Negro sons. She's dead; they've gone away. The pines whisper to Jesus. The Bible flaps its leaves with an aimless rustle on her mound" (7) [9]. The narrator sympathizes with her situation while he is also complicit in her exclusion from the southern town in which she lives. That is, while he laments her situation he is, at the same time, in accord with the tacit agreement that the townspeople reach to build a cabin for her and her mixed-race children in a small strip of land on the outskirts of town between the railroad track and the main road. However, the cabin collapses one day: "Through the dust we saw the bricks in a mound upon the floor. Becky, if she was there, lay under them. I thought I heard a groan. Barlo, mumbling something, threw his bible on the pile. (No one has ever touched it.) Somehow we got away. My buggy was still on the road" (9) [11]. The narrator who is passing by on the road with another townsman is there to witness the fallen structure and hear Becky moan under the rubble, but he does nothing to help and then runs away from the situation. Toomer's use of parenthesis here again reveals the narrator's complicity. In a like manner, the narrator of "Fern" boards the train and heads back North after he walks with her through the cane-brake and there ascertains the severity of her situation as well as his own inability to do anything about it. Similarly, the narrator of "Avey," having failed to communicate his art and his message to her, will likely take flight again from Washington. In other words, the male narrative voices in *Cane* are inclined to flee once they realize that they are caught in the middle of situations that sur-pass their understanding and ability to intervene and effect change. This inclination is also evidenced in the character Dan Moore in "Box Seat" who at the end bolts out of a Washington theater into a black alley and "keeps going on" (69) [67], as well as in the character Lewis in "Kabnis" who runs out of Halsey's base-ment once the horror of the situation becomes too painful and intense for his systematic intellect to bear.

On the other hand, the mixed-race character Paul in "Bona and Paul" does not flee from the complex situation that confronts him in Chicago. Instead, he attempts to understand in a philosophical manner his differentiation and marginalization vis-à-vis the Ameri-can biracial system. Paul, much as Toomer did in 1916, studies physical education at a college in Chicago. Bona is a white female student who attends the same college. She thinks that she is in love with him after she sees him playing basketball in the gymnasium. Paul, however, suspects that Bona is merely fascinated by his racial difference. An attractive mixed-race male, his interaction with Bona parallels the experiences of Avey, Karintha, Fern, and the other mixed-race women in *Cane* who are objectified, marked, limited, and damaged by the normative black-white social gaze. Paul, how-ever, is only vaguely aware of how the biracial system conditions Bona and others to see him as racially different and then prompts them to be fascinated by that difference. He explains to Bona (who accuses him of having "grown cold" and being a "philosopher") that he knows "mostly a priori" that "mental concepts rule" her and that she does not love him (79) [77]. Mental concepts and knowledge that are a priori exist prior to individual experience, but what Paul means here by a priori are the categories, mechanisms, and dictates of a racist culture that a priori mark, limit, and differentiate him and others. Paul comes to an initial and partial understanding of this unconscious, cultural process of racialization through the repetition of painful experiences with women like Bona and in places such as Crimson Gardens.

The Crimson Gardens is a segregated club in Chicago where Bona, Paul, his roommate Art, and his girlfriend, Helen, go on a double date to drink and dance. There amidst a barrage of stares from onlookers in the club:

> A strange thing happened to Paul. Suddenly he knew that he was apart from the people around him. Apart from the pain which they had unconsciously caused. Suddenly he knew that people saw, not attractiveness in his skin but difference. Their stares, giving him to himself, filled something long empty within him, and were like green blades sprouting in his consciousness. There was a fullness, and strength and peace about it all. He saw himself, cloudy, but real. (77) [74]

Paul's realization, however, is not a remedy for his situation and will not help him transcend the material and ideological bounds of a racist nation. Transcendence here might be possible if he had been born and raised outside the American social system like his Norwegian roommate, Art. Paul loves Art (75) [73], and Art truly does not care, as rumor has it, that Paul might be part black. Art, who is a jazz playing "carbon-charged" "purple fluid" (75) [73], also represents the art and the ideals of Young America and the hope of a "transnational" American culture yet to be born. Art, however, (and this might also be read as indicative of Young America) finds himself when push comes to shove angered yet powerless to do anything about the stares and the general racist climate that surrounds Paul in the college and at the Crimson Gardens. Paul though seems to have come to terms with his situation on his own; he is for the moment comfortable in his skin and wants to be with Bona. Ecstatic, he walks back into the Crimson Gardens to shake hands with the black doorman, but when he reemerges back onto the street Bona is gone and so is Art (80). This conclusion implies that if Paul has indeed come to terms with the stares and his mixed racial background and perhaps chanced upon the beginnings of a mixed-race identity as Naomi Zack suggests (136), then his was a deeply subjective and solitary experience, understood by him at that moment and not communicable to a broader audience. In other words, the conclusion confirms the marginal and solitary social position that he occupies. Bona and Art (the art and ideals of Young America) have abandoned him, and he thus finds himself alone in the street at night staring back in the distance at the lights of the Crimson Gardens.

## A Representation of Toomer's Failure

The final piece in *Cane*, "Kabnis," affirms the power of the biracial system in the Jim Crow era to effectively suppress and block sensitive and intelligent mixed race individuals such as Paul and Toomer who struggle to understand, resist, and surpass the limits that their situation imposes on them. "Kabnis" depicts the everyday lived existences of different mixed race individuals in Sempter, a town in Georgia that is thoroughly divided by the black-white color line. "Kabnis" is also an allegory of Toomer's trip to Sparta, Georgia and his attempt to investigate, uncover, and reclaim his literary heritage. Here the reader should not underestimate the significance of Toomer's assertion to Frank that "Kabnis is me" (*Letters* 116). Toomer makes use of the psychological theme of the double, a common feature in the work of turn-of-the century modernist writers such as Joseph Conrad. Lewis and Kabnis are doubles: "Lewis is what a stronger Kabnis might have been, and in an odd faint way resembles him" (*Cane* 97) [95]. Hence, if Kabnis is Toomer, then Toomer is Lewis. Accordingly, Lewis and Kabnis are both racially mixed northerners who find themselves in the South for similar reasons that mirror Toomer's own. Kabnis, whose family was originally from "Georgia" (89) [87], is in search of his southern roots and a stable identity. He is "uprooted, thinning out. Suspended a few feet above the soil whose touch would resurrect him" (98) [96]. In a manner that parallels Toomer's own investigation in Sparta, Lewis walks about town and talks to the townspeople to uncover the buried history of miscegenation and to record the everyday lived realities of mixed-race people such as Halsey and his family. Halsey, who runs his own metal and wood shop, is of all the mixed race characters in "Kabnis" the most adept at coping with the situation and his mixed-blood heritage. In addition, much as Sparta residents typically answered Toomer's questions with silence, denials, and warnings, the line of questioning that Lewis takes annoys the white community and provokes violent threats from anonymous members of the Negro community. In the Jim Crow era, the townspeople of Sempter, like the townspeople of Sparta, are content to live their lives and conduct their business in accordance with the one-drop ideology of the biracial system. Hence, an outsider from the North who tries to stir up "the muck and mire of things" would not be received kindly.

The climatic scene in "Kabnis," the night of drunken debauchery in the cellar below Halsey's workshop, reveals the impasse that Toomer himself reached with the terrors of American history. Halsey's basement, "the Hole" (105) [103], has served the downtrodden and solitary mixed race people of Sempter for many years as a nighttime gathering place in which they wallow in their own abjectness and ease their collective pain with alcohol and sex. Halsey invites Lewis to participate this particular night. Kabnis, Cora, and Stella descend into the Hole with them. In addition, the blind and mute former slave Father John is always present in the Hole to oversee each depraved bacchanal. Having lived through the Emancipation and the Reconstruction, he represents the buried history of miscegenation in the South; he stands as a symbol for the collective sin and denial of miscegenation.

The descent into the Hole also signifies a descent into the human psyche, that of Toomer and that of the mixed-blood collective he represents. As Scruggs and VanDemarr note, here Toomer draws on the tradition of gothic literature to create the imagery and texture of the Hole; he also draws on the detective novel genre to construe the role that Lewis plays (195). In the Hole, Lewis is the detective who believes that his systematic reasoning will yield facts and a final resolution. Lewis is also a manifestation of the calculating and analytical side of Toomer's mind. Kabnis, on the other hand, is a projection of Toomer's sensitive and artistic side. Hence, Kabnis thinks of himself as an "orator" full of "misshapen, split-gut, tortured, twisted words" (*Cane* 111) [109] that he wants to express eloquently and poetically to a broad audience. Indicative of Toomer's own internal conflict while composing *Cane*, Kabnis envies Lewis for his personal qualities, while Lewis seems repulsed by the weakness, insecurity, and sense of self-defeat that he detects in Kabnis' words and mannerisms. Lewis deduces that Kabnis lacks not only a stable identity but also a sense of belonging and a purpose in life. The name "Kabnis" itself which sounds awkward and does not quite fall in line with the grammar of first and last names in American English implies that his existence is socially unintelligible, that his lived reality does not make sense in a black and white social universe. For that reason, Halsey tells Lewis that he has taken Kabnis under his wings to give him a trade and make a man out of him.

In the Hole, Kabnis defends himself against Lewis and Halsey who criticize and ridicule him, but his defiance is short-lived as he surrenders himself to the situation: "Kabnis mutters. Tries to break loose. Curses. Cora almost stifles him. He goes limp and gives up" (112) [109]. At almost the same instant that Kabnis gives up, Lewis finds himself face to face with the terrors of American history, an entangled and complex mess of pathos, cruelty, and ambiguity that plays out in front him in the Hole: "Kabnis, Carrie, Stella, Halsey, Cora, the old man, the cellar, and the work-shop, the southern town descended upon him. Their pain is too intense. He cannot stand it. He bolts from the table. Leaps up the stairs. Plunges through the work-shop and out into the night" (112) [110]. The complexity and intensity of the situation overwhelm Lewis's orderly mind. One can infer that Lewis both flees from this situation and, much as Toomer did in Sparta, boards a train headed back North devoid of any desire to ever go back. As Toomer declares to Frank, *Cane* was his "swan song" because "never again" did he "want a repetition of those conditions . . . which produced *Cane*." For this reason, Toomer and Lewis are content to abandon Kabnis (that part of them) in the cellar where he will continue to flounder in his pathos and uncertainty. Lewis, however, has also suffered a crushing defeat in that he falls miserably short of achieving the purpose of his investigation. It is in this context, that is, in the aftermath of Lewis' failure to untangle the complex situation before him and Kabnis' failure to express this situation poetically to a broad and receptive audience that we can begin to understand Toomer's sudden conversion to Gurdjieffism and his rejection of racial identity.

In other words, we might understand Toomer's sudden conversion to Gurdjieffism as a reaction to his failure to effectively present and communicate the complexities and lived realities, the "suppressed cultural strain" of mixed-blood America through the character sketches, poems, and stories in *Cane*. Through the reception of his work in the publishing industry, in Black Washington, and in White Manhattan, he came to realize that an immense and unbridgeable communication gap existed between the purpose of his project and his intended audience. In light of this painful and frustrating realization, and because his political aspirations had always been stronger than his literary ones, he chose to make *Cane* his swan song. One should not forget here that his literary efforts were borne out of his socialist conviction to influence the masses and change America for the better through both personal and collective action. Hence, his conversion to Gurdjieffism might be read as a decision based on political expediency. Staying close to the conditions that produced *Cane*, as Sherwood Anderson suggested to him, to create more pieces like the ones in *Cane*, would not only have been personally painful and frustrating but would have been politically ineffective and inept. In other words, Toomer arrived at the realization that the "artistic record" of his own hybrid literary heritage would influence no audience let alone lift America into self-knowledge. On the other hand, in Gurdjieffism he thought he had found a doctrine through which he could effectively influence the minds of the masses and thereby create positive change in the American social order. That he was wrong on this account should not diminish our view of him as a political writer and of *Cane* as one of the finest works in American Literature.

### WORKS CITED

Chesnutt, Charles W. *The House behind the Cedars.* 1900. New York: Penguin, 1993.

Frank, Waldo. *Our America.* New York: Boni and Liveright, 1919.

Hutchinson, George. "Identity in Motion: Placing Cane." Smith and Feith 38–56.

Larson, Charles. *Invisible Darkness.* Iowa City: Iowa University Press, 1993.

Locke, Alain. *The New Negro.* New York: Boni and Liveright, 1925.

Michlin, Monica. "Karintha: A Textual Analysis." Smith and Feith 96–108.

Scruggs, Charles. "'My Chosen World': Jean Toomer's Articles in *The New York Call*." *Arizona Quarterly* 52.2 (1995): 103–26.

——— and Lee VanDemarr. *Jean Toomer and the Terrors of American History*. Philadelphia: Penn University Press, 1998.

Smith, Geneviève, and Michael Feith, eds. *Jean Toomer and the Harlem Renaissance*. New Brunswick, NJ: Rutgers University Press, 2001.

Soto, Michael. "Jean Toomer and Horace Liveright; or, A New Negro Gets 'into the swing of it.'" Smith and Feith 162–87.

Toomer, Jean. *Cane*. 1923. Ed. Darwin T. Turner. New York: Norton, 1988.

———. *The Letters of Jean Toomer*. Ed. Mark Whalan. Knoxville: The University of Tennessee Press, 2006.

Williamson, Joel. *New People: Miscegenation and Mulattoes in the United States*. 1980. Baton Rouge: Louisiana State University Press, 1995.

Zack, Naomi. *Race and Mixed Race*. Philadelphia: Temple University Press, 1993.

# JENNIFER D. WILLIAMS

## Jean Toomer's *Cane* and the Erotics of Mourning†

In a 1924 review essay titled "The Younger Literary Movement," W. E. B. Du Bois and Alain Locke praise Jean Toomer for his daring portrayal of black sexuality in *Cane*. They proclaim him the first black writer to challenge the conventions of black genteel literature of the late nineteenth and early twentieth century and its endorsement of Victorian notions of purity, chastity, and domesticity.[1] While these writers of genteel literature sought to restore dignity to black bodies discursively assaulted in mainstream news and literary organs, the ideology of respectability upheld by these texts, as well as the surveillance and policing that reinforced this ideology socially, imposed new forms of sexual repression.[2] By deviating from these

† From *Southern Literary Journal* 40.2 (spring 2008): 87–101. Copyright © 2008 by the Department of English and Comparative Literature at the University of North Carolina at Chapel Hill.

1. These works include William Wells Brown's *Clotel; or, The President's Daughter* (1853), Frances E. W. Harper's *Iola Leroy; or, Shadows Uplifted* (1892), and Pauline Hopkins' *Contending Forces* (1900), among other turn-of-the-century female- and male-authored African American novels. Ann duCille discusses the sociopolitical ramifications of "passionlessness" in these novels in *The Coupling Convention: Sex, Text, and Tradition in Black Women's Fiction* (New York: Oxford UP, 1993).

2. See Evelyn Brooks Higginbotham's *Righteous Discontent: The Women's Movement in the Black Baptist Church, 1880–1920* (Cambridge: Harvard UP, 1993).

conventions, Toomer's work, according to the review, advances a necessary shift in black arts and letters.

That Toomer's depiction of sexually transgressive women marks a literary achievement is certain. However, Du Bois and Locke's serial gloss of these women resembles a seraglio:

> Here is Karintha, an innocent prostitute; Becky, a fallen white woman; Carma, a tender Amazon of unbridled desire; Fern, an unconscious wanton; Esther, a woman who looks age and bastardy in the face and flees in despair; Louise [sic] with a white and black lover; Avey, unfeeling and immoral; and Doris [sic], the cheap chorus girl. These are [Toomer's] women, painted with a frankness that is going to make his black readers shrink and criticize; and yet they are done with a certain splendid careless truth. (289)

Locke and Du Bois imply that liberating "the colored world" from repressed sexual mores can be achieved through liberating black women's bodies. By ascribing an element of realism and "truth" to Toomer's depictions, these authors bestow a certain degree of authenticity to an unbridled black female sexuality.[3] Moreover, the review fails to account for the overlap of desire and loss that occurs on the bodies of black women in *Cane*.[4] Toomer's representations of black women's sexuality neither replicate the exotic primitivism of the Jazz Age nor the nostalgic return of the romantic imagination. Rather, acts of sexual union and conception in *Cane* are marked again and again by traumatic history.

I want to intervene at that critical crossroads in *Cane*, where sexuality and loss intersect at the black female body. I call this coupling of desire and loss an "erotics of mourning" and regard *Cane* as an embodied narrative of a passing era associated with the trauma of slavery. Materializing this passing era in song and/as female embodiment, *Cane* accentuates the role of black female sexuality in modern constructions of blackness. Moreover, Toomer connects anxieties around racial and cultural continuity generated by modernity to the regulation of black female desire.

In "Love and Loss: An Elegy," George E. Haggerty attributes an erotics of mourning to the pastoral elegy, and specifically to the male homoeroticism that is common to the elegy form. I also find

---

3. Du Bois' embrace of these freeing sexual representations had some limitations, however. While he applauded Toomer's efforts and defended Langston Hughes' portrayals of prostitutes and cabaret life against charges of vulgarity, he lambasted Claude McKay's depiction of sexuality and jazz culture in *Home To Harlem*. See A. B. Christa Schwarz, *Gay Voices of the Harlem Renaissance* (Bloomington: Indiana UP, 2003).
4. "Becky," the central figure in one of Toomer's southern vignettes, happens to be white, but as she embodies sexual and racial transgression, her social status as a "white" woman is called into question by the text.

the elegiac connotation of the erotics of mourning suggestive for considering Toomer's use of the landscape of black female sexuality to uncover a history of racial trauma. Yet, Toomer reworks the elegy—as well as its thematic preoccupations with sex and death— and makes it relevant to an African American historical context of slavery, lynching, and migration. In the tradition of the pastoral elegy, Toomer laments modernity's corruption of nature and of folk aesthetics. At the same time, his critique of modernity retains critical ambivalence. He mourns a vanishing "folk spirit" without romanticizing it and attends to the potentially destructive elements of modernity without insisting upon a return to a simpler past.

Since the South for African Americans functions as a site of trauma as well as a symbolic homeland, black pastoralists tend to be less nostalgic than their Anglo American counterparts.[5] Evoking Billie Holiday's performance of "Strange Fruit," for instance, Farah Jasmine Griffin recounts, "[Holiday's] portrayal of the naturally beautiful 'pastoral South,' marred by the realities of burning black bodies, gives meaning and emotion to the descriptions written by [black] novelists" (15). Like Holiday, Toomer "places the black body at the very center of the pastoral."[6] Yet, nearly all of the tortured and violated black bodies in *Cane* are female. Crimes committed against the black female body in *Cane*'s rural settings echo modernity's displacement of nature. Though Toomer feminizes the southern landscape, his treatment of this conventional pastoral trope takes on historically inflected meanings. Throughout *Cane*, violation of the land as/and woman is haunted by the trauma of enslavement and the sexual exploitation of black women that sustained it.

As black women in the book animate the parting soul of slavery, men's desire to have sex with these women denotes a longing for union with the past. This element of longing supports the work of mourning performed by Toomer's text. Imagined by the author as a "swan song . . . a song of an end," *Cane* is suffused with loss and the desire for reclamation (Turner 123). This eroticization of loss is consistent with Freudian constructs of mourning. In his 1917 essay "Mourning and Melancholia," Sigmund Freud defines mourning as "the reaction to the loss of a loved person, or to the loss of some abstraction which has taken the place of one, such as fatherland, liberty, an ideal, and so on" (164). The objective of mourning, according to Freud, is to "work through" loss. To do otherwise, to refuse to

---

5. See Werner Sollors, "Four Types of Writing under Modern Conditions; or, Black Writers and 'Populist Modernism,'" *Race and the Modern Artist*, ed. Heather Hathaway, Josef Jarab, and Jeffrey Melnick (New York: Oxford UP, 2003): 42–53.
6. See Farah Jasmine Griffin, *"'Who set you flowin'?": The African-American Migration Narrative* (New York: Oxford UP, 1995): 15–16. Griffin claims that "Strange Fruit" leaves the gender of the lynched body unspecified, and hence, open to be read as female. I find this observation suggestive in light of the female bodies that occupy *Cane*.

detach from the lost object and, instead, to sustain an identification with loss, is to grieve pathologically, to develop melancholia. Freud returns to melancholia in *The Ego and the Id*. In his revised reading, he attests to the interactive workings between mourning and melancholia and suggests that identifying with the lost object "makes it easier for the object to be given up" or makes mourning possible (*Ego* 19). While Freud does not recant his initial view of melancholia's pathological character, as an agent in the process of mourning, melancholia contradicts its own pathological distinction.[7] Further, the notion of persistent mourning destabilizes temporality. For those who refuse *not* to mourn, who continue to grieve, the lost object lingers as a specter in the ego, ensuring that vestiges of the past persist in the present.

The interaction between mourning and melancholia is suggestive in light of *Cane*'s compatibility with the goals of the New Negro movement of the late nineteenth and early twentieth centuries. For Toomer, as well as for the proponents of a New Negro identity, modernity signaled the death of the "Old Negro," the embodiment of a homogenous southern "folk."[8] Hence, a New Negro identity called for mourning. It required the excavation of a shared past in order to proclaim a collective "new" identity. Toomer's commemoration of a vanishing folk, and particularly his fusion of modernist forms with African American vernacular culture, found *Cane* favorably embraced by proponents of a New Negro movement and designated as the sign of its beginning. While a New Negro identity relied upon the construction of a narrative of continuity rooted in shared origin, however, Toomer offers no promises of rebirth in *Cane*. For New Negro artists and intellectuals, the recovery of black folk culture as a usable past was an attempt to offset the traumas of modernity, such as war, racial violence, dislocation, and alienation. Read through a Freudian lens, then, Toomer's text advocates working through loss whereas a New Negro objective of cultural nationalism might be said to support a sustained engagement with loss. At the same time, the emphasis on black expressive practices of mourning in the New Negro movement and in Toomer's work makes

7. Recent scholarship in American Studies and queer theory has retrieved melancholia as a depathologized structure of feeling and a basis for forming affective political alliances around loss. See, for instance, Douglas Crimp, "Mourning and Militancy," *October* 51 (Winter 1989): 3–18; José Esteban Muñoz, *Disidentifications: Queers of Color and the Performance of Politics* (Minneapolis: U of Minnesota P, 1999); Anne Anlin Cheng, *Melancholy of Race: Psychoanalysis, Assimilation, and Hidden Grief* (New York: Oxford UP, 2000); David L. Eng and Shinhee Han, "A Dialogue on Racial Melancholia" in *Loss: The Politics of Mourning*, ed. David L. Eng and David Kazanjian (Berkeley: U of California P, 2003); and Ann Cvetkovich, *An Archive of Feelings: Trauma, Sexuality, and Lesbian Public Cultures* (Durham: Duke UP, 2003).
8. See Alain Locke's title essay in *The New Negro: Voices of the Harlem Renaissance* (New York: Atheneum Publishing, 1992).

possible a more complex rendering of continuous mourning and its relationship to modern black subjectivity.

The role of the Negro spirituals as a repository of cultural memory is instructive in this regard. Theorizing the sorrow songs as a paradigm for mourning, Paul Anderson's "My Lord, What a Morning" claims black musical traditions as sites of memory where collective traumas can be addressed and possibly repaired. Of Toomer's "Song of the Son," one of the most critically appraised poems in *Cane*, Anderson maintains, "The elegiac poem evokes the 'sorrow songs' as a haunting music that reaches out from the past to confront and challenge the present" (91). The speaker in the poem comes to the soil of his ancestors just in time to capture their "plaintive soul, leaving, soon gone." In tribute, he aims to weave "An everlasting song, a singing tree, / Caroling softly souls of slavery" (12) [16].[9] One could substitute Jean Toomer for the speaker of the poem and *Cane* for his "everlasting song." Anderson spots in the poem's commemoration of the past an opportunity to reconsider distinctions between mourning and melancholia, asserting that Toomer's signature poem "suggests a logic of mourning that parts ways with Freud's ideals for 'working-through' profound losses" (92). Toomer's endeavor to craft an "everlasting song" shores up the practice of cultural mourning as a continual process. I would extend Anderson's observations about "Song of the Son" to the role of music throughout *Cane*. Spirituals and work songs are interspersed throughout the book's narrative prose and short dramas. *Cane*'s religious subtext and plaintive melodies could tag the book itself as a sorrow song. Moreover, the poems nested between vignettes are infused with blues and jazz cadences. *Cane*'s mixing of form and genre in three parts and under an overarching theme resembles a jazz composition. Additionally, the text's geographic movement—from the South to the North and back south again—coupled with consistent references to railroad tracks, train engines, and travelers—is prototypical of blues tropes of migration and modernity. As is also customary for the blues, themes of loss and desire in Toomer's vignettes often transpire in heterosexual love plots.

From the verse that opens the first vignette to the birth-song that closes the last, music features prominently in *Cane* as a site of memory and an intermediary between the past and the present. Music also acts as a structuring device for interrogating dialectical relationships between sexuality and loss. The haunting cadence of folk songs draws attention to the women in Toomer's rural landscape who are objects of male desire and transforms these women into "lost objects" of the past. Women's bodies function metaphorically as songs as well, establishing a female-gendered connection with the past, with the site

9. Page numbers in square brackets refer to this Norton Critical Edition.

of origin. In a letter to his friend Waldo Frank, Toomer establishes a link between the folk song, the black female body, and the black race: "In my own stuff, in those pieces that come nearest to the old Negro, to the spirit saturate [*sic*] with folk-song: Karintha and Fern, the dominant emotion is a sadness derived from a sense of fading, from a knowledge of my futility to check solution. There is nothing about these pieces of the buoyant expression of a new race" (Rusch 24–25). The old Negro represented for Toomer the last tie to a slave past and to the notion of racial purity. "Karintha," specifically, can be read as the severance of a tie to origins, a move that serves a paradigmatic function for the remainder of the text. This originary break assumes the form of a foiled reproduction.

A deceptively beautiful lyric praising Karintha's loveliness overtures what proves to be an eerie account of a girl's transition into womanhood. The lyric proclaims:

> Her skin is like dusk on the eastern horizon,
> O cant you see it, O cant you see it,
> Her skin is like dusk on the eastern horizon
> . . . When the sun goes down. (1) [5]

The portrait of Karintha as dusk assigns her liminal status by alerting readers that what she represents is disappearing. The ellipses that follow make the tale even more ominous. The pause before the last line, the forced interruption of the author's serenade, conceals a secret contained within those few pages.

"Karintha" introduces themes that reoccur throughout the book, such as the passage of time, movement, and death. The unfolding of these themes supports an erotics of mourning as they foreground black women's sexuality as sites of loss. Wishing "to ripen a growing thing too soon," men hasten Karintha's sexual development. Readers witness Karintha transition from a vibrant youth, "a wild flash that told the other folks just what it was to live," to a stationary woman with derision for the men in her community whose privilege of travel and commerce facilitate their journeys to the city and to college and aid their desire to bring Karintha money for sex. These men, who treat Karintha like an exchangeable commodity, model modernity's destructive impulses against nature and folk ideals. The narrative climaxes with an unsuccessful reproduction, either attributable to a stillbirth, abortion, or infanticide. The matter-of-fact statement, "A child fell out of her womb onto a bed of pine-needles in the forest. Pine-needles are smooth and sweet. They are elastic to the feet of rabbits . . . A sawmill was nearby. Its pyramidal sawdust pile smouldered. It is a year before one completely burns," leaves the incident open to varied interpretations (2) [6]. But in accordance with Toomer's notion of *Cane* as a song of an end, the culture associated with a folk past is fading. Hence, sexual acts in

"Karintha," and in the other five sketches in Part One, are punctuated with violence and are most often nonreproductive.[1] These aborted acts of conception stress the impossibility of cultural rebirth, and of mending the ruptures that modernity has wrought.

As evidenced by "Karintha," *Cane* repudiates originary narratives of black racial authenticity through its figurations of black women. Underscoring the gothic elements in *Cane*, Charles Scruggs and Lee VanDemarr's *Jean Toomer and the Terrors of American History* support Karintha's connection to originary blackness by tying the eastern elements in the story to "the myth of origins that lie beyond in Africa" (140). Toomer maps this diasporic genealogy onto the body of Carma as well. "Carma" collapses the black female body and the song into a collective racial past. The vignette's namesake frequently cheats on her husband Bane while he is away working with a contractor. When he confronts her about her infidelity, Carma becomes hysterical, grabs a gun, runs into the canebrake, and feigns suicide. Discovery of his wife's second betrayal, her simulated suicide, drives Bane to madness and murder. Consequently, he ends up on the chain gang. The unnamed male narrator, who first appears as a character in "Becky," reappears in "Carma" to relay the sensational plotline. This speculative narrator—who trails Carma with his eyes as she rides down the road—can only interpret Carma's story; he cannot accurately represent her.

The male author's interpretive authority over female embodiment in *Cane* has garnered understandable criticism from feminist scholars. Janet M. Whyde's "Mediating Forms: Narrating the Body in Jean Toomer's *Cane*" finds that men's interpretive function seizes women's voices and wields a destructive force throughout the text. She claims that Carma's body "becomes the site of conflict of slavery redux, where sexual conflict is transmuted into historical conflict by the hermeneutical usurpation of her body. Like the other women, she disappears by being interpreted, transformed into the physical sign of a unifying abstraction" (46).[2] At the same time, however, Toomer undermines the narrative authority of the male speakers throughout *Cane* by pointing out their complicity within a male public that silences women. He furthers the repressive function of language by reinforcing the role that rumors and gossip play in driving women mad ("Becky"), making them hysterical ("Carma"), and getting them ousted from "polite" society ("Avey"). Toomer's continued self-reflexivity about his interpretive role suggests an awareness of the limits of language and representation.

1. All of the vignettes in Part One, except one, are named after the women they focus on.
2. Also see Laura Doyle, *Bordering on the Body: The Racial Matrix of Modern Fiction and Culture* (New York: Oxford UP, 1994), for a similar critique of *Cane*.

A critique of the way female embodiment gets subsumed beneath male authorship only holds up if language is privileged as the only or best mode of articulation. But words fail in *Cane*. They slip into ellipses and flood over into song. Song wafts like the pine smoke that "curls up and hangs in odd wraiths about the trees, curls up, and spreads itself out over the valley" (2) [6]. Music interrupts narrative continuity as a way to signify what cannot be said. A parenthetical insert in "Carma" sets apart the narrator's description of a woman as "strong as any man" and his recounting of a story described as "the crudest melodrama" (10–11) [15]. The break in the text is both a spatial and temporal interlude that unites the black woman's body with the site of racial origin beyond the Dixie Pike: "She does not sing; her body is a song. She is in the forest, dancing. Torches flare . . . juju men, greegree, witch-doctors . . . torches go out . . . The Dixie Pike has grown from a goat path in Africa" (10) [14]. Carma's singing reverberates throughout the valley to become a song unbound by time and space—a woman's mourning song. Woman embodies the song as well as the sorrow it conveys. The narrator connects that sorrow to the black trauma of diaspora by mapping a trajectory from Africa to Georgia's Dixie Pike. Carma's body, as song, land, and memory, positions her as the site of racial and cultural origin, the locus of loss. Mourning becomes her.

The endeavor for black artists and intellectuals at the turn of the twentieth century to construct a black musical lineage bespeaks a longing to mend those lines of descent ruptured by the Middle Passage, slavery, and migration. By gendering song as female, Toomer supports music's association with natal alienation, or what Nathaniel Mackey terms "wounded kinship." Mackey contends, "Song is both a complaint and a consolation dialectically tied to [natal alienation], where in the back of 'orphan' one hears echoes of 'orphic,' a music that turns on abandonment, absence, loss. Think of the black spiritual 'Motherless Child.' Music is wounded kinship's last resort" (232). Music rescues blackness from originary narratives and locates it in the rifts, breaks, and slippages of identity formation instead. As plaints like "Motherless Child" show, music also offers a language to express incomprehensible grief.

Of course Toomer is not the first to affirm black music's transmission of the unsaid and the ineffable.[3] The mournful cadence of *Cane*'s southern sketches are resonant of Du Bois' interpretation of the "sorrow songs" as "the music of an unhappy people" that "tell[s] of death and suffering and unvoiced longing toward a truer world, of misty wanderings and hidden ways" (267). Toomer's journey

---

3. Paul Gilroy discusses black music as a means of expressing racial trauma in *The Black Atlantic* as well (Cambridge: Harvard UP, 1993).

south and encounter with the spirituals is but one resemblance between *Cane* and *The Souls of Black Folk*. However, Toomer recollects hearing these songs far outside of hallowed concert halls where the refined voices of the Fisk Jubilee singers could be heard performing them:

> A family of back-country Negroes had only recently moved into a shack not too far away. They sang. And this was the first time I'd ever heard folk-songs and spirituals. They were very rich and sad and joyous and beautiful. But I learned that the Negroes of the town objected to them. They called them "shouting." They had victrolas and player-pianos. So, I realized with deep regret, that the spirituals, meeting ridicule, would be certain to die out. With Negroes also the trend was towards the small town and then towards the city—and industry and commerce and machines. The folk-spirit was walking in to die on the modern desert. That spirit was so beautiful. Its death was so tragic. Just this seemed to sum life for me. And this was the feeling I put into *Cane*. (Turner 123)

While both writers regarded the spirituals as a site of cultural memory, Du Bois saw in the Fisk Jubilee Singers' formalization of the folk spirituals a way of sustaining a connection with a lost African ancestry and of using that ancestral past and the shared trauma of slavery as the basis for nation building.[4] Toomer, on the other hand, saw the fading of the field hollers and shouts as evidence of a break with the past and with originary narratives of race. His allusion to Victrolas and player-pianos speaks to modernist forms of black music like blues and jazz. Further, the mention of migration hints toward the tide of black urbanization and modernization that, according to Toomer, would dismantle racial boundaries.

The tide of black migration generated sexual panics among black and white communities. Though fears of miscegenation were common to both groups, a black desire for racial integrity stems, in part, from a history of sexual and racial trauma and cultural loss.[5] The trappings of bourgeois social conventionality, explored in the urban vignettes in Part Two of *Cane*, amplify African American anxieties over cultural dissolution associated with the traumas of migration and modernity. Prior to shifting the setting to black urban geographies, Toomer holds fears of racial amalgamation culpable for sexualized racial violence prevalent throughout the South.

---

4. See Eric J. Sundquist, *To Wake the Nations: Race in the Making of American Literature* (Cambridge: Belnap Press of Harvard UP, 1993).
5. See Hazel Carby, "Policing the Black Woman's Body in an Urban Context" in *Cultures in Babylon: Black Britain and African America* (London and New York: Verso, 1999): 22–39, and Cvetkovich in *An Archive of Feelings*, Chapter Four ("Transnational Trauma and Queer Diasporic Publics").

As lynching was rampant in Georgia during the author's stay there, it is not surprising that it is taken up several times in the text.[6] Toomer addresses or alludes to lynching in the poem "Portrait in Georgia" and the sketches "Becky" and "Blood-Burning Moon" in the first part of *Cane* and returns to lynching in "Kabnis," the final and longest short story in the book. Each of these pieces upsets the triangulated psychosexual drama between black men, white women, and white men that characterizes lynching in our cultural memory. Armed with the myth, bands of vigilantes could fancy themselves heroes charged with protecting white womanhood.[7] Ida B. Wells used her access to the press to overturn popular rationales for lynching. In newspaper articles and pamphlets, Wells documented lynchings of black men who were in consensual relationships with white women and challenged the "chivalry" of white men who could rape black women with impunity.[8]

Toomer takes up interracial intimacies and their tragic outcomes in scenarios that evoke Wells' reports. A short prelude in "Becky" exposes her sexual transgressions and their consequences: "Becky was the white woman who had two Negro sons. She's dead; they've gone away. The pines whisper to Jesus. The Bible flaps its leaves with an aimless rustle on her mound" (5) [9]. Like the aforementioned vignettes, sexual desire initiates this narrative of loss. Even the doubling of mound—as grave pile and as the rise of the female genital area—conflates Becky's sexuality and death. While Toomer does not refer to lynching directly in this sketch, Becky's refusal to reveal the identity of her black lover(s) hints at the violent retribution that would follow this discovery.[9]

"Blood-Burning Moon" bears out these fatal consequences except that the lynching in the story is not the result of a prohibitive sexual encounter. Rather, it follows a deadly battle over masculinity that is rooted in the economics of slavery. A black woman, Louisa, desires and is "loved" by two men, white and black, Bob Stone and Tom Burwell (28) [31]. Bob is the son of the white family Louisa works for and Tom is a black field hand on the Stone estate. Both men claim the right to love Louisa exclusively, but as rumors circulate and each

6. While lynching statistics vary, between 1880 and 1930, according to records compiled by the NAACP and other anti-lynching activists, between 3,337 and 10,000 black people were victims of mob killings. See Sandra Gunning, *Race, Rape, and Lynching: The Red Record of American Literature, 1890–1912* (New York: Oxford UP, 1996): 5.

7. Gunning explores the ways that stereotypes of the black rapist, the white rape victim, the white avenger, and the black woman as prostitute worked together to support popular justifications of lynching (*Race, Rape, and Lynching* 11).

8. See Ida B. Wells-Barnett, *On Lynchings* (New York: Humanity Books, 2002).

9. For example, "Becky" could have been taken from a story Wells published in the *Memphis Ledger* about Lillie Bailey. Bailey was a young white girl who had become pregnant outside of marriage and consequently was taken in at the Woman's Refuge in Memphis. The ladies at the refuge were horrified when Bailey bore a mixed-race child. Bailey refused all attempts to get her to reveal the identity of the child's father. (Wells, *On Lynchings*: 34).

man finds out about his rival, violence ensues. After killing Bob in self-defense, Tom is hunted down by a white mob, lynched, and burned to death. "Blood-Burning Moon" challenges popular narratives of lynching by placing a black woman at the center of the conflict and crafting a black man as a protector. The patriarchal underpinnings of chivalry do not go unnoted in *Cane*. At the same time, Toomer recasts the players in the lynching drama consistent with a history of sexualized racism. White men's rape of black women was as rampant as the lynching of black men. While the unfounded myth of the predatory black male rapist worsened the panics surrounding miscegenation in the post-Reconstruction era, the reality of socially sanctioned sexual abuses against black women by white men went unpunished. Hence, Tom takes for granted that any relationship between Louisa and Bob would be an exploitative one.

The drama of lynching reveals anxieties around race, gender, class, and nation at a moment in which these categories were being recodified. The legislation of race rested upon the regulation of sexual desire through both extralegal forms of violence as well as legal forms of segregation and anti-miscegenation statutes. As state-mandated segregation defined blacks as abject to the "nation," a black collective identity was shaped around shared trauma and loss. Black scholars and artists played a key role in defining and representing a collective blackness. However, these unifying constructs of blackness tended to rely on fantasies of origin and reductive narratives of authenticity, like that of a reified "folk." In spite of Toomer's avowed resistance to originary narratives of race, the tropes of immersion and ancestral reclamation in *Cane* signaled the book's racial "authenticity" for both the orchestrators of the New Negro Movement and the Black Arts Movement.[1] Anticipating the descent into the "blackness of blackness" performed by Ralph Ellison's Invisible Man, however, Jean Toomer's immersion into the South does not substantiate the recovery of an unadulterated folk. Rather, it reveals a blackness rooted in a miscegenated past endemic to the trauma of slavery. Scruggs and VanDemarr go so far as to deem miscegenation "the thing in *Cane* not *named* but always there" (139). Miscegenation, or rather the sexualized racial history that underlies it, is the unspeakable in *Cane*. The site of (racial) origin is resituated as the site of trauma itself.

I find Jennifer DeVere Brody's reading of the moment of descent in *Invisible Man* true for *Cane* as well.[2] Brody claims the "ivory

1. See Henry Louis Gates, Jr., "The Same Difference: Reading Jean Toomer, 1923–1983," in *Figures in Black: Words, Signs, and the "Racial" Self* (New York: Oxford UP, 1987): 196–224.
2. The double meaning of "descent" as a plunge and as ancestry is appropriately telling for this episode.

colored" or "(not) black slave mother" as "the condition of possibility for the birth of (the) blackness of the sun/son," and contends further that "it is she who carries the trace of blackness that gives birth to the trauma experienced and expressed in *Invisible Man*" (689–690). A similar return of the sun/son occurs in "Kabnis," which takes up Part Three of *Cane*. In "Kabnis," the originary rupture that births modern blackness gets articulated through the thematics of obstructed black maternity.[3]

Recalling Toomer's tenure in Sparta, the six-part drama focuses on Ralph Kabnis, a black northerner who heads south to teach.[4] After Kabnis is forced to resign from his post for drinking liquor on school property, he is adopted by black middle-class shop owner and wagon maker Fred Halsey as an apprentice and initiated into the South's racial protocol by the besieged black inhabitants of Sparta who regularly visit Halsey's home. It is one of those frequent visitors, Professor Layman, who confirms Kabnis' fears about lynching by recounting the mob killing of Mame Lamkins:

> White folks know that niggers talk, an they dont mind jes so long as nothing comes of it, so here goes. She was in th family-way, Mame Lamkins was. They killed her in th street, an some white man seein th risin in her stomach as she lay there soppy in her blood like any cow, took an ripped her belly open, an th kid fell out. It was living; but a nigger baby aint supposed t live. So he jabbed his knife in it an stuck it t a tree. An then they all went away. (90) [90]

The story of Mame Lamkins retains many of the details of the lynching of Mary Turner in Valdosta, Georgia, just three years before Toomer's move to Sparta. This notorious mob murder also was discussed widely in the literary circles in which Toomer socialized in Washington, D.C. After Mary Turner publicly protested the lynching of her husband Hayes, the mob set out to "teach her a lesson." They took her to a stream, tied her ankles together, and hung her upside down from a tree, then threw gasoline on her and set her on fire. She was in her eighth month of pregnancy.[5] While she was still alive, one of the men cut open Turner's abdomen, causing her unborn child to fall from her womb to the ground. Another member of the mob

---

3. See Daylanne K. English, *Unnatural Selections: Eugenics in American Modernism and the Harlem Renaissance* (Chapel Hill: U of North Carolina P, 2004).
4. Toomer dedicates this section to Waldo Frank and tells Frank in a letter, "Kabnis is me." See Frederik L. Rusch, *A Jean Toomer Reader: Selected Unpublished Writings* (New York: Oxford UP, 1993): 23.
5. Walter White, "The Work of a Mob," *The Crisis Reader: Stories, Poetry, and Essays from the NAACP's Crisis Magazine*, ed. Sondra Kathryn Wilson (New York: Modern Library, 1999): 345–350.

crushed the infant with the heel of his shoe. To finish their "lesson," the gang fired over a hundred bullets into Mary's hanging body.

Prior to *Cane*'s publication, black women writers, including poet Carrie Williams Clifford and playwright and fiction writer Angelina Weld Grimké protested the lynching of Mary Turner through their art. The lynching drama also was essentially a feminist genre of writing.[6] Unlike popular lynching narratives, black women writers attended to black women's roles as wives, mothers, and community members, thereby drawing attention to women's grief and loss in the aftermath of lynching. Grimké's stories, for instance, bring together the discourse of lynching and that of racial reproduction.[7] The protagonist in "The Closing Door" uses infanticide as a means of resisting racist violence. She refuses to reproduce a black male child for whites to murder. Toomer echoes the tropes of reproduction common to gendered discourses of lynching. Kabnis' frustrated "birth" is a work of art that can capture the "soul" of black southern culture. Longing to "become the face of the South," Kabnis declares, "How my lips would sing for it, my songs being the lips of its soul. Soul. Soul hell. There aint no such thing" (81). Kabnis wants to be the voice of the South, yet his desire to sing for it competes with his alienation from it and his contempt for it. For Kabnis, the beauty of the South is only matched by a horror that cannot be captured in words.

Kabnis' assertion that there is no "mold" to fit the "form" branded into his soul supports the insufficiency of language for bearing witness to traumas as unspeakable as lynching. For Kabnis, the violence of racial history cannot be contained by words unless those words can materialize into flesh, becoming "[m]isshapen, split-gut, tortured, twisted words." Identifying the form branded on his soul with Mame Lamkins and with the unborn child torn from her womb, Kabnis exclaims to his alter-ego Lewis, "I wish t God some lynchin white man ud stick his knife through it an pin it to a tree. An pin it to a tree" (110). Words made flesh. The written narrative of racial history is always already embodied. Reclaiming the past involves remembering the body as a historical text and exploring the tensions that exist between sexual desire and a history of violation.

6. Kathy A. Perkins and Judith L. Stephens' edited volume *Strange Fruit: Plays by American Women* compiles these lynching plays written by women. (Bloomington: Indiana UP, 1998).
7. Grimké revisits the Mary Turner lynching in short stories "Blackness," "The Closing Door," and "Goldie," published in 1919 and 1920 issues of the *Birth Control Review*. See Carolivia Herron, ed. *Selected Works of Angelina Weld Grimké* (New York: Oxford UP, 1991).

WORKS CITED

Anderson, Paul Allen. "'My Lord, What a Morning': The 'Sorrow Songs' in Harlem Renaissance Thought." Homans 83–102.

Brody, Jennifer DeVere. "The Blackness of Blackness . . . Reading the Typography of *Invisible Man*." *Theatre Journal* 57.4 (2005): 679–98.

Du Bois, W. E. B. *The Souls of Black Folk*. 1903. New York: Penguin Books, 1995.

Du Bois, W. E. B., and Alain Locke. "The Younger Literary Movement." *The Crisis* 28 (Feb 1924): 161–62.

Freud, Sigmund. "Mourning and Melancholia." 1917. *General Psychological Theory*. New York: Collier, 1963. 164–79.

———. *The Ego and the Id*. Trans. Joan Riviere. New York: W. W. Norton, 1923.

Griffin, Farah Jasmine. *"Who set you flowin'?": The African-American Migration Narrative*. New York: Oxford UP, 1995.

Haggerty, George E. "Love and Loss: An Elegy." *GLQ: A Journal of Lesbian and Gay Studies*. 10.3 (2004): 385–405.

Homans, Peter, ed. *Symbolic Loss: The Ambiguity of Mourning and Memory at Century's End*. Charlottesville: UP of Virginia, 2000.

Mackey, Nathaniel. "Sound and Sentiment, Sound and Symbol." *Callaloo* 10.1 (Winter 1987): 29–54.

Rusch, Frederik L., ed. *A Jean Toomer Reader: Selected Unpublished Writings*. New York: Oxford UP, 1993.

Scruggs, Charles, and Lee VanDemarr. *Jean Toomer and the Terrors of American History*. Philadelphia P, 1998.

Toomer, Jean. *Cane*. 1923. Introduction by Darwin T. Turner. New York: Boni and Liveright, 1975.

Turner, Darwin T., ed. *The Wayward and the Seeking: A Collection of Writings by Jean Toomer*. Washington, D.C.: Howard UP, 1980.

# EMILY LUTENSKI

## "A Small Man in Big Spaces": The New Negro, the Mestizo, and Jean Toomer's Southwestern Writing[†]

> Taos is an end-product. It is the end of the slope. It is an end-product of the Indians, an end-product of the Spaniards, an end-product of the Yankees and puritans. It must be plowed under. Out of the fertility which death makes in the soil, a new people with a new form may grow. I dedicate myself to the swift death of the old, to the whole birth of the new. In whatever place I start work, I will call that place Taos.
>
> —Jean Toomer, "A Drama of the Southwest (Notes)" (n.d., c. 1935)[1]

A photograph of Jean Toomer taken by his second wife, Marjorie Content, shows him posed at a table with his typewriter before him, replete with a sheet of paper.[2] Content was a noted photographer and this portrait has the posed look of a book jacket. Its composition seems highly constructed: the ream of paper next to the typewriter and the books on the shelf in the background are perfectly placed. The writer is artfully posed with his hand under his chin, as if thoughtfully contemplating his work. Words are barely visible on the sheet of paper exiting Toomer's typewriter; the distance from which this portrait has been taken has obscured them. They appear faint, apparitional, and illegible. The year is 1935, more than a decade after the publication of *Cane* (1923). While this image might be read as contrived, as little more than a fantasy of authorship for a writer who, according to most critical accounts, had already "failed" by this date, the possibility of this photograph

---

† This essay first appeared in *MELUS: Journal of the Society for the Study of Multi-Ethnic Literature of the United States*, issue 33.1 (Spring 2008), pages 11–32, and is reprinted by permission of the journal.

1. Unfortunately Toomer was not in the habit of dating his manuscripts. In *A Jean Toomer Reader*, Rusch suggests that "A Drama of the Southwest" was written in 1935. I can only assume that his notes for this play were written in the same year. The particular quotation I use as an epigraph for this essay looks as though it is extracted from "A Drama of the Southwest" to use as an epigraph for the play itself. These lines, however, do not appear within the typescript of "A Drama of the Southwest" housed at the Beinecke Library, only in Toomer's notes. However, they do appear on several manuscript pages that Toomer labeled "From 'A Drama of the Southwest.'" These lines do not appear in the text of the play, but their recurrence and rewriting seem to emphasize their importance. Throughout this essay, in circumstances such as this where manuscripts are left undated I attempt to date Toomer's archived writings as accurately as possible through textual and contextual clues.

2. This photograph was printed on the cover of the issue of *MELUS* from which this article appeared. For more information on Content see Quasha's collection of Content's work, *Marjorie Content: Photographs*.

as documentary evidence remains. After all, this is the same year that Charles Scruggs and Lee VanDemarr suggest that Toomer's writing reengaged with "a radical analysis of the politics of his time," although "not . . . an open discussion of racial matters" (219).

Like Content's photograph, scholarship on Toomer has continued to represent dichotomously the writer best known for *Cane*. In effect, critics and biographers have created two Jean Toomers. One is the writer of *Cane*, often considered the signal text of the Harlem Renaissance. He is politically engaged, interested in race, and aesthetically experimental. This Toomer looks back to the Southern past and slavery, and views black folk as sources for emergent, modernist, New Negro sensibilities. The other Toomer is post-*Cane* and is not a poet, but a psychologist, philosopher, or spiritual guru. This second Toomer disconnects himself from the New York literary scene of Waldo Frank, *Broom*, or Harlem. He denounces his black heritage, marries white women, and becomes little more than a literary mouthpiece for his spiritual mentor, George Gurdjieff. The promise of Toomer's early experimental writing is thus diminished and he is characterized as never again achieving the "literary merit" of *Cane*. Charles R. Larson, for example, wonders "why Jean Toomer failed as a writer after the publication of that one brilliant work. What diminished whatever potential there was in his later works?" (xiii). These oppositional narratives about Toomer's career have remained relatively untroubled.

Content's photograph, however, raises more than just the question of *whether* Toomer was writing in this period. It also exposes *where* he was writing. This is not an image captured in Sparta, Georgia, in the small cabin adjacent to the school where Toomer acted as substitute principal, a domicile eerily recreated in the "Kabnis" section of *Cane*. It is also not the lush interior of Toomer's childhood brownstone in Washington, DC, its propriety mimicked in the stifling atmosphere of Mrs. Pribby's house in *Cane*'s "Box Seat." Nor is it the Chicago dorm room recorded in "Bona and Paul," perhaps modeled on Toomer's education at that city's American College of Physical Training. Instead, this photograph shows Toomer's books stacked neatly on the imperfectly curved bookshelf of a hand-built adobe house. He writes by the warmth of a distinctive, semi-circular kiva fireplace, a fixture of Pueblo architecture in the New Mexican Southwest. The graceful, rounded pottery of southwestern Indians is displayed on the mantle.

Toomer's time in the Southwest has been excluded from dominant critical narratives of his life and work. The literary footprint of his time in New Mexico exists only in the sparse fragments of Toomer's southwestern writing published in Frederik L. Rusch's *A Jean Toomer Reader: Selected Unpublished Writings*, and in the contributions to the "New Mexico Writers" section of the *New Mexican Sentinel* that have been reprinted and briefly addressed by Tom Quirk and Robert Fleming in *Jean Toomer: A Critical Evaluation.* Most of Toomer's southwestern writing and, indeed, the evidence of his time there, remains archived.[3] To read this archived work and explore Toomer's time in the Southwest complicates previous understandings of Toomer as a writer who never, after *Cane,* returned to "an open discussion of racial matters." When this archive is addressed it reveals that Toomer did, in fact, continue to discuss race, but that this discussion takes a different shape than it did in the locales informing *Cane* and its reception: the rural South, the urban North, and the New York publishing milieu, with its burgeoning attention to black texts. The southwestern archive shifts the critical optic away from *Cane's* fragmented formal qualities, its nostalgic location in a post-slavery historical milieu, and its modernist, New Negro sensibilities—qualities which continue to define Toomer and his literary worth—and towards a more nuanced understanding of the geographical and discursive matrix of race, location, and modernism and modernity proliferating in the interwar US.

Content's photograph relocates Toomer to the Southwest, in an adobe house near Taos. Doing so places Toomer in a space articulate with and yet distinct from the spaces of *Cane* and separates him from the Harlem scene in which he is usually read, however uncomfortably.[4] Informed by geography, his theories of racial formation and his writing about race differ depending on the site of their production and distribution. Despite Toomer's tenuous association with the Harlem scene, *Cane* is often read as the signal text of the New Negro movement, and falls in line with Renaissance obsessions with demarcating black modernity. *Cane* defines a new Negro against the old by juxtaposing the modern against the history of slavery, and also focuses on passing and racial ambiguity, topics rife within Harlem writing and symptoms of a widespread interest in processes of racial definition and categorization. The Southwest provides an alternative to these definitional impulses and is a space where, during this historical moment, racial discourses center not on codification, but on indeterminacy. Here, *mestizaje*, racial mixing, and the modern invention of a futuristic *raza cósmica* develop as modern configurations of race. Concomi-

3. The Jean Toomer Papers are held in the James Weldon Johnson Collection of the Beinecke Rare Book and Manuscript Library at Yale University. I sincerely thank the staff of the Beinecke for their help in retrieving the various unpublished manuscripts I address in this essay. The Works Cited gives a full list of archival location.
4. Here I use the term "articulate" intentionally in a gesture towards Brent Hayes Edwards's spatialized appropriation of Stuart Hall in *The Practice of Diaspora* (11–15).

tantly, in the Southwest Toomer's own racial discourse moves from defining a race against the past to redefining the past in order to imagine the "new American race" of the future.

Toomer lived in the Southwest in sporadic, intermittent stints from 1925–1947. During these sojourns Toomer produced a surprising array of texts. The most substantive are a series of essays about this geographical locale (including "Noises at Night," "New Mexico after India," and "To this land where the clouds fall," all n.d., c. 1940) and a play called "A Drama of the Southwest" (n.d., c. 1935).[5] Toomer also produced a draft called "Sequences" (n.d., c. 1945), comprised of a series of short sketches about the New Mexican space, and an untitled notebook about New Mexico that appears to be the foundation of a novel (n.d., c. 1945).[6] He probably also continued work on his long poem "The Blue Meridian" (which contains southwestern images and was first published in 1936 in *New Caravan*) as well as several other poems that remained unpublished until the compilation of *The Collected Poems of Jean Toomer* (1988).[7] It is likely that he also continued to work on his cryptically-titled autobiography, "Book X." Indeed, much of Toomer's southwestern writing is autobiographical.

Like many other modern writers and artists, Toomer was invited to Taos, New Mexico, for the first time by art patron, socialite, and memoirist Mabel Dodge Luhan, who encouraged Toomer to consider the town for a Gurdjieffian center for spiritual development. Although his work on behalf of Gurdjieff brought him to Taos, Toomer continued to visit New Mexico long after he severed ties with his mentor, believing, perhaps, that New Mexico could provide fulfillment that Gurdjieff could not. When Toomer arrived in the Southwest it was already a landscape crowded with artists and writers. Realist painters such as those involved with the Taos Society of Artists had been active in the region since well before World War I, and the area opened up to modernists after Luhan's arrival in 1917, when she began promoting the space to figures like Willa Cather, D. H. Lawrence, Georgia O'Keeffe, and Andrew Dasburg. Many of these figures represent the southwestern space as dehistoricized and timeless, especially by constructing it in conversation with the paradigm of modern US cities, such as New York.[8] These

5. "To this land where the clouds fall" appears to be the title of an essay catalogued as "Unidentified Draft" in the Jean Toomer Papers. I have retained Toomer's capitalization.
6. Portions of this notebook have been reprinted in *A Jean Toomer Reader* as "The Dust of Abiquiu" (240–48). This essay relies on the archival materials, however, catalogued in the Jean Toomer Papers as "Notebook: Contains Notes about New Mexico."
7. These poems include "Imprint for Rio Grande," "I Sit in My Room," "Rolling, Rolling," "It Is Everywhere," and "The Lost Dancer."
8. Mabel Dodge Luhan's *Edge of Taos Desert: An Escape to Reality* (1934) is perhaps the most flagrant example of this juxtaposition of New Mexico and New York.

modernists construct nostalgic primitivist renderings of the landscape and especially of its indigenous peoples, and present the
Southwest and Pueblo Indians as untouched by modernism's direc-
tive to "make it new."[9]

Nurtured and produced by the New York publishing scene and
literati like Waldo Frank, *Cane* falls in line with these classificatory
impulses through its attention to geography. Although *Cane* has
been claimed as a cosmopolitan text by critics like Scruggs and
VanDemarr, and thereby unyoked from static racial identification,
its structure and force rely on the construction of binary relations
between northern and southern spaces and the black and white
races that are mapped onto them. These oppositions are embedded
in the text's formal characteristics (when, for example, sections are
organized in accordance with their setting) and are also thematically operative. For example, when *Cane* presents mixed-race characters like Paul (in "Bona and Paul") they are ultimately rendered
legible within the contours of tidy black or white scripts. In this
sketch, Paul is first racially ambiguous (which provides the fetishis-
tic allure, the slight hint of danger, for his white date, Bona), but is
ultimately circumscribed to a black identity, exposed through the
juxtaposition of Bona and a black doorman.

When Toomer moves from New York to the Southwest his interest in juxtaposing geography and racial identity remains, but the
relation between spaces and races becomes multiple rather than
double. Like other modernists, there are times when Toomer constructs New Mexico in relation to the "man-made canyons of New
York," such as in his essay "New Mexico after India" (250).[1] This
essay suggests that the Southwest can take on different meanings
depending on from which location one approaches it. Toomer writes
that:

9. Of course this modernist treatment of the Southwest, and indeed the conceptualization of the Southwest itself, is historically situated and contingent. "Southwest" is a
relational term—signifying "southwest of New York" and also "southwest of US modernity." Speaking transhistorically, the term "Southwest" means a different geographical
location at different moments, and is dependent on the westward migration of US
modernity and the changing border with Mexico. The Southwest as we now know it
(the greater Mexican Southwest, the desert Southwest) arguably came into existence
during the early-twentieth century, solidified by events like the achievement of state-
hood for New Mexico and Arizona in 1912. But even now the Southwest remains notoriously difficult to define. As Eric Gary Anderson suggests, doing so may be "less
crucial . . . than a critical sense of the instabilities and limitations of such maps and
the ideological motivations for demarcating in the first place" (6).
1. According to Rusch's *A Jean Toomer Reader*, where "New Mexico after India" has been
most recently printed, this essay was previously unpublished. A published clipping of
it, however, does exist in the Mabel Dodge Luhan Papers, which indicates that it was
initially published in a Santa Fe-based paper called *The New Mexican* on June 26,
1940. See Mabel Dodge Luhan Papers series VI, box 102, folder 2397. Yale Collection
of American Literature. Beinecke Rare Book and Manuscript Library. Yale University,
New Haven.

> In times past, I had always come to New Mexico from the east-
> ern states of America. I had greeted Raton Pass and the land
> extending southwestward and beyond, having in the background
> of my mind the low soft country of the eastern seaboard, the
> prairies of the middle west, commerce, industry, and of course
> the man-made canyons of New York. New Mexico had always
> looked grand, open, sunlit, a summit of ancient earth and his-
> toric peoples. (249–50)

From the East, Toomer suggests, New Mexico becomes a space of
the modernist primitive. Toomer's phrase, the "man-made canyons
of New York," emphasizes the human act of modernization; this site
is set in opposition to the natural, pre-modern canyons of the
Southwest, which—contrary to New York's skyscrapers—evoke the
ancient in the form of their sedimentary layers.

In setting the Southwest against New York like many modern
primitives, Toomer describes the Southwest as atavistic and pre-
linguistic. It becomes a space where he is stripped of language:

> I have never tried to put in words the unique gift of New
> Mexico to me. It is enough that I feel it, I know it, that I recog-
> nize it without need of words. Something of New Mexico came
> to me for the first time fifteen years ago. It was a penetration
> deep under the skin. Ever since then there has existed a spe-
> cial polarization between this human being and the people and
> earth of the Southwest. (252)

The Southwest, which "retains its hold upon [Toomer's] heart as
home" (253), exists not as a linguistic construction, but as a physical
connection. Toomer describes embodiment instead of "words" when
he suggests that the Southwest inspires physical sensations: "I feel
it," he writes, as "a penetration deep under the skin" and in "the
heart." To return to Content's photograph, location, in particular
the hand-built adobe house in Taos, trumps the ghostly traces of
language barely visible on the page exiting Toomer's typewriter. Of
course this tension between language and embodiment is somewhat
paradoxical given that Toomer suggests the abandonment of language within the context of a written document. Nevertheless, it
also deepens the critical and biographical narrative of Toomer's
"failure" as a writer after *Cane* by creating a nexus of language,
geography, and racial belonging. When Toomer recognizes the
Southwest's "penetration deep under the skin," he also describes a
location where he can reconcile, or get "deep under" the complexities of his racial identity (his "skin") in ways that were impossible for
him in New York. Although the Southwest as "home" is described as
having a "hold" on Toomer, his identity, by contrast, becomes flexible and mobile.

Thus Toomer's discussion of the pre-linguistic is divorced from the type of primitivism that attempts to access the pre-linguistic, pre-modern, and essentialized racial otherness. It might ultimately make more sense, then, to read Toomer's lack of words less as an expression of modernist primitivism, and more as an effect of biographical conditions. For those aware of Toomer's struggles to publish after *Cane*, of his expectant letters to acquaintances that insist the next publication is just around the corner, a southwestern essay called "To this land where the clouds fall" laments his "wordlessness":

> Furthermore I am a writer. In any case, that is what I am supposed to be. I, descendant of magicians, am supposed to use words with magical effects. But what words can I use that affect these mountains? Besides, as I have said, this country takes words away from me. Not only do the important words of my vocabulary go, but also the little words of everyday use. Sometimes I can't call to mind the word for some simple thing. Silence is grand, but writers are voluble folk. Who ever heard of a silent writer? (8–9)[2]

Although Toomer's writing of linguistic absence smacks of the kind of primitivism that other southwestern modernists cultivate to inspire modernist aesthetic newness, Toomer's writing in the Southwest often takes a different tack.[3] Instead of participating in the racial reification of modernist primitivism, it provides an alternative to it.

In "New Mexico after India," Toomer describes a feeling of being at home that remains unsatisfied in *Cane*, where both the North and South refuse to house the racially ambiguous. This essay creates a sense of belonging through abandoning a racial binary in favor of a network of geographical and social locations that interlock in the idealized New Mexican landscape. Written after a 1939 trip to India that had failed to provide the spiritual renovation Toomer was seeking, "New Mexico after India" uses the disappointment of India to heighten the experience of actualization he suggests that New Mexico provides. If Toomer imagined the Southwest *only* in conjunction with New York, his vision might be more similar to that of modern primitivists. Instead, Toomer renders the Southwest as an intermedi-

---

2. The pages of this manuscript are unnumbered. Page numbers are included here, though, to indicate the order in which the pages are housed in their archival folder (including blank pages). This is consistent for unnumbered archival texts referred to throughout this essay.
3. As examples of linguistic absence as an effect of modernist primitivism, see Willa Cather's *The Professor's House* and the mummified Indian Mother Eve's frozen, soundless scream, discussed at length in Walter Benn Michaels's *Our America: Nativism, Modernism, and Pluralism*, Mabel Dodge Luhan's infantile renderings of her husband Tony Luhan's English speech in *Edge of Taos Desert*, or D. H. Lawrence's enigmatic Indians in "The Woman Who Rode Away."

ary space between New York and India. He writes, "Compared to
New York the Southwest may seem slow and unchanging. Compared
with the interior of India, the Southwest is in rapid change" (250).
"New Mexico after India" argues that the act of arriving to the
Southwest from India instead of the eastern United States reveals a
much more modern space than he had previously realized. In a
sense, this essay appears to be little more than a ranking of primitiv-
isms, in which his voyage from India to New Mexico reveals that the
latter is more modern than India but less modern than New York.
This trip, writes Toomer, built upon "a background built up of experiences in India, Ceylon, Hong Kong, Shanghai, and Japan," exposes
that "By contrast, even the pueblos seemed to have a touch of the
modern world, the Mexican villages seemed to be growing and
changing as young things grow, and Taos and Santa Fe seemed to be
altering under the same impulse that had created Chicago in some
fifty years" (250). This liminal position between the ancient and the
modern enables Toomer's theorization of racial multiplicity.

"New Mexico after India" describes a multi-ethnic coterie in which
Toomer sees the possibility of racial amalgamation: "The Indian is
upstanding. The Mexican is upstanding. The Negro is upstanding.
The White is upstanding. Let us continue to upstand, and at the
same time bend towards each other on the basis of a common
humanity, and we would become one people in spirit and fundamental aim" (251). This Southwest's ability to function as the nexus for
this kind of multi-racial network has to do with its position somewhere between New York and India in terms of its modernity. India,
he claims, is ruled by the caste system, which he describes as so
ancient and deeply embedded that it is impossible to dissolve. On the
contrary, Toomer's journey to New Mexico from India reveals that
"The Southwest is young" (250), a condition that results in a challenge to "our own complexities, taboos, classes if not castes, racial
prejudices, and knotty problems" (251). Most importantly, Toomer
imagines here a racial mixture made possible at a certain stage of
modernization achieved by the southwestern space.

Contrary to the static images of an eternal primitive, to enter the
Southwest is, of course, to enter a space with very real and palpable
histories of racial and colonial intervention. Discursive outgrowths
of this history, like *mestizaje*, run contrary to early-twentieth-century
impulses towards racial classification proliferating in US urban
centers such as New York. Toomer attends to the region's specific
histories in notes that reveal his interest in a wide variety of sources:
New Mexican tour guide, writer, and folklorist Erna Fergusson's
*Our Southwest* (1940); Mexican American writer, academic, and
League of United Latin American Citizens (LULAC) president
(1941–42) George I. Sánchez's *Forgotten People: A Study of New*

*Mexicans* (1940); anthropologists Adolph F. Bandelier and Edgar L. Hewett's *Indians of the Rio Grande Valley* (1937); and Frank Waters's novel *The Man Who Killed the Deer* (1942).[4] One cannot help but wonder if some of these books are on the shelf in Content's photograph, containing information that reappears in Toomer's allusions and constructs the Southwest as a site for a de-essentialized and flexible racial newness, rather than a region of reified primitivist and modernist aesthetic innovation.

This is the kind of allusion that appears in "Sequences," a series of short impressionistic sketches describing the southwestern landscape, interspersed with somewhat rambling philosophical musings characteristic of the late Toomer. In "Sequences," Toomer refers obliquely to the colonial history of the US Southwest, mentioning Bartholomé de Las Casas and "a certain Spanish priest" in the eighteenth century who, he claims, followed in Las Casas's tradition— likely Miguel Hidalgo. Toomer claims that these figures "came upon a vision of what human life in the new world should be, but who never journeyed far enough to see this particular sky and earth" (4)[5] While this passage may appear rife with the kind of vague spirituality that Rudolph P. Byrd claims "wasted [Toomer's] great talent" (xv), its historical references are not only spiritual. This passage also invests the southwestern racial landscape with a libratory racial identity, as both Hidalgo and Las Casas have been mythologized as anti-racist and anti-imperialist icons—as temporal bookends to the Spanish colonial period and voices of resistance.

Toomer's attention to regional history resonates with other theorizations of race emerging from the Southwest and greater Mexico. In this time period, Latin American discussions of race and nationalism were permeated by reflections upon colonial history and subsequent racial mixing. The voice of Mexican intellectual José Vasconcelos dominates these conversations; Vasconcelos published *La raza cósmica* in 1925, the same year that Toomer first visited Taos. *La raza cósmica* was Vasconcelos's most influential work and the foundational articulation of *mestizaje*. While it is possible that Toomer knew of Vasconcelos through newspaper accounts detail-

---

4. Notes on these texts are contained at the end of Toomer's notebook on New Mexico.
5. Although Rusch has republished this passage, I have chosen to use my own transcription from archival materials and have made some different editorial decisions. For example, Rusch's text reads, "This was discovered in the sixteenth century by an uncommon Spanish priest who underwent transformation, who rose up above himself and came upon a vision of what human life in the New World should be" (253). In the handwritten manuscript containing this passage, Toomer crossed out "seventeenth" and inserted "eighteenth" ("sixteenth," as far as I can tell, does not appear in Toomer's manuscript). In tracing possible historical references in this passage this seems an extremely important difference. It appears likely that Toomer may have written this passage and then gone back to it after checking his facts to correct any errors.

ing his lectures, political activities (including a 1929 bid for Mexican president, with a stridently anti-US platform), translations of his writings, or through Frank's extensive Latin American tours, there is no clear evidence that Toomer used Vasconcelos as a source when studying the Southwest. Regardless, there are clear parallels between Toomer's and Vasconcelos's writings. In a discussion of *Cane*, for example, Tace Hedrick claims that both Toomer and Vasconcelos relied on the image of the hybrid or graft in their racial theorizations (47). When Toomer's writings from the Southwest are taken into account, these parallels become even easier to imagine, existing not only in similar theorizations of racial mixture, but also in their engagement with a cultural geography marked by Spanish colonialism and US imperialism. Both writers are concerned with the processes and products of modernity, and their works contain vague, premonitional spiritualities.

Like Toomer, Vasconcelos roots a theory of racial mixture in Spanish colonialism, which he interprets not as the annihilation of the indigenous, but as the promise of racial mixing. In *La raza cósmica*, for example, he suggests that "Although they [the Spanish] may have thought of themselves simply as colonizers, as carriers of culture, in reality, they were establishing the basis for a period of general and definitive transformation" (9–10). Colonization unwittingly set into motion an epoch of racial mixing through which the cosmic race is born out of a post-colonial modernity: "The days of the pure whites, the victors of today, are as numbered as were the days of their predecessors. Having fulfilled their destiny of mechanizing the world, they themselves have set, without knowing it, the basis for a new period: The period of the fusion and mixing of all peoples" (16). *Mestizaje,* the racial mixture of the "the Black, the Indian, the Mongol, and the White" (9), is an outgrowth of modernization, only possible after "mechanizing the world."

To read Toomer in this mestizo context of the Southwest departs from the usual critical practice of placing him within the Harlem milieu and the New Negro movement. Racial boundaries disintegrate in the Southwest while New York, so often a foil to the Southwest, becomes a space of racial definition. Paradoxically, the interwar US saw increased racial rigidity, as George Hutchinson remarks:

> Indeed, the great irony of Toomer's career is that modern American racial discourse—with an absolute polarity between "white" and "black" at its center—took its most definite shape precisely during the course of his life. The United States would be more segregated at the time of Toomer's death than it had been at the time of his birth, despite the dismantling of some of the legal bulwarks of white supremacy. (53–54)

Legislation such as the 1924 Virginia Racial Purity Act was one aspect of racial codification, but aesthetic and literary publication could also serve this cultural imperative. Narratives of Toomer's career are intrinsically connected to a modern American ethos that seeks to firm up racial categories. These narratives have been well-rehearsed by his biographers and critics, who document, for example, Toomer's opposition to his inclusion in *The New Negro* anthology. Compiled, according to Arnold Rampersad's introduction, to "document the New Negro culturally and socially,—to register the transformations of the inner and outer life of the Negro in America that have so significantly taken place in the last few years," and to enable the Negro to "speak for himself," the book is a (re) definitional project (xxv). Toomer was notoriously uncomfortable with these processes of definition (his letters to Horace Liveright regarding the marketing of *Cane* as a Negro text stand as an excellent example of this discomfort). As Cynthia Earl Kerman and Richard Eldridge suggest, the "new American did not want to be a New Negro" (112), and Toomer insisted that Locke had included his portrait and poem in the volume without permission, effectively disclaiming New Negro identity.

Toomer's rejection of the Harlem Renaissance scene has arguably resulted in a pervasive sense of regret among contemporary academics, but also, notably, among Toomer's New Negro contemporaries. In Langston Hughes's autobiography, *The Big Sea* (1940), he recalls that after *Cane*:

> The next thing Harlem heard of Jean Toomer was that he had married Margery Latimer, a talented white novelist, and maintained to the newspapers that he was no more colored than white—as certainly his complexion indicated. When the late James Weldon Johnson wrote him for permission to use some of his poems in the *Book of American Negro Poetry*, Mr. Johnson reported that the poet who, a few years before, was "caroling softly souls of slavery" now refused to permit his poems to appear in an anthology of *Negro* verse—which put all the critics, white and colored, in a great dilemma. How should they class the author of *Cane* in their lists and summaries? . . . Nobody knew exactly, it being a case of black blood and white blood having met and the individual deciding, after Paris and Gurdjieff, to be merely American. (242–43)

Hughes's lament that Toomer became "merely American" and "Harlem is sorry he stopped writing" (243) reveals that the New Negro movement also participated in a codification of black racial identity, despite the strides it made while "the Negro was in vogue" (as Hughes puts it in the same text). Although the Harlem Renaissance disrupted racist assumptions about blacks and refigured blackness for the modern moment, it also enforced a paradigm that could not delimit Toomer.

For Toomer, the New Negro was limiting because it participated in hegemonic racial discourses that insisted on the blackness of drops of blood. Hughes's recollection references James Weldon Johnson, writer of the foundational *The Autobiography of an Ex-Colored Man* (1912), thereby invoking another central Harlem Renaissance trope: passing. Johnson's novel was an early iteration of the kind of racial crossing that becomes nearly an obsession during the Renaissance. The figure of the "tragic mulatto," pervasive in nineteenth-century texts, shifts to explorations of "passing," a change that temporally maps onto the 1930 removal of "mulatto" from the US census (Schor 91). This removal forces identification as black or white and obscures the US history of miscegenation. Interestingly, the same year that the US removed "mulatto" from the classificatory nomenclature of its census, Mexico removed racial demarcations from its census entirely, a practice that seems to refuse, rather than enforce, racial borders (Vandiver 144). Notably, the 1930 US census also saw the first appearance of the category "Mexican" (Schor 92).

The discourse of racial passing itself participates in the codification of black and white racial identity. While the act of passing appears to disrupt binary constructions of racial identity by demonstrating the binary's permeability, it also tends to show that one can perform blackness or whiteness, but not multiple races simultaneously. In Nella Larsen's *Passing* (1929), for example, Clare Kendry is fluently black and fluently white in separate spheres, but bringing these worlds together risks exposure as a black among whites (in accordance with the "one-drop rule") or as a race-betrayer among blacks. The consequences of this exposure can be as severe as death and can also be delivered by the black community, as the novel's ambiguous conclusion suggests. Similarly, the passer is exposed and punished many times in *Cane*. Early in "Bona and Paul," Paul is a paragon of racial multiplicity, and is enfolded by the mystery of his ambiguous physiognomy: "What is he, a Spaniard, an Indian, an Italian, a Mexican, a Hindu, or a Japanese?" (76). When he is subsequently "outed" by a black doorman his ambiguity dissipates and his race is circumscribed. Mocked by the doorman and abandoned by his white date, Paul suffers both for his race betrayal and his racial subterfuge.

After the publication of *Cane*, Toomer (like his character Paul) could not pass for white; his public persona as its writer called constant attention to his black heritage. Rather than pass, Toomer again and again insisted on his identity as the new American race.

At times Toomer's avowal of this identity seems like an impotent protest against a publishing industry determined to market a Negro writer, a mass media wracked with fear of miscegenation, and a Harlem milieu betrayed by Toomer's literary failure. There is also debate about how well Toomer could pass as black. Recall that Hughes, for example, attests that "certainly [Toomer's] complexion indicated" that he was *other* than black. Critics like Larson insist that despite his grandfather's involvement with figures like Booker T. Washington, "Toomer was raised as a white person" and could never convincingly perform blackness (201). In *Terrible Honesty: Mongrel Manhattan in the 1920s*, Ann Douglas writes briefly of Toomer and Frank's 1922 journey to South Carolina, during which they both, ostensibly, passed as black:

> This was a culture to which well-bred Toomer, raised in cosmopolitan Washington D.C., was almost as great a stranger as Frank. . . . In an extension of the minstrel convention of impersonation, the two men posed in South Carolina as "blood brothers." Frank was accepted by blacks as one of them, just as Toomer would "pass" in later decades and be accepted by whites as white. (79)

*Terrible Honesty* boldly claims that New York was the modern cultural capital of the United States—and, indeed, the world—mainly because of its "mongrelization" of culture in the early-twentieth century. Arguably, however, Douglas's "mongrel Manhattan" is never really mongrel. Instead of racial mixing, Douglas more often describes collaboration and mutual influences among blacks and whites. Passing is itself "emblematic of a wider pattern of trans-race needs and debts" (79). In the passage describing Frank and Toomer's trip to South Carolina, however, Douglas suggests that for Toomer blackness was also a form of passing; physiologically and culturally blackness was as foreign to him as it was to Frank. For Toomer, Douglas's New York and the spaces of *Cane* require passing. Driven by an impulse towards classification, they are not ripe for the arrival of the new American race,

Unlike Clare Kendry's fluency with racial signifiers in *Passing*, which enables her to access both blackness and whiteness (until her exposure and punishment), Toomer was equally illegible as black or as white. Defying this dualistic system, what recourse did Toomer have other than to create a new American race more suited to him? What option was there but to find a racial discourse contradicting that of New York and the modern US? What else could he do but invent a modern paradigm not of passing but of mixing, complicit with the model already being forged in the US Southwest? As Toomer himself writes in his archived notebook about

New Mexico, "If you are in between two worlds, which way?" (19), begging a similar question of location and belonging.[6]

Larson explains that "there were speculations that [Toomer] had chosen to pass as a white person after his second marriage (to a white woman) in 1934" (xii). Although Larson pinpoints Toomer's marriage to Content as the moment when he reportedly begins to pass, Hughes's comment in *The Big Sea* lays the groundwork for these allegations in the cutting reference to Latimer, Toomer's first wife. Their 1931 nuptials provided the occasion upon which Toomer perhaps most famously articulated the birth of the new American race. In an oft-quoted pronouncement that was represented in the mass media as more grandiose than revolutionary, more eccentric than philosophical, he stated:

> There is a new race in America. I am a member of this new race. It is neither white nor black nor in-between. It is the American race, differing as much from white and black as white and black differ from each other. It is possible that there are Negro and Indian bloods in my descent along with English, Spanish, Welsh, Scotch, French, Dutch, and German. This is common in America; and it is from these strains that the American race is being born. But the old divisions into white, black, brown, red, are outworn in this country. They have had their day. Now is the time of the birth of a new order, a new vision, a new ideal of man. I proclaim this new order. My marriage to Margery Latimer is the marriage of two Americans. (Rusch 105)

In this passage, Toomer is clearly *not* attempting to pass, but to theorize a kind of modern American mixed race identity. Toomer envisions his marriage as an accomplishment of this racial redefinition. But rather than clarify his position, his pronouncement was used by the press to decry the evils of miscegenation.

The news media contorted Toomer's statement by focusing, at times, on the same kind of language that Toomer himself uses—in particular, of birth. According to Kerman and Eldridge, the "culmination of this unwanted publicity was in an article in *Time* under 'Races.' Entitled 'Just Americans,' the article focused by innuendo on miscegenation and belittled what appeared to be Toomer's elaborate rationalization for marrying a white woman" (202).[7] Needless to say, articles of this type focus not only on Toomer's drops of black blood, but on Latimer's heritage as well. Even reports of Latimer's

6. When reading this sentence one can hardly help but think of "proto-Chicano" writer Américo Paredes's collection of poetry, *Between Two Worlds*, much of it written during the same period as Toomer's southwestern work, an analogy that once again brings together Toomer with a mestizo Southwest.
7. This *Time* article appeared on March 28, 1932.

death emphasize not only that Toomer is "part Negro," but that Latimer was a descendant of poet Anne Bradstreet and Puritan clergyman John Cotton, rendering her not simply white, but ultra-white ("Margery Toomer" 19). These articles have lurid titles like "Woman Novelist Called by Death: Death Ends Romance of Two Races—White Wife of J. Toomer, Novelist of Negro Blood, Expires in Childbirth." They titillate with their emphasis on childbirth, and Latimer's death becomes an allegory for the threat of miscegenation as the birth of the new American race is literalized in the figure of Toomer and Latimer's child.

Although Kerman and Eldridge claim that black publications, on the contrary, viewed the Toomer-Latimer marriage as "a form of race pride" (202), comments such as Hughes's that "The next thing Harlem heard of Jean Toomer was that he had married Margery Latimer, a talented white novelist, and maintained to the newspapers that he was no more colored than white" have a different tenor. Rather than seeing their marriage as somewhat of a "success," or a source, as Kerman and Eldridge maintain, of "pride," Hughes seems to express a sense of regret and laments Toomer's fate from the perspective of the New Negro. This is not a singular sentiment, as interracial origin stories in the Americas have often inspired dual interpretations. Although discourses of *mestizaje*, for example, were reframed by Vasconcelos as a source of empowerment, they have also been a story of race betrayal. As Marilyn Grace Miller notes, the mythology of *la Malinche* has polarized discussions of *mestizaje* to similar effect. On one hand this figure has been interpreted as traitorous to the Indian and as moving towards assimilation and the loss of indigenous identity. But on the other hand *la Malinche* has been reworked as a radical hybrid. The transmission of Toomer's story of racial mixing—and in some readings, betrayal—maps onto this mythology and figures Toomer as a male *la Malinche* for the New Negro, discursively aligning him, once again, with the geographical space of the greater Mexican Southwest.

Harlem laments the loss of Toomer for literature and for the race when Hughes writes that "Harlem is sorry he stopped writing," making the location of Harlem synonymous with the black race. Toomer's move to the Southwest participates, then, in a spatial betrayal that imbricates his racial betrayal. Far earlier than *The Big Sea*, Hughes had considered the Southwest as a site for the enactment of interracial desire in his poem, "A House in Taos" (1927).[8] Arna Bontemps, among others, has even insinuated that this poem was based on

8. "A House in Taos" was published in 1927 in *Palms*, as the winner of an undergraduate poetry prize judged by Witter Bynner (who had himself been living in New Mexico since 1922). In the same year, it was also published in *Caroling Dusk: An Anthology of Verse by Negro Poets*, edited by Countee Cullen.

rumors of Toomer's time at the home of Mabel Dodge Luhan and her Pueblo Indian husband Tony Luhan, a claim disputed in *The Big Sea* by Hughes (xiv). The poem characterizes Taos as a space for interracial sexuality, describing a multi-ethnic triangulation of desire. Whether lauded as an innovation or denigrated as betrayal, the Southwest is a site of racial mixing. The Toomer-Latimer story epitomizes this and exemplifies Toomer's new American race. This narrative is disciplined by a mass media that adheres to a US racist and misogynist construction of black male predation and white female purity. It is also regimented by a paradigm of racial infidelity and origins stories of mestizo "betrayal"; this paradigm is only made possible by a bifurcated system of racial identity in which "one drop" of black blood signifies the individual's authentic and essential race.

These critiques of Toomer assume that his turn away from blackness is necessarily a turn towards whiteness. But much like Vasconcelos's cosmic race, Toomer's new American race is not about passing. It is not a strategy of whitening or deracination (a term that gestures here towards the invisibility of white racial construction). It is instead a radical re-envisioning of mixed-race identity as enabling and constructive, rather than destructive and degenerate. Positioning Toomer in the Southwest alongside discourses of *mestizaje* allows a rereading of race mixing as more than just a reversal of a binary system; race mixing in fact subverts the system of racial classification. Latimer herself participates in this subversion. In an October 1931 letter, she discusses her role in developing the new American. Surprisingly, perhaps, Toomer is again situated in a dialogic relation with India:

> People in Portage think J. is East Indian. He looks very much like one, that color—beautiful rich skin, gold shade, fine features, and bones, very tall and slender, beautiful mouth, very sleek hair and fine hands. My mother knew about the racial thing and for a time felt quite agitated. Then when she saw that he really is the right person for me she jumped that hurdle and now we are enormously happy. . . . You don't know how marvelously happy I am and my stomach seems leaping with golden children, millions of them. (Kerman and Eldridge 199)

Latimer's letter calls into question the dominant black-white binary by buffering it with India: People *think* Toomer is Indian, which leads to subversion of the "racial thing" and a humanistic lauding of Toomer as simply the "right person." Latimer imagines herself and Toomer as progenitors of a mixed race, populating the world with "millions" of "golden children."

Toomer envisions this fecundity himself. He hints at it most famously in his pronouncement on the occasion of their marriage when he notes his "marriage to Margery Latimer is the marriage of two-Americans" (and where "America," arguably, signifies racial mixing). He expands upon this vision in his New Mexican writing:

> I am one. Here I am I. In these grand spaces I feel grand, with largeness in me, and my body in the world. I tell myself that this geography must in the future as it has in the past produce a great race. I see this future, mountains beyond mountains, and then the sun. I buy land, a large tract. I build a big house and smaller ones. I have fields and cattle. My children grow up. Their children grow up. With my friends and workers I inhabit it, building in New Mexico my world of man. ("To this land" 1)

In this passage, Toomer imagines the Southwest as an ideal homeland for a mixed race subject, much as he does in "New Mexico after India." The spatial is intrinsically connected to the racial. Toomer's "great race," has, as does Latimer's letter, humanistic overtones, and is connected explicitly to the southwestern geography: "Here I am I." The new American race is imagined as springing from the landscape—from Toomer's large tract of land—much as Latimer imagines millions of golden children leaping from her womb. This imagery circumvents many more popular renderings of the Southwest as a barren, desert landscape.

This optimism and emphasis on futurity is undercut, however, by ambivalence. Although Toomer in "New Mexico after India" claims that the Southwest "retains its hold upon [his] heart as home," his failure to settle there permanently is foreshadowed by this ambivalence in his writing of the space. In "A Drama of the Southwest," Toomer's dramatic double, Lewis Bourne, weighs the pros and cons of buying land in Taos, the same land that Toomer critically links to the process of harvesting the new American race.[9] Bourne's ambivalence is based on his suspicions, shared by Toomer in his first-person essays, that the Southwest might become too modern, and that, in short, it might become like New York. In "To this land," Toomer describes an endless deferral of his southwestern land purchase: "My wife [at this time, Content] and I are looking at land. We looked last year. We will look the next. We will look every time we come until we buy" (3). Although the settlement of land is critical to Toomer's regenerative project, he could not quite bring himself to find the perfect tract.

In the same essay, Toomer writes, "I am attracted and repelled, attracted by the actual magnificence of physical New Mexico, attracted by my visions of the potentialities of life here, yet repelled

---

9. The significance of names in Toomer's writing has not been lost on critics, and Toomer's autobiographical Lewis Bourne from "A Drama of the Southwest" is arguably a repetition of the Lewis from the "Kabnis" section of *Cane*.

by a number of trivial matters, all of which I know to be trivial, nevertheless they pester and obsess me as expressions of some deep undiscovered protest" (1). Toomer's language of attraction and repulsion resonates very much with other modernist writing of the Southwest, especially that of Luhan and D. H. Lawrence. These writers describe the Southwest as imbued with a magnetic energy, using terms like "polarization." Recall, too, that this word is also used by Toomer in "New Mexico after India." This language of positive and negative charges also, importantly, describes atomic structures and thus evokes modernization (charged atomic particles, were, after all, first identified in the early-twentieth century).

This scientific language suggests that there is a tipping point for technological modernization brought to the Southwest which threatens the regenerative possibilities of the New Mexican site. The Southwest quickly becomes too modern, emblemized by the building of Los Alamos Laboratory in 1943 with the specific project of creating a nuclear bomb. In "Sequences," Toomer returns to his image of the sloping New Mexican landscape as a metaphor for spiritual and material development. This time, however, he links it to a discussion of the atomic bomb: "Until men are strong in their ascent up the spiritual slope, the existence of atomic energy will block the spiritual climb and enforce still more 'progress' up the material slope. Given men as they now are, its use in society would be an unqualified disaster. It should not be used, except in medicine" (63). At the time "Sequences" was written, the Manhattan Project—its name signifying and spatializing its relation to the paragon of US modernity—was underway a mere sixty-five miles away from Taos. The atomic bomb erupts in doomsday visions among the otherwise pristine landscape that Toomer constructs. In his notebook on New Mexico Toomer writes:

"The mountain will smoke, great winds will come up, the world will be destroyed by fire." So say the old men of the pueblo, some of whom may have true vision and gift of prophecy. Do we not hear the same prediction in different terms from scientists who know the fearful potency of the atomic bomb?

What I do not know is—Do the elders of Taos vision the coming destruction as the end of man, or as the matrix of a new birth? Will resurrection follow this death? And, if so, who will be resurrected? White men? Red men? Black men? An entirely new race? (6)

Despite his apocalyptic tone, Toomer continues to insist that "new men and women are as possible as war. I will hold to the faith that we will be reborn until I see destruction sweep the earth and I am knocked to smithereens" (9). But despite Toomer's "faith" in the possibility of the Southwest for his "entirely new race," the fact remains that he never made New Mexico his permanent home. He never purchased the tract of New Mexican land required as the foundation for the new American race.

Instead Toomer lived the last years of his life in Bucks County, Pennsylvania, where he was asked to define his race at an "inquiry" (as Larson describes it) into whether or not his daughter could attend an all-white school. During the course of this inquiry Toomer was able to convince his audience that he was not black. But neither did he pass as white. However, in Bucks County Toomer was ultimately unable to inhabit his idealized, mixed new American race. During the inquiry he is positioned, once again, in relation to India. A resident of Bucks County interviewed in Larson's *Invisible Darkness* recalls that when he moved to Bucks County he was "told . . . with a straight face, that Mrs. Toomer was married to an East Indian" because "The farmers around here are very narrow. If they thought Mrs. Toomer, white, was married to a Negro, they would make life miserable for both of them. An East Indian they can live with so, remember, Jean Toomer is East Indian" (156). In Bucks County, Toomer's mixed new American race is disabled and he is forced to pass, although not as white. This creates a fissure between Bucks County and New Mexico in terms of Toomer's racial-spatial discourses. For in New Mexico Toomer had described the new American race as arising from the southwestern soil, made fertile through regional history and cultural crosscurrents. In Bucks County, it is the farmers, the tillers of the land themselves, who are "narrow"—so different from the vast southwestern earth.

The consistent mentions of India in Toomer's biography and southwestern writing are often vague and can be, for this reason, frustrating. But they are also revealing. For they not only reinforce the ways in which racial identities become mapped onto spatial locations, but they also suggest that these spaces exist in complex relational networks with one another, calling into question the familiar geographical contours of modernism and modernity. The southwestern space generally considered so antithetical to modernity (and hence so attractive to modernists) is shown to be engaged in processes of modernity not only existent in the local zones that Toomer inhabits as "A small man in big spaces . . . between Taos and Santa Fe" ("Handwritten Notes" 2), but also in Harlem and Greenwich Village; Chicago and Sparta, Georgia; Mexico and India—the complex routes revealed in Toomer's southwestern archive.[1]

---

1. Here I use the term "routes" intentionally, following the direction of James Clifford in his book of the same title, where he suggests that "routes" engender a certain type of ambivalence: "I do not accept that anyone is permanently fixed by his or her 'identity'; but neither can one shed specific structures of race and culture, class and caste, gen-

WORKS CITED

Anderson, Eric Gary. *American Indian Literature and the South-west: Contexts and Dispositions.* Austin: U of Texas P, 1999.

Bandelier, Adolph F., and Edgar L. Hewett. *Indians of the Rio Grande Valley.* Albuquerque: U of New Mexico P, 1937.

Bontemps, Arna. Introduction. *Cane.* By Jean Toomer. New York: Perennial, 1969. vii–xvi.

Byrd, Rudolph P. *Jean Toomer's Years with Gurdjieff: Portrait of an Artist, 1923–1936.* Athens: U of Georgia P, 1990.

Cather, Willa. *The Professor's House.* 1925. New York: Vintage, 1990.

Clifford, James. *Routes: Travel and Translation in the Late Twentieth Century.* Cambridge: Harvard UP, 1997.

Douglas, Ann. *Terrible Honesty: Mongrel Manhattan in the 1920s.* New York: Noonday, 1996.

Edwards, Brent Hayes. *The Practice of Diaspora: Literature, Translation, and the Rise of Black Internationalism.* Cambridge: Harvard UP, 2003.

Fergusson, Erna. *Our Southwest.* New York: Knopf, 1940.

Hedrick, Tace. "Blood-Lines that Waver South: Hybridity, the 'South,' and American Bodies." *Southern Quarterly* 42.1 (2003): 39–52.

Hughes, Langston. *The Big Sea: An Autobiography.* New York: Knopf, 1940.

———. "A House in Taos." *Caroling Dusk: An Anthology of Verse by Black Poets of the Twenties.* Ed. Countee Cullen. New York: Citadel, 1993. 152.

Hutchinson, George. "Identity in Motion: Placing *Cane.*" *Jean Toomer and the Harlem Renaissance.* Ed. Geneviève Fabre and Michel Feith. New Brunswick: Rutgers UP, 2001. 38–56.

Johnson, James Weldon. *The Autobiography of an Ex-Colored Man.* 1912. New York: Hill, 1960.

Jones, Robert B., and Margery Toomer Latimer, eds. *The Collected Poems of Jean Toomer.* Chapel Hill: U of North Carolina P, 1988.

Kerman, Cynthia Earl, and Richard Eldridge. *The Lives of Jean Toomer: A Hunger for Wholeness.* Baton Rouge: Louisiana State UP, 1987.

Larsen, Nella. *Passing.* 1929. New York: Penguin, 1997.

Larson, Charles R. *Invisible Darkness: Jean Toomer and Nella Larsen.* Iowa City: U of Iowa P, 1993.

der and sexuality, environment and history. I understand these, and other cross-cutting determinations, not as homelands, chosen or forced, but as sites of worldly travel: difficult encounters and occasions for dialogue" (12).

Lawrence, D. H. "The Woman Who Rode Away." *Selected Short Stories of D. H. Lawrence*. Ed. James Wood. New York: Modern Library, 1999. 365–98.

Luhan, Mabel Dodge. *Edge of Taos Desert: An Escape to Reality*. 1934. Albuquerque: U of New Mexico P, 1987.

"Margery Toomer, Novelist, Dies in West: Wife of Psychologist was a Descendant of Prominent New England Pioneers." *New York Times* 18 Aug. 1932: 19.

Michaels, Walter Benn. *Our America: Nativism, Modernism, and Pluralism*. Durham: Duke UP, 1995.

Miller, Marilyn Grace. *The Rise and Fall of the Cosmic Race: The Cult of Mestizaje in Latin America*. Austin: U of Texas P, 2004.

Paredes, Américo. *Between Two Worlds*. Houston: Arte Público, 1991.

Quasha, Jill, comp. and ed. *Marjorie Content: Photographs*. New York: Norton, 1994.

Quirk, Tom, and Robert E. Fleming. "Jean Toomer's Contributions to *The New Mexican Sentinel*." *Jean Toomer: A Critical Evaluation*. Ed. Therman B. O'Daniel. Washington, DC: Howard UP, 1988. 65–73.

Rampersad, Arnold. Introduction. *The New Negro: Voices of the Harlem Renaissance*. 1925. Ed. Alain Locke. New York: Touchstone, 1997. ix–xxiii.

Rusch, Frederik L., ed. *A Jean Toomer Reader: Selected Unpublished Writings*. New York: Oxford UP, 1993.

Sánchez, George I. *Forgotten People: A Study of New Mexicans*. Albuquerque: U of New Mexico P, 1940.

Schor, Paul. "Mobilizing for Pure Prestige? Challenging Federal Census Ethnic Categories in the USA (1850–1940)." *International Social Science Journal* 57.183 (2005): 89–101.

Scruggs, Charles, and Lee VanDemarr. *Jean Toomer and the Terrors of American History*. Philadelphia: U of Pennsylvania P, 1998.

Toomer, Jean. "The Blue Meridian." Jones and Latimer 50–75.

———. "Book X." Ts. Jean Toomer Papers series II, boxes 11–12, folders 344–70.

———. *Cane: An Authoritative Text, Backgrounds, Criticism*. Ed. Darwin T. Turner. New York: Norton, 1988.

———. *The Collected Poems of Jean Toomer*. Ed. Robert B. Jones and Margery Toomer Latimer. Chapel Hill: U of North Carolina P, 1988.

———. "A Drama of the Southwest." Ts. Jean Toomer Papers series II, box 44, folder 917. Partially rpt. in Rusch as "Taos Night" 249.

———. "A Drama of the Southwest (Notes)." Ts. Jean Toomer Papers series II, box 44, folder 913.

———. "Handwritten Notes on New Mexico for 'New Mexico after India'" in "New Mexico after India: Notes and Drafts." Ms. Jean Toomer Papers series II, box 48, folder 1011.

————. "I Sit in My Room." Jones and Latimer 83.

————. "Imprint for Rio Grande." Jones and Latimer 81–82.

————. "It Is Everywhere." Jones and Latimer 85–87.

————. Jean Toomer Papers. James Weldon Johnson Collection. Beinecke Rare Book and Manuscript Library. Yale U, New Haven.

————. "The Lost Dancer." Jones and Latimer 39.

————. "New Mexico after India." Rusch, 249–53. Rpt. of "New Mexico after India" in "New Mexico after India: Notes and Drafts." Ts. Jean Toomer Papers series II, box 48, folder 1011.

————. "Noises at Night." Ts. Jean Toomer Papers series II, box 48, folder 1012.

————. "Notebook: Contains Notes about New Mexico." Ms. Jean Toomer Papers series II, box 15, folder 1482. Partially rpt. in Rusch as "The Dust of Abiquiu" 240–48.

————. "Rolling, Rolling." Jones and Latimer 84.

————. "Sequences" in "Sequences: Notes and Drafts." Ms. Jean Toomer Papers series II, box 48, folder 1013. Partially rpt. in Rusch as "Rainbow" 240, "Part of the Universe" 253–57, and "Santa Fe Sequence" 257–58.

————. "To this land where the clouds fall" in "Unidentified Draft." Ts. Jean Toomer Papers series II, box 48, folder 1014.

Vandiver, Marylee Mason. "Racial Classifications in Latin American Censuses." *Social Forces* 28.2 (1949): 138–46.

Vasconcelos, José. *The Cosmic Race / La raza cósmica.* 1925. Trans. Didier T. Jaén. Baltimore: Johns Hopkins UP, 1997.

Waters, Frank. *The Man Who Killed the Deer.* New York: Farrar, 1942.

"Woman Novelist Called by Death: Death Ends Romance of Two Races—White Wife of J. Toomer, Novelist of Negro Blood, Expires in Childbirth." *Los Angeles Times* 18 Aug. 1932: 3.

# NELLIE Y. McKAY

## Jean Toomer, the Artist—An Unfulfilled American Life: An Afterword[†]

Almost two decades have gone by since the rediscovery of *Cane* and Jean Toomer, who wrote that one astonishing book and then disappeared from the landscape of American arts and letters for almost forty years. Published to loud applause in 1923, *Cane* reached only a small self-selected audience, primarily those men and women who

† From *Jean Toomer: A Critical Evaluation*, ed. Therman B. O'Daniel (Washington, D.C.: Howard University Press, 1988). Copyright © 1988 by the College Literature Association. Reprinted with the permission of Howard University Press. All rights reserved.

saw themselves in the avant-garde of American literature. Toomer was described by many as the "most promising Negro author" of his day. However, the promise of such an illustrious beginning was never fulfilled.

Since the late 1960s, a new generation of critics has sought to reinterpret *Cane* and to find answers to the enigmas of Toomer's literary career. During these years of revival, a great deal has been written about both the book and its author by critics who have made pilgrimages to Fisk University to sift through the many thousands of pages of his unpublished manuscripts and by those who have not looked beyond his early unpublished work.

The search for new insights into Cane and for an explanation of Toomer's brief sojourn in the world of letters followed the discovery of his vast collection of unpublished manuscripts shortly after his death in 1967. Housed at Fisk University in Nashville, Tennessee, the collection confirmed that he had continued to write for many years after *Cane* was published in 1923. After 1923, until the early years of the 1930s, a few of his poems and short stories appeared, but his longer literary works, several novels and full-length plays, were subject to numerous rejections from publishers. Changes in his writing style after the publication of *Cane* contributed to his failure to achieve further literary recognition, for by the middle of 1923 Toomer had turned away from the literary muse to search for the meaning of life in religion and philosophy and had sacrificed the art and brilliance that characterized *Cane* for the didacticism of a variety of dogma.

Toomer's obsessive quest for personal harmony was largely responsible for the stylistic changes that he made in his writings. In its pursuit, he came to believe that religion and philosophy held higher potentials for the success of his goal. From his autobiographical writings we know that he expected to find all-inclusive answers to the large questions of human existence through these mediums. When he was twenty-one, he thought he had discovered a source of harmony in socialism but soon found that socialism would not bear the full weight of his need for an "intelligible scheme" to direct his life. Socialism gave way to Buddhist philosophy and Eastern teachings, which gave way to Western literature and art, which, in turn, gave way to the Gurdjieff philosophy, followed by the words of the Holy Men of India, the Society of Friends, and, finally, scarcely a decade before his death at age seventy-three, dianetics (Scientology). None of these, individually, was sufficient to meet the needs of the single system he sought. The grand epiphany he awaited eluded him throughout his life.

When *Cane* was published it was, for many, the beacon that stood at the gateway to the Harlem Renaissance, unsurpassed during that period and for a long time after in its artistic craftsmanship. After a small reprint edition was published in 1927, both the book and its author disappeared from the eyes of their early admirers and critics. In the 1960s, when he was very ill, his wife, Marjorie Content Toomer, turned over his manuscripts to Fisk University. The late Arna Bontemps was chief librarian there at the time, and he had been among the first people to hail Toomer in the early 1920s. His presence at that institution made it a good place for the deposit of the manuscripts. University Place Press, New York, published a third edition of *Cane* in 1967, and in 1969 Harper and Row issued a paperback edition with a new introduction by Bontemps. It was the latter edition that informed the larger public of what had happened to Toomer's star: it had fallen in its ascendency.

*Cane* immediately recaptured its former prestige in the world of letters and propelled itself and its author into the spotlight. This came in the wake of the black revolution of the 1960s, the rise of black studies programs in colleges and universities across the country, and a reawakened interest in the black American's cultural past. *Cane* was mandatory on many reading lists. In a position of preeminence in Afro-American letters, it was unanimously applauded by its new critics as an outstanding depiction of the Afro-American experience. At the same time, scholars had always been intrigued and curious about those issues that might have been responsible for the unfulfilled career of this brilliant writer, and these arose anew.

A study of Toomer's life and work between 1923 and 1967 reveals that this man spent his life searching for the fullest meaning of human existence. However, it was an unsuccessful quest, not only because of his failings but also because of the failings of the world in which he lived. One problem that arose for Toomer early in his brief literary career concerned the link between the success of *Cane* and himself as a "Negro" writer. He never considered himself a Negro, not because he considered himself a white man, but because he aspired in his life and writings to create a synthesis of the many blood lines that flowed through his veins. He aspired, he said, to obliterate the notion of racial superiority or inferiority among a nation of people who were, in a majority proportion, the offspring of many different racial groups. Consequently he rejected the "Negro" writer label in all of its connotations and turned his back on those things that had made the book the splendid achievement it had been. After *Cane* he wrote nothing in which he used, exclusively, those materials related to black American life, but he went beyond this. He deliberately rejected his previous literary ambitions and the modes of expression through which these could have been achieved. His later works were not intended for artistic acclaim. Had the sales of *Cane* been large in 1923 and 1924, his decision to retreat from the literary world might have been different, but, in general, the small sales were not particularly disturbing to him because he had made his withdrawal from that part of his life before the book was published. To his great distress, his later writings went unnoticed because publishers were unsympathetic to the change in his course and to his undisguised discipleship of the Gurdjieff philosophy.

In his heart Toomer was always a philosopher and a mystic. After *Cane* he also wanted to be prophet-priest. He was committed to working toward an America in which all Americans would transcend the errors of past history and move into a new and glorious day of national harmony. In his early writings, he was influenced by Waldo Frank, now one of the forgotten men of American letters, but in the 1920s an influential figure in the group that included Sherwood Anderson, Alfred Stieglitz, Van Wyck Brooks and Randolph Bourne. Frank's philosophy was akin to the creative strivings of the young Toomer.

Toomer broke allegiance with Frank at the same time that he repudiated the merits of art for the salvation of America and Americans. It was then that he turned to Georges I. Gurdjieff, an Eastern mystic who promised his followers that his program would lead them to achieve internal harmony. Toomer was intrigued by Gurdjieff's ideas, for the question of perfect accord between the physical, intellectual, and moral qualities of the human being was one with which he had struggled for a long time. Most of Toomer's writings after *Cane* were products of the Gurdjieff influence, and although his underlying philosophic concerns altered only mimimally between those two periods of his life, there was a marked difference in the way in which he expressed them. The former years were ones of the artist-poet, the latter, those of the prophet-priest. Through all the changes, however, he never gave up the idea of writing as a vocation.

Although there is no question that Toomer's turning away from art was partly connected to his rejection of a racial designation and that it was also partly a rebellion against carrying the burdens of racial and cultural alienation, he was not blameless in his failure as a writer. He read a great deal, and he pondered, but he never formulated his own philosophical theories. He spent his life appropriating whatever was convenient for him from the ideas of others. In a pattern of beginnings and endings, he spent much of his life pursuing ends which never fully materialized for him. He attended half a dozen colleges and universities but never earned a degree, and he adopted a variety of views on how to achieve internal harmony, but all eventually led to disappointment for him. He was led to literary art by his association with Frank and other members of that group. His wish to transcend the "Negro" label led him to the Gurdjieff philosophy and the exploration of higher consciousness, but he discarded this in time because it too failed to fully satisfy his expectations of it. His inability to accept the limitations and failings of human systems and endeavors kept him searching for a perfection that he was never to find. Jean Toomer's failure to fulfill his early promise as a writer is one in which the responsibility must be shared between himself and his society. On his side, in time, his vision, his desire to transcend all limits, lost touch with reality. He died an unhappy man, for he had found no resolution to the dilemma of the human condition. But Toomer's story is not one of only failure, for he was courageous in his personal struggle to strive for the highest ideals of the human imagination, and for this he deserves credit. He was a gifted writer whose vision was of a world in which all people belong to the family of the human race and in which the attainment of spiritual, intellectual, and physical harmony is the ultimate goal to which each should aspire. He was striving to make this a reality. In pursuit of his ideals, he wandered through many doors of inquiry, but sadly, his dream had little chance of fulfillment. The world was not willing to validate his philosophical ideas by publishing his works. Although he could not single-handedly resolve the problem life raised for him, he never turned aside from it. His personal trials reveal that he believed in the potential in himself and in all of America to bring the world closer to the ideal he imagined.

*Cane* and a number of his lesser known pieces are sufficient to prove that Toomer had the eye and the ear of a poet, and he had the gift and genius of an artist. When he turned aside from art it was a great loss for American literature, as well as a tragedy for the man himself. But the larger critical concern that his life raises transcends Jean Toomer or the individual, for it is the universal issue of the artist and society. His failure to achieve his personal goals proves that when any society attempts to place limits on the creative will of the artist there is a tragic loss of cultural vision, and all mankind is poorer for that loss.

# Jean Toomer: A Chronology†

1894 March 29: Nina Pinch-
back marries Nathan
Toomer. December 26:
Nathan Pinchback
Toomer born, Washing-
ton, D.C.

1895 Father, Nathan Toomer,
deserts family.

1896 Nina returns to her
parents' home with infant
son, who is given name
Eugene. Live on Bacon
Street in mainly white
neighborhood.

1899 Nina divorces Nathan.

1901–05 Eugene or "Pinchy"
attends [black]
Garnet School, U
Street.

1905 Fall: Eugene ill. Misses
whole year of school.

1906 Nina marries Archibald
Combes; moves to
Brooklyn with Eugene.
Grandparents sell house
on Bacon Street.

1907 Moves to New Rochelle,
New York.

† From *The Lives of Jean Toomer: A Hunger for Wholeness*, ed. Cynthia Earl Kerman and Richard Eldridge (Baton Rouge: Louisiana State University Press, 1987). Reprinted by permission.

1909  June 9: Nina dies.
      Eugene returns with
      grandparents to live with
      his uncle in Washington.

1910  Enters Dunbar High
      School.

1912  Moves to apartment on U
      Street with grandparents.

1914  January: graduates from
      high school. Summer:
      enters agricultural
      program at University of
      Wisconsin.

1915  January: drops out of
      Wisconsin. Fall: applies
      to Massachusetts College
      of Agriculture; arrives on
      campus but does not
      enroll.

1916  January: Enters American
      College of Physical
      Training in Chicago.
      Explores atheism and
      socialism. Fall: also
      attends classes at
      University of Chicago.

1917  Spring: drops out of
      American College.
      Summer and fall: takes
      classes at New York
      University and City
      College of New York.

1918  Begins intensive reading        "Bona and Paul" written.
      and writing in Chicago,
      Milwaukee, and New
      York. Two jobs, hectic
      schedule.

1919  Physical collapse; recuper-
      ates in Ellenville, New
      York. Back to Washington.

1920  In New York again until fall, devotes self to music and literature; meets Waldo Frank; changes name to Jean Toomer.

Writes "The First American," "Withered Skin of Berries."

1921  In Washington, writes full time, poetry and short stories. Fall: goes to Sparta, Georgia, for two months as substitute principal. December: grandfather dies.

Writes "Meridian Hill—An Autobiographical Story." Finishes "Georgia Night," "Kabnis," and most of his southern sketches.

1922  Close friendship with Waldo Frank, both travel to Spartanburg. Falls in love with Mae Wright. Finishes *Cane* in December. Extols black elements in his background.

Writes *Natalie Mann*. "Song of the Son" and "Banking Coal" published in *Crisis*; "Storm Ending," "Calling Jesus," and "Harvest Song" in *Double Dealer*; "Becky," "Carma," and "Reapers" in *Liberator*; "Face," "Portrait in Georgia," and "Conversion" in *Modern Review*; and "Seventh Street" in *Broom*.

1923  Moves to New York. Meets and falls in love with Margaret Naumburg; estranged from Waldo Frank. Introduced to Gurdjieff philosophy.

*Cane* published. "Fern" published in *Little Review*; "Open Letter to Gorham Munson" in *S4N*; and "Gum" in *Chapbook*. "Withered Skin of Berries" rejected by *Little Review*.

1924  Studies under Orage. Uncle Bismarck dies. Goes to Reno with Margaret Naumburg; attends Gurdjieff's institute at Fontaine-bleau; begins Gurdjieff dance group. Emphasizes concept of "Universal Man."

Finishes "The Negro Emergent." "The Critic of Waldo Frank" published in *S4N*, and "Oxen Cart and Warfare" in *Little Review*.

1925  Begins Gurdjieff work in Harlem. Spends summer with Paul Rosenfeld at

"Easter" published in *Little Review*. Finishes "Values and

York Beach and October at Lake George with Alfred Stieglitz. Visits Mabel Luhan in Taos at Christmas; she urges him to set up Gurdjieff institute there.

Fictions" (rejected for publication).

1926 Breaks with Margaret Naumburg. Mystical experience, beginning at Sixty-sixth Street el station in New York. Summer in Fontaine-bleau and then to Chicago to be a Gurdjieff leader.

1927 Works with groups in Chicago; summer in Fontainebleau.

"Balo" published in *Plays of Negro Life*. Writes "The Gallonwerps" and "The Sacred Factory" (both rejected for publication).

1928 Continues Gurdjieff groups in Chicago; visits York Beach in summer. September: grandmother dies.

"Winter on Earth" published in *The Second American Caravan*; "Mr. Costyve Duditch" in *Dial*. Writes "The Crock of Prob-lems" and "Skilful Dr. Coville" (both rejected).

1929 Continues Chicago groups, summer in Fontainebleau. Decem-ber: falls in love with Emily Otis.

"York Beach" published in *The New American Caravan*; "White Arrow" and "Reflections" in *Dial*; "Race Problems and Modern Society" in *Problems of Civilization*; "American Letter" ("Letter D'Amerique") in *Bifur*. Writes "Transatlantic" and "Essentials" (both rejected). Completes short-story collec-tion "Lost and Dominant," including "Drackman," "Mr. Costyve Duditch," "Love on a Train," "Break," "Easter," "Two Professors," "Mr. Limph Krok's Famous 'L' Ride," "Fronts," "Pure Pleasure," and "Winter on Earth" (rejected for publication).

1930 Gurdjieff visits Chicago; friction with New York group over money for Gurdjieff; Chicago group in uncertain state.

Finishes "Earth-Being—The Autobiography of Jean Toomer" (rejected).

1931 Portage experiment. October 30: marries Margery Latimer. Visits New Mexico.

*Essentials* privately published. Finishes "Blue Meridian" (rejected). Writes "A New Force for Cooperation" and poetry collection "Bride of Air" (both rejected). Writes "Outline of an Autobiography."

1932 The Toomers live in Carmel, California; return to Chicago after adverse publicity. August 16: Margery dies in childbirth; Margery Toomer born.

"Brown River Smile" published in *Pagany,* "As the Eagle Soars" in *Crisis.* Finishes "Portage Potential" and "Caromb" (both rejected).

1933 Lives in Portage with Latimers, collecting Margery's letters. To New York in October and Lake George in December.

Writes "Man's Home Companion."

1934 Gurdjieff in New York, pressing JT for money. JT marries Marjorie Content, September 1 in Taos; Toomers live in New York with young Argie.

"A New Force for Cooperation" published in *Adelphi,* and "The Hill" in *America and Alfred Stieglitz.* Writes "On Being an American"; finishes "Eight-Day World," "The Letters of Margery Latimer" (both rejected).

1935 Breaks with Gurdjieff. Summer in Taos.

Writes "A Drama of the Southwest" and "Book X."

1936 Toomers move to Doylestown, Pennsylvania; JT has plan for a Gurdjieff center.

"Blue Meridian" published in *The New Caravan.* "Lump" written near this time.

1937 Leads group modeled on Gurdjieff work; gives lectures in New York; begins using pen name Nathan Jean Toomer. Uncle Walter dies.

Three meditations published in *New Mexico Literary Sentinel*. Privately publishes *Living is Developing, Work-Ideas I,* and, probably, *A Fiction and Some Facts.* Writes "Talks with Peter," "Psychologic Papers," and "Remember and Return" (all rejected). Begins "From Exile into Being" (works on this until 1946).

1938 Begins attending Friends Meeting.

1939 August to December: Toomers in India in unsuccessful search for spiritual enlightenment.

"Roads, People, and Principles" published in Doylestown *Daily Intelligencer* and also privately published as pamphlet.

1940 January: return to Doylestown. May: JT has kidney removed. August: Toomers join Society of Friends.

Begins "The Angel Begori," "The Colombo-Madras Mail."

1941 JT appointed to four Friends committees in local Meeting.

"Socratic Dialogue" published in *New Mexico Literary Sentinel*. Finishes collection "Blue Meridian and Other Poems" (rejected). Begins "Incredible Journey" (works on until 1948).

1942 Begins work with high school group at Friends General Conference (1942–48). Starts new Gurdjieff group at Mill House.

1943 Health difficulties increasing; gets a "physical reading" from Edgar Cayce. Becomes clerk of Ministry and Counsel Committee, Bucks Quarterly Meeting (1943–48). Much

"These Three" and "Santa Claus Will Not Bring Peace" published in *Friends Intelligencer.*

speaking among Friends
groups (1943–47).
Appointed to Ministry
and Counsel Executive
Committee, Philadelphia
Yearly Meeting
(1943–55).

1944    Becomes adviser to            "The Days Ripen" (poem), "The
        college-age Young             Other Invasion," and "The
        Friends (1944–48). Trip       Presence of Love" published in
        to Midwest for Friends        *Friends Intelligencer*. "From
        General Conference.           Exile into Being" rejected by
                                      three publishers.

1945    Added to Religious Life       "Today May We Do It" and
        Committee headed by           "Keep the Inward Watch"
        Douglas Steere                published in *Friends
        (1945–47).                    Intelligencer*.

1946    Continued widespread          "The Uncommon Man" and
        speaking; asked to write      "Worship and Love" published
        pamphlet on worship.          in *Friends Intelligencer*. "From
                                      Exile into Being" rejected
                                      twice.

1947    Becomes assistant clerk,      *An Interpretation of Friends
        Ministry and Counsel          Worship* published. "Authority,
        Executive Committee,          Inner and Outer," "See the
        Philadelphia Yearly           Heart" (poem), and "Chips"
        Meeting (1947–51).            (aphorisms) published in
        Summer in New Mexico;         *Friends Intelligencer*. "From
        Margery enters George         Exile into Being" and poem
        School in fall.               collection "The Wayward and
                                      the Seeking" both rejected
                                      twice.

1948    More physical difficul-       Two poems, "Prayer" and
        ties; summer in New York      "Here," published in *Friends
        working on Alexander          Intelligencer*.
        Technique. Resigns as
        Young Friends adviser;
        resigns as clerk of
        Ministry and Counsel
        Committee, Bucks
        Quarterly Meeting.

1949  Gives William Penn Lecture at Yearly Meeting. Begins Jungian analysis. Dwindling number of talks to Friends groups. October 29: Gurdjieff dies.

*The Flavor of Man* published. "Spiritual Scarcity" published in *Philadelphia Enquirer.*

1950  Stops analysis, begins exploring dianetics.

"Something More" and "Blessing and Curse" published in *Friends Intelligencer.*

1951  Takes six-week course in dianetics. Gives six-week lecture series at Doylestown Friends Meeting.

Lecture series: "The Persistent Challenge."

1952  Experiments with nutrition and diet. Hears John G. Bennett lecture on Gurdjieff in New York.

Begins writing "Why I Entered the Gurdjieff Work" (works on until 1954).

1953  Recommits self to Gurdjieff work. Attends Gurdjieff groups in New York. Gives course in New Hope, Pennsylvania, workshop.

1954  Continuing abdominal problems. Resigns from Ministry and Counsel Committee, Buckingham Meeting. Attends Louise Welch's Gurdjieff group in Princeton (1954–57). Starts own Gurdjieff group (1954–57).

1955  "Voices for Peace" interview by Doylestown newspaper. Toomers sell Mill House, move to remodeled barn.

1956  Last literary effort.

Writes "First Trip to Fontainebleau."

1957  Ill health makes it
      impossible for JT to
      continue attending or
      leading Gurdjieff groups.

1962  Toomer papers housed at
      Fisk University. JT in and
      out of nursing homes;
      final entry about 1965.

1967  March 30: dies.

1969  *Cane* reissued for first
      time in paperback.

# Selected Bibliography

## Works by Jean Toomer

• indicates works included or excerpted in this Norton Critical Edition.

"Ghouls." *New York Call* 15 June 1919.
"Reflections on the Race Riots." *New York Call* 2 August 1919.
"Americans and Mary Austin." *New York Call* 10 October 1920.
"Song of the Son." *Crisis* 24 (April 1922): 261.
"Banking Coal." *Crisis* 24 (June 1922): 65.
"Storm Ending." *Double Dealer* 4 (September 1922): 146.
"Georgia Dusk." *Liberator* 5 (September 1922): 25.
"Nora" ["Calling Jesus"]. *Double Dealer* 4 (September 1922): 132.
"Carma." *Liberator* 5 (September 1922): 5.
"Becky." *Liberator* 5 (October 1922): 26.
"Fern." *Little Review* 9 (Autumn 1922): 25–29.
"Harvest Song." *Double Dealer* 4 (December 1922): 258.
"Seventh Street." *Broom* 4 (December 1922): 3.
*Cane.* Boni & Liveright: New York, 1923.
"Esther." *Modern Review* 1(January 1923): 50–55.
"Georgia Portraits." *Modern Review* 1 (January 1923): 81.
"Karintha." *Broom* 4 (January 1923): 83–85.
"Blood-Burning Moon." *Prairie* (March–April 1923): 18.
"Gum." *Chapbook* 36 (April 1923): 22.
"Her Lips Are Copper Wire." *S4N* (May–August 1923).
*Kabnis.* First Part. *Broom* 5 (August 1923): 12–16.
*Kabnis.* Second Part. *Broom* 5 (September 1923): 83–94.
"November Cotton Flower." *Nomad* (Summer 1923).
"Open Letter to Gorham Munson." *S4N* 25 (March–April 1923).
"Notations on *The Captain's Doll.*" *Broom* 5 (August 1923): 47–48.
"[Review of] Zona Gale's *Faint Perfume.*" *Broom* 5 (October 1923): 180–81.
"Waldo Frank's *Holiday.*" *Dial* 75 (October 1923): 383–86.
"The Critic of Waldo Frank: Criticism, An Art Form." *S4N* 30 (September–January 1923–1924).
"Oxen Cart and Warfare." *The Little Review* (Autumn–Winter 1924–1925): 44–48.
"Easter." *The Little Review* 11 (Spring 1925): 3–7.
"Balo: A One Act Sketch of Negro Life." *Plays of Negro Life*. Ed. Alain Locke and Montgomery Gregory. New York: Harper and Brothers, 1927.
"Mr. Costyve Duditch." *Dial* 85 (December 1928): 460–76.
"Winter on Earth." *Second American Caravan*. Ed. Alfred Kreymborg, Lewis Mumford, and Paul Rosenfeld. New York: The Macaulay Co., 1928. 694–715.
"Lettre D'Amerique [Letter from America]." *Bifur* 1 (May 1929): 105–14. Rpt. in *Jean Toomer: Selected Essays and Literary Criticism*. Ed. Robert B. Jones. Knoxville: University of Tennessee Press, 1996. 77–85.
"Race Problems and Modern Society." *Problems of Civilization*. Ed. Baker Brownell. New York: D. Van Nostrand, 1929. 67–111.

"Reflections." *Dial* 86 (April 1929): 314.

"White Arrow." *Dial* 86 (July 1929): 596.

"York Beach." *The Negro American Caravan*. Ed. Alfred Kreymborg, Lewis Mumford, and Paul Rosenfeld. New York: The Macaulay Co., 1929. 12–83.

"Brown River Smile." *Adelphi* 2 (September 1931). Rpt. in *Pegany* 3 (Winter 1932): 29–33.

*Essentials: Definitions and Aphorisms*. Chicago: Lakeside Press, 1931.

"As the Eagle Soars." *Crisis* 41 (April 1932): 116.

"The Hill." *America and Alfred Stieglitz: A Collective Portrait*. Ed. Waldo Frank, Lewis Mumford, and Paul Rosenfeld. New York: The Literary Guild, 1934. 295–303.

"A New Force for Cooperation." *Adelphi* (October 1934): 25–31.

"Of a Certain November." *Dubuque Dial* IV (1 November 1935): 107–12.

"The Blue Meridian." *The New Caravan*. Ed. Alfred Kreymborg, Lewis Mumford, and Paul Rosenfeld. New York: The Macaulay Co., 1936. 107–33.

"J.T. and P.B." *New Mexico Sentinel* 20 July 1937: 6.

"Make Good." *New Mexico Sentinel* 20 July 1937: 6–7.

"From a Farm." *New Mexico Sentinel* 31 August 1937: 8.

"Evil." *New Mexico Sentinel* 7 September 1937: 8.

"Good and Bad Artists." *New Mexico Sentinel*, 1937.

*A Fiction and Some Facts*. [A pamphlet], 1937.

*Living Is Developing*. Doyleston, PA: Mill House Pamphlets (Psychological Series No. 1), 1937.

"A Skunk Used as an Example." *New Mexico Sentinel* 17 November 1937: 7.

*Work-Ideas I*. Doyleston, PA: Mill House Pamphlets (Psychological Series No. 2), 1937.

"Imprint for Rio Grande." *New Mexico Sentinel* 12 January 1938: 6.

*Roads, People, and Principals*. Doyleston, PA: Mill House Pamphlets, 1939.

"Socratic Dialogue." *New Mexico Sentinel*, 1941.

"Santa Claus Will Not Bring Peace." *Friends Intelligencer* C (1943): 851–52.

"The Other Invasion." *Friends Intelligencer* 1 July 1944: 423–24.

"The Presence of Love." *Friends Intelligencer* 25 November 1944: 771–72.

"Today May We Do It." *Friends Intelligencer* 13 January 1945: 19–20.

"Keep the Inward March." *Friends Intelligencer* 30 June 1945: 411–12.

"The Uncommon Man." *Friends Intelligencer* 9 March 1946: 147–48.

"Love and Worship." *Friends Intelligencer* 14 December 1946: 695–96.

"Authority, Inner and Other." *Friends Intelligencer* CIV 5 July 1947: 352–53.

"See the Heart." *Friends Intelligencer* 104 (9 August 1947): 423.

"Chips." *Friends Intelligencer* 27 December 1947: 705.

*An Interpretation of Friends Worship*. Philadelphia: Committee on Religious Education of Friends General Conference, 1947.

"Spiritual Scarcity." *Philadelphia Inquirer* 28 March 1949.

*The Flavor of Man*. Philadelphia: Young Friends Movement of the Philadelphia Yearly Meeting, 1949.

"Something More." *Friends Intelligencer* 25 March 1950: 164–65.

"Blessing and Curse." *Friends Intelligencer* CVII 30 September 1950: 576–77.

## *Works about Jean Toomer and* Cane

• indicates works included or excerpted in this Norton Critical Edition.

Ackley, Donald G. "Theme and Vision in Jean Toomer's *Cane*." *Studies in Black Literature* 1.1 (Spring 1970): 45–65.

Antonides, Chris. "Jean Toomer: The Burden of Impotent Pain." Diss. Michigan State University, 1975.

• Abbott, Megan. "'Dorris Dances . . . John Dreams': Free Indirect Discourse and Female Subjectivity in *Cane*." *Soundings: An Interdisciplinary Journal* 80.4 (Winter 1997): 455–74.

Akoma, Chiji Russell. "Between the spoken and the written: Folklore and the Afro-diasporic narrative." Diss. State University of New York at Binghamton, 1998.

———. "'Singing Before the Sun Goes Down': Jean Toomer's *Cane* and the Black Oral Performance Aesthetic." *Folklore in New World Black Fiction: Writing and the Oral Traditional Aesthetics.* Columbus: Ohio State University Press, 2007. 111–30.

Anderson, Paul Allen. *Deep River: Music and Memory in Harlem Renaissance Thought.* Durham: Duke University Press, 2001.

Anonymous. "A Review of *Cane.*" *Boston Transcript* 15 December 1923: 8. Rpt. in *The Merrill Studies in Cane.* Ed. Frank Durham. 31.

———. "Literary Vaudeville: A Review of *Cane.*" *Springfield Republican* 23 Dec 1923: 9a. Rpt. in *The Merrill Studies in Cane.* Ed. Frank Durham. 34.

———. "Books in Brief." The *Nation* 118.3072 (21 May 1924): 591–92.

———. Review. *Dial* 76 (January 1929): 92.

———. Review. *Salient* 2 (February 1929): 18–19.

———. Review. *New Orleans Times-Picayune* 12 April 1931: 30.

———. Review. *Buffalo Courier Express* 21 June 1931.

———. *New York World-Telegram* 17 March 1932: 1.

———. *New York Herald Tribune* 18 March 1932: 9.

———. "Just Americans." *Time* 28 March 1932: 19. Rpt. in *The Merrill Studies in Cane.* Ed. Frank Durham. 15–16.

———. *St. Louis Argus* (March 1932).

———. "Obituary." *New York Times* 18 August 1932: 19.

———. *Baltimore Afro-American* 27 August 1932.

———. *Baltimore Afro-American* 24 August 1934.

———. Editorial. *New York Age* 24 November 1934.

———. *Baltimore Afro-American* 1 December 1934.

Armstrong, John. "The Real Negro." *New York Tribune* 14 October 1923: 26. Rpt. in *The Merrill Studies in Cane.* Ed. Frank Durham. 18–20.

Baker, Houston A., Jr. "Journey Toward Black Art: Jean Toomer's *Cane.*" *Singers of Daybreak: Studies in Black American Literature.* Washington, D.C.: Howard University Press, 1974. 53–80, 107–108.

Baldanzi, Jessica Hays. "Eugenic Fictions: Imagining the Reproduction of the Twentieth Century American Citizen." Diss. Indiana University, 2003.

———. "Stillborns, Orphans, and Self-Proclaimed Virgins: Packaging and Policing the Rural Women of *Cane.*" *Genders* 42 (2005): 39 paragraphs.

Banks, Kimberly. "'Like a Violin for the Wind to Play': Lyrical Approaches to Lynching by Hughes, Du Bois, and Toomer." *African American Review* 38.3 (Fall 2004): 451–65.

Barthold, Bonnie J. *Black Time: Fiction of Africa, the Caribbean and the United States.* New Haven: Yale University Press, 1981.

Battenfeld, Mary. "'Been Shapin Words T Fit M Soul': *Cane,* Language, and Social Change." *Callaloo* 25.4 (Fall 2002): 1238–49.

Bell, Bernard W. "The Afro-American Novel and Its Tradition." Diss. University of Massachusetts, 1970.

• ———. "A Key to the Poems in *Cane.*" *CLA Journal* 14 (March 1971): 251–58.

———. "Portrait of the Artist as the High Priest of Soul: Jean Toomer's *Cane.*" *Black World* 23.11 (September 1974): 4–19, 92–97.

Benson, Brian Joseph, and Mabel Mayle Dillard. *Jean Toomer.* Twayne's US Author Series. 389. Boston: Twayne, 1980.

Birat, Kathie. "'Giving the Negro to Himself': Medium and 'Immediacy' in Jean Toomer's *Cane.*" *Q/W/E/R/T/Y: Arts, Littératures & Civilisations du Monde Anglophone* 7 (Oct 1997): 121–28.

Blackwell, Louise. "Jean Toomer's *Cane* and Biblical Myth." *CLA Journal* 17 (1974): 535–42.

Blake, Susan L. "The Spectatorial Artist and the Structure of *Cane.*" *College Literature Association Journal* 17.4 (1974): 516–34.

Boan, Rudee Devon. "The Black 'I': Author and Audience in African American Literature." Diss. University of South Carolina, 2000.

Boelhower, William. "No Free Gifts: Toomer's 'Fern' and the Harlem Renaissance." *Temples for Tomorrow: Looking Back at the Harlem Renaissance*. Ed. Geneviève Fabre and Michel Feith. Bloomington: Indiana University Press, 2001. 193–209.

• Bone, Robert A. "Jean Toomer's *Cane*." *The Negro Novel in America*. New Haven: Yale University Press, 1958. 80–88.

———. *Down Home: A History of Afro-American Short Fiction from Its Beginning to the End of the Harlem Renaissance*. New York: Putnam's, 1975. 204–38.

Bontemps, Arna. "The Harlem Renaissance." *Saturday Review of Literature* 22 March 1947: 12–13, 44.

———. "The Negro Renaissance: Jean Toomer and the Harlem Writers of the 1920's." *Anger, and Beyond: The Negro Writer in the United States*. Ed. Herbert Hill. New York: Harper, 1966. 20–36.

• ———. Introduction. *Cane*. By Jean Toomer. New York: Harper and Row, 1969.

———. "Remembering *Cane*." *BANC!* 2 (May–June 1972): 9–11.

Borst, Allan G. "Gothic Economics: Violence and Miscegenation in Jean Toomer's 'Blood-Burning Moon'." *Gothic Studies* 10.1 (May 2008): 14–28.

Boutry, Katherine Elizabeth. "Sirens' Song: Literary Representations of the Musical Female." Diss. Harvard University, 1997.

———. "Black and Blue: The Female Body of Blues Writing in Jean Toomer, Toni Morrison, and Gayl Jones." *Black Orpheus: Music in African American Fiction from the Harlem Renaissance to Toni Morrison*. Ed. Saadi A. Simawe. New York: Garland, 2000. 91–118.

Bowen, Barbara E. "Untroubled Voice: Call-and-Response in *Cane*." *Black American Literature Forum* 16.1 (1982): 12–18.

Boyd, Valerie. *Wrapped in Rainbows: The Life of Zora Neale Hurston*. New York: Scribner, 2003.

• Bradley, David. "Looking Behind *Cane*." *The Southern Review* 21.3 (Summer 1985): 682–94.

Braithwaite, William Stanley. "The Negro in American Literature." *Crisis* 28 (Sept. 1924): 210. Rpt. in *The New Negro*. Ed. Alain Locke. New York: Boni and Liveright, 1925. 29–44.

Brannan, Tim. "Up from the Dusk: Interpretations of Jean Toomer's 'Blood-Burning Moon'." *Pembroke Magazine* 8 (1977): 167–72.

Bricknell, Herschell. Review. *Literary Review of the New York Evening Post*, 8 December 1923: 333.

Brinkmeyer, Robert H., Jr. "Wasted Talent, Wasted Art: The Literary Career of Jean Toomer." *The Southern Quarterly: A Journal of the Arts in the South* 20.1 (Fall 1981): 75–84.

• Brown, Sterling A. "Jean Toomer." *Negro Poetry and Drama, and The Negro in American Fiction*. New York: Atheneum, 1969. 67–68.

———, Arthur P. Davis, and Ulysses Lee, eds. *The Negro Caravan*. New York: Dryden, 1941. 15–16.

Bus, Heiner. "Jean Toomer and the Black Heritage." *History and Tradition in Afro-American Culture*. Ed Günter H. Lenz. New York: Campus, 1984. 56–83.

———. "Jean Toomer's *Cane* as a Swan Song." *Journal of American Studies of Turkey* 11 (Spring 2000): 21–29.

Byrd, Rudolph Paul. "Jean Toomer: Portrait of an Artist, The Years with Gurdjieff, 1923–1936." Diss. Yale University, 1985.

———. "Jean Toomer and the Afro-American Literary Tradition." *Callaloo* 8.2 (24) (Spring–Summer 1985): 310–19.

———. "Jean Toomer and the Writers of the Harlem Renaissance: Was He There with Them?" *The Harlem Renaissance: Revaluations*. Ed. Amritjit

Singh, William S. Shiver, and Stanley Brodwin. New York: Garland, 1989. 209–18.

———. *Jean Toomer's Years with Gurdjieff: Portrait of an Artist, 1923–1936.* Athens: University of Georgia Press, 1990.

———, ed. *Essentials: Jean Toomer.* Athens: University of Georgia Press, 1991.

———. "Shared Orientation and Narrative Acts in *Cane, Their Eyes Were Watching God,* and *Meridian.*" *MELUS* 17.4 (Winter 1991–1992): 41–56.

Caldeira, Maria Isabel. "Jean Toomer's *Cane*: The Anxiety of the Modern Artist." *Callaloo* 8.3 (25) (Fall 1985): 544–50.

Cancel, Rafael A. "Male and Female Interrelationship in Jean Toomer's *Cane.*" *Negro American Literature Forum* 5.1 (Spring 1971): 25–31.

Callahan, John F. *In the African-American Grain: Call and Response in Twentieth-Century Black Fiction.* Urbana-Champaign: University of Illinois Press, 1988.

Candela, Gregory Louis. "Melodramatic Form and Vision in Chestnutt's *The House Behind the Cedars,* Dunbar's *The Sport of the Gods,* and Toomer's *Cane.*" Diss. The University of New Mexico, 1982.

Chase, Patricia. "The Women in Cane." *CLA Journal* 14 (March 1971): 259–73.

Chittum, James P. "Sherwood Anderson's *Winesburg, Ohio* and Jean Toomer's *Cane*: A Compatibility of Style and Vision." MS Thesis. Southern Connecticut State University, 1979.

Christ, Jack M. "Jean Toomer's 'Bona and Paul': The Innocence and Artifice of Words." *Negro American Literature Forum* 9 (1975): 44–46.

Christian, Barbara. "Spirit Bloom in Harlem: The Search for a Black Aesthetic during the Harlem Renaissance: The Poetry of Claude McKay, Countee Cullen, and Jean Toomer." Diss. Columbia University, 1970.

Clark, J. Michael. "Frustrated Redemption: Jean Toomer's Women in *Cane,* Part One." *CLA Journal* 22 (1979): 319–34.

Clary, Françoise. "'The Waters of My Heart': Mythe et Identité dans *Cane* de Jean Toomer." *Etudes Anglaises: Grande-Bretagne, Etats-Unis* 50.4 (Oct.–Dec. 1997): 422–33.

Collins, Paschal Jay. "Jean Toomer's *Cane*: A Symbolistic Study." Diss. University of Florida, 1978.

Comprone, Raphael. "Jean Toomer's *Cane*: Language, Desire, and Feminine Jouissance." *Poetry, Desire, and Fantasy in the Harlem Renaissance.* Lanham, MD: University Press of America, 2006.

Cooke, Michael G. "Tragic and Ironic Denials of Intimacy: Jean Toomer, James Baldwin, and Ishmael Reed." *Afro-American Literature in the Twentieth Century: The Achievement of Intimacy.* New Haven: Yale University Press, 1984. 177–207.

Cooperman, Robert. "Unacknowledged Familiarity: Jean Toomer and Eugene O'Neill." *The Eugene O'Neill Review* 16.1 (Spring 1992): 39–48.

Crewdson, Arlene J. "Invisibility: A Study of the Works of Toomer, Wright and Ellison." Diss. Loyola University-Chicago, 1974.

Da-Luz-Moreira, Paulo. "Macunaíma e *Cane*: Sociedades Multi-raciais além do Modernismo no Brasil e nos Estados Unidos." *Tinta* 5 (Fall 2001): 75–90.

• Davis, Charles T. "Jean Toomer and the South: Region and Race as Elements within a Literary Imagination." *Studies in the Literary Imagination* 7 (Fall 1974): 23–37. Rpt. in *Black is the Color of the Cosmos.* Ed. Henry Louis Gates, Jr. New York: Garland, 1982. 235–51. Rpt. in *The Harlem Renaissance Re-Examined.* Ed. Victor A. Kramer. New York: AMS Press, 1987. 185–99.

Davis, Thadious M. *Nella Larsen, Novelist of the Harlem Renaissance: A Woman's Life Unveiled.* Baton Rouge: Louisiana State University Press, 1994.

Dawson, Emma J. Waters. "Images of the Afro-American Female Character in Jean Toomer's *Cane,* Zora Neale Hurston's *Their Eyes Were Watching God,* and Alice Walker's *The Color Purple.*" Diss. University of Florida, 1987.

———. "Eugene (Jean) Pinchback Toomer (1894–1967)." *African American Authors, 1745–1945: A Bio-Bibliographical Critical Sourcebook*. Ed. Emmanuel S. Nelson. Westport, CT: Greenwood, 2000. 408–17.

Deakin, Motley. "Jean Toomer." *American Poets, 1880–1945: First Series*. Ed. Peter Quartermain. Detroit: Gale, 1986. 405–409.

D.E.D. Review. *Brooklyn Life* 68 (10 November 1923): 3.

Dickerson, Mary Jane. "Sherwood Anderson and Jean Toomer: A Literary Relationship." *Studies in American Fiction* 1 (Autumn 1973): 162–75.

Dillard, Mabel M. "Jean Toomer: Herald of the Negro Renaissance." Diss. Ohio University, 1967. Part rpt. in *The Merrill Studies in Cane*. Ed. Frank Durham. 2–10.

———. "Jean Toomer: The Veil Replaced." *CLA Journal* 17 (1974): 468–73.

Dorris, Ronald. "The Bacchae of Jean Toomer." Diss. Emory University, 1979.

———. "Early Criticism of Jean Toomer's *Cane*: 1923–1932." *Perspectives of Black Popular Culture*. Ed. Harry B. Shaw. Bowling Green, OH: Popular, 1990. 65–70.

———. *Race: Jean Toomer's Swan Song*. New Orleans: Xavier Review Press, 1997.

Dow, William. "Jean Toomer's *Cane* and *Winesburg, Ohio*: Literary Portraits from the 'Grotesque Storm Center'." *Q/W/E/R/T/Y: Arts, Littératures & Civilisations du Monde Anglophone* 7 (Oct 1997): 129–36.

———. "'Always Your Heart': The 'Great Design' of Toomer's *Cane*." *MELUS* 27.4 (Winter 2002): 59–88.

———. "'Always Your Heart': Class Designs in Jean Toomer's *Cane*." *Narrating Class in American Fiction*. New York: Palgrave Macmillan, 2009.

• Du Bois, W. E. B., and Alain Locke. "The Younger Literary Movement." *Crisis* 27 (February 1924): 161–63. Rpt. in *The Merrill Studies in Cane*. Ed. Frank Durham. 40–42.

Duncan, Bowie. "Jean Toomer's *Cane*: A Modern Black Oracle." *CLA Journal* 15 (March 1972): 323–33.

Durham, Frank. "Jean Toomer's Vision of the Southern Negro." *Southern Humanities Review* 6 (Winter 1972): 13–22. Rpt. in *The Merrill Studies in Cane*. Ed. Frank Durham. 102–13.

———. "The Poetry Society of South Carolina's Turbulent Year: Self-Interest, Atheism, and Jean Toomer." *Southern Humanities Review* 5 (Winter 1971): 76–80. Rpt. in *The Merrill Studies in Cane*. Ed. Frank Durham. 11–14.

———, ed. *The Merrill Studies in Cane*. Columbus, OH: The Charles E. Merrill Publishing Co., 1971.

Dyck, Reginald. "*Cane* and Its Discontents." *Eureka Studies in Teaching Short Fiction* 1.1 (Fall 2000): 57–73.

Edmunds, Susan. "Tortured Bodies and Twisted Words: The Antidomestic Vision of Jean Toomer's *Cane*." *Grotesque Relations: Modernist Domestic Fiction and the U.S. Welfare State*. New York: Oxford University Press, 2008.

———. "The Race Question and the 'Question of the Home': Revisiting the Lynching Plot in Jean Toomer's *Cane*." *American Literature* 75.1 (March 2003): 141–69.

Egar, Emmanuel Edame. *The Poetics of Rage: Wole Soyinka, Jean Toomer, and Claude McKay*. Lanham, MD: University Press of America, 2005.

Eldridge, Richard [Leete]. "Jean Toomer's *Cane*: The Search for American Roots." Diss. University of Maryland College Park, 1977.

———. "The Unifying Images in Part One of Jean Toomer's *Cane*." *CLA Journal* 22 (1979): 187–214. Rpt. in *Jean Toomer: A Critical Evaluation*. Ed. Therman B. O'Daniel. Washington: Howard University Press, 1988. 213–36.

Ellison, Curtis William. "Black Adam: The Adamic Assertion and the Afro-American Novelist." Diss. University of Minnesota, 1970.

Estes-Hicks, Onita Marie. "Jean Toomer: A Biographical and Critical Study." Diss. Columbia University, 1982.

Fabre, Geneviève, and Michel Feith, eds. *Jean Toomer and the Harlem Renaissance*. New Brunswick, NJ: Rutgers University Press, 2001.

Farrison, W. Edward. "Jean Toomer's *Cane* Again." *CLA Journal* 15 (March 1972): 295–302.

Fahy, Thomas. "The Enslaving Power of Folksong in Jean Toomer's *Cane*." *Literature and Music*. Ed. Michael J. Meyer. New York: Rodopi, 2002. 47–64.

Farebrother, Rachel. "'Adventuring Through the Pieces of a Still Unorganized Mosaic': Reading Jean Toomer's Collage Aesthetic in *Cane*." *Journal of American Studies* 40.3 (Dec. 2006): 503–21. Rpt in *The Collage Aesthetic in the Harlem Renaissance*. Farnham, UK: Ashgate, 2009.

Farland, Maria. "Modernist Versions of Pastoral: Poetic Inspiration, Scientific Expertise, and the 'Degenerate' Farmer." *American Literary History* 19.4 (Winter 2007): 905–36.

Faulkner, Howard. "The Buried Life: Jean Toomer's *Cane*." *Studies in Black Literature* 7.1 (Winter 1976): 1–5.

Favor, J. Martin. "Building Black: Constructions of Multiple African American Subject Positions in Novels by James Weldon Johnson, Jean Toomer, Nella Larsen and George S. Schuyler." Diss. University of Michigan, 1993.

———. "'Colored; Cold. Wrong Somewhere.' Jean Toomer's *Cane*." *Authentic Blackness: The Folk in the New Negro Renaissance*. Durham: Duke University Press, 1999. 53–80.

Fike, Matthew A. "Jean Toomer and Okot p'Bitek in Alice Walker's *In Search of Our Mothers' Gardens*." *MELUS* 25.3–4 (Fall–Winter 2000): 141–60.

Finkel, De Ann Clayton. "Telling Time: Time, Chronology and Change in Sherwood Anderson's *Winesburg, Ohio* and Jean Toomer's *Cane*." Diss. U of Connecticut, 2004.

Fischer, William C. "The Aggregate Man in Jean Toomer's *Cane*." *Studies in the Novel* 3 (Summer 1971): 190–215.

Fisher, Alice Poindexter. "The Influence of Ouspensky's *Tertium Organum* upon Jean Toomer's *Cane*." *CLA Journal* 17.4 (1974): 504–15.

Foley, Barbara. "Jean Toomer's Sparta." *American Literature: A Journal of Literary History, Criticism, and Bibliography* 67.4 (Dec. 1995): 747–75.

• ———. "Jean Toomer's Washington and the Politics of Class: From 'Blue Veins' to Seventh-street Rebels." *Modern Fiction Studies* 42.2 (1996): 289–321.

———. "Roads Taken and Not Taken: Post-Marxism, Antiracism, and Anticommunism." *Cultural Logic: An Electronic Journal of Marxist Theory and Practice* 1.2 (Spring 1998): 11 paragraphs.

———. "'In the Land of Cotton': Economics and Violence in Jean Toomer's *Cane*." *African American Review* 32.2 (Summer 1998): 181–98.

Fontenot, Chester J., Jr. "Du Bois's 'Of the Coming of John,' Toomer's 'Kabnis,' and the Dilemma of Self-Representation." *The Souls of Black Folk One Hundred Years Later*. Ed. Dolan Hubbard. Columbia: University of Missouri Press: 2003. 130–60.

Ford, Karen Jackson. *Split-Gut Song: Jean Toomer and the Poetics of Modernity*. Tuscaloosa: University of Alabama Press, 2005.

Ford, Nick Aaron. "Jean Toomer and His *Cane*." *The Langston Hughes Review* 2 (Spring 1983): 16–27.

• Frank, Waldo. Foreword [to *Cane*]. By Jean Toomer. New York: Boni and Liveright, 1923. Rpt. in *The Merrill Studies in Cane*. Ed. Frank Durham. 18–20.

Fullinwider, S. P. "Jean Toomer: Lost Generation, or Negro Renaissance?" *Phylon* 27.4 (Winter 1966): 396–403. Rpt. in *The Merrill Studies in Cane*. Ed. Frank Durham. 66–74.

Gates, Henry Louis, Jr. "The Same Difference: Reading Jean Toomer, 1923–1982." *Figures in Black: Words, Signs, and the "Racial" Self*. New York: Oxford University Press, 1987. 196–224.

Gayle, Addison, Jr., ed. *Black Expression: Essays by and about Black Americans in the Creative Arts*. New York: Weybright and Talley, 1969.

———, ed. *The Black Aesthetic*. Garden City, N.Y.: Doubleday, 1972.

———. "Strangers in a Strange Land." *Southern Exposure* 3 (Spring–Summer 1975): 4–7.

————. *The Way of the New World: The Black Novel in America.* Garden City, NY: Anchor, 1975. 98–104, et passim.

Gibson, Donald B. "Jean Toomer: The Politics of Denial." *The Politics of Literary Expression: A Study of Major Black Writers.* Westport, CT: Greenwood, 1981. 155–81.

————, ed. *Modern Black Poets: A Collection of Critical Essays.* Englewood Cliffs, NJ: Prentice Hall, 1973. 1–17.

Gloster, Hugh M. *Negro Voices in American Fiction.* Chapel Hill: University of North Carolina Press, 1948. 111, 114, 117, 128–30, et passim.

Goede, William J. "Jean Toomer's Ralph Kabnis: Portrait of the Negro Artist as a Young Man." *Phylon* 30.10 (Spring 1969): 73–85.

————. "Tradition in the American Negro Novel." Diss. University of California, Riverside, 1976.

Golding, Alan. "Jean Toomer's *Cane*: The Search for Identity through Form." *Arizona Quarterly* 39.3 (Autumn 1983): 197–214.

Goldman, Jane. "'Had There Been an Axe Handy': Transatlantic Modernism, Virginia Woolf and Jean Toomer." *European Journal of American Culture* 28.2 (2009): 109–23.

Goodhead, Dokubo M. "Toward a Critical Realist Reading of African and African Diaspora Literatures." Diss. University of Washington, 2008.

Grant, Sister Mary Kathryn. "Images of Celebration in *Cane*." *Negro American Literature Forum* 5.1 (Spring 1971): 32–36.

Grant, Nathan L., Jr. "Jean Toomer and Zora Neale Hurston: Modernism and the Recovery of the Black Male Identity." Diss. New York University, 1995.

————. *Masculinist Impulses: Toomer, Hurston, Black Writing, and Modernity.* Columbia: University of Missouri Press, 2004.

————. "Teaching Jean Toomer's *Cane*." *Teaching the Harlem Renaissance: Course Design and Classroom Strategies.* Ed. Michael Soto. New York: Peter Lang, 2008. 193–99.

Grandt, Jurgen Ernst. "Writing the Blackness of Blackness: African American Narrative and the Problem of Cultural Authenticity." Diss. University of Georgia, 2000.

————. "Shaping Words to Fit the Soul: Afro-Modernism and the Breakdown of Communication in Jean Toomer's *Cane*." *Shaping Words to Fit the Soul: The Southern Ritual Grounds of Afro-Modernism.* Columbus: Ohio State University Press, 2009. 35–54.

Greene, J. Lee. "The Pain and the Beauty: The South, the Black Writer, and Conventions of the Picaresque." *The American South: Portrait of a Culture.* Ed. Louis D. Rubin. Baton Rouge: Louisiana State University Press, 1980. 264–88.

• Gregory, Montgomery. "A Review of *Cane*." *Opportunity* 1 (December 1923): 374–75. Rpt. in *Cane*. Ed. Darwin T. Turner. New York: Norton, 1988. 165–68.

Griffin, John Chandler. *Biography of American Author Jean Toomer, 1894–1967.* Lewiston, NY: Edwin Mellen Press, 2002.

Griffiths, Frederick T. "'Sorcery Is Dialectical': Plato and Jean Toomer in Charles Johnson's The Sorcerer's Apprentice." *African American Review* 30.4 (Winter 1996): 527–38.

Gross, Theodore L. "The Negro Awakening: Langston Hughes, Jean Toomer, Rudolph Fisher, and Others." *The Heroic Ideal in American Literature.* New York: The Free Press, 1971. 137–47.

Guterl, Matthew Pratt. *The Color of Race in America, 1900–1940.* Cambridge: Harvard University Press, 2001.

Guzzio, Tracie Church. "Jean Toomer 1894–1967." *American Writers: A Collection of Literary Biographies: Supplement IX: Nelson Algren to David Wagoner.* Ed. Jay Parini. New York: Scribner's, 2002. 305–22.

Gysin, Fritz. *The Grotesque in American Negro Fiction: Jean Toomer, Richard Wright, and Ralph Ellison* (The Cooper Monographs 22). Bern, Switzerland: Francke, 1975. 36–90, 276–79.

Hajek, Friederike. "The Change of Literary Authority in the Harlem Renaissance: Jean Toomer's *Cane*." *Literarische Diskurse und historischer Prozess: Beiträge zur englischen und amerikanischen Literatur und Geschichte.* Ed. Brunhild de la Motte. Potsdam, GDR: Pädagogische Hochschule 'Karl Liebkneckt', 1988. 106–114. Rpt. in *The Black Columbiad: Defining Moments in African American Literature and Culture.* Ed. Werner Sollors and Maria Diedrich. Cambridge: Harvard University Press, 1994. 185–90.

Hall, Chekita Trennel. "The Blues as a Paradigm of Cultural Resistance in the Works of Gloria Naylor." Diss. Bowling Green State University, 1995.

Hall, Fred. "*Cane* by Jean Toomer: Theater Review." *Atlantic Voice* (27 April–3 May 1985): 6.

Han, Jaehwan. "The Postcolonial Imagination: Race, Identity, and (Post)coloniality in Selected African-American Fiction." Diss. Indiana University of Pennsylvania, 2004.

Harmon, Charles. "*Cane*, Race, and 'Neither/Norism'." 32.2 *Southern Literary Journal* (Spring 2000): 90–101.

Harris, Leonard, and Charles Molesworth. *Alain L. Locke: The Biography of a Philosopher.* Chicago: The University of Chicago Press, 2008. 170–75.

Harris, Trudier. "The Tie That Binds: The Function of Folklore in the Fiction of Charles Waddell Chesnutt, Jean Toomer, and Ralph Ellison." Diss. The Ohio State University, 1973.

Hart, Robert C. "Black-White Literary Relations in the Harlem Renaissance." *American Literature* 44 (January 1973): 612–28.

Hawkins, Stephanie L. "Building the 'Blue' Race: Miscegenation, Mysticism, and the Language of Cognitive Evolution in Jean Toomer's 'The Blue Meridian'." *Texas Studies in Literature and Language* 46.2 (Summer 2004): 149–80.

Hayden, Robert, David J. Burrows, and Frederick R. Lapides. *Afro-American Literature: An Introduction.* New York: Harcourt Brace Jovanovich, 1971. 3, 5–12, 110, 303.

Hedrick, Tace. "Blood-Lines That Waver South: Hybridity, the 'South', and American Bodies." *Southern Quarterly: A Journal of the Arts in the South* 42.1 (Fall 2003): 39–52.

Helbling, Mark. "Jean Toomer and Waldo Frank: A Creative Friendship." *Phylon* 41 (1980): 167–78.

———. "Sherwood Anderson and Jean Toomer." *Negro American Literature Forum* 9 (1975): 35–39.

Henton, Jennifer E. "Twain, Du Bois, Toomer and Hurston: Reading American Literature and Reading Race." Diss. University of Delaware, 2001.

Hicks, Granville. "Balm in Gilead." *Hound & Horn* 3 (January–March 1930): 276–80.

Holmes, Eugene C. "Jean Toomer—Apostle of Beauty." *Opportunity* 10 (August 1932): 252–54, 260.

Howell, Elmo. "Jean Toomer's Hamlet: A Note on *Cane*." *Interpretations* 9 (1977): 70–73.

Hughes, Langston. "The Negro Artist and the Racial Mountain." *The Nation* 122 (23 June 1926): 692–94.

• ———. "Gurdjieff in Harlem." *The Big Sea: An Autobiography.* New York: Knopf, 1940. 241–43.

———. "The Twenties: Harlem and its Negritude." *African Forum* 1 (Spring 1966): 11–20.

Hunter, Raymond Thomas. "Black Naturalism: A Philosophy and Technique Used by Black Novelists in the First Half of the Twentieth Century." Diss. Wayne State University, 1978.

• Hutchinson, George B. "Jean Toomer and the 'New Negroes of Washington'." *American Literature* 63 (December 1991): 683–92.

———. "Jean Toomer and American Racial Discourse." *Texas Studies in Literature and Language* 35.2 (Summer 1993): 226–50. Rpt. in *Interracialism:*

*Black-White Intermarriage in American History, Literature, and Law.* Ed. Werner Sollors. Oxford: Oxford University Press, 2000. 369–90.

———. *In Search of Nella Larsen: A Biography of the Color Line.* Cambridge: Harvard University Press, 2006.

Ickstadt, Heinz. "The (Re)Construction of an American Cultural Identity in Literary Modernism." *Negotiations of America's National Identity, II.* (Transatlantic Perspective Series) Ed. Roland Hagenbüchle, Josef Raab, and Marietta Messmer. Tübingen, Germany: Stauffenburg, 2000. 206–28.

Ikonné, Chidi. "*Cane*: A Sexual Revolution That Failed." *Black Culture and Black Consciousness in Literature.* Ed. Chidi Ikonné, Ebele Eko, and Julia Oku. Ibadan, Nigeria: Heinemann, 1987. 23–31.

• Innes, Catherine L. "The Unity of Jean Toomer's *Cane*." *CLA Journal* 15 (March 1972): 306–22.

Jackson, Blyden. "Jean Toomer's *Cane*: An Issue of Genre." *The Twenties: Fiction, Poetry, Drama.* Ed. Warren French. Deland, FL: Everett/Edwards, 1975. 317–33.

———. *The Waiting Years: Essays on American Negro Literature.* Baton Rouge: Louisiana State University Press, 1976. 189–97.

Jacques, Geoffrey. "A Change in the Weather: Modernist Imagination, African American Imaginary." Diss. City University of New York, 2004.

Jayasundera, Ymitri. "Transatlantic Convergence of Englishness and Americanness: Cultural Memory, Nationhood, and Imperialism in Twentieth Century Modernist Fiction." Diss. University of Massachusetts Amherst, 2001.

Johnson, James Weldon. "Race Prejudice and the Negro Artist." *Harper's Magazine* 157 (1928): 769–76.

———. *Black Manhattan.* New York: Knopf, 1930. 274.

———. *Along This Way.* New York: Viking, 1968. 375–76.

• Jones, Gayl. "Blues Ballad: Jean Toomer's 'Karintha'." *Liberating Voices: Oral Tradition in African American Literature.* Cambridge: Harvard University Press, 1991. 70–78.

Jones, LeRoi. "Philistinism and the Negro Writer." *Anger, and Beyond: The Negro Writer in the United State.* Ed. Herbert Hill. New York: Harper, 1966. 51–61.

———. "The Myth of a 'Negro Literature'." *Home: Social Essays.* New York: Morrow, 1966. 105–15.

Jones, Norma Ramsey. "Africa, as Imagined by Cullen & Co." *Negro American Literature Forum* 8 (Winter 1974): 263–67.

Jones, Robert Butler, Jr. "Symbolist Aesthetics in Modern American Fiction: Studies in Gertrude Stein and Jean Toomer." Diss. The University of Wisconsin-Madison, 1981.

———. "Jean Toomer as Poet: A Phenomenology of the Spirit." *Black American Literature Forum* 21 (Fall 1987): 275–87.

———, ed. *The Collected Poems of Jean Toomer.* Chapel Hill: University of North Carolina Press, 1988.

———. *Jean Toomer and the Prison-House of Thought: A Phenomenology of the Spirit.* Amherst: University of Massachusetts, 1993.

———, ed. *Jean Toomer: Selected Essays and Literary Criticism.* Knoxville: University of Tennessee Press, 1996.

Josephson, Matthew. "Great American Novels." *Broom* 5 (Oct. 1923): 178–80.

Joyce, Joyce Ann. "Gwendolyn Brooks: Jean Toomer's 'November Cotton Flower'." *Say That the River Turns: The Impact of Gwendolyn Brooks.* Ed. Haki R. Madhubuti. Chicago: Third World Press, 1987: 80–83. Rpt. in *On Gwendolyn Brooks: Reliant Contemplation.* Ed. Stephen Caldwell Wright. Ann Arbor: University of Michigan Press, 1996. 182–85.

Julien, Claude. "The Eye That Cannot/Will Not See: Location and Intertextuality in Jean Toomer's 'Becky'." *Journal of the Short Story in English* 5 (Autumn 1985): 23–31.

Jung, Udo O. H. "'Spirit-Torsos of Exquisite Strength': The Theme of Individual Weakness vs. Collective Strength in Two of Toomer's Poems." *CLA Journal* 19 (December 1975): 261–67. Rpt. in *Jean Toomer: A Critical Evaluation*. Ed. Therman B. O'Daniel. Washington, D.C.: Howard University Press, 1988. 329–35.

———. "'Nora' is 'Calling Jesus': A Nineteenth-Century Dilemma in an Afro-American Garb." *CLA Journal* 21 (1977): 251–55. Rpt. in *Jean Toomer: A Critical Evaluation*. Ed. Therman B. O'Daniel. Washington, D.C.: Howard University Press, 1988. 293–96.

Kerblat-Houghton, Jeanne. "Mythes Ruraux et Urbains dans *Cane* de Jean Toomer (1894–1967)." *Mythes Ruraux et Urbains dans la Culture Américaine*. Aix-en-Provence, France: University de Provence, 1990: 67–77.

Kerlin, Robert T. "Singers of New Songs." *Opportunity* IV (May 1926): 162. Rpt. in *The Merrill Studies in Cane*. Ed. Frank Durham. 42–43.

Kerman, Cynthia E[arl]. "Jean Toomer?—Enigma." *Indian Journal of American Studies*, (7-i) 67–78.

———, and Richard Eldridge. *The Lives of Jean Toomer: A Hunger for Wholeness*. Baton Rouge: Louisiana State University Press, 1987.

Kodat, Catherine Gunther. "Southern Modernists in Black and White: Jean Toomer, Allen Tate, William Faulkner, and Zora Neale Hurston." Diss. Boston University, 1994.

———. "To 'Flash White Light from Ebony': The Problem of Modernism in Jean Toomer's *Cane*." *Twentieth Century Literature* 46.1 (Spring 2000): 1–19.

Kesteloot, Lilyan. "Negritude and Its American Sources." *Boston University Journal* 22 (Spring 1974): 54–64.

Kopf, George. "The Tensions in Jean Toomer's 'Theater'." *CLA Journal* 17 (June 1974): 498–503.

Kousaleos, Peter G. "A Study of the Language, Structure, and Symbolism in Jean Toomer's *Cane* and N. Scott Momaday's *House Made of Dawn*." Diss. Ohio University, 1973.

Kraft, James. "Jean Toomer's *Cane*." *Markham Review* 2 (1970): 61–63.

Kramer, Victor A. "'The Mid-Kingdom' of Crane's 'Black Tambourine' and Toomer's *Cane*." *CLA Journal* 17 (1974): 486–97.

Krasny, Michael. "The Aesthetic Structure of Jean Toomer's *Cane*." *Negro American Literature Forum* 9.2 (Summer 1975): 42–43.

———. "Jean Toomer's Life Prior to *Cane*: A Brief Sketch of the Emergence of a Black Writer." *Negro American Literature Forum* 9 (Summer 1975): 40–41.

Kuenz, Jane Ellen. "Producing the New Negro: The Work of Art in the Harlem Renaissance." Diss. Duke University, 1995.

Kulii, Elon A. "Literature, Biology and Folk Legal Belief: Jean Toomer's Kabnis." *The Language Quarterly* 25.3–4 (Spring–Summer 1987): 5–7, 49, 54.

Kutzinski, Vera M. "Unseasonal Flowers: Nature and History in Plácido and Jean Toomer." *The Yale Journal of Criticism: Interpretation in the Humanities* 3.2 (Spring 1990): 153–79.

Lairet, Dolores Person. "Echos Thématiques, Structuraux et Stylistiques dans *Cane* de Toomer et Cahier . . . de Césaire." *Francographies: Bulletin de la Société des Professeurs Français et Francophones d'Amérique* 2 Spécial (1993): 41–57.

Lamothe, Daphne Mary. "Ethnographic Discourse and Creole Consciousness and Culture in Harlem Renaissance Literature." Diss. University of California, Berkeley, 1997.

———. "*Cane*: Jean Toomer's Gothic Black Modernism." *The Gothic Other: Racial and Social Constructions in the Literary Imagination*. Ed. Ruth Bienstock Anolik and Douglas L. Howard. Jefferson, N.C.: McFarland & Co, 2004. 54–71.

Larson, Charles R. "Reconsideration: *Cane* by Jean Toomer." *The New Republic* 174 (19 June 1976): 30–32.

————. *Invisible Darkness: Jean Toomer and Nella Larsen*. Iowa City: University of Iowa Press, 1993.

Lasker, Bruno. "Doors Opened Southward." *Survey* 51 (Nov. 1923): 190–91. Rpt. in *The Merrill Studies in Cane*. Ed. Frank Durham. 29–30.

Lemke, Sieglinde. "Interculturalism in Literature, the Visual and Performing Arts during the Harlem Renaissance." *Double Crossings/EntreCruzamientos*. Ed. Mario Martín Flores and Carlos von Son. Fair Haven, NJ: Nuevo Espacio, 2001. 111–21.

Lewis, David Levering. *When Harlem Was in Vogue*. New York: Knopf, 1981.

Lieber, Todd. "Design and Movement in *Cane*." *CLA Journal* 13 (Sept. 1969): 35–50.

Lightweis-Goff, Jennifer. "'Blood at the Root': Lynching as American Cultural Nucleus." Diss. University of Rochester, 2009.

Lindberg, Kathryne V. "Raising *Cane* on the Theoretical Plane: Jean Toomer's Racial Personae." *Cultural Difference and the Literary Text: Pluralism and the Limits of Authenticity in North American Literatures*. Ed. Winfried Siemerling and Katrin Schwenk. Iowa City: University of Iowa Press, 1996. 49–74.

• Littel, Robert. "A Review of *Cane*." *New Republic* 26 December 1923: 126. Rpt. in *The Merrill Studies in Cane*. 32–33. Ed. Frank Durham. Rpt. in *Cane*. New York: W. W. Norton & Company, 1988. 169–70.

Littlejohn, David. "Before *Native Son*: The Renaissance and After." *Black on White: A Critical Survey of Writing by American Negroes*. New York: Grossman, 1966. 58–60. Rpt. in *The Merrill Studies in Cane*. Ed. Frank Durham. 100–102.

Locke, Alain. "Negro Youth Speaks." *The New Negro: An Interpretation*. Ed. Alain Locke. New York: Albert and Charles Boni, 1925. 47–53.

————, ed. *The New Negro: An Interpretation*. New York: Albert and Charles Boni, 1925. Rpt., New York: Johnson Reprint Corporation, 1968. 49, 96–104, 136–43, 415.

————. *Four Negro Poets*. New York: Simon Schuster, 1927. 5–6.

————. "Self-Criticism: The Third Dimension in Culture." *Phylon* 11 (Fourth Quarter 1950): 391–94.

Luskey, Matthew Christian. "Modernist Ephemera: Little Magazines and the Dynamics of Coalition." Diss. University of Oregon, 2003.

• Lutenski, Emily. "'A Small Man in Big Spaces': The New Negro, the Mestizo, and Jean Toomer's Southwestern Writing." *MELUS* 33 (Spring 2008): 11–32.

Lynch, Suzanne Marie. "Symbols of Racial Possibilities: Perspectives on Nella Larsen, James Weldon Johnson, and Jean Toomer." MA Thesis. Florida Atlantic University, 1999.

MacKethan, Lucinda H. "Jean Toomer's *Cane*: A Pastoral Problem." *Mississippi Quarterly* 28.4 (1975): 423–34.

Mackey, Nathaniel. "Sound and Sentiment, Sound and Symbol." *Callaloo* 10.1(30) (Winter 1987): 29–54.

Macon, Wanda Celeste. "Adolescent Characters' Sexual Behavior in Selected Fiction of Six Twentieth Century African-American Authors." Diss. The Ohio State University, 1992.

Manora, Yolanda. "'She was in the Family Way': The Dialectics of Modernity and Maternity in Jean Toomer's *Cane*." *Obsidian* 8.1 (Spring 2007): 51–73.

Martin, Odette. "*Cane*: Method and Myth." *Obsidian* 2 (Spring 1976): 5–20.

Marvin, Tom. "Jean Toomer's 'Kabnis'." *Explicator* 67.1 (Fall 2008): 43–45.

Mason, Clifford. "Jean Toomer's Black Authenticity." *Black World* 20 (Nov. 1970): 70–76.

Matthews, George C. "Toomer's *Cane*: The Artist and his World." *CLA Journal* 17 (1974): 543–59.

McKay, Nellie Y. "Jean Toomer, the Artist: A Portrait in Tragedy." Diss. Harvard University, 1977.

————. *Jean Toomer, Artist: A Study of His Literary Life and Work, 1894–1936*. Chapel Hill: University of North Carolina Press, 1984.

———. "Jean Toomer." *Afro-American Writers from the Harlem Renaissance to 1940*. Ed. Trudier Harris and Thadious M. Davis. Detroit: 7Letras, 1987. 274–88.

• ———. "Jean Toomer, the Artist—An Unfulfilled American Life: An Afterword." *Jean Toomer: A Critical Evaluation*. Ed. Therman O'Daniel. Washington, D.C.: Howard University Press, 1988.

McKeever, Benjamin F. "*Cane* as Blues." *Negro American Literature Forum* 4.2 (July 1970): 61–63.

McNeely, Darrell Wayne. "Jean Toomer's *Cane* and Sherwood Anderson's *Winesburg, Ohio*: A Black Reaction to the Literary Conventions of the Twenties." Diss. The University of Nebraska-Lincoln, 1974.

Mellard, James M. "Solipsism, Symbolism, and Demonism: The Lyrical Mode in Fiction." *Southern Humanities Review* 7 (Winter 1973): 37–51.

Miller, R[uth] Baxter. "Blacks in His Cellar: The Personal Tragedy of Jean Toomer." *The Langston Hughes Review* 11.1 (Spring 1992): 36–40.

Mintz, Steven. "Jean Toomer: A Biographical Sketch." *BANC!* 2 (May–June 1972): 1–3.

Mitchell, Carolyn A. "Henry Dumas and Jean Toomer: One Voice." *Black American Literature Forum* 22.2 (Summer 1988): 297–309.

Momplaisir, Francesca M. "The Re-visioning of Goddesses: Revisionist Poetics in African Diaspora Women Writers' Re-creations of Black Women Characters from Black Male Authored Canonical Texts." Diss. New York University, 2004.

Moore, Lewis D. "Kabnis and the Reality of Hope: Jean Toomer's *Cane*." *North Dakota Quarterly* 54.2 (Spring 1986): 30–39.

• Munson, Gorham B. "The Significance of Jean Toomer." *Opportunity* 3.33 (September 1925): 262–63.

Nicholls, David. "Conjuring the Folk: Modernity and Narrative in African America, 1915–1945." Diss. The University of Chicago, 1995.

———. *Conjuring the Folk: Forms of Modernity in African American*. Ann Arbor: University of Michigan, 2000.

———. "Jean Toomer's *Cane*, Modernization, and the Spectral Folk." *Modernism, Inc.: Body, Memory, Capital*. Ed. Jani Scandura and Michael Thurston. New York: New York University Press, 2001. 151–70.

Nitta, Keiko. "Jean Toomer, *Cane* (1923)." *Eigo Seinen/Rising Generation* 154.7 (Oct. 2008): 388–91.

Nower, Joyce. "Foolin' Master." *Satire Newsletter* 7 (Fall 1969): 5–10.

Nwankwo, Nkem. "Cultural Primitivism and Related Ideas in Jean Toomer's *Cane*." Diss. Indiana University, 1983.

O'Daniel, Therman B., ed. *Jean Toomer: A Critical Evaluation*. Washington, D.C.: Howard University Press, 1988.

Ohnesorge, Karen Jane. "Inscription and Vision: Gender- and Race-Inflected Subjectivity in Late Twentieth-Century Intersections of Image and Text." Diss. The University of Kansas, 2005.

———. "Cane Fields, Blues Text-ure: An Improvisational Meditation on Jean Toomer's *Cane* and Jean-Michel Basquiat's *Undiscovered Genius of the Mississippi Delta*." *The Funk Era and Beyond: New Perspectives on Black Popular Culture*. Ed. Tony Bolden. New York: Palgrave Macmillan, 2008. 107–24.

Ortiz-Monasterio, Ignacio. "Jean Toomer's 'Kabnis' and the Language of Dreams." *Southern Literary Journal* 38.2 (Spring 2006): 19–39.

Oxley, Thomas L. G. "The Negro in the World's Literature." *New York Amsterdam News* 28 March 1928. Rpt. as "The Black Man in the World of Literature." *Philadelphia Tribune*, 25 June 1936.

Pabst, Naomi. "Blackness/Mixedness: Contestations over Crossing Signs." *Cultural Critique* 54 (Spring 2003): 178–212.

Parham, Marisa. "Event Horizons: Notes on Memory, Space and Haunting." Diss. Columbia University, 2004.

Parsons, Alice Beal. "Toomer and Frank." *The World Tomorrow* 7 (March 1924): 96.

Peckham, Joel Bishop, Jr. "Exploding the Bordered Text: Transgressive Narrative in the American South." Diss. The University of Nebraska-Lincoln, 1999.

———. "Jean Toomer's *Cane*: Self as Montage and the Drive toward Integration." *American Literature* 72.2 (June 2000): 275–90.

• Pellegrini, Gino Michael. "Jean Toomer and *Cane*: 'Mixed-Blood' Impossibilities." *Arizona Quarterly: A Journal of American Literature, Culture, and Theory*, 64.4 (Winter 2008): 1–20.

Petesch, Donald. "Jean Toomer's *Cane*." *Postmodern Approaches to the Short Story*. Ed. Farhat Iftekharrudin, Joseph Boyden, Joseph Longo, and Mary Rohrberger. Westport, CT: Praeger, 2003. 91–96.

Rampersad, Arnold. *The Life of Langston Hughes*. Vol. I. New York: Oxford University Press, 1986.

———. *The Life of Langston Hughes*. Vol. II New York: Oxford University Press, 1988.

Ramsey, William M. "Jean Toomer's Eternal South." *Southern Literary Journal* 36.1 (Fall 2003): 74–89.

Rand, Lizabeth A. "'I Am I': Jean Toomer's Vision Beyond *Cane*." *CLA Journal* 44.1 (September 2000): 43–64.

Rankin, William. "Ineffability in the Fiction of Jean Toomer and Katherine Mansfield." *Renaissance and Modern: Essays in Honor of Edwin M. Moseley*. Ed. Murray J. Levith. Sarasota Springs, NY: Skidmore College, 1976. 160–71.

Reckley, Ralph, Sr. "The Vinculum Factor: 'Seventh Street' and 'Rhobert' in Jean Toomer's *Cane*." *College Language Association Journal* 31.4 (June 1988): 484–89.

Redding, Saunders. "The New Negro." *To Make a Poet Black*. Chapel Hill: The University of North Carolina Press, 1939. Rpt. in *The Merrill Studies in Cane*. Ed. Frank Durham. 51–53.

• Reilly, John M. "The Search for Black Redemption: Jean Toomer's *Cane*." *Studies in the Novel* 2.3 (1970): 312–24.

Rice, H[erbert] William. "Repeated Images in Part One of *Cane*." *Black American Literature Forum* 17 (1983): 100–105.

———. "An Incomplete Circle: Repeated Images in Part Two of *Cane*." *College Language Association Journal* 29.4 (June 1986): 442–61.

———. "Two Work Songs in *Cane*." *Black American Literature Forum* 23.3 (Fall 1989): 593–99.

Richardson, Riche Deianne. "Black Southern Displacements: On Regional Edge in African American Literature and Culture." Diss. Duke University, 1998.

Riley, Roberta. "Search for Identity and Artistry." *CLA Journal* 17 (1974): 480–85.

Robinson, Joyce Russell. "The Shadow Within: Du Boisian Double Consciousness in Five African American Novels (Pauline E. Hopkins, Jean Toomer, Ralph Ellison, Richard Wright, Toni Morrison)." Diss. Emory University, 1991.

Rochette-Crawley, Susan Marie. "Marginal Genre, Major Form; the Twentieth Century Short Story and Theories of the Marginal and Minor." Diss. The University of Wisconsin-Madison, 1994.

Rohweder, John. "'Blood-Burning Moon': Louisa's Story." *MAWA Review* 11.2 (Dec. 1996): 84–88.

Rohrberger, Mary. "The Question of Regionalism: Limitation and Transcendence." *The American Short Story: 1900–1945: A Critical History*. Ed. Philip Stevick. Boston: Twayne, 1984. 147–82.

• Rosenfeld, Paul. "Jean Toomer." *Men Seen: Twenty-four Modern Authors*. New York: Dial, 1925. 227–33. Rpt. in *The Merrill Studies in Cane*. Ed. Frank Durham. 93–95.

Rusch, Frederik L. "'Every Atom Belonging to Me as Good Belongs to You': Jean Toomer and His Bringing Together of the Scattered Parts." Diss. State University of New York, Albany, 1976.

———. "Form, Function, and Creative Tension in *Cane*: Jean Toomer and the Need for the Avant-Garde." *MELUS* 17.4 (Winter 1991–1992): 15–28.

————, ed. *A Jean Toomer Reader: Selected Unpublished Writings*. New York: Oxford University Press, 1993.

Sanders, Mark A. "American Modernism and the New Negro Renaissance." *The Cambridge Companion to American Modernism*. Ed. Walter Kalaidjian. Cambridge: Cambridge University Press, 2005. 129–56.

Saunders, James Robert. "Sonia Sanchez's Homegirls and Handgrenades: Recalling Toomer's *Cane*." *MELUS* 15.1 (Spring 1988): 73–82.

Schultz, Elizabeth. "Jean Toomer's 'Box Seat': The Possibility for 'Constructive Crises'." *Black American Literature Forum* 13 (Spring 1979): 7–12. Rpt. in *Jean Toomer: A Critical Evaluation*. Ed. Therman O'Daniel. Washington, D.C.: Howard University Press, 1988. 297–310.

Scruggs, Charles W. "The Mark of Cain and the Redemption of Art: A Study in Theme and Structure of Jean Toomer's *Cane*." *American Literature* 44.2 (May 1972): 276–91.

————. "Jean Toomer: Fugitive." *American Literature* 47 (March 1975): 84–96.

• ————. "Textuality and Vision in Jean Toomer's *Cane*." *Journal of the Short Story in English* 10 (Spring 1988): 93–114.

————. "The Photographic Print, the Literary Negative: Alfred Stieglitz and Jean Toomer." *Arizona Quarterly: A Journal of American Literature, Culture, and Theory* 53.1 (Spring 1997): 61–89.

————. "The Reluctant Witness: What Jean Toomer Remembered from *Winesburg, Ohio*." *Studies in American Fiction* 28.1 (Spring 2000): 77–100.

————. "Jean Toomer and Kenneth Burke and the Persistence of the Past." *American Literary History* 13.1 (Spring 2001): 41–66.

————, and Lee VanDemarr. *Jean Toomer and the Terrors of American History*. Philadelphia: University of Pennsylvania Press, 1998.

Sergeant, Elizabeth. "The New Negro." *The New Republic* 46 (12 May 1926): 371–72.

Shaw, Brenda Joyce Robinson. "Jean Toomer's Life Search for Identity Realized in *Cane*." Diss. Middle Tennessee State University, 1975.

Shaw, Phil. "Jean Toomer and Carl Van Vechten: Identity, Exploitation, and the Harlem Renaissance." MA thesis. University of Denver, 2009.

Sherrard-Johnson, Cherene. "The Geography of the Mulatta in Jean Toomer's *Cane*." *Portraits of the New Negro Woman: Visual and Literary Culture in the Harlem Renaissance*. New Brunswick, NJ: Rutgers University Press, 2007. 107–42.

Shigley, Sally Bishop. "Recalcitrant, Revered, and Reviled: Women in Jean Toomer's Short Story Cycle, *Cane*." *Short Story* 9.1 (Spring 2001): 88–98.

Simrill, Spenser. "What's in a Name? A Mystical and Symbolic Reading of Jean Toomer's 'Kabnis'." *Langston Hughes Review* 16.1–2 (Fall 1999–Spring 2001): I: 89–104.

Snaith, Anna. "C. L. R. James, Claude McKay, Nella Larsen, Jean Toomer: The 'Black Atlantic' and the Modernist Novel." *The Cambridge Companion to the Modernist Novel*. Ed. Morag Shiach. Cambridge: Cambridge University Press, 2007. 206–23.

Solard, Alain. "The Impossible Unity: Jean Toomer's 'Kabnis'." *Myth and Ideology in American Culture*. Ed. Regis Durand. Villeneuve d'Ascq: U de Lille III, 1976. 175–94.

————. "Myth and Narrative Fiction in *Cane*: 'Blood-Burning Moon'." *Callaloo* 8.3 (25) (Fall 1985): 551–62.

• Sollors, Werner. "Jean Toomer's *Cane*: Modernism and Race in Interwar America." *Jean Toomer and the Harlem Renaissance*. Ed. Geneviève Fabre and Michel Feith. New Brunswick, NJ: Rutgers University Press, 2001.

Somerville, Siobhan Bridget. "The Same Difference? Passing, Race, and Sexuality in American Literature and Film, 1890–1930." Diss. Yale University, 1994.

Soto, Michael. "Literary History and the Age of Jazz: Generation, Renaissance, and American Literary Modernism." Diss. Harvard University, 1999.

Spofford, William K. "The Unity of Part One of Jean Toomer's *Cane*. *Markham Review* 3 (1972): 58–60.

Stein, Marian L. "The Poet-Observer and 'Fern' in Jean Toomer's *Cane*." *Markham Review* 2 (1970): 64–65.

Steinecke, Ann. "Revolt from the Village: Place and Anxiety in Modern American Fiction." Diss. University of Maryland, College Park, 1996.

Stepto, Robert B. *From Behind the Veil: A Study in Afro-American Narrative*. Urbana: University of Illinois Press, 1979.

Story, Ralph Dewitt. "Master Players in a Fixed Game: An Extra-Literary History of Twentieth Century Afro-American Authors. 1896–1981." Diss. University of Michigan, 1984.

Taylor, Clyde. "The Second Coming of Jean Toomer." *Obsidian* 1 (Winter 1975): 37–57.

Terris, Daniel. "Waldo Frank, Jean Toomer, and the Critique of Racial Voyeurism." *Race and the Modern Artist*. Ed. Heather Hathaway, Josef Jarab, and Jeffrey Melnick. New York: Oxford University Press, 2003. 92–114.

Thompson, Chezia Brenda. "Hush, Hush—Somebody's Callin' Ma Name: Analyzing and Teaching Jean Toomer's *Cane*." Diss. Carnegie Mellon University, 1985.

Thompson, Larry E. "Jean Toomer: As Modern Man." *Harlem Renaissance Remembered*. Ed. Arna Bontemps. New York: Dodd, Mead, 1972. 51–62.

Thompson-Cager, Chezia. *Teaching Jean Toomer's 1923 Cane*. New York: Peter Lang, 2006.

Thornton, Jerome E. "'Goin' on de Muck': The Paradoxical Journey of the Black American Hero." *College Language Association Journal* 31.3 (Mar 1988): 261–80.

Thurman, Wallace. "Negro Artists and the Negro." *New Republic* 52 (31 August 1927): 37–39.

———. "Nephews of Uncle Remus." *Independent* 119 (24 September 1927): 296–98.

Trevitte, Chad. "Marks of Damaged Life: Re-Reading Modernity in Twentieth Century American Fiction." Diss. University of North Carolina, Chapel Hill, 2004.

Trudell, Shane Willow. "Meridians: Mapping Metaphors of Mixed-Race Identity." Diss. University of Florida, 2004.

• Turner, Darwin T. "The Failure of a Playwright." *CLA Journal* 10 (June 1967): 308–18.

———. "Jean Toomer's *Cane*: A Critical Analysis." *Negro Digest* 18.3 (Jan. 1969): 54–61.

———. *In a Minor Chord: Three Afro-American Writers and Their Search for Identity*. Carbondale: Southern Illinois University Press, 1971.

———. "An Intersection of Paths: Correspondence Between Jean Toomer and Sherwood Anderson." *CLA Journal* 17 (June 1974): 455–67.

———. Introduction. *Cane*. By Jean Toomer. New York: Liveright, 1975.

———, ed. *The Wayward and the Seeking: A Collection of Writings by Jean Toomer*. Washington, D.C.: Howard University Press, 1980.

———. *Cane: An Authoritative Text, Backgrounds, Criticism*. New York: Norton, 1988.

Twombly, Robert C. "A Disciple's Odyssey: Jean Toomer's Gurdjieffian Career." *Prospects: Annual of American Cultural Studies* 2: 437–62.

Van Doren, Carl. "Negro Renaissance." *Century Magazine* 111 (Mar. 1926): 635–37.

Van Mol, Kay R. "Primitivism and Intellect in Toomer's *Cane* and McKay's *Banana Bottom*: The Need for an Integrated Black Consciousness." *Negro American Literature Forum* 10.2 (1976): 48–52.

Wagner-Martin, Linda. "Toomer's *Cane* as Narrative Sequence." *Modern American Short Story Sequences: Composite Fictions and Fictive Communities*. Ed. J. Gerald Kennedy. Cambridge, England: Cambridge University Press, 1995. 19–34.

Waldron, Edward E. "The Search for Identity in Toomer's 'Esther'." *CLA Journal* 14 (March 1971): 277–80.

• Walker, Alice. "The Divided Life of Jean Toomer." *In Search of Our Mothers' Gardens*. San Diego: Harcourt Brace Jovanovich, 1983. 60–65.

———. "In Search of Our Mothers' Gardens." *In Search of Our Mothers' Gardens*. San Diego: Harcourt Brace Jovanovich, 1983. 231–43.

Wallace, Carolynn Reid. "Jean Toomer: Death on the Modern Desert." Diss. The George Washington University, 1981.

Wardi, Anissa Janine. "The Mark of '*Cane*': A Vernacular Study of Jean Toomer's African American Pastoral in Narratives of Gloria Naylor, Ernest Gaines, and Toni Morrison." Diss. Syracuse University, 1999.

———. "The Scent of a Sugarcane: Recalling *Cane* in The Women of Brewster Place." *CLA Journal* 42.4 (June 1999): 483–507.

———. "Divergent Paths to the South: Echoes of *Cane* in Mama Day." *Gloria Naylor: Strategy and Technique, Magic and Myth*. Ed. Shirley A. Stave. Newark: University of Delaware Press, 2001. 44–76.

Watkins, Patricia. "Is There a Unifying Theme in *Cane*?" *CLA Journal* 15 (March 1972): 303–305.

Weaks-Baxter, Mary. "The Dawn of Direct and Unafraid Creation: Jean Toomer and his *Cane*." *Reclaiming the American Farmer: The Reinvention of a Regional Mythology in Twentieth Century Southern Writing*. Baton Rouge: Louisiana State University Press, 2006. 57–78.

Webb, Jeff. "Literature and Lynching: Identity in Jean Toomer's *Cane*." *ELH* 67.1 (Spring 2000): 205–28.

Welbon, Anita. "Healing the Wounds: The Power of Art in Twentieth-Century African-American Novels." Diss. Vanderbilt University, 1997.

Welch, William. "The Gurdjieff Period." *BANC!* 2 (May–June 1972): 4–5.

Westerfield, Hargis. "Jean Toomer's 'Fern': A Mystical Dimension." *CLA Journal* 14 (March 1971): 274–76.

Whalan, Mark. "Jean Toomer, Technology, and Race." *Journal of American Studies* 36.3 (Dec. 2002): 459–72.

———. " 'Taking Myself in Hand': Jean Toomer and Physical Culture." *Modernism/Modernity* 10.4 (Nov. 2003): 597–615.

———, ed. *The Letters of Jean Toomer, 1919–1924*. Knoxville: University of Tennessee Press, 2006.

• ———. "Jean Toomer and the Avant-Garde." *The Cambridge Companion to the Harlem Renaissance*. Ed. George Hutchinson. Cambridge, England: Cambridge University Press, 2007. 71–81.

———. *Race, Manhood, and Modernism in America: The Short Story Cycles of Sherwood Anderson and Jean Toomer*. Knoxville: University of Tennessee Press, 2007.

Whittaker, Joseph. "Metaphors of the Underground in Contemporary African-American Literature." Diss. The Pennsylvania State University, 1998.

Whyde, Janet M. "Mediating Forms: Narrating the Body in Jean Toomer's *Cane*." *Southern Literary Journal* 26.1 (Fall 1993): 42–53.

Wilks, Jennifer. "Writing Home: Comparative Black Modernism and Form in Jean Toomer and Aimé Césaire." *MFS Modern Fiction Studies* 51.4 (Winter 2005): 801–23.

• Williams, Jennifer D. "Jean Toomer's *Cane* and the Erotics of Mourning." *Southern Literary Journal* 40.2 (Spring 2008): 87–101.

Withrow, Dolly. "Cutting Through Shade" [Jean Toomer's "Reapers"]. *CLA Journal* 21 (September 1977): 98–99.

Woodson, Jon. *To Make a New Race: Gurdjieff, Toomer, and the Harlem Renaissance*. Jackson: University of Mississippi Press, 1999.

Woolfork, Lisa Gail. "Trauma and Racial Difference in Twentieth-Century American Literature." Diss. The University of Wisconsin-Madison, 2000.

Wright-Cleveland, Margaret E. "White is a Color: Race and the Developing Modernism of Jean Toomer, Ernest Hemingway, and William Faulkner." Diss. The Florida State University, 2009.

Yellin, Michael Joseph. "Jean Toomer and Waldo Frank: Literary Modernism and the Ambivalence of Black-Jewish Identification." Diss. Lehigh University, 2007.

Zamberlin, Mary F. "Rhizosphere: Gilles Deleuze and Minor American Literature and Thought." Diss. University of Washington, 2003.